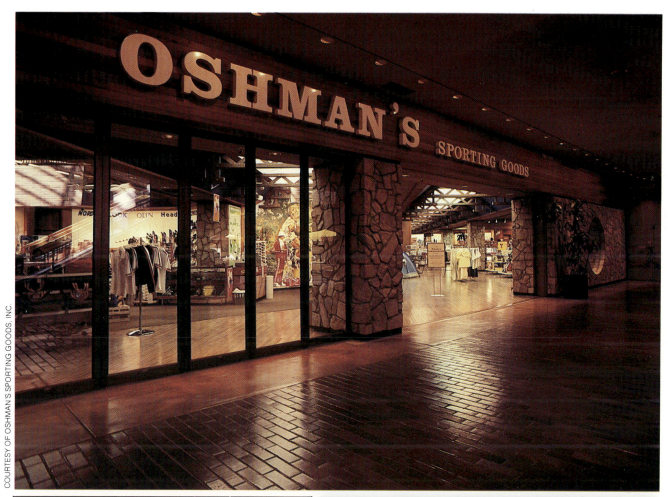

INTRODUCTION TO BUSINESS

JOHN M. IVANCEVICH
College of Business Administration
University of Houston

HERBERT L. LYON
College of Business Administration
University of Houston

DAVID P. ADAMS
Business Administration Department
Oakland Community College

WEST PUBLISHING COMPANY
St. Paul   New York   Los Angeles   San Francisco

A study guide has been developed to assist you in mastering concepts presented in this text. The study guide reinforces concepts by presenting them in condensed, concise form. Additional illustrations and examples are also included. The study guide is available from your local bookstore under the title, *Study Guide to Accompany Introduction to Business*, prepared by Curtis G. Mason.

Design: Janet Bollow
Copyediting: Susan Weisberg and Jay Stewart
Illustrations: Brenda Booth
Cover photograph: Tom Tracy
Production coordination: Janet Bollow Associates
Composition: Dharma Press

Library of Congress Cataloging in Publication Data

Ivancevich, John M.
  Introduction to business.

  Bibliography: p.
  Includes index.
  1. Industrial management—United States. 2. Business enterprises—United States. I. Lyon, Herbert L. II. Adams, David P. III. Title.
  HD70.U519 1983   658   82-21777
  ISBN 0-314-69656-3
  1st Reprint—1983

CONTENTS IN BRIEF

CONTENTS

FINANCING AND INSURING BUSINESS   307
PROFILE IN BUSINESS   Amadeo Peter Giannini   307

PART FIVE

CHAPTER 15
MONEY AND
BANKING   309

ON THE JOB
Moving into the New World
of Diversified Banking   310

BUSINESS CLOSE-UP
Business, But Not as Usual   315

BUSINESS CLOSE-UP
A Retailer Gets into
Financial Services   320

BUSINESS CLOSE-UP
Electronic Banking
Becomes a Reality   325

CHAPTER   16
SHORT- AND
LONG-TERM FINANCING   329

ON THE JOB
Sue's Salon   330

PREFACE

Business organizations are a major force in our society. They are our primary source of goods and services, income, and jobs. The practical value of business to individuals and society is tremendous.

Introduction to Business has been written for the student who must live and earn a living in a world influenced by business. The book presents a balanced view of American free enterprise and business organizations—their strengths, weaknesses, successes, failures, problems, trends, and challenges. The result is a realistic picture of how businesses operate and of the people who are the most important resources in making them work.

An introductory business course usually provides the first opportunity for students to examine the nature and characteristics of business. In presenting business in a thorough, interesting, and realistic manner, this book has a number of objectives:

OBJECTIVES

- *Educational objectives.* To provide thorough basic knowledge about business for both business and nonbusiness students. An increased awareness of business operations can evoke enthusiasm, understanding, and appreciation.
- *Environmental objectives.* To bring into clear distinction the conflicting environmental forces that influence the effectiveness of business. Owners, suppliers, customers, unions, government, competition, and the workforce make demands that businesses must consider. The book makes the reader aware of the difficulties involved in satisfying these numerous and often conflicting demands.
- *Decision-making objectives.* To illustrate the complexities involved in making a business work. Managers must make choices among different courses of action. Any time a choice is made, there is some risk of not succeeding as well as the chance of succeeding. Being able to make decisions is the key to operating a business and is therefore a major learning objective.
- *Vocabulary enrichment objectives.* To introduce clear and concise definitions of business terms. A good vocabulary will help students understand and interpret business news and information found in daily newspapers and magazines and on radio and television.

■ *Vocational objectives.* To increase the student's awareness of careers in business. By learning about the many challenging and rewarding careers, students may be encouraged to seek more information about entering the world of business.

We believe that the materials in the *Introduction to Business* package make the book and its supplements achieve the six objectives in an exciting and readable way.

THE BOOK'S FORMAT

A glance at the table of contents will show that the book covers the important functional areas of business. Part One develops ideas about business, the nation's economy, and government-business relationships. Part Two discusses management and organization. Part Three focuses on personnel and human resources, and labor–management relations, and production. Part Four covers marketing, and Part Five deals with financing and insuring business. Part Six covers such important business tools as accounting, statistics, and computers. Part Seven, international law, ethics, and the future of business are discussed.

A common thread throughout the twenty-four chapters is the emphasis on practical application. We have drawn on our experiences as managers, employees, consultants, educators, trainers, and business-management seminar leaders to provide many of the examples in the resource materials used throughout the book.

Each chapter begins with a set of learning objectives and an "On the Job" vignette. These short vignettes present a real-world situation appropriate to the chapter's topic. At the close of each chapter is a summary of its main points. Each chapter also includes student practice assignments—issues to analyze and consider, and short case studies. These assignments will help the student accomplish the six educational objectives.

At the end of Parts One through Six are sections discussing careers. The appendix presents a career package—a set of materials to help readers understand the necessary steps and ingredients for finding a job. The career materials include facts, statistics, and information about many of the available careers in business.

DISTINCTIVE FEATURES

We have worked especially hard to provide distinctive materials that will make the reading and the course enjoyable. Some of the distinctive features of the book are:

■ A practical, applications orientation
■ "On the Job" examples to introduce realism into the content of each chapter, with "On the Job Revisited" text references to these examples
■ "Business Close-Ups"—specific examples of business in action, the people involved, and the final outcomes
■ An emphasis on decision making and its central role in business firms
■ A view of business in America that shows both positive and negative attributes

- Detailed, thorough career information that can help job searchers
- A chapter on small business and franchising with up-to-date information
- A chapter on business law and ethics
- A chapter on international trade
- A chapter on information systems and computers that readers with minimum exposure to these areas can appreciate and understand
- An extensive glossary of key terms

The business activities cited in the text place a special premium on the importance of reaching decisions. Decision making is the most important task of each person involved with business, whether as a customer, owner, employee, or creditor. In selecting a career, the student must make a number of decisions about what training and education is needed, what companies offer the best opportunities, and how best to begin a career. A person who is considering starting a small business, buying an ongoing business, or purchasing a franchise makes decisions. And managers in business organizations must constantly make decisions.

In most chapters, the decision-making theme is further reinforced by asking the reader to consider real business cases in companies such as Apple Computer, General Motors, AT&T, Romac, Honeywell, and Coy Brewery. The case studies present situations involving some business principle, concept, or topic. Two or more questions after each case provide the reader with some direction for analyzing the case.

The instructor is an important resource person for students, serving as a moderator, referee, facilitator, and information source all at the same time. As in the business world, there is little room in analyzing the case studies for loose comments that can't be supported by logical thinking and analysis. Thus, the instructor leading discussions should require that a systematic program of analysis be followed. Listed below are steps that students can use to analyze the case studies, make decisions, and meet the quality of analysis expected by the instructor.

A SPECIAL NOTE ON THE END-OF-CHAPTER CASES

1. *The Preliminaries*
   a. Read the entire case to acquire a general impression of the issues involved.
   b. Think about the chapter topics that relate to the case.
2. *The Specifics*
   a. Reread the case and identify the specific problems that it illustrates. Don't stop at identifying the symptom; get to the major problems.
   b. Examine the questions and provide detailed answers. Support your response with facts that were covered in the chapter.
   c. Place yourself in the role of the main individuals discussed in the case, and consider what you would do in a similar situation.
   d. Consider how the problems presented in the case could be avoided in the future.
3. *Presenting a Case to the Class*
   a. Summarize the main issues and identify the main characters in the case.

b. Clearly identify the main problem and illustrate how it became the key problem.

c. Present your responses to the end-of-case questions.

d. Discuss how the chapter material helped you analyze the case. Show how you logically reached your conclusions.

e. Ask for questions or ask if any classmates identified a different problem or answered the questions differently.

PACKAGE

A complete package of supplements has been prepared to accompany INTRODUCTION TO BUSINESS which emphasizes content, quality, teachability, and thoroughness. The components of the package are:

■ **Instructor's Manual**

Part One Learning Objectives; Chapter Preview; Chapter Lecture Resource Notes for Your Class Presentation; End of Chapter Questions and Answers; Suggested Additional Questions for the Chapter; Suggested Transparencies for This Chapter; Suggested Term Paper Topics for This Chapter; End of Chapter Cases.

Part Two Business Forms

Part Three Film Guide

■ **Transparencies** Over 100 transparency acetates to highlight material presented in the chapters.

■ **Lecture and Additional Transparency Enrichment Pack** Two additional lectures per chapter with additional complementary transparencies.

■ **Student Enrichment Guide** A self-paced learning resource to help students reinforce principles and content in the text and become more involved with business.

■ **Test Bank** A set of 1800 test questions organized by topic.

■ **Business Profiles** A series of high-interest articles discussing a variety of real life firms, their background, managers, and products.

ACKNOWLEDGMENTS

We are indebted to many people who have provided suggestions for improving this text. The suggestions have surely made this a better book. In particular, we would like to sincerely thank the following reviewers of the manuscript.

Edwin C. Aronson, Golden West College
Jim Baylor, Riverside City College
Clara Buitenbos, Pan American University
Van L. Bushnell, Southern Utah State College
Mel Choate, N. Seattle Community College
Bob Cross, Saint Petersburg Junior College
Les Dlabay, Illinois State University
Sally Ferguson, Southern Illinois University
Andrea Freling, Ferris State College
Ed Goodin, University of Nevada, L.V.
Susan Harrison, Parkersburg Community College

James Hovendick, San Jacinto College
Donna Meyer, Antelope Valley College
Van Miller, University of New Mexico
Jim Morgan, West Los Angeles College
Neal Nixon, Montana State University
P.E. Phillips, University of Akron
Pablo Ulloa, El Paso County Community College
William Weller, Modesto Junior College

In addition, we would like to express thanks to the managers, employees, union leaders, and entrepreneurs who work in business organizations and provide the goods and services that we all enjoy and consume. Without them and the business events that occur every day, this book would not have meaning. It is people who provide the human touch and spirit to the buildings, warehouses, and offices in a business.

A NOTE TO STUDENTS

We have written a book about business specifically for students. Your learning, future role in business, and enjoyment in reading were our major considerations in preparing the text. We want to admit openly that we are excited about business in a free enterprise society, and we hope our excitement will become evident and contagious as you read the book.

Introduction to Business is being used in your present class, but you can also consult it in the future. It is a resource book that surveys the field of business. Reading the book will not qualify you as an expert in all business activities. No one person can ever hope to master the many phases and activities of business. However, if you read and learn the material contained in this book, there will be few areas of business to which you have not been exposed. We wanted to make this exposure alive, up-to-date, and practical. We hope that, after completing the book, you will feel we were successful.

It takes certain writing and integration skills to survey the field of business in one book. It takes an even greater skill on the student's part to sort out, carefully weigh, and evaluate this survey. Your experience, imagination, and reading ability will all play major parts in what you acquire from this book. Let us know your impressions, your likes and dislikes, and your overall feelings about *Introduction to Business*. Your feedback will help us make improvements. Thank you for allowing us to provide you with this *Introduction to Business*.

John M. Ivancevich
Herbert L. Lyon
David P. Adams

PROFILE IN BUSINESS

John H. Johnson (1918-   )

"I feel that if we've done anything at all, we've made black people proud to be black. And if we've done nothing else, that's enough."

I can't say I had a very happy childhood," recalls John Johnson, raised in Arkansas as an only child. His father died in a sawmill accident when John was six. "But it wasn't an unhappy childhood. . . . I had no contact with the world outside, and when you have nothing to compare with, you aren't aware that you should be unhappy." Johnson attended segregated schools in Arkansas City, where one teacher supervised several grades and there was no Negro high school. John repeated eighth grade to stretch his schooling an extra year.

During the Depression, the family moved to Chicago's South Side, where Johnson swept through high school. An honor student, president of the student council and his class, managing editor of the newspaper, business manager of the yearbook, he was invited to address an Urban League banquet honoring outstanding high-school seniors. The president of Supreme Life Insurance Company was a featured speaker. He hired Johnson as an office boy and arranged a scholarship for part-time study at the University of Chicago.

Supreme Life was something of a watering hole for young blacks on the rise. As assistant to the president, Johnson edited a monthly digest of company, local, and national news for blacks. Reader response within the company encouraged him to

BUSINESS: THE ECONOMY AND RESPONSIBILITIES

launch a similar publication for general circulation. With his mother's furniture for collateral, he borrowed $500 for a promotional mailing to 20,000 Supreme Life policyholders. About 3,000 of them became charter subscribers to the *Negro Digest*, intrigued by regular features like "My Most Humiliating Jim Crow Experience" and "If I Were a Negro" (written by white contributors). When Eleanor Roosevelt wrote an article pondering what her life might be like if she were black, the *Digest's* circulation jumped to 150,000.

His first publication had been patterned loosely after *Reader's Digest*. His second adopted the picture format of *Life* and the credo "to provide positive images of blacks in a world of negative images." The first issue of *Ebony* appeared on Chicago newsstands in November 1945, focusing on black achievements and success stories. Glamorous women decorated the pages for returning GIs. Many blacks have criticized *Ebony's* relentless upbeat, its reluctance to tackle hard social and economic issues. Johnson is more concerned with mirroring the aspirations of a growing black middle class. "When we started, success might have meant big cars and mink coats and fancy houses—material evidences. Now it might be raising a family, overcoming a racial handicap, or sending your kids to college." Johnson convinced major advertisers that his picture magazine provided direct access to a ripe new market, and *Ebony* was secure. By the mid-1970s, circulation ran well above one million, and ad revenues topped $10 million.

Meanwhile, *Negro Digest* meta-morphosed into a literary journal, *Black World*. Johnson has launched a few other publications for the black market, some successful, some not. A "true confessions" magazine called *Tan* matured into a women's journal, then became a show-business magazine called *Black Stars*. Johnson keeps one ear to the ground and a firm hand on all his publications, bending them to carefully targeted readerships.

In 1962 Johnson started publishing books. The Johnson Publishing Company also owns a Chicago radio station and Fashion Fair, a lucrative cosmetics business developed from *Ebony* fashion shows. The growth of John H. Johnson's communications empire is inseparable from the emergence of a black American middle class.

CHAPTER 1

BUSINESS AND SOCIETY

LEARNING OBJECTIVES

After studying this chapter, you should be able to:

Discuss what is meant by the term *business* in a society such as the United States.

Describe the business and economic meanings of the term *profit*.

Explain why it is important to study and be knowledgeable about business.

Illustrate the important role played by people in businesses.

Compare various eras of business growth and development from the colonial system to the present day.

KEY TERMS

Bartering
Business
Business transaction
Business enterprises
Business profit
Opportunity costs
Economic profit
Mercantilism
Recession
Inflation

THE MAN WHO TURNS MISTAKES INTO BARGAINS FOR CONSUMERS

Some manufacturers in the trade call Sy Syms an undertaker, but in practice he is an "off-pricer." Undertaker, off-pricer, business person, or whatever else he may be called, Syms is selling just about every type of clothing he can lay his hands on.

Syms has built an enormous new distribution center in the New Jersey Meadowlands where he sells brand-name apparel at prices well below

Adapted from Walter McQuade, "The Man Who Makes Millions on Mistakes," *Fortune*, September 6, 1982, pp. 106–116.

wholesale. Off-pricers buy excess brand-name clothes inventories at before-wholesale prices, keep their selling expenses down, and can consequently sell at very low prices to consumers. In fact, Syms's prices are about half what the same clothes sell for in specialty shops.

No matter what his more conventional competition calls him, Syms's business is one of the fastest growing in the clothing business. He now has ten stores in eastern cities from Boston to Fort Lauderdale. Last year, Syms sold around $115 million

off-price brand-name clothes for a profit of $10 million. The key to his success is selling clothes that customers recognize for bargain prices. One of Sym's goals is to produce an educated consumer because that is his best customer.

Sy Syms represents one meaning of the word *business* as it is used in America today. Certainly he understands the value of making a profit and the role people play in business. All of these ideas are discussed in this chapter.

This book is about business as it exists in society. The business environment is dynamic because of the continual changes in social, technological, economic, governmental, and human forces. Attempting to observe and pinpoint these changes is like trying to find the famous needle in the haystack. The needle is there, but it is difficult to locate. Similarly, changes are dificult to recognize because they are always occurring. And in many cases, changes in consumer demand, wages and prices, career mobility, and resource availability are subtle.

Business is everywhere, and it has made our standard of living what it is. This in itself is sufficient reason to study business. A person who is uneducated in basic business principles, issues, and concepts may well be uncomfortable conducting such everyday activities as buying groceries, paying bills, reading newspapers, and traveling by automobile or bus. A person with a low "business IQ" usually is not able to function in our society without frustration and anxiety.

Studying business can help us become better, safer, and more intelligent consumers of goods and services. Most of us have a limited amount of income to spend, so we must make decisions about what to buy. By using the best information possible, we can get the maximum benefit from business transactions.

Business, like the rest of society, is dynamic and always changing. New laws are passed, prices are raised, new products are introduced, old products are modified, our style of living and needs and values are changing. Coping with these and other changes requires an understanding of business and its environment.

Unless we understand how business works in our society, we can develop misconceptions. There are still many people in America who believe that (1) most large business corporations earn a 20 percent profit on sales; (2) large business organizations outnumber small businesses; (3) most business careers are not challenging and interesting; and (4) most employees of businesses are motivated solely by increased pay or economic rewards. These incorrect assumptions and attitudes frequently result in unprofitable business transactions.

Finally, understanding business can help us uncover possible careers. There are numerous career opportunities in large and small businesses. Learning about the different forms of business (sole proprietorship, partnership, and corporation), business functions (marketing, production, accounting, and finance), and management and nonmanagement tasks can help us make career choices. Then we can develop the educational and experience base that will give us a better chance of succeeding.

WHY STUDY BUSINESS?

Years ago, when our ancestors began to barter, business became a reality. Our ancestors discovered that producing everything one needs requires doing some undesirable work. They also discovered that individuals have various traits, needs, and skills. If a person specialized in a particular job, like making shoes or growing corn, the surpluses produced could be

BUSINESS: WHAT IS IT?

BARTERING
The exchange of goods without using money.

BUSINESS
Means of exchanging goods, services, or money for a profit.

BUSINESS TRANSACTION
Exchanging a product for money.

BUSINESS ENTERPRISE
An organization involved in exchanging goods, services, or money to earn a profit.

bartered for other desirable goods. This early exchange of goods, without using money, was called **bartering**.

Today, business—as conducted in the United States, Canada, Great Britain, West Germany, and Japan—is more complicated than bartering shoes for corn. It is more complicated because of the environment and the human elements in modern society. However, **business** can still be defined as the exchange of goods, services, or money for mutual benefit or profit.

When an organization such as General Motors (GM) exchanges a Chevrolet Celebrity for money, it is involved in a **business transaction**. GM hopes to earn a profit by being involved in the transaction. The car buyer hopes to receive a dependable vehicle to drive to work and to use for leisure.

Today in the United States, more than 14 million business organizations of all sizes are involved in exchanging goods and services for a profit. These **business enterprises** aim to earn a profit as a result of the exchange of goods, services, or money. We are all affected in some way by the activities of business enterprises. We sleep on products made by business, eat food processed by business, and read newspapers published by business.

So what does business involve? In the sense that business involves the exchange of goods, services, or money for mutual benefit, we are all involved in business. In addition, business enterprises, such as Pizza Hut, Household Finance, and Kroger's are involved in exchanging goods, services, and money to earn a profit. Thus, business correctly and necessarily includes both mutual benefit and profit.

The Objectives of Business Enterprise

A number of objectives are important in the conduct of business. Lists of business objectives generally include such factors as survival, growth, and social responsibility.

Survival is an obvious objective. No other objectives can be accomplished if the business enterprise does not survive.

Growth is an objective because business does not stand still and because there is something American and attractive about increased development. The growth of IBM and McDonald's are often used as examples of business success accomplished through growth.

Finally, in recent years, meeting social responsibilities has been recognized as an important objective. Businesses, like each person in society, must accept their responsibilities in the areas of pollution, discrimination, and conservation.

Although survival, growth, and social responsibility are important objectives, the profit objective also plays a major role in business. Profit means different things to different people because of their values, attitudes, and perceptions, so we will look at it more carefully.

The Businessperson's View of Profit

BUSINESS PROFIT
The sum remaining after subtracting all the costs, including taxes, from the revenue received for selling a product or service in the market.

Typically, a businessperson calculates profit by subtracting all the costs, including taxes, from the revenue received for selling a product or service in the market. This is referred to as **business profit**. For example, the franchise owner of a fast-food restaurant like Burger King or Steak & Ale subtracts all expenses (for supplies, staff, property, advertising, and so on) from all income to determine the business profit.

Successful business organizations receive a profit because they effectively meet the needs and demands of customers for their goods and services. Basically, profits reward a business enterprise for effectively conducting a number of activities, listed below.

- *Risk taking.* The business takes some risks by entering a new market or by competing head-on with stiff competition. For example, Toyota invested millions of dollars in promoting and selling small cars in the United States. Today, this Japanese corporation is the largest small-car seller in the U.S. market.
- *Evaluation of demand.* Business organizations that evaluate consumer needs and demands and move efficiently into a market can earn substantial profits. Xerox in the photoreproduction industry, Apple Computer in personal home computers, and McDonald's in fast foods are examples of companies that have made accurate assessments of consumer demands and thereby have received satisfactory profits.
- *Efficient management.* A major cause of business failure is improper or inadequate management of people, technology, materials, and capital. Efficient planning, organizing, controlling, directing, and staffing can earn satisfactory profits. Some of the most profitable large corporations are also considered well-managed businesses. Included in this category are General Electric, Polaroid, Baker International, Levi Strauss, Minnesota Mining and Manufacturing, and Procter & Gamble. These and other well-managed corporations and smaller businesses earn, on the average, around 5 percent a year on total sales. Of course, business profit rates vary greatly by industry, size of business, managerial effectiveness, and location of the business.

The Economist's View of Profit

The economist, like the businessperson, subtracts expenses from income to find profit. But the economist also considers **opportunity costs**, the amount of profit a business gives up by using human, technological, and capital resources in some specific way. For example, the owner of a small florist shop pays herself a salary of $10,000 for operating the business. But suppose she could earn $15,000 working for a large wholesale florist supply house. Her opportunity cost is $5000. The economist would include this $5000 as a cost of operating the florist shop. Thus, **economic profit** is earned income minus both actual expenses and opportunity costs.

One practical difficulty with the economist's view of profit is calculating opportunity costs. It is often hard to put a dollar value on lost opportunity. The businessperson's view of profits is possible to calculate and thus more realistic. Therefore, this book will emphasize business profit.

OPPORTUNITY COSTS
The amount of profit a business gives up by using human, technological, and capital resources in some specific way.

ECONOMIC PROFIT
Earned income minus both actual expenses and opportunity costs.

THE BUSINESS ENVIRONMENT

The study of business involves paying attention to business as it functions in a dynamic environment. The astute business executive or owner must understand the impact of environmental factors. In addition, business affects the environment. Through their actions, business people can influence economic policies, shape social attitudes, develop new technologies, and alter the political process. Exhibit 1–1 depicts the relationship

EXHIBIT 1-1
Business in a Dynamic Environment

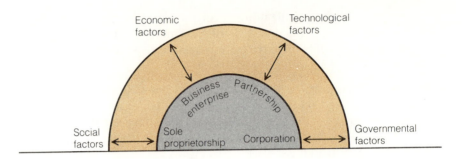

between environmental forces and business. (These forces and the internal dimensions of business—such as management, marketing, finance, and control systems—will be treated throughout this book.)

Economic Factors

Threats from competitors, the availability of natural resources, profits, sales volume, and other similar aspects are all considered economic factors. In essence, economic factors are any forces that have an economic effect on the business.

An important and often overlooked economic factor is land. Economically, land involves not only space but also the natural resources of the land, such as gas, oil, iron ore, copper, and coal. America has been fortunate enough to have enough land (space and natural resources) to fulfill the needs and wants of its citizens. But is important to note that land alone does not guarantee an enjoyable quality of life. Effective business management and decision making must be combined with land and other economic factors.

Social Factors

Social attitudes, values, education, and birth rate are examples of social factors that affect business. Changes in these and similar factors have a direct influence on sales and on profits earned. For example, if attitudes continue to shift toward a more relaxed lifestyle and people continue to have money to spend, there will be a growing market for certain leisure goods and services.

Technological Factors

The new technologies available to businesses have a significant effect on consumer demand and purchasing patterns. And as technology changes, businesses must make some changes. Microwave ovens, personal computers, fiber optics, and solar and nuclear energy have all been developed through technological advancement. Business, through research and development, has initiated many of these advances.

Governmental Factors

Local, state, and federal governments can do much to encourage or protect business through tariffs, tax incentives, low-interest loans, and investment in research and development. On the other hand, government may vigorously enforce antidiscrimination laws, antitrust laws, laws against consumer deception, and pollution control requirements. Thus, the governmental force can be either supportive or restrictive.

The human element is the foundation of business. Business needs people as owners, consumers, employees, and managers. People need business for goods, services, and jobs. It does not matter whether business is conducted in Mexico, Canada, or China. Businesses may be conducted differently, and the objectives of businesses may differ, but the universal element in all business activities is people.

THE HUMAN ELEMENT: THE FOUNDATION OF BUSINESS

Owners

The people who own a business, as well as those who invest some money in a business, do so because they expect to earn a profit. Most of the giant corporations, such as General Motors, Tenneco, General Mills, and Beatrice Foods, are owned by large numbers of people. General Motors has approximately 1.2 million stockholders, and Tenneco has about 232,000. In making decisions, the professional managers in business organizations need to consider the owners and what they expect from the business.

Employees

The employees provide the skills and abilities needed to market a product or service and to earn a profit. Most employees expect to receive an equitable wage or salary and to be given gradual increases in the amount they are paid for the use of their skills and abilities. A business enterprise must have a committed and effective team of employees in order to compete with other businesses.

Consumers

In the American marketplace, the target of business activity is consumers. The business enterprise attempts to satisfy consumer needs and desires while earning a profit. One of the first jobs of the businessperson is to find out what the consumer population needs and desires. Consumers in growing economic systems, such as Japan, West Germany, Canada, and the United States, seem to want more and better products and services. They want better automobiles, better homes, more luxuries, and better leisure equipment.

Because consumers continually want more and better things, new businesses are formed and other businesses make adjustments to accommodate the demand. When there is a need or desire for products or services, a business can earn a profit by supplying it promptly and efficiently. Businesses attempt to keep up with the changes in consumers' needs and desires. This is certainly risky, because consumer wants may change quickly. The uncertainty and risk involved in reading consumer needs and wants provide a challenge to the business decision maker attempting to earn a profit.

Business Managers

The businessperson responsible for operating the business may be the owner (an owner-manager) or may be employed by the owner (a professional manager). One thing both types of business manager have in common is that they seek to achieve the objectives of profit, growth, survival, and social responsibility.

The owner-manager sets his or her own objectives, whereas a professional manager attempts to achieve objectives set by others. The professional manager is responsible and accountable to the owners of the business, who judge the manager's performance by examining how well their objectives have been accomplished over a period of time.

A BRIEF HISTORY OF AMERICAN BUSINESS

You may ask why we should study the history of business and business people. After all, the past is gone and finished. But looking back at the historical development of business and some important business leaders may help us understand business in today's environment. Furthermore, the future directions of business may become clearer if we understand the past.

American business leaders have built the most successful economic system that any nation has had. This success story arises from the three basic freedoms, sufficient natural resources, hard-working and intelligent people, and outstanding business leadership. American business leaders have displayed their talents in organizing businesses, managing human resources, financing business, marketing goods and services, and using information resources. Our country's business leaders are tops because of their ceaseless drive and motivation toward excellence.

Mercantilism

MERCANTILISM
A system of state power with public authority controlling and directing the country's economic life.

To understand the forces behind the founding of the American colonies, one must understand the economic thought of the times. The doctrine of mercantilism stressed the development of a strong economic state. **Mercantilism** is a system of state power, with public authority controlling and directing the nation's economic life. This economic philosophy led the governments of European nations—especially those of England, France, Spain, and Portugal—to do everything possible to increase the power and wealth of the country. The basic tenets of mercantilism were that a nation should:

- Be as self-sufficient as possible.
- Sell more goods to foreigners than were purchased from foreigners in order to increase the mother country's wealth.
- Accumulate gold and silver bullion because these served as a measure of the country's wealth and power.
- Establish colonies, which served as sources of raw materials or precious metals as well as a market for finished goods.

The Wealth of Nations

Adam Smith, a professor at the University of Edinburgh in Scotland in the late 1700s, was one of the most prominent critics of the mercantilist philosophy. Unlike the mercantilists, Smith wanted to place individuals and their needs at the focal point of the economy. He felt that individuals' pursuit of their own best interests would lead a nation to attain its goals. His book *Inquiry into the Nature and Causes of the Wealth of Nations* (1776) presented many of his views. Smith believed:

- People do their best when they reap the rewards of hard work and intelligence and suffer the penalties of laziness. (He favored the use of profits as a means of providing individual incentive and initiative.)
- People should be free to conduct business or seek work that provides them with the greatest reward for their efforts.
- What serves the individual also serves society. The pursuit of individual

self-interest leads to the best allocation of the nation's resources and thus to the maximum satisfaction of people's needs.

The enemy of human freedom at that time was assumed by Smith to be the state—the internationalist, mercantilist government that imposed tariffs, granted monopolies, levied taxes, and above all sought to improve what was best left to itself.[1] So Smith argued for free competition among all producers. But free competition can exist only if the government follows a policy of laissez-faire. This policy encourages government to leave business and the economy alone. Only on rare occasions, in order to prevent monopolies, should a laissez-faire government interfere with the operation of the economy. Instead, the economy is guided by the "invisible hand" of competition. This was the key to Smith's philosophy: if government stayed out of the economy and allowed businesses and consumers to pursue their own best interests, competition among producers would keep prices low while generating the goods demanded by consumers.

Though many of Adam Smith's suggestions have been practiced in the United States, the concept of laissez-faire has generally been rejected. Government officials have ignored Adam Smith's advice that the economy operates best when left alone and have actively sought to improve its operation. Today, government involvement covers numerous areas, including

Price regulation

Truth in advertising

Maintenance of product quality

Highway construction

Regulations of the rates and services of railroads, trucking companies, public utilities, and airlines

Automobile safety, emission, and mileage standards

Pollution standards

Many of these topics are covered in later chapters.

Although what we call the Industrial Revolution began about 1769, it did not make its appearance in America until 1790. In that year, a young apprentice mechanic, Samuel Salter, was able to construct the machinery necessary for the textile mill. His mill in Rhode Island was America's first true factory. When Eli Whitney invented the cotton gin in 1793, the expansion of cotton production was sufficient to support several cotton mills.

Whitney made another significant contribution to the industrialization of America: interchangeable parts. In 1798, he won a contract to build 10,000 muskets for the American government. He immediately set out to build a plant and design the new musket. He first divided the work to be accomplished among his workers (each one specialized in a particular task). Next, he designed highly accurate machinery to make the parts. Because this machinery worked with such great accuracy, it enabled unskilled workers to do the work of skilled workers. Finally, by using templates,

The Industrial Revolution in the United States

he was able to manufacture thousands of interchangeable pieces. In setting up his factory, he used the specialization of labor that Adam Smith had described and, through tight quality control, was able to use unskilled workers to produce a product of high quality.

These were the beginnings of industrial life in the United States, but this changed drastically after the Civil War ended in 1865. Improvements in rail and steamship transportation closed the gap between producer and consumer. It became possible to sell products to a large market scattered over wide geographic areas rather than being restricted to sales in small local markets. In addition, the factory system expanded and began to influence all aspects of life. In fact, America began to shift from a predominantly rural society to an urban one.

To service the expanding markets, a new type of business was necessary. The general store or the small mill could not service a market that was geographically dispersed. It became increasingly evident that only a larger, more efficient business operation could deal with the demands of larger markets. Producers needed better distribution systems, transportation, warehouses, production capabilities, and managerial skills.

The Pre-Depression Years

The period from the end of the nineteenth century to the Great Depression in 1929 were years of growth in the oil, steel, and financial industries. Other industries, such as tobacco, meat, and copper, were also growing. For example, in the early nineteenth century, meat processing had been quite primitive, done either at home or by local butchers. But around the turn of the century, a major industry based on hogs and cattle was created through the business spirit, risk taking, and knowledge of men like Philip Armour, Gustavus Swift, and Michael Cudahy.

The prosperity of the 1920s resulted from a number of factors. One important cause was the profits made in stock market speculation. People were putting money into the stock market, often on credit. They would buy some stock and then use the stock as a security pledge to obtain a loan to buy even more stock. This method worked well when stock prices were increasing. But when prices dropped drastically, as they did in the period following the Black Monday of October 28, 1929, the bottom fell out. The extent of the financial collapse is indicated in Exhibit 1–2. Note, for instance, how Radio Corporation of America lost 98 percent of its stock market value in three years.

The Great Depression

The Depression of 1929 –1941 will be ingrained in the minds of Americans for generations to come. Even today, many decisions made by President Reagan are affected by his experiences during the Depression. The poverty, tragedy, and unemployment that prevailed have had no equal. During the period from October 1929 to the early 1940s, unemployment hit 25 percent of the work force, or about 13 million people; the value of the goods and services produced in the country was cut in half; and stock market prices fell 80 percent. The hopes and dreams that marked the 1920s came suddenly to an end.

Although the crash of the stock market in 1929 was a major factor leading to the Great Depression, other factors helped. These included:

COMPANY	1929 (HIGH)	1932 (LOW)
Consolidated Cigar	$115	$ 2½
Erie Railroad	93½	2
General Foods	82	20
General Motors	91	8
New York Central	256	9
Radio Corporation of America	115	2½
Southern Railway	165	2½
U.S. Steel	261	21
Wright Aeronautical	150	4

From Gordon V. Axon, *The Stock Market Crash of 1929* (New York: Mason and Lipscomb, 1974), pp. 93–94.

EXHIBIT 1-2
Selected Stock Prices in the Depression Era

- The actions of the Federal Reserve System
- Installment buying
- Overproduction of consumer goods and decline in investment
- Speculation

The crash of the stock market came early in the Depression, and its effects were not as significant as the waves of bank failures that were to follow. The first came in October 1930, the second in March 1931, and the third in the last quarter of 1932.[2] In each case, banks failed because investors panicked. In the poor business climate, investors became fearful that the banks would collapse and stood in lines to withdraw their funds. Because banks did not (and still don't) keep on hand 100 percent of the cash that is deposited (they make loans to other people with the money of their depositors), they could not pay back all their depositors at once and thus went bankrupt. Millions of Americans lost their life savings in the bank failures.

The New Deal Years

When Franklin D. Roosevelt became president of the United States in 1933, the economic system of the Western world was paralyzed. One-fourth of the workers in the United States were unemployed, production of goods and services was down by half, and corporate profits were off by two-thirds. Roosevelt made America's economic problems the focal point for both domestic and foreign policy. The policies of the New Deal centered in two areas: unemployment and banking reform.

Solving the unemployment problem proved very difficult. Roosevelt proposed, and Congress passed, a series of acts dubbed the alphabet acts because everyone referred to them by their initials. The National Industrial Recovery Act (NIRA), for example, brought labor, management, and consumers together to set prices and wages and to regulate output. The New Deal policies of Roosevelt seemed to work, but 20 percent of the work force, or almost 9 million Americans, were still unemployed in 1939.

World War II and the Postwar Period

It wasn't until the start of World War II that the nation's economic troubles started to ease up. Unfortunately, economic problems were replaced by wartime fears.

War production meant that Uncle Sam was the principal consumer of goods. Various industries modified their facilities to produce tanks, weapons, tools, military clothing, airplanes, ships, and other wartime equipment. The government's total wartime expenditure (1941–1945) was about $347 billion. As a result, such consumer goods as shoes, tires, clothing, gasoline, and meat became scarce and had to be rationed.

After World War II, there was some fear that peace would again bring depression. But these fears were unfounded. The economy continued to expand because of:

■ A backed-up demand for consumer goods resulting from the limits placed on consumption during the war
■ Built-up purchasing power resulting from individual savings during the war
■ Plant and equipment expansions created by the war
■ An efficient and ready-to-work labor force
■ The population explosion during the ten years following the war
■ The emergence of new or modernized industries and processes—natural gas, plastics, electronics, data processing, aluminum, and aeronautics

The 1950s to the Present

RECESSION
When the level of economic activity declines for at least a six-month period.

INFLATION
The rise in the average level of prices for all goods and services in a particular time period.

In the 1950s, the economy continued to expand. There were four recessions during the 1950s and 1960s, but they were mild. When the level of economic activity declines for at least a six-month period, the economy is said to be in **recession**. Employment and the production of goods and services are generally down during a recession. It was during the 1950–1982 period that Americans enjoyed new shopping malls, high-technology consumer goods such as microwave ovens, new educational opportunities, improved health care, and many other new commodities and services. At the same time, Americans became quite familiar with the term **inflation**, which refers to a period of rising prices, or a decline in the purchasing power of the dollar (the dollar buys less).

In the 1960s and 1970s, the government examined the inflation problems facing citizens and began to play a larger role in the economy. The New Frontier of President John F. Kennedy and the Great Society of President Lyndon B. Johnson meant more government involvement in business. A major part of the New Frontier concept was the notion of cutting personal income tax to stimulate consumption, investment, and employment and to hold inflation at a reasonable level. The Great Society programs included providing medical aid to older Americans, improving product safety, and improving housing. These programs meant that the federal government poured more dollars into the economy. Even President Reagan's New Federalism involves more government spending. Through these and other programs, the government has become more involved in business.

THE BOOK'S FORMAT

The seven distinct parts of the book are portrayed in Exhibit 1–3. Part One will set the tone for the rest of the book. Chapter 2 presents the economic foundation for American business. Chapter 3 examines the relationship of business, government, and society. Part Two discusses forms of business

THE FORMAT OF *INTRODUCTION TO BUSINESS*

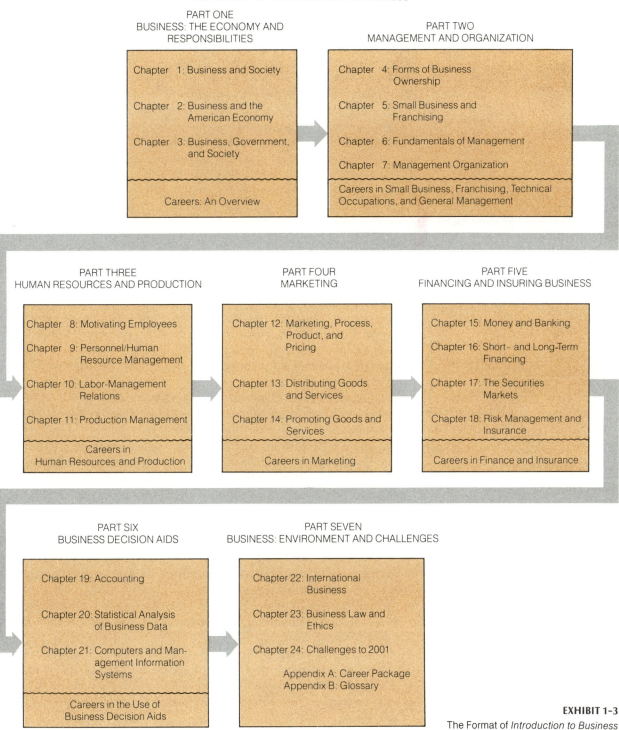

PART ONE
BUSINESS: THE ECONOMY AND
RESPONSIBILITIES

Chapter   1: Business and Society

Chapter   2: Business and the
American Economy

Chapter   3: Business, Government,
and Society

Careers: An Overview

PART TWO
MANAGEMENT AND ORGANIZATION

Chapter   4: Forms of Business
Ownership

Chapter   5: Small Business and
Franchising

Chapter   6: Fundamentals of Management

Chapter   7: Management Organization

Careers in Small Business, Franchising, Technical
Occupations, and General Management

PART THREE
HUMAN RESOURCES AND PRODUCTION

Chapter   8: Motivating Employees

Chapter   9: Personnel/Human
Resource Management

Chapter 10: Labor-Management
Relations

Chapter 11: Production Management

Careers in
Human Resources and Production

PART FOUR
MARKETING

Chapter 12: Marketing, Process,
Product, and
Pricing

Chapter 13: Distributing Goods
and Services

Chapter 14: Promoting Goods and
Services

Careers in Marketing

PART FIVE
FINANCING AND INSURING BUSINESS

Chapter 15: Money and Banking

Chapter 16: Short- and Long-Term
Financing

Chapter 17: The Securities
Markets

Chapter 18: Risk Management and
Insurance

Careers in Finance and Insurance

PART SIX
BUSINESS DECISION AIDS

Chapter 19: Accounting

Chapter 20: Statistical Analysis
of Business Data

Chapter 21: Computers and Management Information
Systems

Careers in the Use of
Business Decision Aids

PART SEVEN
BUSINESS: ENVIRONMENT AND CHALLENGES

Chapter 22: International
Business

Chapter 23: Business Law and
Ethics

Chapter 24: Challenges to 2001

Appendix A: Career Package
Appendix B: Glossary

EXHIBIT 1-3
The Format of *Introduction to Business*

and management and organizations. In Part Three human resources issues such as motivation, personnel, and labor-management relations and production are discussed. Part Four covers marketing in business. Part Five addresses the financial aspects of business. Part Six analyzes accounting, statistical procedures, and computers and management information systems. Finally, Part Seven describes the international aspect of business law and ethics and the future directions of the American business system.

These parts and the supplemental materials accompanying the book are intended to help the reader become more aware of business in our society. We are the ones who permit businesses to operate. Therefore, our awareness and understanding of business enterprise is essential.

SUMMARY

- Business involves the exchange of goods, services, or money for mutual benefit.
- The main objectives of businesses are to survive, grow, and meet their social responsibilities.
- Profits are important to business. Profits represent the difference between the money received from selling a product and all the costs, including taxes, involved in making the product.
- Many forces influence the business environment and include social factors, economic factors, technology, and governments. These forces are all external to any business enterprise.
- The human element is the foundation of business because people make things happen in business. Owners, employees, consumers, and managers are the key human elements in business.
- The growth of the American economy and business in general has not been smooth. Many events have had an impact on American business, including the Industrial Revolution, the Great Depression, the New Deal, World War II, and the Vietnam War. Events such as strong economic growth, high inflation rates, and high unemployment rates are all related to these important events.

ISSUES TO CONSIDER AND ANALYZE

1. Why is business more complex today than a hundred years ago?
2. What should a business owner's profit amount be? Should there be a set amount of profit for a business?
3. Examine some industries and determine the average or typical profit margins for business owners.
4. Mercantilism as an economic doctrine was attacked by Adam Smith in 1776. Do any elements of the mercantilist philosophy remain in the United States?
5. Adam Smith felt that government was responsible for creating monopolies. Can you think of any monopolies in America that were not created by the government?
6. Do you think America could have another Great Depression? Why or why not?
7. Why are people the main element to consider when discussing business?
8. What were the objectives and the result of the New Deal?
9. Is business profit or economic profit the way you look at profits? Why?
10. Provide some examples of government involvement in business.

NABISCO PLUS STANDARD BRANDS EQUALS FOOD COLOSSUS

CASE FOR ANALYSIS

Business constantly changes. Some businesses grow, and other businesses die as the conditions under which they operate change. Often businesses must change just to survive. However, some change because change is to their benefit. This is the reason Nabisco and Standard Brands merged in July 1981 to form Nabisco Brands, America's fourth-largest food processor, with sales of $5.8 billion.

In style and way of doing business, the two companies were considered completely different. Nabisco was an old-line American company that was viewed as stodgy. Standard Brands, on the other hand, was considered youthful and slick. Some executives said the marriage could not work. In fact, there were occasional eruptions, and some executives did leave. As Chairman of the Board Robert Schoeberle said, "Not everybody can grow in our flowerpot."

Even so, the two companies had much in common. Each owned some of America's best known food products: Ritz crackers, Oreo cookies, Planter's peanuts, and Baby Ruth candy bars. The companies even had the same customers, the same form of advertising using the same theme, and the same type of promotions. Perhaps this is why the merger was so successful: it was logical and natural, and, in the opinion of Nabisco Brands, consumers would benefit. First of all, the merged company is more streamlined and has more efficient distribution methods. This helps to hold food prices down because distribution costs are lower. Some product lines were consolidated, and only the strongest selling brands survived. The merger and these changes made it easier for food stores to deal with company salespeople and reduced retailer costs.

There were many opportunities for the new company to capitalize on the respective strengths of the two individual companies. For example, Standard Brands is very strong in certain international markets, for example, Latin America. Nabisco products can now be introduced into these mass growth markets very quickly. On the other hand, Nabisco is strong in European and Japanese markets, which often take years to develop. Standard Brands can piggyback on Nabisco's strength in Europe and Japan and enter these markets quickly. The "new" company is an economic giant and moving force in both international and domestic food markets. The combined company can penetrate these two markets more quickly than if each had to start from scratch.

New product introductions should increase because of Standard Brands' outstanding research department, yet Nabisco has the distribution to get these new products to consumers, with three thousand direct salespeople to move products into grocery stores. There is probably no food market the new company will not be able to penetrate. Together, they may become the world's leader in food processing in the next decade. By combining their strengths, the new company—Nabisco Brands—is bigger and richer.

Adapted from "Stodgy Nabisco, Slick Standard Brands Mesh vs Food Colossus," *Houston Chronicle,* April 9, 1982.

QUESTIONS

1. Do you agree that consumers can benefit from the merger of the two companies into Nabisco Brands? Explain your answer.
2. What do you think would be the objectives of the "new" company?

CHAPTER 2

BUSINESS AND THE AMERICAN ECONOMY

LEARNING OBJECTIVES

After studying this chapter, you should be able to:

Explain the meaning of the term *economics.*

Identify various types of economic resources.

Discuss how people's needs and wants are met.

Compare different economic systems.

Explain why profits are important to business.

Discuss the role of entrepreneurs in the American economy.

KEY TERMS

Economics
Natural resources
Capital resources
Labor resources
Needs
Wants
Economic system
Communism
Profit motive
Socialism
Capitalism
Profit
Resource markets
Product markets
Gross national product
Inflation
Productivity
Profit
Profit motive
Entrepreneurs

FRESH SHOP SUPERMARKET, INC.

Jose Guerra managed a large Los Angeles supermarket for fifteen years. During that time he determined that about 60 percent of his customers bought their groceries in one store and their fresh foods in another. Guerra believed that a speciality supermarket featuring only quality fresh foods and providing first-class service could make a good profit. He decided to open such a specialty supermarket with four departments: delicatessen, bakery, meats, and produce. Prices would be competitive with regular supermarkets.

Guerra was certain he had a good idea, but he was uncertain about how to acquire the money needed to open Fresh Shop Supermarket. He initially needed about $65,000 for operating expenses and $240,000 for inventory and display equipment. Guerra believed in his idea enough to invest his total savings of $55,000. It was not enough just to have a good idea. Guerra had to believe in his idea enough to sell other people, so they would be willing to invest their money in the project too. The remainder of the necessary money was provided by five Los Angeles investors, each

of whom was given part ownership in Fresh Shop Supermarket, Inc. Like Guerra, these investors took a risk, hoping they would make a profit in the new business.

Fresh Shop Supermarket was started to meet the needs and wants of shoppers desiring first-class service. In making the decision to open the store, Guerra became an entrepreneur—that is, he put up part of the money needed to start the business. The individual entrepreneur has played, and continues to play, an important role in the growth of the American economy.

Understanding economics is important for every person. High taxes, unemployment, and high prices are only a few economic issues that are headlines in today's news. Each of these issues affects us directly. For example, citizens are constantly asked to pay increasing taxes to support government programs and national defense efforts. Because most people must work for money to provide a living, unemployment creates serious economic problems. Retired people often have trouble meeting their living expenses because their retirement income does not keep up with rising prices. Each of these three different situations illustrates the importance of economics in our daily life.

Though no single definition of economics satisfies everyone, a concise understandable definition is:

Economics is the study of how a society (people) chooses to use scarce resources to produce goods and services and allocate them to people for their consumption.

This definition raises certain key points that are important to understanding economics. These key points are (1) using scarce resources, (2) producing goods and services, and (3) allocation.

A nation's resources are divided into three broad areas: natural, capital, and labor. **Natural resources** are provided by nature in limited amounts; they include crude oil, natural gas, minerals, timber, and water. Natural resources must be processed before becoming a product or being used to produce other goods or services. For example, trees must be processed into lumber before they can be used to build homes, shopping malls, and schools.

Capital resources are goods produced for the purpose of making other types of goods and services. Some capital resources, called *working capital,* have a short life and are used up in the production process. They include fuel, raw materials, paper, and money. Long-life capital resources, which can be used repeatedly in the production process, are called *fixed capital.* Examples of fixed capital resources are factory buildings, record-pressing machines, electronic computers, and railroad cars. Jose Guerra needed both working capital and fixed capital to open Fresh Shop Supermarket, Inc.

Labor resources represent the human talent of a nation. To be of value in the labor force, individuals must be trained to perform either skilled or semiskilled work. For example, some people must have extensive training to be mechanical engineers, whereas others need only a little training to operate a gasoline station pump. This collection of human talent is the most valuable national resource. Without human resources, there would be no productive use of either natural or capital resources.

AN OVERVIEW OF ECONOMICS

ECONOMICS
The study of how a society chooses to use scarce resources to produce goods and services and physically distribute them to people for consumption.

National Resources

NATURAL RESOURCES
Economic resources provided by nature in limited amounts. They must be processed before being used to produce goods and services or being made into a product.

CAPITAL RESOURCES
Goods produced for the purpose of making other types of goods and services.

LABOR RESOURCES
A nation's human talent; people making up the labor force.

Needs and Wants

NEEDS
Goods and services people must have to exist.

WANTS
Goods and services people would like to have but do not need for survival.

A nation's resources are used to meet people's needs and wants. **Needs** are goods and services people must have simply to exist. **Wants**, on the other hand, are things they would like to have but do not absolutely need for survival. Such items as food, clothing, shelter, and medical care are needs; video recorders, cassettes, fashionable clothes, and luxury vacations are wants.

A person's wants can be unlimited; as soon as one want is satisfied, another one is created. Even wealthy people tend to have unlimited wants. Henry Ford was once asked how much money it would take before a person would stop wanting more. He reportedly answered, "Just a little bit more."

Considering that people have many vital needs plus an almost unlimited list of wants, is it possible to satisfy all of the population's needs and wants? The answer is *no*. It is an economic fact that a nation's resources are limited. We all know, for example, that the supply of oil and natural gas in the United States is a limited natural resource. Even the amount of capital resources, such as corporate stocks and bonds that can be raised during a specific time, is limited.

Because we live in a world in which the quantity of all resources is limited, we must make choices about how these scarce resources are to be used. To make these choices, we have to answer three fundamental economic questions:

- *What goods and services will be produced, and in what quantities?* What industrial goods and what consumer goods will be produced? Apartments or new houses? Railroad cars or large trucks?
- *How will goods and services be produced, and by whom?* For instance, will energy be produced from coal, natural gas, or nuclear power?
- *Who will use the goods and services?* When the goods and services are divided, who is to benefit from their use? Rich or poor? Families or single people? Old or young?

These questions are basic to the operation of any economy. The answers depend on the roles of free enterprise and government in the economy and on the nation's political system, which greatly influences the economic system of a nation. Answers to these three basic questions provide a picture of how a nation's economic system works.

COMPARING ECONOMIC SYSTEMS

ECONOMIC SYSTEM
The process by which labor, capital, and natural resources are organized to produce and distribute goods and services.

An **economic system** is the manner in which labor, capital, and natural resources are organized to produce and allocate goods and services to meet people's needs and wants. The three major economic systems today are communism, socialism, and capitalism. Often these words are used incorrectly to refer to political systems. These are economic systems that are influenced by political systems. In general, the politics that influence each system are too broad to discuss in detail in this book; however, we will look at the three economic systems briefly.

When a government is run by a single political party that owns and controls all of a nation's economic resources, the system is called **communism**. This system is often referred to as *social ownership of property,* meaning that individual ownership is denied and there is a community sharing of all wealth. All important economic decisions are made by a government-controlled central planning unit. Consumers usually can buy what they want when goods are available, but they have no say about what goods will be made available.

What is called communism today is not what was called communism in the nineteenth century. Today's version is more a form of socialism ruled by a single political group, the Communist Party. In the USSR and the People's Republic of China, the world's two largest communist countries, there is limited private ownership of property, including land. In a communist economy there is seldom any direct competition among businesses, nor is there a strong public emphasis on earning a profit. Nevertheless, the **profit motive** is used in communism to make the economic system work better. "Profits" are used to expand the nation's capital and to provide the economic incentive needed for managers and workers to exceed government-set production quotas.

Like communism, **socialism** stresses government ownership of economic resources and coordinated economic planning. However, there are several important differences. First, socialism may permit private ownership of some basic industries, with strict government controls. Normally, however, basic industries—for example, steel, electronics, coal, and communications—are owned by the government. Smaller businesses are owned by individuals. Second, the marketplace is used to supplement government planning of production and distribution. This means that, through purchases in the marketplace, consumers can influence decisions about what goods and services will be produced. Governments currently using forms of socialism include France, Sweden, West Germany, and the United Kingdom.

A third major economic system is **capitalism**, or private enterprise. The system is characterized by private ownership of capital, freedom of economic choice, and competition among businesses seeking a profit. Under capitalism, consumers play an important role in economic decision making through their purchases in the marketplace. Their purchases in effect represent "economic votes" for products sold in the economic system.

A capitalistic system guarantees certain basic rights. One is the right to private ownership of capital such as land, buildings, and inventions. This *right to private property* is often considered the most basic right of capitalism. Because of private ownership, an individual also has the right to any income produced by the property.

Two other important rights of capitalism are freedom of choice and freedom of enterprise. *Freedom of choice* means that people have the right to buy or to reject any product, and to decide where to work and whether or not to invest. Thus, people cast economic votes every time they make

Communism

COMMUNISM
A type of economic system in which the government run by a single political party controls all of a nation's economic resources.

PROFIT MOTIVE
The willingness to risk time and money in business ventures with the hope of making a profit.

Socialism

SOCIALISM
A type of economic system that stresses government ownership of economic resources and coordinated economic planning.

Capitalism

CAPITALISM
One type of economic system, often called free enterprise or private enterprise. It is characterized by private ownership of capital and competition among businesses seeking a profit.

PROFIT
The difference between business income (revenue) and business expenses (costs); what is left after all costs of making and selling a product, including taxes, are subtracted from its selling price.

economic decisions in the free market. *Freedom of enterprise* means that businesses and individuals with the capital may enter essentially any legal business venture they wish. This important feature of capitalism permits individuals to seek out profit-making business opportunities.

Any business or individual can earn a profit under capitalism if a useful good or service is produced. **Profit** is what is left when all the costs of making and selling a product, including taxes, are subtracted from its selling price. Businesses and individuals do not have a *right* to make a profit. Profit is a reward to a business for using scarce economic resources efficiently. Consumers must consider a good or service reasonable in price, quality, and value before a profit can be made.

Competition is yet another important part of capitalism. Businesses must compete in the free market with other firms selling the same product or similar products. Because of competition for consumer dollars, businesses have to be aware of what consumers want to buy. If they ignore consumer wishes, they are likely to lose sales, which directly affects the amount of business profits. If a business consistently loses money and makes no profit, it will fail and close its doors. Consequently, competition among businesses generally provides consumers with lower prices, more services, and improved products. The 1982 ticket price wars in the airline industry are an example of how fierce competition among businesses can grow.

Capitalism is the economic system found in the United States, although the U.S. economy is not pure capitalism. A more apt description of the system is "mixed" capitalism. Capitalism becomes mixed when government establishes operating guidelines and laws for businesses to follow. For example, one important federal law requires a variety of safety rules to be followed on construction jobs. The economic system is also mixed when government competes directly with business. Governments can compete with businesses in such areas as medical research, electric power generation, and communication. The United States Postal Service is an example of a government business that competes with private businesses like Federal Express and United Parcel Service.

The form of economic system that is most appropriate for a nation depends on several things, including cultural factors and the level of available economic resources. It is unlikely that capitalism would be appropriate for a nation with a low level of education, limited capital, and few natural resources. Capitalism normally works best with an educated people capable of making their own economic decisions. In fact, capitalism encourages people to take the initiative to become better educated and to make their own decisions.

Exhibit 2–1 summarizes major features of the three economic systems we have discussed. Exhibit 2–2 presents a comparison of the American and Soviet economies. The various economic measures used show that, on balance, the American economy outproduces the Soviet economy.

THE AMERICAN ECONOMY

The American economy began to develop shortly after the landing of the *Mayflower*. It was largely a barter economy. For example, farmers traded tobacco and potatoes for the services of a blacksmith. Bartering was com-

CHUCK E. CHEESE AND THE SINGING ROBOTS

In 1972, with $500 capital, Nolan Bushnell started a company named Atari. The company's product was a video game called Pong. Bushnell's interest in video games originated when he was an engineering student at the University of Utah. By 1975 a home version of Pong was developed, and Sears Roebuck & Company bought 100,000 games. A few months later Atari was bought by Warner Communications, and Bushnell personally received around $15 million in cash and debentures.

The entrepreneurial spirit of Nolan Bushnell has surfaced again in a company called Pizza Time Theater, Inc. The concept combines fast foods and electronics in a self-service pizza parlor that doubles as a game arcade.

Adapted from Peter W. Bernstein, ''Atari and the Video-Game Explosion,'' *Fortune*, July 27, 1981, pp. 40–46.

While people wait for their pizza, they may plug quarters into video game machines located in the arcade. In addition to the games, Pizza Time Theater, Inc. features a stage show of singing computerized rubber robots every eight minutes. One of the featured robots is a rat called Chuck E. Cheese. Others include Harmony Howlette, a country-and-western coyote who sounds like Loretta Lynn, and a French Pig named Madame Oink.

In 1981 there were forty-four Pizza Time Theater locations. Bushnell, with an eye on the future, expects to have a thousand restaurants in operation by 1985. In fact, Bushnell predicts that someday Chuck E. Cheese will be better known than Mickey Mouse. This is not an unreasonable ambition for an entrepreneur who turned $500 into a personal fortune of around $70 million in ten years.

mon because colonial America did not have an acceptable money system. What money the settlers had returned to England to pay for goods bought from England, leaving the colonies ''money poor.'' To help solve this problem, the settlers tried substitutes for money. Goods and farm commodities were given fixed economic values, resulting in what was called *commodity money*. But the commodity money system didn't work well, and bartering became the widely accepted method of exchange.

By the middle 1700s, major economic activity in America consisted primarily of fur trading, agriculture, shipbuilding, fishing, banking, and land speculation. During the American Industrial Revolution in the mid-1800s, the economy became industrialized, and agriculture began to use machines for farming. New machines were developed, large ships were built, ship canals were dredged, and railroads were constructed on a massive scale.

During the early 1900s, the United States became one of the world's leading industrial powers. With World Wars I and II, the nation developed into the most powerful economic system in the world. In the period since World War II, rapid technological development made the economy increasingly complex. Technology made it possible for the United States to land people on the moon, to build powerful electronic computers, and to develop laser surgery techniques for the human eye and brain, among other accomplishments.

ECONOMIC CHARACTERISTIC	COMMUNISM	SOCIALISM	CAPITALISM
Ownership of productive resources	Business is owned and managed by the state.	Basic industries are state owned, with individuals owning many smaller businesses.	Most businesses are owned by individuals.
National economic goals	Goals are set by state-controlled central planning agencies.	Some goals are set by private business, but goals for basic industries are determined by the government.	Goals are determined by consumers and individual businesses in a competitive marketplace. Government involvement is limited.
Role of consumer	Consumer choice is limited by state control of prices and income earned.	Consumers have to accept market prices set by the government and are constrained by wage guidelines.	Consumers are free to buy whatever is available and are limited only by their income, their credit, and the availability of products.
Role of workers	Choice of job is limited by the state, and all wages are set by the state. Workers have no right to strike.	Workers may choose a job in a government or industry, or own or work in a smaller business. The right to strike is often limited.	Workers may choose where to work. They have freedom to strike in most cases.
Major advantages	The nation's economic resources can be used for a limited number of national goals. Wages are held down so the state can build more capital. Employment is stable because almost all people are assigned government-controlled jobs.	Unemployment is low because people can be put to work in government-owned businesses or work programs. There is relatively direct control of the nation's economic resources.	Individuals are free to try a new job or enter a business to make a profit. Financial and social rewards can be great for a person who is successful.
Major disadvantages	No incentive for the individual to be creative or to take a financial risk. Limited choices are available to labor, consumers, and management. The economic system is inefficient.	A low incentive in government-owned businesses for workers to be highly productive. Economic inefficiency is not uncommon.	Economic growth is not stable and moves in cycles. Competition in business creates some economic waste. Unemployment may be relatively high because of limited government jobs.

EXHIBIT 2-1
Major Economic Systems

EXHIBIT 2-2
A Comparison of Two Economies—
U.S.A. and U.S.S.R.

FACTOR/PRODUCT	MEASURE	U.S.A.	U.S.S.R.
Gross national product	Dollars	$2.9 trillion	$1.4 trillion
Population	—	230 million	268 million
Energy use per person	Tons of coal	12.4	6.1
Computer products sold	Dollars	$58.2 billion	$9.2 billion
Oil production	Barrels/day	8.6 million	12.8 million
Steel production	Metric tons	100.8 million	148.0 million
Autos produced	—	6.4 million	1.3 million
Farm workers	% of work force	3 percent	24 percent
Meat produced per person	Pounds	256	126
Grain produced per person	Pounds	2552	1571

Adapted from "Communism: The Great Economic Failure," *U.S. News & World Report*, March 1, 1982, p. 33.

The United States has developed the world's largest economy. To understand the basic parts of the American economy we can look at the model in Exhibit 2–3. This model is a simplification of our real economic system, including only the broadest parts of the economy. It does not include the government.

Look at Exhibit 2–3 and note the difference between resource markets and product markets. **Resource markets** are places where economic resources—natural, labor, technology, and capital—are bought and sold. The New York Stock Exchange where money is invested in companies, is a capital resource market. The employment ads in local newspapers are another example of a resource market, where labor is bought and sold. **Product markets** are the thousands of markets in America where the outputs of business—goods and services—are sold to consumers. Consumers pay for goods and services with money. This type of consumer expenditure is called *retail sales*. Money payments that businesses receive from retail sales are their business revenue.

Where do consumers get the money to spend for goods and services? Exhibit 2–3 shows that consumer households supply economic resources to the resource markets. People provide labor through work, invest their money in businesses (capital), and sell natural resources to businesses in return for money. The money paid to people for these economic resources is what they use to purchase goods and services. To businesses, however, money paid to consumers is an expense.

Two distinct types of economic resource flows are illustrated in Exhibit 2–3. The flow of economic resources and products is shown by the inner circle. The inner circle flows counterclockwise, showing that economic

How Does the Economy Work?

RESOURCE MARKETS
Places where economic resources are bought and sold.

PRODUCT MARKETS
Places where consumers and businesses buy the output of businesses.

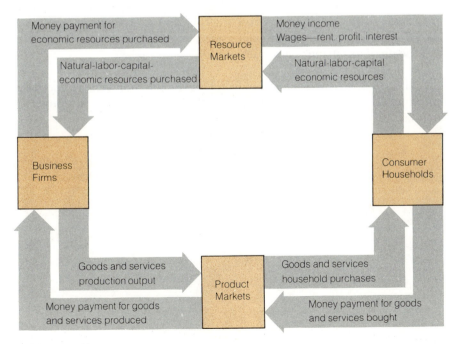

EXHIBIT 2–3
Flow of Money and Products in the American Economy

resources move from consumers to businesses and then return to consumers as finished goods and services. Money flow, on the other hand, is shown by the outer circle. This clockwise flow of money begins when firms pay consumers for the economic resource they purchase. Consumers use their money to purchase the goods and services produced by businesses. These two economic flows take place continuously and at the same time. As long as consumers spend all their money, the flow of money into and out of consumer households is equal.

This simple model does not address all facets of a capitalist economy. For example, the model does not show that some consumers save part of their income. And it has no way to account for high inflation and high unemployment rates. In reality, it takes both government intervention and the action of free markets to help correct these two major economic problems.

What Does the Economy Produce?

GROSS NATIONAL PRODUCT
GNP represents the total money value of all goods and services produced by a nation during a specific time period.

The American economy produces thousands of different types of goods and services, ranging from electronic games, jet aircraft, skyscrapers, homes, and autos to open-heart surgery, sporting events, and rock concerts. How well the American economy works as it produces these goods and services can be determined partly from the **gross national product** (GNP). The GNP represents the total money value of all goods and services produced in a specific time period. Dividing GNP by total population yields a per-capita GNP. A country with a high per-capita GNP is usually better off economically than one with a low per-capita GNP.

Exhibit 2–4 shows America's per-capita GNP for various years since 1950 in current dollars. Current dollars means the per-capita GNP is not adjusted for inflation. Inflation is the rise in the average level of prices for all goods and services in a particular time period. Since 1929, per-capita GNP has increased almost fourteen times. During the same period, the population has approximately doubled. Because the economy is expanding faster than the population is growing, America's standard of living and the economic well-being of its citizens continues to rise.

Current Economic Concerns

Even though America's standard of living is high, inflation and productivity are important economic concerns. These two concerns can combine to seriously lower our nation's standard of living.

EXHIBIT 2–4
Per-Capita GNP for Selected Years
(current dollars)

Year	GNP (IN BILLIONS)	POPULATION (IN THOUSANDS)	PER-CAPITA GNP
1950	$ 286.5	152,271	$ 1,882
1960	506.5	180,671	2,803
1970	992.7	204,879	4,845
1976	1,718.0	215,152	7,985
1977	1,918.0	216,880	8,844
1978	2,156.1	218,717	9,858
1979	2,413.9	220,584	10,943
1980	2,627.4	227,020	11,573
1981	2,925.5	224,950	13,005

When the price of food, gasoline, or medical service goes up, that is not necessarily bad. After all, a higher price means more money for someone. It is bad, however, when the general level of all prices goes up. That is inflation, meaning that everybody's money buys fewer goods and services. For example, a family of four earning $10,000 in 1970 had to earn $22,477 in 1981 to maintain their 1970 buying power. The amount of money soared, creating an illusion that people almost always improve their standard of living. However, actual buying power did not increase.

Productivity is one way to help control inflation. **Productivity** is a measure of the relationship between what is produced and what is used to produce it—in other words, the relation of output to input. When a person produces more output with the same amount of input, that represents a gain in productivity. Productive workers can be paid more wages without causing inflation because they are producing more. Traditionally, America has had a high productivity growth rate—at least until the 1970s. Then our productivity growth rate slowed at a time when inflation rates started rising. These two factors have combined to seriously affect our economy and our standard of living. Exhibit 2–5 shows how America's productivity growth rate compared with that of other industrialized nations between 1973 and 1978. The only nation with a lower productivity growth rate was the United Kingdom (0.3 percent). This trend must be reversed if America is to strengthen its economy, improve the quality of life of its citizens, and compete with other nations in world business.

PRODUCTIVITY
A measure of the relationship between what is produced and what is used to produce it (output/input).

Even with inflation and productivity problems, it is fair to conclude that America's economy is large and expanding. But how has this particular country become the dominant economic power of the world? Many factors played a part. First, North America has an abundance of natural resources. Second, the industriousness of the people who settled America was important. But perhaps most important was the profit motive.

The profit motive means that people are willing to risk their time and money in a business venture with the idea that they might make a profit. Profit is the difference between a business's income and its expenses. When expenses are greater than income, there is no profit. Millions of individuals invest money in stocks, bonds, small businesses, and franchises with the hope of earning a profit. The profit motive is central to the operation of America's economic system. Yet profit is one of the most misunderstood aspects of capitalism.

Profit is a valuable source of new capital that is used to build new plants and buy machinery. For example, U.S. Steel is constructing a new mill in Pennsylvania to meet steel demand in 1985. This new mill will require about $3 billion of new money or capital investment. U.S. Steel borrowed the $3 billion to build the steel mill and will repay the loan from the profits it expects to make from the mill. This means that, out of each dollar of profit, U.S. Steel may spend twenty-five cents to repay the loan.

In addition to new plant construction and plant expansions, profit helps to pay for the development of new products, technological innovations,

THE PROFIT MOTIVE

EXHIBIT 2–5
International Comparison of Productivity Growth Rates 1973–1978

COUNTRY	AVERAGE ANNUAL PERCENTAGE INCREASE
United States	1.5
Belgium	6.3
Canada	2.8
Denmark	4.5
France	5.1
Germany	5.1
Italy	2.5
Japan	3.3
United Kingdom	0.3

Source: Productivity Perspectives (Houston: American Productivity Center, 1980), p. 44.

THAT'S PRODUCTIVITY

People have worn stockings for thousands of years, so it would be easy to assume there was no way left for manufacturers to improve production. Not so, at least in the American hose industry! Even though technology in the industry has remained essentially unchanged for centuries, American manufacturers increased their productivity by 13 percent in 1980.

In the 1970s innovations in raw materials and manufacturing literally transformed the $4.6 billion industry into a semiautomated, highly competitive state. Over one-third of the manufacturers and workers have left the industry

Adapted from Gwen Kinkead, "Socko Productivity," *Fortune*, September 1980, pp. 72–74.

since 1970. At the same time, productivity increased 200 percent. High-speed machines were substituted for both people and old equipment. Industry capacity doubled, but with half the machines and the same number of people. New machines produce a leg-shaped panty-hose every 75 seconds just to meet the consumer demand of 1 billion pairs a year.

All of these gains in productivity have helped keep the price of panty-hose down. In 1971, a pair of panty-hose cost $1.10. In 1981, the average price was $1.09. More than anything else, the sheer magic of high-speed knitting has turned the hosiery industry into a productivity champion that benefits the consumer.

and the creation of new jobs. In fact, creating new jobs for workers is one of the most important things that profits do. Without profits, businesses would not expand and create new jobs. Profits from private companies have also been used to redevelop large downtown areas of such major cities as Chicago, Dallas, Detroit, Houston, New York, Phoenix, and San Francisco. The development of the Houston Center in downtown Houston (Exhibit 2–6) is an example. When completed in 1990, this urban development will have used about $3 billion of private capital to redevelop thirty city blocks of land.

Some people raise objections to businesses making a profit, whereas others feel that business firms should be able to make as large a profit as possible. One solution is for a business to make a "fair and reasonable profit." The problem is to determine exactly what is fair and reasonable. Most American businesses presently make a profit of about a nickel or less on every dollar of sales. Is that fair and reasonable? Congress faced this issue when drafting legislation for a national energy policy. Much of the controversy involved the price that oil companies could charge for natural gas and oil. Congress passed a "windfall profits," or excess profits, tax to hold profits down. But what is a excess profit to one person is not to another. It is unlikely that the controversy can ever be resolved to everyone's satisfaction. The important point is that we must accept the idea of profit, at some level, if America's economic system is to continue providing jobs for people.

EXHIBIT 2–6
The Houston Center, a Joint Venture between Cadillac Fairview Urban Development, Inc., and Texas Eastern Corporation

The profit motive encourages **entrepreneurs**, people who set up and manage a business and assume the financial risks involved in an effort to make a profit. This is exactly what Jose Guerra did when he raised the money needed to open Fresh Shop Supermarket. Businesses started by entrepreneurs are normally small and are likely to produce special types of goods or services. This is the type of business Atari was when Nolan Bushnell started it in 1972. By concentrating on a special niche in the market, such as video games, entrepreneurs can compete in an economy dominated by large corporations. Another example is the group of small, special-service computer companies that now prosper alongside the computer-industry giants. Apple Computer is an example of these businesses that provide smaller computers, special services, and component parts that complement the products of large computer companies.

In the short economic history of America, there have been millions of entrepreneurs. Entrepreneurs have had significant impact on the shape of the economy and our quality of life. Many entrepreneurs, on the basis of a single new idea or invention, have started a business that eventually grew into a corporate giant. Some well-known entrepreneurs of this type include B.F. Goodrich (rubber industry), Henry Ford (automotive industry), John D. Rockefeller (oil refining), and Richard Sears (retailing). The past actions of other entrepreneurs, although not as well known, could touch your life now.

Consider the man on a family vacation who could find no convenient, reasonably priced lodging near the highway. Thinking other travelers would patronize a system of motels located near exits on the nation's new interstate highway system, Kemmons Wilson borrowed money and built the first Holiday Inn. From this single motel, Holiday Inns has become the world's largest hotel corporation.

ENTREPRENEURS AND PRIVATE ENTERPRISE

ENTREPRENEURS
People who set up and manage a business and assume the financial risks involved in the effort to make a profit.

On the Job Revisited

In June 1980, Robert E. "Ted" Turner started the Cable News Network (CNN) in Atlanta. Turner raised over $60 million from investors and banks to start a business that would compete with established, well-financed corporations. The risks in this new venture were very great, but the possible rewards were also very great. Turner currently needs over $2 million a month to pay CNN's employees and other operating costs until cable subscribers are great enough to sustain the network. Even if CNN should prove to be a colossal failure, Ted Turner is an entrepreneur and risk taker setting the trend for television news in the future. With the growth in cable television, however, it is not likely CNN will fail.

Entrepreneurs are not always successful. Consider the case of Clarence Saunders, who developed the idea of a self-service supermarket. In 1916 Saunders opened the first Piggly Wiggly store, a venture that made many millions of dollars for him and other people during the 1920s. The stock market crash in 1929 destroyed most of his personal fortune, but later in life Saunders attempted a comeback with another major innovation. Shortly after World War II, he opened a completely automated retail food store in Memphis called the Keedoozle. Saunders's approach to grocery shopping was not successful because it was too advanced for its time. Technology in 1948 was unable to meet the demands of a fully automated grocery store. Moreover, consumers were unwilling to buy groceries without first touching the products. Technological problems and lack of consumer acceptance made Saunders's last effort a financial failure. Today, however, this type of store is operated in Japan.

Some people who have been successful entrepreneurs include Ray Kroc of McDonald's (hamburgers); Mary Wells Lawrence, founder of the Wells, Rich, Green, Inc., advertising agency; Hugh Hefner of Playboy Enterprises; and John Johnson, publisher of *Ebony* magazine. They all have at least one characteristic in common—they are highly motivated individuals who were willing to take risks. Some of this motivation may be personal psychology, but the potential to make a profit is no doubt the moving force.

Entrepreneurs who want to develop new or improved consumer and industrial products for a profit today face exceptional opportunities. For example, Ramy Shanny raised $65 million to form Inesco, Inc., in San Diego. Inesco will produce miniature nuclear fusion reactors for a market that may have a $60 billion potential. This makes the profit potential close to 10,000 to 1 on a venture that has about a 50–50 chance of success. Certainly Shanny is a risk taker.

The two essential requirements of an entrepreneur—foresight and the willingness to risk capital—have remained unchanged over time. Many of today's new entrepreneurs will join those of past decades in advancing the standard of living for the people of the United States.

SUMMARY

- Economics is the study of how people decide to use their nation's scarce resources to produce goods and services and allocate them for consumption.
- The major types of economic resources are natural, labor, and capital resources.

■ Needs and wants of consumers are satisfied by using one or more of the nation's economic resources to produce the goods and services people need or want to consume.

■ Needs are things people must have to survive. Needs include food, clothing, shelter, and medical care.

■ Wants are not needed for survival. The list of wants is unlimited.

■ The three major economic systems are communism, socialism, and capitalism.

■ A modified version of capitalism is used in the United States.

■ Profit represents the difference between what a business takes in (revenue) and what it costs to operate (expenses).

■ Profits are important to business because they provide some of the money businesses need to expand and increase the number of jobs.

■ Profits are also used to pay people for investing their money in a business.

■ Entrepreneurs are important to the American economy because they take economic risks with their capital. Many new jobs are created by the successful new businesses started by entrepreneurs.

ISSUES TO CONSIDER AND ANALYZE

1. Explain why the American economic system can be thought of as a system of flows. Identify the major parts of the economic system and show how the parts relate to one another.
2. Compare and contrast the three different economic systems used by various world nations.
3. What three major economic questions does every society have to answer?
4. Explain why profit is so important to the survival and growth of the American economic system.
5. What is the fundamental role of the entrepreneur in the American economic system?
6. People often say that little opportunity is left in America for people who want to develop new products and services. Other people say there is more opportunity for the entrepreneur now than at any time in our history. Which position do you agree with? Why?
7. Develop a brief report that explains the advantages and disadvantages of government ownership of business.
8. Explain this statement: If telephone companies were not regulated monopolies, people would have to pay more for telephone service.
9. What are the basic rights that citizens have under the free enterprise system? Which right is the most important?
10. Does business have a right to make a profit? Explain.

PRODUCTIVITY AT BURGER KING

CASE FOR ANALYSIS

Making a profit in the fast-food business is difficult, a fact that Burger King management faces every day. Many factors can affect profits, but many corporate executives say productivity is what the game is all about.

Time is an important factor at Burger King. Nobody cares about how many hamburgers can be made between 11:00 P.M. and 6:00 A.M. But demand is so intense at lunch and around 6:00 P.M. that, if you can make more, you can sell more.

In order to increase production, productivity, and profits, Burger King uses time-and-motion studies on all employee movements. The goal is to produce more hamburgers faster with less labor input. Sometimes this means spending capital for machines to add to the production process.

One specific problem Burger King faced was how to increase rush-hour productivity at the drive-in window. Two ideas were suggested in a management meeting. First, the drive-in window could be redesigned to add a second lane and window to serve more cars. This would require a redesign of standard company building plans. A second idea was to move the bell hose, which rings inside when a car drives over it, back ten more feet from the window. This additional distance would permit the employee sufficient time to be ready to take the order when the car stopped. It was estimated that an additional thirty cars per hour could be serviced at a Burger King drive-in window with this simple change.

QUESTIONS

1. Which suggestion do you think is likely to have more positive impact on productivity and profits? Why?
2. Does serving an additional thirty cars per hour affect the production lines inside? If so, how?

Adapted from Edward Meadows, "How Three Companies Increased Their Productivity," *Fortune*, March 10, 1980, pp. 92–101.

CHAPTER 3

BUSINESS, GOVERNMENT, AND SOCIETY

LEARNING OBJECTIVES

After you have studied this chapter, you should be able to:

Discuss the formation and powers of the Interstate Commerce Commission.

Define antitrust legislation and restraints of trade.

Explain the major sections of the Sherman and Clayton acts.

Identify the most important consumer legislation.

Explain why we have pollution.

Identify the major types of environmental problems.

KEY TERMS

Rate discrimination
Antitrust legislation
Restraint of trade
Merger
Predatory price cutting
Per se violation
Interlocking directorates
Cease and desist orders
Fair-trade agreements
Collusive contracts
Cartel
Administrative law
Zero population growth (ZPG)

LEARNING TO LIVE WITH GOVERNMENT

Noreen Conolly graduated from her local university with a liberal arts degree. She had taken courses in economics and business but was more interested in philosophy and social issues. In particular, she was greatly influenced by a philosophy teacher who was very much in favor of individualism.

After a few jobs she didn't really like, Noreen began working at a small public relations firm that handled accounts from middle-sized firms in her region. A couple of years later, one of those firms, Diversified Industries, Inc., offered her a job. They wanted her to do public rela-tions and government liaison work for them. Noreen wasn't sure she could handle the task but decided to take a chance.

She quickly found that her tasks were time consuming and covered much broader issues than when she worked for the public relations firm. As a diversified conglomerate deal-ing in various areas of both manufac-turing and services, her company was constantly having to answer to government regulatory agencies for problems concerning pollution, employee relations, and certain trade practices. Noreen discovered that in today's business world the individualistic spirit espoused by her college philosophy teacher was being threatened. Noreen also found her-self faced with the difficult task of convincing the media that her com-pany's high profits were justified.

Noreen spent many nights pour-ing over government regulations and reports pertaining to Diversified In-dustries' activities. She was certain that the tide would change in favor of less government regulation soon be-cause her firm (and probably many others) was slowly finding it more and more difficult to do business in a world of increased government regulation.

The business firm of today does not exist in a vacuum. Business leaders cannot consider that their only task is to maximize profits for the benefit of the company's shareholders. They cannot even consider that all the company needs to do is provide products that consumers continue to buy. The business firm of today must cope in a world where (1) government regulations at all levels influence the way products are made, serviced, and advertised; how employees are paid and treated; and how consumers are satisfied; and (2) the management of the firm is expected to engage in socially responsible activities, even though the term *corporate social responsibility* has never been objectively defined. It's tough to be in business today. How can the owner/manager of the typical business firm satisfy the sometimes conflicting demands emanating from shareholders, government, and consumers?

Government enters into the activities of business whenever they relate to environmental problems, consumer problems, and monopoly problems. In this chapter, we will treat only the most important areas of government regulation of business:

Regulation pertaining to interstate commerce

Regulation of monopolies

Consumer protection

The environment

GOVERNMENT REGULATION— INTERSTATE COMMERCE

The basis for federal government control over economic activities is a so-called *commerce clause* in the Constitution that states: "The Congress shall have the power to . . . regulate commerce with foreign nations, and among the several states. . . ."[1]

From this base, the federal government has extended its control over business and the economy. Exhibit 3-1 provides a summary of some of the more significant legislation affecting business.

The Interstate Commerce Commission Act, 1887

One of the first major moves of the federal government to control business practices was the passage of the Interstate Commerce Commission Act in 1887. The act created the Interstate Commerce Commission (ICC), whose function was to prevent **rate discrimination** by the railroads. At that time, railroads with a monopoly on the freight transportation between two cities were able to charge shippers excessively high prices as there was no other effective means of transportation. When two or more railroads were in competition for freight traffic between two cities, however, rates were pushed to low levels. When rates fell below costs, the railroads began to cut back on service, maintenance, and investment, which led to increased downtime for equipment, a higher accident rate, and poor schedules. In either case, the shipper was the loser.

RATE DISCRIMINATION
Discrimination in railroad rates in which the per-pound, per-mile charge differed according to whether competition existed on a particular route. Also, rate discrimination sometimes involved charging different prices to different companies for the same service.

[1] The United States Constitution, Article 1, Section 8. The last section of this article states that Congress shall have the power to "make all laws which shall be necessary and proper for carrying into execution the foregoing powers."

DATE	LAW	MAJOR PROVISIONS
1887	Interstate Commerce Commission Act	Regulates unfair railroad practices; sets up Interstate Commerce Commission (ICC)
1890	Sherman Antitrust Act	Prohibits monopolies or attempts to monopolize and combinations or conspiracies in restraint of trade
1906	Pure Food and Drug Act	Deals only with issues involving misbranding
1906	Meat Inspection Act	Establishes minimum standards of sanitation for production
1914	Federal Trade Commission Act	Establishes Federal Trade Commission (FTC) and makes unfair methods of competition illegal
1914	Clayton Act	Amends Sherman Act; outlaws price discrimination, tying contracts, purchase of competitor's stock, and interlocking directorate where effect may be to substantially lessen competition
1936	Robinson-Patman Act	Prohibits price discrimination on goods of like grade and quality
1938	Wheeler-Lea Amendment	Strengthens the FTC Act; makes false advertising of food, drugs, etc., illegal
1938	Food, Drug, and Cosmetic Act	Strengthens 1906 act by giving jurisdiction over items not misbranded but potentially dangerous to health
1950	Cellar-Kefauver Antimerger Act	Gives increased authority to FTC; outlaws purchase of competitor's plant and equipment
1966	National Traffic and Motor Vehicle Safety Act	Sets motor vehicle safety standards
1968	Consumer Protection Credit Act (Truth-in-Lending)	Requires creditors to provide a statement of finance charges and annual percentage rate when individuals apply for credit
1970	Fair Credit Reporting Act	Requires consumer credit reporting agencies to use reasonable measures to guarantee the accuracy of credit information. Consumers who are denied credit must be given access to the substance of all information in the reporting agency's file
1972	Consumer Product Safety Commission Act	Establishes the Consumer Product Safety Commission, which has the power to set safety standards for consumer products and to require warnings by manufacturers
1977	Magnuson-Moss Warranty Act	Requires simple, complete, and conspicuous language concerning information about warranties
1978	Fair Debt Collection Practices Act	Regulates debt collection practices, making it unlawful for debt collectors to call at unusual times and to harass individuals.

Specific regulations in the areas of consumer legislation, labor law, banking and financial markets, and marketing are covered in other chapters.

EXHIBIT 3-1
Development of Government Regulation

This situation led Midwestern farmers (through their grange associations) to push state governments for passage of laws to control the abuses of the railroads. Originally organized as fraternal groups, grange associations became politically active in the late 1800s and did succeed in getting laws passed in several states. These laws were ineffective, though, because a railroad could change its rates as soon as it crossed state lines. After several years of battle in Congress and increased public pressure, the Interstate Commerce Commission Act was passed in 1887.

Though the ICC was initially established to watch over the activities of the railroads, its powers have since been expanded to include all forms of bus, truck, inland waterway, and pipeline traffic operating in interstate commerce. In addition to ensuring that rates charged by these carriers are reasonable, nondiscriminatory, and published, the agency protects the public interest in other ways. Some of its other functions are:

- Setting safety standards for equipment and personnel. This provision has undoubtedly reduced the number and severity of accidents in the regulated industries.
- Approving requests for the extension or discontinuation of service. In this role, the ICC helps protect against the higher costs of too many competitors in a market and ensures that rural areas of the country will have some available means for shipping goods.
- Regulating combinations between companies in the regulated industries. For example, when two railroads want to merge, they must seek ICC approval.

The recent trend toward deregulation of industry in the United States is causing a reduction in the ICC's power.

Our government attempts to foster competition in the economy. To this end, numerous efforts have been made to legislate against business practices that seemingly destroy the competitive nature of the system. This is the general idea behind antitrust legislation: If the courts can prevent collusion among sellers of a product, then monopoly prices will not result; there will be no restriction of output if the members of an industry are not allowed to join together in **restraint of trade**. The competitive solution to the price–quantity problem is one in which the price of the item produced is equal to its cost to society. Monopoly, on the other hand, leads to a restriction in output and higher prices.

The first antitrust law in the United States was passed during the period of the greatest **merger** movement in American history. A large number of firms were monopolizing and merging, or joining with other firms. When a number of firms merged, the business organizations were then called *trusts*. A copper trust, a steel beam trust, an iron trust, a sugar trust, a coal trust, a paper bag trust, and the most famous of all, the Standard Oil trust, were formed. There was an increasing public outcry for legislation against these large trusts.

The Sherman Antitrust Act, passed in 1890, was the first attempt by the federal government to control the growth of monopoly in the United States. The most important provisions of that act are:

Section 1 Every contract, combination in the form of trust or otherwise, or conspiracy, in restraint of trade or commerce among the several states, or with foreign nations, is hereby declared to be illegal.

Section 2 Every person who shall monopolize, or attempt to monopolize, or combine or conspire with any other person or persons to monopolize any part of the trade or commerce . . . shall be guilty of a misdemeanor.

Notice how vague this particular act really is. No definition is given for the terms *restraint of trade* or *monopolization*. Despite this vagueness, however, the act was used to prosecute the infamous Standard Oil trust.

ANTITRUST POLICY

RESTRAINT OF TRADE
Any action that impedes the free flow of commerce, such as an agreement among producers to restrict output or to split up geographical sections of the country in which each of them will sell the particular product.

The Sherman Act

MERGER
The joining together of two firms into one firm.

Standard Oil of New Jersey was charged with violations of Sections 1 and 2
of the Sherman Antitrust Act. This was in 1906, when the company controlled over 80 percent of the nation's oil-refining capacity. Among other
things, Standard Oil was accused of both **predatory price cutting** to drive
rivals out of business and obtaining preferential price treatment from the
railroads for transporting Standard Oil products, thus allowing Standard to
sell at lower prices.

After conviction by a district court, the company appealed to the
Supreme Court, which ruled that Standard's control of and power over the
oil market created "a *prima facie* presumption of intent and purpose to
maintain dominancy . . . not as a result from normal methods of industrial
development, but by means of combination." Here, the word *combination*
meant taking over other businesses and obtaining preferential price treatment from railroads. The Supreme Court forced Standard Oil of New Jersey
to break up into many smaller companies.

This ruling came about because the judges felt that Standard Oil had
used "unreasonable" attempts at restraining trade. The Court did not come
out against monopoly per se. The fact that Standard Oil had a large share of
the market did not seem to matter; rather, according to the Court, the
problem was the way in which Standard acquired that large market share.
In any event, antitrust legislation was used to break up one of the largest
trusts in the United States at that time.

The Clayton Act

The Sherman Act was so vague that, in 1914, a new law was passed to
sharpen its antitrust provisions. Called the Clayton Act, this law prohibits
or limits a number of very specific business practices, which again were felt
to be "unreasonable" attempts at restraining trade or commerce. Some of
the more important sections of that act are:

> *Section 2* [It is illegal to] discriminate in price between different purchasers
> [except in cases where the differences are due to differences in selling or
> transportation costs].
>
> *Section 3* [Producers cannot sell] on the condition, agreement or understanding
> that the . . . purchaser . . . shall not use or deal in the goods . . . of a competitor or
> competitors of the seller.
>
> *Section 7* [Corporations cannot hold stock in another company] where the
> effect . . . may be to substantially lessen competition.

The above activities mentioned in the Clayton Act are not necessarily
illegal. In the words of the law, they are illegal *only* when their effects "may
be to substantially lessen competition or tend to create a monopoly." It
takes the interpretation of the courts to decide whether one of the activities
mentioned actually has the effect of "substantially" lessening competition.
On the other hand, there is an additional provision in the Clayton Act that
represents a **per se violation**—one that is *always* or by definition illegal. This
activity is **interlocking directorates**. It is illegal per se for the same individual to serve on two or more boards of directors of corporations that are
competitive and are worth more than $1 million. The very existence of this
interlock is enough to allow the government to prosecute.

The Federal Trade Commission Act was designed to prevent certain unfair competition and to specify acceptable competitive behavior. In particular, it was supposed to prevent predatory cutthroat pricing—that is, overly aggressive competition that tends to eliminate too many competitors. One of the main features of the act was the creation of the Federal Trade Commission (FTC). That commission is charged with the power to investigate unfair competitive practices. It can do so on its own or at the request of firms that feel they have been wronged. When "unfair methods of competition in commerce" are discovered, the commission can issue **cease and desist orders**—orders that require a firm to stop a particular action immediately. In 1938, the Wheeler-Lea Act amended the 1914 Federal Trade Commission Act. The amendment expressly prohibits "unfair or deceptive acts or practices in commerce." Following up on that act, the FTC engages in what it sees as a battle against false or misleading advertising and the misrepresentation of goods and services for sale in the marketplace.

In 1936, Section 2 of the Clayton Act was amended by the Robinson-Patman Act. The Robinson-Patman Act was aimed at preventing producers from driving out smaller competitors by means of discriminatory price cuts—that is, charging some customers less than others. The act has often been referred to as the "Anti-Chain Store Act" because it was meant to protect *independent* retailers and wholesalers from "unfair discrimination" by manufacturers.

The Robinson-Patman Act was the natural outgrowth of increasing competition that independents faced when manufacturers and mass distributors started to develop after World War I. The essential provisions of the act are as follows:

1. It was made illegal to pay brokerage fees unless an independent broker was employed. Often chain stores would demand a brokerage fee as a form of discount when they purchased large quantities of their products directly from the manufacturer instead of going through a broker or wholesaler. Thus, payment of a brokerage fee as a form of discount was considered to give unfair advantage to chain stores over independents, who had to use a broker or wholesaler.
2. It was made illegal to offer concessions such as discounts, free advertising, promotional allowances, and so on to one buyer of a product if the same concessions were not offered to all buyers. This provision was an attempt to stop large-scale buyers from obtaining special deals that would allow them to compete "unfairly" with small buyers.
3. Other forms of discrimination, such as quantity discounts, were also made illegal whenever they "substantially" lessened competition. Price discrimination as such was not illegal if, in fact, price differences were due to differences in costs or were "offered in good faith to meet an equally low price of a competitor."
4. It was made illegal to charge lower prices in one location than in another, or to sell at "unreasonably low prices" if such marketing tech-

The Federal Trade Commission Act of 1914

CEASE AND DESIST ORDERS
Orders from a government agency that require a firm or firms to immediately stop a particular action. Usually cease and desist orders are applied to so-called unfair methods of competition and commerce.

The Robinson-Patman Act

niques were designed to "destroy competition or eliminate a competitor." Thus, so-called predatory pricing was outlawed.

Exemptions to the Antitrust Laws

There are numerous antitrust acts, many of which serve to exempt certain business practices from antitrust legislation. In effect, exemptions from antitrust laws foster monopolies and monopoly practices. Nonetheless, the industries affected have had such powerful lobbying forces in Congress that they have been able to obtain these exemptions. Here we list a few exemptions that have been important on the American industrial scene.

THE MILLER-TYDINGS ACT AND THE McGUIRE ACT   In 1937, the Miller-Tydings Act was passed as an amendment to Section 1 of the Sherman Act. The new act allowed individual states to permit so-called **fair-trade agreements** by which the manufacturer specified a listed, or fair-trade, price below which no retailer could offer the product. Portions of this act were declared invalid by the Supreme Court in 1951. In 1952, Congress passed the McGuire Act, which restored those portions taken out by the Supreme Court the year before. In 1977, the McGuire Act was rescinded, and fair-trade agreements, at least for the moment, are no longer with us.

FAIR-TRADE AGREEMENTS
Agreements by which the manufacturer specifies a minimum, or fair-trade, price, below which all retailers cannot sell the product. Another name for a fair-trade agreement is a resale price maintenance agreement.

SMALL BUSINESSES   Small businesses are allowed to engage in certain concerted, or joint, activities without violating the antitrust laws. This legislation started with the Small Business Act of 1953.

OIL MARKETING   In 1935, the Interstate Oil Compact was passed. It allows states to determine quotas on oil that will be marketed in interstate commerce.

FOREIGN TRADE   Under the provisions of the 1918 Webb-Pomerane Act, American exporters can engage in cooperative activity.

LABOR AND AGRICULTURE   Labor and agricultural organizations are exempted from the Sherman Antitrust Act by Section 6 of the Clayton Act. Agriculture's exemption from antitrust legislation is further extended by the Capper-Volstead Act (passed in 1922), the Cooperative Marketing Act (passed in 1926), and certain provisions of the Robinson-Patman Act. Labor's exemption was strengthened by the Norris-LaGuardia Act of 1932. In other words, individuals may act in concert in legal ways, even though they are actually restraining trade in agriculture and in labor markets.

Enforcement of Antitrust Laws

The enforcement of antitrust laws has been rather uneven. Of course, there have been many spectacular cases brought and won by the government, such as the case against the electrical companies' conspiracy in the early 1960s. Use of the Sherman Act did allow the government to break up the Standard Oil trust, and the government also broke up the American Tobacco Company. It can be argued that antitrust laws are effective in preventing the enforcement of **collusive contracts**—agreements among firms that may restrict the free flow of commerce. Hence, the existence of

COLLUSIVE CONTRACTS
Agreements among firms that in some way restrict the free flow of commerce. Collusive contracts may involve restricting output or setting minimum prices.

antitrust laws makes it hard to prevent cheating by cartel members. The term **cartel** is often applied to any association of firms attempting to restrict the market in order to benefit themselves via higher profits. A member of a cartel is a firm that participates in a collusive agreement to restrict production, share specific markets, or keep prices at a specific level.

Governmental efforts to avert problems of monopoly have concentrated on preventing mergers. Today, large firms must first seek permission from the Justice Department before merging. The Justice Department will indicate whether it feels any antitrust laws would be violated if such mergers were to take place. Often, the Justice Department will deny the merger on the grounds that it will seriously lessen competition.

Clearly, the political climate in Washington will determine how aggressive the government is in pursuing antitrust problems. For example, shortly after Ronald Reagan was elected president, several large antitrust cases were settled in one way or another. American Telephone & Telegraph agreed to give up its ownership and control of some twenty-two regional telephone systems in exchange for being able to compete in the computer and telecommunications fields. The decade-old case against IBM was dropped by the Justice Department. And a lengthy FTC case against large cereal manufacturing companies was dropped. Perhaps by the time you read this, a new administration will be in power, and the trend will be reversed.

Noreen Conolly recently found herself in a turmoil at the office. Diversified Industries, Inc., was attempting to buy an out-of-state firm that manufactured and serviced electric generators. Just when the deal was about to go through, the Federal Trade Commission stepped in and issued a legal order (injunction) preventing the merger. The FTC argued that Diversified Industries was threatening potential competition by buying out the firm. The FTC felt that if Diversified purchased the electrical generator manufacturing company, it would not then enter the business at a later date with a totally new, competing firm started from scratch. Therefore, *potential* competition would be eliminated if Diversified bought the existing company now.

Noreen really couldn't understand the logic of the FTC, but, after some research, she found that the FTC had prevented numerous mergers using the same argument. When she was required to issue press releases concerning the anticompetitive effects of the attempted merger, Noreen stuck to her guns. She argued for her company that the electrical generator manufacturing firm was having cash-flow problems and might go out of business if it wasn't purchased by Diversified. She found quite a few sympathetic reporters in her area, but some were still worried about the growth of Diversified. They were concerned that the conglomerate strength of the company might bestow superior abilities on any firm it purchased and consequently lessen competition in the industry.

Besides trying to prevent business combinations that are in restraint of trade, federal legislation also attempts to protect consumers from unscrupulous business practices.

CARTEL
A group of firms joined together by a collusive agreement in order to restrict output and raise prices to increase the profits of the member firms.

On the Job Revisited

CONSUMER PROTECTION

The Pure Food and Drug Act, 1906

The Pure Food and Drug Act of 1906 was adopted only after several decades of public concern about food adulteration and patent-medicine frauds. Support for the act was led by Dr. Harvey Wiley of the Agriculture Department, who had cataloged 1400 pages of documented cases of food adulteration. In February 1906, Upton Sinclair published his book *The Jungle*, which highlighted the working conditions in the Chicago stockyards. The book, an immediate best-seller, moved President Theodore Roosevelt to take the lead in the fight for passage of the act.

Passed in June 1906, the Pure Food and Drug Act sought to protect consumers' health as well as their purses. The act prohibited the interstate commerce of both misbranded and adulterated food and drugs. Generally speaking, the act was reasonably effective in barring the extremes of dangerous adulteration. However, the protection against misbranding and misrepresentation was very weak.

During the proceedings for a new bill, a shocking tragedy occurred. In 1937, the manufacturer of Elixir Sulfanilamide decided to produce the drug in liquid as well as capsule form. The new drug, although safe in capsule form, became lethal in liquid form. Almost 100 people were killed by the drug before the FDA could act. It seized the remaining stock, enough to kill 3720 people, and prosecuted the manufacturer. This tragedy provided the final impetus for passage of a bill that increased the powers of the FDA.

The Food, Drug, and Cosmetic Act, 1938

The Food, Drug, and Cosmetic Act of 1938 expanded the 1906 act. It added cosmetic and therapeutic devices to the list of regulated items, made sanctions more severe, and strengthened the definitions of adulteration and misbranding of food and drugs. With the sulfanilamide tragedy in mind, Congress also required that information on new drugs be filed with the FDA for testing before the drugs were introduced to the market. These provisions were tightened further by the Kefauver-Harris Drug Amendments in 1962. But the law failed to curb the false advertising claims of manufacturers. This job was left to another piece of consumer legislation.

Other Consumer Legislation

The Wheeler-Lea Amendment to the Federal Trade Commission Act was passed in 1938. The Federal Trade Commission Act had made false advertising illegal, but the courts interpreted this to mean that false advertising was illegal only if it hurt competitors. The Wheeler-Lea Amendment gave the FTC the power to forbid not only "unfair methods of competition" but also "deceptive acts or practices" in the sale of goods in general.

A variety of other acts have been passed in the consumer interest. Some acts that require accurate labeling of products include:

- Wool Products Labeling Act, 1939
- Fur Products Labeling Act, 1951
- Flammable Fabrics Act, 1953
- Federal Hazardous Substances Labeling Act, 1960
- Fair Labeling and Packaging Act, 1966

Others deal with consumer finances:

- Consumer Credit Protection Act, 1968 (truth-in-lending)
- Fair Billing Credit Act, 1975

SMOKING, THE SURGEON GENERAL, AND YOU

It's been years since the U.S. surgeon general indicated that smoking is positively linked to lung cancer. It's been quite a while, too, since the head of the Consumer Product Safety Commission offered to the press a startling conclusion: he had the legal right to ban cigarettes. The turmoil that followed that statement didn't last very long, however, because the head of the Consumer Product Safety Commission backed down. More than a decade ago, Congress, convinced that smoking was indeed injurious to the nation's health, banned cigarette commercials on radio and TV. In 1981, the surgeon general came up with a correlation between smoking and three more types of cancer. Government intervention in this area has had some effect. The per-capita consumption of smoking is down 7 percent from its peak year in 1973, when the "average" American smoked 4148 cigarettes per year. By the middle of 1982, the estimate was 3840.

That doesn't mean that the cigarette industry has gotten smaller, though. In 1958, 470 billion cigarettes were produced. In 1981, 734 billion were produced. In 1982, the tobacco industry contributed $57 billion to the gross national product, an amount equal to one-fourth of the entire defense budget. That figure includes tobacco picking, trucking, the manufacture of matches, and advertising. A "mere" $14 billion is spent directly on tobacco products. The fact is, the government's campaign against smoking hasn't been overwhelmingly effective. A lot of people are not yet convinced that smoking causes cancer, and so they continue to take risks. Numerous lawsuits continue to be brought against individual firms and the industry, but no court has yet awarded a claim for damages against a tobacco company.

The Tobacco Institute—an educational and lobbying group for the tobacco industry—would like to get the American public to stop singing the ditty: "Ashes to ashes and dust to dust; if the Marlboros don't get you, the Winstons must."

Adapted from "Big Smokey," *Forbes*, April 26, 1982, p. 56.

Finally, some laws attempt to protect the consumer from products that may be hazardous:

- Cigarette Labeling Act, 1966
- Child Protection and Toy Safety Act, 1969
- Public Health Smoking Act, 1970
- Consumer Product Safety Act, 1972

The framers of the United States Constitution were very concerned about giving too much power to any one branch of the federal government. Consequently, they built into the Constitution a system of checks and balances to ensure that any one branch of the government did not become too powerful. Legislative power was reserved for Congress. Since then, however, Congress has allowed federal agencies (which are part of the executive branch) to write laws, interpret them, and enforce them. Where

THE REGULATORY COMMISSIONS

ADMINISTRATIVE LAW
That body of rules and regulations set down by administrative agencies, such as the Federal Trade Commission, the Interstate Commerce Commission, and the Food and Drug Administration. Law that is generated by agency rulings rather than by the legislature.

EXHIBIT 3-2
Jurisdiction of State
Regulatory Commissions

INDUSTRY	NUMBER OF STATES HAVING COMMISSIONS
Railroads	49
Telephone	49
Common-carrier trucks	48
Gas utilities	47
Telegraph	47
Electric utilities	46
Contract-carrier trucks	45
Gas pipelines	28
Water carriers	25
Oil pipelines	23
Air transport	18

On the Job Revisited

there are no court decisions or written laws governing a specific type of business conduct being considered by an agency, the agency may make a ruling that is binding on business. The only alternative open to the business manager is an expensive court appeal. If the decision is not overturned, it becomes binding and is called **administrative law**.

A few of these agencies (ICC, FTC, and FDA) have already been discussed. Many other federal agencies have profound effects on the operations of large and small businesses. In addition, many state governments have similar agencies that regulate or control the activities of business. The jurisdiction of the state commissions is briefly summarized in Exhibit 3-2.

The regulatory agencies are supposed to serve as economic monitors for the industries they regulate. They determine which firms can enter the industry, what services will be provided, and what rates will be charged. But some critics contend that these agencies do a poor job of protecting the consumer and actually encourage the monopolistic activities they are supposed to prevent. Such critics point out that the working relationships that can develop between an agency and the industry it is supposed to regulate often tend to ease the burden on the industry rather than the consumer.

Critics further suggest that regulators are too often political appointees who either lack qualifications for the job and display little interest in it or are taken directly from the industries they regulate. In either case, critics contend, the public gets the short end of the stick. Every American family pays about $2000 per year in higher prices because of unnecessary and wasteful regulation.

A case in point is the ICC's past rule barring truckers from cutting rates in order to fill their empty trucks on return trips. The consequences of this action are obvious: truckers purchase more trucks than they need, and fewer than 50 percent of the truckers have full loads in both directions. The end result is higher rates, more traffic congestion, and higher levels of air pollution and energy consumption.

The only way to correct these and other problems, contend the critics, is to revamp the regulatory commissions. Although there is tough opposition from the commissions, Congress, and the regulated industries, it appears that changes will continue to take place. Some industries might be better off with less government regulation.

Part of Diversified Industries' activities involves their medium-sized chain of retail food markets. Diversified has a central warehouse from which it ships food to the six markets it owns. On numerous occasions, the trucks (owned by Diversified) come back to the warehouse empty. One of the managers of the trucking division decided to take advantage of this unused capacity and offered to ship, at relatively low rates, some merchandise for dealers in the area. Nothing much happened until a local trucking company found out. It got the State Utility Commission to intervene on behalf of the Interstate Truckers' Associaton. They argued that Diversified's trucks were not common carriers and therefore had no legal right to transport other companies' products.

As soon as the injunction was issued to prevent Diversified's activities, Noreen was bombarded with phone calls from the press. They wanted to

SNAP, CRACKLE, AND POP

The case seemed clear-cut. The major cereal manufacturers were preventing competition simply by generating millions and millions of dollars of advertising, thereby preventing outsiders from entering the industry. The FTC brought suit more than a decade ago against the so-called Big Three—Kellogg, General Mills, and General Foods. Those companies did and still do control 80 percent of the ready-to-eat cereal market.

The theory behind the FTC's attack was novel. It was called the *shared monopoly theory* of anticompetitive business practices. The FTC's attorneys had argued that the three cereal companies acted as one monopolistic concern even without directly conspiring to set prices or limit the competition. The FTC called it a tacit understanding and charged that this tacit understanding kept cereal prices high and stopped competitors from entering the business.

This shared monopoly theory was novel because it involved a situation in which there was no active collusion among the firms. The FTC's attorneys contended that Kellogg was the price leader and that it, and it alone, determined cereal prices. General Mills and General Foods simply followed suit. In addition, it was contended that the Big Three excluded competitors by controlling the amount of shelf space in grocery stores. Finally, the FTC staff charged that the Big Three promoted a "bewildering profusion of trade names," such as Trix, Kix, Froot Loops, and Fruity Pebbles. Small firms found it prohibitively expensive to introduce their own brands. The estimated cost to breakfast cereal buffs of these supposed anticompetitive actions was a staggering $1.2 billion between 1958 and 1972.

In 1982, a new chairman of the FTC, James Miller, took a different view of the situation. He directed the FTC to formally end this controversial antitrust case. Another FTC commissioner, Patricia Bailey, said that the FTC should not undertake to restructure an industry "without a clear supportive signal from the Congress."

Not surprisingly, the cereal makers crackled with excitement at the news. Kellogg chairman William LaMothe said that "the suit has been an expensive and wasteful cloud hanging over our company. We applaud the decision."

Adapted from "FTC Drops 10-year-old Antitrust Suit against the Three Largest U.S. Cereal Makers," *The Wall Street Journal*, January 18, 1982, p. 6.

know what Diversified was going to do. Noreen was aware of an increasing national mood in favor of deregulation, and she strongly recommended that her superiors fight the case in court. In presenting the company's side of the story, she argued brilliantly that the only real loser was the consumer, since higher prices were a direct result of the inefficiency of the current shipping system. There was no reason to have empty trucks rolling around when they could be filled with goods that needed to be distributed.

Environmental problems have existed from the beginning of time. Today, however, there is a serious problem because of the limits of the earth's capacity to absorb increasing levels of pollution generated by both businesses and consumers. Reducing pollution and protecting the environment

BUSINESS AND THE ENVIRONMENT

are important problems facing our society today. Government has imposed all sorts of regulations to minimize the impact of undesirable by-products from today's production processes.

Causes of Pollution

The pollution in our environment can be traced to many factors, but three are of prime importance: the increasing size and concentration of the population, the affluence of the consumer, and the development of new technologies.

POPULATION   Population is a major factor in environmental deterioration. Although the United States is close to experiencing zero population growth, forecasters anticipate that the population will continue to grow at least until the turn of the century. **Zero population growth (ZPG)** is defined as 2.1 children per child-bearing couple. As the people of the postwar baby boom begin having children to replace themselves, the potential for another baby boom exists. In addition, medical science predicts that it will be possible to add another fifteen years to life expectancy. Thus, people will be living longer at the same time that more children are being born. These two factors combined will cause the population to grow from about 225 million people today to about 270 million by the year 2000.

ZERO POPULATION GROWTH (ZPG)
A situation in which the average annual increase in the population is zero. This will occur when every child-bearing couple has exactly 2.1 children.

In addition to the size of the population, large concentrations of people in urban areas pose serious problems. Cities face problems of traffic congestion, excessive noise, air pollution, and overloading of sewage treatment facilities (which causes water pollution). The damaging effects of a large and concentrated population on the environment are endless.

CONSUMER AFFLUENCE   The American consumer has enjoyed, with minor exceptions, a period of rising income ever since the Depression of the 1930s. These higher income levels have enabled more people to demand additional products and also to replace those products more frequently. This has placed an increasing burden on solid-waste disposal systems.

Year after year, some American businesses attempt (through advertising) to convince consumers that they need newer, better, and bigger products. Many consumers now throw out the old and bring in the new even when the old would have worked just fine. Short-range decision making of this kind has prompted some people to suggest that business should begin to "unsell" or "demarket" many products. This unselling has already begun in some industries. For example, oil companies and public utilities have begun to encourage consumers to conserve energy. Unfortunately, many of the products demanded by newly affluent consumers—cars, air conditioners, dishwashers—require large amounts of energy. They increase the pressure on energy resources and also potentially increase the level of pollution.

TECHNOLOGY   Finally, technology has in many cases had a detrimental effect on the environment. There are thousands of new chemicals; some will not easily decompose, and others may cause cancer. The overall effect is to increase the amount of pollutants in the environment and raise the possibility for some type of environmental disaster. Although technology has caused some of our pollution problems, it also offers the promise of allowing society to control its pollutants and live in harmony with the environment.

One of the most destructive changes in the environment has been the increase in pollution. Pollution affects nearly every aspect of our physical world.

Types of Environmental Problems

AIR POLLUTION   Industry, consumers, and governments continuously add to the contamination in the air. Although the amount of air pollution has been reduced in recent years, there is still cause for concern. Air pollution can be caused by automobiles, smoking, forest fires, incinerators, and industrial plants. Carbon monoxide from automobile exhaust reduces the amount of oxygen in the blood. When the oxygen level of the blood is reduced, stamina and ability to concentrate decrease. Thus, high levels of carbon monoxide in the air reduce one's performance in the classroom and on the athletic field. Other sources of air pollution, such as hydrocarbons and sulfates, irritate the lining of the lungs, increasing the likelihood of such respiratory diseases as lung cancer, emphysema, and asthma. Furthermore, air pollution endangers not only human health but also agricultural crops, trees, and other living things.

WATER POLLUTION   A second major form of pollution is water pollution. For years, cities and industrial plants along waterways have been dumping raw sewage and waste materials into our rivers, lakes, and streams. The assumption was that flowing water could cleanse itself. In recent years, this assumption has not proven true. In fact, pollution levels have increased, although in some places (for instance, the Houston Ship Channel), water quality has improved a great deal. The overall picture is still a bit dismal. Exhibit 3-3 is a list of the rivers in the United States that have sections so polluted they are not fit for swimming.

Some river segments officially rated as unswimmable in part for at least 50 percent of the year because of pollution*:

Big Sioux River in South Dakota	Missouri River (lower portion)
Catawba River in South Carolina	Monocacy River in Maryland
Cedar River in Iowa	North Platte River in Wyoming
Chattahoochee River in Georgia	Red River in Louisiana
Connecticut River in Connecticut	Rio Grande in New Mexico
Des Moines River in Iowa	Roanoke River in Virginia
Grand River in Michigan	Susquehanna River in Pennsylvania
James River in Missouri	Tar River in North Carolina
Jordan River in Utah	Yazoo River in Mississippi
Mississippi River (Rock Island to Cairo, Ill.)	Yellowstone River in Montana

From Environmental Protection Agency.

*River segments are rated as too polluted for safe swimming when bacteria counts at sampling stations rise to levels considered hazardous to health. Typically, pollution is highest near cities, while headwaters, tributaries, and other stretches may be swimmable.

EXHIBIT 3-3
Pollution in U.S. Rivers

On the bright side, researchers at Michigan State University have developed a kind of superwater out of polluted water. The polluted water is first used to grow edible underwater vegetation at several times the normal rate. Once the plants have removed most of the pollutants, the water is pumped into a second pond. Because of the high oxygen content introduced by the plants, fish in the pond grow at several times their normal rate. This process cleans up the water and provides vegetation and fish for a hungry world.

SOLID WASTE   Our affluent society casts off a great many solid wastes: automobiles, cans, bottles, plastic containers, tires, newspapers, and human and animal waste. These wastes can be put in the four major categories shown in Exhibit 3–4. Agricultural waste accounts for over 50 percent of the 4.4 billion tons of solid waste produced in the United States each year. Mineral wastes account for 38 percent; residential, commercial, institutional, and industrial wastes account for only a small portion of the total. But this small percentage is responsible for a large amount of the highly toxic waste that causes the most damage to the environment.

On the Job Revisited

Pollution control affects managerial decisions. For example, the phone hasn't stopped ringing in Noreen Conolly's office. Diversified decided to close down the paper mill that it had been operating for the last twenty-two years. According to the company, it was no longer profitable to run the mill. The hundreds of families that would be affected by loss of employment couldn't accept that. They went to the governor and to the press. It just didn't seem right that a plant that had existed for so long should be closed down on such relatively short notice. Noreen's job was to satisfy both the press and the governor's office that Diversified had no choice.

When she started to look into the actual numbers, Noreen found out why the decision had been made. Increasingly strict regulations governing the amount of harmful by-products that could be emitted from the plant's production process could not be ignored. It was costing Diversified more and more to produce the same quantity of paper every year. Finally, the rate of return on the investment in the company was less than it would be if Diversified simply closed the place down, took its loss, and invested the remaining monies in government bonds. Given the ups and downs in that business, it didn't seem right to Diversified's managers to use shareholder and investment dollars to earn a rate of return that wasn't even as high as the return on a government bond.

Noreen decided to issue a news release explaining that someone always has to pay for the cost of pollution control. In this case, consumers would end up paying higher prices for paper products because there would be one less supplier, and the employees in the area would definitely lose out. But that's the price that society has decided it must pay for a cleaner environment. Nothing in this world is free, certainly not clean air and clean water.

Solid-waste disposal can at times be an embarrassing problem. The Federal Reserve Bank in San Francisco, for many years, disposed of its solid waste (old currency) by burning the material in the incinerator. When the

EXHIBIT 3-4
Sources of Solid Wastes
(in millions of tons)

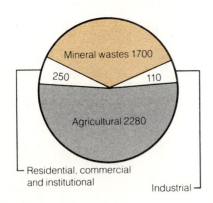

Mineral wastes 1700
250   110
Agricultural 2280
Residential, commercial and institutional
Industrial

Environmental Protection Agency cited the bank for polluting the air over San Francisco, it was faced with the problem of finding a better means of disposal. The choices were to put pollution control equipment on the incinerator or to install a grinder. After some investigation, the bank discovered that the pollution equipment would not fit in its existing facility and that, although the grinder would fit, it might vibrate enough to crack the foundation of the bank building.

In Boston, the General Electric Company powers its plant by burning an unusual fuel. Garbage is collected from surrounding communities and burned to generate 4500 BTUs of heat energy per pound, one-third the energy of coal. The company's savings are estimated to be 14 to 16 million gallons of oil per year. Garbage power may provide a partial solution to both the solid-waste disposal problem and the energy shortage.

NOISE   In 1977, noise pollution became an important issue, especially to many people in the New York City area. With the arrival of the British-French supersonic plane Concorde, New Yorkers were up in arms over the supposed high noise level of the plane.

High noise levels affect the nervous system, and continued high levels of noise can lead to hearing loss. Every individual has a different tolerance for noise, however, which makes it difficult to set specific standards. In spite of these problems, the federal government has set the allowable noise levels in most industrial plants at 85 decibels. This is about equal to the sound of a heavy truck accelerating 50 feet away. Estimates are that about 50 percent of American manufacturing workers are exposed to this level of noise or higher. The cost to reduce the noise level for those workers will be about $4 billion.

An even bigger problem may be to reduce the level of noise pollution in the country in general. Some of the sounds above 85 decibels are a New York subway station, a shout at 1 foot, a jet takeoff at 2000 feet, and a disco. In an effort to reduce noise pollution, several major cities—including Baltimore, Boston, San Francisco, and New York—have adopted noise codes. The New York code even includes specifications for the amount of time ice cream vendors can play their jingles.

Who Will Pay for Cleaning the Environment?

What percentage of the responsibility for cleaning up the environment should business, government, or individuals assume? Should they pay equal amounts? How long should businesses and governments have to stop polluting? What will happen to individuals who lose their jobs when the plants they work in are closed down because of pollution violations? What should be done to compensate consumers who cannot get electrical power because the construction of power plants is halted on environmental grounds? It seems reasonable to assume that, although we will all pay to clean up the environment, we will not all pay equal amounts. Some of us will be asked to give up much more than others.

The Council on Environmental Quality has prepared an estimate of the cost of cleaning up America over the next ten years. The total reaches $371 billion. Of that, $195.5 billion, or 52.7 percent, will be used to fight air pollution, and $158 billion will be needed to fight water pollution.

Only 4.6 percent, or $17 billion, will be used to fight noise and solid-waste pollution.

The funds for fighting pollution will come from both business and government. But the American people will actually pay the entire $371 billion. The government will most likely raise its share through added taxation. Business will pass on its cost to consumers in the form of higher prices; to its employees, in the form of lower wages; or to its owners, by returning less on their investment. Thus, we all have a financial stake in the effort to clean up the environment.

SUMMARY

■ The basis for federal government control over the majority of economic activities in our economy is the commerce clause in the Constitution. Article 1, Section 8 allows the Congress to regulate commerce among the several states and to make all laws that are necessary for carrying out this power.

■ The first major piece of federal regulatory legislation was the Interstate Commerce Act of 1887, which was designed to prevent continuing rate discrimination by railroads. The ICC's power was expanded to include not only rate regulation but the setting of safety standards and the approval of extension or discontinuation of service by common carriers.

■ Antitrust legislation at the federal level was introduced through the Sherman Act of 1890, which was designed to prevent restraints of trade and the injurious effects of monopoly. The Sherman Act was used in 1906 to break up the Standard Oil trust.

■ Because the Sherman Act was so vague, the Clayton Act was passed in 1914. Among other things, it prohibited price discrimination and interlocking directorates. The latter were deemed a per se violation, one that is always illegal.

■ The Federal Trade Commission Act of 1914 established the Federal Trade Commission, which has the power to issue cease and desist orders where unfair methods of competition in commerce are discovered.

■ The Robinson-Patman Act, or the " Anti-Chain Store Act," was put into effect to protect independent retailers and wholesalers from unfair discrimination by manufacturers. Among other things, it made virtually any type of discrimination in price, quality, or service illegal. Predatory pricing was, in essence, outlawed whenever it was designed to destroy competition or eliminate a competitor.

■ Among the many exemptions to the antitrust laws are those that cover small businesses, oil marketing, foreign trade, labor unions, and agriculture.

■ The first major piece of consumer protection legislation was the Pure Food and Drug Act of 1906, which prohibited the interstate commerce of misbranded and adulterated food and drugs. This act was expanded in 1938 to include cosmetics and therapeutic devices. The 1938 act also strengthened the definitions of adulteration and misbranding of food and drugs. The Kefauver-Harris Drug Amendments of 1968 further strengthened the act by requiring that the effectiveness of drugs be shown before they could be put on the market.

■ Numerous regulatory commissions exist in the United States in order to protect both consumers and producers. These commissions have the power to issue rulings that have the effect of law. These rulings are referred to as administrative law. In the past few years, regulatory agencies have come under fire for too much regulation. Indeed, we are now living, perhaps temporarily, in a period of deregulation.

■ The three most important causes of pollution in our environment are the increasing size and concentration of our population, the affluence of the consumer, and the development of new technologies.

■ A cleaner environment requires a sacrifice, and that sacrifice will come out of the people's pockets, for ultimately the cost of a cleaner environment is passed on to the consumer by government and business.

1. What is the historical-legal basis for all federal government regulation of economic activities?
2. What was the principal reason for the passage of the Interstate Commerce Commission Act in 1887?
3. Why did the Congress feel it necessary to supplement the Sherman Act with the Clayton Act in 1914?
4. Name some common restraints of trade and how they affect the consumer.
5. List the most common exceptions to the antitrust laws and explain their effects on the consumer.
6. What is the major method by which regulatory agencies affect economic activity?
7. If we attained zero population growth, would we eliminate all pollution? Why or why not?
8. Who pays for the cleanup of our environment?

ISSUES TO CONSIDER AND ANALYZE

LISTERINE: TELL IT LIKE IT IS

CASE FOR ANALYSIS

In the case of *Warner-Lambert* v. *Federal Trade Commission* (FTC), the FTC had issued an order requiring the firm to cease and desist from advertising its product, Listerine mouthwash, as a preventive cure for the common cold. The FTC also directed Warner-Lambert to indicate in all future advertisements that "Contrary to prior advertisement, Listerine will not help prevent colds or sore throats or lessen their severity." The FTC involvement in corrective advertising was upheld by the circuit court of appeals.

In the Warner-Lambert case, the government—through the FTC—was involved in what is now called corrective advertising. Listerine has been on the market since 1879, and Warner-Lambert has always claimed that the product had a beneficial effect. The FTC found that Listerine did not in fact alleviate colds or sore throats because it contained insufficient amounts of therapeutic ingredients to do any good.

The court ruled that Listerine's advertisements in the past were false and that consequently the FTC did have the power to prescribe corrective advertising. On the other hand, Warner-Lambert felt that the government was meddling in business matters and was violating the firm's rights under the First Amendment.

The FTC was considered to be acting in the public interest. Warner-Lambert was ordered to spend $10 million on advertising to correct the false impression of the therapeutic benefits associated with Listerine that was given to the public through its original advertisements.

QUESTIONS

1. Should the government be involved in corrective advertising cases such as the Listerine situation? Why or why not?
2. How is the public interest served by FTC involvement in cases such as this one?

AN OVERVIEW

Choosing a career is one of the most important decisions affecting your future. Some careers require certain skills and training. For example, if you want to be a manager, you probably would benefit from several years of study in college. Other career choices are not quite so demanding educationally.

One factor that should affect your career choice is the number of available jobs. Unfortunately, this factor is difficult to assess, but many workforce planning studies are available to help you. These are published by the U. S. Government Bureau of Labor Statistics and are in most public and college libraries. You owe it to yourself to learn what types of jobs are likely to be available when you enter the work force. It is reasonable to assume that many new career choices will be open in the next several years in both business and government.

The following questions may help you select college courses and evaluate career opportunities:

▪ How do my personal values and interests compare with the careers available?
▪ What areas of employment are likely to have the greatest career opportunities?
▪ For what career areas does my college education prepare me?

▪ How do earnings in different careers compare?
▪ What are the typical working conditions in different careers?
▪ How much education is necessary for employment and advancement in various careers?

These questions are not easy to answer, but, in your own interest, you should consider them seriously. But remember that the answers may change over time because economic conditions and your personal interests constantly change. Skills that are needed today may be in low demand ten years in the future.

OPPORTUNITIES IN BUSINESS

The opportunities for interesting and varied careers in business are very bright for the foreseeable future. Both the natural expansion of existing jobs and the creation of jobs in new industries will provide them. During the last twenty years of this century, entirely new industries are likely to develop, and they will provide many career opportunities. Consider the computer industry. In 1945, few people would have thought that in only twenty years more than a million people would be employed directly or indirectly as a result of the computer. It is very likely that in the next few years new inventions or new

needs for additional services will have a similar impact on business. Entirely new industries will be created because of technological advances or changes in human values that redirect our nation's energies.

The U. S. Department of Labor has prepared a forecast of job opportunities by broad occupational groups through 1990, using 1978 as the base year. Exhibit I–A shows that, by 1990, job opportunities in the United States will expand 21 percent. Growth in new industries will account for 30 percent of total new jobs. There will also be more opportunities for people seeking professional and managerial jobs. These jobs require both a college education and technical competence, but they are also likely to be the highest paying jobs.

OPPORTUNITIES IN GOVERNMENT

Government service, one of the nation's largest fields of employment, provides jobs for about 1 out of 6 employed persons in the United States. State or local governments (county, city, township, school district, or other special division) now employ 5 out of 6 government workers.

Government employees (federal, state, and local) represent a large portion of each state's work force.

	PROJECTED		
OCCUPATION GROUP	1978 Employment (thousands)	1990 Employment (thousands)	Change
White-collar workers	47,200	58,400	26.2%
Professional/technical workers	14,200	16,900	19.0
Managers and administrators	10,100	12,200	20.8
Salesworkers	6,000	7,600	26.7
Clerical workers	16,900	21,700	28.4
Blue-collar workers	31,500	36,600	16.2
Craft and kindred workers	12,400	14,900	20.2
Operatives	14,400	16,600	15.3
Nonfarm laborers	4,700	5,100	8.5
Service workers	12,900	16,700	29.4
Farm workers	2,800	2,400	−14.3
Totals	94,400	114,100	20.9%

From U.S. Department of Labor, Bureau of Labor Statistics, *Occupational Outlook Handbook* (Washington, D.C.: U.S. Government Printing Office, March 1980), pp. 20–23.

EXHIBIT I–A
Projected Employment by Major Occupations

acquire new values. Each of us goes through stages of growth, development, and uncertainty in a career. This process of change continues throughout life.

You will probably begin the first stage of your career with a limited amount of work experience. Thus, it is important to become informed about the potential careers that are available in the functional areas of business, which include marketing, accounting, finance, and production. In addition to knowing about career opportunities in business, you must learn about yourself. You need to determine what your goals are and what career might help you reach these goals. This is often a difficult process, but there are ways to get at the problem.

First, you should give serious thought to your own preferences regarding a career. You should also talk to people involved with career and guidance counseling in your college. Most career counseling centers provide tests that help you to gain objective appraisals of your skills, attitudes, and aptitudes. The test results and professional evaluation may cause you to rethink your job preferences. Managers of college placement offices are also a valuable source of information about jobs. They are usually aware of current job market conditions and future job trends. But you must make the final choice.

They work in large cities, small towns, even in isolated places such as lighthouses and forest ranger stations. A small number of federal employees work overseas.

Government employment is expected to grow more slowly than the average for all industries through the 1980s. Public concern about rising tax burdens is expected to produce pressure for restraint in government spending at all levels, slowing growth of government employment. Furthermore, a slower than average growth of state and local government employment is expected because of declining public school enrollments. Public school employees and teachers are hired by local governments and paid for by taxes raised in the community.

CAREER PLANNING

Career choice can be thought of as a two-stage process: (1) learning about job opportunities, and (2) learning about yourself. By making an effort to get information on these two points, you will be able to make a better career decision. Careers don't just happen in most cases. Preparing for future jobs requires developing a systematic career plan.

Even with a career plan, you are likely to change jobs and organizations more than once during your life because your personal goals will change. Even the best of plans must be altered when conditions warrant. The main reason people change their career plans is that they change in ambition, develop new skills, and

JOB OPPORTUNITIES

There are two major objectives in learning about job opportunities. First, you want to know what jobs are available in the job market. Second, you want to become informed about the nature of these jobs.

Your college placement office is an excellent place to start when you want to find out what jobs are available. People in such offices should have current and accurate information about employment possibilities. Your teachers and people in business should also be able to assist you in learning about the local, national, and international job market.

Learning about the nature of jobs is more difficult than finding out what jobs are available. There is no sure or easy way to do this. One place you can begin is by reading publications that discuss jobs and positions. Two such publications are:

■ *Encyclopedia of Careers and Vocational Guidance*, 4th ed. New York: Doubleday, 1978. Volume 2, *Careers and Occupations*, describes different occupations.

■ *Occupational Outlook Handbook*, Washington, D.C.: U.S. Department of Labor, Bureau of Labor Statistics. This book, published annually, contains information about jobs, educational requirements, and incomes.

This textbook also will introduce you to career possibilities in the different areas of business. For example, you will read about careers in marketing, finance, banking, accounting, and computers. After reading the career sections, you will have some idea of the characteristics, requirements, and future opportunities in these areas of business. But this material will present only the most basic information.

Perhaps the most important thing you can do to prepare for a career is to maintain sufficient educational breadth to take advantage of new career opportunities. Routine jobs are most vulnerable for elimination because computers can take over such work. For this reason, education may be far more important than narrow, technical training for today's business student.

PROFILE IN BUSINESS

Mary Kay Ash

The "Powder Puff General" transformed thousands of bored homemakers into an efficient, intensely loyal army of businesswomen.

Her mother left the house each morning at 6 A.M. to run the family's Houston restaurant, and Mary Kay, age seven, cared for her invalid father. That early independence and the image of a hard-working woman generated one of the fastest growing commercial ventures in America, but it took a while.

Kay was an honor student in high school, but college seemed remote and too expensive. "I got married instead," she says. But then the draft during World War II left her with three small children on a gravel street in the wrong part of Houston. She took a part-time job selling household products at parties in homes. Thirteen years and one divorce later, she transferred to another direct-sales company, World Gifts. In eleven more years, she was national training director, but that seemed to be the limit for her at World Gifts. "At some point, you reach that golden door marked 'Men Only.'" When she spent a year training a man who was then appointed her boss, making twice her salary, Mary Kay "retired"—briefly.

Remarried in the same year she left World Gifts, 1963, Mary Kay Hallenbeck and her new husband devised a direct-sales cosmetics operation that would celebrate the womanpower other companies restrained. She bought formulas for skin-care products from the granddaughter of a hide tanner. She drew

PART TWO

MANAGEMENT AND ORGANIZATION

up lists of everything that the firms she had worked for had done right and wrong, added her corrections, and talked nine friends into giving the Mary Kay Cosmetics sales pitch a try. "Exactly one month to the day before we were due to open, my husband dropped dead at the breakfast table. I saw the world collapsing around me."

But her two sons, one of whom is now the firm's president, rallied behind her. They trained "consultants" in Mary Kay's keenest sales techniques and no-nonsense skin-care program, sold them $65 product kits, and sent them off into a clog-pored Middle America ripe for "beauty show parties." There is no cold canvassing in Mary Kay's operation. A consultant arranges parties for four or five interested women in the prospective customers' own homes, where everyone relaxes but

peer pressure is intense. As they increase sales and recruit more consultants, Mary Kay's saleswomen become directors, senior directors, and area directors, collecting commissions on their own sales and those of their recruits. To lure consultants up this ladder, Mary Kay Ash (remarried again) drapes each rung with gift-rewards: typewriters, telephone-answering devices, color TVs, mink coats, diamond rings, portraits of Mary Kay. As many as 6500 diamond rings have been distributed in a single month. But the ultimate reward, for top area directors with annual retail sales exceeding $100,000, is one year's use of a pink Cadillac, the company hallmark.

One courtesy never extended to consultants is credit. "A woman in direct sales with no business background will sell $300 worth . . . forget

the company store and shop and spend it. Two weeks later when it's time to pay, there's no money. And you get an out-of-state hot check." Consultants pay hard cash for their own inventory.

In 1981, Mary Kay's sales force numbered over 40,000 throughout the United States, Canada, and Australia. Twenty-five percent of them converge annually for a three-day sales seminar and awards program, usually held in Dallas, Ash's home town and headquarters. These gatherings resemble religious revivals more than corporate conventions, with much singing and many tearful testimonials by glazed homemakers transformed into resourceful, independent businesswomen.

Mary Kay Ash sells more than cosmetics.

CHAPTER 4

FORMS OF BUSINESS OWNERSHIP

LEARNING OBJECTIVES

After studying this chapter, you should be able to:

Discuss the advantages and disadvantages of the major forms of business—sole proprietorship, partnership, and corporation.

Describe the differences between a general and a limited partner.

Explain the different types of corporations that operate in the U.S. economy.

Compare the extent of liability to owners of a sole proprietorship, a partnership, and a corporation.

Illustrate what is meant by the term *double taxation* of corporate stockholders.

KEY TERMS

Sole proprietorship
Unlimited liability
Partnership
General partnership
Limited partnership
Joint venture
Syndicate
Business trust
Corporation
Charter
Proxy
Double taxation
Subchapter S
   corporation
Merger
Consolidation
Cooperative
Savings and loan
   associations

LIVING AND WORKING AS PARTNERS

Not so long ago, Bill and Nancy Riemer had what many might call a comfortable life. Nancy had been a fashion retailer for eighteen years in an Indianapolis clothing store. Bill was a middle manager for Vitro Laboratories. They owned two small cars and a home well on its way to being paid for, and together they earned over $44,000 a year. What they did not have, both agreed, was a great deal of satisfaction with their jobs. They both felt burned-out, tired, and bored.

Then, in the summer of 1979, they visited friends in Mesa, Arizona, where it dawned on them that they needed a change in their comfortable life. Bill and Nancy looked at a number of business opportunities and thought about different forms of businesses—sole proprietorship, partnership, and corporation. After about three months of considering their life and what it would take to run a business, they bought a women's clothing store in Prescott, Arizona, for about $80,000. To do so, they formed a partnership. It was a form of business that was easy to start, they could combine their skills, and it had some tax advantages over a corporation.

Since its beginning, the business has required both Bill and Nancy to put in at least 60 hours each per week. They have had some business disagreements. In addition, they have been short of cash to expand the store's line of clothing. Despite these problems, Bill and Nancy claim that they are happier than ever before and excited about owning their own business.

Bill and Nancy are enthusiastic about life. Everything is not perfect and not what they thought it would be, but they have found many new challenges. They now know from experience that forming a partnership has its advantages and disadvantages. They made a carefully thought-out decision to leave corporate life for their own business. You have to know who you are and what you want before taking a major step like Bill and Nancy's.

The year was 1947, and Frank Gorell was playing the French horn for the Broadway opening of *Annie Get Your Gun*. On the stage, the vibrant Ethel Merman belted out, with authority, "There's No Business like Show Business," while Gorell, down in the orchestra pit, worried about the storm window business.

Gorell was a career concert musician, although he always claimed to be a businessperson at heart. In 1947, he invested all his savings in a new venture—a storm window manufacturing business. He felt that this was a new product people needed. By night, he played for *Annie Get Your Gun*; by day, he sold storm windows through his corporation.

Now in his sixties, Gorell is president of Season-all Industries, a $30-million manufacturer of custom-made storm and replacement windows. As Gorell tells it, there are some 40 million U.S. homes more than twenty years old. Their windows can seldom be replaced by standard-size windows. Season-all dealers take a customer's measurements, which are then forwarded to a plant where the window is made. With the energy crisis, Season-all is a growing corporation.

The Gorell success story is possible for any person in the American business system.[1] Of course, not every business can be as successful as Season-all. But everyone in the United States can start a business or become an owner of a business.

Anyone who wants to start a business may choose from three basic forms of private ownership: sole proprietorship, partnership, and corporation. Frank Gorell chose to form a corporation. Another person in a similar situation may have elected to form a proprietorship. Bill and Nancy Riemer selected a partnership. There is no "right" or "correct" form of business ownership, and it's possible to convert from one type of ownership to another.

SOME INITIAL GUIDELINES

In the United States today, there are about 11 million sole proprietorships, 1 million partnerships, and 2 million corporations. Each form of business ownership has advantages and disadvantages. If you are planning to go into business, you need to review these pros and cons and determine which form of ownership is best suited for you. The guidelines that can help you make a decision about the type of ownership will be discussed throughout this chapter.

A person considering business ownership should examine the following factors:

- *Capital requirements.* The amount of funds necessary to finance the operation
- *Risk.* The amount of personal property a person is willing to risk by starting the business
- *Control.* The amount of control the owner exercises
- *Managerial abilities.* The managerial ability needed to plan, organize, and control the business
- *Time requirements.* The time needed to operate the business and provide guidance to the employees
- *Tax liability.* The taxes a person must pay because of the business

SOLE PROPRIETORSHIPS

SOLE PROPRIETORSHIP
A business owned and managed by one individual.

The oldest and most common form of private business ownership in the United States is the sole proprietorship. A **sole proprietorship** is a business owned and managed by one individual. The owner may have help from others in operating the business, but the sole proprietor is the boss; he or she "is" the company.

Typically, the sole proprietor is the owner of a small service or retail operation, such as a beauty shop, hardware store, bakery, or restaurant. The sole owner, often aided by one or two employees, operates a small shop that usually caters to a group of regular customers. The owner is usually an active manager, working in the shop every day.

The capital (money) needed to start and operate the business is normally provided by the owner, through personal wealth or borrowed money. The sole proprietor controls the operations, supervises the employees, and makes most of the decisions. It is the managerial ability of the owner that usually accounts for the success or failure of the business.

As Exhibit 4–1 indicates, approximately 11 million individuals operate sole proprietorships in the United States. The largest number of sole proprietors are in agriculture, forestry, and fisheries, and in services. Although sole proprietorships make up about 78 percent of all businesses in the United States, they account for only about 8.3 percent of all sales, as Exhibit 4–2 shows. Corporations, on the other hand, account for about 14 percent of all businesses but about 87 percent of total sales. Partnerships make up about 8 percent of all businesses and account for about 4 percent of total sales.

Advantages of a Sole Proprietorship

Many people have the desire to be their own boss. This goal can be accomplished by forming a sole proprietorship. There are other advantages as well.

Ease of starting. Any person can start a sole proprietorship with a minimum number of problems. For example, Irene Pappas wanted to start a bakery in Tarpon Springs, Florida. She decided that a sole proprietorship

EXHIBIT 4–1
Forms of Business Ownership in Various Industries

INDUSTRY	NUMBER OF BUSINESSES (IN THOUSANDS)		
	Proprietorships	Partnerships	Corporations
Agriculture, forestry, and fisheries	3,177	121	66
Mining	71	22	19
Construction	994	69	215
Manufacturing	224	28	231
Transportation, communication, and public utilities	385	17	85
Trade	2,265	193	673
Wholesale	307	29	238
Retail	1,862	164	433
Finance, insurance, and real estate	895	476	433
Services	3,303	227	517
All industries	11,346	1,153	2,242

Adapted from U.S. Department of Commerce, Bureau of the Census, *Statistical Abstracts of the United States*, 1981, p. 535.

was best for her needs. No general laws prohibited Irene from starting the bakery, but she needed a food permit from the Tarpon Springs Health Department. She also needed a $100 occupational license, from the Florida Department of Revenue, to operate her bakery.

Once Irene received the food permit and paid the license fee, she began operations. By contrast, a partnership usually must pay a legal fee for drawing up articles of partnership, a legally binding agreement. A corporation must pay an incorporation fee to the state in which it is chartered and legal fees for filing all the documents needed to incorporate.

Total control. Irene, as the owner, had total control over the operations of the bakery. She was the boss who made final decisions.

As the sole owner, Irene worked as many hours as she wanted. This freedom indicates the control she had over daily operations and decisions. Of course, if Irene decided to take every other afternoon off to play tennis, an employee would have to be present to operate the business, or the doors would close.

Participation in profits and losses. All the profits earned or losses incurred by operating the bakery were Irene's. In contrast, partners share profits and losses. In states that permit one person to own a corporation, ownership of profits and losses is comparable to that in the sole proprietorship.

Use of managerial ability. Irene had everything to lose or gain from her efforts. The possibility of personal losses generally encouraged Irene to devote time, energy, and expertise to the bakery's operation, and success depended largely on the efficient use of her abilities. Thus, Irene had to use her own managerial abilities or pay someone else who had managerial expertise. Either way, full credit for success or blame for failure belonged to Irene.

Secrecy. Irene, like other individuals who don't own a business, filed information on income, expenses, hours worked, and other items required by income tax regulations. This information typically is not made available to the public. Any other information, such as the special formula for her delicious Greek pastries, did not have to be shared with the public because Irene was a sole proprietor.

Tax breaks. A major advantage of the proprietorship over the corporation is that the business pays no income tax. Instead, Irene paid taxes as an individual on all her income earned from the bakery. A corporation pays taxes on profits, and its owners, the stockholders, pay taxes on their dividends. Therefore, Irene as a sole proprietor paid no taxes on business profits.

Ease of dissolving. If Irene were to decide to dissolve the proprietorship for personal, health, financial, or any other reasons, there would be no legal complications. If, after owning the bakery for three years, she decided to close the business, she would be free to do so. As long as she had paid all the outstanding bills, her decision would be all that is needed to close the bakery. Irene would not even have to consult with a partner.

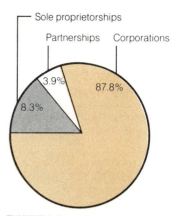

EXHIBIT 4–2
Business Sales of U.S. Organizations. (From U.S. Department of Commerce, Bureau of the Census, *Statistical Abstracts of the United States*, 1981, p. 534.)

Disadvantages of a Sole Proprietorship

If there were only advantages associated with the sole proprietorship, a person organizing a business would have little to consider. But the realities of the business world are never so simple and certain.

UNLIMITED LIABILITY
Obligation of investors to use personal assets, when necessary, to pay off debts to business creditors; a disadvantage of sole proprietorships and partnerships.

Unlimited liability. The law provides that Irene's total wealth may be used to satisfy the claims of the bakery; this is called **unlimited liability**. For Irene, this means that practically everything she owned could be sold to pay any debts for operating the bakery. For example, if Irene's bakery failed, she might have to sell her personal jewelry or automobile to pay business debts that couldn't be paid by the liquidation or sale of such business assets as bakery ovens and a cash register.

Difficulty in raising capital. Irene's investment in the bakery was limited to personal wealth. The amount she could borrow to operate the business was also limited by her personal wealth. If she had a large estate, Irene would have little problem borrowing money. Generally, businesses requiring large amounts of capital are not formed as sole proprietorships. Few individuals can affort $200 to $300 million to build a gas pipeline or to operate a specialty airline.

Limitations in managerial ability. Irene must have or get all the know-how needed to manage the shop. Operating a bakery needs someone with planning, organizing, controlling, marketing, financial, motivational, and customer-relations skills. Irene is unlikely to have all these abilities herself. Indeed, it's a rare individual who has this range of needed expertise. However, many of these managerial abilities can be bought. For example, Irene could hire an accountant to keep the books and an advertising consultant to help promote her bakery goods.

Lack of stability. Death, illness, bankruptcy, or retirement of the owner terminates the proprietorship. Irene's business could be sold to others, but the bakery as organized would cease to exist.

PARTNERSHIPS

PARTNERSHIP
A business owned by two or more people.

GENERAL PARTNERSHIP
A partnership in which at least one partner has unlimited liability; a general partner has authority to act and make binding decisions as an owner.

LIMITED PARTNERSHIP
A partnership with at least one general partner and one or more limited partners who are liable for loss only up to the amount of their investment.

It is not unusual for a business to have a small beginning as a sole proprietorship, later expand into a partnership, and finally become a corporation. Many corporate giants like J. C. Penney, H. J. Heinz, and Ford Motor Company started as sole proprietorships. The Uniform Partnership Act, Section 6, defines a **partnership** as "an association of two or more persons to carry on as co-owners of a business for profit."[2] Thus, it is similar in many respects to a sole proprietorship. One major difference is the number of owners.

A partnership can be based on a written contract or oral agreement that is voluntary and legal. The law regards individuals as partners when they act in such a way as to make people believe that they are operating a business together.

There are about 1 million partnerships, of various types, in the United States. Some of the types can be identified by name; others cannot. The two major types are the general and the limited partnership. A **general partnership** is a business with at least one general partner (see below) who has unlimited liability for the debts of the business. A **limited partnership** has at least one general partner and one or more limited partners.

DO YOU REALLY WANT TO TAKE THE PLUNGE?

A question-and-answer session with an expert on starting sole proprietorships reveals some important information. Gene C. Walker is such an expert, and here is some of what he has to say.

Q. Does the idea of starting a business still hold great appeal?

A. It certainly does. That is evident from Dun & Bradstreet figures showing that 530,000 businesses were started in 1980.

Q. How prepared are most people to enter business?

A. Miserably. Some people find themselves technically or emotionally unprepared to be the creator of ideas, the boss, the person who has to meet the Friday-night payroll. Others start businesses in fields in which they have no experience at all. Their chances for success are slim.

Q. How does a person know if he or she has what it takes to go into business?

A. Ultimately, you really can't be sure until you've taken the plunge. However, it's good to ask some soul-searching questions. How badly do I want to be on my own? How much am I willing to sacrifice my time and energy? How many burdens am I willing to put on my family? If you want to work only 9 to 5, the business probably won't survive much beyond the time when your first seed money runs out.

Adapted from "Starting a New Business," *U.S. News & World Report*, July 13, 1981, pp. 75–76.

The General Partner

Regardless of the percentage of the business that he or she owns, a *general partner* has the authority to act and to make binding decisions as an owner of the business. The general partner is potentially liable for all the debts of the business, although partners generally share profits and losses. By contrast, the sole proprietor is always liable for such debts. The agreement reached between partners usually specifies the plan for sharing profit and loss.

With the authority to act as an owner, a general partner can engage the partnership in binding agreements. Unless a partnership agreement prevents a general partner from making such agreements, the partnership is responsible for all actions of each owner.

Limited Partners

All partnerships must have at least one general partner. They can also have limited partners. A limited partner can be *silent* (known as an owner but takes no active role in management), *secret* (takes an active role but is not publicly known), *dormant* (takes no active role and is not publicly known), or *nominal* (lends his or her name but takes no active role and does not invest any money). A limited partner is liable for loss only up to the amount of capital invested. Thus, if a limited partner invests $20,000 in the business, he or she is liable for only that amount.

The Partnership Contract

It is sound business practice, although not required, that a partnership agreement be written and signed. Such a contractual agreement is referred to as *articles of partnership*. Written articles of partnership can prevent or minimize misunderstandings at a later date. Although oral partnership agreements are perfectly legal, they tend to be difficult to recreate and are open to misunderstandings. The proof of an agreement can be captured in the written articles of partnership.

The main features of a written partnership agreement include:

- The name of the business partnership
- The type of business
- The location of the business
- The expected life of the partnership
- The names of the partners and the amount of investment each is making
- The procedures for distributing profits and covering losses
- The amount partners will withdraw for services
- The procedure for funds withdrawal
- The duties of each partner
- The procedures for dissolving the partnership

Advantages of a Partnership

On the Job Revisited

Like the sole proprietorship, the partnership has some advantages and some disadvantages. Bill and Nancy Riemer in this chapter's "On the Job" carefully weighed each of these advantages and disadvantages before purchasing their clothing store. Some of the advantages of a partnership listed below may outweigh the disadvantages associated with a sole proprietorship.

More capital. In the sole proprietorship, the amount of capital is limited to the personal wealth and credit of the owner. In a partnership, the amount of capital may increase significantly. A person with a good idea but little capital can look for a partner with the capital and/or credit standing to develop and market the idea.

Combined managerial skills. In a partnership, people with different talents and skills may join together. One partner may be good at marketing, and the other may be an expert in accounting and financial matters. The combination of these skills could make the business a success.

Ease of starting. Because a partnership involves a private contractual arrangement, it is relatively easy to start. It is nearly as free from government regulation as a sole proprietorship is. The cost of starting a partnership is low and usually involves only a modest legal fee for drawing up a written agreement. An oral agreement is sufficient but not recommended. Bill and Nancy Riemer had a lawyer friend set up the legal framework for their clothing store.

On the Job Revisited

Legal status. Over the years, legal precedents for partnerships have been established through court cases. The questions of rights, responsibilities, liabilities, and partner duties have been covered. Thus, the legal status of the partnership is understood, and lawyers can provide sound legal advice on partnership issues.

Tax advantages. The partnership has some potential tax advantages over a corporation. In a partnership, as in a sole proprietorship, the owners pay taxes on their business earnings, but the partnership as a business doesn't pay income tax. In 1971, the federal government reduced the income tax ceiling for earned income to 50 percent, which is less than the ceiling for business income. As a result, sole proprietors and partners have a tax advantage over corporation owners.

There are also disadvantages associated with the partnership form of business. These must be weighed against advantages before making a decision on forming a partnership.

Disadvantages of a Partnership

Unlimited liability. Each general partner is liable for the partnership debts. Suppose that Bill and Nancy's partnership fails with outstanding bills of $60,000. This amount must be paid by someone. If Bill doesn't have the personal assets to pay off the debt and Nancy does, she has to pay off the debts. This is one reason for choosing partners carefully.

On the Job Revisited

Potential conflicts. Although decisions made by several people (partners) are often better than those made by one, there is a potential danger in two or more people deciding on some aspect of the business. Power and authority are divided, and the partners will not always agree with each other. As a result, poor decisions may be made. Disagreements between partners make decision making more time consuming because a compromise or agreement must be reached before action can be taken.

Instability. If a partner dies or withdraws from the business, the partnership is dissolved. A new partnership or some other form of business organization must be legally established.

Investment withdrawal. A person who invests money in a partnership may have difficulty withdrawing the investment. It is much easier to invest in a partnership than it is to withdraw. The money is typically considered a "frozen investment" and is used in the operation of the business.

Limited capital availability. The partnership may have an advantage over the sole proprietorship in the availability of capital, but there is no comparison between a partnership's and a corporation's ability to raise capital. In most cases, partners have a limited capability and are not able to compete in businesses requiring large outlays. The amount of capital a partnership can raise depends on the personal wealth of the partners and their credit ratings. It also depends on how much they are willing to invest in the partnership.

Besides proprietorships and partnerships, there are a few other forms of ownership that do not require incorporation. These forms are used by people who want to join together to accomplish various objectives without going to the trouble of forming a corporation.

OTHER UNINCORPORATED FORMS OF BUSINESS

Joint Ventures

JOINT VENTURE
Similar to a partnership except that actual management is delegated to one person and the venture usually lasts for only a short time.

A temporary partnership, usually set up for a specific purpose and for a short period of time, is a **joint venture**. It is an association of persons who combine their money, efforts, knowledge, and ability for the purpose of carrying out a single business operation to make a profit. For example, ten investors may join together to buy 100 acres of land on the outskirts of a growing city such as San Diego. The land is to be held for five years. During this time, it will be developed into a subdivision, and lots will be sold to home builders. When the lots are all sold, the joint venture will end.

Over the short duration of the joint venture, each participant has the same legal position as a general partner. But in most joint ventures, the managerial decisions are made by one participant. The joint venture differs from the general partnership in that it is not a continuing business.

Syndicates

SYNDICATE
A business that engages in financial transactions. Members can sell their ownership interest to buyers of their choice.

An association of two or more individuals or businesses for a particular business purpose is a **syndicate**. In most cases, syndicates engage in financial transactions. Unlike a joint venture, a syndicate need not be dissolved after the transaction is completed. The members of a syndicate can sell their ownership interest to buyers of their choice. In a partnership, the remaining partners can veto a new partner.

A common type of syndicate is the underwriting syndicate, a group of investment banking companies formed for the purpose of selling a large issue of corporation stocks. The managerial decisions are in the hands of the group that forms the synidcate.

Business Trusts

BUSINESS TRUST
A business that holds title to securities for investors.

A **business trust** is often used to hold securities for investors. In general, a trust allows the transfer of legal title to a property to one person for the use and benefit of another. The original name for this form of business was the *Massachusetts trust*, because it was created in that state when the laws did not allow corporations to buy and sell real estate.

Under the business trust, a trustee or group of trustees is legally permitted to do business. The trustees issue shares, called *trust certificates*, to investors. These shares show that the holder has transferred funds to a trustee and has the legal right to benefit from the success of the trust investments. Shareholders have no right to vote for trustees or to have a voice in management, but they do have the right to sell their trust certificates to a buyer of their choice.

CORPORATIONS

CORPORATION
A business that is a legal entity separate from its owners.

Some industries, such as automobile manufacturing, computer manufacturing, oil refining, and natural gas production, require millions of dollars to operate a business. The only way such vast sums of money can be put together is by attracting numerous investors. The unincorporated forms of business—the proprietorship and the partnership—are not attractive enough to investors who do not want to make decisions or to be actually involved in managing the firm. The **corporation**, by contrast, provides a form of business ownership whereby owners spread over a wide geographical area can hire professional managers to operate the business. In the eyes of the law, the corporation is an artificial being, invisible, and intangible. It has the rights of a legal person—it can own property, purchase goods and services, and sue other individuals or corporations.

The corporate form of business organization accounts for about 87 percent of the total sales (over $3000 billion) of U.S. businesses. There are over 1.9 million profit-oriented corporations of all sizes. In addition, there are many corporations that are not conducted for profit and that do not have private owners or stockholders. These nonprofit corporations conduct their business in the areas of government (for instance, the U. S. Postal Service), education, health (a public-health clinic), religion, and charity (the March of Dimes).

The Formation of a Corporation

The legal status of a corporation stems from a **charter**, which is a state-issued document authorizing its formation. In 1830, New York extended the use of the corporate form to businesses, and by the early 1860s, most of the other states granted corporation charters.

CHARTER
A state's written agreement giving a corporation the right to operate as a business.

Most states require that at least three persons join together to form a corporation. They fill out an application form for a charter (articles of incorporation) which is reviewed by state officials. An example of a corporation application for the state of Minnesota is presented in Exhibit 4–3.

After the charter has been granted, the incorporators and all subscribers or the owners of the stock of the business meet and elect a board of directors. They also approve the bylaws of the corporation, if this is a state requirement. The board of directors then meets to elect the professional managers and to make any other decisions needed to start the business.

The corporation has many relationships with various groups. Included in the corporation's domain of operation are stockholders, creditors, customers, and employees. Exhibit 4–4 presents the corporation's range of relationships. The actual owners of the business, as shown in Exhibit 4–4, are the stockholders who have invested their money. The corporation is run by professional managers who plan, organize, control, and direct the activities needed to sell goods and/or services to customers. It is also the managers who decide what property to purchase, what human resources to hire, and where to borrow needed funds.

Types of Corporations

When we think about business corporations, our attention usually centers on the giants that are listed annually in *Fortune's* "Directory of the 500 Largest U.S. Industrial Corporations." This listing includes over 130 firms with assets of more than $1 billion. Included in this list of giants are such well-known corporations as U.S. Steel, Mobil Oil, General Motors, IBM, Tenneco, and Westinghouse Electric. Each of these corporations is profit-oriented. The ten largest U.S. corporations are listed in Exhibit 4–5.

Many state universities and many religious organizations are nonprofit corporations. Such government corporations as the National Aeronautics and Space Administration and the Tennessee Valley Authority exist only to provide services to the public. Exhibit 4–6 lists these and other types of corporations that operate in the United States.

Running the Corporation

A corporation is managed by a board of directors elected by the stockholders or owners. Directors are assumed to be free to make their own judgments on all matters presented to them. The directors do not make judgments for one group of owners. They make judgments in the best

EXHIBIT 4-3
A Sample Articles of Incorporation

ARTICLES OF INCORPORATION

OF

_____
(name of corporation)

We, the undersigned, of full age, for the purpose of forming a corporation under and pursuant to the provisions of Chapter 301 Minn. Statues, known as the Minnesota Business Corporation Act, and laws amendatory thereof and supplementary thereto, do hereby associate ourselves as a body corporate and adopt the following Articles of Incorporation:

ARTICLE I

The name of this corporation is: _____

Note: The corporate name must end with "Incorporated," "Inc." or "Corporation" or contain "Company" or "Co." not immediately preceded by "and" or "&."

ARTICLE II

The purposes of this corporation are: _____
_____
_____
_____
_____

ARTICLE III

The period of duration of corporate existence of this corporation shall be:
_____

Note: The duration may be perpetual or for a specified period of time.

ARTICLE IV

The location of the registered office of this corporation in this state is:
_____

Note: Give street or post office address, city or town, county and zipcode number.

ARTICLE VI

The amount of stated capital with which this corporation will begin business is:
_____

Note: The stated capital must be at least $1000.

ARTICLE VII

The total authorized number of shares of par value is: _____
and the par value of each share is: _____
The total authorized number of shares without par value is: _____
_____

ARTICLE VIII

The description of the classes of shares, the number of shares in each class, and the relative rights, voting power, preferences and restrictions are as follows: _____
_____

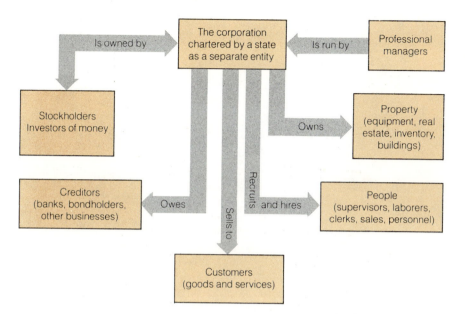

EXHIBIT 4-4
The Domain of the Profit-Oriented Corporation

interest of all owners. Thus, they are in most cases elected because of their business ability.

The directors are elected by the stockholders; usually, each share of common stock entitles the stockholder to one vote (see Chapter 13 for discussion of stock). For example, George Kinncaid of Saginaw, Michigan, owns ten shares of General Electric voting stock and is therefore eligible to cast ten votes. In many cases, stockholders vote by proxy. A **proxy** is a written statement signed by the stockholder allowing someone else to cast his or her number of votes. Usually the proxy permits a member of the board of directors to cast the votes.

Once the board is elected, it must put together the best possible team of managers to run the day-to-day operations. The board of directors decides

PROXY
A written statement signed by a stockholder of a corporation allowing someone else to cast his or her number of votes.

EXHIBIT 4-5
Ten Largest U.S. Industrial Corporations

RANK		COMPANY	SALES	ASSETS		EMPLOYEES	
'81	'80		($000)	($000)	RANK	NUMBER	RANK
1	1	Exxon (New York)	108,107,688	62,931,055	1	180,000	8
2	2	Mobil (New York)	64,488,000	34,776,000	3	206,400	6
3	3	General Motors (Detroit)	62,698,500	38,991,200	2	741,000	1
4	4	Texaco (Harrison, N.Y.)	57,628,000	27,489,000	5	66,728	49
5	5	Standard Oil of California (San Francisco)	44,224,000	23,680,000	7	43,281	101
6	6	Ford Motor (Dearborn, Mich.)	38,247,100	23,021,400	8	404,788	2
7	9	Standard Oil (Indiana) (Chicago)	29,947,000	22,916,000	9	58,665	64
8	8	International Business Machines (Armonk, N.Y.)	29,070,000	29,586,000	4	354,936	4
9	7	Gulf Oil (Pittsburgh)	28,252,000	20,429,000	11	58,500	65
10	11	Atlantic Richfield (Los Angeles)	27,797,436	19,732,539	13	54,200	75

Source: From "The 500 Largest Industrial Corporations," *Fortune,* May 3, 1982, pp. 260–279.

EXHIBIT 4-6
Types of Corporations

TYPE	DESCRIPTION	EXAMPLES
Private	Attempts to earn a profit	General Electric, Tenneco
Public	Owned and run by the government	NASA, Tennessee Valley Authority
Closed	Stock held by only a few owners and not actively sold on the stockmarket	Dallas Cowboys, Brunswick, Hughes Aircraft, Mars Candy, Hallmark Cards
Open	Stock held by numerous people and actively sold on the stock market	W. R. Grace, General Mills
Municipal	Cities and townships that carry out business	San Diego, California; Knoxville, Tennessee
Nonprofit	Service organization incorporated for limited-liability status	Notre Dame University, Boy Scouts of America
Single-individual	Individually owned business incorporated to escape high personal income tax rate	Johnny Carson Clothing, Inc.

for or against the recommendations submitted by the officers of the corporation. Although the board is the final authority, it usually responds to requests and recommendations that are made by the professional managers.

The stockholders are the actual owners. They have the right to inspect the books and papers of the business, the right to attend stockholders' meetings, the right to vote on certain matters (such as mergers), and the right to share in the profits earned. Even if John Jones owns 3000 shares and Nancy Wilcox owns only 2 shares, they have the same rights. Many stockholders are uninterested in the rights of ownership except for the privilege of sharing in the profits by receiving dividends. This may be just as well, because if decisions had to be based on the opinions of all owners, the business would stand still. Of all U.S. corporations, American Telephone & Telegraph has the largest number of stockholders, with over 3 million owners. General Motors has about 1.2 million owners, and IBM has the third-largest number of stockholders, with about 740,000.

Advantages of a Corporation

The power and presence of corporations in American business suggest that they have certain advantages over other forms of business ownership.

Limited liability. A person investing funds in a corporation receives shares of stock and becomes an owner. In a corporation, the liability of the stockholder equals the amount of funds invested. Thus, if the business is forced to liquidate, each owner loses only the amount of money he or she has invested.

Skilled management team. The board of directors is responsible for hiring professional managers, and the owners delegate their power of operating the business to these managers. Professional managers are

THE ROCKEFELLERS ARE OWNERS IN A BIG WAY

A rare look into the holdings of the Rockefeller family was provided during 1974 congressional hearings on the nomination of Nelson Rockefeller as vice president of the United States. The total value of the family's investment came to a little over $1 billion. The Rockefeller ownership of corporations was also interesting. The family's ownership in some corporations was as follows:

	Total Number of Shares	Market Value
Exxon	2,288,171	$156,700,000
IBM	384,042	72,600,000
Mobil	1,762,206	63,600,000
General Electric	509,952	19,400,000
Rockefeller Center	1,125,000	98,300,000
Merck	455,100	30,000,000

	Total Number of Shares	Market Value
Coca-Cola	62,200	3,900,000
Eastman Kodak	535,973	38,400,000
J. C. Penney	40,596	1,700,000
Standard Oil of California	3,410,148	83,300,000

Members of the Rockefeller family are some of the owners of these corporations. Even though they own so many shares, they have no different rights or privileges of ownership than the person who owns a single share of stock.

Adapted from ''What the Rockefellers Own,'' in *Everybody's Business*, edited by Milton Moskowitz, Michael Karz, and Robert Levering (New York: Harper & Row, 1980), p. 867.

trained and experienced career executives. They may own shares of stock in the business, but usually they do not own enough to control the corporation.

Transfer of ownership. Stockholders have the right to sell their shares of a corporation's stock to whomever they please, barring a legal restriction on some closed corporations. These shares of ownership can be sold whenever the stockholder desires and at the price the buyer is willing to pay. Thus, stockholders can freely buy and sell shares of stock. The investment flows easily and is not frozen. This right to sell shares of stock gives corporations the ability to attract large numbers of stockholders.

Greater capital base. As previously stated, the size of a proprietorship or partnership is limited to the amount of capital that one or several people have available and are willing to invest. But the corporation can attract capital from a large number of investors by selling shares of stock.

Stability. State law varies, but a corporation can usually be chartered to operate indefinitely. The death, retirement, or sale of stock by stockholders need not dissolve the business. The corporation's policies may be altered by the sale of large blocks of stock, but the business will go on. Nor will the death or retirement of the president of the board or the chief executive officer stop the corporation from doing business.

Legal entity. A corporation can purchase property, make contracts, or sue and be sued in its corporate name. These characteristics distinguish it most clearly from other forms of business organization. As Justice Marshall of the U.S. Supreme Court stated, a corporation is "an artificial being." This legal status allows the stockholders to have limited liability.

Disadvantages of a Corporation

As was true with the other forms of business organization, the corporation has some disadvantages. Some of the more obvious ones follow.

Difficulty of starting. Establishing a corporation involves applying for a charter from a state. Each state has its own set of laws, and these must be considered before deciding where to incorporate. The chosen state then reviews the application and issues a charter that specifies various restrictions on operations.

Lack of ownership control. The individual stockholder has little control over the operations of the corporation except to vote for a slate of individuals for the board of directors. The buying and selling of shares of stock is the only real control an owner has.

Taxation. In addition to an annual franchise tax in the state of incorporation, an annual payment is required by most states for the right to operate as a corporation. There are no such fees charged to a proprietorship or partnership. In some states, there are also corporate state income taxes levied on income earned within the state. The taxes are at lower rates than federal taxes.

At the federal level, the corporation has to pay taxes on its profits. The minimum rate of tax on the first $25,000 of corporate profit has varied over the years. In 1983 the rate is 15 percent; it is 18 percent in the $25,000–$50,000 range; 30 percent in the $50,000–$75,000 range; and 40 percent in the $75,000–$100,000 range. Profit in excess of $100,000 is taxed at a rate of 46 percent. The stockholders must also pay income tax on the dividends they receive through ownership. This practice of taxing corporate income and dividends is referred to as **double taxation**.

Under present tax laws, a small corporation with ten or fewer owners can elect to be taxed as a partnership. These smaller corporations are identified as **Subchapter S corporations** (see discussion later in this chapter) because they are identified in Subchapter S of the Internal Revenue Code. A comparison of how federal income taxes apply to the three forms of business ownership appears in Exhibit 4–7.

Government involvement. State and federal governments have the right by law to exercise certain control on, and to require certain reports from, businesses. For example, a corporation cannot conduct its business in a state it isn't registered in.

A corporation organized under the laws of one state (Delaware) or country is called, within that state or country, a *domestic* corporation. When such a business operates in another state (for example, Illinois) or country, it is called a *foreign* corporation. Foreign corporations doing business in several states must obtain a certificate of authority from each state. Some states require a foreign corporation to deposit bonds with the state treasurer to protect anyone who might suffer loss by reason of some action by the corporation.

DOUBLE TAXATION
Taxing a corporate owner's money twice by taxing it as income of a corporation and as dividends of the individual owner.

SUBCHAPTER S CORPORATION
A corporation with ten or fewer owners; files an income tax return as a partnership to take advantage of lower tax rates.

ITEM	PROPRIETORSHIP OR PARTNERSHIP	LARGE CORPORATION (ALL EARNINGS PAID TO OWNERS)	SUBCHAPTER S CORPORATION (10 OR FEWER OWNERS)*
Sales (annual)	$500,000	$500,000	$500,000
Expenses	400,000	400,000	400,000
Before-tax profit margin	100,000	100,000	100,000
Tax on business	0	25,750[†]	0
After-tax profit margin	100,000	74,250	100,000
Tax on owner(s)[‡]	45,000	33,413	45,000
Owners' after-tax share of earnings	55,000	40,837	55,000

*Taxed similarly to a partnership.
[†]Tax base is 15 percent on first $25,000 of profit, 18 percent on next $25,000, etc., see page 76, and 46 percent on profit above $100,000.
[‡]Using tax base of 45 percent on income earned.

EXHIBIT 4-7
Federal Income Taxes Applied to Forms of Business

Lack of secrecy. A corporation must make available to each stockholder an annual report. In a closed corporation, the few reports circulated usually won't get into the hands of nonowners. But when a large number of reports are issued, the reports become public knowledge. These reports present data on sales volume, profit, total assets, and other financial matters. The public disclosure of these data gives competitors and other outsiders a view of the financial condition of the corporation.

Lack of personal attention. In most corporations except the small ones, management and ownership are separate. This can result in a lack of personal interest in the success of the corporation. If the managers are also stockholders, the lack of personal interest is often minimized. It is assumed that employees who are also owners will work harder for the success of the business, but the accuracy of this assumption is an individual matter. Most managers have pride in their work and want any business they are involved with to succeed.

Credit limitations. Banks and other lenders have to consider the limited liability of corporations. If a corporation fails, its creditors can look only to the assets of the business to satisfy claims. For partnerships, the creditors can rely on personal assets of the partners to pay off business debts.

From 1945 to 1970, the United States economy underwent a growth cycle that resulted in the creation of larger corporations. Today, the largest five hundred corporations control over 70 percent of the assets and profits in the United States. Two procedures that have led to this creation of corporate giants are the merger and the consolidation.

A **merger** occurs when two or more corporations combine their assets. In the case of two business firms, one ceases to exist. The continuing corporation operates the business and typically assumes all the absorbed corporation's debts and liabilities.

THE MERGER AND CONSOLIDATION BINGE

MERGER
The combination of two or more corporations and all their assets; all but one cease to exist.

A WAVE OF CORPORATE TOGETHERNESS

The growing wave of giant mergers has raised old fears about the dangers of concentrating too much power in the hands of a few corporate chiefs—and new questions about whether their smaller competitors can survive. Many experts argue, however, that; economic conditions being what they are, bigger business is both inevitable and—in some cases—desirable. The growing scarcity of resources, the cost and challenge of new technology, the accelerating pace of economic change, and foreign competition are forcing many companies to seek both opportunity and salvation in size.

Another reason for the increase in mergers is that business corporations want to insulate themselves against uncertainty. Instability in the world and other political and governmental uncertainties are feeding the urge to merge. Some of the largest mergers are the following:

	Value	Date
DuPont and Conoco	$7.2 billion	1981
Elf Aquitane and Texas Gulf	2.7	1981
Seagram and Conoco	2.6	1981
Kuwait Petroleum and Santa Fe International	2.5	1981
Freeport Minerals and MCMO Ran Oil & Gas	2.3	1981
Nabisco and Standard Brands	2.0	1980
Dart Industries and Kraft	2.4	1980
Schering and Plough	1.4	1980

Value is the amount of cash paid by the firm (first one listed) that acquires or merges with a second firm. For example, DuPont paid $7.2 billion to Conoco stockholders and Elf Aquitane paid Texas Gulf stockholders $2.7 billion.

An important question for everyone to think about is whether the merged giant corporation can really be managed efficiently? What do you think? When is a giant corporation too big?

Based on "DuPont's Great Lead," *Newsweek*, July 20, 1981, p. 52; and "Is Business Getting Too Big?" *Newsweek*, July 20, 1981, p. 53.

CONSOLIDATION
A combination of two or more corporations to form a new corporation.

Consolidation is the joining together of two or more corporations to form a new corporation. The new corporation takes over the property, rights, powers, and obligations of the old corporations. When the Pontiac, Oldsmobile, Buick, and Cadillac Corporations joined together in 1917 to form General Motors, a consolidation took place.

The total number of mergers and consolidations has decreased throughout the 1970s. But because the average size of the deals has risen, the overall dollar amounts are significant. The total value of just the 50 largest mergers in 1981 came to more than $49 billion—the highest volume since 1969, when a total of $24 billion worth of merger deals occurred in the United States.[3]

The most popular merger candidates these days have been energy-related and natural-resource companies. General Electric's acquisiton of Utah International enables it to get hold of the latter company's coal resources. ARCO acquired Anaconda and took over its copper reserves.[4] Note that many of the largest mergers in 1981 involved oil companies.

The corporation is certainly the dominant form of incorporated ownership, but a number of other widely used incorporated forms of business have unique advantages. Four of these are Subchapter S corporations, cooperatives, savings and loan associations, and professional service associations.

The Subchapter S corporation is a tax-option business. That is, it can be taxed like a partnership, as Exhibit 4–7 showed. The Subchapter S corporation cannot have more than ten shareholders, each of whom must sign a form agreeing to be taxed as a partnership. A business with more than 20 percent of its income from rents, dividends, or royalties doesn't qualify. As a rule of thumb, this method of taxation has a distinct advantage for a business operating at a loss, because the loss is shared and is immediately deductible on the tax returns of the shareholders. In the case of profits, the corporate tax rate is avoided.

An organization in which a group of people collectively own and operate all or part of their business is a **cooperative** (co-op). The co-op is often found where a large number of small producers can band together to become more competitive. Such well-known brands as Sunkist oranges and Sun Maid raisins are the property of food-producer cooperatives that joined to market the products grown by many members.

More than 5500 producer co-ops do business in the United States, with annual sales of over $16 billion. In addition, approximately 7500 farmer-owned buying co-ops purchase machinery, fertilizer, seeds, materials, and so on at a rate of over $4 billion annually. Farm co-ops have increased their annual revenues from $25 billion in 1970 to over $57 billion today. Until recently, farm co-ops were generally unknown to the public. For example, Kansas City–based Farmland Co-op, owned by some 500,000 farmer members, had sales of approximately $1.8 billion in 1980. Other billion-dollar co-ops are Associated Milk Producers, Grain Terminal Association, and Land O'Lakes.

Dividends are paid to co-op members in proportion to the amount of goods that each member has bought or sold through the cooperative. These *patronage dividends* are considered a refund of overpayments rather than a distribution of profits.

A disadvantage of co-ops is that, as they grow larger, they become more visible to the public. And if the public questions their market power, they may lose their special status under the law.

Savings and loan associations are corporations that operate in much the same manner as savings banks. The owner of an account is given a pass-book in which deposits and withdrawals are noted. About 30 percent of the 5500 savings and loan associations in the United States are incorporated under federal law; the remaining 70 percent have state charters.

In a mutually owned savings and loan association, both savers and borrowers are members. Members elect a board of directors to manage the association. The assets of these associations consist of shares bought by over 40 million buyers. Most of the capital of this form of business is invested in local home mortgages.

OTHER INCORPORATED FORMS OF BUSINESS

Subchapter S Corporation

Cooperatives

COOPERATIVE
A business in which a group of owners or buyers join together to operate the business.

Savings and Loan Associations

SAVINGS AND LOAN ASSOCIATION
A business in which savers and borrowers are members. Most of the business's money is invested in local home mortgages.

Professional Service Associations

Traditionally, the professional services of doctors, lawyers, dentists, and the like could be performed only by individuals and not by corporations. Impersonal corporate entities were not allowed to provide personal-care services. But in late 1969, the Internal Revenue Service agreed that organizations of professional people, organized under professional association laws, could be treated as corporations for tax purposes. Thus, the tax advantages of profit sharing and pension plans, not available to private persons and partnerships, could be made available to professional service association members.

SUMMARY

■ Each form of business has advantages and disadvantages.

The sole proprietorship is easy to start, the owner controls it, it can be easily dissolved, and it receives tax breaks. On the other hand, the owner has unlimited liability, has difficulty raising capital, and has limited skills.

The partnership is easy to start, usually has more capital than the sole proprietor, and receives some tax breaks. However, a partner has unlimited liability, money is "frozen," and there is room for conflicts.

A corporation owner has limited liability, can transfer ownership, and relies on managers to run the business. However, owners have little control and are double-taxed.

■ If a person has to use his or her wealth to satisfy claims of creditors of a business, this is called unlimited liability. Sole proprietors and partners have this type of liability.

■ The corporation is an artificial being in the eyes of the law. If you own a part of a corporation, you have limited liability. You are risking only what you invested.

■ The government practice of taxing corporate income and owner dividends is called *double taxation*. The owner is taxed twice—on both income and dividends.

ISSUES TO CONSIDER AND ANALYZE

1. List some of the corporations that you have business dealings with on a regular basis.
2. In what ways do a corporation and a cooperative differ?
3. Why is it recommended that, in starting a partnership, a firm set of articles of partnership be established?
4. What is the difference between a general and a limited partner?
5. Consider your own financial situation and goals. What business form is most compatible with your interests and resources?
6. What is a Subchapter S corporation?
7. Why is it important to understand the term *unlimited liability*?
8. Why is there a potential limit of available managerial abilities in a sole proprietorship?
9. What fields of business are suitable for a sole proprietorship?
10. What is the difference between a merger and a consolidation?

APPLE COMPUTER, INC.: A SUCCESS STORY

Steven Jobs is, at twenty-six, the chairman of the board of Apple Computer, Inc., a business that has surged from sales of $2.7 million in 1977 to sales of approximately $600 million in 1982. Jobs is a businessman who had an idea, took some risks, made some timely decisions, and now has a thriving corporation on his hands. It didn't just happen; he and a few of his friends made it happen.

One of Job's best friends, Stephen Wozniak, had some technical skills and ideas about computers. They pooled their talents in the early 1970s and built what they called easy-to-use computers. These pint-size computers were smaller than a portable typewriter, but they could do the feats of much larger computers. Wozniak was the technical genius, and Jobs was able to see the marketing potential of the computers. The two friends raised $1300 to open a makeshift production line. They then decided to form a corporation, which Jobs called Apple Computer, Inc.

Jobs moved around California raising money. A. C. Markkula, a former marketing manager at Intel, a computer chip manufacturer, became very interested in Apple, Inc. When he offered his expertise and $250,000 of his own money, Jobs and Wozniak made him an equal owner in the business. Markkula was able to arrange a credit line with the Bank of America and persuaded others to invest money in Apple.

From the start, the Jobs, Wozniak, and Markkula team did almost everything right. They developed a spiffy, attractive model called Apple II. They also wrote clear, concise instruction manuals that made the machine easy for consumers to use.

In addition to working hard to develop new products, Apple will now have to prove that it has the management talents needed in a firm that has joined the ranks of the Fortune 500. Though Wozniak remains a major shareholder, he has dropped out of company business. Markkula plans to retire by 1984 to spend more time with his family. Jobs, who had the vision to build one of America's foremost companies from a hobbyist's toy, must show that he has the foresight and ability to guide a major corporation. Apple went from an idea, to a partnership, to a public corporation in a very short time.

QUESTIONS

1. Why do you think Jobs and Wozniak decided to become a corporation?
2. What abilities are needed to guide a corporation like Apple?
3. What risk did A. C. Markkula take when he decided to join Jobs and Wozniak in forming Apple, Inc.?

Based on "The Seeds of Success," *Time*, February 15, 1982, pp. 40–41.

CHAPTER 5

SMALL BUSINESS AND FRANCHISING

LEARNING OBJECTIVES

After studying this chapter, you should be able to:

Discuss ways of becoming an owner of a small business or a franchise.

Develop your own personal assessment to determine if you have what it takes to run a small business.

Explain some of the reasons many small businesses fail.

Identify the steps to take before entering a franchise agreement.

Compare the advantages and disadvantages of owning a small business and a franchise.

KEY TERMS

Small business
Small Business
   Administration
MESBIC
Franchising
Franchisee
Franchisor
Cancellation provision
Exclusive handling

THE ENTREPRENEURIAL SPIRIT BURNS BRIGHT

Starting with $9,500 of her own money last August, Marilyn Einhorn produced and sold three thousand high fashion women's bathing suits by February. Her customers included such big name stores as Burdines, Macy's, and Bonwit Teller.

Einhorn, twenty-two, graduated from the University of Delaware with a degree in fashion design and merchandising. With the savings she put aside from custom designing evening wear while she studied, Marilyn went to New York looking for a job. She couldn't find one, but she met Tom Cizk of Cizk Manufacturing, a contractor of swimwear, who taught her about the business. Every penny

Marilyn had went into fabric. All her other expenses were financed on sixty-day credit.

She took her goods on the road and went door to door. Soon orders began to roll in. Marilyn did everything herself: selling, sewing, buying. Her day was an around-the-clock whirlwind.

She formed Mee (her initials) Swimwear in October, and she was the sole owner. When banks declined to finance her, Marilyn went to the Small Business Administration and applied and received a women's mini-series loan of $20,000 at 9 percent.

Mee bathing suits retail for $40 to

$62, and Marilyn sells them for about half that. She was able to pay off her loan in six months and is now designing a second line. She plans to have sales reps around the country and will open outlets in Europe next year.

Marilyn always wanted to operate her own business. She had an entrepreneurial spirit and was willing to take some risks. She can be proud of her accomplishments. In Marilyn's case, the future is bright and failure is not even a part of her vocabulary. In this chapter starting a business like Marilyn's is a major topic.

Many of the most publicized corporate giants began as small businesses and grew large through effective management. For example, Coca-Cola began when a pharmacist brewed a batch of syrup that tasted good; a restaurant owner named Colonel Sanders owned a small cafe that served "finger-lickin'good" chicken; and a salesperson named Ray Kroc discovered a tasty hamburger in California that he turned into the McDonald's burger.

What characterizes small businesses? The Small Business Act of 1953 defines **small business** as "one which is independently owned and operated and not dominant in its field of operation." The act authorized the Small Business Administration (SBA) to use a number of yardsticks to identify a small business. For example, in lending money to small businesses, the SBA has established the following limits for qualifying:

■ *Retailing and service.* $1 million to $5 million annual sales, depending on the industry.
■ *Wholesaling.* $5 million to $15 million annual sales, depending on the industry.
■ *Manufacturing.* 250 or fewer employees. If employment is more than 250 but fewer than 1500, a size standard for a particular industry is used.

These criteria suggest that smallness depends on your point of view. You may consider Marshall Field's (a department store company that started in Chicago) small in comparison to Sears. But compared to many other department store companies, Marshall Field's is large. Therefore, it is correct to say that a small business is one that is not dominant in its industry and that can be started with a moderate investment for that industry.

Smallness should not be equated with not making a contribution to the economy. Here are some facts about small businesses in the U. S.:

■ They provide nearly 60 percent of the total employment in business.
■ More than 90 percent of all corporations are small—including farms.
■ Small businesses account for about 43 percent of the gross national product of the United States.
■ Small businesses account for nearly $8 of every $10 made by construction firms.
■ Eighty percent of all American businesses employ fewer than 10 people.

SMALL BUSINESS
A business that is independently owned and operated and not dominant in its field of operation.

BECOMING A SMALL-BUSINESS OWNER

Many people imagine themselves running their own business, making the key decisions, and earning a profit. Becoming a small-business owner can provide these opportunities. There are three ways to become a small-business owner: by taking over a family business, buying an already operating business, or starting a new business.

Children have often taken over the family business. In most cases, the employees of small bakery, barber, grocery, and butcher shops were the children of the owner. They learned the business by working with their parents. In some situations, the children learned well and were motivated to continue the business. In other cases, the parents forced the business on the children, and the results have included parent–child conflict and business failure.

Some people buy out an operating business. The buyer and seller work out a contractual agreement involving the inventory, equipment, and price. The details of this purchase agreement should also be spelled out in a legal contract between the buyer and seller.

The third method of becoming a small-business owner, starting a business from the ground up, requires hard work and careful planning. Without solid planning, a new owner is likely to be swamped by the first wave of problems. Getting all the information needed to do a good job involves hard work. The new owner will have to study materials about products and markets, consult with professional and business experts, and perhaps attend seminars and workshops for a quick education about managing a small business. These actions are very important, because a new business has no previous customers or business records as an established business does.

TYPES OF SMALL BUSINESS

In every industry, there are successful small businesses. Small-business owners operate manufacturing plants, salad restaurants, computer stores, yogurt stores, day-care centers, skating rinks, retail stores, computer production plants, construction firms, accounting offices, printing plants, record stores, and hundreds of other businesses. However, small business is more concentrated in some areas of the economy than in others.

Manufacturing

There are thousands of small manufacturing businesses. Included in this category are printing shops, steel fabricating shops, recreational equipment plants, clothing manufacturers, cabinet shops, furniture shops, and bakeries.

The manufacturing business involves converting raw materials into products needed by society. Therefore, the owner must understand production and marketing and how these business functions complement each other. About 30 percent of all manufacturing businesses are considered small.

Service

The service sector contains a diversity of firms; there are hundreds of service business opportunities. Approximately 40 percent of all businesses in the United States specialize in selling services to consumers. Service businesses include:

- *Business services.* Businesses that provide service to other business organizations—accounting firms, advertising agencies, blueprint services, tax consultants, collection agencies, and so on
- *Personal services.* Includes barber and beauty shops, baby-sitting agencies, piano teachers, laundries, and travel agencies
- *Repair services.* Includes automobile repair, jewelry repair, appliance repair, furniture repair, plumbing repair, and truck repair services
- *Entertainment and recreation services.* Includes racetracks, motion picture theaters, amusement parks, golf courses, and bowling alleys
- *Hotels and motels.* Includes the operation of hotels, motels, and recreational vehicle (RV) camps

With the growth of available leisure time and the rise in consumer spending power, individuals, families, and other businesses are expected to increase their use of service firms. The 62 million Americans who produce services in 1981 are expected to increase to an estimated 68.6 million by 1985.[1]

The wide array of service businesses suggests a number of common characteristics. First, most small service firms offer one or, at most, a few major services. The accountant specializes in taxes, the jewelry repair shop fixes watches, and the tall men's clothing store sells suits for men who are over six feet tall.

Second, the majority of small service businesses do not keep large amounts of supplies or inventory on hand. They purchase the materials or goods they need when there is a demand.

Third, because services are consumed immediately, suppliers of services operate on a cash-and-carry or partial-payment-in-advance basis. The plumber wants to be paid when the repair is made.

Fourth, service businesses rely on human ability. They sell such intangibles as income tax knowledge or the ability to make kitchen cabinets that are attractive and functional. This ability adds value to what the customer or client receives—a completed income tax form or a beautiful kitchen cabinet.

Finally, the majority of small service businesses are sole proprietorships. This is consistent with the other characteristics of small business, such as specialized expertise, little need for large inventory, and application of knowledge and craft ability.

Wholesaling

Wholesaling involves the activities of persons (or firms) who sell to retailers, other wholesalers, or industrial firms. Wholesale trade consists mainly of small businesses. Firms with fewer than 100 employees are responsible for more than 75 percent of the industry's paid employment. In fact, very small firms—those with fewer than twenty employees—have 41 percent of the total employment.

Merchant wholesalers sold over $700 billion worth of goods in 1980. Small wholesale firms sell a wide range of products, including groceries, supplies, machinery, appliances, grain, and fruits and vegetables. These businesses serve as a link between manufacturers and retailers or industrial users.

Retailing

Retailers are merchants who sell goods to ultimate consumers, that is, to us. The giants of retailing include Sears Roebuck, Safeway Stores, J. C. Penney, and S. S. Kresge. Small, local retail businesses sell many of the same products as these giant business corporations. There are corner drugstores, shoe stores, grocery stores, restaurants, jewelry stores, and hardware stores in almost every populated location in the United States.

THE ENTREPRENEURIAL SPIRIT

Despite the risks of starting a small business, some people are still willing to take a chance. An *entrepreneur*, as we saw in Chapter 2, is a person who sets up and manages a business and assumes the financial risks involved in the effort to make a profit.

JENO'S SON IS LIKE HIM

Michael Paulucci's father founded Jeno's Pizza. Michael, like his father, had his own entrepreneurial drive and desire. He started in the family business as a salesman in 1969. He then spent one year in advertising and gradually moved through different sectors of the company. He became chairman of Jeno's, Inc., in 1979.

Michael and his father had few problems working together. Says Michael, "He's always let me operate pretty much on my own." This doesn't mean that differences of opinion never exist. Michael always wanted to open a hamburger, sandwich, and steak specialty restaurant. This type of food was outside the boundaries of the Paulucci family's specialty—pizza. Jeno didn't want his son to go into this kind of restaurant. However, with $600,000 in personal funds, Michael bought an 1889 warehouse in Duluth, Minnesota, refurbished it, and opened his first Grandma's restaurant.

Despite his father's pleas and because of Michael's own entrepreneurial drive, Grandma's has been a success. It now has revenues of over $2 million annually and a staff of 100, and a second Grandma's is being planned.

The "can do" attitude of Michael is what made Jeno Paulucci a successful entrepreneur. Jeno's ideas, spirit, drive, work ethic, and self-confidence served as a model for young Michael. The good personal relationship between Jeno and Michael also helped the younger Paulucci develop into the businessman he is today.

From Michael Beky, "Born and Bred Entrepreneurs," *Venture*, March 1981, pp. 36ff.

Is there an entrepreneurial type, a kind of person suited for managing a small business? The entrepreneur appears to need many of the same characteristics as the successful manager at IBM, W. R. Grace, or Kellogg's. That is, he or she must be intelligent, honest, dependable, mature, articulate, and a leader. In addition, the entrepreneur seems to be an individualist willing to go his or her own way rather than accepting or identifying with something that others have built, such as a large corporation. Other characteristics of the entrepreneur are an intense need for accomplishment, a readiness to discover new challenges, an ability to deal with unusual situations, and a persistent enthusiasm for hard work despite setbacks. Entrepreneurs are pioneers who enjoy each step on the way to achieving important objectives.

Self-Evaluation: The Personal Questions

No family member, business consultant, or business owner can tell you that you should become a small-business owner or an entrepreneur. You must make the final decision.

Are you ready to run a small business? An important starting point is determining your goals in life. Then you must match these goals with the benefits associated with the type of business you are considering. There are other important questions to ask yourself, including:

■ Are you a self-starter?
■ Do you like other people?

■ Can you lead others?
■ Are you well organized?
■ Are you a decisive decision maker?
■ Do you enjoy hard work and long hours?
■ Do you stick with a project?
■ Can you handle pressure?
■ Can you communicate well?
■ Do you understand planning, organizing, and controlling?
■ Do you learn from past mistakes?
■ Are you in excellent health?

If you had to answer *no* to any of these questions, you probably need to think through your plans to operate a small business. Of course, this is only a checklist of questions and not a final answer. But honest answers to these kinds of questions can help a person face the real world of operating a small business.

Some Potential Benefits and Costs

There are potential benefits and costs associated with any business venture. One important benefit for many entrepreneurs is the personal gratification from operating one's own business. The entrepreneur can exercise all of his or her talent and can do so with some degree of independence. Some entrepreneurs also can obtain power by operating their own business. Another benefit of starting a small business is financial gain. The financial return from a successful small business can be substantial.

On the other hand, there are some potential and actual costs associated with operating your own business. There is a chance that the initial investment will be lost. Not all risks in the business are controlled by the entrepreneur. Fashion changes, government regulations, competition, and labor problems may threaten the business. There is also a tendency in some businesses toward irregular income. During the first six months of many potentially profitable firms, the owner may receive zero profits. Being in business for yourself also means long hours. There is generally less time for recreation and the family. These are important parts of life, but sometimes they must be sacrificed to operate the business successfully.

STARTING A SMALL BUSINESS

Starting any business requires some careful investigation and planning. An excellent guide to use for these initial steps is the Small Business Administration's *Checklist for Going into Business* (Small Marketers Aid No. 71). Assistance in starting any business is also available from the International Entrepreneur's Association in Santa Monica, California. No matter what the business, certain general steps must be taken in planning a new business. Let us look at them briefly.

Establishing Business Objectives

A successful business owner must establish objectives in order to have a sense of purpose and direction. These objectives can focus on personal development, size of operation, type of product, number of employees, and profit margin. The objectives can be specified for the next five years or any other appropriate time span.

Securing Licenses and Permits

Each state and local community has requirements for business organizations. In some communities, certificates and licenses are necessary. An entrepreneur who plans to sell vacuum cleaners door-to-door will in most cases need a vendor's permit. Barbers, hair stylists, real estate agents, and all positions in the medical field require occupational permits. A few businesses require federal licenses: meat processors, radio and TV stations, and investment advisory services. It is important to check carefully what licenses, certificates, and permits are needed to operate the business you're considering.

Determining Personnel Requirements

On the Job Revisited

A successful manager must plan for the types and number of employees needed to operate the business. These considerations should be weighed against the availablity of personnel. For example, clothing store owners like Bill and Nancy Riemer (see Chapter 4) need salesclerks to service customers.

Determining Site

The small-business owner must decide where to locate the business and whether to build or lease the physical facilities. Factors that should be considered in choosing a location are availability of and access to workers (if needed), traffic patterns and volume, and relationship to the market. A good market relationship means there are enough customers in the area to keep the business going.

In deciding whether to build or lease, you must consider space requirements for future expansion. Long-run sales and profit objectives must be spelled out at the start so that the location and build or lease decisions can be made with the objectives clearly established.

Planning a Marketing Approach

In order to sell a product or service, the small-business owner needs to build a favorable image, effectively use channels of distribution, and determine a competitive price. The owner who lacks ability in these areas must seek professional expertise. Hiring consultants can be expensive: some management and marketing consultants charge up to $900 per day plus expenses. Other sources, such as the Small Business Administration, don't charge for management counseling except for the consultant's out-of-pocket expenses.

Preparing Budgets

On the Job Revisited

The budget is an instrument of planning and control. It helps the owner plan how to use scarce resources and keep watch over their actual use. The most important budgets for a small-business owner are the *operating budget*—a budget that allows the owner to compare budget activities with actual costs—and the *cash-flow budget*—a statement of what cash will be needed to pay expenses and where the cash will come from to pay them. Marilyn Einhorn had to prepare the operating and cash-flow budgets for her swimwear business. Though she wasn't an accountant, Marilyn still needed to be able to keep track of costs, expenses, and cash flow.

Identifying Sources of Funds

After the budgets are prepared, an owner must locate potential sources of funds. The small-business owner's ability to raise funds is one of the major determinants of the size and type of business that will result. There is no

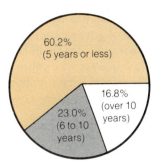

EXHIBIT 5-1
Business Failures by Age of Firm

Source: The Business Failure Record: 1978 (New York: Dun & Bradstreet, 1979).

one best source of funds, but some sources that need to be continually monitored are personal funds, commercial banks, insurance companies, and the Small Business Administration. Marilyn Einhorn was able to receive a women's miniseries loan of $20,000 from the Small Business Administration. Without this money, her business dream couldn't come true.

On the Job Revisited

SMALL-BUSINESS FAILURES

Not every small manufacturing, service, wholesaling, or retailing business is a success. The rate of small-business failures fluctuates from year to year because of economic conditions and other factors, but the average rate of failure within five years after the business starts has been over 50 percent. The initial five-year period provides a stiff test of the business owner's managerial ability. Exhibit 5–1 shows the percent of business failures by age of the firm.

Aside from the relatively few small-business failures caused by fraud, neglect, and uncontrollable disasters like floods and earthquakes, the root cause is usually poor management. Poor management is reflected in a number of ways; some of the ways are presented in Exhibit 5–2.

PLANNING OVERSIGHTS	USE OF INADEQUATE BUSINESS METHODS
Not able to detect market and competitive changes	Poor record keeping
Poor knowledge of economics	No credit controls
No plans for emergency situations	No inventory control system
Inadequate financial planning	Inability to hire help
MANAGERIAL CHARACTERISTICS	**UNDERFINANCING**
Unwillingness to work hard and long hours	Lack of funds to buy adequate stock and equipment
Lack of ability to deal with people	Lack of funds to buy merchandise when discounts are available
Failure to delegate responsibility and tasks	Lack of funds to hire personnel
Unwillingness to learn the business from the ground up	

EXHIBIT 5-2
Poor Management Causes of Small-Business Failures

THE SMALL BUSINESS ADMINISTRATION

SMALL BUSINESS
ADMINISTRATION (SBA)
An independent agency of the federal
government, created in 1953 for the
purpose of protecting the interests of
small-business owners.

The **Small Business Administration (SBA)** is an independent agency of the federal government. It was created in 1953 for the purpose of protecting the interests of small-business owners. Big-business interests are promoted in Congress by well-organized lobbies, which work to create an atmosphere that is favorable for big business. But small businesses did not have this type of lobby power, and for this and other reasons the SBA was created.

SBA Loans

One important function of the SBA is to provide loans. If a small-business owner needs more money, the SBA can help. In general, the SBA will lend money to an entrepreneur only after he or she has been turned down by private lenders.

The SBA loans money on a term basis; that is, the money must be paid back within a specified number of years. SBA *direct loans*, from the agency's own funds, are made to small businesses. SBA *participating loans* supplement loans from banks. Another SBA loan is the *guaranteed loan*. The money comes from a bank, but the SBA guarantees to pay 90 percent of the loan if the owner defaults or can't pay.

SBA Managerial Assistance

The SBA has an Office of Management Assistance that aids people who want to develop their managerial skills. In fact, SBA loan approvals often require applicants to take action to improve their abilities; the SBA Office of Management Assistance is often used for such assistance.

The SBA sponsors management training courses that stress the fundamentals of management. Typically, the courses run for three or four weeks, one night a week. The agency also sponsors short, one-day updating courses that cover the latest tax, investment, and legal developments.

Minority Business and the SBA

The most popular minority-owned businesses are owner-operated restaurants, beauty parlors, barber shops, newspaper–magazine stores, and grocery stores. But in the United States, with about 38 million minority citizens, the number of minority-owned businesses is disproportionately small. This may be due to lack of funds, inexperience, inability to obtain credit, and/or lack of interest in business.

The last ten years have seen society emphasize racial equality, equal economic opportunity, and minority ownership of businesses. The business community, government, and a large portion of society are promoting minority ownership. Large corporations are making an effort to buy from and support minority-owned businesses. For example, Xerox helped a black organization start a business to produce transformers that Xerox purchases for its own operations.

In cooperation with the U.S. Department of Commerce, the SBA has instituted programs that assist small businesses owned and managed by the socially or economically disadvantaged. Such disadvantages may arise from cultural, social, or chronic economic circumstances or background. The category includes, but is not restricted to, blacks, native Americans, Mexican Americans, Asian Americans, and Eskimos.

Congress passed the Small Business Investment Act of 1958 to make it easier for small firms to get needed long-term capital to finance their growth. This act authorized the SBA to license *small-business investment companies* (SBICs). An SBIC is a privately owned and privately operated company licensed by the SBA to furnish loans to small firms.

SBICs dedicated to assisting small firms owned and operated by minority-group members are called *minority-enterprise small-business investment companies* (MESBICs). A **MESBIC** is owned and operated by established industrial or financial concerns, private investors, or business-oriented economic development organizations. Minority owners can ask for financial and managerial support from a MESBIC.

William Madison is the owner of Kelly Chemical Company in Chicago, which sells hair-care products to the black market. Madison expanded his sales force and improved the packaging and advertising of the firm's shampoos, conditioners, and hair relaxers. His plans cost about $1 million. He raised the money from a number of MESBICs. He felt that, without this needed influx of money, the firm couldn't compete in the Chicago area.[2]

MESBIC
Acronym for minority-enterprise small-business investment company. Such a company is owned and operated by established industrial or financial concerns, private investors, or business-oriented economic development organizations.

An attractive business opportunity for many people is to obtain a franchise and become the owner of a restaurant, motel, service station, beauty salon, or other business. Ray Kroc, chairman of McDonald's Corporation, states: "Franchising has become the updated version of the American dream."[3] Franchising has helped thousands of Americans to become owners of their own businesses.

During the last few decades, there has been a boom in this type of business. It is estimated that $50 billion a year—27¢ of every dollar spent on food in the United States—now goes to buy meals away from home.[4] A small amount is spent in formal, or "white tablecloth," restaurants. Much of the 27¢ is spent in chicken, hamburger, beef, fish, taco, and pizza franchise businesses.

Of course, the 600,000 franchise units in the United States include many other forms of business beside fast-food restaurants. Franchising, a booming field, cuts across forty industries ranging from motels and automobile dealers to campgrounds. Franchise sales in 1982 were approximately $384 billion, or about 37 percent of all retail sales.[5] Some of the hottest areas in franchising are real estate and convenience stores. About 8000 independent real estate firms have become franchised members of a half-dozen new nationwide chains. The dominant chain is Century 21 Realty of Irvine, California, which has signed up more than 5000 outlets.

What, exactly, is **franchising**? One definition that is fairly accurate and informative is the following:

> *Franchising* is a system for the selective distribution of goods and/or services under a broad name through outlets owned by independent businessmen called "franchisees"; although the franchisor supplies the franchisee with know-how or brand identification on a continuing basis, the franchisee enjoys the rights to profit and runs the risk of loss. The franchisor controls the distribution of his goods and/or services through a contract which regulates the activities of franchisees, in order to achieve standardization.[6]

FRANCHISING

FRANCHISING
A system for selective distribution of goods and/or services under a brand name through outlets owned by independent business owners.

HAMBURGERS AROUND THE WORLD

Over the past twenty-five years, McDonald's has done to restaurant food what Henry Ford did to automobiles a generation earlier. Ray Kroc, the driving force behind McDonald's, didn't invent the product—he just figured out how to mass-produce it uniformly. You can walk into a McDonald's and get a hamburger, french fries, and a shake inside of 50 seconds, and the meal will taste just the same in Tampa as it does in Phoenix—or, for that matter, Tokyo.

There are now more McDonald's outlets (about 5100) alone in the United States than there were fast-food restaurants in 1950. Out of every fast-food dollar Americans spend, McDonald's gets $.20. For every *one* Burger King Americans eat, they consume *three* McDonald's. The consumption rate is *one* Wendy's for every *ten* McDonald's.

A primary reason for the presence of McDonald's is Ray Kroc. In 1954, he met Maurice and Richard McDonald, who ran a hamburger stand in San Bernardino, California. Kroc was amazed at the stand's business. He approached the brothers about franchising the operation. They were leery of the fast-talking salesman from Chicago. But Kroc was persistent, and the brothers finally gave in. Kroc headed back to Des Plaines, which is near Chicago, and opened his first McDonald's.

By 1960, when Kroc bought out the McDonalds for $2.7 million, there were about 250 McDonald's across the United States. Kroc is now worth at least $250 million.

Adapted from Milton Moskowitz, Michael Lutz, and Robert Levering, eds., *Everybody's Business* (New York: Harper & Row, 1980), pp. 128–132.

FRANCHISEE
The independent owner of a franchise outlet who enters into an agreement with a franchisor.

FRANCHISOR
The licensing company in the franchise arrangement.

This definition points up the crucial elements of a franchise business: (1) a contractual agreement between the **franchisee** (person) and **franchisor** (the company); (2) a branded product or service (for example, car mufflers or Nautilus exercise equipment); (3) operation by a businessperson for the purpose of earning a profit; and (4) monitoring by the franchisor so that standard procedures and a standardized product or service are used.

The Franchise World

Many people assume that franchising is of recent origin. This is not so. Two early franchise operations in the United States were Coca-Cola, which first supplied its syrup to franchised bottlers around 1900, and Rexall Drug Stores, which started around 1902. Other examples of early franchise pioneers included automobile dealerships and gasoline stations. Gasoline companies entered the franchising field around 1930:

> The stuff that makes the car go, namely gas, went in franchising sometime later, about 1930, to be precise. Up until then the oil companies had been operating their own stations. A few of them began to license dealers and in the period from 1930 to 1935, the practice spread until it became for all intents and purposes the sole method employed to distribute gasoline.[7]

In the 1950s, franchising spread across the United States. In fact, 90 percent of all franchise companies doing business today started in the early 1950s.

Franchise opportunities touch every type of business. Some current examples of franchised businesses are motels, fast foods, drugstores, variety stores, repair shops, dry-cleaning services, laundromats, employment agencies, car-rental services, pet shops, duplicating services, diet programs, home-cleaning services, and training programs. This list in no way exhausts all the possible franchise opportunities.

According to a recent U.S. Department of Commerce booklet, franchise sales of goods and services were expected to reach a total of over $384 billion in 1982, an increase of over 100 percent since 1973 reported sales of $161.9 billion. Exhibit 5-3 indicates the 1981 level of franchising.

WHO EATS AT HOME?   An obvious sign of the popularity of franchising is the numerous fast-food outlets lining the highways and lurking in shopping malls. Today there are over 60,000 fast-food restaurants in the United States, many of which are franchise operations. They serve everything from special flavors of ice cream to hot dogs.

McDonald's has an international network of 5100 restaurants that sell a billion hamburgers every five months. It is the biggest food-franchise operation in the world, with sales of about $2 billion in 1981.

Kentucky Fried Chicken has 5300 stores, which have total sales of about $1.2 billion. It serves 2.3 billion pieces of chicken a year—enough to provide eleven pieces for every man, woman, and child in the United States.

H. Salt, Esq., a chain of fish-and-chips restaurants, belongs to the Kentucky Fried Chicken chain, which in turn belongs to Heublein, Inc. Burger King, which probably ranks third in size among the fast-food franchises, is part of the Pillsbury Company, which owns Steak & Ale Restaurants and Poppin' Fresh Pie shops. Burger Chef belongs to General Foods.

In the fast-food franchising business, there appears to be a trend for the company to own the units. Many units in the two largest chains, McDonald's and Kentucky Fried Chicken, are owned by the company. A study indicates that Kentucky Fried Chicken earns more profit from the company-owned stores than it does from franchised units. The same study reported that two-third of McDonald's profits come from the 2000 units it

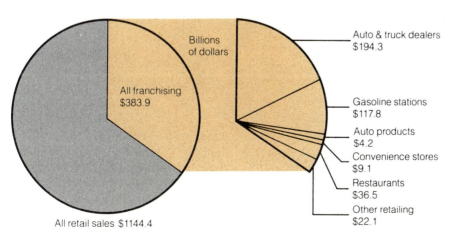

All franchising $383.9

Billions of dollars

Auto & truck dealers $194.3

Gasoline stations $117.8

Auto products $4.2

Convenience stores $9.1

Restaurants $36.5

Other retailing $22.1

All retail sales $1144.4

EXHIBIT 5-3

Volume of Franchise Sales in 1982 (in billions). (From *Franchising in the Economy 1980–1982*, U.S.Department of Commerce, 1982, p. 12.)

owns.[8] Company-owned units promise greater control, fewer legal problems, and more rapid responsiveness to other fast-food competitors. These advantages make company ownership versus franchisee ownership of the store more attractive.

The Franchising Agreement

Each franchise organization enters into a contractal agreement with each franchisee. These contracts may differ in a number of areas, such as the capital needed, the training provided, the managerial assistance available, and the size of the franchise territory. But there are a number of common points found in most franchise contracts. The franchise buyer normally pays an initial fee to the company and agrees to pay the franchisor a monthly percentage of sales. In exchange, the franchisee has the right to sell a standard product or service.

CAPITAL TO ENTER   In almost every franchise, the franchisee must invest some money. The amount can vary from a few thousand dollars to many thousands. Some examples of the different initial fee requirements appear in Exhibit 5-4.

A McDonald's franchise can require as much as $200,000. For example, purchasing a McDonald's franchise could require a cash down payment of $75,000. This money is used to cover the landscaping and opening costs, license fee, site development fee, equipment down payment, signs, and security deposit. If the franchise costs $200,000 and the cash down payment is $117,500, the balance of $82,500 must be financed through private sources. The McDonald's corporation does not lend money or guarantee loans. The company will provide a site, build the restaurant, and develop the parking lot. The operator pays rent on a twenty-year lease.[9]

Another example is Midas, Inc., which is famous for installing automobile muffler systems. A person purchasing this franchise needs $20,000 for inventory, equipment, signs, furniture, fixtures, and lease deposits. There is no fee charged for obtaining the franchise.

EARNINGS FOR AN OWNER   Most purchasers of franchises enter the business to earn money. In fact, the owner and the company both want to earn money. Earnings are a measure of the success of the franchise. If the business is to be successful, it must be well managed, provide good products or services, and obtain repeat customers.

EXHIBIT 5-4
Approximate Franchise Fees for Some
Well-Known Franchises

FRANCHISE NAME	MONEY NEEDED
Holiday Inns of America	$250,000 to 400,000
McDonald's	60,000 to 200,000
Burger King	45,000
A & W International	37,000
Aamco Automotive Transmissions	35,000
Kampgrounds of America	30,000 to 50,000
Goodyear Tire and Rubber	25,000 to 75,000
Rexall Drug Company	15,000 and up
Putt-Putt-Golf Courses of America	10,000 to 30,000

PASS THE EGGROLLS, TACOS, AND LASAGNE—PLEASE

Tacos, eggrolls, and lasagne may never replace hamburgers as standard American fast-food fare, but ethnic eating places are increasing their share of the restaurant franchise market. The Department of Commerce does not list ethnic restaurant franchises as a separate category yet, but things may change in the future.

Trends in ethnic restaurant franchises are apparent in what is available for prospective franchisees. Some of the ethnic restaurants that seem to be catching on are the following:

Charlie Chan: A $20,000 franchise fee, and total investment is about $115,000; about 30 restaurants now open. Multiple franchises are not encouraged.

La Rosa's: A regional Italian-style family restaurant serving pizza, pasta, sandwiches, complete dinners; 42 franchises are operating in Ohio and Kentucky. Franchise fee is $10,000, and total investment is $150,000. Restaurants average $410,000 per year in gross sales.

Taco Time: Has about 240 franchises operating. Ownership of at least five franchises is required; franchisees pay $150,000 for an area license that covers a minimum of five stores, plus a $10,000 fee per store. Average gross sales per unit are about $300,000 per year.

Chelsea Street Pub: Offers international food, drink, and entertainment in an English pub setting. Franchise fee is $30,000, and total investment is about $200,000. Franchisor charges a 5 percent royalty fee and a 2 percent advertising fee. An average unit, open six days per week, grosses about $1 million in sales annually.

Adapted from ''Franchise Facts,'' *Venture*, July 1981, p. 52.

The franchisor begins to earn money from the cash down payment. In some cases, there is a franchise fee that must be paid before certain rights of operation are granted. The franchisor also requires some type of royalty payment on gross sales. The amount of royalty or share of the proceeds paid to the franchisor differs from company to company. McDonald's requires a 3 percent royalty on gross sales. A Kentucky Fried Chicken franchisee pays the company a 5 percent royalty based on gross sales (total sales receipts).

No matter what the percentage of royalty, franchisees often dislike paying profits to someone else.

Royalities have one negative aspect—a psychological one. It is only human nature for a man to feel some pain when he sees part of the fruit of his labor go to someone else. Paradoxically, this pain may become more intense as the franchise operation gets more successful. The franchisee may be making many thousands of dollars, but so is the franchisor. It may hurt.[10]

Being involved and working hard to make the franchise a success and then being required to share the earnings deflates the ego of some franchisees. In addition, the franchisee may view the sharing of profits as inequitable. He or she does all the work, and the franchisor takes a share of the earnings.

THE CONTROL FACTOR   Many who consider entering into a franchise contract assume that they will be their own boss. This assumption is only partially accurate. The franchisor exercises a significant amount of control over the franchisee. This control is brought to bear in such areas as: (1) real estate ownership, (2) territorial restrictions, (3) cancellation provisions, and (4) required exclusive handling.

Some franchise companies own the real estate, select the site of the business location, and build the facility. These companies then lease the facility to a franchisee. This arrangement is exemplified by Exxon, Shell, Gulf, and Texaco. These companies often select the location for a service station and build it according to their specifications. McDonald's, Pizza Hut, and Mr. Steak are other organizations that own the site and the building.

A second type of control is placing restrictions on the selling territory of the franchisee. A selling territory is a geographical zone, for example, a three-square-mile area on the east side of Los Angeles. However, a number of court cases have made it difficult for a supplier (franchisor) to limit the area within which a merchant seller (franchisee) can operate. In a publicized court case involving Schwinn Bicycle Company, the Supreme Court ruled against territorial restrictions.[11] The Schwinn ruling has discouraged some franchisors from imposing rigid limits on franchisee territories, but most franchisors try to protect franchisees by spacing them far enough apart to prevent customer crossover between units. However, today's consumer is mobile, so franchise spacing often doesn't matter.

CANCELLATION PROVISION
The contract provision giving a franchisor the power to cancel an arrangement with a franchisee.

The **cancellation provision** in a contract is a powerful control device. Gasoline companies often issue operators of service stations a one-year franchise. If the operator is not considered successful by some company standards, the franchise agreement can be canceled after that time. This provision can force operators to run the business as directed by the franchisor.

EXCLUSIVE HANDLING
A form of control in which a franchisor requires the franchisee to purchase only supplies that are approved by the franchisor.

A fourth type of control involves **exclusive handling**. The franchise unit must stock only those brands or items that are permitted by the franchisor. A precedent-setting court case involved Standard Oil Company of California. Dealers of Standard Oil were not permitted to buy and stock tires, batteries, or accessories from suppliers that were not specifically approved by Standard Oil. The Supreme Court ruled that this requirement reduced competition and was in fact illegal.

Advantages of Owning a Franchise

Although there are problems with the franchise business, there are also reasons that it appeals to people. A person who has never owned or managed a business needs guidance to operate successfully. This guidance can be provided by a well-run franchise organization. In addition, a franchisor can provide a brand name, proven products or services, and financial assistance.

Guidance.   A glaring weakness in small businesses is the lack of managerial ability (see Exhibit 5–2). A person with limited managerial skills may be able to get by in a large organization because he or she is just one of many managers. But no one can cover up for or "carry" a franchise manager.

Many franchisors try to overcome managerial deficiencies or inexperience by providing some form of training. For example, McDonald's has an intensive nineteen-day course for owners and operators at Hamburger University in Elk Grove, Illinois. The school provides instruction in management decision making (with an emphasis on quality, service, and cleanliness), beverages, buns, and carbonation. Kentucky Fried Chicken operates a training school for improving management skills that is called Chicken University. A & W trainees study gooology (preparation of burger dressings), thermal mixology (coffee and hot chocolate), and fryocracy (french frying).

Brand name.   The investor who signs a franchise agreement acquires the right to use a nationally promoted brand name. This identifies the local unit with a recognized product or service. Travelers recognize the Holiday Inn sign, the golden arches of McDonald's, and the Century 21 signs. These features and characteristics are brought to the attention of potential consumers through national promotion—in a survey of school-children, 96 out of 100 could identify Ronald McDonald correctly.[12]

A proven product.   The franchisor can offer the franchisee a proven product and method of operating the business. The product or service is known and accepted by the public: customers will buy Kentucky Fried Chicken, Midas automobile mufflers, Gulf gasoline, and H & R Block income tax counseling.

Financial assistance.   By joining a franchise company, the individual investor may be able to secure financial assistance. Start-up costs of any business are often high, and the prospective investor usually has limited funds. And, as Chapter 4 mentions, the sole proprietor generally has a limited credit rating, which can make it difficult to borrow needed funds. In some cases, association with a well-established franchisor—through its reputation and its financial controls—may enhance the investor's credit rating with local banks.

Disadvantages of Owning a Franchise

As with any business venture, some disadvantages are associated with franchising. Many of these were mentioned briefly earlier in this chapter. Some of the more pressing negative features of franchising are the costs, lack of control, and inadequate training programs offered by some unscrupulous promoters.

Costs.   As already mentioned, franchisees must pay franchise fees. If it were possible to earn the same income independent of the franchisor, the investor would save the amount of these fees. However, the franchisor can provide training, guidance, and other forms of support that would otherwise cost money. Thus, the franchisee is paying for the opportunity to share in these forms of support.

External control.   The Standard Oil, Schwinn, and other cases have recently eased some of the franchisor's rigid control over the franchisee. Nevertheless, a person who signs a franchise agreement still loses some independence. The franchisor, in order to operate all of the franchise outlets as a business, must exercise some control over promotional activities, financial records, hiring, service procedures, and managerial development. Even though these controls may be useful, they are typically unpleasant to the person who wants independence. In the best of circumstances, the franchisee is at most semiindependent. In a sole proprietorship, the owner is totally independent.

Weak training programs. Some franchisors have developed excellent training programs. Even competitors concede that the McDonald's training experience is outstanding. But some promoters promise sound training programs and never deliver. In other cases, the training programs are weak—too brief and staffed by trainers who do not have instructional skills. The facilities are sometimes unsuitable for proper learning and development.

Evaluating the Franchise Opportunity

Because of the nature of franchising in the United States, it is important to evaluate an opportunity carefully before signing an agreement. The large number of franchise companies makes the evaluation task difficult.

An important first step is to know where to look for information. These are some of the available publications:

- *The 1982 Franchise Annual*, Dixon, E. L. Jr., ed., Lewiston, New York: Info Press, 1982.
- *Franchising in the Economy 1980–1982*, Washington, D.C.: U.S. Department of Commerce, 1982.
- *Franchise Opportunities Handbook*, Washington, D.C.: U.S. Department of Commerce, August 1981.
- *The Info Franchise Newsletter*, Lewiston, New York: Info Press, 1982 (monthly report).
- *Franchising Today*, 3106 Diablo Avenue, Hayward, California 94545. Bimonthly magazine.

With these and other sources in hand, the person interested in franchising can learn about contractual arrangements, fees, royalty sharing, government regulations and protection, training availability, and managerial skills required.

A second step is to be aware of potential problems. Franchise holders have registered complaints against some franchising companies. The main complaints seem to be:

- Misrepresentation of earnings to franchisees
- Misrepresentation of training activities
- Too much control over prices and management
- Whimsical terminations of franchise agreements

A number of these complaints are handled by the Federal Trade Commission, and there is some public sentiment to subject franchising to federal laws. However, the prospective franchise owner's best defense is to personally investigate the franchise company in detail before signing an agreement.

SUMMARY

- There are three ways that a person can become a small-business owner—by taking over a family business, buying an already operating business, or starting a new business.

■ A small business can provide an owner with independence, power, and a sense of accomplishment.

■ Before starting your own small business, you should ask yourself some questions about yourself and your intentions. Learn about yourself before taking the first step.

■ Small businesses fail largely because of planning oversights, managerial flaws, use of inadequate business methods, or underfinancing.

■ A person can purchase a business franchise from many different kinds of franchising companies.

■ Before entering a franchise agreement, consider the capital required, how much you can earn, the type of control the franchisor has, and whether you will get any assistance from the franchisor.

■ A franchise can offer advantages such as guidance from experienced people, a brand name, a proven product, and financial assistance.

1. Ask a few small-business owners why they started or bought their businesses. Consider their answers in the light of this chapter.
2. What are some of the risks involved in operating a small business?
3. In what fields are small-business operations important in your city or town?
4. Why might a prospective franchisee want to hire a lawyer?
5. How does the SBA help minority business owners?
6. Why are the problems of small business different from those of such large corporations as Shell Oil, IBM, and General Mills?
7. Why does the royalty paid to a franchisor create some psychological problems for franchisees?
8. What in your opinion will be the future of franchising in Canada? Japan?
9. Why is the brand name an important issue in franchising?
10. Prepare a list of some of the small-business and franchise failures that have recently occurred in your city or town. Explain some likely reasons the failures occurred.

ISSUES TO CONSIDER AND ANALYZE

"COY": A NEW BEER ON THE BLOCK

CASE FOR ANALYSIS

Billed as the "first great international beer brewed in America," Coy International Private Reserve hit the shelves of New Orleans in February 1981. Entrepreneur Neal Kaye, Sr. (pronounced *coy*) and his son have now rolled the beer into six states. The senior Kaye worked twenty-five years as an executive of the Jos. Schlitz Brewing Co. Kaye, Sr., and his son split the start-up costs of the new beer 50–50.

After Kaye, Jr., approached his father with the idea of producing his own brand of beer, he sat down with a brewmaster to work out the flavor. "This product is aimed at a heavy beer drinker. I wanted a product that had a combination beer and ale taste."

Rather than operate their own brewery, the Kayes commissioned Pearl

Adapted from Phil Fitzell, "A Label of Their Own," *Venture*, July 1981, pp. 46–47.

Brewing Co. of San Antonio to produce the beer, using Kaye's formula and packaging design. If demand exceeds Pearl's production capacity, the Falstaff Brewing Co. plant in Galveston, Texas, will handle the overflow.

Coy hit the streets of New Orleans, its test and home market, in February, selling 7000 cases in its first two weeks. The beer sold at $1.59 a six-pack, versus premium beers at $2.09 and private-label beers at $1.49. The Kayes expect Coy to be distributed through twenty-six wholesalers in six states, including Louisiana, Texas, New Mexico, and Arizona.

Whether Coy beer catches on remains to be seen. So far the Kayes seem to be using their talents and understanding of how to operate a business to gain a foothold in the tough beer market.

QUESTIONS

1. Why do you think the Kayes decided to use Pearl and, if needed, Falstaff to produce their Coy beer?
2. Do you think that the Kayes will make money during their first year of operation? Why?

CHAPTER 6

FUNDAMENTALS OF MANAGEMENT

LEARNING OBJECTIVES

After studying this chapter, you should be able to:

Define the meaning of management.

Explain the managerial functions of planning, organizing, staffing, directing, and controlling.

Discuss the difference between leadership and management.

Illustrate the different levels in the managerial hierarchy.

Identify the various pressures that a manager faces in reaching decisions.

KEY TERMS

Management
Objective
Managerial hierarchy
Management principle
Authority
Responsibility
Accountability
Leadership
Contingency approach
Planning
Organizing
Staffing
Directing
Controlling
Role

MANAGING MADE THE BUSINESS BLOOM

Bill Waslinski stared gloomily out his office window at 1000 acres of cultivated roses, hollies, junipers, azaleas, and evergreens. The rows of thriving plants were a major part of the year's inventory for the Holly Hill Company, a $12 million nursery business he managed. But instead of flowers and bushes, Waslinski could see little more than management problems multiplying like weeds all around him. The nursery's sales were lagging, employees were quitting, competition was everywhere, and Waslinski's desk looked like a warehouse of papers.

With a growing sense of frustration, Waslinski received even more bad news in the mail. He'd been summoned for jury duty, just when management problems were at the highest frenzy—spring delivery season. No solutions—just problems.

He was behind in his planning, organizing, directing, staffing, and controlling responsibilities as a manager. His management style was to do the job "myself." But Holly Hill was just getting too big for Waslinski to manage by himself.

Wasklinski finally realized that he'd have to change his management style to survive. The first step was to relieve himself of the company's day-to-day operations. Middle-level and lower level managers were given the authority, responsibility, and accountability to do the day-to-day nursery jobs. With these managers handling the daily business, Bill Waslinski was now finally free to do the one job he'd been neglecting—acting in the role of a top executive, the president of Holly Hill.

Bill believes that, with his change in management style, Holly Hill is now a much healthier company. He states, "I've got six good managers (middle and lower) who run the daily business. They do a better job in their own areas than I could ever hope to do myself. They're well paid, but they've each brought back far more in profits, productivity, and morale than they cost. I finally saw the trees in the forest and learned to be a top-level manager of a business."

In this chapter, many of the things Bill Waslinski learned about managing in a business will be discussed. The fundamentals of managing a business are exciting and challenging. Managing other people is unlike any other job because it is so filled with change, challenge, and excitement. You can't rest on yesterday's successes.

The success or failure of any business, large or small, depends largely on the competence of a management team or a manager. Bill Waslinski found out how important his management style was to the success of Holly Hill nursery. It is estimated that about nine out of ten business failures can be traced to managerial incompetence or inexperience. Some analysts also claim that most organizational failures in health care, government, education, and religion can be traced to poor management. According to Peter Drucker, a management consultant and educator,

> Our society has become, within an incredible short fifty years, a society of institutions. It has become a pluralistic society in which every major social task has been entrusted to large organizations—from producing economic goods and services to health care, from social security and welfare to education, from the search for new knowledge to the protection of the natural environment . . . [and] it is the managers and management that make institutions perform.[1]

We don't have to look far to find examples of management failures. The U.S. Congress in 1979 authorized $1.5 billion to help bail out the Chrysler Corporation. A major reason for Chrysler's problems was poor managerial decisions in the past. Not only had Chrysler made some poor decisions, but management reacted very slowly to environmental changes—the public demand for smaller cars.[2]

It isn't hard to find other examples that point up the importance of managing effectively. But we should not lose sight of the fact that managers are only human. They have personal goals, expectations, and needs, just as nonmanagers do. Managers also have individual strengths and weaknesses. There is no ideal or perfect set of behaviors, attitudes, and beliefs that will make a manager successful. Nor is there a "correct" way to manage. There are only actions appropriate for specific situations.

So what is management? **Management** is the process of planning, organizing, staffing, directing, and controlling an organization's human, financial, and material resources to accomplish its goals. In addition, management is a team of people who get things done through other people. In fact, most of an organization's employees do nonmanagerial work. Receptionists, file clerks, computer programmers, and bank tellers are all nonmanagers.

Is management a profession? If a profession is an occupation that serves others, then we can consider management a profession. But if a profession is a field of expert knowledge that requires licensing, graduate study, and certification—such as medicine and law—then management is not a profession. There is, however, a body of knowledge in the field of management. Over the years, various procedures and processes have been used by managers to reach organizational goals. A knowledge of past management practice can be useful when applied to organizational problems today. Thus, academic training can prove useful, although managers are evaluated on the basis of job performance and not according to the degree they earned in college or at some special training institute.

MANAGEMENT
The process of planning, organizing, staffing, directing, and controlling an organization's human, financial, and material resources to accomplish its goals. The process itself is carried out by a team of managers who get things done through other people.

THE ROLE OF OBJECTIVES

OBJECTIVE
A specific result or target to be reached by a certain time.

Businesses are started and operated to survive and earn a satisfactory profit. These are two generally accepted objectives of businesses. **Objectives** are desired results or targets to be reached by a certain time. Objectives are specific, state what is to be accomplished, and indicate when it will be achieved.

One procedure for setting objectives is the *cascade approach*, in which objectives are set from the top level of management down. This process provides direction to lower-level managers. In the cascade approach, the objectives are started at the top.

1. A clear statement of organizational purpose is issued.
2. Long-range goals are developed from this statement.
3. The long-range goals are converted into specific performance objectives for departments.
4. Objectives are then developed for each subunit in each department.
5. Within the subunits, challenging but attainable personal objectives are set.[3]

We should be aware that organizations and individuals have a network of multiple objectives, potentially conflicting. Business firms must be concerned with social responsibilities as well as profits. Individuals have personal lives and families in addition to careers. Hewlett-Packard, a leading producer of electronic instruments, is an organization with multiple objectives. After examining the Hewlett-Packard objectives in Exhibit 6–1, think about the definition of an objective. Are the Hewlett-Packard objectives specific, do they state what is to be accomplished, and do they indicate when it will be achieved?

Organizational Objectives

General Motors, the giant producer of automobiles, painfully suffered the loss of a portion of its market in the early 1970s. The energy crunch hurt sales of medium-size and large cars, the type of auto associated with the

EXHIBIT 6-1
Hewlett-Packard's Objectives

Customer:	To provide products and services of the greatest possible value to our customers, thereby gaining and holding their respect and loyalty.
People:	To help Hewlett-Packard people share in the company's success, which they make possible; to provide job security based on their performance; to recognize individual achievements; and to ensure the personal satisfaction that comes from a sense of accomplishment in their work.
Management:	To foster initiative and creativity by allowing the individual great freedom of action in attaining well-defined organizational and personal objectives.
Citizenship:	To honor corporate obligations to society by being an economic, intellectual, and social asset to each nation and community in which the company operates.
Profit:	To achieve sufficient profit to finance company growth and to provide resources needed to achieve other corporate objectives.

From *Public Annual Report*, Hewlett-Packard, 1981.

success of General Motors. In order to recapture the share of the market it lost, GM set a goal of selling 60 percent of all domestically manufactured cars.[4] It reduced the weight of most models by 700 to 1000 pounds and intended to reduce the length of cars a few inches without reducing their interior. By 1980, cars under 3500 pounds accounted for about 50 percent of GM sales, as compared to 20 percent in 1976. GM's objectives were specific.

The Northeast Insurance Company relies on its sales force to sell policies. In 1981, the sales team decided to set an objective of capturing 5 percent of the Chicago–Calumet Region market by 1986. This ambitious five-year objective means that the sales department will have to increase its market share from 2 percent to 5 percent in only five years.

Departmental Objectives

The operations department of Scott Manufacturing, Inc., of Milwaukee is divided into three teams. Each team includes technicians, operators, and material-handling personnel and has an informal leader and a nickname. These teams compete to be the most productive group in the department without sacrificing the quality of the product.

Subunit Objectives

Each team sets goals for specific quantities and quality and outlines, to some extent, a plan for achieving the objectives and a set of target dates. At Scott, the informal group, or subunit, sets objectives; the organizational and departmental objectives described above are set within the framework of a formal organization.

Donna Miller had been a bank teller for three years at Lansing Ridge Road Bank in San Diego. She wanted to earn a college degree so she could become a loan officer in the bank. But whenever she planned to attend school, some personal problem, such as an illness or a lack of money, prevented Donna from starting.

Individual Objectives

After four of Donna's closest friends started their college education, she finally began to outline a set of objectives. She established September as the starting date to enroll in school. If she were accepted and passed the courses, she could receive a business degree within three years. During her years in school, she would be able to borrow at least $8000 to pay for a room in the student dormitory and for tuition.

Objectives serve as targets for managers at the top of an organization as well as for those managers who work with operating employees. They are the specific guideposts around which managers become a team. If the objectives are clear, challenging, meaningful, and measurable, the organization has the standards available to judge whether managers at all levels in the hierarchy are using their authority, responsibility, and accountability efficiently.

The local Jack-in-the-Box or Baskin Robbins franchise has a simple managerial hierarchy: a store manager, an assistant manager, and a number of counter sales personnel. This hierarchy is also called a *chain of command*. In contrast, Newport News Shipbuilding Corporation has a president, five

THE MANAGERIAL HIERARCHY

vice presidents, department heads, project managers, and over 1200 first-line supervisors. All managers have various amounts of authority, responsibility, and accountability. They exist at different levels of what is referred to as the **managerial hierarchy**.

MANAGERIAL HIERARCHY
The levels of management in an organization. Typically there are three distinct levels—top, middle, and supervisory.

Exhibit 6-2 presents a pyramid diagram of a managerial hierarchy. The pyramid is used for many medium-size and large-size businesses because it indicates the number of managers at each level and the authority relationships among them.

Three levels of management are shown in the pyramid: top, middle, and supervisory. Top managers have more authority in decision making than middle managers; middle managers have more authority in decision making than supervisory managers. Some titles typically associated with the various levels are also shown in Exhibit 6-2.

Top Management

At the top of the management pyramid is the president and other managers who are engaged primarily in charting the overall mission, strategy, and objectives of the business. The top-management team must be skilled in planning product distribution, recruiting key personnel, and developing plans. In addition, those at the top often are asked to represent the organization in community activities, dealings with the government, and seminars and the like at educational institutions. They function externally for the business and are important spokespersons for everything the company is attempting to accomplish.

The obligations and responsibilites of top managers in large organizations are numerous. Consequently, the monetary rewards are often relatively large. The pay of top managers—including base salary, bonus, and other monetary considerations—is often in six figures. The effective top manager is also very mobile. At least one out of five executives moves to a new geographic location each year. Many top-level managers move from one company to another. Thus, the question is not whether the top-level manager will move, but where and when.

EXHIBIT 6-2
The Three-Level Management Hierarchy

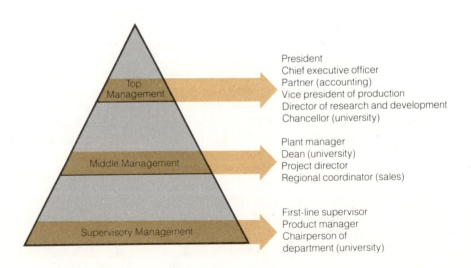

TOP MANAGEMENT MEANS TOP DOLLAR, 1980

The highest paid top managers receive large annual salaries and bonuses for their expertise, talent, and managerial skill. In fact, on top of the salary and bonus of many top managers, organizations are paying long-term income awards. These awards are often based on some measure of corporate profitability and can be cashed in after about five years.

Nine of the top twenty-five executives are the following:

			Salary	Bonus	Salary & Bonus	Long-Term Income	Total
					(In Thousands of Dollars)		
Robert A. Charpie	President	Cabot	—	—	$ 799	$2531	$3330
C. C. Gavin, Jr.	Chairman	Exxon	640	275	915	2145	3060
David S. Lewis	Chairman	General Dynamics	400	55	455	2557	3012
Robert Anderson	Chairman	Rockwell International	415	450	865	1164	2029
Donald P. Kelly	President	Esmark	—	—	1647	314	1961
J. R. Lesch	President	Hughes Tools	—	—	418	1452	1870
Pierre Gousseland	Chairman	AMAX	405	360	765	936	1701
Ray A. Burke	Sr. Vice President	Union Oil of California	224	286	510	1031	1541
Rawleigh Warner, Jr.	Chairman	Mobil	498	530	1028	427	1455

Robert A. Carpie, president of Cabot Corporation—a diversified, energy-oriented company—became the highest paid U.S. executive, with total annual compensation hitting $3.3 million. The inclusion of long-term income makes direct comparisons from year to year difficult. Also, some long-term income figures are not always available. Listed below are a few more top executive salaries of organizations that many of [Business Week's] readers do business with.

			Salary	Bonus	Salary & Bonus	Long-Term Income	Total
					(In Thousands of Dollars)		
Thomas A. Murphy	Chairman	General Motors	$400	$400	$800	—	$800
W. T. Beebe	Chairman	Delta Airlines	—	—	350	—	350
J. Paul Austin	Chairman	Coca-Cola	462	300	762	—	762
August A. Busch, III	Chairman	Anheuser-Busch Co.	—	—	606	—	606
William S. Sneath	Chairman	Union Carbide	452	268	720	12	732
Fred L. Turner	Chairman	McDonald's	—	—	375	—	375
H. A. Shaub	President	Campbell Soup	151	167	318	1	319
William S. Paley	Chairman	CBS	315	250	565	88	653

From "Pay at the Top Mirrors Inflation," Business Week, May 11, 1981, pp. 58–78.

Middle Management

The middle level of the management hierarchy includes plant supervisors, college deans, project directors, and regional sales coordinators. These managers receive the broad overall strategies, missions, and objectives from top managers and translate them into specific action programs. The emphasis is on implementing the broad organizational plans. Basically, the middle manager is a conduit between the top policy makers (top management) and the supervisory personnel who are responsible for producing products and/or services so that the company achieves its objectives.

Supervisory Management

The third level of management, the supervisory level, is directly responsible for the minute details needed to coordinate the work of nonmanagers. Supervisors must work directly with employees and motivate them to perform satisfactorily. The supervisor in a factory, the departmental chairperson in a college, and the product manager in a marketing department must translate the overall corporate goals into action plans. This level of management is the link between managers and nonmanagers. The best top-level objectives must eventually meet the test of reality at the supervisory level.

The cornerstone that separates the three levels of management from nonmanagers is decision making. Managers at any level, performing any managerial function and applying any management principle, must make decisions. Top managers must determine the overall direction of the company. The middle manager must decide how to implement the overall plan at the supervisory level: How should the plan be communicated? How should the supervisors be motivated? When should the supervisor be informed about the overall plans? The supervisor must decide how to motivate employees and reward the best performers.

Operating Employees

The managerial hierarchy in Exhibit 6–2 shows only managers. The majority of employees in medium-size and large-size business organizations do nonmanagerial work. The bank teller waits on customers, the salesperson sells dresses to a customer, and the machinist works on equipment that produces units that the company sells. Therefore, the pyramid is complete only with a foundation that shows all the employees who are not performing managerial duties. These are the *operating employees*.

MANAGEMENT PRINCIPLES

MANAGEMENT PRINCIPLE
A guideline that serves to help managers make decisions.

Management principles are guidelines for managerial decision making at the three levels in the managerial hierarchy—top, middle, and supervisory. Principles are rather obvious in the physical sciences. For example, if you mix two parts hydrogen and one part oxygen, the result is H_2O, or water. But management principles are not so specific and absolute; they merely serve as a basis for action. Some of the better developed principles in management are division of labor, organizational structure, authority, responsibility, and accountability.

**Division of Labor:
Specialization**

Today, many people do specialized work. The owner of a fast-food franchise specializes by providing a limited menu to customers; a mortgage-loan officer in a bank specializes by reviewing and granting a specific type of loan; and a nuclear-valve salesperson sells only a specific type of product. Specialization has many advantages.

Organizations attain specialization by dividing labor vertically or horizontally. *Vertical* division of labor involves dividing work from the bottom level (the plant worker, the bank teller) to the top level (the president). One outcome of vertically dividing work is the creation of a chain of command. The chain of command—the hierarchy from the top to the bottom—is actually a system of authority.

Horizontal division of labor means specializing job duties for each employee so that he or she can become efficient in performing a job. The advantages of the horizontal division of labor are assumed to be:

■ The efficient use of a manageable number of skills
■ Easier training to prepare for a job
■ More practice per skill, which results in greater efficiency
■ A more structured and routine job

Horizontal division of labor can cause managers some problems. For example, a job that consists of tightening one type of screw for eight hours is highly specialized, and some people would consider it boring and degrading. Some workers want to be challenged by their job, and they may be highly dissatisfied with a job they consider boring. High levels of dissatisfaction may result in excessive absenteeism and turnover and consequently, in lost productivity. Lost productivity increases costs and lowers profits.

Work can also be divided on the basis of function, product, geography, or market. Employees are often placed in such *functional* areas as production, marketing, personnel, and finance. Departments in many companies reflect division by function. The *product* division of labor is used by such companies as General Motors: one executive is in charge of the Chevrolet Division; another is responsible for the Oldsmobile Division. *Geographical* division of labor is used especially by businesses concerned with marketing or production that requires a fixed location. The famous Macy's chain of department stores has New York and San Francisco divisions, among others. Finally, some businesses set up *customer-based* divisions—say, a consumer-products division and an industrial-products division.

Some organizations use a number of these divisions of labor. For example, top-level executives may be divided on the basis of function (production, personnel, marketing, finance); the vice president of production may be responsible for producing goods in the United States, Canada, and Australia (geographical division); the U.S. production manager may be responsible for producing goods for consumers or industrial users. Management decides whether to use a particular division of labor or some combination only after carefully evaluating experience, research, pro and con arguments, and objectives.

Organizations have both formal and informal structures, frameworks within which the manager must make decisions. These structures are patterns of relationships among people and the positions they occupy.

Organizational Structure

Therefore, organizational structure is the pattern or network of relationships among various positions and position holders.

Formal structure is the specified, on-paper pattern of organizational positions and their accompanying responsibilities and authority. *Informal structure* springs up within the formal structure when employees interact on the job. A group of employees from one department who eat lunch together is likely to have an informal structure quite different from the formal structure.

The structures within a business organization provide a system of communications and satisfaction for employees, and they encourage efficiency. The lack of a proper organizational structure can result in chaos and inefficiency because it is through the organization's structure that a hierarchy is established. More about organizational structure will be presented in the next chapter.

Authority, Responsibility, and Accountability

AUTHORITY
The right to use resources to encourage people to perform and accept orders.

Authority is the right to use resources for encouraging performance and the basis through which the manager makes decisions. Formal authority is the right to give orders and the power to have employees respond so that organizational objectives can be accomplished. Power and authority are best understood as separate factors, although power may be considered the application of formal authority.

People derive power from greater knowledge, a strong personality, or a special skill. And power is a two-way process. For example, a manager may control subordinate opportunities for a pay raise, but subordinates indirectly determine the manager's chances for a raise. Subordinates must perform well for the manager to be considered effective. Thus, power flows between managers and subordinates. It reflects the political realities of a business organization and is an informal way to encourage people.

Several other kinds of authority exist. A person may be considered an authority because of special knowledge. Authority can also exist in a given situation, as when a special problem occurs and a particular manager takes over to correct it. The manager assumes authority because of the situation. And in some cases, people have authority because thay occupy a position. Bill Waslinski is an example of a person who occupies a position of authority because he is the president of Holly Hill Nursery.

Holding a position does not automatically provide the authority needed to do the job. If subordinates don't accept the authority of a superior, then he or she has lost the "right" to encourage employees to perform more effectively.

On the Job Revisited

An important part of authority is knowing when to delegate it. In a company such as Zenith Radio, the authority to operate the business lies with the chief executive officer (CEO). Although the chief executive officer is subject to the influence of the board of directors, he or she is the primary authority center. The board of directors has delegated to the CEO the authority to run Zenith. The CEO in turn must delegate to others, and these in turn to others. Eventually, the proper amounts of authority are in the hands of employees who need it to carry out Zenith's work. *Delegation*, then, is the process by which authority is distributed throughout the business.

The delegation of authority does not occur automatically. Rather, it is a planned distribution. The superior may assign duties to subordinates or grant them permission to do something. By delegating, the manager is, in effect, creating the organizational structure.

The manager who has authority and power must report to a superior. This means that the manager is responsible for using the authority based on the position. **Responsibility,** then, is the obligation of a subordinate to perform duties required by the immediate superior. **Accountability** refers to the fact that people with authority and responsibility are evaluated by their immediate superiors. Accountability directs the manager's attention to what the superior expects. Anyone who accepts a managerial position in a business organization also accepts authority, responsibility, and accountability. The manager who uses authority, responsibility, and accountability effectively will be a leader.

RESPONSIBILITY
Obligation of a subordinate to perform duties required by an immediate superior.

ACCOUNTABILITY
Requirement that a person with authority and responsibility be held accountable to a person above him or her in the managerial hierarchy for any actions.

LEADERSHIP AND MANAGEMENT: SETTING THE RECORD STRAIGHT

LEADERSHIP
The process of influencing the activities of an individual or group toward accomplishing objectives.

Leadership and management are not the same. Management has been defined as the process of planning, organizing, staffing, directing, and controlling that is carried out by a team of managers. Management involves working with and through individuals and groups to accomplish objectives. **Leadership** is the process of influencing the activities of an individual or group toward accomplishing objectives. A person can exert leadership with or without such official titles as manager, director, supervisor, or chairperson. Therefore, management and leadership are not interchangeable terms. A person can be considered a manager because of his or her position, but an effective leader is the person who can achieve important objectives. Bill Waslinski was certainly a manager. But until he made some changes, his approach to leadership left a lot to be desired. Remember, leadership is the process of influencing others toward the accomplishment of objectives. Some managers are just not able to effectively influence subordinates. Of course, if this goes on for some time, the manager may have to be replaced.

Some managers are more effective—better leaders—than others. But why? Some believe that determining the traits of effective leaders is the answer to the leadership puzzle. Studies of such traits as height, appearance, energy level, personality, and intelligence have shown that leader effectiveness cannot be accurately predicted from traits.

Since the trait approach has proven unreliable, there has been more interest in studying leader behavior. Managers and behavioral researchers have attempted to determine what effective leaders *do*. They have identified different leadership styles, including:

- *Autocratic.* Make most decisions and tell followers what to do.
- *Democratic.* Consult with subordinates before making decisions.
- *Free-rein.* Allow subordinates to make most decisions.
- *Adaptive.* Attempt to provide the type of style required by subordinates. Some subordinates want to be told, others want to consult, and others want to make decisions.

CONTINGENCY APPROACH
A leadership approach that attempts to determine which style of leadership will work best in a given situation.

The evidence suggests that the best style to use in leading others depends on the leader and the situation. This recent and most popular view of leadership is called the **contingency approach** because it attempts to determine what will work best in a given situation. According to Dr. Fred E. Fiedler, a behavioral researcher, consultant, and educator who advocates this approach, the best style for a given situation depends on:

■ *Leader–member relations.* The relationship between the leader and the group (is the leader liked, respected)
■ *Leader power.* The formal power and authority of the position (president, director, first-line supervisor)
■ *The job task of subordinates.* The nature of the job (routine or nonroutine; assembly-line workers or research chemists)[5]

Fiedler has developed a framework that matches these three situational variables with the best style—whether relationship- or task-oriented. For example, if an office manager is well liked by subordinates and has a moderate amount of power, and the subordinates' jobs are routine, a task-oriented style of leadership should achieve the best results. The situational mix provides the key to which style will be most effective. Fiedler and others have researched eight different mixes over the past twenty-five years. Exhibit 6–3 summarizes some cases that illustrate the match between situation mix and leadership style.

Today, managers and researchers are giving most of their attention to the situational nature of leadership. Most agree that there is no "best" leadership style. The challenge is to find the style that best fits the situation. What works at Quaker Oats Co. is not necessarily going to be effective at Nabisco, Inc.

EXHIBIT 6–3
Situation Mix-Leadership Style Match for Best Results

SITUATION	LEADER–MEMBER RELATIONS	POSITION POWER	JOB TASKS	LEADERSHIP STYLE FOR BEST RESULTS
Popular supervisor on assembly line at Ford Motor Company	Good	High	Routine	Task-oriented. Leader directs closely and is respected.
Unpopular machine shop supervisor at Black & Decker	Poor	High	Routine	Relations-oriented. Although power is in the hands of the leader, followers can block its use. Thus, work on improving relations is needed.
Popular director of research laboratory at Baxter Laboratories	Good	High	Nonroutine	Task-oriented. Less task-oriented than first situation, but needs some direction because of nonroutine tasks.
Unpopular appointed leader of informal group to investigate new product design at Bechtel Engineering	Poor	Low	Nonroutine	Task-oriented. Has little power and is disliked. Best hope is to concentrate on investigating the new product design.

The exhibit highlights four of the situational mixes that have been extensively researched by Fiedler and others. Fiedler and others have studied leaders in business organizations, the military, athletic teams, the government, and educational organizations.

In discussing the process of managing and leading within a business organization, it is important to study the functions of management. Functions are what the management team does. Instead of using a team, Bill Waslinski tried to *be* the team at the Holly Hill nursery. He found out that all of the management functions have to be coordinated. The five major functions of management are planning, organizing, staffing, directing, and controlling. Though we will discuss them separately, in practice, these functions are performed simultaneously.

When managers plan, they project a course of action for the future, attempting to achieve a systematic set of business actions aimed at achieving objectives. Thus, **planning** essentially means deciding in advance what is to be done. Of course, plans alone do not bring about desired results; but without a plan and a set of objectives, managerial actions are likely to produce confusion. Planning is a task that every manager must do every day.

The work of planning is basically mental. Planning demands thinking things through logically. Managers should think before acting and act in light of facts rather than best guesses.

One reason for such famous business failures as the Edsel, the Penn Central Railroad, and Daniel Boone Chicken was faulty planning or no planning at all. In the early 1970s, the Daniel Boone Chicken franchise tried to compete head-on with Kentucky Fried Chicken but failed to secure proper sites or to train store managers. In addition, it couldn't secure the money needed to properly operate the fast-food stores over the long haul.

There are many reasons why a manager must plan. For one thing, planning helps provide the coordination needed to do the job. Planning helps assure that things will get done, but it can also show the manager when things may not get done and why they were not done right. Planning also helps the manager determine who will do what job, how long it will take to do the job, and what resources are needed to get the job done.

Indicators of poor planning are found in almost every business organization. They include unmet schedules, idle employees, busywork for subordinates, and duplication of work.

THE PLANNING PERIOD   For what length of time should a manager plan? A distinction is generally made between short-range and long-range planning, but the definition of these terms depends on the manager's position in the hierarchy, the kind of business operation, and the kind of industry. Most managers, however, consider short-range planning to encompass a period of up to one year. Long-range planning usually means more than a year.

For activities in some departments, the manager can plan three to six months in advance. For example, in planning for preventive equipment maintenance in a production department, a three-month schedule may be developed. For most lower-level supervisors, the planning period is likely to be for a week or a day. Short-range planning is involved in staffing a production-line work station, Some employees must be at the station every day; thus, staffing plans are a daily consideration.

MANAGEMENT FUNCTIONS

Planning

PLANNING
The management function of establishing objectives and developing plans to accomplish them.

REQUIREMENTS OF GOOD PLANS   Good plans must first be realistic. Objectives that are impossible to meet may create confusion and dissatisfaction among employees. Second, managers should provide back-up plans in case the original plans fail. Third, managers should collect all the relevant information needed to complete the plan. A plan that is based on incomplete information usually fails. Fourth, planning requires coordination. Managers simply can't plan by themselves. A marketing manager needs to coordinate plans with the production manager. Finally, planning demands creativity. Simply dusting off and using last month's or last year's plan means not making progress. Managers must continually search for better ways to accomplish objectives. New ideas need to be considered and logically evaluated.

Organizing

ORGANIZING
The management function of grouping people and assignments so that the job tasks and the mission can be properly carried out.

The **organizing** function of management consists of grouping people and assigning activities so that the job tasks and the mission can be properly carried out. The establishment of the managerial hierarchy is the foundation of the organizing function. Specific details of organizing will be discussed in the next chapter.

Staffing

STAFFING
The management function of selecting, placing, training, developing, and compensating subordinates.

The **staffing** function includes the selection, placement, training, development, and compensation of subordinates. A manager's staffing activities also include the evaluation and appraisal of performance. Specific details about this function are covered in Chapter 9.

Some managers believe that staffing activities are the sole responsibility of the personnel department. But because managers are directly affected by staffing decisions, they should become involved. Line managers can be aided by the personnel department but typically do not give up the final responsibility for staffing.

Directing

DIRECTING
The management function of initiating action.

Directing is the managerial function that initates action. It means issuing directives, assignments, and instructions. Directing also means building an effective group of subordinates who are motivated to perform. It means getting subordinates to work to accomplish objectives.

The directing function is a part of any manager's job, but the time and effort managers spend in directing vary with their position in the managerial hierarchy, the number of assigned subordinates, and the type of job activities being performed. For example, the first-line supervisor spends most of the day directing subordinates, whereas the president spends significantly more time in other activities.

Generally speaking, the manager may choose from many directing styles. Styles of directing are similar to the leadership styles discussed earlier. Two such styles of direction are the autocratic and the democratic.

The *autocratic*, close style of supervision means providing subordinates with detailed job instructions. The manager structures or specifies exactly what is to be done and when the work is due. The manager using this style delegates as little authority as possible. The autocratic manager assumes that he or she should do the planning and make the necessary decisions.

Some employees respond positively to the autocratic style. On the other hand, some employees tend to lose interest and lack initiative when working for an autocratic manager. In some cases, individuals or even groups of subordinates may actively resist and may develop hostilities toward the autocratic manager.

Under certain circumstances and with certain employees, autocratic direction may be necessary. Employees with skill deficiencies, lack of experience, or various personality traits want firm and structured direction. Some feel that general supervision is no supervision at all.

The opposite of autocratic direction is *democratic*, general supervision. The essential feature of this approach is that the manager consults with subordinates about job activities, problems, and corrective actions. The manager using the general approach seeks help and ideas. The democratic approach does not lessen the manager's formal authority because decision-making power rests with the manager.

For democratic management to be successful, the manager must be enthusiastic and honest in using it, and the employees must want it. If a subordinate believes that a superior "knows best," there is little likelihood that the person will be motivated to perform better under the general supervision style.

Probably the best reason for considering the democratic style is that, if subordinates participate in a job-related decision, they are apt to be more enthusiastic about performing the job. (Because of participation in decision making, participants generally become very supportive of the final decisions enacted. Their efforts and participation result in trying hard to make the decision a success.)

Democratic supervision is not the same as no supervision at all. It requires that subordinates be given job assignments, but the assignments are linked primarily to the employees' understanding of what results are expected. The assignments are not specific and detailed. They are, however, result-oriented. Challenging objectives may exert a degree of pressure on subordinates, but this pressure is quite different from close supervision. The subordinate participates in setting the objectives or at least discusses the goals before they are finalized.

Controlling

Controlling is the managerial function of checking to determine whether employees are following plans and if progress is being made, and of taking action to reduce discrepancies. The core idea of control is to make modifications in behavior and performance when deviations from plans are discovered. Planning, organizing, staffing, and directing are the initial steps for getting the job done. Controlling is concerned with making certain that plans are being correctly implemented. Supervisors who delegate their responsibility should take care to control because they always maintain the ultimate responsibility for the work that is delegated.

CONTROLLING
The management function of checking to determine whether employees are following plans and whether progress is being made, and of taking action to reduce discrepancies.

The process of control has four basic steps:

1. Setting standards for time, quality, quantity, and so on
2. Measuring performance (results)
3. Comparing performance to standards
4. Making necessary modifications

A standard indicates to employees what is expected. For example, a management team may set a standard for producing two acceptable units a day or for achieving industrial sales of $50,000 a month. Ideally, standards are measurable and easy to understand. But how are standards set for an accountant or personnel manager? Standards in these and other staff areas are often somewhat fuzzy attempts to determine the important functions in the departments.

An important part of a manager's job is to monitor performance so that problems can be pinpointed. Once performance is assessed and compared to the standards set earlier, a course of action can be started. Of course, too much measurement can be expensive and can alienate the people being monitored. It is important for each person involved in the control checks to understand their importance.

In many cases, managers develop clear standards and monitor results but fail to make the necessary corrections. If standards are not being met, the manager must search for the problem, find it, and correct it.

The entire control process is spelled out in Exhibit 6-4. An important phase of organizational control is the feedback that occurs. If performance is acceptable, no modification is needed; if performance is unacceptable, objectives will not be met, so modifications are needed.

THE MANAGER'S ROLES

ROLE
A set of expected behaviors. A manager has three major roles as a conduit, processor, and decision maker.

In carrying out the five major management functions, managers perform various roles. A **role** is a set of expected behaviors. For example, a man may play the role of a father. As such he serves as a role model or a person who is looked upon as a good example. As a role model, the father is expected to be kind, understanding, helpful, and provide a good example to his child. Similarly a manager is expected to serve a number of roles and to be a good role model.

First, the manager serves as a *conduit,* or linking person, because of the position held in the managerial hierarchy. Second, the communications that flow to and from the manager make it necessary for him or her to process information. Third, the fact that a manager is a conduit and communicator means that decisions must be made. Managers are the key

EXHIBIT 6-4
The Control Cycle and Requirements

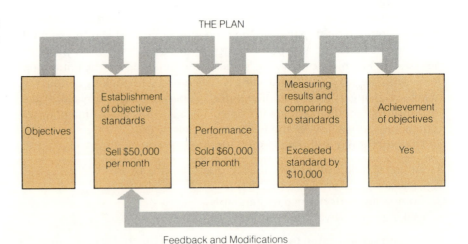

THE PLAN

Objectives

Establishment of objective standards

Sell $50,000 per month

Performance

Sold $60,000 per month

Measuring results and comparing to standards

Exceeded standard by $10,000

Achievement of objectives

Yes

Feedback and Modifications

SOME SPECIAL TRAITS OF EXECUTIVE ROLE MODELS

Is there something special about a role model? A person who stands out above others is a role model. What distinguishes the people who run businesses from those who never reach the top? A need for power seems to be an attribute of many of the top role models in business. Some examples of the power need are captured in profiles of a few executives:

John W. Hanley, chief executive of Monsanto Company, recalled that even he felt the urge "just to see if you could persuade people to do what you wanted them to do." Working part-time at a soda fountain, he would use high-pressure tactics to make his customers take an egg in their malted milk shakes.

Donald N. Frey worked his way up from laboratory researcher to group vice-president of the Ford Motor Company by the age of 44—but that wasn't enough. "I just have to run a whole business," he explained. "I'm not happy unless I'm dealing with all the pieces." He went on to become chief executive of Bell and Howell.

From "What Makes Tycoons Tick?" *Nation's Business*, June 1981, pp. 60–64.

Robert Beck of Prudential Insurance says he likes "the chance of being able to work with an organization that can influence things. When this kind of company decides on a course of action, it can be a force for good. I like being a part of it. That turns me on."

In addition to power many executive role models have a need for competitive situations. Some consider power as no more than winning. Competition is an extension of the urge for power.

Persistence is also an important trait. Some feel that persistence is more important than intelligence for the man or woman who hopes to reach the top. "Men of high intellectual caliber are often strikingly ineffectual," according to Peter F. Drucker, the renowned management educator, consultant, and philosopher. "They often fail to realize that a single insight is not in itself achievement and performance. They may never have learned that insights become effective only through hard, systematic work."

decision makers in organizations. These aspects of managing are referred to as roles—behaviors associated with the position.

Bill Waslinski performed each of these roles at Holly Hill. As president, he was a conduit to other managers. He also was a processor of vital information—sending and receiving. The decision-making buck stopped at Bill's desk. He had the final say and responsibility for decisions—big and small.

On the Job Revisited

The manager must be in frequent contact with others to fulfill the organization's objectives. This daily activity requires the manager to lead subordinates. Each time a manager influences an employee to work a little harder, to have confidence in the organization, or to report minor problems before they become major ones, he or she is performing as a conduit from management to operating employees. Leadership is essential for influencing the behavior and performance of employees. An important feature of influencing others is, of course, the ability to communicate confidence and mutual respect.

The Conduit Role

119

The Processing Role

The manager is the "nerve center" or focal point of a group. He or she should have a total picture of the group, its strengths and weaknesses, and its needs. This knowledge enables managers to process information flowing to and from the group and to feed it the relevant information. For example, the manager may receive word that a community-action group will file a legal suit against the company for polluting the environment. This information may be considered premature or inaccurate by the executives of the organization, and they may ask managers to discuss this with their subordinates. Managers would need to assure the subordinates that, to date, no legal action had been taken and that the problem will be handled by top management. The manager also would inform the group of the organization's official position on the rumor.

The Decision-Making Role

The position of the manager in the hierarchy requires the acceptance of responsibility for decision making. The manager, as a conduit and processor of information, must take bits of information from various sources, interject a personal opinion, consider the present situation, analyze the resources available, and tie this all together before reaching a decision. The exact mix of factors that must be considered before reaching a decision is different for every situation. But the decisions must be made by the manager, and the manager must make decisions under pressure.

THE PRESSURES AND CHALLENGES OF MANAGING

Managers agree that all members of the management team make decisions under pressure. Pressure inevitably has some influence on the decisions made by a manager. For example, Jim Strader is a plant superintendent for General Mills. He has been asked to find a new supervisor for the maintenance department. Many forces act on Jim during the decision-making process, including the company owners, the maintenance department employees, the union, the government, the job requirements, past company hiring practices, salary requirements, and personal values. Exhibit 6–5 outlines the sources of pressure on Jim and their expectations. The pressures highlighted in the table don't exhaust the potential sources of pressure that have to be considered. Furthermore, some of the pressures are more important than others and have to be dealt with before others.

From a practical point of view, the pressures affecting decision makers often force managers away from the ideal style. The manager who can always make perfectly sound decisions would be theoretical, reflective, systematic, diagnostic, moralistic, and thorough, but such characteristics can rarely be used to the fullest in managerial situations. The pressures and realities of business management—employees quitting, absenteeism, poor employee training for the job, occasional morale problems, employee distrust because of job insecurity, dissatisfaction with various job features, and the like—often require a style other than the ideal. Recall that Bill Waslinski didn't use an ideal style, and he got himself into trouble. He had to make a drastic change in his style.

On the Job Revisited

PRESSURE SOURCE	EXPECTATIONS OF PRESSURE SOURCE
Owners	A committed manager
	An experienced manager
	A profit-maximizing manager
Employees	An equitable manager
	A hard-working manager
	A manager who will present their grievances forcefully
Union	A fair manager
	A manager who has worked with unions previously
	A manager who will listen to grievances
Government	Insurance that all qualified minority group members are considered
	A fair and unbiased selection process
Job requirements	An experienced manager
	A college education
	A knowledge of mechanical packaging equipment
Past hiring practices	First opportunity to fill vacancies to present employees
Salary requirements	Pay between $18,000 and $20,000 to selected manager
Jim's values	Giving job to Jack Connors, present employee
	Second preference is Don Buhl, also a present employee
	Not liking to work with noncollege candidates or candidates who have difficulty expressing themselves

EXHIBIT 6-5
Pressures that Affect
Jim Strader's Selection

SUMMARY

■ Management is the process of planning, organizing, staffing, directing, and controlling an organization's human, financial, and material resources to accomplish its goals. The process is carried out by a team of technical managers who get things done through other people. Objectives provide the direction for an organization. They are the desired results or targets that should be reached by a certain period of time.

■ The managerial hierarchy consists of three levels of management—top, middle, and supervisory. Managers have varying amounts of authority, responsibility, and accountability based on their position in the hierarchy.

■ Management principles are guidelines for managerial decision making. Some of the more developed principles include the division of labor; the formal organizational structure; and authority, or the right to give orders and use power to influence others.

■ Leadership and management are not the same. A person can be a leader without having an official position or title such as vice president of production.

■ According to behavioral researcher Dr. Fred E. Fiedler, the best style of leadership depends on leader–member relations, leader power, and the job tasks of subordinates.

■ The five major functions of management are planning, organizing, staffing, directing, and controlling.

Planning involves developing a set of actions to achieve objectives.

Organizing consists of grouping people and assigning activities so that job tasks and the mission can be carried out.

Staffing involves the selection, placement, training, development, and compensation of subordinates.

ISSUES TO CONSIDER AND ANALYZE

1. What did Bill Waslinski mean when he said, "I finally saw the trees in the forest and learned to be a top manager of a business"?
2. The captain of a sailing craft definitely must plan, organize, and control. Explain why the captain would have to engage in these management functions?
3. Why must organizations of any size be concerned with and involved in the managerial processes of planning, organizing, staffing, directing, and controlling?
4. What role models do you use when thinking about the work of managers?
5. What types of pressures, besides those in Exhibit 6–5, do managers face?
6. What recent business successes can be traced to the work of managers?
7. Is authority given to a manager?
8. Do you consider yourself an adaptive leader? Why or why not?
9. Explain the main differences in managerial activities for a manager practicing autocratic supervision and one practicing democratic supervision.
10. Is management a profession?

CASE FOR ANALYSIS   GENERAL MOTORS GROWS THEIR OWN MANAGERS

Anyone familiar with the General Motors (GM) of the 1960s can't help but wonder whether the GM of 1983, 1984, or 1985 will be the same company. The complacent giant that used to dominate its industry by sheer size is now an aggressive, inventive product leader. GM accomplished this out of self-renewal not by sacking old management and breaking with the past, but through continuity. Its system for developing and making the best use of its people has continued to produce managers who are willing and able to manage in a changing environment.

GM's top executives have created a culture that produces a lot of job security for managers. More than managers of most other organizations, they feel assured that they will advance on their merits. If they carry out the functions of management efficiently, GM managers believe that they will continue to be employed. This sense of security seems to free GM managers—particularly those on their way toward the top—to dedicate them-

Adapted from Charles G. Burck, "How GM Stays Ahead," *Fortune*, March 9, 1981, pp. 48–56.

selves to the objectives of the company. They can concentrate on the high-priority objectives instead of politicking to advance their careers.

The GM management team is close-knit. GM boasts that it hires fewer people from outside than any other major U.S.corporation. Two-thirds of GM's managers never worked for anyone else. Managers come to GM and become a part of it—and then it's like an important part of their lives.

GM even starts grooming future managers while they're still teenagers. The teenagers are students at General Motors Institute in Flint, Michigan. This is the only accredited U.S. college owned and operated by a company. Its graduates include GM's last three presidents, and currently four of its top fifteen executives. The students learn about management principles, functions, and roles. The five-year program takes forty-eight weeks per year—work and study alternate in twelve-week shifts.

GM believes that managers who are knowledgeable, loyal, and skilled at working with people are the core of success. Maintaining a loyal management cadre requires allowing managers to do their jobs. GM has this philosophy and continually works at sustaining it by keeping good managers and training future managers.

QUESTIONS

1. Why is it necessary for a large company like General Motors to have a close-knit managerial team?
2. What do you think about GM's program of grooming future managers in the General Motors Institute?
3. Would you go to work for GM as a manager? Why?

CHAPTER 7

MANAGEMENT ORGANIZATION

LEARNING OBJECTIVES

After studying this chapter, you should be able to:

Define terms such as organizing, organization structure, and functional authority.

Describe centralized versus decentralized decision-making authority.

Illustrate a matrix structure.

Compare the advantages and disadvantages of functional, product, and territorial structures.

Explain how various principles of organization can be used by managers.

KEY TERMS

Organizing
Organization structure
Informal organization
Line authority
Staff authority
Functional authority
Centralization
Decentralization
Organization chart
Principle
Principle of unity of
    command
Scalar principle
Principle of span of
    control
Principle of functional
    similarity
Functional structure
Product structure
Territorial structure
Matrix structure

HELP! HELP! I NEED ADVICE ABOUT ORGANIZING

Joy Flynn is a management consultant in Denver specializing in helping managers organize their business. When she started her business ten years ago, there were some snickers. Critics felt that she would go broke —after all, everyone knows how to organize a business. They were wrong. Joy now employs ten consultants and an office staff of eighteen people. Below is an example of how Joy operates. It's a telephone call from a close friend, Bud Grandscio from Little Rock, Arkansas.

Joy: Hi, Bud. How is everything in Arkansas?

Bud: Not bad, Joy. I wanted to talk a little more about my business growth problem. You know, that sounds funny. My business is growing, and I think I have a problem.

Joy: Refresh my memory, Bud. You just purchased six King Sooper Save Stores in Arkansas, and you already own seven Grandy supermarkets.

Bud: Right. I'm now trying to put together a structure to coordinate these thirteen stores in the Arkansas-Tennessee area. I've been looking at some management books, but they only offer principles and some basic structures. Not much help.

Joy: Bud, what we will have to do is look at a number of things: (1) what you are trying to accomplish—your objectives; (2) your time frame to accomplish the objectives; (3) how you are organized now; (4) what resources—people, financial, equipment—you have available; and (5) what kind of competitive environment you are operating in.

Bud: Let me think over these questions. Can you visit with me in Little Rock next Thursday? I'd much rather work with you and not one of your consultants. I want to put an organization structure together.

Joy: I have a tight schedule, but I'll be in your office at 10:00 A.M. Remember to have my questions answered. It will give our meeting a good start.

In this chapter we'll consider the kind of issues raised in Joy's questions to Bud.

In the previous chapter we stated that **organizing** is the management function of assigning activities and grouping people so that the activities can be carried out. In other words, it is the process of designing and developing a structure that will aid managers in accomplishing objectives. When a business grows from a one-person operation to one with employees, organization is necessary. Increasing size causes specialization, more personal interactions, and differing viewpoints. Rather than a single owner doing everything, the growing business has employees with assigned tasks. Some type of organizational structure is needed for things to run smoothly and in a coordinated manner. This chapter looks at how organizing occurs in a business. Some crucial decisions must be made. Structure doesn't just happen; managers must plan and implement the way a business will be organized. Bud Grandscio certainly knows that structures don't just appear.

In organizing a business, an individual or a group must decide what each person will do and how much authority each will have. The **organization structure** is the arrangement of the work to be done. The organization's structure is intended to help the business accomplish its objectives. There is really no "one best" way to organize.[1] The "how to organize" decision for a particular business depends upon a lot of different factors, including size, market, personnel, competition, history, and financial resources available. General Motors is organized on the basis of product—Cadillac, Chevrolet, Buick, Oldsmobile, and Pontiac. Macy's department store is organized on the basis of geography—East Coast, West Coast, and so on. Gulf Oil Corporation is organized on the basis of functions to be performed—marketing, production, exploration, chemicals.

Simply copying the organization structure of another business is not a good practice. What works for IBM doesn't necessarily work for Honeywell or Apple. There are differences between businesses in their markets, objectives, and resources. Nevertheless, there are a few points that all managers can keep in mind when organizing the business. These are the kind of points that Joy Flynn asked Bud to think about before their meeting.

In the last chapter, we said that objectives are desired results or targets. The multiple objectives of a business provide the direction for those organizing the firm. They provide the framework for hiring the type of human resources needed.

It is important to have clearly stated, meaningful, and challenging objectives and specific targets. The objectives give meaning to the business and what it is attempting to accomplish.

Organization, department, subunit, and individual objectives must fit together. This means that the efforts of individual employees must be coordinated, or woven together. Managers and leaders can be the coordinators if they are respected and skilled in integrating the efforts of their subordinates or followers. Any organization structure, no matter how

---

ORGANIZING
The managerial function of grouping people and assigning activities so that the resulting structure will aid in accomplishing objectives.

ORGANIZATION STRUCTURE
The arrangement of work to be done in a business.

SOME BASIC POINTS

On the Job Revisited

Clarity of Objectives

Coordination

LOOK OUT FOR NO.1! THE STRUCTURE IS IN PLACE

In the 1980s, International Business Machines (IBM), which has long been No. 1 in the computer business, is ready to unveil a new program that will make it even bigger and stronger. In the 1970s, many critics mentioned how IBM had missed many market opportunities. John R. Opel, IBM's president since 1974, wants to make sure that IBM misses no opportunities.

The organization structure and its response to market opportunities will help Opel do the job. IBM has changed from a functional to a more mixed product–dominated structure. In structuring for the push in the 1980s, IBM has emphasized having a structure that is especially responsive to customer requests and providing customer service. Opel is a marketing man and knows that IBM must service customers. He believes that a structure that uses multiple arrangements can respond more quickly to market demands and needs.

Since IBM is so big, some of the structural changes are difficult to put a finger on. However, a good example is what happened to the once-separate General Systems and Office Products divisions. They were first pulled together under the General Business Group. Then Informational Records and General Technology were also brought in under the General Business Group. One result of this consolidation was to control the fighting and competition among the divisions. Now product and pricing decisions are made at the top level of management. IBM has moved to a more centralized authority to make pricing and product decisions in the General Business Group divisions.

Whether the move to more centralized authority will be good for IBM employees (there are over 340,000 of them) and the profit margin is difficult to say at this time. Many IBM watchers believe that IBM now has the organization structure in place to do what it wants.

Adapted from "No. 1's Awesome Strategy," *Business Week*, June 8, 1981, pp. 84–88.

complicated, requires someone or some group to work continually on coordinating the activities of others. Managers should not underestimate the effort that must go into coordination.

Understanding Formal and Informal Organization

INFORMAL ORGANIZATION
A network of personal and social relationships that emerge when people work together.

There are really two distinct organizations that influence employees. The formal organization is the one put together by management, created by the individuals with authority, responsibility, and accountability. The formal organization is the one that is displayed in the organization chart (more on this a little later) of the business.

An informal organization exists in every business. The **informal organization** is not planned or shown on an organization chart; it is a network of personal and social relationships that emerge when people work together.

Informal organizations develop because people who work together form relationships. In the past, managers tried hard to abolish the informal organization, but these attempts were futile. The informal organization is a network that serves a purpose for employees. It exists in every organization because people want it and use it to exchange opinions, information, and attitudes.

Formal authority is the right to give orders. In effective organizations, managers delegate authority. The organization structure can provide the framework for such delegation. When managers find that they do not have the time to perform their jobs, it is often a sign that they have failed to delegate properly. When subordinates become frustrated in meeting their responsibilities, it may mean that they are not clear about what authority has been delegated to them.

Organization structure determines the pattern for delegation of authority. It helps to establish a common understanding between the superior and subordinate about the degree and type of authority that is delegated. Three types of authority are used in organization structural arrangements—line, staff, and functional. Managers should understand these distinctions in order to know how much decision-making freedom they have.

Line authority. Each position in the managerial hierarchy has direct authority over lower positions in the hierarchy. A manager with line authority is the unquestioned superior for all activities of his or her subordinates.

Staff authority. This is advisory authority. A person with staff authority studies a situation and makes recommendations, but has no authority to take action. For example, a person studies possible sites for a new plant location. The results of the study would be submitted to a group or person with the authority to make the site location decision.

Functional authority. This uses staff specialists and provides them with limited areas of authority. The specialist is able to take action and make decisions within limited areas without involving line managers.

The backbone of most organization structures is line authority. Staff and functional authority supplement the line manager's authority. In structuring a business, managers may use each of these types of authority. Exhibit 7-1 summarizes some of the advantages and disadvantages of each of these forms of authority.

Another important consideration is the amount of authority to delegate. When only a small amount of authority is delegated, a business is called **centralized**. In a centralized business, a relatively small number of managers make the decisions and hold most of the power and authority.

The opposite of a small management group making decisions is referred to as a **decentralized** business. That is, authority is delegated to more (lower) levels of management. The delegation of authority in centralized versus decentralized businesses is presented in Exhibit 7-2. The exhibit points out a few of the advantages and disadvantages associated with each type of delegation.

Organizations move back and forth along the continuum. For years, Sears was a centralized business, but in the 1950s and 1960s it changed to a more decentralized business. Today Sears has moved back toward being a more centralized business again. Around 1980, Sears executives declared that they wanted closer control of decision making. In other words, Sears management wanted authority centralized.

Delegation of Authority

LINE AUTHORITY
Unquestioned authority to make decisions and take action.

STAFF AUTHORITY
An advisory type of authority in which a person studies a situation but has no authorized authority to take action.

FUNCTIONAL AUTHORITY
Authority to take action in limited areas.

Centralization and Decentralization of Authority

CENTRALIZATION
All, or nearly all, of the authority to make decisions is retained by a small group of managers.

DECENTRALIZATION
When a significant amount of the authority to make decisions is delegated to lower-level managers.

EXHIBIT 7-1
Some Advantages and Disadvantages of Line, Staff, and Functional Authority

ADVANTAGES	DISADVANTAGES
Line authority	
Everything is kept simple.	Neglects advisors.
Authority is spelled out in a hierarchy.	Overloads line managers.
Encourages quick action.	Requires very talented line managers.
Staff authority	
Enables experts to be used.	Confusing to some employees.
Frees line managers to do day-to-day activities.	Creates line–staff conflicts.
Is good training ground for line managers.	Places staff in subservient role.
Functional authority	
Line managers do not have to do decision making.	Relationships are more complex.
Uses expert knowledge.	Difficult to coordinate.
Trains future executives.	

EXHIBIT 7-2
The Decentralized–Centralized Continuum of Authority

Maximum delegation of authority ———————————————— Little or no delegation of authority

| 1 | 1 | 1 | 1 | 1 |

Decentralized operation ———————————————— Centralized operation

| 1 | 1 | 1 | 1 | 1 |

DECENTRALIZED	CENTRALIZED
Advantages	**Advantages**
Places decision making closer to the action.	Uniformity of policies.
Allows more people to use their skills.	Helps avoid duplication of effort.
Helps develop managers for the future.	Decisions are uniform.
Disadvantages	**Disadvantages**
Coordination is more difficult.	Great demands on a few managers.
Capable managers not always available for the role.	Reduces sense of involvement.
Lack of uniformity of policies.	Gives large amount of power to a few managers.

The **organization chart** is a graphical device that presents a picture of the formal structure of a business. Organization charts are nothing more than maps of positions, people, and their authority relationships. Exhibit 7–3 illustrates a simple line authority chart. Each position is represented by a box (with a title), and the flow of authority is represented by straight lines. One of the first things Joy Flynn will ask Bud Grandscio is to see his current organization chart. The chart will provide her with a quick picture of the current structure of Grandy supermarkets.

The organization chart shows authority, the location of responsibility, and whom subordinates report to in accounting for their actions. It does not show the exact communication patterns because it can't picture the informal relationships and organization. A worker communicating directly with the president, for example, would represent informal organization.

Exhibit 7–4 illustrates a structure expanded to include the three forms of authority. The legal counsel is a staff position advising the president on legal matters. The functional special project director has a direct line of limited authority to the project A engineer supervisor. This supervisor can receive directives from the special project director without checking or going through the middle-level manager.

Any organization chart will probably need continual updating. Organization charts offer only a general view of the formal structure at a specific time. Changes in the environment, personnel, resources, size, and technology necessitate keeping the chart up to date. And remember—even if it is fairly up to date, the organization chart doesn't show the informal organization.

You may now be asking, "Are delegation of authority, charts, and formal and informal organizations all there is to organizing?" No, some principles of organizing have been found through practice and experimentation. These principles were considered in the structure of large businesses like

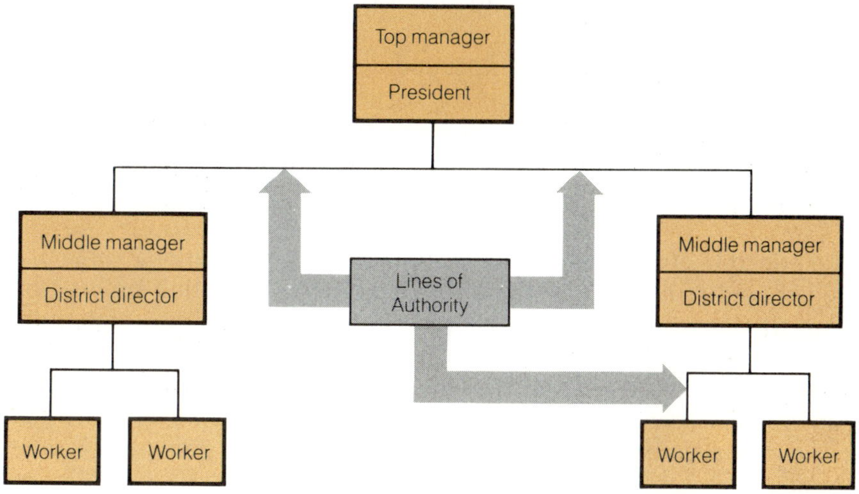

The Organization Chart

ORGANIZATION CHART
A map of positions, people, and their formal authority relationships in the organization.

PRINCIPLES OF ORGANIZATION

EXHIBIT 7-3
Organization Chart:
Line Authority.
Lines of authority are pointed out simply for information and would not appear on a real organization chart.

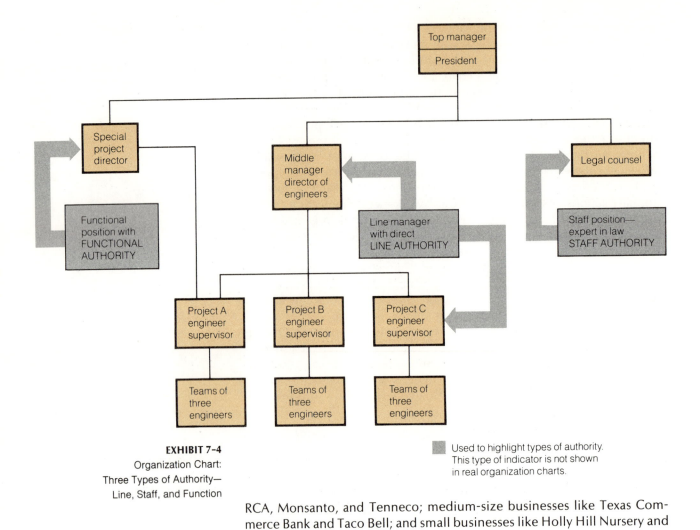

EXHIBIT 7-4
Organization Chart:
Three Types of Authority—
Line, Staff, and Function

PRINCIPLE
A guideline that managers can use in making decisions.

RCA, Monsanto, and Tenneco; medium-size businesses like Texas Commerce Bank and Taco Bell; and small businesses like Holly Hill Nursery and Joliet Jake's Auto Repair Center.

A **principle** is a guideline for decision making. Principles are not laws etched in stone. Sometimes they are used exactly as they are stated, whereas other times principles are modified or completely ignored. In general, those responsible for organizing keep a number of organizational principles in mind. Since there are numerous principles available to consult, we have selected only a few of the more popular ones as illustrations. These are the kind of principles that Joy will be describing to Bud.

Principle of Unity of Command

PRINCIPLE OF UNITY OF COMMAND
The principle that no member of an organization should report to more than one superior.

The **principle of unity of command** states that no member of an organization should report to more than one superior. Conflicting orders from different superiors should be guarded against because they violate the principle of unity of command. Subordinates need to know from whom they receive the authority to make decisions and do the job. This principle can be followed in a pure line authority organization. However, when staff or functional authority structures are used, the unity of command is often violated.

The **scalar principle** states that authority and responsibility should flow in a clear, unbroken line from the highest to the lowest manager. Since there is a managerial hierarchy, the importance of the scalar chain from top to bottom is obvious. Breaking the chain results in uncertainty, frustration, and confusion.

An extension of the scalar principle is the notion that authority should equal responsibility. For example, suppose a production supervisor at Dow Chemical has been assigned the responsibility to purchase new plant equipment. It would be important for this supervisor to have the authority to determine what price should be paid for the new equipment. Without this authority, how could the supervisor be held responsible for the decision?

The **span of control** is the number of subordinates reporting to a supervisor or "boss." This principle says there is a limit to the number of subordinates one superior should supervise. Often managers using the span of control principle specify an exact number of subordinates. This is unrealistic because some supervisors can handle more subordinates than others. The optimum span of control depends on many factors, such as the type of subordinates, the nature of the job, the supervisor's skill in handling subordinates, the situation, and the time available to do the job.

In general, highly skilled subordinates require less supervision than the less skilled. This permits the supervisor to have a *wide* (also called *short*) span of control—that is , a larger group of subordinates reporting to him or her. A large group of highly skilled technicians in a research and development unit of DuPont can be supervised by a single manager. On the other hand, an open heart surgery team at Michael Reese Hospital in Chicago involves highly skilled subordinates but a *narrow* (also called *tall*) or *small* span of control. Thus, the optimum span of control depends on many factors. There is no universal set of numbers; there are only general suggestions to examine the total picture—the managers, subordinates, job, resources, and time available.

Most activities in an organization are arranged into what are called *departments*. The arrangement is based on the **principle of functional similarity**; for example, the product departmental units of General Motors—Chevrolet, Buick, Oldsmobile, Pontiac, and Cadillac. The logic of this principle is that putting together people who are working on the same product or task is efficient. They can share feelings, beliefs, and suggestions, and hopefully a teamwork spirit can develop and grow.

This principle states that the levels in a managerial hierarchy should be kept to a minimum number. As the levels or layers of management increase, a number of problems become greater. Communication, message distortion, personal contact, and feeling a part of a team are factors addressed by this principle. The more levels of management, the longer the communication chain. This means more potential for message distortion. Moreover, there is less contact between top management and the lower levels as the distance from top to bottom increases. Finally, people feel

Scalar Principle

SCALAR PRINCIPLE
The principle that authority and responsibility should flow in a clear, unbroken line from the highest to the lowest manager.

Principle of Span of Control

PRINCIPLE OF SPAN OF CONTROL
The principle that limits the number of subordinates reporting to a supervisor.

Principle of Functional Similarity

PRINCIPLE OF FUNCTIONAL SIMILARITY
The principle that work should be arranged on the basis of similarity.

Principle of Minimizing Levels of Management

more isolated as these distances between levels increase, and there is a loss of the team spirit, of pulling together.

Principle of Flexibility

The environment of every business is dynamic and changing. Inflation, consumer demands, and government regulations are just a few of the environmental changes. The organizational structure must be flexible enough to permit changes in arrangements to meet environmental changes. This means that any structure should be developed with change in mind. Because change is inevitable, structures must be flexible enough to not destroy the continuity of the business. Sears, Procter & Gamble, the IBM are three well-known businesses that have been able to adapt their structures to meet change. These and other successful businesses are able to adapt because their organizational structures permit change.

These six principles of organization are by no means the only ones.[2] These are a few principles that offer managers the means by which to build an organization that can compete and adapt. The principles also permit managers to put together specific forms of organization structure to meet their particular needs. The principles of organization are the building blocks for constructing a formal organization structure.

THE ORGANIZATION STRUCTURE DECISION

A person involved in organizing a business should identify the business's objectives, the types of people working for the business, the technology, and the environment in which the business operates. If you've ever been in a house in which the rooms are poorly arranged or are too small, you know the importance of the notion that "form follows function." That principle is also important in making organization structure decisions. People making structure decisions need to examine the functions before selecting a form (that is, the structure).

On the Job Revisited

Joy Flynn has asked Bud Grandscio to prepare answers to her questions. She is trying to encourage him to work through his plans logically. Care in planning for the structure will result in a more efficient arrangement for Bud's supermarkets. Joy is asking Bud to practice the "form follows function" idea.

Numerous forms of structure are available to managers. Again because of space limitations, we have selected only a few for discussion here. We have selected the forms that are the most popular and widely used in business organizations.

Functional Structure

FUNCTIONAL STRUCTURE
A structure with units or departments arranged so that each has a different set of activities and responsibilities.

The **functional structure** sets up units or departments so that each has a different set of activities and responsibilities. In a manufacturing firm, this would mean that engineering, manufacturing, and marketing would be separate departments. In a hospital, functional structure would include departments of nursing, housekeeping, medical records, radiology, and so forth. A functional structure for a county hospital is shown in Exhibit 7–5.

Advantages. The functional structure orients people in the department toward a specific set of activities. The engineer focuses on engineering

DIFFERENT STROKES FOR DIFFERENT FOLKS

General Electric (GE) is a complex company because it manufactures a large range of products. GE was one of the pioneers of decentralization, and it made a great effort to adhere to the notion that "authority should equal responsibility." In the past decade, the balance of power has shifted away from department managers toward the central office.

Liberty Mutual Insurance Company is a nationwide organization of 13,000 people providing all kinds of insurance to business and personal policyholders. The distinction between line and staff is hazy. Each major function—underwriting, operations, claims, loss prevention, and sales—tends to consider itself of greatest importance. A sign in one sales office says, "Sales is not the most important department, it is the only department."

The home office functional departments are powerful for good reason. Liberty Mutual wants to control the quality of service. However, because Liberty Mutual is nationwide, it is also structured on the basis of territories. This sometimes complicates things. It is not always clear who is really the stronger supervisor—the regional managers or the local functional managers.

Johnson & Johnson is a conglomerate with more than seventy-five subsidiaries around the globe. The company produces the familiar Band-Aids, baby products, pharmaceuticals, and so forth. The subsidiaries are divided into eight groups, each headed by a person who is chairman of the board of the five to twenty companies in that group. Companies within each group typically share either geographic location or a similiarity in product line.

Each subsidiary at Johnson & Johnson is organized as if it were an independent company. The full-time salaried executives of each subsidiary constitute its board of directors.

International Telephone and Telegraph (ITT) prides itself on developing what it believes is the best system yet devised to give direction and control to a complex conglomerate organization. A large number of company presidents report to the chief executive's office. ITT has an auditing staff also reporting to the chief executive. In addition, a matrix (discussed later in this chapter) parallels the operating companies. For example, there is a vice president of receivables and a vice president of inventories who monitor individual company operations in their respective areas. Thus, they can initiate questions and make reports on excessive accounts receivable or stocks of supplies in individual subsidiaries.

work, and the salesperson works on marketing activities. These functional experts become even more skilled in their areas. Research shows that the functional structure has advantages for a firm operating in a relatively stable (unchanging or slowly changing) environment.[3] Petrochemical companies like Gulf, Shell, and Exxon operate in a normally stable environment. Few product line changes occur year after year, so they use basically the functional structure.

Disadvantages. The functional structure deemphasizes the exchange of ideas and cooperation with other departments. The boundary between, say, marketing and engineering is imaginary, but it seems like the Great Wall of China. This happens because each department is evaluated on the basis of its own performance. Knowing they will be evaluated this

EXHIBIT 7–5
Functional Structure in a Hospital

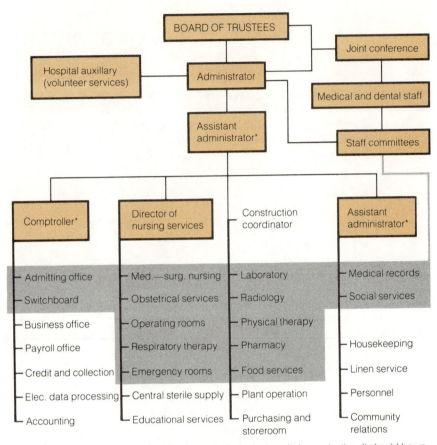

This chart reflects the line responsibility and authority in the hospital organization. It should be understood, however, that a great part of the work of the hospital is accomplished through informal interaction between the identified services and functions. These functional working relationships are encouraged. Where there is difference in understanding or when changes in procedure are required, the line organization should be carefully observed.

*Area directors.

way, managers concentrate on department matters intead of overall organizational objectives.

If the business's objectives and environment demand cooperation across departments. the functional structure becomes an obstruction. Problems arise that have no single departmental solution. What happens is that the problems go unresolved or the buck is passed or problems are pushed up to top management.

In summary, functional structures are best suited for businesses with a relatively stable environment like Exxon's. The Exxon-type organization takes advantage of technical expertise. On the other hand, in an environment like that of IBM, with numerous product line changes, a functional structure would lack flexibility. There is little reason for departments to cooperate and work together in a functional arrangement.

Businesses producing a wide variety of products often establish a **product structure**. Product structure was used as early as 1927 by Procter & Gamble (P&G). A new company soap, Camay, was not selling. A young executive, Neil McElroy (who later became the president of P&G), was assigned to give his exclusive attention to increasing the sales of Camay. This he did by using product managers. Soon afterward P&G added other product managers.

Today many firms, especially those in the food (for example, General Foods), toiletries (Gillette), and chemical industries (Dow), use product structures. General Foods uses a product structure in its Post Division. There are separate managers in charge of cereals, pet foods, and beverages. Exhibit 7–6 presents an outline of the General Foods Post Division.

Advantages. The product structure fixes responsibility with the managers for a product or product line. A success or failure of Post Toasties is the responsibility of the general manager of cereals. This means that product managers devote all their energy and skill toward the targets of containing product costs, meeting schedules, and earning a profit. Instead of a department orientation, as with the functional structure, there is a product target.

In addition, the product structure encourages creativity. One study found that businesses with product structures were more successful in creating and selling new products than were businesses without product structures.[4] The product structure also is flexible enough to cope with changing environments. People have to cooperate so that the product performs well.

Disadvantages. The price of the product structure can be high. Product managers often are not given enough authority to carry out responsibilities. They have to spend a lot of time coordinating activities so that people work together efficiently. This means less time for planning. They often are told that they are like minipresidents, but in fact they are usually only referees and low-level coordinators.

Managers have also found that, compared to employees in functional structures, employees in product structures are more insecure and anxious about unemployment and personal development.[5] Perhaps this is the result of product structures used in relatively unstable, unpredict-

Product Structure

PRODUCT STRUCTURE
An organization structure in which a manager is placed in charge of and has responsibility for a product or product line.

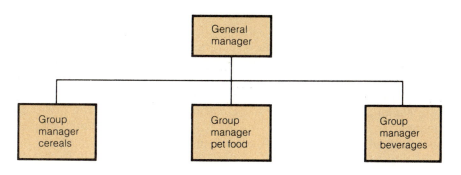

EXHIBIT 7–6
Outline of General Foods Post Division: Product Structure

able environments. The environment rejects products, even certain kinds of packages and names of products. This unpredictability is sometimes too much for those working in product structures. Did you know that General Food's Postum was first rejected when it was called Monk's Brew and Elijah's Manna was a flop until it was renamed Post Toasties?

Territorial Structure

TERRITORIAL STRUCTURE
The organization structure in which units are divided on the basis of territory or geographical regions.

The **territorial structure** divides units on the basis of territory. When adjustments to local conditions, markets, or resources are important, the territorial structure has advantages because it can fix responsibility on the basis of territory.

Merchandising organizations such as Macy's, Sears, and J. C. Penney have found territorial structure attractive. A&P, Safeway, and Kroger also have territorial division structures coupled with centralization of certain functions such as purchasing and distribution. Exhibit 7-7 outlines the territorial structure of Macy's department stores.

Each division shown in Exhibit 7-7 would operate like an independent business. The division managers would have the authority to take advantage of regional cost, resource, and competitive conditions. Territorial differences can be coped with more effectively. In the early 1970s Kentucky Fried Chicken did not respond quickly enough to territorial differences and for a long time lost a significant share of the southern U.S. market. Church's Chicken found out that the southern market preferred crispy crust chicken. Kentucky Fried Chicken failed to pick up this preference and continued to make one kind of chicken—noncrispy. The result was a shift in customer market share to Church's. If Kentucky Fried Chicken had been set up in a territorial structure, they may have been faster in their response to Church's.

Matrix Structure

MATRIX STRUCTURE
Arrangement of activities in both function and product (or project) units. There are both functional and product managers, with varying degrees of authority over the work performed by the same people.

The 1950s and 1960s brought a shift from functional to product structures. In the 1970s, there was a sharp increase in the use of what is called a **matrix structure**. A matrix starts as a functional structure. Then another structure, organized by product, or project, is overlaid or integrated with the functional structure.[6] The result is that employees are assigned to both a functional department (permanent home) and a particular product or project (temporary home). Exhibit 7-8 illustrates a matrix structure. Five functional departments and three projects that are staffed by employees from the departments are shown.

Why the matrix, an obvious violation of the principle of unity of command? You may recall that both the functional and the product structures had weaknesses. The functional structure was weak in emphasizing the exchange of ideas and cooperation, though it did permit specialists to interact and strive for technical excellence. The product structure was weaker at encouraging job security, though it was strong at inducing cooperation, adhering to schedules, and controlling costs. The matrix is designed to gain the strengths of both the functional and the product structures while avoiding the disadvantages of either.

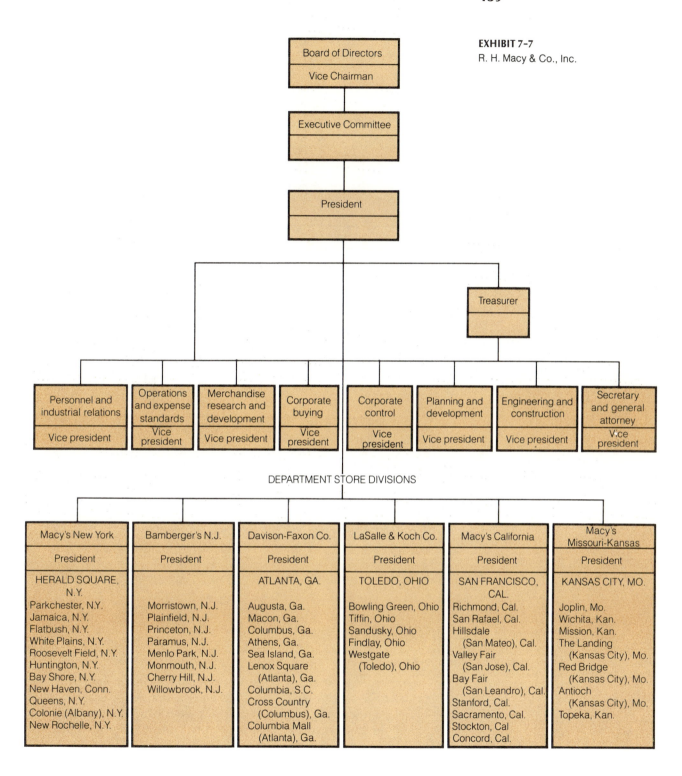

EXHIBIT 7-7
R. H. Macy & Co., Inc.

Board of Directors — Vice Chairman

Executive Committee

President

Treasurer

Personnel and industrial relations — Vice president

Operations and expense standards — Vice president

Merchandise research and development — Vice president

Corporate buying — Vice president

Corporate control — Vice president

Planning and development — Vice president

Engineering and construction — Vice president

Secretary and general attorney — Vice president

DEPARTMENT STORE DIVISIONS

Macy's New York — President
HERALD SQUARE, N.Y.
Parkchester, N.Y.
Jamaica, N.Y.
Flatbush, N.Y.
White Plains, N.Y.
Roosevelt Field, N.Y.
Huntington, N.Y.
Bay Shore, N.Y.
New Haven, Conn.
Queens, N.Y.
Colonie (Albany), N.Y.
New Rochelle, N.Y.

Bamberger's N.J. — President
Morristown, N.J.
Plainfield, N.J.
Princeton, N.J.
Paramus, N.J.
Menlo Park, N.J.
Monmouth, N.J.
Cherry Hill, N.J.
Willowbrook, N.J.

Davison-Faxon Co. — President
ATLANTA, GA.
Augusta, Ga.
Macon, Ga.
Columbus, Ga.
Athens, Ga.
Sea Island, Ga.
Lenox Square
   (Atlanta), Ga.
Columbia, S.C.
Cross Country
   (Columbus), Ga.
Columbia Mall
   (Atlanta), Ga.

LaSalle & Koch Co. — President
TOLEDO, OHIO
Bowling Green, Ohio
Tiffin, Ohio
Sandusky, Ohio
Findlay, Ohio
Westgate
   (Toledo), Ohio

Macy's California — President
SAN FRANCISCO, CAL.
Richmond, Cal.
San Rafael, Cal.
Hillsdale
   (San Mateo), Cal.
Valley Fair
   (San Jose), Cal.
Bay Fair
   (San Leandro), Cal.
Stanford, Cal.
Sacramento, Cal.
Stockton, Cal
Concord, Cal.

Macy's Missouri-Kansas — President
KANSAS CITY, MO.
Joplin, Mo.
Wichita, Kan.
Mission, Kan.
The Landing
   (Kansas City), Mo.
Red Bridge
   (Kansas City), Mo.
Antioch
   (Kansas City), Mo.
Topeka, Kan.

EXHIBIT 7–8
Matrix Structure Design

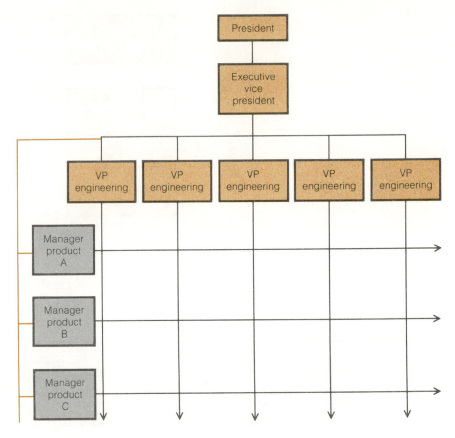

Matrix structures have been used in the following organizational types:

Manufacturing	*Service*
Aerospace	Banking
Chemicals	Insurance
Electronics	Retailing

Professional	*Nonprofit*
Accounting	Hospitals
Consulting	United Nations
Law	Universities

The matrix structure is good at responding to three conditions. First, it may be necessary to respond to two equally important environmental pressures. Aerospace firms like General Dynamics and Boeing must meet technical requirements and customer cost constraints. The functional manager may argue for more money to improve the product technically, while the project manager may argue for meeting budget constraints. The dual focus of technical and cost interests is possible in the matrix structure.

Second, requirements for communication among employees may exceed the capacity of a traditional structure. Environmental uncertainty, complexity of the work, and interdependence across departments increase as a business grows and diversifies its products and markets. The traditional functional structure does not encourage cooperation and a total team spirit. What is needed is a structure that encourages the sharing of information. The sole department is not the best orientation; the total system or project is the key.

Third, performance, cost, and time pressures require greater sharing and use of resources. When talented engineers, physicists, computer specialists, and other skilled professionals are in scarce supply, it becomes important for several groups, projects, or units to share the talent and resources. Placing limited resources in only one department results in a monopolization of the resources. In the matrix structure, talent and resources can be moved from project to project. Priorities for the use of the limited resources are measured against the overall business objectives and interests. The matrix makes this shifting of resources an easier task.

SOME PROBLEMS WITH MATRIX STRUCTURES.   If the matrix always worked for every business, it would be more widely used. There are, however, some problems with the matrix. Some of the most frequently cited problems include:[7]

1. Confusion about who reports to whom, and when
2. Power struggles between functional and product managers
3. "Groupthink," or too much group decision making
4. "Meetingitis," or just too much time wasted in one meeting after another
5. "Papermills" are produced. In order to assure cooperation and coordination, there is a tendency to put it down in writing. The result is a seemingly endless papermill.

The advantages of the matrix structure seem to outweigh its problems. Nevertheless, this type of organization structure is not for everyone. The two-boss manager in the matrix must be very good at working with people. Remember the two-boss manager is a direct contradiction to the principle of unity of command. Would you be able to work with two bosses—one functional and one product? Think about some of the conflicts you might face. Suppose they both wanted you to attend an important meeting at 10:00 A.M. or wanted you to attend training seminars on the same date, one in Los Angeles and one in Boston?

The Multiple Structure

We have been discussing forms of structure as if they were an either/or choice. In fact, businesses are free to use any form or combination of structures. The Post Division of General Foods uses a product structure, and other departments and divisions are organized on the basis of function and territory.

EXHIBIT 7-9
IBM Corporate Organization.
(Reprinted with permission of
International Business Machines
Corporation.)

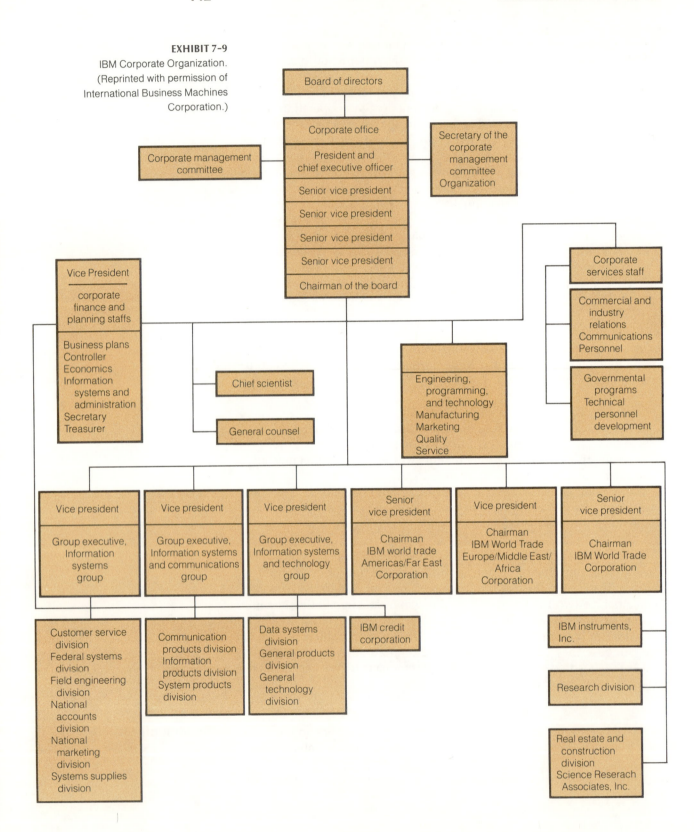

Large organizations, particularly, are likely to use multiple structures. Study the organization chart of IBM in Exhibit 7–9. What do you find? Functional, product, and territorial structures can be seen. Marketing and manufacturing are functional units. The data processing (DP) product group is using a product structure. IBM Europe is a territorial structure.

SUMMARY

■ There is no one best way to organize a business. Managers need to match what is best for their business with a flexible structure that can adapt or be adapted to change.

■ Before any attempt is made to organize, managers should work with clear objectives, understand that coordination is important, be aware that formal and informal organizations exist, and understand what is meant by delegation of authority.

■ Line, staff, and functional authority are three forms of authority found in business organizations.

■ Organizations vary in their degree of centralization or decentralization of authority.

■ Principles of organizing are used to help make better structure decisions. Some of these principles are:

Unity of command. Subordinates should report to no more than one supervisor.

Scalar. Authority and responsibility should flow in a clear and unbroken line from the highest to the lowest manager. An extension of this principle is that authority should equal responsibility.

Span of control. There is a limit to the number of subordinates who should report to a supervisor.

Functional similarity. Activities (work) should be arranged on the basis of similarity.

Minimizing levels of management. Levels in the managerial hierarchy should be kept to a minimum.

Flexibility. Structure should be flexible enough to permit easy change.

■ A functional structure sets up units or departments so that each has a different set of activities and responsibilities.

■ Product structure involves grouping activities on the basis of product or product line.

■ Territorial structure divides units on the basis of geographical territory.

■ The matrix structure, which became popular in the 1970s, is a combination of a functional and a product structure. The result is that subordinates have a functional boss (their permanent home is in the functional unit) and a product boss (a temporary home).

■ More and more organizations have found that a multiple structure is best for them. That is, each of the various departments may be structured differently.

ISSUES TO CONSIDER AND ANALYZE

1. If you were managing a group of research and development professionals, would you use a wide or a narrow span of control? Why?

2. Why would large organizations such as Eastman Kodak, Boise Cascade,

and U.S. Gypsum tend to use multiple forms of organizational structure?

3. Why is the matrix structure called a two-boss situation?
4. Why do informal organizations exist within formal organizations?
5. Why is it important before organizing a business to have clearly stated objectives?
6. What can happen if a manager has too little authority to carry out responsibilities?
7. Is the scalar principle used by the president of the United States? Explain.
8. In what type of business would a product structure be used?
9. Can you think of any business that has totally centralized authority?
10. When does a staff manager have line authority to take action in limited areas of responsibility?

CASE FOR ANALYSIS   **AT&T REORGANIZES ALONG MARKET LINES**

Historically, American Telephone & Telegraph Company (also called the Bell System) was a prime example of a regulated monopoly protected by law. However, technological advances in the field combined with regulatory and judicial decisions whittled away at AT&T's markets. Home telephones, communications equipment for business, private transmissions lines—all are no longer protected pieces or a regulated monopoly.

AT&T's management observed the changes in their environment and decided to convert the organization from a regulated monopoly to an aggressive company. AT&T is a monster in size, with twenty-three operating companies and over 900,000 employees. Many employees resisted changing such a large company's orientation. Hard-liners were opposed to many of the structural changes and were hard to convince. Size alone and the previous relative independence of the operating companies were assumed to be two reasons for the resistance to change.

The catalyst for change was a consulting report compiled by McKinsey & Co., a world-renowned management consulting firm. The McKinsey report proposed that AT&T lacked the necessary communication, authority, and accountability systems for addressing customer needs. In essence, AT&T was not able to convert customer needs into products and services. The company was suited structurally, philosophically, and behaviorally to operate in a regulated monopoly market. The consultants recommended that AT&T set up a new marketing department at headquarters, focus on markets where competition was gaining a foothold, and upgrade the quality of its sales force. McKinsey told AT&T to rid itself of a monopoly mentality and adopt a marketing approach.

The reorganization plans have been in place for over a year, and there are still signs of resistance to change. In fact, some of the telephone companies in the AT&T system have decided to rewrite plans concerning the internal structure and operation.

QUESTIONS

1. Could any reorganization plan be implemented in a company like AT&T without receiving criticism and resistance? Why?
2. What does it mean to say that AT&T was structurally, philosophically, and behaviorally suited to operate in a regulated monopoly market?

CAREERS IN SMALL BUSINESS, FRANCHISING, TECHNICAL OCCUPATIONS, AND GENERAL MANAGEMENT

A business career doesn't necessarily require being part of the management of a large corporation. There are many other ways to find a niche for yourself in the world of work. Exhibit II–A shows some of the fast- and slow-growing career areas in business and technical fields.

SMALL BUSINESS AND FRANCHISING

Some people claim that small business firms are vanishing and soon will be extinct. They assume that the small firm is the powerless victim of big business corporations that are taking everything over. Historical data indicate that the small-business segment of the economy has grown less rapidly than big business, but it is far from extinct. In every industry, there are successful small firms. Small-business entrepreneurs operate florist shops, coal mines, construction firms, restaurants, gift shops, sporting goods stores, and many other businesses. In the future, the opportunities for owner-managers should increase as citizens have more disposable income to spend. This should increase the demand for goods and services furnished by independents (sole proprietors) and franchises.

The skills, abilities, and personal characteristics of owner-managers

The U.S. Department of Labor expects the economy to create more than 20 million new jobs during the 1980s. In addition, about 47 million jobs will open up as workers retire, die, or leave the labor force.

The Department's Bureau of Labor Statistics makes its projections for specific occupations on the basis of its model of the economy in 1990. Bureau officials caution that the projections are based on generally optimistic assumptions about the nation's economy in the decade ahead.

Using the forecasting tools available, here are some of the occupations that the Department of Labor thinks will grow *faster* than average and others that will grow *slower*.

Faster-than-Average Business and Technical Growth

Accountants ■ bank clerks, officers, and tellers ■ business machine repairers ■ clerical workers ■ computer programmers ■ computer technicians ■ dispensing opticians ■ EKG and EEC technicians ■ engineering and science technicians ■ health-services administrators ■ hotel housekeepers ■ industrial machinery repairers ■ insurance claims representatives ■ maintenance electricians ■ medical record technicans ■ occupational health and safety workers ■ real estate agents and brokers ■ receptionists ■ retail sales ■ statisticians ■ systems analysts ■ travel agents ■ welders

Slower-than-Average Business and Technical Growth

Bowling-pin machine mechanics ■ credit managers ■ forge shop occupations ■ food technologists ■ hotel managers ■ keypunch operators ■ locomotive engineers ■ office machine operators ■ postal clerks ■ securities sales workers

Fast-Growing but Competitive

Actuaries ■ city managers ■ emergency medical technicians ■ forestry technicians ■ labor relations workers ■ urban and regional planners

For more information, see the *Occupational Outlook Handbook* published by the Bureau of Labor Statistics, U.S. Department of Labor, 200 Constitution Avenue, N.W., Washington, D.C., 20210.

exert a powerful influence on the fortunes of small companies. Therefore, you must determine whether you have the characteristics needed for success in a small business. The

EXHIBIT II–A

Fast-Growing versus Slow-Growing Occupations

following list of characteristics is important in your self-analysis:

- A need for independence
- Willingness to work long hours
- A high degree of self-confidence
- The ability to coordinate activities without becoming frustrated
- A need to use every skill to solve problems
- The ability to react quickly to change
- An understanding of laws, regulation, and rules

Each person considering going into a small business should conduct a thorough self-analysis along these lines.

The self-analysis will lead to another important choice—whether to be an independent small-business owner or to buy a franchise. Franchising (see Chapter 5) has been one of the most rapidly expanding areas of business activity in recent years. The options for independent and franchise business that appear to be most popular and are expected to remain so in the near future can be classified as follows:

- *Retailing.* Food, appliances, hardware, clothing
- *Service.* Auto repair, plumbing, electric work, floor covering, janitorial service
- *Wholesaling.* Jobbers, brokers, distributors, manufacturing agents
- *Consulting.* Management, investment, marketing, land use, engineering, government
- *Manufacturing.* Metals, plastics, food processing

This list doesn't exhaust all possibilities, but it does indicate the wide range of opportunities available.

The person who has the necessary personal characteristics has many options available in either independent business or franchising.

Small-business owners advertise when they plan to sell a share of the business. These ads generally point out the purchase price, the type of business, and the location. Anyone interested in buying an ongoing business should do a lot of checking on the reputation of the business, the past successes and failures of the business, and the reason the current owner is planning to sell.

TECHNICAL OCCUPATIONS

A lot of people think that a business career is designed only for college graduates. This isn't necessarily true. There is a meaningful job for people interested in working. In fact, jobs are in abundance in many areas of the country for people who are technically trained. The scientific revolution started by the launching of space satellites in 1957 has created many career opportunities for technicians. The government and businesses of all sizes need technicians. Qualified technicans can earn twice the salary of an average high school graduate who is not qualified. With one or two years of post–high school education and training, a qualified technician can join business organizations, government agencies, and health institutions.

A technician is a person who works with engineers, scientists, and other professionals. The technician makes things happen by converting a theoretical model or idea into action. Some of the technical jobs that can be found in business organizations are:

- *Air conditioning and heating.* Help design home, office, and laboratory air conditioning and heating arrangements
- *Construction.* Suggest and work on projects that house business operations
- *Electronic data processing.* Process and analyze business data by using computer systems
- *Health.* Work in business organizations to improve the quality of work life
- *Instrumentation.* Work on devices so that business organizations can control pollution and minimize ecology problems
- *Office.* Provide accounting, financial, and legal secretarial assistance to business executives
- *Environmental control.* Recommend programs for conserving limited natural resources and controlling waste disposal

Many excellent junior and community colleges, technical institutes, and vocational schools offer programs that help an individual become a qualified technician. In one or two years, these schools can develop a person to the point where he or she can earn a good living. If you are interested in receiving more detailed information on technical careers, contact the following:

- National Association of Trade and Technical Schools
1601 18th Street, N.W.
Washington, D.C. 20009

- Accrediting Commission for Business Schools
United Business Schools Association
1730 M Street, N.W.
Washington, D.C. 20036

■ Occupational Education Project
American Association of
Junior Colleges
One DuPont Circle
Washington, D.C. 20036

Exhibit II–B presents some salary information for a number of technical occupations. These are just four of the possible occupations available to a person who is technically trained and educated.

Machine tool operators. There are about 540,000 machine tool operators in the United States. They are skilled workers who operate a variety of machines. Besides shaping metal, they must know how to calculate precise measurements (sometimes down to a millionth of an inch) so that the pieces they produce will be perfect. They work in a noisy area and must stand for long hours. It is estimated that about 2000 new openings a year for the next decade will be available for machine tool operators.

Maintenance machinists. These are repair experts trained to fix a variety of machines. When something breaks down, they must find and correct the problem. Usually they serve an apprenticeship of about three or four years. Over 150,000 people are maintenance machinists, and there is a need for about 1000 new machinists a year.

Millwrights. Millwrights install machinery for the production of metal parts, textiles, and printing. This work involves building platforms for machines, reading blueprints, using installation tools (such as power tools), and di-

CITY	MACHINE-TOOL OPERATORS	MAINTENANCE MACHINISTS	MILL-WRIGHTS	TOOL-DIE MAKERS
Atlanta	N/A	$ 9.71	$10.84	$10.47
Boston	$ 7.58	8.65	7.72	9.39
Chicago	9.84	10.02	10.78	10.55
Detroit	11.29	11.00	11.27	11.33
Houston	N/A	10.46	10.55	9.98
Los Angeles	N/A	10.98	N/A	10.63
New York	N/A	9.83	N/A	8.77
Philadelphia	9.25	9.91	10.01	10.20
San Francisco	N/A	10.88	N/A	12.34

Source: Bureau of Labor Statistics, *Area Wage Surveys,* 1981.

EXHIBIT II–B
Average Hourly Wages of Machinists in Nine Cities

recting cranes and other equipment. The training and education of a millwright can take as long as eight years, but usually it involves a four-year course of study and classroom practice. There are about 95,000 millwrights and a need for about 1000 new ones a year.

Tool and die makers. Tools and dies are the parts of equipment used by other machinery workers to mass produce metal parts. Tool makers produce the fixtures that hold metal while it is being shaved and measuring devices to gauge the precision of the parts produced. Die makers produce metal forms or dies for stamping pieces out of metal. Many tool and die makers become tool designers and may also open their own tool and die businesses. About 170,000 people are now employed as tool and die makers, and about 1000 new jobs will be available each year through the next decade.

Exhibit II–C presents some advertisements for technicians. The want ads of most newspapers list many job opportunities for technicians needed by business organizations.

GENERAL MANAGEMENT

One of the most varied and widespread career areas in business is management and supervision. Managers in both the private and public sectors effectively run the United States. Career paths in management in a private organization could look something like what is shown in Exhibit II–D.

Few college graduates start at the top level of management. They must start at the bottom of the firm, prove that they can do the job, and slowly work their way up the management ladder. Realistically, a college graduate is hired for his or her management potential, not immediate skills. Exhibit II–E describes the general features of an entry-level management assignment.

Most organization charts of profit-oriented businesses indicate four main functions: production, accounting, finance, and marketing. The career opportunities in these four functional areas are covered in other sections of this book. But a number of positions in business and

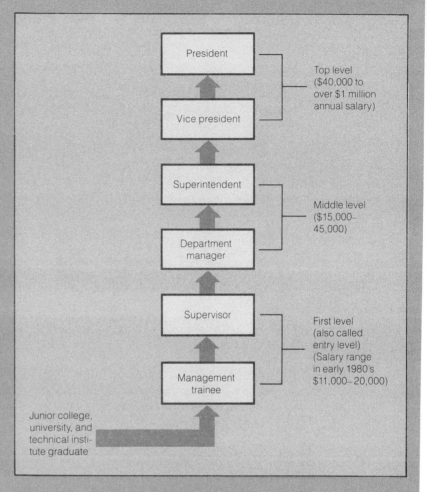

EXHIBIT II-D

General Management Career Paths

public service don't fit neatly into these four categories. The people working in these areas are managers with skills and abilities in general management.

Job Opportunities: Management

The future holds promising prospects for young, ambitious beginners in management. Currently, there is a decline in the number of potential executives in the 35- to 55-

EXHIBIT II-C

Some Job Advertisements for Technicians

year-old range. It is predicted that, by 1985, there will be 60,000 graduate degrees awarded in business. But this will not be enough to fill all the management vacancies. One source of management talent will be women. Today, at the executive level, men outnumber women 60 to 1. About 5.6 percent of all management or administrative jobs are now held by women. Certainly more women will enter management because business needs them and their talents.

Definition

The entry-level assignment is designed to introduce the person to the organization and hasten the transfer from an academic setting to an employment setting. The assignments are not lifelong commitments, but they do provide career direction. They often open doors to career opportunities unavailable with no experience.

Purpose

Whether a formal training program or one of the more common direct-placement assignments, the entry-level assignment is used to

- Assist in determining the best career path within an organization
- Expose the typical problems encountered by employees in the position
- Introduce the people the new employee must work with, both inside and outside the organization
- Enable the new employee to begin applying and using skills as soon as possible
- Evaluate potential

The entry-level assignment is a technique employers use to introduce the organization and smooth the new employee's entrance into it. Entry-level assignments are not meant to hold people indefinitely.

EXHIBIT II–E
Entry-Level Managerial Assignments

Unless women and minorities move into management jobs at all levels, many organizations will face the prospect of overburdened, burned-out, and overworked managerial employees.

Women managers make on the average about $6,000 a year less than their men counterparts. This kind of difference will have to be corrected if organizations are going to attract more women into management. A survey of the top fifty industrial firms in the U.S. is quite revealing. Women make up less than 5 percent of the managers earning $40,000 or more.[1] Some women figure that, if they can't get a break in management, they'll work for themselves. There were 1.9 million self-employed women in 1979, a 43 percent increase over 1972.[2]

The facts indicate that qualified, ambitious, energetic men and women of every ethnic background will be needed to manage businesses in private and public industry. A few want ads shown in Exhibit II–F illustrate how managerial candidates are recruited.

NOTES

[1]Listed in John W. Wright, *The American Almanac of Jobs and Salaries* (New York: Avon, 1982), p. 712.
[2]Wright, p. 715.

MANAGEMENT CAREER

Immediate Openings
Salary Open
Increases based on
Performance
Profit Sharing
Blue Cross
Major Medical
Retirement Plan
Paid Vacations

If you have supervisory experience, and enjoy public contact, our management training program is a good place to start your career in our growing, national company. Our expansion program has created many openings and opportunities for career minded individuals.

Knowledge of bowling and the recreation industry is helpful. A High School education is required, and some college is advantageous.

SUPERMARKET MANAGEMENT

Tech Food Markets, the "Value Leader" is looking to increase its store management team. If you would like to join our organization, we welcome the opportunity to talk to you. If you have had at least two years experience as a Store Manager or Assistant Store Manager for a supermarket chain, consider yourself a professional, and are looking for a good future, this may be your opportunity!

If you are interested please submit your resume.

GENERAL MANAGER
Restaurant Operations

Bonanza International restaurants has a career opportunity for General Manager, responsible for 3 to 5 restaurant operations. Requires individual with successful multi-unit experience; heavy emphasis in the following areas:

- Merchandising, Marketing/Advertising
- Finance/Accounting
- Management Development

Organized, innovative, "ready-to-set-the world on fire" people, please contact us . . . we will offer you good benefits, salary commensurate with background, and opportunity for professional growth. Please write to:

Corporate Staffing
WATKINS
Watkins International
1701 S. Central Expwy.
Detroit, Michigan
An equal opportunity employer M/F

THEATRE MANAGEMENT OPPORTUNITIES

With progressive motion picture theatre company. Rapid advancement for the theatre career minded person.

Call after 3 p.m.:
Mr. Young—NW Village Cinema
—466-3533
Mr. Wilson—Southmore Cinema
—473-3007
or write:
Universal Corporation
2150 W. 18th #18
Dallas, Tx. 77008

SUPERVISOR
Retail Loan Operations

Unique and challenging position for an individual seeking advancement in a professional environment. This supervisor will assume responsibility for control of work procedures and the motivation and development of personnel in Retail Loan Operations.

This position requires a minimum of two years supervisory experience of at least 6 people and a knowledge of banking installment loan operations, including an accounting background and a familiarity with on-line data systems. The successful candidate will have good oral and written communication skills and the ability to interface well with customers and management.

We offer free life and health insurance, a profitable investment program and transportation subsidies.

Inquire by calling Dean Arnold at 757–6387 or by applying in person at the Wilcox Building, 9th floor, 1010 Yates Ave., Columbia, S.C.

EXHIBIT II–F
Advertisements for Jobs
in General Management and Supervision

151

PROFILE IN BUSINESS

Don Hoodes
(1926–   )

Chicago Tribune Photo

On hot Friday afternoons in the summer, his voice is likely to ring out over the company intercom: "Put down your pens or your tools, get your suits, and out to the pool!"

Thirteen years ago, Don Hoodes was fired for insubordination from a company making rotary air compressors. He decided to form his own competitive firm, Sullair Corporation, on the premise that employees treated with respect and generosity will repay the company handsomely. The experience of Sullair offers dramatic proof that they do.

Four hundred employees at the company's main factory and offices in Michigan City, Indiana, establish their own work schedules. Most of them put in a ten-hour day, four days a week. "There is no whistle when people can stop for ten minutes for a cup of coffee or to go to the bathroom," says one Sullair executive. "A guy takes a break when his back hurts him a little." There are also no plant supervisors. But there is an Olympic-size swimming pool, a sauna, a squash court, a basketball court, indoor and outdoor tennis courts, and a picnic ground, all on the company premises and all open to employee family members. At about 4 o'clock each afternoon, a company pub opens up for those who have finished work to serve themselves from a well-supplied bar.

PART THREE

HUMAN RESOURCES AND PRODUCTION

Earlier they dined at the Cafe la Bastille, the company cafeteria, where a meal of Cornish game hen, candied yams, and pasta pilaf costs less than a dollar.

All this and quite a bit more is subsidized by a firm that still maintains a comfortable profit margin. In the mid-1970s, after ten years in business, Sullair had captured 30 percent of the rotary air compressor market, and sales were up 40 percent annually, to the level of $50 to $60 million. "There's a certain spirit —I don't know what it is exactly—but a down-to-earth philosophy here," explains a Sullair employee. The work gets done and done well, with a consistent sense of individual re-sponsibility. Employee turnover averages 1 percent a year.

Several Sullair subsidiaries, including one in Australia and another in Germany, flourish under the same liberal policies. They are all small operations, no doubt a key to this kind of easy-going success. Outstanding employees are encouraged to set up their own affiliated businesses, "and they tend to run the same way we do," reports Sullair's senior vice president. "If you call them on a Friday afternoon, they may be sitting around the office having a little party."

All employees enjoy profit sharing, and Hoodes has instituted an employee stock-ownership plan. The company picks up the full tab for medical and dental insurance and drug prescriptions. Two local supermarkets have arranged 10 percent discounts for Sullair employees. Nearly everyone commutes to Sullair by car, so when gas prices shot up, Hoodes built a company gas station and held the price per gallon at a quaint 35¢ (maintained by a $3000-a-month company subsidy).

Security analysts ponder how Sullair can support such effusive fringe benefits and keep increasing profits. A company official just shrugs and smiles. "We try to treat everybody equally. That's our basic philosophy."

CHAPTER 8

MOTIVATING EMPLOYEES

LEARNING OBJECTIVES

After studying this chapter, you should be able to:

Define what is meant by the term *motivation*.

Discuss the role of managers in creating conditions that are favorable for motivating employees.

Compare and contrast the different approaches to motivating employees.

Identify how job enrichment uses motivation theory in redesigning a job.

Illustrate the impact of the famous Hawthorne studies on the use of motivation programs.

Explain B. F. Skinner's view of motivation.

KEY TERMS

Motivation
Need hierarchy
Physiological need
Safety need
Social need
Esteem need
Self-realization need
Personality
Theory X
Theory Y
Work motivation model
Hawthorne studies
Job enrichment
Management by objectives
Behavior modification
Reinforcer
Positive reinforcer
Negative reinforcer
Punishment
Quality circles

THE MOTIVATION PUZZLE
IS TOUGH TO SOLVE

The manager, Tina Martinez, was really stumped. Joe Garza and Mike Welson, two of her subordinates, looked exactly alike on paper. Both were in their early thirties, had good solid work experience in every phase of their machinist jobs, and were considered hard workers. However, about six months earlier, Joe's performance really hit rock bottom. In contrast, Mike's performance was excellent as usual. Rejects of Joe's work kept showing up, and he seemed burned-out and bored. Tina was puzzled because Joe and Mike were her two superstars. She called Mike in for a talk and found out nothing. She then tried Joe, and he wasn't very helpful either. He simply apologized for not doing the job.

Tina had to do something about the situation. Her first action was to sit down and think about the people and situation facing her. She made a list of questions about Joe Garza:

Is Joe sick?
Does Joe have personal (at home) problems?
Is Joe getting tired of his job?
Why is this showing up at this time?

These were simply Tina's thoughts; she wasn't thinking precisely in terms of motivation or Joe's internal feelings and needs. Motivational problems occur within a person. Joe's feelings and needs at this time could be the culprit in this performance lag puzzle. Joe should have been performing as he always had, but something had gone haywire.

One person who can help repair the problem is Tina. She needs to look at what this chapter has to say about motivation, needs, personality, and ways of creating a positive motivational atmosphere for subordinates. And she needs to "tease" Joe into expressing his feelings. Unless Tina solves the motivation puzzle, Joe Garza may have to be asked to leave the organization. This is the most serious kind of decision managers can face.

One of the most difficult tasks facing managers like Tina Martinez is motivating employees. Because managers are responsible and accountable for meeting important organizational objectives, they must be concerned about the performance of employees in such important tasks as painting an automobile on an assembly line, writing a computer program, or selling a microwave oven to a customer. Successful business managers must create an atmosphere that motivates employees to use their skills and abilities. When a skilled employee like Joe Garza is not performing up to his capabilities, is this a motivation problem? Yes, it probably is.

Motivation is the way drives or needs direct a person's behavior toward a goal. It concerns the level of effort one puts forth to pursue specific goals. A manager is not able to observe the motivation process directly since it occurs internally; managers observe behaviors and then reach conclusions about a person's motivation. For example, Tina knows that Joe and Mike have similar skills and work experience to perform well. Mike has continued to complete his work, but Joe recently has begun to slip. She concludes that Mike is motivated, but Joe is not motivated. Why? That's the motivation puzzle Tina is attempting to answer.

Generally speaking, rewards and punishments are the tools managers use to motivate employees. The variety of rewards that employees can receive in exchange for their effort (motivation) can be classified as extrinsic and intrinsic. *Extrinsic* rewards are those external to the work itself. They are administered by someone else, such as a manger. Examples of extrinsic rewards include pay, fringe benefits, recognition, and praise. *Intrinsic* rewards are related directly to performing the job. In this sense, intrinsic rewards are often described as self-administered. Examples of intrinsic rewards include feeling good about accomplishing an objective and being able to make decisions without consulting a supervisor. On the other hand, punishment involves taking something away from a person or administering an undesirable consequence for a particular behavior. For example, a frequently tardy worker would be punished if because of tardiness his pay for the time missed was deducted from his paycheck. Both types of rewards appear to produce higher levels of performance than punishment does. Communicating and administering rewards and punishments are part of the manager's job in creating the best motivational atmosphere.

Motivation is goal oriented, and it works this way: First, there is tension in the person created by unfulfilled needs. A *need* indicates a deficiency; for example, when you are hungry, you have a need for food. Second, the person starts a search to find a reasonable solution that will satisfy unfulfilled needs. Third, when some of the needs are fulfilled and some of the goals accomplished, the process begins again. Exhibit 8–1 illustrates the goal-oriented process of motivation.

Unless they have some idea about the motivation process, it is almost impossible for managers to create the atmosphere their subordinates need to perform efficiently. As Peter Drucker, a recognized management educator and consultant, has stated: "No matter how authoritarian the insti-

THE MOTIVATION PROCESS

MOTIVATION
The way drives or needs direct a person's behavior toward a specific goal. It concerns the level of effort one puts forth to pursue the goal.

EXHIBIT 8-1
The Process of Motivation

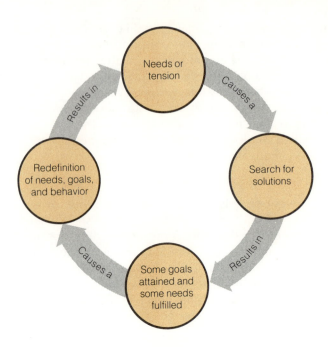

tution, it has to satisfy the ambitions and needs of its members and do so in their capacity as individuals. . . ."[1]

THE NEED HIERARCHY

A popular theory of human needs that helps us understand motivation is called the **need hierarchy**. Psychologist Abraham Maslow identified five basic needs that explain the internal motivation process: physiological, safety, social, esteem, and self-realization needs.[2]

Types of Needs

The needs Maslow identified fall into a hierarchy or arrangement of power to motivate behavior, as illustrated in Exhibit 8-2. Each higher order need becomes active and motivates a person only when lower level needs are fulfilled. Each person is assumed to have needs in each of these categories. Examples of job satisfiers that can fulfill the needs are also included in Exhibit 8-2.

PHYSIOLOGICAL NEED
Biological need for food, air, water.

PHYSIOLOGICAL NEEDS   The starting point for understanding motivation is the **physiological need**. The person who is hungry or tired is thinking about food or sleep, not work. But when physiological needs become fulfilled, food and sleep lose their power to motivate.

SAFETY NEED
Workers' need to be financially secure and protected against losing their jobs.

SAFETY NEEDS   If the physiological needs are relatively well fulfilled, the **safety needs** become important. Workers are concerned about being protected against losing their jobs and being financially secure when they

THE TIMES ARE 'A CHANGIN'

Why is performance lagging in many organizations? Is it poor equipment, poor leadership, or inefficient management? These are all likely answers to the question. Another explanation that is growing in popularity is that the values of people have changed. People born from 1946 through the early 1960s are entering the work force in growing numbers. They are joining with different value systems than workers of yesterday. Daniel Yankelovich, who heads the research firm of Yankelovich, Skelly & White, describes the younger generation as being more concerned with personal growth, self-realization, and enjoyment of work and leisure.

Based on interviews with 3500 families, Yankelovich contends that 40 percent of the labor force is composed of workers who belong to new work-value groups. One new-value group dislikes formal job structures and rejects money as a substitute for fulfillment; the primary objective of the second group is to earn money not for the sake of money but to buy a certain lifestyle. Once that is achieved the group tends to hold back on the job.

These type of changes in society and values have changed the way managers look at motivation. The employee of today is less submissive, more self-confident, and critical of inequities in pay, managerial favoritism, and overall treatment. These changes signal the need for changes in the way managers work to create an atmosphere to motivate subordinates. Money, job enrichment, and behavior modification could be useful in helping managers motivate people if they fit the person's needs and the organizational goals. The notion of fit is in, while the idea that money can buy loyalty, production, and morale is being seriously questioned.

A more enlightened view of worker psychology is what is needed in the 1980s. The new view stresses individual differences and the fact that many but not all employees want to involve themselves in their jobs. Worker involvement in companies like Procter & Gamble, General Foods, Xerox, Ohio Bell, Shaklee Corp., and Polaroid is being accomplished by self-managed work teams, quality circles, labor–management committees, and job enrichment committees devoted to redesign jobs to help workers satisfy their needs. Some quotes emphasize management's new thoughts on motivation:

William A. Ayers (employee-Shaklee Corp.) working on a self-managed work team—"You have a sense of owning the job, and it makes you want to do a better job."

Sidney Harman (chairman of Harman International Industries) interested in creating a motivational atmosphere—"It was my conviction I [was responsible for] the development of people who worked for me. You can't create this kind of program as a surrogate for speedup. You do it because it's right."

Alfred S. Warren, Jr. (industrial relations vice-president of General Motors) some general views—"We're still living in the 1930's world, paying for the use of a worker's hands and not what he can offer mentally. One of the most dehumanizing assumptions ever made is that workers work and managers think."

Adapted from "The New Industrial Relations," *Business Week*, May 11, 1981, pp. 85–98.

retire. This set of needs can be satisfied by the creation of seniority systems, pensions, and insurance plans. As with the physiological needs, once a major portion of the safety needs are satisfied, the next level of needs becomes more important.

SOCIAL NEEDS Employees want to belong and to interact with other employees. Thus, the friendly behavior of individuals in small groups

EXHIBIT 8–2
The Maslow Need Hierarchy
and Job Satisfiers

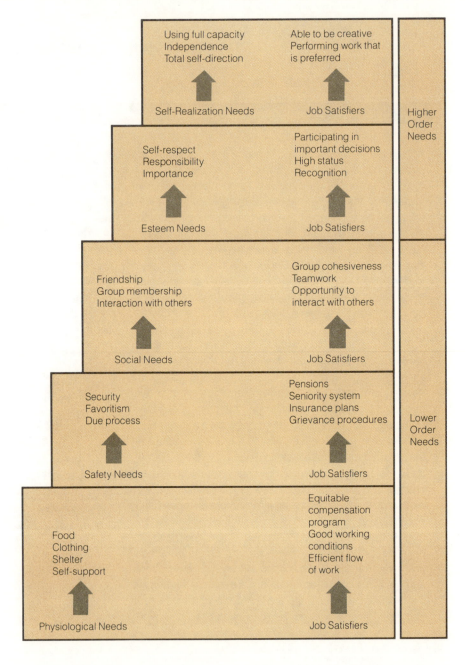

SOCIAL NEED
The need to belong and to interact with
other people.

within organizations is a major source of satisfaction for **social needs**. In a small group, individuals support and encourage one another; as a by-product they get a sense of being an accepted member of the group. Once the social needs are significantly satisfied, they begin to lose their power to motivate.

ESTEEM NEED
The need for self-respect and respect
from others.

ESTEEM NEEDS   The **esteem needs** are needs for self-respect and respect from others. An important part of this need set is that an employee's work efforts and output must be recognized and appreciated by others. When the need for esteem is strong, the individual will often set difficult goals, work hard to achieve the goals, and receive recognition for these efforts. Accomplishing goals and the recognition that results lead to feelings of self-esteem and confidence.

SELF-REALIZATION NEEDS   The top of the need hierarchy is **self-realization**, the ability to display and use one's full potential. This need takes over when an adequate level of satisfaction has been reached in the other four needs. A person who reaches self-realization has come close to using his or her full set of skills.

Maslow noted that self-realizing people display certain characteristics:

- They tend to be serious and thoughtful.
- They focus on problems outside themselves.
- Their behavior is unaffected and natural.
- They are strongly ethical.[3]

Reaching a level of complete self-realization rarely occurs.

Most people think of artists, composers, and scientists as seeking self-realization. Because people work to satisfy more basic needs, managers often overlook the self-realization need. Certainly, it's hard to achieve self-realization while working if other needs are not being adequately satisfied. But everyone is capable of partially satisfying the self-realization need.

Maslow's need hierarchy provides a useful framework for managers. Of course, employees differ in the intensity of their needs. Some people have an intense security need that will dominate their behavior no matter what managers do. Others are more strongly influenced by their esteem needs. There is no standard program for managers to follow when attempting to encourage a high level of motivation. Differences in personal background, experience and education are so powerful that conditions that work for one individual may not work for another.

Every person's personality is unique. **Personality** describes a set of traits that an individual possesses. These traits usually are displayed in the manner by which the person attempts to satisfy needs. Each person inherits physical and mental traits. These traits influence how others act toward and feel about us. For example, a person who is taller than others may be ridiculed or teased, which could damage his or her self-esteem. Cultural background is another factor. Our friends, family, and teachers influence our feelings of worth and confidence. In addition, the environment we were raised in influences our personality development. The quality of life in our neighborhood or town, the type of education we received, and the economic conditions we faced as youngsters all shape personality.

A manager can do little about the hereditary, cultural, and environmental influences on a subordinate's personality. But it is important for managers to understand how personality can influence internal motivation. People who are not satisfied with their self-image or with the way others respond to them will be motivated to bring about changes. If the

SELF-REALIZATION NEED
The highest need in the Maslow hierarchy; the need to maximize the full range of one's potential and skills.

Personality

PERSONALITY
The way a person acts, feels, and responds to people and situations.

On The Job Revisited

manager can create conditions that will make these changes positive for the individual and for the business organization, then everyone can benefit. Think about Tina and what she needs to know about Joe's personality. By working with Joe, she probably already knows a lot about his background and personality. This knowledge will help Tina come up with a plan to get Joe back in the groove. In addition, Tina would probably focus on such traits as Joe's dependability, emotional stability, moodiness, and style of interacting with others. She would be comparing these traits before, when Joe seemed motivated, with now, when he is not motivated.

THEORY X AND THEORY Y

THEORY X
Managerial assumptions that employees dislike work, responsibility, and accountability and must be closely directed and controlled to be motivated to perform.

THEORY Y
Managerial assumptions that employees want to be challenged, like to display creativity, and can be highly motivated to perform well if given some freedom to direct or manage their own behavior.

Although managers should try to understand needs and personality, they often don't. Douglas McGregor, a professor of management, introduced two theories of managerial style, referred to as **Theory X** and **Theory Y**, to explain this phenomenon.[4]

Theory X managers are assumed by McGregor to view the average employee as:

- Disliking work and finding ways to avoid it as much as possible
- Responding to threats of punishment or control because of the dislike of work
- Avoiding responsibility because of a lack of ambition
- Wanting to be directed and have security

A problem with making these assumptions about people is that they can become self-fulfilling. If a manager believes Theory X, he or she will probably create conditions to satisfy the physiological and safety needs, closely controlling and supervising subordinates. Of course, some employees respond favorably to this style, but others feel frustrated, experience anxiety, and have high degrees of conflict. Their goals for self-esteem and self-realization can't be achieved.

Theory Y, on the other hand, is a set of managerial assumptions that results in looser control and more delegation of authority. The Theory Y manager assumes that the average employee:

- Enjoys work and does not want to avoid it
- Wants to achieve organizational goals through self-directed behavior
- Responds to rewards associated with accomplishing goals
- Will accept responsibility
- Has initiative and can be creative in solving organizational problems
- Is intellectually underutilized

According to McGregor, Theory Y assumptions reflect a managerial emphasis on human growth and development instead of coercive authority.

Theory X and Theory Y indicate two extremely different positions—one emphasizing an autocratic management style and the other a democratic management style. Many workers are now demanding Theory Y behavior from managers. They want to satisfy some of their social, esteem, and self-realization needs on the job, and Theory X–oriented management behavior only produces frustration and anxiety. On the other hand, some workers don't respond well in a Theory Y–oriented organization. However, because of our democratic political heritage, the idea of Theory Y is more appealing to most people. Nevertheless, some job situations call for autocratic controls. The key is the manager. He or she must review the people involved and the situation.

A WORK MOTIVATION MODEL

In the 1950s, Frederick Herzberg, a social psychologist and consultant, proposed a **work motivation model** that is still extremely popular among business managers.[5] Herzberg surveyed accountants and engineers, asking them to describe when they felt good or bad about their jobs. He found that one set of job and personal factors produced good feelings and that another created bad feelings.

Hygiene Factors

One set of factors Herzberg called *hygiene factors* (also called maintenance factors by some). These factors, if present and available, are essential to maintain job satisfaction, although they cannot motivate an employee. The hygiene factors include:

- Salary
- Job security
- Working conditions
- Status
- Interpersonal relations with peers and supervisors
- Technical supervision
- Company policies

WORK MOTIVATION MODEL
A model proposed by social psychologist Frederick Herzberg. He found in his research that a set of job factors, which he called *hygienes*, were essential to maintain high job satisfaction. These factors included salary, job security, and working conditions. Another set of factors, called *motivators*, included recognition, responsibility, and advancement opportunities.

These hygiene factors, if absent or inadequate, cause job dissatisfaction. Herzberg believes that by providing these factors, managers can prevent job dissatisfaction but cannot motivate employees to perform any better.

Motivator Factors

The second set of factors were described by Herzberg as *motivators* of on-the-job behavior. They include

- Achievement
- Recognition
- Advancement
- The job itself
- Growth opportunities
- Responsibility

The hygiene factors deal with external features of the job. Motivators are job content–oriented or specifically tied to the job itself. The employee appreciates the hygiene and motivator factors at different times. For example, the employee takes a pay check (hygiene factor) to a bank and cashes it and receives some satisfaction when the money is received. While actually performing the work, the employee can receive and enjoy such motivators as responsibility, recognition, and growth opportunities. These and other motivator factors make up the fabric of the job.

Maslow and Herzberg Compared

Maslow's need hierarchy and the Herzberg work motivation model have many similarities, as Exhibit 8–3 shows. The lower level needs are similar to the hygiene factors. These needs are adequately satisfied for many employees, but some have not adquately fulfilled their lower level needs. In

EXHIBIT 8-3
The Need Hierarchy and Work
Motivation Model: Similarities

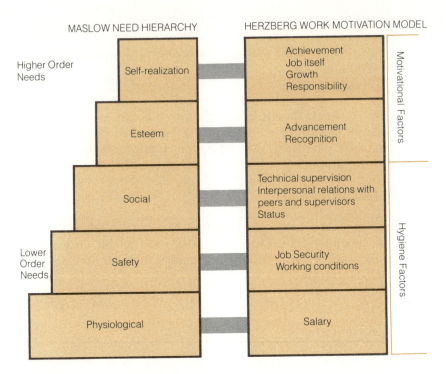

MASLOW NEED HIERARCHY   HERZBERG WORK MOTIVATION MODEL

Higher Order Needs
Self-realization — Achievement / Job itself / Growth / Responsibility
Esteem — Advancement / Recognition
Social — Technical supervision / Interpersonal relations with peers and supervisors / Status
Lower Order Needs
Safety — Job Security / Working conditions
Physiological — Salary

Motivational Factors
Hygiene Factors

their situation, hygiene factors may be motivators. Managers today pay more attention to the higher level needs, or motivator factors.

Although Herzberg's model is very popular and makes common sense, it has been criticized. Some critics remind us that the original study group from which the model was developed included only engineers and accountants. These two occupational groups are not representative of most employees (for instance, mechanics, lathe operators, clerks, typists) in business organizations. However, Herzberg cites a number of other studies that used nurses, supervisors, scientists, food handlers, and assemblers and found results similar to the original study that used only engineers and accountants.

Other critics have questioned the manner in which Herzberg collected his information. They believe that his method of asking questions influenced the way the accountants and engineers responded. Despite these criticisms, the work motivation model is used by many managers as it is logical and uses language that managers understand.

THE HAWTHORNE STUDIES

HAWTHORNE STUDIES
A series of experiments at a Western Electric plant from 1927 to 1932. The studies found that work groups significantly affect the way workers behave and perform.

The **Hawthorne studies** were conducted from 1927 to 1932 at a Western Electric plant in a suburb of Chicago.[6] The team of Harvard University researchers included Elton Mayo, Fritz Roethlisberger, and William Dickson. This series of experiments is the single most important historical foundation for the behavioral study of employees.

In an illumination experiment, employees were divided into two groups. One group was placed in a test room where the intensity of lighting was varied, and the other group worked in a room with constant lighting over the time of the experiment. When light levels were raised, production increased; when light levels were lowered, production still increased. Puzzled, the researchers decided to change working conditions. They introduced shorter rest periods, longer but fewer rest periods, and other changes. Once again, no matter what change was introduced, production still improved.

The researchers next interviewed many of the employees involved in the study, asking questions about their reactions to working conditions. The researchers found that a change in morale occurred because the employees felt responsible. They also felt good about being a part of the experiment. Labor turnover stopped, and absences were drastically reduced. One employee who had been absent eighty-five times in the thirty-two months before the experiment went for sixteen months without an absence.

A second experiment, which lasted for only sixteen weeks, was designed to measure the effect of group incentive plans on productivity. Although economic incentives were offered for increased productivity, the members of the group set informal production quotas that would allow most group members to work at a comfortable pace. The power of the informal group, not the economic incentive, was controlling production.

The Hawthorne findings offered no perfect answers or specific programs for managers. But the studies showed that informal groups can influence productivity. In the first experiment, productivity increased through group pressure, but it was restricted by group pressure in the second experiment. Both experiments used highly cohesive or tight-knit groups.

The major difference in the two experiments was the supervisory style used. In the first, general supervision was used. The employees stated that they had "freedom" and were "treated" well. In the second experiment, a closer supervisory style was used.

There were other dissimilarities. The employees were women in the first experiment, men in the second. The second room was set up specifically for the experiment and, unlike the first room, involved no researcher-introduced changes. In the first room, the researchers produced changes in lighting and rest periods.

Regardless of the differences, the Hawthorne studies showed how group characteristics and type of supervision, among other things, influence motivation and productivity. Although the studies have been interpreted in different ways, one message is clear: managers attempting to create a favorable climate for motivation need to consider the group and its own style of supervision. Tina's list of questions shows that she was concerned about her style of managing, but she paid no attention to how the group affected Joe. Maybe she needs to find out if the group is having any influence on Joe's performance problems.

On the Job Revisited

The group incentive plan in the Hawthorne studies did not motivate the employees as expected. This and other studies show that there is no magic formula for providing employees with the interest and desire to perform well, although some programs are better than others. It is the manager's job to find the best motivational trigger for his or her group and situation. For

MOTIVATIONAL APPROACHES IN BUSINESS ORGANIZATIONS

some, money is a key, whereas for others a clear set of objectives is the best way to motivate.

Money

The economic value of money allows employees to satisfy unfulfilled needs. The belief that money is and should be a strong motivator is deeply rooted in our society. Nevertheless, one researcher estimates that as few as 10 percent of the hourly nonmanagerial workers in the United States respond to financial incentive plans by producing to capacity.[7] The other 90 percent do not produce more, even though greater productivity means more money.

Do professional employees, like accountants, lawyers, managers, and scientists, respond to financial incentives? Many professionals assume that job success—and financial reward—results largely from individual effort. But today some professionals who are dissatisfied with their financial rewards seek other solutions. In fact, some engineers and scientists have joined unions to improve their financial rewards.

In considering money as a motivator, managers need to recognize the variables that affect its power. One is the employee's control of the work environment. A professional employee like an engineer, who generally has more control over work pace than the production-line worker, often will not work harder for more money. Other variables are the employees' needs, the employees' backgrounds and experiences, and the nature of the job.

Unfortunately, it is very difficult for a manager to determine all these variables. Finding out these things is what Tina is attempting to do. Managers can use such diagnostic tools as interviewing, counseling, and attitude surveys, but even with these tools, the manager must use experience, intuition, and listening skills to put together the best motivational money package.

Job Enrichment

JOB ENRICHMENT
An approach that involves redesigning a job to increase the satisfaction and motivation of workers. It incorporates variety, feedback, and autonomy in the job.

In his work motivation model, Herzberg introduced **job enrichment**. It is a method intended to increase the motivation and satisfaction of employees and to improve production through job design. By adding more motivators to the job, job enrichment can make work meaningful, stimulating, and challenging. The employee comes to view the job as a lot like play.

The first step in job enrichment is to determine the characteristics of a job that increase motivation.[8] Consider the Little League baseball player practicing hitting at the batting cage. Practicing hitting is meaningful because it will improve performance. The ballplayer is fully responsible for anything hit in the batting cage. And soon after the ballplayer swings, he or she has knowledge of how well the ball is hit. The "psychological feelings" of the ballplayer that result are important in determining his or her motivation.

The same is true for an employee doing a job. That is, there must be on each job:

- *Meaningfulness.* The work must be perceived as worthwhile.
- *Responsibility.* The employee must be personally responsible for any effort expended.

■ *Knowledge of results.* The employee must receive, on a regular basis, feedback about how well he or she is performing.

When these three conditions are present, a person usually feels good about the job and his or her contribution. These good feelings motivate the person to continue to do well. But if one of these three conditions is missing, the internal feeling (motivation) drops off dramatically.

Research studies indicate that five job characteristics create good psychological feelings about a job. These characteristics can be enriched by a manager. Three of the five characteristics contribute to the meaningfulness of a job:

■ *Skill variety.* The degree to which a job requires a worker to perform activities that are challenging
■ *Task identity.* The degree to which the job requires the completion of a "whole" piece of work. For example, building an entire generator has more task identity than just placing a flywheel on the generator as it passes by on a conveyer belt
■ *Task significance.* The degree to which the job is significant to the organization or other individuals

A fourth job characteristic leads an employee to experience more responsibility: *Autonomy* is the degree to which the job gives the worker freedom, independence, and leeway to carry out what is required. The fifth job characteristic, *feedback,* is the degree to which a worker gets information on his or her effectiveness in carrying out the job.

Such organizations as AT&T, Saab-Scandia, Volvo, and General Foods have reported using job enrichment to motivate employees. They have redesigned or changed job characteristics for various employees or groups. Like all sound motivation programs, job enrichment must be used selectively. The user must consider the situation, the job, and the people involved (see Exhibit 8–4). Usually, if the organization supports enrichment, more employees desire the job changes. Management must also provide enough time for the approach to be understood.

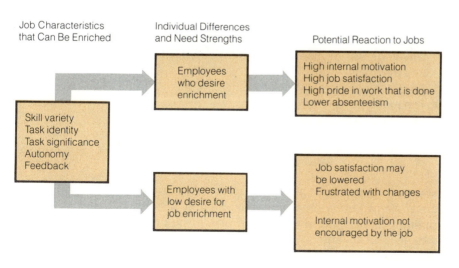

EXHIBIT 8–4
Job Characteristics, Individual Differences, and Reactions

Management by Objectives

MANAGEMENT BY OBJECTIVES (MBO) A popular motivational technique that involves superiors and subordinates setting objectives for the subordinate that will cover a specified period of time. The emphasis is on results accomplished.

Another popular motivation technique is called **management by objectives (MBO)**. MBO has existed for over twenty years and has been used by thousands of organizations around the world. According to Peter Drucker, management by objectives will motivate the user because setting objectives stimulates the individual to work harder.[9] A manager and subordinates, individually or as a group, define areas of responsibility in terms of the results expected. The goals of the organization are translated into individual goals and are established as objectives that will be met at a specified time. Both parties focus on the goals, the actual results achieved, and the differences between goals and results. Thus, MBO is an attempt to specify goals and encourage employee participation in the setting of some standard. MBO requires careful planning so that realistic goals are set.

The MBO approach is an effective motivational tool as well as a program that encourages planning, organizing, directing, and controlling. Wells Fargo Bank uses MBO primarily as a planning and control technique. On the other hand, Tenneco uses a goal-setting program to encourage managerial self-development.

Whatever MBO is used for, it is based on certain assumptions. These assumptions are that individuals perform better when (1) they have a clear target, such as challenging goals; (2) they have some input into the goals that are set; and (3) they receive feedback on how they are doing.

The emphasis of MBO in most organizational programs is on results, or the end product of the process itself. But this does not mean that the manager can sit idly by while subordinates work hard to accomplish goals. Typically, managers meet with subordinates over the course of the goal period (usually one year) to reexamine the goals. If changes are necessary, they are made. Managers in some MBO programs meet separately with each subordinate at the start of the goal period, during the period, and at the end to evaluate progress. This extra effort is needed to make the program successful.

Like other motivational programs, MBO is not always a 100 percent success. Some of the problems and pitfalls associated with MBO are:

- Failure to provide proper feedback
- Lack of support from top management
- Unwillingness of managers to allow subordinates to participate in setting the goals
- Failure to reward good performance
- Too much paperwork
- Use of MBO as a "whip" to control employees more closely
- Focus on only organizational or job goals, excluding personal goals
- Failure to communicate the overall objectives of the MBO program

Many of the problems and pitfalls occur because MBO is assumed to be the answer to every organizational problem. It is not. Managers must still carefully analyze the problem and match the motivational procedure to the situation at hand.

THE LEADING BEHAVIORIST SPEAKS ABOUT BEHAVIOR

There is too much emphasis in the world on trying to get people to do things by threatening them with punishment rather than by offering them positive rewards. This is the view of B. F. Skinner, one of the world's leading psychologists. His theories of human behavior have had wide influence, and have many of his colleagues upset with what he preaches.

Listed below in concise form are some of Skinner's views. Think about them in terms of motivation at work. Do you agree or disagree? Why?

Human behavior is determined wholly by environment and not by unfulfilled needs. External work conditions and individual experiences explain the behavior of an employee.

Decisions are never really left up to people. Their own bodies were not left to them; they were born with those. Their families were not left to them; they inherited those.

Money is not a natural reinforcer. No one works on Monday morning because he or she is reinforced by a paycheck on Friday afternoon. The employee who is paid by the week works during the week to avoid losing the standard of living that depends on a weekly wage.

When a *response* occurs (good performance) and is reinforced (praised), the probability that it will occur again in the presence of a similar kind of reinforcement is increased.

Supervision by *positive reinforcement* changes the whole atmosphere of the work space and produces better results. A constantly critical position on the part of the supervisor encourages bad morale, absenteeism, and job changing. You get the work out, but at a high price.

Skinner is a behaviorist, which means that he seeks explanations of human behavior not in the mind but outside. This view differs significantly from Maslow's need hierarchy. Who do you think is more correct—Maslow or Skinner?

Adapted from ''An Interview with B. F. Skinner,'' *Organizational Dynamics,* Winter 1973, pp. 31–40.

Behavior modification is the application of a set of learning principles, called operant conditioning, developed by psychologist B. F. Skinner.[10] Behavior modification grew out of the idea that changing the attitude of a person does not necessarily improve performance. Instead, the person's behavior must be changed. This is best done by changing the environment in which the person behaves.

Skinner believes that the way people behave is a function of heredity, past experiences, and the present situation. Managers can control only the present situation. Therefore, Skinner recommends that managers consider these two points: (1) If an act (behavior) is followed by a pleasant consequence (say, a pat on the back), it probably will be repeated; and (2) if an act is followed by an unpleasant consequence, it probably will not be repeated. It is the job of the manager to design the present situation so that good performance results.

The manager can shape the behavior of subordinates by controlling the **reinforcers**. A reinforcer is a consequence of behavior that can improve the likelihood that the behavior will or will not occur again. According to

Behavior Modification

BEHAVIOR MODIFICATION
Application of learning principles, called operant conditioning, to motivation. The basis is the proposition that behavior depends on its consequences—if consequences are favorable, the behavior will probably be repeated.

REINFORCER
A consequence of behavior that improves the chances it will occur again or, in the case of a negative reinforcer, will not occur again.

POSITIVE REINFORCER
Something preferred by a worker, such as praise for a job well done.

NEGATIVE REINFORCER
A method to discourage certain behaviors; for example, reprimand for not finishing a job on time.

On the Job Revisited

PUNISHMENT
Providing an undesirable consequence (taking away some pay) for a particular behavior (reporting to work late two times within a month).

Skinner, the most immediate behavior before the reinforcement is used to relate performance and rewards. For example, praise—a **positive reinforcer**—given after an employee completes a job on time may increase the occurrence of finishing work on time. A **negative reinforcer**—a reprimand—for not finishing on time may also increase the likelihood of work being done on time By finishing on time, the employee creates a situation in which the supervisor will not issue a reprimand. The reprimand is considered a negative reinforcer.

Tina Martinez could go a long way toward solving the Joe Garza problem by finding out what reinforcers he prefers. It will be difficult at this time because Joe is going into a shell, but it is worth the effort to ask him about reinforcers or preferred rewards.

Punishment influences behavior by presenting something that is distasteful or withdrawing something liked. For example, a manager says something rude to an employee and receives disapproval from other managers. If the disapproval is unpleasant enough, the manager's rudeness is less likely to occur in the future. Another kind of punishment takes something pleasant away. Suppose Nick Ruiz, a project engineer, is assigned temporarily to a group that is important to him. Because Nick frequently arrives late to work for the new assignment, he is placed back in a regular work group. Nick is not able to work with the group he likes because of his tardiness. He has been punished.

There is a difference between punishment and negative reinforcement. In negative reinforcement, an act that allows the person to avoid some unpleasant event (supervisor's reprimand) is reinforced by removing the unpleasant event. In punishment, one of two things happens: (1) An unpleasant event (group disapproval) follows a behavior (rude remark), or (2) a pleasant event (being a member of a group) is taken away after a behavior (tardiness).

Managers applying behavior modification on the job:

1. Identify the elements of a job that are observable and measurable.
2. Measure how frequently behaviors occur.
3. Positively reinforce the person when a correct behavior occurs.

These procedures have met with some success at Emery Air Freight Corporation. Emery personnel load containers with packages and ship them by air. Management assumed that containers were always being loaded to capacity but a check found that containers were being fully loaded only 45 percent of the time. A list of employee activities and goals for filling containers was developed. Results were recorded in terms of container use so that team results could be compared. By providing feedback, correcting deficiencies, and providing recognition for good performance, management increased container capacity.

Like other motivation programs, behavior modification has been criticized. Some individuals criticize it because they view it as a technique that Skinner transferred to humans after conducting trial experiments with animals such as pigeons. Critics claim that employees are not pigeons and do not respond like them. Another criticism is that behavior modification is too artificial. The employee who receives reinforcement should know why

THE NEW MOTIVATIONAL KID ON THE BLOCK: QUALITY CIRCLES

A concept that was born in the late 1940s is sweeping across North America from Toronto to San Diego. It is called the *quality circle*. Small teams of eight to twelve employees and supervisors meet in a nonhierarchical setting and solve problems. The quality circle is a motivational approach that first started in Japan, where it has been used with great success.

Today over 500 American companies including General Motors, Honeywell, Ford, Westinghouse, and Bethlehem Steel have set up quality circles. A typical quality circle has eight to twelve volunteers. They receive several hours of training on how to gather and use data—skills they put to work solving problems. They meet on company time.

An underlying theme of quality circles is that workers not only want to improve their work life and conditions but also want jobs that give them a sense of self-realization and esteem. They want to show what they know and can do. The quality circle (QC) is the stage that gives workers the opportunity to 'show.''

A QC at the General Motors assembly plant in Tarrytown, New York, is given credit for preventing the closing of the plant. In the early 1970s, the plant was plagued by violence and absenteeism. The quality of its cars was poor, and each year employees filed 2500 to 3000 grievances. Then workers and supervisors became involved in QC discussions that centered on solving problems. Everything improved—morale, quality of output, and grievances, which fell sharply to only about 40 a year. Now the plant's producing GM's X cars and has a new lease on life.

Some companies reward the ideas coming from QCs handsomely. For example, Northrop passes on 10 percent of any dollar savings to the QC that comes up with a usable job-related suggestion, and the team decides how to divvy up the money. But most companies believe that the employee's biggest reward is to show what he or she knows and can do. Workers appreciate being treated like people with skill, intelligence, and experience. QCs are a motivational tool that can help some individuals, groups, and organizations improve performance.

Adapted from, "The Far Side of Quality Circles," *Management Review*, October 8, 1981, pp. 16–17; and "How to Do It Better," *Newsweek*, September 8, 1980, p. 59.

he or she receives a reward. In most behavior modification programs, positive reinforcers often are provided without an explanation. The complexity of the work environment often leaves no time to explain their use. Finally, there is a manipulative aspect to behavior modification. Behavioral consequences are controlled, and people are forced to change behavior by the manager instead of on their own initiative. This approach is not consistent with the theme that people should act freely. The need for self-realization is not recognized, and this is considered dehumanizing.

A LAST LOOK AT TINA'S MOTIVATION PUZZLE

After reading this chapter, Tina would have some ideas about how to proceed with Joe Garza. She knows that motivation is Joe's problem. There are individual and organizational factors that can be causing the problem. The individual factors include needs, goals, personality, and ability; the organizational factors could include pay, job security, the job itself, and even Tina's supervisory style.

On the Job Revisited

Tina must figure out what Joe wants. Asking him, his co-workers, and others who know him is a common way to find out. Tina can then use this information to select or put together a reward package for Joe. The rewards may include the kind of things discussed by Maslow, Herzberg, and Skinner. That is, they could include giving Joe a more challenging job assignment; allowing him to participate more in job-related decisions; praising Joe's good performance more frequently; assuring Joe that his job is secure; recommending that Joe be allowed to attend a training program to help him improve his technical expertise; or improving Joe's working conditions.

As we learned in this chapter, not all persons are motivated to the same degree by one set of motivators. Tina understands that Joe and Mike differ in cultural background, rewards they prefer, and ambition. As a result of such differences, Tina must tailor the motivation program as much as possible to Joe. Her job is to find out what Joe's needs are and then design the best program possible to help him satisfy these needs. This is one reason a management job is so challenging.

Tina can't forget about her other subordinates and concentrate only on Joe. She must work hard to help each subordinate put forth his or her best effort in order to achieve organizational objectives. This is the role that manager's play in motivating employees. It's difficult, challenging, and time consuming, but when a manager succeeds in helping subordinates put forth their best effort, the results are gratifying and worth all the hard work. The ideas of Maslow, Herzberg, Skinner, and others can help managers like Tina design individually based motivation packages.

SUMMARY

- Motivation is a process that goes on inside each of us. No manager can directly observe a subordinate's motivation. All a manager can do is observe behavior and then reach conclusions about whether a subordinate is motivated.
- The motivation process is set off by unfulfilled needs that a person attempts to satisfy. By accomplishing goals, the person fulffills those needs.
- Maslow's need hierarchy is one way of looking at motivation. It assumes that people have a hierarchy of needs, from physiological to self-realization, which they attempt to satisfy.
- Personality is the central basis of how a person acts, feels, and responds to the world. It is shaped by heredity, culture, and the environment.
- Managers have the challenging task of identifying needs and personality. They can also determine how their particular style of managing influences behavior. McGregor suggests that some managers are Theory X types, and others are Theory Y types. The Theory X manager seems to be concerned with helping subordinates satisfy lower level needs. The Theory Y manager works on satisfying higher level needs. This suggests that managers probably need to practice some Theory X and some Theory Y.
- Herzberg's theory of motivation uses managerial language and instructs managers that motivators should be used to create a more positive work

environment. Motivators are conditions such as providing employees with increased responsibility, more advancement opportunities, and more recognition for good work.

■ The Hawthorne studies at the Western Electric plant brought attention to the important role that groups play in motivating employees. The work group is a force that can certainly influence individual behavior.

■ Four motivational approaches indicate that theory can be put into practice. Money, job enrichment, management by objectives, and behavior modification are applications of theory and principles. However, people are so different in many respects that an approach such as paying incentives or enriching a job must be applied with caution. The person and the situation are factors that must be cautiously weighed before managers take motivational steps.

1. If behavior modification is such a promising motivational approach, why isn't it used by more managers?

2. Why is motivation considered a challenging part of a manager's job?

3. Is it correct to assume that a motivational approach that works with one employee will be just as successful with another employee? Why or why not?

4. What is a quality circle? Where can it be used?

5. Why is respect between a manager and a subordinate so important when objectives are being established for the subordinate?

6. Is money a motivator? Explain.

7. A student stated that needs do not change over time. Do you agree? Why or why not?

8. The chapter suggests that managers need to analyze the situation carefully before using a particular motivational approach. Why?

9. Can managers directly observe motivation? Explain.

10. Why is it so difficult for managers to determine what will motivate employees to a high performance level?

ISSUES TO CONSIDER AND ANALYZE

WORKERS' VOTE ON RAISES AT ROMAC

CASE FOR ANALYSIS

About nine years ago, in response to a lot of pressure to unionize, Romac—a pipe-fitting plant in Seattle—really stepped out ahead of the pack. The company agreed to let employees themselves decide who should get a raise by voting on the matter. This is really a daring experiment to boost productivity. The company believes that money is a motivator of productive behavior.

Here's how the plan works. A new employee at Romac can request a hike after a six-month probationary period by completing a form. On the form, the employee lists his or her current pay level, previous raise (if any), the requested raise (the average is 20 to 40 cents per hour), and why he or

Adapted from "Want a Raise? Take a Workers' Vote!" *Personnel,* September–October 1980, pp. 43–44.

she deserves the raise. The employee then goes on the "board." His or her name, hourly wage, and photograph are posted for six consecutive working days, during which time the other employees can observe his or her performance. At election time, the majority rules. Executives and managers don't get to vote, but they can veto any raise that is granted. The veto has not been used since the plan started.

Romac president Manfred McNeil admits that, at the beginning, managers showed little enthusiasm for the plan. Some managers feared the company would go bankrupt. Others questioned allowing workers the privilege of determining raises. On the other side, workers like the involvement in such an important decision. A wage increase at Romac says that an employee is doing well on the job in his or her own opinion, in the company's opinion, and in the opinion of co-workers.

The importance of top management support of the plan is now being debated at Romac. Some believe that the plan would work today, after nine years, even without support from the top. Others believe that top management support creates a positive motivational atmosphere. If management vetoed everything the workers voted on, there would be a return to the "us against them" mentality.

QUESTIONS

1. Is top management's support really needed in the Romac "voting a raise" plan? Why?
2. Why would a company like General Motors or Procter & Gamble have a lot of problems setting up and using a Romac type of "voting a raise" plan?
3. Could poor economic times put the Romac raise plan in jeopardy? Explain.

CHAPTER 9

PERSONNEL/HUMAN RESOURCE MANAGEMENT

LEARNING OBJECTIVES

After studying this chapter, you should be able to:

Discuss the view that personnel/human resource management (P/HRM) is both a staff function and a line responsibility.

Explain the activities conducted by the various divisions of a personnel department—employment, training and development, wage and salary management, and employee benefits and services.

Define some of the legal requirements of the Civil Rights Act of 1964 and the Equal Employment Opportunity Act of 1972.

Identify the roles that the government plays in each phase of P/HRM.

Illustrate the various steps followed in recruitment and placement of personnel.

Compare P/HRM activities in large- and small-business organizations.

KEY TERMS

Personnel/human
   resource management
Human resource planning
Recruitment
Job analysis
Job description
Job specification
Equal Employment
   Opportunity Commission
Civil Rights Act
   of 1964
Equal Employment
   Opportunity Act of 1972
Affirmative action
   program
Training
Management development
Performance appraisal
Wages
Salaries
Benefits
Services
Occupational Safety
   and Health Act

A DIFFICULT DECISION: WHOM TO HIRE?

Curt Dalsec is the director of personnel/human resource management of Wingflight, Inc., a medium-size manufacturer of machine tools and parts for the automotive, steel, and aircraft industries. The company is located in Hammond, Indiana, a city about 15 miles from Chicago. High unemployment in the Chicago area has really had an impact on the programs Curt is in charge of. For example, when word leaked out into the community that Wingflight was looking for machinists, mechanics, and apprentice technicians, the result was over 285 job applicants.

Wingflight has a reputation of being a good employer. Wages are fair; fringe benefits and services are competitive; and the firm hates to lay off employees. Of course, there have been some layoffs, but not as many as those in other similar firms in the Chicago area.

The recent rumor about Wingflight looking for some new workers was true. Because of new contracts received from Lockheed, Ford, and Republic Steel, Curt and other Wingflight executives decided to hire about eight machinists, six mechanics, and twelve apprentice technicians. Curt was faced with the job of reviewing 285 application blanks. Not only did he have to review the applicants, he eventually had to make some difficult selection decisions—whom to hire and whom not to hire! In tough economic times, Curt felt bad about having to turn down some qualified people, but there just were not enough openings.

Curt developed a screening and orientation process that included the following steps:

1. Review the job applications. He and two assistants would do this independently and check their evaluations. He would consider the Equal Employment Opportunity Act (1972) in making this screening decision. This Act (which amended the 1964 Civil Rights Act) forbids discrimination on the basis of race, color, religion, sex, or national origin.

2. Interview the better candidates.
3. Administer valid and reliable skill and aptitude tests.
4. Conduct background checks on candidates.
5. Have supervisors interview the candidates who made it to this point.
6. Provide job offers and have new hirees take a medical examination.
7. Conduct orientation training.
8. Establish six-month probationary performance review process for new hirees.

Curt certainly had enough candidates. His problem was to find the best from the group and to also comply with the spirit of the law. He worked hard, and so do other personnel/human resource employees. Their jobs, responsibilities, and contributions to a firm will be clearly displayed in this chapter.

To meet the challenges of managing and motivating subordinates, managers must understand the potential of human resources and then secure, retain, and develop these resources.[1] This is the foundation of personnel/human resource management (P/HRM).

The management of any unit or department in an organization—marketing, finance, accounting, personnel—involves the accomplishment of objectives through use of the skills and talents of people. Thus, P/HRM is considered both a line management responsibility and a staff function.

In business organizations of any size—large, medium, or small—human resources must be recruited, compensated, developed, and motivated. The small organization typically cannot afford to have a separate P/HRM department that continually follows the progress of individuals and reviews the accomplishment of goals. Each manager is responsible for using the skills and talents of employees. Larger firms usually have a P/HRM department that can be a source of help to line managers. In either case, much of the work in recruitment, compensation, and performance appraisal must be finalized and implemented by managers.

THE PERSONNEL/ HUMAN RESOURCE MANAGEMENT FUNCTION

The personnel program at General Electric serves the needs of the organization and facilitates the accomplishment of GE's objectives. But their program would probably not be well suited for Glidden Paint Company or Wingflight, Inc., without modifications. Each company develops its own P/HRM program after considering such factors as size, type of skills needed, number of employees required, unionization, clients and customers, financial posture, and geographic location.

The success of the P/HRM program also requires the cooperation of managers, because it is they who must interpret and implement policies and procedures. Line managers must translate into action what a P/HRM department provides. Without managerial support at the top, middle, and lower levels, P/HRM programs cannot succeed. Therefore, it is important that managers clearly understand how to mesh their responsibilities with those of the P/HRM department.

Personnel/human resource management can be defined as the process of accomplishing organizational objectives by acquiring, retaining, terminating, developing, and properly using the human resources in an organization. The notion of accomplishing objectives is a major part of any form of management. Unless objectives are regularly accomplished, the organization ceases to exist.

PERSONNEL/HUMAN RESOURCE MANAGEMENT
The process of accomplishing organizational objectives by acquiring, retaining, terminating, developing, and properly using the human resources in an organization.

The acquisition of skilled, talented, and motivated employees is an important part of P/HRM. The acquisition phase involves recruiting, screening, selecting, and properly placing personnel. Curt Dalsec is faced with an acquisition and screening problem at Wingflight, Inc.

Retaining competent individuals is important to any organization. If qualified individuals regularly leave a company, it becomes necessary to seek new personnel continually. This costs money and is time consuming. The opposite of retention is, of course, termination, which is an unpleasant part of any manager's job. Employees occasionally must be terminated for breaking rules, failing to perform adequately, or job cutbacks. The procedures for such terminations usually are specified by a P/HRM staff expert or are covered in a labor–management contract.

Developing personnel involves training, educating, appraising, and generally preparing personnel for present or future jobs. These activities are important for the economic and psychological growth of employees. Self-realization needs cannot be satisfied in an organization that does not have an efficient set of development activities.

The proper use of personnel involves understanding both individual and organizational needs so that the full potential of human resources can be employed. This part of personnel management suggests that it is important to match individuals over time to shifts in organizational and human needs.

P/HRM in larger organizations such as IBM, General Mills, Xerox, or Ford is performed in a staff department like the one shown in Exhibit 9-1. Remember, however, that each company organizes its department according to its own set of needs and objectives.

THE EMPLOYMENT DIVISION

An organization can only be as effective as the people who operate the business. Thus, acquiring the necessary people to operate the business is the first phase of any P/HRM program. This phase is carried out by the employment division.

In carrying out the activities of the employment division, managers throughout the organization need to establish human resource plans. Recruitment, selection, placement, and other employment actions stem from this planning.

EXHIBIT 9-1
An Example of a Personnel/Human Resource Management Department

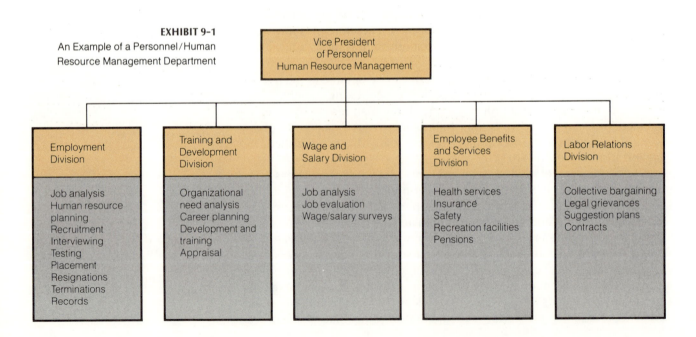

Vice President of Personnel/ Human Resource Management

Employment Division	Training and Development Division	Wage and Salary Division	Employee Benefits and Services Division	Labor Relations Division
Job analysis Human resource planning Recruitment Interviewing Testing Placement Resignations Terminations Records	Organizational need analysis Career planning Development and training Appraisal	Job analysis Job evaluation Wage/salary surveys	Health services Insurance Safety Recreation facilities Pensions	Collective bargaining Legal grievances Suggestion plans Contracts

WHAT DID YOU SAY?

The field of personnel/human resource management (P/HRM) is like other professional disciplines in that a jargon or special vocabulary has been developed. Physicians have their own language, and so do lawyers and computer programmers. For those outside the field, this vocabulary or set of code words is hard to understand.

The following list is meant to be read in good humor. It has been created by P/HRM specialists who have read one too many reports or have spent one year too long doing all the jobs facing them.

Term	The Double-Talk P/HRM Meaning
Average employee	Not too bright
Active socially	Drinks heavily
Exceptionally well qualified	Made no major blunders—yet
Shows great promise	Related to the boss
A keen analyst	Thoroughly confused
Not the desk type	Did not go to college
Tactful with superiors	Knows when to keep mouth shut
Meticulous	A nit-picker
Has leadership qualities	Is tall or has a loud voice
Exceptionally good judgment	Lucky
Takes pride in work	Conceited
Strong principles	Stubborn
Concientious	Scared
Of great value to the firm	Gets to work on time

Adapted from E. James Brennan, "Personnel Jargon," *Personnel Journal*, July 1981, p. 526.

Human resource planning involves estimating the size and makeup of the future workforce. This process helps the organization acquire the right number and kinds of people when they are needed. Experience indicates that, the longer the period predicted, the less accurate the prediction. Other complicating factors include changes in economic conditions, fluctuations in the labor supply, and changes in the political environment.

Formal and informal approaches to human resource planning are used. For example, some organizations use mathematical projections. Data are collected on such topics as the supply of resources, labor-market composition, demand for products, and competitive wage and salary programs. From these data and previous records, statistical procedures are used to make predictions. Of course, unpredictable events can alter past trends, but somewhat reliable forecasts can be made.

Human Resource Planning

HUMAN RESOURCE PLANNING
The steps taken in estimating the size and makeup of the future workforce.

On the Job Revisited

Wingflight, Inc., and Curt Dalsec didn't know that they would receive contracts from Boeing, Ford, and Republic Steel. The firm had to do the best it could to meet the increased demand for its products. In Curt's case, he had an abundance of people looking for jobs.

Estimating from experience is a more informal forecasting procedure. Department managers may be asked for opinions about future human resource needs. Some managers are confident in planning, whereas others are reluctant to offer an opinion or are just not reliable forecasters.

The J. C. Penney Company, a large retail merchandiser, plans its human resource needs from information supplied by each retail store. Penney's develops five-year consumer-demand projections for each position in the organization. Personnel needs in management are supplied primarily through promotion, because experienced employees have low turnover and clearly defined career paths. The company recruits recent college graduates for lower level managerial and staff positions. All J. C. Penney managerial employees are called associates to give them a stronger sense of commitment to the organization, and each employee is evaluated on potential for being promoted. These evaluations give the company a readily available company-wide inventory of human resources. A computer is used to match present and anticipated vacancies with available associates.

Recruitment

RECRUITMENT
Steps taken to staff an organization with the best qualified people.

Recruitment is an essential step in staffing an organization. Its primary objective is to acquire the best qualified applicants to fill vacancies. However, even before acquiring applicants, it is necessary to clearly understand the job that needs to be filled. The methods and procedures used to acquire an understanding about jobs is called *job analysis*. It was through job analysis that Curt and other Wingflight executives decided on the kind of people to hire.

JOB ANALYSIS
The procedures for determining the tasks that make up a job and the skills, abilities, and responsibilities an employee needs to do the job.

JOB DESCRIPTION
A statement that furnishes information about a job's duties, technology, conditions, and hazards. Data for preparing the description come from the job and analysis.

JOB SPECIFICATION
A statement derived from the job analysis about the human qualifications needed to perform the job.

SOURCES OF JOB INFORMATION **Job analysis** is the process of determining the tasks that make up the job and the skills, abilities, and responsibilities an employee needs to successfully accomplish the job. The information for obtaining the facts about a job are shown in what are called a **job description** and a **job specification**. The relationship between these is shown in Exhibit 9-2.

An efficient job analysis program provides information that is used by every division within the personnel department. For example, to recruit and select effectively, it is necessary to match qualified personnel with job requirements. The full set of job information is provided by the description and specification. Another example involves the establishment of proper rates of pay. If equitable pay systems are to emerge, it is necessary to have a complete job description. An example of a job description is provided in Exhibit 9-3.

EQUAL EMPLOYMENT OPPORTUNITY COMMISSION
A government commission that enforces laws that attempt to provide equal opportunities for employment without regard to race, religion, age, creed, sex, national origin, or disability.

LEGAL ASPECTS OF RECRUITING Individuals responsible for recruiting are faced with legal requirements. For example, a certain percentage of minority group members and women must now be recruited for positions that have seldom been filled by these people. These requirements are enforced by laws administered by the **Equal Employment Opportunity Commission**

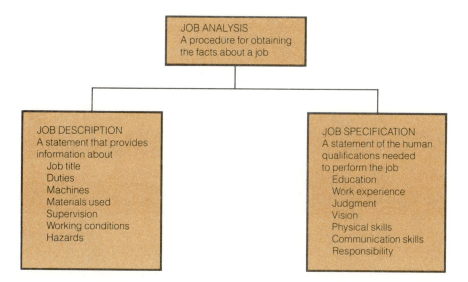

EXHIBIT 9–2
Sources of Job Information

(EEOC). The federal government attempts to provide equal opportunities for employment without regard to race, religion, age, creed, sex, national origin, or disability through Title VII of the **Civil Rights Act of 1964** and the **Equal Employment Opportunity Act of 1972**. These laws have broad coverage and apply to any activity, business, or industry in which a labor dispute would hinder commerce. The laws also cover state and local governments, governmental agencies, and agencies of the District of Columbia.

Some of the specific provisions of the Equal Opportunity Act of 1972 are the following:

CIVIL RIGHTS ACT OF 1964
An act that makes various forms of discrimination illegal. Title VII of the act spells out the forms of illegal discrimination.

EQUAL EMPLOYMENT OPPORTUNITY ACT OF 1972
A law that has specific provisions about equal opportunities for employment.

■ It is unlawful for an employer to fail or to refuse to hire, or to discharge, any individual or otherwise to discriminate against any individual with respect to compensation, conditions, or privileges of employment because of race, color, religion, sex, age, or national origin. This applies to applicants for employment as well as current employees.

■ Employers may not limit, segregate, or classify employees in such a way that would deprive them of employment opportunities because of race, color, age, religion, sex, or national origin.

■ The EEOC now has the power to file action in a federal district court if it is unable to eliminate alleged unlawful employment practices by the informal methods of conference, conciliation, and persuasion.

■ Employment tests may be used if it can be proven that they are related to the job or promotion sought by the individual. Tests should be validated for each company.

■ No discriminatory statements may be included in any advertisements for job opportunities.

The EEOC attempted at first to encourage employers to follow the guidelines of the law. Now the EEOC is more aggressive and asks employers to prepare **affirmative action programs**. This means that the em-

AFFIRMATIVE ACTION PROGRAM
A program in which an employer specifies how the company plans to increase the number of minority and female employees.

EXHIBIT 9-3
Job Description

Job: New Products Manager
    Victoreen Electronics
    Palos Park, Illinois (Plant)

The New Products Manager reports directly to the Vice President of Product Planning.

The New Products Manager plans, organizes, and directs the development and testing of electronic products produced for industrial customers of the organization.

Responsibility Domain

A. Plans from worksheet to final production all electronic products requested by the Vice President of Product Planning.
B. Establishes appropriate project teams to carry out plans within time and budget constraints.
C. Provides managerial guidance and counseling to project team leaders on all phases of the project.
D. Develops adequate quality testing for all newly developed products.
E. Prepares cost/benefit analysis on each project assigned.

Supervision Domain

- Project leaders (3)
- Operational engineers (15)
- Process technicians (3)
- Apprentice operational engineers (3)
- Accountant/economist (1)
- Draftsperson (1)
- Secretary (1)

Coordination Domain

A. Coordinates activities with each New Products Manager through preparation of prework planning document.
B. Coordinates with Purchasing Department in arranging for the purchase of necessary materials to complete projects.
C. Coordinates with Personnel Department in arranging for proper recruiting, selection, training and development, and compensation of employees within the supervision domain.

	January 2, 1983
Job Description Completed	_____
Prepared by Job Analyst	_____
	Frank Sopcich
Accepted by Vice President of Product Planning	_____
	Janet Luby
Filed by Vice President of Personnel	_____
	Claude Saunders

ployer must spell out how the company plans to increase the number of minority and female employees. If EEOC investigators do not like the distribution of employees, they can propose adjustments. The employer may then state why these adjustments can or cannot be made. Wingflight has always tried to meet the spirit of the law. This is why Curt is being so careful in screening the recruits who want to work for Wingflight.

On the Job Revisited

Even if the EEOC does not get involved with an employer, an individual may sue if he or she feels that discrimination is taking place. The number of complaints of job discrimination has increased from 8800 in 1966 to over 20,000 in 1981.[2] At present, the EEOC is bringing approximately 300 suits per year against employers.

For example, hiring practices by airlines have been the subject of two important court decisions. One held that female gender is not a bona fide occupational qualification for the job of cabin flight attendant. Another held that an airline's policy that stewardesses must be single is unlawful. No other female employees were subject to the policy, and there was no formal policy restricting employment to single male stewards. Another court has ruled it illegal to fire a female employee because she is pregnant and unmarried. A sex discrimination case against a New York law firm was settled, before a court ruling, when it agreed to recruit, hire, and promote women attorneys on the same basis as men.

The legal procedures regarding equal employment opportunities and recruitment are important to employers. Business organizations have to adjust to and work with these laws. Although adjustments are sometimes difficult, they seem to be a better alternative than becoming involved in a long and costly court battle. Providing equal opportunities to all qualified job applicants makes sense both legally and morally. The vast majority of managers in business organizations believe that all citizens have a right to any job they can perform reasonably well after a reasonable amount of training.

RECRUITING ACTIONS   If needed human resources are not available from within the company, outside sources must be tapped. A well-known firm such as General Mills has a file on previous applicants who wanted employment. Even though these applicants were not previously hired, they frequently maintain an interest in working for a company with a good reputation and image. By careful screening of these files, some good applicants can be added to the pool of candidates.

Advertisement in newspapers, trade journals, and magazines is a means to secure new applicants. Such an advertisement is presented in Exhibit 9–4. Responses to advertisements are received from qualified individuals and some who are unqualified. Occasionally, a company will list a post office box number and not provide the company name. This form of advertisement is called a *blind advertisement*. Blind ads are used to eliminate the necessity of contacting every applicant. However, a blind ad does not permit the company to use its name or logo, which is a form of promotion.

One of the most important sources for recruiting lower level managers is the college campus. Many colleges and universities have placement

Career Openings in Management

Ground-floor growth opportunity in new circulation branch
operations. Good pay as you train as a District Sales Manager.
Start immediately.

Supervisory and/or business experience desirable.
Prefer two years of college.

• Medical insurance
• Mileage allowance
• Fringe benefits
• Paid vacation

Call for appointment,
Personnel Department, between 10 a.m. – 12 and 1 – 3 p.m.
332-2981 Ext. 531

McCorey Distributing Corporation
Nashville, Tennessee

An Equal Opportunity Employer. M/F

centers that work with organizational recruiters. The applicants read advertisements and information provided by the companies and then are interviewed. The most promising students are invited to visit the company, where other interviews are conducted.

In locating experienced employees, organizations can use private employment agencies, executive search firms, or state employment agencies. Some are no-fee agencies, which means that employers pay the fee, if there is one, instead of the applicant. An organization is not obligated to hire any person referred by an agency, but the agency is usually informed when the right person is located.

EMPLOYEE SELECTION AND PLACEMENT

The selection and placement of personnel begins with a need for human resources and depends on legal requirements. Discriminatory practices in recruiting, testing, and offering a job are illegal, as stated in the Civil Rights Act of 1964 and the Equal Employment Opportunity Act of 1972.

The selection process is a series of steps that starts with the initial screening and ends with the orientation of newly hired employees. Exhibit 9-5 is a flow diagram showing each step in the process. Preliminary interviews are used to screen out unqualified applicants. This screening is often the first personal contact an applicant has with a company. If the applicant passes the preliminary screening, he or she usually completes an application blank. The steps spelled out in Exhibit 9-5 are what Curt Dalsec is following, almost to the letter, at Wingflight, Inc.

On the Job Revisited

The application blank is used to obtain information that can be used in reaching an employment decision. It is important that the questions on the blank can, even in a general sense, predict job success. The appropriate questions are usually developed after a careful job analysis is completed. The application form should be complete enough and yet concise enough to provide necessary information and not a jumbled mass of unnecessary information.

Applications

Interviews are used throughout the selection process, but there are three basic interviewing steps. First, interviewers must acquaint themselves with the job analysis. Second, they must analyze the information on application blanks. Third, interviewers need to ask questions that can add to what is included on the application blank. While performing these three interviewing steps, the interviewer must be courteous, create a favorable atmosphere, and provide the applicants with information and a positive image of the organization.

Interviews

For years, selection tests have been widely used to screen applicants.[3] Widespread use of tests started with World War II, when the Army Alpha Test was used to measure intelligence. The installation of a sound testing program is costly and time consuming, and it must be done by experts. Just because a test has been useful for selecting sales personnel in one company is no reason to believe that it will be just as useful in another company.

Testing

The advantages of a sound testing program include:

■ *Improved accuracy in selecting employees.* Individuals differ in skills, intelligence, motivation, interests, and goals. If these differences can be measured and if they are related to job success, then performance can be predicted to some extent by test scores.
■ *An objective means for judging.* Applicants answer the same questions under the same test conditions, so one applicant's score can be compared to the scores of other applicants.
■ *Information for present employee needs.* When tests are given to present employees, they can provide information about training, development, or counseling needs. Thus, they can objectively uncover needs.

Despite these advantages, tests have become controversial in recent years. Important legal rulings and fair-employment codes have resulted in strict procedures for developing tests. The following criticisms have been directed at testing programs:

■ *Tests are not infallible.* Tests may reveal what people can do but not what they will do.
■ *Tests are given too much weight.* Tests cannot measure everything about a person. They can never be a complete substitute for judgment.
■ *Tests discriminate against minorities.* Ethnic minorities, such as blacks and Mexican-Americans, may score lower on certain paper-and-pencil tests than whites. Title VII, Equal Employment Opportunity, of the Civil Rights Act of 1964, prohibits employment practices that artificially discriminate against individuals on the basis of test scores.

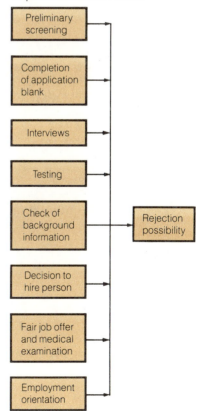

EXHIBIT 9–5
Steps in the Selection Process

Despite the problems, controversies, and costs involved, tests are widely used. Testing is a part of the employment process, one of the tools that can help the manager make decisions. In summary, test results provide some usable information, but they do not provide a total picture of how well the person will perform.

The Hiring Decision

After the preliminary screening—evaluating the application blank, interviewing, and testing—the company may decide to make an offer. If so, a background check is usually made. The background check verifies information by consulting references. Usually this information is obtained by letter, by telephone, or in person. One important group of references is previous employers; the company tries to gather facts about the applicant's previous record of job performance. Under the Fair Credit and Reporting Act, the prospective employer is required to secure the applicant's permission before checking references.

When the reference check yields favorable information, the line manager and an employment division representative meet to decide what the offer will be. The offer is usually made subject to successful completion of a physical examination. This examination can be conducted by a company physician or a doctor outside the organization. The objective is to screen out people whose physical deficiencies might be expensive liabilities and to place people on jobs they are physically able to handle.

On the Job Revisited

Wingflight used physicians in Hammond to conduct very thorough physical examinations of job candidates. Last year 6 out of 134 new hires failed the Wingflight physicals. Unfortunately, they were screened out and not hired.

TRAINING AND DEVELOPMENT

Training and development programs include numerous activities that inform employees of policies and procedures, educate them in job skills, and develop them for future advancement. The importance of the training and development program to the organization cannot be overemphasized. Through recruitment and placement, good employees can be brought into the company, but they need continual education and development so that their needs and the objectives of the organization can be achieved simultaneously.

Orientation

Most large companies have a formal orientation program for employees. Although most new employees usually know something about the organization, they often do not have specific information about the working hours, pay, parking, rules, facilities, and so on. The P/HRM department is usually the coordinator in providing orientation information, but the immediate supervisor is the key to the process. The supervisor must eventually establish a cordial relationship with the new employee that will encourage communication.

Training Programs

Training is a continual process of helping employees perform at a high level that begins the first day a person starts to work. It may occur at the place of work or at a special training facility, but it should always be supervised by experts in the educational process.

To be effective, a training program must accomplish a number of objectives. First, it must be based on organizational and individual needs. Training for training's sake is not the objective. Second, the objectives of training should spell out what problems will be solved. Third, all training should be based on sound theories of learning. This is a major reason that training and management development is not something for amateurs. Finally, training must be evaluated. Evaluations can determine whether a training program is working.

LOCATING PROBLEMS Before a training program can be developed, problem areas must be pinpointed. Organizations can use a number of techniques to identify problems, including reviewing safety records, absenteeism, data, job descriptions, and attitude surveys to see what employees think about their jobs, bosses, and the company.

SETTING OBJECTIVES Once training needs have been identified, objectives need to be stated in writing. These objectives provide a framework for the program. The objectives need to be concise, accurate, meaningful, and challenging.

There are usually two major categories of objectives—skills and knowledge. Skill objectives focus on developing physical abilities; knowledge objectives are concerned with understanding, attitudes, and concepts.

CONDUCTING PROGRAMS A large variety of methods are available for reaching the skill and knowledge objectives. Such factors as cost, time available, number of persons to be trained, background of trainees, and skill of the trainees determine the method used. Some of the more widely used training methods are:

- *On-the-job training.* A supervisor or other worker may show a new employee how to perform the job.
- *Vestibule training.* This is a term used to describe training in a classroom or away from the actual work area.
- *Classroom training.* Numerous classroom methods are used by business organizations. The lecture or formal, organized presentation is one method. A conference or small discussion group gets the student more involved than the lecture method.

Training is generally associated with operating employees; management development is associated with managerial personnel. **Management development** refers to the process of educating and developing selected personnel so that they have the knowledge, skills, attitudes, and understanding needed to manage in future positions. The process starts with the selection of a qualified individual and continues through that individual's career.[4]

The objectives of management development are to ensure the long-run success of the organization, to furnish competent replacements, to create an efficient team that works well together, and to enable each manager to use his or her full potential. Management development may also be nec-

TRAINING
A continual process of helping employees perform at a high level. Training may occur on the job or at a special training facility.

Management Development

MANAGEMENT DEVELOPMENT
The process of educating and developing selected personnel so that they have the knowledge, skills, attitudes, and understanding needed to manage in the future.

essary because of high executive turnover, a shortage of management talent, and our society's emphasis on lifelong education and development.

DEVELOPMENTAL METHODS   There are two main ways employees can acquire the knowledge, skills, attitudes, and understanding necessary to become successful managers. One is through formal development programs; the other involves on-the-job development.

On-the-job programs include:

- *Understudy programs.* A person works as a subordinate partner with a boss so that eventually he or she can assume the full responsibilities and duties of the job.
- *Job rotation.* Managers are transferred from job to job on a systematic basis. The assignment on each job generally lasts about six months.
- *Coaching.* A supervisor teaches job knowledge and skills to a subordinate. The supervisor instructs, directs, corrects, and evaluates the subordinate.

These on-the-job development plans emphasize actual job experience. They are used to increase the manager's skill, knowledge, and confidence.

Formal management development programs are often conducted by training units within organizations or by consultants in universities and specialized training facilities around the country. In the very large corporations, such as General Electric, Westinghouse, International Harvester, and AT&T, full-time training units conduct regular management development courses. For example, one major course offered at General Electric, called the Advanced Management Course, is designed for the four highest levels of management. It is conducted over a period of thirteen weeks, and its content includes business policy, economics, social issues, and management principles.

PERFORMANCE APPRAISAL
A procedure used by managers to assess performance and inform the employee of their expectations and opinions.

PERFORMANCE APPRAISALS   Another aspect of development involves the **performance appraisal**. Managers can use appraisal programs to communicate their expectations and to work with subordinates to improve personal deficiencies. Most employees want to know how well they are performing, and appraisals provide a basis for reviewing their performance. Appraisals also give employees a chance to discuss their career plans with their supervisor.

If properly handled, formal performance appraisals can help supervisors and subordinates develop mutual trust, respect, and understanding. But in order to develop these positive characteristics, performance appraisals must be divorced from the review of salary.

Perhaps the oldest performance appraisal technique is the rating plan. Usually the supervisor is supplied with a printed form for each person to be rated and is asked to circle or check the phrase that best describes the individual on the particular trait. Exhibit 9–6 is a sample rating scale. This type of scale is easy to use, but it has serious disadvantages. First, scoring the scale is difficult. Second, it doesn't tell which traits are most important. Third, ratings usually cluster around the more positive statements. Finally, this system doesn't tell a manager how to help subordinates correct deficiences.

Date of appraisal: _____   Average score this year _____

Employee: _____   Average score last year _____

Job title: _____

Department: _____

Length of job tenure: _____

Please rate this employee on each of the following. Circle the score that best represents your opinion of the employee.

Ratings

1 = Unacceptable	Quantity of work	1 2 3 4 5
2 = Below acceptable	Quality of work	1 2 3 4 5
3 = Acceptable	Attitude	1 2 3 4 5
4 = Good	Dependability	1 2 3 4 5
5 = Superior	Cooperation	1 2 3 4 5
	Creativity	1 2 3 4 5
	Accepting responsibility	1 2 3 4 5
	Technical job knowledge	1 2 3 4 5

Comments about employee: _____

_____

Supervisor's signature: _____

Date: _____

EXHIBIT 9–6
Rating Scale Used by
Excelsior Products, Inc.

A newer approach to performance appraisal is the *assessment center.* This approach was started by the work of Dr. Douglas Bray at American Telephone and Telegraph.[5] Employees undergoing appraisal are observed in a variety of activities: participating in group discussions, conducting interviews, and solving case problems. Trained assessors (line managers) at a higher level than the employees performing these exercises—but not their immediate supervisors—evaluate six to twelve people over two or three days. At the end of the exercises, the supervisors meet to discuss and evaluate the promotion potential of each person. The supervisors prepare an evaluation report, which may be shared with the participants, which summarizes each person's strengths and weaknesses and makes recommendations for further development. At least 1000 different companies, such as General Electric, Tenneco, Sears, Standard Oil of Ohio, and J. C. Penney, now use assessment centers. At AT&T alone, approximately

40,000 persons are assessed this way each year. The main advantage is that the team of trained assessors can make valid evaluations and appraisals because it is not personally associated with the employees but is familiar with the requirement of the positions.

WAGE AND SALARY MANAGEMENT

In modern society, money is important both economically and psychologically. Without money, a person can't buy the goods and services that make life comfortable. Money is also equated with status and recognition. Because money is so important, employees are quite sensitive about the amount of pay they receive and how it compares to what others in the company and in society are earning. It is important for employees to believe that they are being fairly compensated for the time, effort, and results they provide the employer.

Employee Compensation

WAGES
Compensation based on the time an employee works or number of units produced.

SALARIES
Compensation based on time, but the unit of time is a week, a month, of longer.

The most common system by which operating or nonmanagerial employees are compensated is **wages** based on time increments or number of units produced. Blue-collar workers traditionally have been paid at an hourly or daily rate, although some blue-collar employees are now being paid biweekly or monthly. Employees who are compensated on a weekly or longer schedule are paid **salaries**. Hewlett-Packard is one organization that has eliminated the daily rate of pay and now considers all personnel at all levels to be salaried employees.

WAGES Some organizations try to motivate employees to improve performance by paying on the basis of the number of units produced. This is called a piecework system. Piece rates are calculated by dividing the hourly wage for the job by the number of units an average employee is expected to produce in an hour. For example, if the rate of pay is $5 per hour and the average employee is expected to produce twenty-five units per hour, then the piece rate is $.20 per unit. If a worker produced forty pieces under this plan, he or she would earn $8 for the hour.

A daily rate of pay is easier than a piece rate to understand and use because time standards and records of the employee's output are not needed. Unions generally prefer the daily rate of pay over systems that involve piecework or incentive payments. This preference is based on the belief that a piecework system tends to reduce a group orientation. By being paid on the basis of individual effort, a worker can produce at any level he or she wants to. The union prefers to encourage group solidarity and a united front.

Many factors help determine the wage rate for a nonmanagerial job. Wages for certain jobs are affected by the availability of and demand for qualified personnel, although unions and the government may hinder the effects of supply and demand. Unions, for example, can prevent employers from lowering wage rates through strike threats and contract agreements, even when qualified personnel abound.

The existing wage rates in competing companies or in the community also help determine wage rates. Organizations typically conduct wage surveys to assess hourly rates, piecework or other incentive rates, and fringe benefits offered by other organizations. If the wage rates of an organization are too low, it may not continue to attract qualified personnel. Wing-flight conducts an annual wage survey of the Hammond area to keep them competitive.

Over the past forty years, inflation has greatly affected wage rates. For example, in 1982 the average weekly pay of a steelworker was $500.50. This represents $54.67 more a week than was earned in 1981. However, after allowing for inflation, the change actually represented a $6.53 loss in real earnings. Wages have been raised periodically just to maintain a comfortable standard of living for workers. These adjustments have been related to the Consumer Price Index (CPI), which measures changes in the general price level for all goods and services.

In many organizations, the relative worth of a job and the wage adjustments for it are determined by using *job evaluation* systems. A job is compared with others within the organization or with a scale. Under the ranking method, all jobs are ranked, from highest to lowest, on the basis of skill, difficulty, working conditions, contribution to goods or services, or other characteristics. This is a simple plan but not totally objective. The personalities of the current job holders often distort rankings. Nor are unions enthusiastic about job evaluation. With such a system, the union negotiator has almost no role to play.

Wage and salary administration, like other areas of P/HRM management, has been the target of various laws. For instance, full-time employees must be paid at least $3.35 per hour. Since the first minimum wage law enacted in 1938, the rate has risen over 1000 percent, from $.25 to $3.35 as of January 1, 1981. In addition, the Fair Labor Standards Act (1930) forbids the employment of minors between sixteen and eighteen years of age in such hazardous occupations as coal mining, logging, and woodworking. And the Equal Pay Act (1963) forbids employers to pay employees differently on the basis of sex. Women performing the same work as men must receive the same wage or salary. AT&T was required to pay $6,300,000 to 6100 women employees whose pay had suffered because of their sex.[6] The act does not prohibit compensation differences based on seniority, merit, or performance.

SALARIES   Salaried employees are assumed to have more influence over the way they perform their jobs than are employees who are paid wages. But in developing an equitable compensation system for executives, a similar approach is used: Comparisons are made, surveys are conducted, the supply-and-demand of candidates is analyzed, and the job duties and responsibilities are analyzed.

One method developed specifically for evaluating middle- and top-management positions was initiated by Hay Associates. First, analysts evaluate each position from information provided in the job description. Three factors are analyzed: job know-how, problem solving, and accountability. Then, through a statistical procedure, the evaluation for the jobs in a particular company are converted to the Hay control standards, a special ranking system. Hay Associates publishes annual surveys showing the compensation practices of a number of companies for jobs of similar

IS THERE INJUSTICE IN PAY PLANS?

Today, American women working full time earn only about 60 percent of what men earn. In an effort to close this gap, there has been a growing movement in the last few years to have the widely accepted concept of equal pay for equal jobs expanded to include equal pay for comparable jobs.

In one Supreme Court case in 1981, it was ruled that a sex discrimination suit may be brought under the 1964 Civil Rights Act. The suit involved Washington County, Oregon, prison matrons claiming sex discrimination because male prison guards, whose jobs were somewhat different, received substantially higher pay. The county had evaluated the men's jobs as having 5 percent more "job content" than the female jobs, and paid the males 35 percent more.

Although this Supreme Court ruling does not mention comparable worth, it permits women to bring suit on the grounds that they are paid lower than men holding comparable jobs. Prior to this ruling, there was confusion in lower courts on the issue of "comparable job" pay discrimination.

In another case, several hundred union employees of the City of San Jose, California, walked off their jobs for nine days over the comparable worth issue. A survey found that women's jobs paid less than men's jobs of comparable worth. One eye-opening example is that senior librarians, typically female, earned 27 percent less than senior chemists, typically male, although the two jobs were rated comparably by the city. The union and the city settled the strike on July 14, 1981, with the city agreeing to pay $1.45 million in raises for several hundred female employees to make their pay more equitable with male employees.'

Other comparable worth cases that should cause some pause for thought are these:

- Nurses working for the City of Denver, Colorado, starting at $1000 per year less than painters, tree trimmers, and tire-service men
- Women handling health and beauty aids for a division of Super Valu Stores, Inc., in western Pennsylvania, eastern Ohio, and northern West Virginia, being paid $3500 less than men handling perishable food
- Clerical employees at the University of Northern Iowa, Cedar Falls, being paid less than janitors and groundkeepers

Other common inequity examples are teachers being paid less than garbage collectors, social workers less than bus drivers, and secretaries less than laborers. These traditional female jobs are paid less. Is that fair? This is what the argument of equal pay for comparable jobs is all about. What is your opinion?

Adapted from Ann Miller, *Women, Work, and Wages: Equal Pay for Jobs of Equal Value,* Report to EEOC (Washington, D.C.: National Academy of Sciences, September 1, 1981).

control standards. All Hay clients use the same evaluation method, so they can compare management salaries.

Benefits and Services

BENEFITS
Financial payments made by an employer over and above the base wage and salary compensation.

SERVICES
Nonmonetary programs provided by companies to employees.

Benefits and services are forms of supplementary compensation. They represent monetary and nonmonetary payments over and above wage and salary rates. **Benefits** are financial in nature, whereas **services** are employer-supplied programs, facilities, or activities (e.g., parks, gymnasiums, housing, transportation) that are considered useful to employees.

If benefits and services are to yield a return to the employer and provide something positive to employees, they must be developed and used systematically. Too often, the so-called fringes are improperly installed. It is important to determine what benefits and services are preferred by employees and what resources are available to meet these preferences, and then select the best package within the means of the company. Some of the important points to consider in developing a benefit and service package for employees is its ability to:

- ■ *Attract and retain competent personnel.* Employees and candidates looking at opportunities evaluate the total compensation package—wage plus fringes or salary plus fringes. One reason for Wingflight's popularity is that people in the community see the firm as having a competitive compensation package.

- ■ *Satisfy security needs.* Through a sound program of benefits and services, an organization can satisfy employees' security needs, including retirement income, disability income, death benefits, medical and dental protection, and educational assistance. These needs may be too expensive for employees to provide themselves.

- ■ *Meet government regulations.* Federal and state laws require companies to support such benefits as unemployment compensation and survivors' insurance. The states provide unemployment compensation to people who are unemployed and seeking employment. These benefits are typically provided for at least twenty-six weeks.

The benefits and services offered to employees are significant. The average firm pays about 33 percent of its payroll to benefits. A breakdown of this payment appears in Exhibit 9–7.

Some benefits are provided because of union–management bargaining. Procter & Gamble and Nunn-Bush Shoe Company have a guaranteed annual wage (GAW). These plans guarantee employees a certain number of weeks of employment, but strike periods are not covered in the program. Companies with employees in the United Auto Workers union provide supplemental unemployment benefits (SUB). The guaranteed annual wage and supplemental unemployment benefits are negotiated by labor and management as a part of the collective bargaining process. For example, the contract would require company contributions to a fund that supplements the unemployment compensation available to employees from federal and state sources or both.

As a result of the efforts of unions, employees, the government, insurance companies, and society in general, the **Occupational Safety and Health Act (OSHA)** became a law on April 28, 1970. The Act directs the Secretary of Labor to enforce safety and health standards in over 4 million businesses and for over 57 million employees. The core of the act may be the system of standards that must be met. For example, OSHA has set a limit for industrial noise of 90 decibels where there is eight hours of exposure per day. OSHA puts special emphasis on improving safety conditions in the five industries with injury rates more than double the national average of 15.2 disabling injuries per million employee hours worked. These industries are longshoring (69.9 injuries per million employee hours), meat and meat products (43.1), roofing and sheet metal (43.0), lumber and wood products (34.1), and miscellaneous transportation equipment (33.3).

OCCUPATIONAL SAFETY AND HEALTH ACT (OSHA)
An act to protect the health of employees. Employers must furnish work places free from recognized hazards to life and health.

EXHIBIT 9-7
Weekly Employee Benefit Costs
by Industry, 1980

	Per employee per week
All industries	$117.00
Manufacturing:	
Petroleum industry	203.42
Chemicals and allied industries	114.10
Primary metal industries	143.73
Transportation equipment	142.29
Machinery (excluding electrical)	127.15
Electrical machinery, equipment and supplies	121.02
Fabricated metal products (excluding machinery and transportation equipment)	119.46
Printing and publishing	114.50
Food, beverages and tobacco	111.69
Stone, clay and glass products	110.94
Instruments and miscellaneous products	108.50
Rubber, leather and plastic products	106.96
Pulp, paper, lumber and furniture	104.37
Textile products and apparel	67.96
Nonmanufacturing:	
Public utilities	158.42
Banks, finance and trust companies	112.08
Miscellaneous nonmanufacturing industries (research, engineering, education, government agencies, construction, etc.)	109.81
Insurance companies	106.83
Wholesale and retail trade	80.96
Hospitals	74.13
Department stores	70.31

"Employee Benefits," *Nation's Business*, December 1981, p. 76.

Enforcement of OSHA standards is accomplished through a system of inspectors, citations, and penalties. Labor Department representatives may enter any business, at a reasonable time, to inspect the health and safety conditions. They may also question the employer, employees, or employee representatives. Criminal penalites can go as high as $20,000 and/or one year in prison. Four categories of violations may result from an inspector's visit:

- *De-minimus.* A minor violation not directly job related
- *Nonserious.* A minor violation that is job related; can result in a penalty of up to $1000
- *Serious.* One in which there is a chance of serious injury or death; can result in a penalty of over $1000

■ *Imminent danger.* One in which there is almost the certainty that serious injury or death will occur; penalty assessed by the federal courts

■ Personnel/human resource management (P/HRM) is the process of accomplishing organizational objectives by acquiring, retaining, terminating, developing, and properly using the human resources in an organization.

■ A personnel/human resource department in a business firm (usually a medium-sized or large firm) typically includes employment, training and development, wage and salary, employee benefits and services, and labor relations divisions.

■ Human resource planning is an important P/HRM activity that involves estimating the size and makeup of the future workforce.

■ Job analysis is an important process used in P/HRM to determine the tasks that make up the job and the skills, abilities, and responsibilities an employee needs to successfully accomplish the job.

■ The federal government attempts to provide equal opportunities for employment without regard to race, religion, age, creed, sex, national origin, or disability through Title VII of the Civil Rights Act of 1964 and the Equal Employment Opportunity Act of 1972.

■ Selection for employment is a process with a number of hurdles a candidate must pass. The steps in the process include application blanks, interviews, tests, reference checks, and a medical examination.

■ Training and development programs are used to inform employees of policies and procedures, educate them in job skills, and develop them for future advancement.

■ Management development refers to the process of educating and developing selected personnel so that they have the knowledge, skills, attitudes, and understanding needed to manage future positions.

■ Nonmanagerial employees are usually paid wages on the basis of time worked. Managerial employees are usually paid salaries or on the basis of a weekly or monthly rate.

■ A job evaluation system is used to compare jobs or to determine the relative worth of one job compared to another job.

■ Benefits and services are forms of supplementary compensation. Benefits are financial (insurance protection); services are programs provided by the employer (a gymnasium).

1. Discuss with a small-business owner the types of personnel/human resource management activities he or she engages in. What did you find out?

2. What is the difference between a job description and a job specification?

3. How active is the government in the P/HRM activities conducted by a business organization?

4. Why is testing such a controversial part of the selection sequence?

5. What is an assessment center, and how can it be used by an organization?

6. What is the union view of job evaluation systems? Why?
7. Do experts in P/HRM need to use what are called scientific procedures? Explain.
8. An individual was overheard making the following statement: "Because we are such a small company, there is little need to be concerned about P/HRM." What do you think about this statement?
9. Why are organizations so interested in benefits and services for employees?
10. Why is management development an important part of a P/HRM program?

CASE FOR ANALYSIS   **HONEYWELL: THE COST VERSUS BENEFITS OF RECRUITING ENGINEERS**

Honeywell is a leading advanced electronics firm that must actively recruit electrical engineers. A major problem Honeywell faces is that there are not enough electric engineers to fill existing job vacancies. The company had to develop a program that dealt with the shortage problem. David Nelson is Honeywell's manager of selection and placement. He believes that he has a plan to attack the electrical engineer shortage problem. This case offers a concise version of Dave's plan.

First, Honeywell would survey a large sample of electrical engineers (students as well as employees in industry). The objective of the survey was to measure (1) overall awareness of Honeywell, (2) familiarity with Honeywell, (3) perceptions of Honeywell as an employer, and (4) personal characteristics of electrical engineers. A telephone survey was used because it provided a high response rate, rapid results, and an ability to talk with respondents.

A questionnaire was then developed to gather additional information. To measure awareness of Honeywell, respondents were asked to name companies in the advanced electronics field and companies with the most noticeable advertising. To measure familiarity with Honeywell, respondents were asked to list Honeywell's services, products, and technological accomplishments. To measure Honeywell's reputation as an employer, respondents were asked to (1) rate the desirability of Honeywell and several competitors as employers, (2) rate how well Honeywell provides the benefits of a good employer, (3) name companies they would like to work for if they changed employers, and (4) rate their interest in working for Honeywell.

This plan was generally supported by the Personnel/Human Resource Management Department at Honeywell. However, some employees of Honeywell and some competitors consider it too costly and too much like marketing. The marketing complaint centers on the notion that in engineering and other professions like medicine and law it is not accepted

*Adapted from Rich Stoops, "A Marketing Approach to Recruitment," *Personnel Journal*, August 1981, p. 608.

practice to advertise. Professionals are considered by some to be above the procedures used by marketing such as advertisement.

Despite some complaints, Dave believes that he is on the right road to help correct the shortage problem. He believes that unless something is done now, Honeywell will be caught short in the human resource area in a few years.

QUESTIONS

1. Of what value to Honeywell will be the information gained from the telephone and questionnaire surveys?
2. How would you rate Dave Nelson's plan? Is it sound? Can it benefit Honeywell?
3. What about the complaints about Dave's plan? Do you agree or disagree with them? Why?

CHAPTER 10

LABOR-MANAGEMENT RELATIONS

LEARNING OBJECTIVES

After studying this chapter, you should be able to:

Discuss why unions appeal to some employees but are resisted by other employees.

Explain the key issues facing unions in the United States.

Illustrate the main features of the Wagner, Taft-Hartley, and Landrum-Griffin acts.

Identify the different types of union shops and what is meant by a right-to-work law.

Define the main steps in the collective bargaining process and the roles played by union and management in reaching agreement.

Compare such common union weapons as strikes, boycotts, and picketing and discuss their use to coerce and influence management decisions about bargaining concessions.

KEY TERMS

Guaranteed annual wage
Yellow-dog contract
Industrial union
Craft union
AFL-CIO
Business representative
Union steward
Injunction
Wagner Act
National Labor Relations Board
Taft-Hartley Act
Landrum-Griffin Act
Sweetheart contract
Restricted shop
Open shop
Agency shop
Preferential shop
Union shop
Right-to-work laws
Closed shop
Collective bargaining
Grievance
Strike
Boycott
Hot-cargo agreement
Lockout
Mediator
Arbitrator

THE UNION PRES:
KNOWLEDGEABLE AND HARD-NOSED

Tony Olympia is a union leader at the Maddox Machine and Tool plant in Duluth, Minnesota. At age eighteen, after quitting school, Tony followed his father into the plant. He eventually became a heavy-duty crane operator. At twenty-six, he was elected as a shop steward, and four years later he became president of the local United Steelworkers (USW) union. The Duluth local union now has about 4500 members.

The local administration of the union is now a full-time job for Tony. He is paid a salary from the local treasury. His job involves handling administrative details, conducting union meetings, enrolling new members, investigating membership complaints, and, along with international representatives, negotiating local contracts with employers.

Another important part of Tony's job is to talk with the members. He spends a lot of time meeting at the union hall, in his home, at members' houses, or any convenient place just to talk shop. He knows members' fears, concerns, and dreams.

Tony believes that in the past decade unions have become too friendly and ''buddy-buddy'' with management. He prefers to keep an arm's length distance from managers and to negotiate hard for his members. He feels that you can't be tough and hard-hosed with someone if you're too friendly. In a recent session with managers from Huggins Fabricating Company, he really got irritated when the union vice president, a shop steward, and the union financial secretary went to lunch with two management negotiators. Tony called the union officials into his office the next day and told

them about his feelings. He wants the union to be united, solid, and hard-nosed in every contact with management. Tony sees the world as us (the union) against them (management).

Although Tony never finished high school, he has enrolled in adult education and training seminars on economics, law, labor relations, communication, marketing, advertising, and government relations. He feels that education, either through a formal system or self-taught, is a must for any union leader. The future of unions in America depends on having informed leaders. Tony feels that informed leaders can meet the challenges of the 1980s and keep unions in an important and powerful position to meet the coming changes in society.

Even before the Declaration of Independence, skilled artisans joined together to provide their families with financial aid in the event of illness or death. Today, over 20 million blue- and white-collar employees, like Tony Olympia, have joined together in unions. Their philosophy is the same: in joining together, there is strength. In fact, a *union* is a group of employees who have joined together to achieve present and future goals that deal with employment conditions.

The power of employees joined together shows at the bargaining table, when union and management meet to discuss numerous issues. Many of the P/HRM decisions discussed in Chapter 9 are influenced by union-management bargaining agreements. Employers in unionized organizations must often consult with union officials before taking actions that affect union members. In addition, many nonunionized companies have a workers' committee or council that managers consult before taking action on some job issues. Their policies and practices may affect employees' interest in unionizing.

One important job of a union is to negotiate and administer the workers' contract with the employer, which covers wages, hours, and the conditions of employment. This is a significant part of Tony Olympia's job as president of the local United Steelworkers Union in Duluth. But there are many other attractive features of union membership, and these appeal to different segments of the workforce.

First, many employees want some assurance that their jobs will exist in the future. They do not want to be fired or arbitrarily laid off because of a personality clash with the manager or some unpredictable economic recession. Unions, through collective bargaining, continually discuss and debate the issue of job security.

Second, people need to socialize and be part of a group. Unions meet these needs by bringing together people with similar interests and goals. Through meetings, social events, educational programs, and common projects, unions build a strong bond of friendship and team spirit.

Third, a safe and healthy place to work is important to employees. Unions in the United States and Canada have pushed hard for good working conditions. This well-publicized emphasis on improved working conditions appeals to employees who are considering a union.

Perhaps one of the strongest motives for joining a union is that it provides employees with a communication link to management. This link enables them to express dissatisfactions and disagreements about the job, management, and other issues. One such link is the grievance procedure detailed in the union–management contract.

Finally, compensation is an important reason for working. Employees want to receive a fair day's pay for good work and good fringe benefits. They are very concerned with receiving pay and fringe benefits that are competitive in the community.

A few unions have secured **guaranteed annual wages** (GAW) or guaranteed annual employment for members. The best known plans are Procter & Gamble's, Hormel's, and Nunn-Bush's. These plans guarantee regular employees a certain amount of money or hours of work. The

WHY DO SOME PEOPLE JOIN UNIONS?

GUARANTEED ANNUAL WAGES
A plan that guarantees an annual wage or employment for members covered by the plan. The objective of the plan is to provide economic security.

purpose of the GAW is economic security. Most companies oppose this type of guarantee because they are concerned about continuing to pay workers when sales are down.

Unions exist because management has not satisfied the total set of employees' needs and wants. It seems impossible for any management to continually satisfy every need and want, but some companies, such as IBM, have not been unionized. IBM has worked at making wages, salaries, fringe benefits, and other programs very attractive to employees. This concerted effort has probably been one of the main reasons IBM employees have not decided to join unions.

A BRIEF HISTORY OF AMERICAN LABOR UNIONS

Unions have existed in the United States since the colonial era. They originally functioned as fraternal societies providing help for members. Today, most unions are part of national organizations, most of which are affiliated with the AFL-CIO (American Federation of Labor–Congress of Industrial Organizations).

Early Unions

Employers successfully resisted the earliest efforts to organize unions. An 1806 court ruling made it a "conspiracy in restraint of trade" for workers to combine or exert pressure on management. In effect, unions were illegal until 1842, when the Massachusetts Supreme Court, in *Commonwealth* v. *Hunt*, decided that criminal conspiracy did not apply if unions did not use illegal tactics to achieve goals.

Even then, employers still resisted by discharging employees who joined unions. It was also easy for employers to have employees sign **yellog-dog contracts**, signed statements that promised the employee would not form or join a union. Employers also obtained court injunctions against strikes.

Early unions promoted social reform and free public education. Some of the more militant groups—like the Molly Maguires from the Pennsylvania coal mines—were considered socialist or anarchist. They were involved in rioting and bloodshed initiated by both employers and union members.

YELLOW-DOG CONTRACT
A statement signed by an employee promising that he or she will not form or join a union.

A More National Approach

The turbulent 1870s and 1880s brought growing recognition of the labor union approach to social and economic problems. These experiences helped solidify the union movement and encouraged the development of a nationwide organization.

The first union federation to achieve significant size and influence was the Knights of Labor, formed around 1869. This group attracted employees and local unions from all crafts and occupational areas. In general, there are two types of unions, industrial and craft. **Industrial union** members are all employees in a company or industry, regardless of occupation. **Craft union** members belong to one craft or to a closely related group of occupations. The strength of the Knights was diluted because it failed to integrate the needs and interests of skilled and unskilled, industrial and craft members.

A group of national craft unions cut their relationships with the Knights of Labor around 1886 to form the American Federation of Labor (AFL). They elected Samuel Gompers of the Cigar Makers' Union president. At first, the

INDUSTRIAL UNION
A union in which all members are employees in a company or industry regardless of occupation.

CRAFT UNION
A union in which all members belong to one craft or to a closely related group of occupations.

AFL restricted membership to skilled tradespeople, but it began to offer membership to unskilled employees when the Congress of Industrial Organizations began to organize industrial employees.

Growth in the union movement from 1886 to 1935 was slow. The government's attitude toward union organizing was neutral, indifferent, or opposed. But with the passage of federal laws in the 1920s and 1930s that gave protection to the union organizing process, union membership began to grow. Thus, formal law helped unions grow during their formative years. From 1933 to 1947, union membership grew from 3 million to 15 million.

In 1935, the Congress of Industrial Organizations (CIO) was formed by John L. Lewis, president of the United Mine Workers, in cooperation with a number of presidents of unions expelled from the AFL. The CIO was formed to organize industrial and mass-production employees. The AFL organized craft employees, like machinists, bricklayers, and carpenters; the CIO wanted to organize craft and unskilled employees within an industry, like assembly line workers, machinists, and assemblers.

Competition for new union members led to bitter conflicts between the AFL and CIO, but in 1955 they merged. The structure of the present **AFL-CIO** is shown in Exhibit 10–1. The majority of national and international labor unions now belong to the AFL-CIO, although a number of unions, representing over 4 million members, are unaffiliated. Such large and powerful unions as the Teamsters and the United Auto Workers are not affiliated with the AFL-CIO.

To attract and retain members, unions have concentrated their efforts on issues that employees are concerned about. These issues are an important part of the motivational forces influencing employees to unionize.

Many organizations have searched for and found technological advances that result in increased productivity. In some cases, technological advances have displaced workers, many of whom belonged to unions. For years, unions resisted technological changes that displaced labor. However, as it became apparent that improvements in productivity were the only way to increase compensation and remain competitive, many unions changed their attitude about technology. Some, such as the United Auto Workers, the United Steelworkers, and the United Rubber Workers, now support technological improvement and work with management representatives to minimize the displacement and improve the quality of work life. They bargain for compensation for displaced workers, retraining, and relocation assistance for laid-off employees.

Labor unions support the principle of equal rights for all people regardless of race, sex, creed, or national origin. Furthermore, as employers, unions must comply with the provisions of the 1964 Civil Rights Act. In the West and Southwest, for example, equal opportunity for migratory workers has been a rallying point for union organizing efforts. But one dilemma that unions face, along with management, is finding enough jobs for those who are capable and willing to work.

AFL-CIO
The merged body of the American Federation of Labor (craft union members) and the Congress of Industrial Organizations (industrial union members).

ISSUES FACING UNIONS

Unemployment

Social Dilemmas

EXHIBIT 10-1

Structure of the AFL-CIO

From U.S. Department of Labor, Bureau of Labor Statistics, *Director of National Unions and Employee Associations, 1971.* Bulletin 1750 (Washington, D.C.: Government Printing Office, 1971), p. 6.

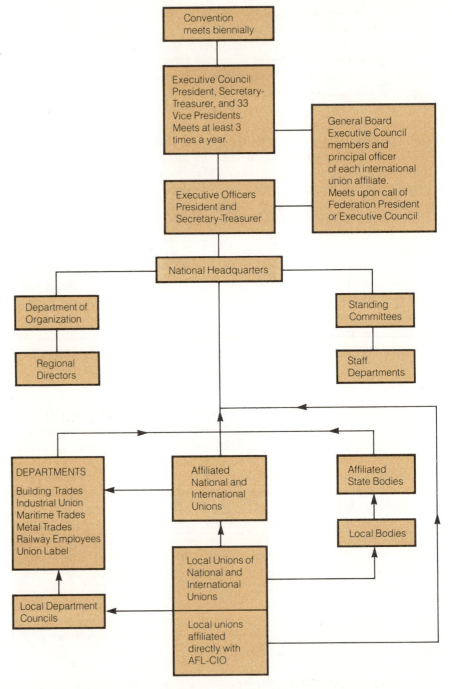

Quality of Life   Improving members' overall quality of life is an important goal of the union movement. Organized unions like the United Auto Workers have supported the national health security act, the fight against poverty, housing development, care for the aged, and a guaranteed minimum standard of living for every person in society. The union believes that such programs, which improve the life of all citizens, are the responsibility of business, government, and labor.

THE UNION IS ADVERTISING

The network commercial begins with a woman, who appears to be an executive, entering her office. As orchestra music fills the background, the shot switches to show that she's a classroom teacher at school. A lyrical message follows: "Sharing each and every day, and caring to help you on your way."

Paid for by the National Education Association, the commerical appears regularly on television. The NEA, a union-like professional group, and many unions are turning to advertising and promotion to help brighten their occasionally shabby images. "The use of professional advertising by labor unions has doubled in the past couple of years," says Victor Kamber, whose Kamber Group is a consultant to the AFL-CIO's building and construction trades department, "and the number of union leaders talking about it is probably up tenfold."

Much of the advertising aims to correct "misconceptions" about union members. "Lots of people have the feeling that labor is just out for the next buck," says Lee White, public affairs director of the Communications Workers of America. Last year, the union started running nationwide TV commercials showing, for example, that a telephone switchman also may be a volunteer coach of a neighborhood basketball team.

This year, the United Brotherhood of Carpenters and Joiners of America began some image-building because, as a spokesperson says, "The general public has a confused image of labor. They see mostly television stories about strikes and dissension." The union is running a TV spot showing a carpenter cutting out the union emblem with a jigsaw and placing it on a wooden map of North America. The message: "We're building the 20th Century."

The International Ladies' Garment Workers' Union, which during the 1930s produced a pro-union musical hit on Broadway, sponsored the first national union TV campaign in 1975. To encourage shoppers to shun imported clothing, the union commercial asked them to "look for the union label." Wilbur Daniels, the union's executive vice president, concedes that "the problem hasn't gone away." But, he says, as "a voice in the wilderness," the union "helped the public and the legislative branch recognize the existence of the problem."

Most ad-minded unions can't afford national TV advertising, so they concentrate on local broadcasting instead. In Buffalo, N.Y., a group of 20 building trades unions, after several years of radio advertising, expanded into local television this year. "We're trying to tell people about the social things we do, like charitable work," a spokesperson says.

On a different track, the International Association of Machinists and Aerospace Workers has started monitoring TV news and entertainment programs for anti-union content. After an initial reading, the union charged that the three major networks favored "corporate positions" over union positions.

Before organizing employees in Tucson and Salt Lake City recently, the union took out local TV and newspaper ads, hired professional pollsters to solicit the views of potential members, and computerized its mailings. "I'm not claiming that was the only reason we were successful out there," a spokesperson says, "but it sure helped."

In addition to its national TV advertising, the union is considering sponsorship of national cable TV programs on such topics as taxes, the economy, and collective bargaining.

Adapted from Robert S. Greenberger, "More Unions Try Slick Advertising to Educate and Influence the Public," *Wall Street Journal*, September 30, 1980.

The most significant increase in union membership occurred from 1933 to 1947. This growth occurred after the Depression, a time when public sentiment was antimanagement. Unions became more powerful with the added members. In 1933, there were only 3 million union members, accounting for about 7 percent of the total labor force. The number of union

Membership

members continued to increase until 1956, declined until 1963, and started to grow slowly until it reached 21 million workers in 1981, or about 20 percent of the total labor force and 28 percent of nonagricultural employment.

The ten largest U.S. unions and their memberships are presented in Exhibit 10–2. The three largest unions, with memberships of more than a million each, are the Teamsters, Auto Workers, and Steelworkers. Exhibit 10–3 shows the degree of unionization by industry type. For example, at least 75 percent of the blue-collar employees in transportation are unionized, whereas fewer than 25 percent of local government employees are unionized.

The organizational and recruiting efforts of unions have varied according to changes in economic, social, and political conditions. New membership drives will probably occur in the public sector, which includes military personnel, police, and firefighters; among professionals, including teachers, medical personnel, athletes, and lawyers; among employees in service industries; and among agricultural workers.

On the Job Revisited

Tony Olympia wants to recruit another 1000 members for his local union in the next year. He is working with the international union drawing up a campaign that will accomplish his goal. Hard work and working within the law are needed to get the job done.

Unions are very interested in attracting public employees. A 1962 executive order by President John F. Kennedy, which was strengthened by

EXHIBIT 10–2
The Ten Largest Unions in the
United States

UNION	AFFILIATION	MEMBERS
Teamsters, Chauffeurs, Warehousemen and Helpers of America, International Brotherhood of	Independent	1,888,895
Automobile, Aerospace and Agricultural Implement Workers of America, International Union, United (UAW)	Independent	1,358,354
United Food and Commercial Workers	AFL-CIO	1,076,000*
Steelworkers of America, United	AFL-CIO	964,000
State, County and Municipal Employees, American Federation of	AFL-CIO	889,000
Electrical Workers, International Brotherhood of (IBEW)	AFL-CIO	825,000
Machinists and Aerospace Workers, International Association of	AFL-CIO	664,000
Carpenters and Joiners of America, United Brotherhood of	AFL-CIO	619,000
Laborers' International Union of North America	AFL-CIO	627,406
Service Employees' International Union	AFL-CIO	575,000

Source: AFL-CIO Department of Research, 1980.
*Retail Clerks and Meatcutters merged in 1979 to form this union.

NOT JUST UMPIRES BUT ALSO PLAYERS YELL STRIKE!

The 1981 strike by major-league baseball players cost 26 baseball clubs about 1.25 million dollars a day in ticket revenues, and the 650 players had to forgo about $600,000 a day in salaries. The union in professional sports has become a powerful force. Sports unions handle many of the same chores of other unions—negotiating for minimum salaries, fringe benefits, and working conditions and handling grievances, postretirement career guidance, and financial counseling.

Although sports unions do not negotiate salaries for a specific player, they help set the ground rules for player trades and acquisitions. They have also been a force in the salary area. In baseball, average salaries have climbed 656 percent—from $22,500 to $70,000—since 1966.

Today unions are finding more acceptance among players and owners. However, union leaders concede that they are having trouble convincing the fans, especially when strikes are involved. Some fans feel that athletes are spoiled and overpaid for playing games. The future of unions in professional sports is safe. The ire of fans in the future, however, is something that the athletes, union leaders, and owners will have to face more and more as disputes turn into strikes. Some of the fans' displeasure is based on average earnings for four-to-six month seasons. The facts about these salaries are spelled out below.

PRO ATHLETES AND THEIR UNIONS

BASEBALL	FOOTBALL	BASKETBALL	HOCKEY	SOCCER
Major League Baseball Players Assn.	National Football League Players Assn.	National Basketball Players Assn.	National Hockey League Players' Assn.	North American Soccer League Players Assn.
Executive Director: Marvin Miller	Executive Director: Edward Garvey	General Counsel: Lawrence Fleisher	Executive Director: R. Alan Eagleson	Executive Director: John Kerr
Members: 650	Members: 1,496	Members: 650	Members: 375	Members: 500
Average earnings: $170,000	Average earnings: $80,000	Average earnings: $186,000	Average earnings: $108,000	Average earnings: $30,000
Dues: $720	Dues: $760	Dues: $750 (1981–82 season)	Dues: $900	Dues: $480

Adapted from "Unions in Professional Sports," *U.S. News & World Reports*, July 20, 1981, pp. 57-58.

amendments in 1969 and 1971, set up a form of collective bargaining for federal government employees. As a result, public employee unions have become the fastest growing labor groups in the country.

In the past, professors, teachers, nurses, doctors, athletes, and other professionals have considered themselves above union goals, procedures, and tactics. Yet these groups have recently begun to recognize union gains

EXHIBIT 10-3
The Degree of Union Organization
in Selected Industries

75 percent and over

Transportation	Paper
Contract construction	Electrical machinery
Ordnance	Transportation equipment

50 percent to less than 75 percent

Primary metals	Manufacturing
Food and kindred products	Fabricated metals
Mining	Telephone and telegraph
Apparel	Stone, clay, and glass products
Tobacco manufacturers	Federal government
Petroleum	Rubber

25 percent to less than 50 percent

Printing, publishing	Machinery
Leather	Chemicals
Furniture	Lumber
Electric, gas utilities	

Less than 25 percent

Nonmanufacturing	State government
Textile mill products	Trade
Instruments	Agriculture and fishing
Service	Finance
Local government	

Adapted from U. S. Department of Labor, Bureau of Labor Statistics (Washington, D. C.: Government Printing Office, 1977), pp. 70–71.

and adopt union tactics. The National Education Association (teachers) has over 1.4 million members, the American Nurses' Association has about 200,000 members, and the Fraternal Order of Police has 147,000 members.[1]

The strike by major-league baseball players in the summer of 1981 and the professional football players in the fall of 1982 indicated the degree of union muscle in professional sports. Besides baseball and football, unions now represent all professional athletes in basketball, hockey, and soccer. Even jockeys and rodeo contestants are organized.[2]

Another area that unions are attempting to unionize is agriculture. These organizing efforts are especially intense in the grape, lettuce, citrus, and cotton regions of California.

In addition to these new organizing efforts in industries and professions, unions are also attempting to attract white-collar, female, and black employees. Because of boredom and frustration in many white-collar jobs, some employees have considered unionizing. In the past, white-collar employees identified more with management practices and antiunion ideals and philosophy.

The proportion of working women who are members of labor unions is declining. However, the number of female union members is increasing.

The Coalition of Labor Union Women, an alliance of blue-collar working women, was formed in 1974 to end sex discrimination in wages and hiring. It also is attempting to elect more women as union officials. With more women officials, other women might believe that unions welcome them and need their abilities and skills. However, much work needs to be done in organizing women. There are approximately 45 million women in the workforce, but in 1981 only about 4.6 million were members of unions.

Black employees are another fast-growing segment of the workforce and a target of union organizers. In 1980, there were approximately 2.7 million black trade unionists. However, blacks have not been represented in union management in proportion to their membership. Furthermore, several unions have been found guilty of discriminating against blacks. Both blacks and women are demanding more say in union decisions, and they will certainly acquire additional power as unions attempt to increase their membership.

Resistance to Unions

Despite well-planned and systematic organizing efforts, about 80 percent of the total labor force, or 80 million workers, still are not unionized. One reason is that many people distrust unions. Some people believe that unions stand against individualism and free enterprise. They feel that people should get ahead on their own skills and merits. They resent the unions' position in favor of collectivism and the use of seniority in personnel decisions involving promotions, layoffs, and pay increases.

Many professionals resist unions because they view them as a blue-collar enterprise. Doctors, lawyers, and professors assume that they should not be associated with blue-collar tactics and behavior. This attitude is somewhat contrary to some of the actions of such professional associations as the American Medical Association (AMA). Some claim that the most powerful *union* in the United States is the AMA.

Some employees resist unions because they identify with management values and practices. Management typically does not support union tactics. These nonmanagers may be considering their aspirations to be a part of management when they resist union organizing efforts.

THE STRUCTURE AND MANAGEMENT OF UNIONS

Many unions are large organizations with management, leadership, and financial control problems similar to those faced by business firms. National union headquarters employ staff economists, engineers, attorneys, accountants, wage and salary experts, and professional managers.

The National Union

The constitution of the national union establishes the rules, policies, and procedures under which the local unions may be chartered and become members. Each national union exercises some control over the local unions. These controls usually deal with the collection of dues, the admission of new members by the local, and the use of union funds. The national also provides the local unions with support for organizing campaigns, strikes, and the administration of contracts. There are over 100 national union organizations and about 80,000 local unions.

The Local Union

The labor movement has its foundation in the local craft union. The local has direct influence over the membership. Through the local, members exercise their complaints and pay the dues that support the national union.

The activities of locals are conducted by officials elected by the members. The elected officials include a president, vice president, secretary-treasurer, business representative, and committee chairpersons. Elected officials of local unions often have full-time jobs in addition to their regular union duties.

BUSINESS REPRESENTATIVE
A union official who is responsible for negotiating and administering the labor agreement and for settling problems that may arise in connection with the contract.

In many local unions, the **business representative** is the dominant person. In Tony Olympia's union, he has the title of *president*, which is the same as the title *business representative*. The major responsibilities of the business representative are to negotiate and administer the labor agreement and to settle problems that may arise in connection with the contract. The business representative also collects dues, recruits new members, coordinates social activities, and arranges union meetings.

UNION STEWARD
Person who represents the interests of local union members in their on-the-job relations with managers.

The **union steward** represents the interests of local union members in their relations with managers on the job. In the auto industry, the steward (called a *committee person*) devotes full time to solving disputes that arise in connection with the union–management labor contract.

Managing the Union

The job of managing a union is challenging and time consuming. Union officials need to be dedicated, willing to work long hours, able to counsel members on personal problems, and skilled in influencing people. This combination of skills and abilities must also be obvious to members; tenure in office, especially at the local level, depends on projecting a favorable impression. Officers must run periodically for reelection. Tony Olympia has been in the president's chair for eight years and plans to run again next year. Some problems that he and other union officers face are member apathy, financial control, and recruitment of new members.

On the Job Revisited

It is common knowledge that the majority of union members are apathetic about attending union meetings and voting on contracts or strike decisions. Thus, it is difficult for union officials to encourage members to take their union responsibilities more seriously. At the United Steelworkers monthly meeting in Duluth, Tony estimates that only about 80 out of the 4500 members attend regularly.

Unions are financed through dues, fines, and initiation fees collected at the local level. But union members resist high assessments. Union officials must convince members that, unless the union has a sound financial base, it won't have the power to secure favorable labor agreements. A majority of union members pay dues that come out to roughly two hours' wages per month, and two major unions—the Steelworkers and Automobile Workers—have set their monthly dues at exactly this two-hours level. Initiation fees are paid once and tend to be in the $25–$75 range. The dues and initiation fees for all American unions total about $3 billion a year.

The drive to organize more employees always faces union officials. Without new members, unions don't have the strength to carry out tactics to satisfy the needs, preferences, and interests of the membership. Developing effective organizing drives is the responsibility of local and national unions alike.

The union–management pattern of interaction is governed by state and federal laws. These laws have evolved through common law and through rulings by the National Labor Relations Board and the courts. Figuratively speaking, these laws have swung back and forth like a pendulum, at one time favoring management and at another time favoring unions.

In the 1930s, the federal government became involved in labor disputes outside the railroad industry. The Norris-La Guardia Act, also called the Anti-Injunction Act, passed in 1932, limited the powers of federal courts to stop union picketing, boycotts, and strikes. **Injunctions**, court decrees to stop union activities, had provided employers with an easy way to hinder union activities. The Norris-La Guardia Act also made the yellow-dog contract unenforceable.

The National Labor Relations Act, better known as the **Wagner Act**, was passed in 1935. The stated purpose of the Act was to encourage the growth of trade unions and restrain management from interfering with this growth. This Act made the government take an active role in union–management relationships by restricting the activities of management. Five unfair labor practices specified in the Wagner Act are summarized in Exhibit 10-4.

The power to implement the Wagner Act was given to a three-person **National Labor Relations Board (NLRB)** and a staff of lawyers and other personnel responsible to the board. The board sets up elections, on request, to determine if a given group of workers wishes to have a union as a bargaining representative. The board also investigates complaints of unfair labor practices.

The Wagner Act was considered pro-labor. In order to swing the pendulum back toward management, in 1947 Congress passed the **Taft-Hartley Act** (also called the Labor–Management Relations Act), which amended and supplemented the Wagner Act.

The Taft-Hartley Act guaranteed employee bargaining rights and specifically forbade the five unfair employer labor practices first established in the Wagner Act. But the Act also specified unfair union labor practices. The union was restrained from such practices as those shown in Exhibit 10–5.

LABOR LEGISLATION

Early Labor Law

INJUNCTION
Court order that prohibits the defendant from engaging in certain activities such as striking.

The Wagner Act

WAGNER ACT
A law that made collective bargaining legal and required employers to bargain with the representatives of the employees. The law is also referred to as the National Labor Relations Act.

NATIONAL LABOR RELATIONS BOARD (NLRB)
A group that investigates cases of alleged unfair labor practices by employers and unions and holds elections to determine whether groups of employees want to be unionized.

The Taft-Hartley Act

TAFT-HARTLEY ACT
A labor law, passed in 1947, that prohibits the closed shop, requires unions to bargain in good faith, and makes it illegal for a union to discriminate against employees who don't join the union.

EXHIBIT 10-4
Unfair Labor Practices According to the Wagner Act

- To interfere with, restrain, or coerce employees in the exercise of their rights to organize
- To dominate or interfere with the affairs of a union
- To discriminate in regard to hiring, tenure, or any employment condition for the purpose of encouraging or discouraging membership in any union organization
- To discriminate against or discharge an employee because he or she has filed charges or given testimony under the Wagner Act
- To refuse to bargain collectively with representatives of the employees, that is, to refuse to bargain in good faith

EXHIBIT 10-5
Union Unfair Labor Practices

■ To restrain or coerce employees in the exercise of their right to join or not to join a union except when an agreement is made by the employer and union that a condition of employment will be joining the union, called a union security clause authorizing a union shop

■ To cause an employer to discriminate against an employee other than for nonpayment of dues or initiation fees

■ To refuse to bargain with an employer in good faith

■ To engage, induce, encourage, threaten, or coerce any individual to engage in strikes, refusal to work, or boycott where the objective is to

force or require any employer or self-employed person to recognize or join any labor organization or employer organization

force or require an employer or self-employed person to cease using the products of or doing business with another person, or force any other employer to recognize or bargain with the union unless it has been certified by the NLRB

force an employer to apply pressure to another employer to recognize a union. Examples are: picketing a hospital so that it will apply pressure on a subcontractor (Food Service, Maintenance, Emergency Department) to recognize a union, or forcing an employer to only do business with others, such as suppliers, who have a union, or picketing by another union for recognition when a different one is already certified

■ To charge excessive or discriminatory membership fees

■ To cause an employer to give payment for services not performed (featherbedding)

The Landrum-Griffin Act

LANDRUM-GRIFFIN ACT
Labor law passed in 1959 that requires unions and employees to file financial reports with the secretary of labor and that requires certain activities to ensure that the union is operated democratically.

In view of the corruption found in some unions, Congress assumed that the individual union member was still not adequately protected by the labor laws in existence. Therefore, in 1959 Congress passed the **Landrum-Griffin Act**, which is officially designated the Labor-Management Reporting and Disclosure Act. It was designed to regulate the internal affairs of unions.

This Act, referred to as the bill of rights of union members, gave every union member the right to (1) nominate candidates for union office; (2) vote in union elections; and (3) attend union meetings. Union members also had the right to examine union accounts and records. In addition, the union was required to submit an annual financial report to the secretary of labor. Employers had to report any payments or loans made to unions, their officers, or members. This portion of the Act was to eliminate what are called **sweetheart contracts**, under which the union leaders and management agree to terms that work to their mutual benefit but maintain poor working conditions for other employees.

SWEETHEART CONTRACT
Agreement between union leaders and management to terms that work to their mutual benefit but maintain poor working conditions for other employees.

Labor unions stress the importance of job security for members. Labor legislation also addresses the issue of union security. And union security is a major reason for trying to increase union membership. Unions want to increase their security by requiring all employees to join the union once it is elected as the legitimate bargaining agent. Instead of pushing the notion of higher wages, Tony Olympia emphasizes the job security a worker gains by being a member of the union.

In some elections, the union is voted in by a slim margin. In such cases, some employees obviously don't want to join the union. Different types of union shops have developed as a result, and they represent various degrees of union security.

RESTRICTED SHOP   When management tries to keep a union out without violating any labor laws, a **restricted shop** exists. A restricted shop is an attitude rather than a formal arrangement. Management may try to provide wages and fringe benefits that make the union and what it can offer unattractive. This is a legal effort to make the union's organizing ineffective.

It is illegal to create a restricted shop by dismissing employees who want to unionize; trying to influence employees who are thinking about starting a union; or promising rewards if the union is voted down. These activities could result in legal action against management.

OPEN SHOP   An **open shop** is one in which there is neither a union present nor a management effort to keep the union out. The employees have total freedom to decide whether or not they want a union. This type of shop is a prime target for union organizing efforts.

AGENCY SHOP   In the **agency shop**, all employees pay union dues whether or not they are members of the union. This means that no employee is a "free rider." Everyone pays dues for the services of an organized union even though some employees are not members. However, nonunion members are generally required to pay only a fair share of the costs associated with collective bargaining.

PREFERENTIAL SHOP   In the **preferential shop**, the union is recognized, and union members are given preference in some areas. For example, in the hiring of new employees, union members are given preference over nonunion members. This type of preference may also be given in such areas as promotion and layoff. Many of these preferential decisions are in violation of the Taft-Hartley Act. If there is an excessive amount of preferential treatment, a closed shop may exist, which is also prohibited by the Taft-Hartley Act.

UNION SHOP   The **union shop** requires the employee to join a union after being hired. An employer may hire any person, but within a certain period of time the employee must join the union if he or she is to keep the job. Under the Taft-Hartley Act, this period of time can be no shorter than

UNION SECURITY

On the Job Revisited

RESTRICTED SHOP
A company whose management tries to keep a union out without violating any labor laws.

OPEN SHOP
A company in which employees don't have to join a union or pay dues, but can decide without pressure whether to become union members.

AGENCY SHOP
A company where all employees pay union dues, whether or not they are union members.

PREFERENTIAL SHOP
A company that recognizes the union and gives some preference to union members in hiring in some areas.

UNION SHOP
A company that requires employees to join the union after being hired.

RIGHT-TO-WORK LAWS
State laws requiring that two people doing the same job be paid the same wages, whether or not they belong to the union.

thirty days. But under the Landrum-Griffin Act, this period can be shortened to seven days in the construction industry only. Most union–management labor contracts provide for the union shop.

The Taft-Hartley Act allows states to forbid union shops by passing what are called **right-to-work laws**. Under these laws, two persons doing the same job must be paid the same wages, whether or not they belong to the union. The union believes this is unfair, because the nonunionized employees pay no dues but share in the benefits won by the union. Twenty states have right-to-work laws, as shown in Exhibit 10–6. The percentage of the nonagricultural labor force that is unionized is also shown.

CLOSED SHOP
A company that hires only workers who are members of the union; illegal under the Taft-Hartley Act.

CLOSED SHOP   The **closed shop** requires that a new employee be a union member when hired. The union itself provides labor to the organization. Although this type of shop is illegal, modified closed shops are found in the construction, printing, and maritime industries. For example, an ironworkers' union hall sends out union members to construction sites on request. A nonunion member has little chance to be sent from a union hall to a job because the union's business agent makes the assignments. Union members elect the business agent, while the nonunion members have no vote.

EXHIBIT 10–6
Right-to-Work States

LEGEND
■ States with 'right to work' laws
□ States without 'right to work' laws   Data as of 1982

Whenever employee–employer relationships involve unions, collective bargaining establishes, manages, and enforces contractual agreements between the parties. The Taft-Hartley Act instructs that it is an unfair labor practice for the employer to refuse to bargain collectively with chosen representatives of a duly certified labor union. The Landrum-Griffin Act states that it is an unfair practice for the representatives of a labor union to not bargain in good faith with an employer. The current national policy, then, is that employees and employers must bargain in good faith to work out employment issues and disputes.

Collective bargaining is a process by which the representatives of the business firm meet and attempt to work out a contract with union representatives. *Collective* means only that representatives are attempting to negotiate an agreement. *Bargaining* is the process of cajoling, debating, discussing, and threatening to bring about a favorable agreement for those being represented.

The collective bargaining process and the final agreement reached are influenced by many variables. Exhibit 10-7 identifies some of the variables

COLLECTIVE BARGAINING

COLLECTIVE BARGAINING
Negotiation of a labor contract by union and management. The parties sit down, discuss, debate, and sometimes threaten in an attempt to get a final contract favorable to their side.

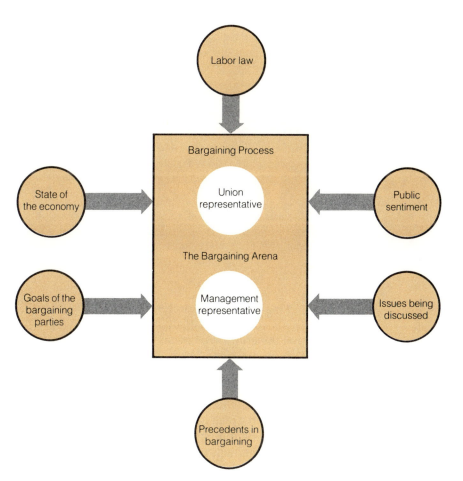

EXHIBIT 10-7
The Forces Influencing
the Bargaining Process

GIVEBACKS AND ORGANIZING EFFORTS: THE UNION IN THE 1980s

"It's getting tougher and tougher to negotiate a decent settlement," says the United Automobile Workers president, Douglas Fraser. A number of times, his union has made major contract concessions to keep Chrysler Corporation out of bankruptcy. Last time these "givebacks" totaled $622 million. Givebacks were not even in the vocabulary of union leaders until the late 1970s and early 1980s.

The phenomenon of giving up hard-won wages and benefits is now a troublesome reality facing many labor leaders. But the facts of life—unemployment, plant shutdowns, layoffs, sluggish productivity, and automation—point to few alternatives. President John Sweeney of the Service Employees Union states, "A union should seek the best possible contract for its members. But you have to keep the employer healthy or you negotiate yourself out of a job."

In a healthy business economy, high labor costs can be absorbed. But when business slumps, as it has in many industries in recent years, employees have less room to maneuver. The union has to give ground in some cases.

To keep Consolidated Rail Corporation from being sold to its competitors, employees gave up 200 million dollars a year in raises. Meat-packers in Baltimore took wage cuts to save their jobs. These are just a few of the examples of "givebacks" that occurred in 1981.

For most unions, winning pay increases is still a major goal. However, occasionally the push to achieve the goal is disastrous. In 1981 members of the Professional Air Traffic Controllers Organization (PATCO) rejected a contract in late July. Union bargainers went for broke and threatened an illegal strike (they were government employees) unless demands for higher pay and more time off were met. The government negotiators refused and the union struck. The result—some 12,000 PATCO members were fired.

It has not been all downhill for unions. The Communications Workers recently won bargaining rights for 11,500 state-employed office workers in New Jersey. The Teamsters and the UAW report gains in signing up workers outside of the trucking and auto industries. In a massive organizing campaign the AFL-CIO is spending close to $2 million on a project to organize workers in the fast-growing Houston area.

Union leaders hope that success in Houston will give momentum to other organizing efforts in the South. An earlier organizing effort in the Los Angeles area netted AFL-CIO unions more than 400,000 new members. The union's leadership knows that there is strength in numbers and the union can ill afford to see their ranks decline.

Adapted from "Unions on the Run," *U. S. News & World Report*, September 14, 1981, pp. 61–65.

influencing the union and management representatives. For example, the state of the economy affects collective bargaining. The firm's representative must consider whether the company can pay an increased wage based on current and expected economic conditions. In 1981, unions began to agree to roll back wages and fringe benefits granted in better times. United Airline employees took an 8 percent pay cut, and General Tire and Rubber employees agreed to a 4 percent cut.[3] Thus, each of the forces shown in Exhibit 10–7 involves a union and a management response. Each side of the collective bargaining table will be influenced by such factors as the economy and the environment, but perhaps in different ways.

In early 1982, the United Auto Workers and General Motors (GM) reached an agreement designed to save GM $3 billion. Both management and union representatives sat across the bargaining table and considered plant shutdowns, termination of long-tenured employees, foreign competition in the auto market, and the economic recession. Under the agreement, GM's 320,000 U. S. autoworkers had their wages frozen (no raises would be given for thirty months), gave up nine paid personal holidays per year, and deferred their June, September, and December cost-of-living allowance increases in 1982.In exchange, GM cancelled four announced plant closings, agreed to a two-year moratorium on plant closings, improved benefits for laid-off workers, and provided workers with a profit-sharing program.[4]

The actual process of collective bargaining involves a number of steps: (1) prenegotiation; (2) selecting negotiators; (3) developing a bargaining strategy; (4) using the best tactics; and (5) reaching a formal contractual agreement.

Prenegotiation

In collective bargaining, both sides attempt to receive concessions that will help them achieve their objectives. As soon as a contract is signed by union and management, both parties begin preparing for the next collective bargaining session. Thus, the importance of careful prenegotiation preparation cannot be overemphasized. Tony Olympia plays a big role in helping the international union negotiator know what to bargain hard for at the table.

On the Job Revisited

In the prenegotiation step, both parties typically prepare economic data and reports that can be used to help support arguments or issues raised. Particularly valuable to negotiators are Bureau of Labor Statistics surveys on wage rates for various occupations, industries, and labor markets.

The Negotiators

On the management side of the bargaining table may be any one of a number of people, including the P/HRM director, the executive vice president, or the company lawyer. Or management may field a team of negotiators, so that all forms of expertise are present. Typically, the team consists of a personnel/human resource management expert, a lawyer, a manager or vice president with knowledge of the entire business organization, and an economist.

The union also uses a team approach. The union team generally consists of business agents, shop stewards, the local union president, and, when the negotiation is very important, representatives from national union headquarters. When industrywide bargaining is taking place, as in the automobile industry, the chief negotiator is a representative from the national union.

Mapping the Strategy

Because the labor ageement must be used for a long period of time, it is important to develop a winning strategy and tactics. The strategy is considered to be the plan and policies that will be pursued at the bargaining table. Tactics are the specific actions taken in the bargaining sessions. It is important to spell out the strategy and tactics because bargaining is a give-and-take process with characteristics of a poker game, a political campaign, or a heated debate.

On the Job Revisited

Tony's strategy is to pay "hard ball" from the start. Let management know the union means business. The fact that some plants have closed around Duluth has mellowed Tony a little. He doesn't want the firms with union members to close down. He still plays "hard ball," but he compromises more than in the past.

Tactics

Tactics are calculated actions used by both parties. Occasionally, tactics are used to mislead the other party. But they are also used to secure an agreement that is favorable to either management or the unions.

In one case, General Electric used a tactic called Boulwareism (named after the person who developed it). GE's management worked out an offer that was final and presented it to the union. No matter how heated or long negotiations became, the offer was final. The National Labor Relations Board ruled that the Boulware tactic was a failure to bargain in good faith. GE appealed this decision and won in the lower courts. However, the U.S. Supreme Court informed GE that it could not give one best offer but had to start lower in order to permit the union to obtain benefits and save face with the membership.

A commonly used tactic of the union is to attempt to have management reach agreement clause by clause. Each clause is agreed to before the next clause is discussed. This tactic focuses on separate points instead of the total package and is usually resisted by management.

Another tactic used by both sides is the attempt to wear down the other side through long marathon sessions. This tactic relies on fatigue to weaken the other side.

The Contract

The union–management contract designates the formal terms of agreement. The average contract covers two or three years and varies from a few typewritten pages to well over a hundred pages, depending on the issues covered, the size of the organization, and the union.

The labor contract is divided into sections and appendices. The sections that can be and are covered in some labor agreements are listed in Exhibit 10–8. The exhibit shows that a major part of the contract is concerned with such employment issues as wages, hours, fringe benefits, and overtime.

EXHIBIT 10–8
Content of a Labor Agreement

▓ Purpose and intent of the parties	▓ Seniority
▓ Scope of the agreement	▓ Safety and health
▓ Management	▓ Military service
▓ Responsibilities of the parties	▓ Severance allowance
▓ Union membership and checkoff	▓ Savings and vacation plan
▓ Adjustment of grievance	▓ Supplemental unemployment
▓ Arbitration	benefits program
▓ Suspension and discharge cases	▓ S.U.B. and insurance
▓ Rates of pay	grievances
▓ Hours of work	▓ Prior agreements
▓ Overtime—holidays	▓ Termination date
▓ Vacations	▓ Appendices

Adapted from United States Steel Corporation and the United Steelworkers Union, "Labor Agreement."

Day-to-day compliance with contract provisions are an important responsibility of the first-line manager, who works closely with union members. As the representative of management, the first-line manager must discipline workers, handle grievances, and prepare for such actions as strikes.

Most contracts agree that management has a right to discipline workers. But any discipline in a unionized firm must follow legal due process. If an employee or union challenges a disciplinary action, the burden of proof rests on the company. Often management will lose a case that is arbitrated (settled by an impartial third party) because improper disciplinary procedures have been followed.

Many union–management contracts specify the types of discipline and the offenses for which corrective action will be taken. Some of the infractions that are typically spelled out are:

- *Incompetence.* Failure to perform the assigned job
- *Misconduct.* Insubordination, dishonesty, or violating a rule such as smoking in a restricted area
- *Violations of the contract.* Initiating a strike when there is no strike clause, for example

The contract should list penalties for such infractions. Inconsistent application of discipline is sometimes a problem. Violators must be disciplined similarly. When one employee is reprimanded for regularly arriving at work late but another with a similar tardiness problem is discharged, discipline is being applied inconsistently.

Consistent, prompt, and reasonable discipline programs are what union and management representatives attempt to spell out in the contract. One strategy is to use a progressive program. Repeated or more serious violations result in penalties of increasing severity. The sequence of progressive discipline might be:

1. An oral caution and a note in the personnel file of the employee
2. A written reprimand that becomes a part of the file
3. A short, two-day to one-week suspension
4. A demotion to the next lower job position
5. A long, one- to three-month suspension
6. A discharge

The emphasis in this approach should be on developing within the total work force a willingness to obey and follow rules and regulations. The goal is to encourage employees to follow rules because they want to and not because they are afraid of the progressively severe penalties.

A **grievance** is a complaint about a job that creates dissatisfaction or discomfort, whether it is valid or not. The complaint may be made by a single employee or by the union. It is important to note that, although the validity of the grievance may be questionable, it should be handled correctly. Even if an employee files an official grievance that seems absolutely without support, the manager should still handle it according to formal contractual provisions.

ADMINISTERING THE CONTRACT

Discipline

Grievances

GRIEVANCE
Complaint about a job that creates dissatisfaction or discomfort, made by an employee or the union.

Grievance procedures are usually followed in unionized companies, but they are also important channels of communication in nonunionized organizations. In the unionized organization, the contract contains a clause covering the steps to be followed and how the grievance will be handled. The number of steps varies from contract to contract. But a labor union is not essential for establishing a procedure.

Exhibit 10-9 illustrates a four-step grievance procedure used in a unionized company.

1. The employee meets with the supervisor and the union steward and presents the grievance. Most grievances are settled at this point.
2. If the grievance is not settled at step 1, there is a conference between middle management and union officials (a business agent or union committee).

On the Job Revisited

3. At this point, a top management representative and top union officials (for example, the union president, like Tony Olympia) attempt to settle the grievance. Last year Tony was involved in seventeen grievances that reached the third step.
4. Both parties (union and management) turn the grievance over to an arbitrator who makes a decision. Arbitration is usually handled by a mutually agreed upon single individual or a panel of an odd number. In 1980, 17,062 labor disputes were filed with the Labor Arbitration Association.[5]

Although most grievances are handled at step 1, there are a number of important principles for managers to follow. They should (a) take every grievance seriously; (b) work with the union representative; (c) gather all information available on the grievance; (d) after weighing all the facts,

EXHIBIT 10-9
A Grievance Procedure

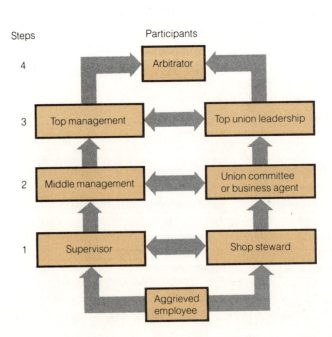

provide an answer to the employee voicing the grievance; and (e) after the grievance is settled, attempt to move on to other matters.

A **strike** is an effort to withhold employee services so that the employer will make greater concessions at the bargaining table. The strike, or a potential strike, is a major bargaining force used by the unions. However, the total amount of working time lost to strikes has been decreasing. In 1980, the total came to 33,000 worker-days compared to 48,000 in 1974.[6]

Before a union strikes, it needs to consider the legality of striking, the members' willingness to endure the hardships of a long strike, and the employer's ability to operate the organization without union members. The greater the employer's ability to operate the organization, the less chance the union will have of gaining the demands it makes.

Tony Olympia feels that in bad economic times the strike is less of a weapon. Unions have to back off a little to help the firm survive. He does feel, however, that management has to be watched carefully. He is not convinced that managers always level with unions about the firm's financial position. Tony says, "A lot of times they cry wolf while they are laughing all the way to the bank."

There are a number of different types of strikes, including:

- *Economic strike*. Based on a demand for better wages or fringe benefits than the employer wants to provide.
- *Jurisdictional strike*. Exists when two unions argue over who has the right to perform a job. For example, bricklayers and ironworkers may both want to install steel rods in doorways. The rods are made a part of the brickwork and are needed to hold up heavy steel doors. If either group strikes to force the employer to grant the work to its members, a jurisdictional strike occurs. This type of strike is illegal under the Taft-Hartley Act.
- *Wildcat strike*. An unapproved strike that may suddenly occur because one union subgroup has not been satisfied by a grievance decision or by some managerial action. The union leaders do not sanction this type of strike.
- *Sitdown strike*. When employees strike but remain in the plant. Such strikes are illegal because they are an invasion of private property.

When any strike occurs, management must be able to function during the work stoppage, and the company must be protected from strike sabotage.

Management should also be aware of picketing procedures. The union hopes to shut down the company during a strike, so it may place members at plant entrances to advertise the dispute and discourage persons from entering or leaving the buildings. Peaceful persuasion through the formation of a picket line is legal, but violence is not. Picketing may also take place, without a strike, to publicize union viewpoints about an employer.

Another type of union pressure is the **boycott**. In a primary boycott, union members do not patronize the boycotted firm. A secondary boycott occurs when a supplier of a boycotted firm is threatened with a union strike unless it stops doing business with the boycotted company. A special type of boycott is the **hot-cargo agreement**. Under this agreement, the

Strikes

STRIKE
A union weapon used to get management to make concessions. It involves withholding employee services from the employer.

On the Job Revisited

BOYCOTT
A bargaining tactic whereby the union attempts to get people or other organizations to refuse to deal with the employer.

HOT-CARGO AGREEMENT
Agreement between management and union that workers may avoid working with materials that come from employers that have been struck by a union; a form of boycott; illegal except in the clothing and construction industries.

employer permits union members to avoid working with materials that come from employers who have been struck by a union. This type of boycott is illegal except in the construction and clothing industries.

Management's response to these union pressures may be to continue operations with a skeleton crew of managerial personnel, to shut down the plant, or to lock the employees out. The **lockout** is an effort to force the union to stop harassing the employer or to accept the conditions set by management. Lockouts are also used to prevent union work slowdowns, damage to property, or violence related to a labor dispute. Many states allow locked-out employees to draw unemployment benefits, thereby weakening the lockout. In practice, the lockout is more of a threat than a widely practiced weapon of management.

Occasionally, disputes between union and management become serious but do not reach the strike or lockout stages. Often a third party becomes involved. The third party may be a fact-finding group appointed by the government or the two parties, a mediator, an arbitrator, or a mediator-arbitrator. A fact-finding group investigates the issues and makes a public report. The public declaration often causes the parties to become less antagonistic or extreme.

A **mediator** tries to get the two parties to reason and works at improving the communication between the parties. The mediator does not make a decision but attempts to stimulate the parties to reach an agreement. Most mediators are supplied by state and federal governments, but any mediator must be accepted by both union and management.

An **arbitrator** is a third party who collects information, listens to the positions taken, and makes a binding decision. Union and management must comply with the decision. Most labor contracts provide for use of an arbitrator in grievance procedures, as shown in Exhibit 10–9.

When a mediator-arbitrator enters the situation, both parties know the mediator-arbitrator will make a ruling if they do not reach a solution. Recently, in the baseball strike of 1981 and nursing strikes in Chicago, Trenton, and Boston, mediator-arbitrators were used. In these situations, the mediator was able to get the parties in the disputes to reach an agreement.[7]

National Emergencies

If a strike or lockout is widespread or occurs in a crucial industry, it could pose a threat to the nation's economy and security. For example, if the airline, trucking, or rail industries were shut down for a sufficient time, such vital services as food distribution, the movement of medical supplies, or the delivery of military repair parts could be threatened.

The president of the United States can take action that resolves such strikes and lockouts. The Railway/Labor Act and the Taft-Hartley Act provide the mechanisms that are employed in national emergency situations. For example, if there is no contract agreement and a strike or lockout could threaten the nation's welfare or security, the president can (1) direct the attorney general to obtain a court order (an injunction) preventing the strike or lockout for eighty days; (2) appoint a board of inquiry to study the impasse and make recommendations; and (3) order the Federal and Conciliation Service (FCS) to attempt to mediate the dispute. The FCS is a

LOCKOUT
Management pressure tactic that involves denying employees access to their jobs.

MEDIATOR
Third party to a labor dispute, who tries to get union and management to reason and works at improving communication between them.

ARBITRATOR
Third party to a labor dispute who makes the final binding decision about some disputed issue.

division of the Department of Labor that provides mediation and conciliation services when an impasse exists in contract negotiations.

If the impasse is still not settled by the sixtieth day, the inquiry board is
reconvened. After the board reports the employer's final offer, the National
Labor Relations Board conducts a secret ballot election among the employees. If the employees vote not to accept the offer, the attorney general
must ask the federal court to dissolve the injunction The union has a legal
right to strike after this eighty-day "cooling-off" period.

The national emergency provisions have been used, on the average,
about once a year in the past ten years. The most recent use of them was by
President Carter in the coal miners' strike of 1977–1978. However, after only
ten days (not eighty), the judge ruled that the attorney general had not
been able to prove that the strike posed a threat to the nation's economy.[8]

SUMMARY

- Unions have existed in the United States since the colonial era. Today most members are in unions affiliated with the AFL-CIO.
- Unions attract employees because of security, social opportunities, communication links to management, and compensation advantages.
- To attract members, unions have focused their attention on unemployment, equal rights, and quality of life.
- Today, in a workforce of about 102 million, 21 million workers belong to unions. The largest union, with about 1.9 million members, is the Teamsters.
- Some people resist unionization because they resent the unions' position in favor of collectivism instead of individualism; some people consider unions too blue collar–oriented.
- Unions are structured on a national and a local level. At the local level, business representatives, like a president, are in charge of activities.
- The Norris-La Guardia Act of 1932 limited the powers of federal courts to stop union picketing, boycotts, and strikes.
- The Wagner Act of 1935 was passed to encourage the growth of trade unions and to restrain management from interfering with this growth.
- The Taft-Hartley Act forbids unfair union practices.
- The Landrum-Griffin Act of 1959 was designed to regulate the internal affairs of unions.
- Collective bargaining is a process by which the representatives of the business firm and the union meet and attempt to work out a contract. The contract designates the formal terms of agreement and usually covers responsibilities of the parties, rates of pay, hours of work, vacations, arbitration, and grievance procedures.
- A grievance is a complaint about a job made by a worker.
- A strike is an effort by employees to withhold services so that the employer will make greater concessions at the bargaining table.

ISSUES TO CONSIDER AND ANALYZE

1. What are the main objectives of the major labor laws that influence labor union and management relations?
2. What will unions have to do to increase their membership in the mid and late 1980s?

3. Do you believe that unions have too much power? Explain.
4. It has been claimed that union and management representatives at collective bargaining sessions must be actors who put on a performance. What does this mean?
5. Why is the prenegotiation phase of the collective bargaining so important?
6. Interview a professional (doctor, lawyer, accountant, engineer) and ask about his or her impressions of unions.
7. How does public sentiment influence union–management relations?
8. What does a union officer like Tony Olympia need to consider before encouraging members to go out on strike?
9. What is the difference between a strike and a secondary boycott?
10. Why is the work of the mediator-arbitrator called "mediation with muscle"?

CASE FOR ANALYSIS   **THE UNITED AUTO WORKERS UNION ATTEMPTS TO ORGANIZE A PLANT IN THE SOUTH**

They made a Hollywood movie about Norma Rae, who battled to bring the union into a textile plant. On the other side of the fence are workers who battle to keep unions out. Rusty Jones is such an employee from Decatur, Alabama. He didn't want the General Motors Saginaw Steering Gear Divisions organized by the United Auto Workers (UAW). GM Decatur is a five-year-old facility that employs 1500 workers, with 2500 more jobs in prospect when a new building opens soon.

The UAW had just won much-publicized elections at GM plants in Louisiana and Oklahoma. The move to organize GM Decatur started when some workers began sporting T-shirts and caps with UAW insignia. Jones decided to join with other antiunionists and meet the T-shirt and caps gimmick with a keep-the-union-out T-shirt and cap campaign.

Jones believes that the UAW's organizing interests lie primarily in collecting more dues. He states that employees already receive good wages and all the medical and insurance fringes offered to union workers. He doesn't see anything that the union can offer.

The first election at the plant resulted in a 714 to 667 union loss. Quickly the UAW charged unlawful antiunion practices to the National Labor Relations Board. After a hearing, a second election was held. The UAW lost the second vote by a close 690 to 675 margin. Again charges about the antiunion campaign were filed. Now a third election is going to be run.

The Jones forces versus the UAW forces are out beating the bushes seeking support for their positions. A Jones supporter states, "Unions are just out for themselves today, and they're damaging the country. Hell, they've helped price the American auto industry out of the market." On the other side, the union is encouraged by the second election tally. A leader stated, "When we come within fifteen votes of winning an election

Adapted from Jeff Blyskal, "Beating the UAW—Three Times," *Forbes*, March 2, 1981, pp. 37–38.

here in the South, . . . we've got everything in our favor." The union also feels that, when workers start to get laid off, they'll be crying for a union.

Rusty Jones still feels that the union is not needed. He believes that no money can buy the workers at GM Decatur. The smooth union organizers, according to Jones, ". . . thought they were dealing with a bunch of rednecks who would just fall in line and join." They learned that Decatur wasn't like union country up North and out East.

QUESTIONS

1. What did Rusty Jones mean when he stated that all the union was interested in was collecting more dues?
2. Even though the union lost the second election, the leadership seemed optimistic. Why?
3. Is Rusty Jones a hard-core union buster? Explain.

CHAPTER 11

PRODUCTION MANAGEMENT

LEARNING OBJECTIVES

After studying this chapter, you should be able to:

Discuss the meaning of inputs, processes, and outputs in the production process.

Explain why technology is important to production.

Illustrate how the production department relates to other departments in organizations.

Explain the importance of planning, layout, and control to the production process.

Illustrate the major activities of production control.

Discuss the purpose of quality control.

Identify the relationship between production and the environment.

KEY TERMS

Production
Production management
Technology
Materials requirement
  planning (MRP)
Plant layout
Process layout
Product layout
Fixed-position
  layout
Production control
Aggregate production
  planning
Production schedule
Inventory control
Quality control

ROBOTS DON'T NEED COFFEE BREAKS

Chico Samoff is a production supervisor for a company that builds control valves and pumps for the chemical industry. The company—New England Controls, Inc.—has put together a management construction committee responsible for bringing their new plant on line. The availability and quality of a labor force to operate two production shifts in the modern plant is one of the committee's major concerns.

On the day shift, Samoff wants to use sixty people to operate and perform routine maintenance in the plant. He favors using three people on the second shift, along with some computerized robots. Equipped with computer brains and armlike projections and grippers, the robots can perform many tasks normally done by people. Samoff says these robots can play a big role in boosting New England Controls' productivity because they can do 90 percent of the new plant's jobs. Besides, Samoff says, "Robots don't ask for coffee breaks."

There are two other important reasons for using the robots. First, the robots will do jobs people do not like to do. For example, 90 percent of the routine welding can be done by robots. Second, there will be no trouble with the labor union because the robots will be used on a late night shift. Most of New England Controls' employees do not want to work at that time. Even though buying the robots will be expensive, most committee members agree with Samoff's views about using them in the new plant.

Having an adequate labor force and developing a productive plant layout are important management considerations anytime a new plant is built. These and other factors, such as technology, production planning, and control, are among the most important production management decisions any business makes.

The goods and services in our economy are created through production. **Production** is the process of changing inputs into goods and services that people and organizations want or need. At New England Controls, Inc., Chico Samoff supervises the production of chemical pumps and control valves.

Each day we consume goods and services labeled "made in U.S.A." that have been produced by one or more production systems. Production plays such an important part in our lifestyle that it would be difficult to over-emphasize its role in America's economy. The significance of production can be shown by looking at two important natural resources—crude oil and natural gas. These two natural resources provide the petrochemicals that serve as building blocks for hundreds of goods we all use. For example, they are the source of nearly 50 percent of our fertilizers, over 50 percent of our fibers, 80 percent of our rubber, and 100 percent of our plastics. Exhibit 11-1 shows the link between these two natural resources, production, and our quality of life.

For years, people assumed that many resources like natural gas and oil could be found in limitless supply. Now we know that the supply is not limitless and that all resources must be used carefully and efficiently. Production management plays a major role in helping us use our resources efficiently. **Production management** includes the activities concerned with the efficient use of economic resources and their conversion into finished goods and services.

The basics of the production process, using the important product of iron and steel as an example, are presented in Exhibit 11-2. These two major products of such companies as U.S. Steel, Republic Steel, and Jones and Laughlin are used as inputs for many products made by other businesses. Iron and steel are used in producing railroads, bridges, buildings, barns,

PRODUCTION
Process of changing inputs into goods and services that people want.

PRODUCTION MANAGEMENT
Activities concerned with the efficient use of economic resources and their conversion into finished goods and services.

THE BASICS OF PRODUCTION

Natural Resource	Petrochemical Form	Product	Area of Life Affected
Natural gas	Propane	Wire coating	Communication
		Recording tapes	Entertainment
		Aspirin	Health
		TV cabinets	Entertainment
	Ethane	Auto parts	Transportation
		Golf ball covers	Recreation
		Carpets	Housing
	Methane	Tires	Transportation
		Anesthetics	Health
		Dresses	Clothing
	Butane	Toys	Recreation
		Coats	Clothing
		Paints	Housing
		Fertilizers	Food
		Phonograph records	Entertainment
	Benzene	Adhesives	Construction
		Furniture	Housing
Crude oil		Printing ink	Education
	Xylene	Insecticides	Food

EXHIBIT 11-1
The Link between Resource, Production, and Quality of Life

EXHIBIT 11-2
Steelmaking: From Inputs
to Finished Products

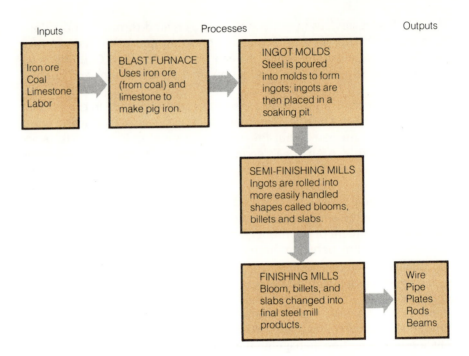

Inputs — Processes — Outputs

Iron ore
Coal
Limestone
Labor

BLAST FURNACE
Uses iron ore
(from coal) and
limestone to
make pig iron.

INGOT MOLDS
Steel is poured
into molds to form
ingots; ingots are
then placed in a
soaking pit.

SEMI-FINISHING MILLS
Ingots are rolled into
more easily handled
shapes called blooms,
billets and slabs.

FINISHING MILLS
Bloom, billets, and
slabs changed into
final steel mill
products.

Wire
Pipe
Plates
Rods
Beams

hardware, nails, furniture, tin cans, refrigerators, and tractors. The Boeing 767s pictured in Exhibit 11–3 use the output of steel mills as well as rubber, plastics, and other materials.

After a product is produced, it is checked to make sure quality standards have been met. After finished goods (output) pass a final quality inspection, some are shipped immediately to consumers. Those that are not shipped immediately are stored in inventory. In either case, finished products become available so that the marketing function can be carried out.

Some production processes follow the same flow shown in Exhibit 11–2 but do not produce a physical good. For example, when a tired traveler checks into a motel to rest for the night, the motel performs a service by providing a comfortable place for the traveler to sleep. Fire departments produce services when they put out fires in a home. Producing services, like producing physical goods, requires inputs, conversion processes, and quality inspections. But services are intangible and cannot be placed in inventory. Examples of selected services produced by different organizations are shown in Exhibit 11–4. It is important to realize that the service production processes noted in Exhibit 11–4 contain only some of the most essential production inputs. The list of inputs is incomplete without many other managerial and economic resource inputs.

TECHNOLOGY AND PRODUCTION

TECHNOLOGY
New ideas and inventions and their
application to increase America's
production and productivity.

New technology is important both for improving the efficiency of production and for providing new products. **Technology** comprises the new ideas and inventions that may be used to increase America's production efficiency and productivity. There is often a long lag from the time a technology is discovered until its actual application. For example, the technology for shale-oil extraction has been well known for some time,

EXHIBIT 11-3
The Final Steps in Production

EXHIBIT 11-4
Services Produced in Business
Organizations

ORGANIZATION	BASIC INPUTS	CONVERSION PROCESS	OUTPUT
Motel	Tired people, comfortable beds, hot water, quiet rooms, food	An environment and sufficient time for people to use the physical facilities	Rested and relaxed people
University	High school graduates, teachers, classrooms, laboratories, textbooks, library	Providing information, knowledge, and skills to people	Educated and trained people
Hospital	Patients, physicians, nurses, medicine, special equipment, housekeeping supplies	Delivering health care to people	Healthy people
Fire department	Fire fighters, trucks, ladders, hose, axes, water, ropes, saws	Putting out a burning fire that is a threat or is damaging property and life	Extinguished fire
Restaurant	Food, waitresses, chef, hungry customers, physical environment	Well-prepared and nicely served food in an enjoyable environment	Pleased customers

Many airline passengers in the United States are saying hello to lasagne and fettuccine and goodbye to meat and potatoes thanks to Marcella Vitaline Aitken. In 1977 Aitken sold Eastern Airlines on the idea of serving pasta prepared according to her own special recipes to their customers. Eastern Airlines now purchases over 150,000 in-flight meals per month. Since starting the business, Aitken has signed many other companies including Western Airlines and Ozark Airlines. She estimates that her business soon will be serving over 25,000 in-flight meals per day.

To accomplish this production feat, Aitken's company purchased a $55,000 Italian pasta-making machine. The machine mixes the ingredients, kneads the dough, and is capable of producing everything from fettuccine to macaroni. But that's not all. The machine also cooks the pasta, stuffs it with meat or cheese, and cuts the food into individual servings. This new machine doubles production capacity while reducing labor costs by more than 60 percent. High productivity rates and strict cost controls have been the keys to Aitken's success in building pasta making into a very profitable $6 million business.

Adapted from Susie G. Nazem, ''Mamma Marcella Takes to the Air with Pasta Power,'' *Fortune*, August 27, 1979, p. 118.

but cheaper sources of crude oil were readily available. With the rapid increase in crude oil prices, the application of shale-oil technology in western states became economically feasible.

Modern technology gives us new production methods and products that improve our standard of living. Automobiles, television, microwave ovens, neurosurgical equipment, and abundant food supplies are the direct result of modern technology. The monorail used to move people from exhibit to exhibit in Disneyland is one example of applying technology to transportation. Technologies for the 1980s seem to be even more promising. Examples include computers operating on light instead of electricity, ceramics replacing steel, and scopes that permit doctors to watch human brains in the process of thinking. Exhibit 11-5 summarizes some of the important new technologies and how they may affect our way of life in the 1980s. For example, imagine robots doing much of routine production work, freeing people to do more creative work! This is one reason Chico Samoff wanted to use robots in the new plant being built by New England Controls, Inc. Even if new technology does improve the efficiency of production processes, production departments will continue to work with people in other departments of a business.

PRODUCTION AND THE BUSINESS ORGANIZATION

When producing goods and services, the production department becomes involved with almost every other department in an organization—some departments more than others. For example, the marketing department influences production decisions at General Mills by providing estimates of how much Wheaties or Cheerios is likely to be sold. Information about new product ideas, customer quality requirements, customer evaluation of existing products, and new orders also are channeled through marketing to the production department.

The purchasing department is closely involved with all production decisions because purchasing buys the inputs needed to produce goods and services. For example, the purchasing department at Ford Motor Company buys the steel and plastic used in autos. In a service organization such as a police department, purchasing is responsible for acquiring the inputs needed to provide the service of public protection. Purchasing also helps to determine what specific items need to be purchased to meet engineering specifications, when they are to be delivered, and how the organization's raw-material inventory is to be managed. In addition, the purchasing department is a good source of ideas for locating lower cost suppliers of materials used in the production process.

Production managers must operate efficiently if the firm is to succeed. To be efficient, managers like Chico Samoff must pay attention to the cost of input materials, the cost of labor, and the cost of maintaining the physical plant. The accounting department, by keeping accurate records, helps to monitor and control the cost of producing goods and services. For example, the production department at U.S. Steel Co. is concerned about the costs of producing a ton of rolled steel. Likewise, Massachusetts General Hospital administrators must have a good estimate of what it costs to use an operating room for different types of medical operations.

Production, like other important business functions, employs people. The personnel department helps by providing a flow of qualified people to operate the production process. A personnel department typically recruits people, trains new employees in certain aspects of the business, handles labor relations, and institutes safety programs that help avoid production accidents.

PRODUCTION AREA	NEW TECHNOLOGY	APPLICATION
Electronics	Optical computers	Replace electronic computers
Knowledge engineering	Artificial intelligence	Robots doing basic production work
Materials	High-performance ceramics	Replace many metals in auto and jet engines
Surface science	Catalytic reaction	Reduce corrosion in steel parts and save energy on moving parts
Biotechnology	Genetic engineering	Improve food production, human health, and medical science

Source: "Technologies for the '80s," Business Week, July 6, 1981, pp. 48–56.

EXHIBIT 11–5
Significant New Technologies

CUMMINS BETS A BILLION

For decades, Cummins Engine Company has been the leading builder of diesel engines that power those eighteen-wheelers roaring down American highways. Today, Cummins sells almost 50 percent of the engines that power America's heavy-duty trucks. This represents more than twice the sales of its closest competitor.

With a sales record like this, it would be easy to get comfortable with your market lead. But Cummins is not taking it easy. Executives believe the future of truck engines will be for smaller, shorter-haul trucks, and the diesel engine is a natural for this market.

In the next few years, Cummins Engine Company plans to spend more than $1 billion to expand its plants and seek new engine markets. Over $500 million of this needed expansion will come from profits and the remainder from bank loans.

There is no guarantee Cummins will be right with its plan. But, if it is, the company will become stronger, bigger, and more profitable. It will pull well ahead of its competitors and dominate the diesel engine market. In a sense, you can say that Cummins executives are betting the future of the company in the amount of $1 billion. Certainly this is a bet where the stakes are high!

Adapted from *The Wall Street Journal*, July 31, 1981, p. 21.

The production department is dependent on many other departments in a business, including industrial engineering, finance, and research and development. The important point is that production must receive information and assistance from within and outside the organization to function properly.

MANAGING THE PRODUCTION PROCESS

We have seen that production is a complex process requiring almost daily direct contact with the other departments of an organization. Thus production management, managing raw materials and their conversion into finished products, is no simple matter.

Production management involves three essential activities. Planning the production process is the first of the activities. Here, decisions are made about the nature of the product to be produced; the location of the plant; and the method of assembling the raw materials, labor, and warehouses needed to produce a product.

Second, decisions are made about how the production process is to be laid out. Layout decisions involve the design and installation of the plant and machines required to do the best job in the production process. During layout, the flow of work through the production process is also decided. These are decisions that Cummins Engine Company has to make as its plant is expanded.

The third production management activity is controlling and operating the production process. Here the goal is to make sure that the production process runs smoothly. Important production control decisions include production scheduling and inventory control.

A major part of production planning is determining exactly what to produce, when to schedule a production run, what inputs to buy, and how to control material and labor costs. These are joint decisions, usually shared by several departments, including production, marketing, and finance, Computer technology can be applied to production planning decisions in the form of **materials requirements planning (MRP)**. MRP is a computer-based method that develops schedules for the inputs needed to produce a product, the amounts of inputs needed, and the dates when orders for inputs should be placed. The logic of MRP is to balance the quantity of inputs purchased with the demand for the final product.

Two major responsibilities of the production department in new product decisions are (1) to convert new product ideas into actual products and (2) to build the plants needed to make the product. New product planning, which is essentially a marketing department responsibility, is explored in more detail later in this book.

Providing the plant for new production can involve several basic alternative decisions. First, the business may continue to produce in the present plant and subcontract to fill new product orders. Second, the present plant can be expanded, if possible, to accommodate the new product. Third, the present plant can be kept and a new plant built in addition. Fourth, the present plant can be sold and the entire production relocated to a new site.

If a new plant is to be built, several factors must be considered in selecting the plant location. For example:

- *Location of markets.* Where are the people who will buy the goods produced in the new plant? If transportation costs for moving the product to the market are high, then locating the plant near markets is advisable. Some businesses, such as dairies, bakeries, and produce stores, locate near markets because their finished products will spoil quickly. Finished products that are bulky, heavy, or fragile are normally produced close to their markets. Local beverage bottling plants like those for Coca-Cola and Pepsi-Cola are examples of this type of product.
- *Location of supplies.* Where will the inputs for the production process come from? Seafood canning companies locate near the source of fish because fish are perishable. Auto assembly plants often are located in regions that produce many of the component parts of an auto. For example, the Ford Motor Company plant in South Chicago is close to U.S. Steel and Republic Steel plants. This helps keep transportation costs down and ensures a steady supply of component parts.
- *Transportation facilities.* Fortunately, transportation is available throughout most of the United States. Transportation plays a signifiant role in the selection of a specific plant location. For example, businesses that ship fresh flowers from Hawaii must be located near air freight handlers and an airport.
- *Availability of labor.* Where will workers come from? In addition, the levels of skill and education, productivity, the extent of unionization, and the cost of living for workers must be determined. In some in-

Production Planning

MRP
A computer-based method that develops schedules for the inputs needed to produce a product, the amounts of inputs needed, and the dates when orders for inputs should be placed.

stances, an adequate labor force is not available when a decision is made to locate a plant in a specific place. Jones and Laughlin Steel faced this problem when it built a new steelmill in Hennepin, Illinois, a town of about 500 people. But because well-paying jobs were available, workers were willing to move to the new plant site. Many furniture plants moved into the South because of the availability of large numbers of semiskilled laborers and lower wage rates. These were important considerations in making the furniture industry profitable. Having an adequate labor force was important to Chico Samoff. He felt the use of robots in the late night shift was one way to get a qualified labor force that would help make the new plant profitable and productive.

On the Job Revisited

- *Living conditions.* The climate must be agreeable enough so that workers are willing to remain in the location. This factor has contributed to the rapid growth of new plant locations in the West, Southwest, and Southeast. In addition to climate, the overall living conditions of a community are important. Some factors normally considered include fire and police protection, traffic problems, schools, parks and public recreation, cultural activities, and the attitude of the community toward the new plant.

Choosing a plant location is difficult because so many factors—economic, social, and political—must be evaluated carefully. A business seldom finds the ideal plant location. Managers must weigh all the positive and negative factors and make the best decision possible.

Plant Layout

PLANT LAYOUT
Process of arranging machines, determining where people will work, and arranging service facilities so that a plant may produce products.

A most important part of managing the production process is laying out the plant. **Plant layout** decisions include machine arrangement, deciding where people will work, and the location of service/maintenance facilities. The primary objective of any plant layout decision is to arrange all the elements to make the plant productive by getting the greatest possible production at the lowest cost.

To get a high rate of production, managers must achieve several specific objectives. For example, in the dairy industry, materials-handling machines are used to move the milk from the cow to the consumer without human hands touching the milk. It is not always possible to achieve all the objectives shown in Exhibit 11-6. Production managers frequently have to make do with a limited quantity of machines, buildings, materials, and employees.

EXHIBIT 11-6
Plant Layout Objectives

SPECIFIC OBJECTIVE	MANAGEMENT GOAL
Minimize materials handling	To reduce the cost of moving materials through the plant
Reduce hazards that affect employees	To make the plant safer for workers
Balance the production process	To avoid bottlenecks in production
Reduce machine interference	To cut noise, heat, fumes, and other factors that interfere with employees
Increase employee morale	To make the job more enjoyable
Use space effectively	To get the most return from the space available for production
Use labor effectively	To keep the employees doing productive jobs with little idle time

There are three important and useful types of plant layout. The **process layout** is used for products that can be made in a series of separate steps. Examples of such products include custom-made furniture, machine tools, and prefabricated buildings. A major advantage of the process layout is flexibility, but the process is not designed for a high volume of output.

The **product layout** is used for products that are produced in large volumes or made in a continuous process. A refinery is an example of a product-layout plant. Products of this type include gasoline, chemicals, and paper. A disadvantage of the product layout is that the line can often be shut down if only one machine breaks down.

A third layout, the **fixed-position layout**, is less common because all the production materials must be brought to one place (see Exhibit 11–3). Aircraft carriers, supertankers, dams, and office buildings are made in a fixed-position layout. An important advantage of this method is that highly skilled workers can complete large parts of the project. For example, when building nuclear aircraft carriers in the Newport News, Virginia, shipyards, one group of workers comes to the construction site and is able to install the ship's total power plant.

An ideal plant layout for producing all products does not exist. Production managers must consider several factors in deciding on a specific layout for a product. The object is to make plant layout as manageable and productive as possible. Major factors that must be considered in the decision are the types of material used, the types and skills of people employed, the location and types of necessary production machines, and the nature of support services.

The major activities that are part of **production control** are aggregate production planning, production scheduling, and inventory control. Production control activities normally are used to support the actual production process, which means production control is usually a staff function.

Aggregate production planning involves planning for a specific time period, say, six months to one year. General plans are developed for the business's total production requirements, as opposed to day-to-day plans. The basic objective of aggregate production planning is to choose a combination of plant, employees, and materials that can best produce the needed goods and services. Airlines such as United, Continental, Pan Am, and Delta continuously engage in aggregate planning to accommodate peak business seasons like Christmas. Without making sure equipment and employees are available, they would have no practical way to meet the demands of Christmas travel.

A **production schedule** is a timetable for doing certain jobs and using specific materials and machines. A production schedule puts the aggregate production plan to work by detailing the exact workload for a specific week. Therefore, a production schedule represents the implementation stage of the production management process. The schedule is very important to all businesses that produce complex products, such as computers, automobiles, and medical equipment. For example, producing Honeywell computers requires that hundreds of circuits, switches, and

---

PROCESS LAYOUT
Plant layout used for products that can be made in a series of separate steps.

PRODUCT LAYOUT
Plant layout used for products that are produced in large volumes or made in a continuous process.

FIXED-POSITION LAYOUT
Plant layout that requires all the production materials to be brought to one location.

Production Control

PRODUCTION CONTROL
Activities that support the production process through aggregate production planning, production scheduling, and inventory control.

AGGREGATE PRODUCTION PLANNING
Planning by business to determine total production requirements for a specific time period.

PRODUCTION SCHEDULE
A production timetable for doing certain jobs and using specific materials and machines.

component parts be available at the right time. An accurate production schedule helps managers determine what parts are needed at different stages of assembly and to plan to have the needed parts in the proper quantity at the proper time.

Investment in inventories, even with good production planning and scheduling, represents a lot of money. Some inventories, particularly those of large firms, involve millions of dollars. Therefore, the proper inventory control results in large dollar savings. **Inventory control** is based on the idea of having adequate supplies of materials available to meet production requirements while minimizing the financial costs of stocking the inventory. Without adequate inventories on hand, goods cannot be produced. Lost production means orders cannot be filled, and customers can be lost. Being able to meet delivery dates is an important consideration to a firm's customers. Carrying an adequate inventory can be expensive because money tied up in an inventory cannot be used for other purposes. Carrying an inventory also means the business will incur additional warehouse expenses, insurance costs, and taxes. All of these expenses are called the *inventory carrying cost* because they are related to goods carried in inventory.

INVENTORY CONTROL
Maintaining adequate supplies for production while keeping the costs of carrying inventory down.

Quality Control

Even with good production management, some finished products will not be produced satisfactorily. This may result from normal human error, machine problems, or poor-quality raw materials. Because of possible production mistakes, the quality of the finished product must be frequently checked. Inspection must be an important part of the production process. Poor-quality parts will be found earlier in the process, thus saving the cost of expensive repairs. Good inspection raises the final quality level and saves the firm money.

Many companies take pride in producing a quality product. For example, the Zenith Radio Corporation used the slogan "The quality goes in before the name goes on" in national advertising campaigns. Ford Motor Company stresses the same idea with the phrase "Quality is Job #1" in their national advertising campaign. **Quality control** is the attempt to assure both management and the company's customers that its products have been designed, produced, and marketed to meet high standards. In this broad perspective, quality control requires information from the engineering, production, and marketing departments. In our discussion, quality control will be restricted to production.

QUALITY CONTROL
Process by which business assures both management and customers that its products have been designed, produced, and marketed to meet high standards.

In this more narrow context, there are three important reasons for having a quality control program: to check the quality of production inputs, the work in process, and the final output. This helps to ensure the organization's ability to produce a high-quality good or service.

The objective of *input quality control* is to find poor-quality inputs before costly production operations begin. For example, Miller Brewing Company checks the hops, grain, and malt before the brewing process for Lite Beer starts. This helps avoid producing a batch of beer that cannot be sold to consumers because of poor-quality raw materials.

Second, certain standards must be maintained in the production process. For example, General Motors assembly lines that produce J-Cars must use uniform parts that meet certain specified quality standards. *Process quality control* makes sure standards are met in process. Unless the assembly parts fit and work together correctly, the auto production line will shut down. If the doors don't fit the openings in the body or the steering wheel doesn't fit the steering column, General Motors cannot produce J-Cars.

The third major reason for production quality control is to make sure products meet customer specifications. If products do not meet customer needs, orders will be canceled. For example, The Lyon's Paw produces expensive custom-dyed silk flowers for business offices. If the silk dyes do not blend with the office color schemes, then the businesses will not accept the flowers. To be successful, the company must produce custom silk flowers to meet the color specifications. *Output quality control* is the key to ensuring a quality product.

Quality control programs are not restricted to manufactured goods. Services also must meet certain standards. This is the way a service-producing organization makes sure customers are satisfied. A happy customer is more likely to come back. The problems of poor-quality service range from potential customer dissatisfaction to serious financial losses and even customer death.

PRODUCTION AND THE ENVIRONMENT

The pollution problems in our society are caused by all of us because everyone contributes to environmental pollution. Wastes are generated as a by-product of both the production and the consumption of goods and services. Production processes result in liquid wastes, air pollution, solid wastes, and noise pollution.

Business and other organizations, by expanding production capability, have contributed to environmental problems. The problems with wastes and air quality become even more severe when faulty technology is used;

EXHIBIT 11–7
Examples of Quality Control and Consumer Service

SERVICE PROVIDER	INSPECTION AREA	WHAT TO LOOK FOR	PROBLEMS WITH POOR QUALITY
Hospital	Laboratory test	Reading accuracy	Inaccurate medical diagnosis
Insurance company	Claims	Claim accuracy	Financial loss to company, customer complaints
Bank	Checking accounts	Transaction accuracy, overdrawn accounts	Unhappy customers, possible loss to bank on overdrafts
Stockbroker	Buying margin	Adequate cash reserves	Violation of law, customers suffering serious financial losses
Motel	Housekeeping	Cleanliness of facilities	Unhappy customers who will not use the motel again
Restaurant	Food service	Quality of food and method of serving	Customer dissatisfaction, poor restaurant image
Doctor	Medical staff	Accuracy of diagnosis, competitiveness in surgery service	Patient death or injury, malpractice lawsuits, poor physician image

that is, when the machines and equipment are environmentally inefficient. The effort to control automobile emissions is an example of an attempt to control pollution in a product with a technology that is considered faulty by some people.

Some businesses have tried to clean up environmental problems caused by their production process. Instead of responding to laws or governmental regulations, firms such as U.S. Steel have simply taken action. At the U.S. Steel plant in Baytown, Texas, water is recycled within the plant. The water that is processed picks up oil, metal scale, and heat in the steel-making operation, but it can be reused if the pollutants are removed in various filtering and cooling steps. Some chemical businesses, such as Dow Chemical Company and Shell Chemical Company, put back into streams water that is cleaner than when it was removed for production. Even so, environmental controls are part of the production process and will remain so for many years.

An increasing number of companies are adopting policies and programs to protect the environment from the wastes and pollutants given off in the production process. Many of these programs, like the U.S. Steel recycling effort, conserve important and scarce resources. Managers in mature business firms have developed sound attitudes about the production process and its waste pollutants.

SUMMARY

- Economic resources in the form of production inputs are combined by various productive processes to make the output used to satisfy the needs and wants of consumers.
- Technology plays an important role in almost all production processes because new ideas and inventions increase America's productive capacity.
- The production department cannot function alone in a business. It is tied very closely to decisions made in the marketing and finance departments regarding customer wants and company resources.
- The main functions of production management include production planning, production layout, and production control.
- Production control, usually a staff job, supports the production process. Major production control activities include aggregate production planning, production scheduling, and inventory control.
- Quality control is the key to assuring management and consumers that products have been designed, built, and marketed to meet high standards.
- The three primary types of quality control involve checking inputs before they are used, checking products while they are being produced, and inspection of finished products.
- Production has in impact on our environment, and the impact can be either good or bad. Today many businesses, both large and small, are working hard to avoid environmental problems and even to improve the environment by leaving it in better shape than when the business started using it.

1. Refer to Exhibit 11-3. Give some examples of inputs used in the exhibit and explain what is meant by the creation of form utility (refer to Chapter 2 for a review of form utility).
2. Explain how the marketing department influences decisions made in the production department.
3. Which type of plant layout is likely to be used for the following products?
   a. Dining room table
   b. Antibiotics
   c. J-Car
   d. Video tape recorder
   e. Airplane
   f. Unleaded gasoline
4. Explain the difference between aggregate production planning and a production schedule.
5. Explain the purpose of quality control and discuss three forms of quality control.
6. Explain how the inventory control objectives of minimizing dollar inventory investment and striving for economical purchasing are contradictory.
7. The location of markets and the location of supplies are two important considerations in any plant location decision. Indicate which would be more important in locating a plant to produce the following products:
   a. Custom-made cabinets
   b. Lumber
   c. Motels
   d. Concrete drain pipes
   e. Frozen orange juice
   f. Hospitals
8. Select some natural resource or raw material and explain how that material is transformed by production to play an important role in our daily life. Use Exhibit 11-1 as a guide.
9. Purchasing materials used in a production process at the lowest possible cost may be a questionable purchasing policy. Why?
10. If quality control is left to a production worker who is paid on an incentive system based only on quantity produced, the worker is likely to have high standards in judging the production output. True or False? Explain.

CHIPS THAT SEE AND MEASURE

Seeing things more clearly has long been a fascination of people. The telescope, microscope, and television are three examples of people's attempts to see things more clearly.

Adapted from Gene Blyinsky, "And Now, Chips that Can See," *Fortune*, August 10, 1981, p. 161.

Modern technology has provided yet another new way to see things with unheard of clarity. The imager chip made of silicon has astounding visual capabilities. The chip collects light eighty times more efficiently than regular photographic film. In fact, a submarine can take a picture at night of another ship four miles away using only starlight.

The chip can also see and measure with extreme precision. This makes it possible to control production operations more effectively, resulting in more final output. For example, lumber-mill operators have directed the proper cutting of logs into lumber by eye for years. By this method of production control, a 12-inch log sometimes would be cut into a 4-by-4 piece of lumber. Now logs are sized up by imager-chip cameras linked to computers. The end result is more lumber per log using less labor to do the cutting.

The medical equipment industry uses imager chips to measure the plastic barrels of insulin syringes. This product must be made with high precision so that insulin dosages may be properly dispersed. The old approach to quality control was to sample and discard entire batches of syringes when a bad one was found. Now each syringe is checked and the defective ones discarded. This is accomplished because a camera equipped with an imager chip can take 2000 pictures per second.

The future of imager chips production is very bright for the next twenty years. Some people believe that the 1980s will be the decade of solid-state imager chips.

QUESTIONS

1. Explain how imager chips can be used by manufacturing businesses to increase their production efficiency. Give two specific industrial examples.
2. If the 1980s will be influenced by the imager chip, do you think the technology can be used to improve the efficiency of the U.S. Postal Service? Explain or give an example.

CAREERS IN HUMAN RESOURCES AND PRODUCTION MANAGEMENT

PERSONNEL AND LABOR RELATIONS MANAGEMENT

Many personnel opportunities are available to college graduates with proper training and academic preparation. Government agencies, educational institutions, health delivery systems, and businesses need personnel management expertise. In large organizations, the personnel department may employ twenty people. Usually, five units operate in the personnel department: labor relations, recruitment, training, wage and salary, and benefits and services. Exhibit III–A shows some of the job opportunities in personnel and labor relations.

The *labor relations unit* is involved in collective bargaining, arbitration hearings, and handling grievances. Members of this unit must understand the labor–management contract. Thus, they must be familiar with labor legislation, economics, and bargaining strategy and tactics. If you are interested in this line of work, you should take courses in these areas. You may even want to earn an undergraduate or graduate degree with an emphasis on industrial relations or law.

The *recruitment unit* is responsible for attracting people to work in the company. Its members may prepare job descriptions and job specifications, develop and administer

tests, interview applicants, check on people's backgrounds, and submit a pool of qualified applicants to managers seeking new employees. This unit is also involved in helping managers develop and implement appraisal procedures so that employees know how well they are performing. Courses in statistics, industrial psychology, and personnel management should be included in your degree program if you are interested in the recruitment unit.

The *training unit* needs people who understand how to evaluate employees and apply learning theory and the techniques associated with organizational and management development. An undergraduate or graduate degree that permits you to take courses in the behavioral sciences, psychology, research methods, and learning theory is good if you are preparing to seek employment in the training unit.

The *wage and salary unit* plans and administers a wage and salary system. Members of the unit must meet with managers, conduct wage and salary surveys, and understand laws and regulations. Thus, college preparation in survey techniques, labor economics, and labor law is important.

Personnel in the employee *benefits and services unit* handle benefit programs, which include health, life, and disability insurance and pension

plans. They also coordinate such services as the cafeteria, snack bars, health and recreational facilities, and counseling for employees nearing retirement. A background in general management and insurance would provide knowledge that this unit could use.

Personnel workers in government agencies generally do the same kind of work as those in large business firms. But public personnel workers deal with employees whose jobs are governed by civil service regulations. This means that personnel workers in government pay a significant amount of attention to job analysis and the interpretation of competitive examination scores for employment.

Most employers try to fill beginning positions in personnel with college graduates who have the potential to move into high-level management jobs. Some seek graduates who have majored in personnel or labor relations; others prefer a graduate with a general business major. Still other employers believe that a liberal arts education is best for a person interested in personnel work. Most seem to want the person to have at least a college degree.

New personnel employees usually begin working in on-the-job training programs. They are asked to analyze and classify applicants to interview, or employees to counsel on retirement or insurance. After a

PERSONNEL ASSISTANT

- Keeps management abreast of current manpower and turnover statistics for a worldwide company of 4,500 employees;
- Controls paperflow to and from the Personnel Department and the payroll and computer operations;
- Monitors authorizations for personnel changes for 450 Division Headquarters employees, ensuring accuracy and adherence to company policy; and more.

QUALIFICATIONS:

—50 plus wpm typing skills.
—Experience with a computerized personnel records system desirable but not necessary.
—Degree not required.

Brooks, a leader among petroleum industry service companies, offers this career opportunity to an individual familiar with various aspects of the personnel function, some of them being: record keeping, salary policy, statistical reporting, payroll and computer interfacing. This position offers the right person a great deal of visibility and recognition in a progressive organization, as well as competitive starting salary and an excellent benefits program.

EMPLOYMENT MANAGER
Multi-Plant, Growth Oriented Career Opportunity in Recruitment

We are one of the leading apparel companies with an immediate position for the individual with at least 4 years of personnel recruitment and generalist experience. This position will require about 30% travel time throughout the southeast and offers competitive income commensurate with your experience, a generous benefits program and excellent growth potential. Headquarters is in a small mid-South college town.

FOR CONFIDENTIAL ATTENTION, PLEASE SEND YOUR RESUME TO:

LEADER BOX 1810
An Equal Opportunity Employer m/f

DIRECTOR LABOR RELATIONS

A growing, New York based company that is a division of a large FORTUNE 500 company with sales nationwide and overseas needs an individual to fill a new staff position. Candidate must have a college degree and a minimum of 5 years experience in Industrial Relations with emphasis on:

— Labor contract administration and negotiations.
— Preparation of arbitration briefs.
— Representing company in NLRB hearings.
— Preparation and instruction of courses in labor relations and labor law application for Supervisors and Foremen.

Legal training is preferred with an ability to take a strong leadership role at all levels within the organization. Excellent compensation and benefit package. Resume, including salary history, should be submitted in confidence to:

MAST BOX M1011
Equal Opportunity Employer

EXHIBIT III–A
Advertisements for Jobs in Personnel and Labor Relations

training period of six months to two years, the person is given a permanent assignment in one of the units. The career path up the personnel ladder is usually quicker if the individual can communicate effectively. Writing and speaking skills are essential for the trainee and the experienced personnel employee.

The number of workers in personnel and labor relations is expected to grow faster than the average for all occupations through 1990. Management must meet the demands of employees for supportive and effective personnel programs. Recent legislation has also stimulated a greater demand for qualified personnel employees who understand occupational safety and health, equal employment opportunities, and pensions.

JOB OPPORTUNITIES:

Personnel

About 400,000 people are employed in the area of personnel/human resource management. Annual salaries range from $10,000 for clerks to $100,000 for vice presidents in large corporations. Exhibit III–B shows the annual salary ranges in personnel departments in small organizations (those with fewer than 4000 employees). Brief job descrip-

EXHIBIT III–B
Annual Salary Ranges in Small
Personnel Departments (1980)

TITLE	NORMAL SALARY RANGE	MAXIMUM
Top Personnel/Industrial Relations Position	$34,000–42,500	$60,300
Manager of Personnel	26,600–31,000	40,500
Employment and Recruiting Supervisor	21,900–25,000	33,500
Interviewer	16,300–17,800	20,800
Equal Employment Opportunity Specialist	21,300–23,100	29,900
Labor Relations Specialist	29,400–35,000	42,000
Labor Relations Representative	23,100–26,100	28,800
Compensation and Benefits Administrator	24,200–29,000	46,700
Wage and Salary Analyst	18,600–20,000	22,900
Benefits Administrator	16,600–19,200	25,600
Security/Safety Specialist	23,200–26,400	30,700
Training Supervisor Specialist	23,100–26,800	36,888
Personnel Assistant	13,500–15,300	18,500
Plant/Branch Office Personnel/Industrial Relations Manager	26,000–28,200	37,500

Source: 1980 American Society for Personnel Administration, *Hansen Salary Survey of Personnel and Industrial Relations Positions* (1980). Reprinted with permission.

tions of the kind of jobs available in personnel are presented in Exhibit III–C.

The role of personnel/human resource management is increasing in response to legislation, early retirement, and interest in the quality of work life. Opportunities in this area should expand in both private and public business for people with knowledge of government regulations, statistics, and training and development.

For more information on careers and salaries in the personnel and labor relations field, write to

- American Society for Personnel Administration
18 Church Street
Berea, Ohio 44017
- International Personnel Management Association
1313 E. 60th Street
Chicago, Illinois 60637
- Director of Personnel
National Labor Relations Board
1717 Pennsylvania Avenue, N.W.
Washington, D.C. 20570
- American Society for Training and Development
P.O. Box 5307
Madison, Wisconsin 53705

PRODUCTION

In most industrial organizations, the production function requires the largest number of employees. Production involves the management of people and machines, and managerial, supervisoral, quality control,

EXHIBIT III-C   Examples of Personnel Jobs

Top Personnel/Industrial Relations Positions. Title is usually Director, Vice-President, or Department Manager. Has responsibility for all areas and aspects of personnel and industrial relations department; originates, develops, implements, and coordinates policies and programs. Also monitors activities affecting all company operations at all locations. Possible responsibility for community and public relations matters.

Manager of Personnel. Is in charge of daily routines of personnel department, including recruiting and employment, compensation and benefits administration, training, and employee services. May oversee office services encompassing personnel functions.

Employment and Recruiting Supervisor. Responsible for a variety of areas, including recruiting and placement procedures, training programs and tests, attainment of Equal Employment Opportunity (EEO) goals, and terminated employees.

Interviewer. Involved in all phases of screening prospective employees; also processes changes in employee status and conducts exit interviews.

(continued on p. 246)

Equal Employment Opportunity Specialist. Is responsible for the effective and lawful carrying out of the corporate Affirmative Action/Equal Employment Opportunity programs. Conducts internal audits of corporate practices to identify possible violations, and compiles and submits required AAP/EEO statistical reports.

Labor Relations Specialist. Is responsible for good labor–management relations, formulates the company's labor relations policy in accordance with top management's approval. Also represents management in labor relations, including collective bargaining negotiations.

Labor Relations Representative. Participates in and advises management concerning relationships with labor unions representing company employees. Researches and evaluates labor relations trends.

Compensation and Benefits Administrator. Except for top management's programs, is responsible for compensation and benefit programs for all employees. Implements programs to maintain the company's competitive posture while being cost-effective. Advises employees on benefit programs and implements benefit coverage.

Wage and Salary Analyst. Prepares standardized job descriptions; evaluates positions, determines grades, and prepares records of the evaluations. Conducts compensation surveys and participates in compensation surveys conducted by other companies.

Benefits Administrator. Administers benefit programs. Advises employees on eligibility for programs. Maintains benefit records and implements benefit coverage.

Security/Safety Specialist. Assists Personnel Manager in ensuring compliance with OSHA and developing employee safety programs. Trains foreman and worker groups in safety procedures. Records and reports on lost-time accidents. May supervise security guards.

Training Supervisor/Specialist. Is responsible for training and educational programs in connection with management development, on-the-job training, and employee orientation. Records training activities and employee progress and monitors programs' effectiveness. Senior personnel in this position may design and develop in-house programs.

Personnel Assistant. Responsible for wide variety of activities which may include interviewing, wage and salary record keeping, assisting with training, safety, benefits, or other personnel services.

Plant/Branch Office Personnel/Industrial Relations Manager. Responsible for effective administration of personnel programs in one or more domestic plant/branch office facility in accordance with established policies and procedures. Participates in collective bargaining in unionized plants. Also responsible for OSHA compliance and employee safety. Possibly does recruiting and hiring of nonmanagement personnel.

Source: American Society for Personnel Administration, *Hansen Salary Survey of Personnel and Industrial Relations Positions* (1980). Reprinted with permission.

Exhibit III–C, continued

purchasing, and materials management positions are available. An entry-level production job for a college graduate is line supervisor. The line supervisor would supervise people who operate machines and is often responsible for supervising production runs, designing budgets, and motivating subordinates.

A staff production job for a beginner might be assistant quality assurance manager. This job is designed to help prevent product deficiencies and to detect and correct any that are found. The assistant quality assurance manager samples, inspects, and tests products.

The inventory manager's job is to have the right amounts of inventory available when needed. The inventory manager works closely with the purchasing and traffic managers. The purchasing manager is responsible for forecasting supply and price trends, getting the best deal for the firm, and enforcing purchasing policies. The traffic manager deals mainly with securing delivery of purchased materials. He or she routes traffic, traces shipments, secures equipment to ship goods, and works hard to get the most favorable freight rates for the firm.

Overall, career opportunities in production areas are increasing faster than average, according to the Bureau of Labor Statistics. Production positions and some of the career paths are shown in Exhibit III–D.

Job Opportunities: Production

Exhibit III–E presents a few of the job opportunities found in the production area. Overall, career opportunities in production areas are increasing

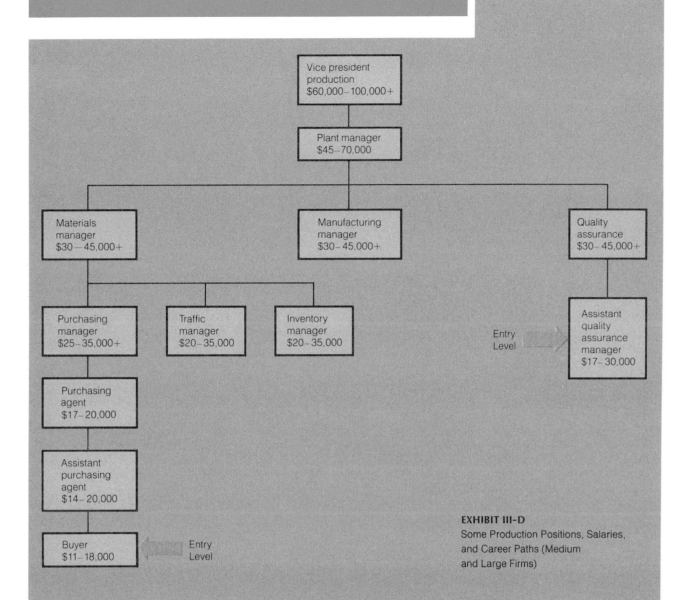

Vice president
production
$60,000–100,000+

Plant manager
$45–70,000

Materials
manager
$30–45,000+

Manufacturing
manager
$30–45,000+

Quality
assurance
$30–45,000+

Purchasing
manager
$25–35,000+

Traffic
manager
$20–35,000

Inventory
manager
$20–35,000

Entry
Level → Assistant
quality
assurance
manager
$17–30,000

Purchasing
agent
$17–20,000

Assistant
purchasing
agent
$14–20,000

Buyer
$11–18,000 ← Entry
Level

EXHIBIT III-D
Some Production Positions, Salaries,
and Career Paths (Medium
and Large Firms)

faster than average. Jobs in purchasing provide numerous opportunities in government agencies, hospitals, educational institutions, and manufacturing firms. Graduates of two-year programs will find most of their opportunities in small firms. Especially high demand is predicted for individuals with technical backgrounds to work in companies that manufacture complex items such as industrial engines and electronics equipment.

Another area in which demand is strong is quality assurance. Consumers want good and safe products. The government insists on safe products. Thus, numerous opportunities exist for inspectors of products (quality assurance experts). Exhibit III–E presents a few of the job opportunities found in the production area.

For additional career information on production opportunities contact:

■ American Production and Inventory Control Society
Suite 504 Watergate Building
2600 Virginia Avenue, N.W.
Washington, D.C. 20037
■ American Society for Quality Control
161 West Wisconsin Avenue
Milwaukee, Wisconsin 53203
■ National Association of Purchasing Management
11 Park Place
New York, New York 10007

PROFILE IN BUSINESS

Kemmons Wilson
(1913-   )

He couldn't find a decent motel between Memphis and Washington—so he built his own.

Charles Kemmons Wilson was nine months old when his father died and his mother moved from Arkansas to Memphis, Tennessee. To support her family, she took jobs as a dental assistant and an auditor's bookkeeper. When Wilson was fourteen, running drugstore deliveries after school, he was struck by a car. One leg was fractured and permanently shortened, forcing him out of school for a year. Later, his mother was hospitalized, and Wilson quit high school to support her.

Determining to start his own business, he bought a secondhand popcorn machine and rented a corner of the local movie house. In six months he was earning more than the theater management, who canceled his lease and sent Wilson on his way with $50 for the popper. That $50 bought five secondhand pinball machines, which Wilson installed in drugstores and restaurants. Profits went into

more machines. When he was twenty years old, Wilson built a house for $1700 and used it as collateral for a $3000 bank loan. Later he sold the house for $6500 and built more. Eventually, his holdings included seven Memphis movie houses, one of which he, his wife, and his mother operated to hold down the payroll. Meanwhile, he had picked up the regional Wurlitzer jukebox distributorship and a small airplane in which he took people for $1 skyrides.

When the United States entered World War II, Wilson sold all his properties for $250,000 and invested in war bonds. While he was stationed at the Memphis Municipal Airport, waiting to go overseas with the Air Transport Command, he built nine two-family houses to rent to servicemen, leaving the project in his mother's hands. In the China-Burma-India theater of operations, he flew C-47 transports over "the Hump," a notorious route across the Himalayas.

Back in Memphis after the war, Wilson lost $100,000 with an Orange Crush distributorship, his only unsuccessful venture. He turned back

PART FOUR

MARKETING

to more familiar enterprises, buying movie theaters in St. Louis and Louisville, building houses and apartments. His involvement in the construction business prompted him to join a lumber and hardware supply firm as vice president.

When he was thirty-eight years old and a prosperous businessman, Kemmons Wilson took his wife and five children in the family station wagon for a trip to Washington, D.C. On route they stayed in motels that grated on Wilson's nerves—dreary, uncomfortable, and overpriced, with no restaurants nearby. He bristled at paying extra for children who had brought their own bedrolls so that all seven Wilsons could share the same room. After the trip, Wilson designed the motel he had been unable to find between Memphis and Washington. It had 120 brightly colored rooms (each with a telephone and air conditioning), a restaurant, a swimming pool, a dog kennel, parking facilities, a babysitting service, and no charge for kids sharing their parents' room. The architects drawing up his plans called the motel Holiday Inn, after a 1942 movie, and the name stuck.

Within two years, by 1953, there were four Holiday Inns on the main routes into Memphis.

With visions of a national chain of Holiday Inns, Wilson approached "the biggest thinking man" he knew—Wallace Johnson, a fellow Memphis builder with national contacts. They incorporated Holiday Inns of America in 1954, with Wilson as chairman of the board, Johnson as president, and Dottie Wilson, Wilson's mother, as vice president. They invited prominent builders from around the country to Memphis and offered them franchises: a $500 fee to build and operate a Holiday Inn according to the plans of the four originals, with supervision and regular inspection by the parent company. Each franchise paid a royalty per room, half of which was put into national promotion.

In 1957, the company went public, issuing 120,000 shares of stock at $9.75. Over the next fifteen years, each of those shares increased to $800. Today over 1500 Holiday Inns have spread through every state and more than twenty-five other countries. The company receives

thousands of requests for new franchises annually, about 200 of which are granted, each for a $15,000 franchise fee and 6 percent royalties on rented rooms.

Kemmons Wilson's influence is still felt at Holiday Inns of America, and the Memphis headquarters supplies and monitors every motel. All managers attend the Holiday Inn University, part of a two-campus complex of corporate offices encompassing a shopping center, banks, restaurants, a theater, a post office, and the offices of a growing family of subsidiaries. The Inn Keepers Supply Company handles purchasing for all Holiday Inns. Holiday Press is one of the largest printing operations in the South. The Institutional Mart of America functions as a national supermarket of goods and services for institutional developers. It grew out of the business of supplying more than a thousand Holiday Inns.

Wilson's prosperity is reflected in his Holiday Inn motto: "It's a wonderful world."

CHAPTER 12

MARKETING: PROCESS, PRODUCT, AND PRICING

LEARNING OBJECTIVES

After studying this chapter, you should be able to:

Explain the meaning of *marketing*.

Discuss the marketing process used in the United States.

Identify the major parts of the marketing mix.

Discuss how a product is part of the marketing mix.

Explain the role of pricing in the marketing mix.

KEY TERMS

Marketing
Utility
Marketing concept
Market
Consumer market
Industrial market
Market segmentation
Marketing mix
Marketing strategy
Product
Convenience goods
Shopping goods
Specialty goods
Product life cycle
Price

CALCARE GOES INDUSTRIAL

Tony Captino was finishing two years of school at Bridgeview Community College. He had taken courses in business, including some in marketing. Tony wanted to start a new division in a very large floor covering store he worked for in Los Angeles. The new division—a professional carpet cleaning service for businesses and homes—would be located in central Los Angeles and called Calcare Carpet Service.

Calcare's service would be high quality, stressing honest pricing, convenience, deep-cleaning action, fast drying time, and guaranteed satisfaction. In fact, Calcare would not leave a job until the customer was completely satisfied. No other carpet cleaning service in Los Angeles offered this guarantee. The idea behind the new division was to produce a carpet service that customers wanted and needed.

Tony planned to concentrate initially on small businesses, with the idea of expanding into the home market. Since Los Angeles is a large city, the total small-business market was too big for Calcare to serve. Tony started by dividing the city into geographic areas and soon realized that some geographic areas contained more small businesses than others. These larger areas offered good sales potential, and Tony selected three such areas as Calcare's target markets. His marketing effort was restricted entirely to these three high-potential areas.

The approach to marketing Tony used was planned out and carefully executed. The importance of this kind of planning will become clear as you read this chapter. We will discuss the marketing process, the nature of a product, and how the market price can be set. We will also look at ways that managers like Tony can divide large markets into smaller and more similar target markets.

Wherever people live, trade develops. Wherever trade develops, people try to figure out what other people want to buy and what they are willing to pay for it. This is what marketing is about. Marketing is part of human nature and an important part of our economy.

Marketing is an important part of the well-being and standard of living in Western industrialized nations. We are all involved in marketing something—a skill, a product, or a service. In addition, many people make a living by becoming directly involved with marketing.

The success of organizations from the size of General Motors to the mom-and-pop grocery store depends to a great extent on marketing. Most people are aware from television that General Motors actively markets its products. But organizations like the small mom-and-pop stores, the Girl Scouts, the American Cancer Society, universities, and political parties also engage in marketing.

With so many organizations marketing, it is easy to see why many definitions of marketing have developed. Some definitions consider only businesses and physical products. But a complete view of marketing is much broader. One broad view defines **marketing** as

> the exchange among individuals and organizations that attempts to satisfy both the needs and wants of people and the organization's marketing objectives.

This broad view of marketing has a focus on organizations—both profit and nonprofit—and on the needs and wants of people. A short list of goods, services, and concepts that are often marketed to meet people's needs and wants appears in Exhibit 12-1. This list gives you an idea of the types of items that are marketed and why there are so many different approaches to marketing.

MARKETING
The exchange among individuals and organizations that attempts to satisfy both the needs and wants of people and the organization's objectives.

CREATING CONSUMER UTILITY

Marketing, like production, has an output that creates utility. **Utility** is the ability of any good or service to satisfy consumer wants or needs. In production, the output is usually tangible; in marketing, the output can be intangible. The utility created by the two processes is different.

Utility can be divided into four major types: form utility, place utility, time utility, and ownership utility. Production creates form utility by converting a raw material into a usable product. For example, refining crude oil into gasoline makes the raw material more useful by changing its form. Oil refineries in New Jersey create form utility. But gasoline has no utility to consumers unless it is available for purchase (ownership utility) where (place utility) and when (time utility) they want it. Marketing makes gasoline available to consumers for purchasing and in the process creates place, time, and ownership utilities. This is the way marketing produces an intangible output of economic value to consumers.

UTILITY
The ability of a product or service to satisfy consumer wants or needs.

THE MARKETING CONCEPT

Even though marketing is the key to creating consumer satisfaction, marketing has not always been a central part of American business. The "era of marketing" started about 1950. Rather than just selling what was produced,

EXHIBIT 12-1
Examples of Goods, Services, and Concepts Marketed in the United States

GOODS	SERVICES	CONCEPTS
Car	Security service	Join the army
Video recorder	Eye examination	Do not shoplift
Fast food	Law enforcement career	Buy union
Baseball ticket	Dental work	Give to the United Fund
Health food	Child care	Do not litter
Rolled steel	Pet grooming	Stop smoking
Firetruck	Typing	Conserve energy

MARKETING CONCEPT
A business philosophy that consumer preferences for goods and services are important in determining what is to be produced.

businesses began trying to find out what consumers wanted to buy. The Pillsbury Company, which sells packaged baking mixes, was the leader in adopting this marketing orientation by trying to satisfy its customers with products they wanted at a reasonable profit. This orientation, called the marketing concept, is now a way of doing business for many organizations. The heart of the **marketing concept** is that consumer preferences for goods and services are important in determining what is to be produced by a business. Tony Captino applied the marketing concept when he started Calcare Carpet Service. He was concerned with producing a carpet service that customers wanted, needed, and would buy.

ELEMENTS OF MARKETING
The Process

Marketing is affected by many factors as goods and services move from producers to consumers. The model in Exhibit 12-2 shows some important factors that affect the flow of products from producers to consumers. These are some of the more important factors that influence marketing.

EXHIBIT 12-2
The Marketing Process

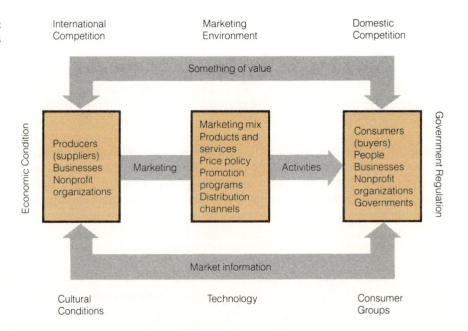

Marketing brings together the two main forces of exchange—producers (suppliers) and consumers (buyers). Notice in Exhibit 12-2 that *consumers* may be individuals, businesses, nonprofit organizations, and governments. This is a broad use of the word *consumer*. The same broad use applies to *producers*, which may include a manfacturer of a good (auto or videodisc), a wholesaler or retailer (grocery supplier or pizza restaurant), a service business (theater or car rental), or a nonprofit organization (transit authority, hospital, university, or opera).

The consumers listed in Exhibit 12-2 represent a market. A **market** is a group of people or organizations that buys a particular good, service, or concept. Markets can be divided into consumer markets (people) and industrial markets. **Consumer markets** consist of people who buy goods and services for their own use, called *consumer goods*. Examples of consumer goods include tape decks, fast foods, cars, and clothes.

In an **industrial market**, goods are sold that are used to produce other products for resale. Rolled steel bought by Ford Motor Company to produce cars is an example of an industrial good. Some goods can be put into either category, depending on how they are used. A microcassette recorder you may use to record a speech is a consumer good. If the same recorder is used by an Aetna Insurance Company agent to record information about a policy claim, then it is an industrial good.

Most markets can be divided into groups of consumers with similar characteristics. Dividing a total market into similar groups is called **market segmentation**. Recall that Tony divided or segmented the Los Angeles area into smaller, similar target markets for professional carpet care service. Almost all consumer and industrial markets can be segmented because it is difficult to produce a product that *all* consumers and businesses like. Some important characteristics that can be used to segment consumer markets are population, income, age, sex, and ethnic background. Exhibit 12-3 shows how the major products bought by people vary with their ages. The different age groups represent target markets for different goods and services. For example, younger adults (20–34 years) are heavy buyers of furniture, cars, clothing, and housing.

In order to "hit" target markets, producers usually develop a marketing mix (see Exhibit 12-2). The **marketing mix** consists of four parts: (1) product, (2) price, (3) promotional activities, and (4) place decisions. These are the aspects required to move a product from producer to consumer.

Marketing a product involves much more than just selling. A business manager makes decisions for each part of the marketing mix to compete for individual consumers. Making these decisions is the core of marketing management. By combining the parts of the marketing mix, managers develop a **marketing strategy**, the blueprint a business uses to compete in its various target markets or market segments. The marketing strategy becomes a guide for combining the parts of the marketing mix in the market.

Determining how to combine these parts requires a knowledge of target markets. The target markets represent marketing opportunities that are best found after careful analysis of the organization's markets. For exam-

Consumer and Industrial Markets

MARKET
A group of people or organizations that buys a particular good, service, or concept.

CONSUMER MARKET
People who buy goods and services for their own use.

INDUSTRIAL MARKET
Market for goods that are used to produce other products for resale.

MARKET SEGMENTATION
The process of dividing a total market into similar groups.

The Marketing Mix

MARKETING MIX
The combination of elements—product, price, promotional activities, and distribution channels—that affect the selling of a product.

MARKETING STRATEGY
The blueprint a business uses to compete in its various target markets or market segments.

EXHIBIT 12-3
Products Purchased by or for
Various Consumer Age Groups

AGE	NAME OF AGE GROUP	MERCHANDISE PURCHASED
0–5	Young children	Baby food, toys, nursery furniture, children's wear
6–19	Schoolchildren (including teenagers)	Clothing, sports equipment, phonograph records, school supplies, food, cosmetics, used cars
20–34	Young adults	Automobiles, furniture, houses, clothing, recreational equipment, purchases for younger age segments
35–40	Younger middle age	Larger homes, bigger autos, second cars, new furniture, recreational equipment
50–64	Empty nest	Recreational items, purchases for young marrieds and infants
65 and over	Retired	Medical services, travel, drugs, purchases for younger groups

Adapted from Louis E. Boone and David L. Kurtz, *Foundations of Marketing* (Hinsdale, Ill.: Dryden Press, 1980), p. 87.

ple, Eastman Kodak conducted a thorough marketing analysis before entering the self-developing camera and film market. Their analysis showed the present status and an estimate of the future status of the market. It is important to look at the future because market conditions always change.

Combining the parts of the marketing mix is a big job, even though the parts of the mix are under the producer's control. Points that must be addressed in developing a marketing strategy are shown in Exhibit 12-4. For example, consider a manager attempting to answer the following questions: What is the exact nature of the product that is to be sold, as seen by possible consumers? What is the price policy? How many dollars should be spent on the program? What channels of distribution will be used? These and similar questions pose major challenges to the skill and creativity of a manager.

All the parts of the marketing model in Exhibit 12-2 that we have considered so far have been under the control of either the producer or consumer. For example, producers determine what price to charge, and consumers decide if the product is worth the price. But a number of factors are beyond the control of producers or consumers. Such factors as competition, government regulation, and technology form what is called the *marketing environment*. These external factors are beyond the total control of an organization or individual, so producers and consumers must adapt to them. One way producers attempt to adapt is through the type of product they offer for sale.

PRODUCTS

PRODUCT
A good or service that satisfies
consumers.

A **product** is any good or service that satisfies a consumer need or want. The product is an important part of a business's marketing mix, so the product and marketing strategy are closely interrelated. Because customers and products vary, a single marketing strategy may not work well for all products. The type of strategy used depends in part on the type of product being marketed.

To make it easier to develop a good marketing strategy, products have been classified in different ways. One way is according to the type of user the product is intended for. As Exhibit 12-5 shows, the two main categories are consumer and industrial users. The carpet cleaning service run by Tony Captino is an example of a service that can be classified as an industrial or consumer service.

Exhibit 12-5 also shows that products can be divided into goods and services, each with its own classification scheme. Consumer goods can be divided into convenience, shopping, and specialty goods. **Convenience goods** are goods often bought with little shopping effort, such as newspapers, chewing gum, cigarettes, soap, and milk. **Shopping goods** are goods for which consumers normally compare price, quality, and style, such as furniture, autos, color televisions, and microwave ovens. Goods with unusual characteristics are called **specialty goods**. These goods, which are usually expensive, include special occasion clothing, fine wines, artwork, and antique furniture.

Industrial goods can also be divided into three different categories—capital, basic, and support goods. *Capital goods* include fixed-plant (machine tools, computers, buildings) and productive equipment (trucks, cars, typewriters, portable drills). These goods are used in manufacturing and never become part of the final product. *Basic goods* enter directly into the production process. Examples include raw materials (coal, lumber), semimanufactured goods (sheet steel, flour sold to bakeries), and component parts (electric motors, original tires). *Support goods* are consumed in the operation of the organization but do not become part of the finished product—for instance, operating supplies (pencils, adding machine tape) and maintenance items (paint, grease, brooms, cleaning materials).

Classifying Products

On the Job Revisited

CONVENIENCE GOODS
Goods bought with little shopping effort.

SHOPPING GOODS
Goods for which consumers normally compare price, quality, and style.

SPECIALTY GOODS
Goods with unusual characteristics that are usually expensive.

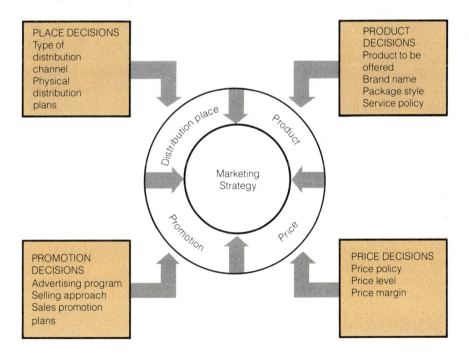

EXHIBIT 12-4
Marketing Strategy and Marketing Mix

PLACE DECISIONS
Type of distribution channel
Physical distribution plans

PRODUCT DECISIONS
Product to be offered
Brand name
Package style
Service policy

Distribution place
Product
Marketing Strategy
Promotion
Price

PROMOTION DECISIONS
Advertising program
Selling approach
Sales promotion plans

PRICE DECISIONS
Price policy
Price level
Price margin

EXHIBIT 12-5
Product Classification Scheme

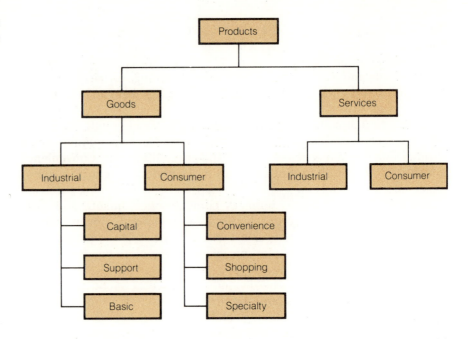

Classifying services is more difficult than classifying goods. Often it is hard to tell a service from a good. For example, are energy sources like electricity and natural gas goods or services? A restaurant is a service even though it serves a product—food. Services need to be classified and understood because service industries now employ over 50 percent of the labor force, and the figure will grow.

One way to classify services is on the basis of the buyer. According to this scheme there are two major classifications: industrial and consumer buyers, as Exhibit 12-5 shows. Consumer services include personal and recreational services (tennis lessons, hairstyling, movies) and household services (electricity, garbage collection, lawn care, insurance, telephone). Industrial services represent a larger variety of services. Industrial users include businesses, governments, farmers, and mines, to name just a few. Some of the services used by industry are transportation, private consulting, employee training programs, and accounting audits.

Product Life Cycle

PRODUCT LIFE CYCLE (PLC)
Evolutionary stages of a product in the marketplace, from introduction to withdrawal.

Products, like people, go through a series of stages that occur no matter how a product is classified. The stages in a product's life, from introduction to its complete withdrawal from the market, is called the **product life cycle** (PLC).

The stages of the PLC are shown in Exhibit 12-6. The PLC stages appear to be divided evenly, but the time a product spends in each stage and the length of the life cycle may vary substantially. For example, the complete PLC for microwave ovens may be twenty to twenty-five years; the PLC for the hula hoop was only about one year. All products go through a complete PLC but at different rates.

The importance of the product life cycle in developing a marketing strategy can be illustrated by considering the black-and-white television

FEDERAL EXPRESS GOES AIR MAIL

Federal Express introduced a new product in 1981—the first privately delivered air mail letter. The product is named the "Overnight Letter," and a two-ounce letter can be delivered overnight in America for $9.50. This head-to-head competition with Uncle Sam was made possible when the Postal Service changed the rules to let private carriers deliver letters if they were "extremely urgent."

With this important rule change now final, Federal Express expects to deliver about 100,000 Overnight Letters a day by 1985. At that time, the company's revenues are projected to be around $2 billion a year.

The Overnight Letter will likely be a very successful new product for Federal Express. The company is the industry's low-cost operator, and its price of $9.50 is the industry's lowest. This means competitors will have a very difficult time matching Federal's price and making a profit. Competitors have a choice: enter the letter business and have a hard time making money or let Federal Express have the business. The second option puts Federal Express in a good position because businesses like to use the same carrier to ship both letters and small packages.

Even with the competitive edge the Overnight Letter gives the company, management is still looking ahead. Federal is trying to get fifteen low-power TV stations to beam private business messages. Management is now preparing for the next revolution—electronic mail.

Adapted from Geoffry Colvin, "Federal Express Dives into Air Mail," *Fortune*, June 15, 1981, pp. 106–108.

set, which is now in the decline stage of its PLC. The pricing, promotion, and distribution efforts required to sell this product today differ significantly from those used when it was introduced in the late 1940s.

INTRODUCTION During the introduction stage of the black-and-white television set, consumers typically knew little about the new product. Sales volume and profits were both low, and profits for some firms were even negative (see Exhibit 12-6). The main objective in this stage was to create demand for the new product called television.

GROWTH The growth stage was characterized by a rapidly rising sales volume due to high product awareness and consumer acceptance. Between 1960 and 1970, everyone was aware of television, and almost every family owned a set. Profits increased rapidly in this stage, and new businesses (domestic and foreign—the Japanese with Panasonic, Sony, etc.) entered the market. Each business tried to create a preference for its brand.

MATURITY During this stage, sales leveled off and started to decline. Intense competition led to lower product prices and a substantial decline in profits. Television set prices dropped from $200 for a 19-inch set in 1965 to prices of $130 in the 1970s. The general nature of the maturity stage of the PLC is "dog-eat-dog," resulting in a decline in the number of pro-

EXHIBIT 12-6
Stage in the Product Life Cycle

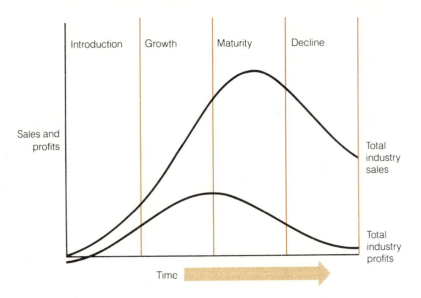

ducers. Only the economically strong producers survive this marketplace *shakeout*. This happened in the pocket calculator market with Casio, Texas Instruments, and Sharp becoming domininant market forces. As the market for personal computers matures, the same situation will develop. In all probability, Apple Computers will be one of the surviving companies.

DECLINE   In the decline stage, sales continue to fall. The decline is due partly to a change in consumer preferences and partly to the increased number of substitute products (color television). There is a continuous flow of new products entering the market, any of which may be a substitute for a product currently in the decline stage of its PLC.

PLC and the Marketing Mix   Knowing a product's position in its PLC can help managers develop marketing plans. For example, as a product reaches the maturity stage, managers must develop ways to deal with price declines and intense competition. Two ways to deal with these market conditions are (1) to concentrate on brand promotion and (2) to make a product different from the competition (for instance, introduce remote control switches for the black-and-white television) in the consumer's mind. Making the product different can be done through improving service policy, adding features to the product, and changing the product's physical design. For example, Casio sells an electronic calculator that lets the user conduct boxing matches between calculations, an added feature.

PRICING   Deciding the price to charge for a product is one of the most important and difficult decisions managers make. To consumers, price is a very visible part of the marketing mix. For example, in early 1982, the new Chrysler Corporation was advertising on television that it was holding the line on some model prices to fight inflation in America, thereby announcing its price to millions of people.

Price is the exchange value of any product to buyers where the exchange value is converted into money. The key to this definition is *exchange value*, which represents what a buyer is willing to pay for a product. Exchange value varies from one buyer to another; it is determined by each individual buyer. The decision to buy or not buy a product proves whether the product's price and its value to a buyer are equal.

There are several reasons why it is not easy to set a product's price. The want-satisfying power of products is different, depending on the individual consumer. The amount of money available to spend varies among consumers. The cost of doing business is not the same for all organizations, and higher costs must be covered by higher prices. Setting a product's price requires managers to strike a balance between price and costs. Therefore, managers use the marketing mix and some pricing objectives to guide their efforts to achieve this balance.

Organizations usually have more than one *pricing objective* that influences a product's price. For example, while trying to maintain high profits in the short run, a business may also seek to build a high-quality, prestige product image. Another organization may not worry about the long run and simply charge what the traffic will bear. For products with a short product life cycle, like a hula hoop, this is a good pricing objective.

There are several types of pricing objectives. As you can see in Exhibit 12-7, making a profit and maintaining the economic growth are two important pricing objectives. But there are many others. As shown in Exhibit 12-8, pricing objectives can generally be put into three broad categories: profit objectives, volume objectives, and status quo objectives.

PROFIT OBJECTIVES   Making a profit is the main idea of capitalism. This makes setting a product's price so that a reasonable profit can be maintained an important objective. This is especially true in today's economy, in which maintaining a reasonable profit margin is often difficult.

Profit is the difference between revenue and cost (profit = revenue − cost). Revenue is the result of multiplying price by the quantity sold (revenue = price × quantity sold). By raising or lowering the price, it is possible to affect the amount of profit earned. This is done through revenue. Raising the price is *not* always profitable. Is it profitable to raise the price by 7 percent only to have the quantity sold fall by 12 percent? The answer is *no*. So in setting the price, managers must be aware of how sensitive the quantity sold is to price increases or decreases.

Some organizations try to make the most profit possible at the expense of all else, including customer loyalty. This objective is called profit maximization. Profit maximization usually requires an organization to give up attracting large numbers of loyal customers, yet loyal customers provide the base for long-run profits. Thus, the profit maximizing pricing objective leaves the door open to stiff competition. Profit maximization, as a pricing objective, is largely restricted to economic theory, but it may be applied in special business situations. For example, a parking lot owner can charge very high prices for parking spaces near a football stadium on the day of a

The Meaning of Price

PRICE
The exchange value of any product to buyers where the exchange value is converted into money.

Pricing Objectives

EXHIBIT 12-7
Selected Pricing Objectives

Get maximum long-run profits
Encourage growth
Get maximum short-run profits
Build traffic
Be regarded as fair by customers
Maintain price-leadership
Create interest and excitement
    about the item

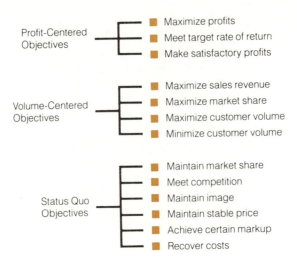

EXHIBIT 12–8
Classification of Pricing Objectives

Profit-Centered Objectives
- Maximize profits
- Meet target rate of return
- Make satisfactory profits

Volume-Centered Objectives
- Maximize sales revenue
- Maximize market share
- Maximize customer volume
- Minimize customer volume

Status Quo Objectives
- Maintain market share
- Meet competition
- Maintain image
- Maintain stable price
- Achieve certain markup
- Recover costs

football game. On other days, the owner may not be able to give parking spaces away.

Many organizations reach for a target rate of return when a product's price is set. A target rate of return may apply to either capital investment or total sales volume. Using this objective, an acceptable rate of return is determined, and a price is set that will likely permit the rate of return to be reached.

The goal of after-tax rates of return can vary substantially among organizations, often ranging from 8 to 20 percent. How realistic these figures are today is questionable. Current business practices indicate that target rates of return on investment are most likely to serve as guides for pricing decisions. The reason is that managers may not attempt to separate pricing decisions from other types of organizational decisions.

"Satisfactory profits," or some "acceptable level" of profit, may be an organization's profit objective. In this case, prices are administratively set after the cost of producing a product is determined. Of course, what is "satisfactory" will change over time. For example, a 6 percent after-tax profit may have been adequate in the mid-1960s. With an inflation rate of 8 to 12 percent, after-tax profits must significantly exeed 12 percent to attract the capital necessary to keep the organization running.

VOLUME OBJECTIVES.   Volume-centered pricing objectives are normally used to maximize market share, number of customers, or sales revenue. Maximizing sales revenue does not always lead to increased profit, so it is seldom used by organizations today.

Currently, more emphasis is placed on getting a greater proportion of customers. *Market share*, the ratio of customers to total number of people in a market, is one indicator of how an organization is doing relative to its competition. Market share is a better indicator than sales volume alone. Maximizing the number of customers means penetrating the market and getting a broad base of loyal, profitable customers. Increasing market share is based on the idea of getting and keeping long-run profits for the organization.

THE COST OF PRICE FIXING

Price fixing has been illegal in the United States for over ninety years, ever since the Sherman Antitrust Act was passed. Price fixing means that businesses find schemes to keep prices at artificially high levels rather than letting market forces set prices.

Two well-known ways of fixing prices include rigging bids and making agreements with competitors on minimum market prices. Other ways are less obvious. In one case, the U.S. Justice Department reported companies used a coded system of innocent-looking numbers to pass price information. In fact, the code system was designed to give the appearance of price competition—not price fixing.

Price fixing is costly; at least it has been since 1961. In a case involving the electrical equipment industry, the courts put seven executives in jail and fined twenty-nine companies almost $2 million. The largest fines were paid by General Electric Co. ($437,500) and Westinghouse Corp. ($375,000). This sent out a loud message to business: price fixing doesn't pay. It costs dearly if you're caught.

Although some executives have been guilty of price fixing, most executives resist the practice. Some resist even to the point of resigning their jobs. Some businesses, like the Weyerhauser Co., have started educational programs for their employees that explain what price fixing is and why it is illegal. The educational program includes mock grand jury proceedings using company attorneys in very real situations. Other businesses, including Allied Corp. and Textron, Inc., practice "preventive law" because they do not want to willfully violate the law.

Adapted from Bruce A. Jacobs, "Price Fixing: Is It Worth the Risk?" *Industry Week*, August 24, 1981, pp. 43–48.

STATUS QUO OBJECTIVES   Growth and change in market conditions may not always be good for all organizations. For example, IBM and General Motors have been involved in antitrust actions, and the actions may continue if market shares for their products increase significantly. These businesses are seemingly threatened because they do their job well. Smaller businesses may also be content to maintain small, profitable market shares. Gaining an additional market share may be expensive and difficult and, once achieved, may not increase profits. Organizations that do not especially want to alter a favorable set of market conditions won't favor action-oriented pricing objectives. Instead, they will favor status quo objectives, which use price to maintain present market conditions.

Maintaining an organization's current market position can mean different things. It may mean maintaining the existing market share or maintaining stable prices. Some organizations do not want to be a market leader, so they adopt a pricing strategy of meeting the competition's price. Other organizations are interested in maintaining their existing market image. For example, it is unlikely that a discount carpet store could easily change its image and sell high-priced oriental rugs. In fact, if the discount business is profitable, the store would not want to change its image.

Although managers use price as part of their marketing mix, they do not have complete freedom in setting price. Three things affect the degree of management control over pricing decisions.

Price and the Marketing Mix

First, the marketing environment exerts influence through general economic, social, political, and legal conditions. For example, politics have influenced past decisions to raise steel prices. Successful attempts to force rollbacks in price increases were made by Presidents John F. Kennedy and Jimmy Carter. In Kennedy's case, the government launched an investigation of the U.S. Steel Company's decision to raise prices. The real problem was that prices were raised across the board rather than on specific types of steel. After the rollback, certain prices were quietly raised, and within a year all the increases were made.

Second, a manager's freedom to set price can be restricted by external conditions, such as the total market demand for a product, the degree of competition in the market, the actions of raw material suppliers, and government actions. For example, Brazil, a major supplier of coffee beans, significantly raised the tax on exported coffee in 1976. This new tax, coupled with a smaller than usual supply and strong market demand, caused the retail price per pound of coffee to more than triple. Initially, the demand for coffee held, but soon American consumption began to decline. Coffee prices also started to decline as the forces of supply and demand began to work. Nevertheless, a long-term decline in coffee consumption began and has continued into the 1980s.

Third, internal forces affect pricing decisions. The characteristics of the product, the nature of the marketing mix, and the organization's resources and cost structure can affect pricing decisions. For example, a product's stage in its life cycle heavily influences where market price is set.

Organizations usually consider price to be a very important element in the marketing mix. Although price is under the control of the managers, the freedom to set a market price is often restricted. These restrictions come from both inside the organization and external market forces. For example, if the demand for home insulation exceeds available supply, the price of insulation can be raised and people will pay the price. If the reverse market condition is true, then insulation price is difficult, if not impossible, to raise. Managers must be flexible and set price according to a product's market demand and the availability of product supply.

SUMMARY

- Marketing is important to everyone's well-being and to almost all organizations.
- The output of marketing is the creation of utility, especially place, time, and ownership utilities.
- The marketing concept causes an organization to focus on satisfying consumer wants and needs.
- Market segmentation is the key to dividing markets into similar groups of buyers who purchase similar products.
- The marketing mix consists of four parts: product, price, promotion, and distribution. The marketing strategy is the blueprint used to combine the parts in order to compete in market segments.
- A product is any good or service that satisfies consumers.
- The four stages of the product life cycle are used to decide how to

combine the parts of the marketing mix. The mix depends on which stage a product is in.

- Price is the exchange value of any product to buyers when the exchange value is converted into dollars.
- Price is an important part of the marketing mix because it is so highly visible and it is what people pay for a product.
- The three major groups of pricing objectives are (1) profit objectives, (2) volume objectives, and (3) status quo objectives.
- Managers must be flexible and set price according to a product's market demand relative to the available supply.

1. Develop your own definition of marketing, using your own words and ideas. Compare your definition with the one in the text.
2. Select a product you recently bought and list the specific needs and/or wants this product was to satisfy. Describe the marketing activities required to make the product available to you.
3. Explain how the marketing process creates utility for you, using the product you selected in question 2 as an example.
4. Prepare a list of ten goods and ten services you have purchased in the last month. Classify the goods as convenience, shopping, or specialty goods, and give your reason for the classification. Is it possible to classify some of the services as either a good or a service?
5. Classify the following industrial goods according to the scheme shown in Exhibit 12–5. Explain your choice of classification.
   a. Rolled sheet steel
   b. Copying equipment
   c. Lumber
   d. Fleet of executive cars
   e. Word-processor ribbons
6. What are the major parts of the marketing mix? How do the parts of the mix relate to one another?
7. What is the relationship between a product's exchange value and its want-satisfying power?
8. Consider the statements "Cook with gas" and "Conserve energy," which are concepts promoted by public and private utilities. Indicate which stage of the product life cycle these two concepts are in.
9. Use your own experience to set a fair market price or price range for the following consumer products.
   a. Ticket to the NCAA basketball final game
   b. Hairstyling at a local shop
   c. Rent for an apartment near your college campus
   d. Automatic car wash
10. Why do you think a business would ever use a pricing objective other than to get the maximum profit on a good or service? Refer to Exhibit 12–8 for possible pricing objectives.

ISSUES TO CONSIDER AND ANALYZE

CASE FOR ANALYSIS   **FARBERS' PRESTIGE SUPERMARKETS**

The supermarket industry is a slow-growth business with annual sales of over $230 billion. John Rosenberg, president of Farbers, Inc., was looking for a new marketing strategy to make the company more profitable. After several meetings, Ann Earls, Marketing Director, suggested a radical supermarket marketing strategy. She proposed to build a prestige supermarket featuring wide carpeted aisles, soft lights, chandeliers, and music. Her idea is to cash in on high-grade grocery shopping, featuring fresh, exotic, and high-quality foods. The target market for this store is young, affluent, nutrition-conscious customers.

The marketing strategy is to stress high-turnover perishable foods to offset the slower moving exotic foods like fresh papayas and prime cuts of meat. Earls estimates she can turn Farbers's inventory forty-five times a year versus the industry average of twenty-five times. By selling service and ultra high-quality foods, she thinks the affluent family market segment will "trade-up" to the prestige supermarket. If the marketing strategy works, Earls estimates profits at Farbers could jump 35 percent per year.

Rosenberg realizes the profit potential is large, but the risk is also large. These prestige supermarkets will carry high labor costs and high store rents. So, he is not certain about Earls's new idea. There are other ways to improve profits, and Rosenberg is considering starting a rigid cost control program for the existing stores. He is of the opinion this is the sure way to increase profits.

QUESTIONS

1. What do you think of Earls's marketing strategy, especially if profit growth is part of Farbers's overall business plan?
2. Which approach would you recommend to Rosenberg? Explain your reasoning.

Adapted from "A New Twist: Supermarkets with All the Frills," *Business Week*, August 17, 1981, p. 122.

CHAPTER 13

DISTRIBUTING GOODS AND SERVICES

LEARNING OBJECTIVES

After studying this chapter, you should be able to:

Explain what a *channel of distribution* is and why it exists.

Discuss the basic channels of distribution used to move consumer and industrial products.

Classify the different types of marketing intermediaries.

Discuss the issues regarding the cost of distributing products to final users.

Explain the major transportation modes used in our country's physical distribution system.

KEY TERMS

Channel of distribution
Marketing intermediary
Wholesaler
Retailer
Independent wholesaler
Agent wholesaler
Wheel of retailing
Scrambled merchandising
Physical distribution
Private carriers
Contract carriers
Common carriers

FRAKES FURNITURE COMPANY

Frakes Furniture Company is a large furniture manufacturer located in North Carolina. The company makes a wide variety of living room and dining room furniture that is sold throughout the United States. One reason Frakes has been successful in reaching several large market segments is its very strong and loyal distribution network. Some retailers in the channel of distribution have sold Frakes's furniture for almost fifty years. Independent wholesalers in Jacksonville, Seattle, and Kansas City have been associated with Frakes's channel of distribution for forty years. Three of the retail stores located in New York City, Chicago, and Boston are owned by Frakes. Twelve other wholesale distributors are owned by Frakes.

Moving furniture through this nationwide channel of distribution to consumers requires vast knowledge about the network of wholesalers and retailers. It is also necessary to know when to use different types of contract and common carriers. Esther Walters has this knowledge because she works in the shipping department at Frakes. Her major job is to route furniture shipments to their destinations at the least cost. Sometimes speed is important, so Esther has to decide whether to use a contract carrier or air freight. To make these distribution decisions, Esther must understand the advantages and disadvantages of different modes of transportation.

In this chapter, we will discuss the various types of wholesalers and retailers found in channels of distribution. We will also consider the different modes of transportation that are used to physically move goods through the distribution channel. Finally, we will compare the characteristics of the different transportation modes.

Producing products and setting their prices are important, but only part of the total marketing mix. The gap that exists between producers and consumers must be bridged before consumers can buy a product. The purpose of distribution is to bridge that gap, so it is an important part of the marketing mix. The main job of distribution is to create time, place, and ownership utility by making products available for purchase by consumers when and where they want them.

CHANNELS OF DISTRIBUTION

Distribution is marketing to many people. Organizations must get their products into the hands of users, so every organization performs some distribution function. For example, Coca-Cola uses supermarkets, convenience stores, vending machines, fast-food outlets, and restaurants to distribute Coke. Black & Decker distributes power tools through retail outlets, department stores, hardware stores, and discount stores. Services produced by cities, including transit, trash collection, and police protection, are useless without departments to distribute them. Almost every public and private organization is somehow involved with distribution.

All consumers are touched by distribution. The fact products are available to final consumers when and where they are wanted does not happen accidentally. Organizations plan and develop ways to deliver their products to users. A **channel of distribution** is the path a product and its title of ownership take in moving from producer to final consumer. The path links together all the organizations directly involved in marketing a product.

CHANNEL OF DISTRIBUTION
The path a product and its title of ownership take in moving from producer to final consumer.

Why Do Channels of Distribution Exist?

Suppose there are only four consumers and four producers in a market, as shown in Exhibit 13–1. Each consumer has direct contact with every producer, which represents the shortest route between any producer and any consumer. Thus, there are sixteen direct contact points in this market. Imagine what would happen if direct distribution were used nationwide. As the number of producers and consumers expanded, the possible contacts would expand into the trillions!

An alternative to direct distribution is indirect distribution, which puts an organization or person in the distribution path between producers and consumers. This person or organization, called a **marketing intermediary**, helps the movement of products between producers and consumers. A marketing intermediary may be an agent, wholesaler, retailer, or a com-

MARKETING INTERMEDIARY
A person or organization that helps the movement of products between producers and consumers.

EXHIBIT 13–1
Direct Distribution from Producer to Consumer

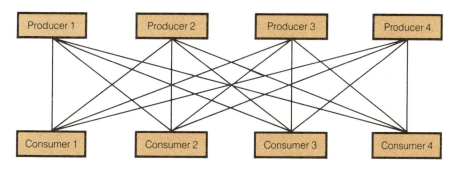

EXHIBIT 13-2
Indirect Distribution from
Producer to Consumer

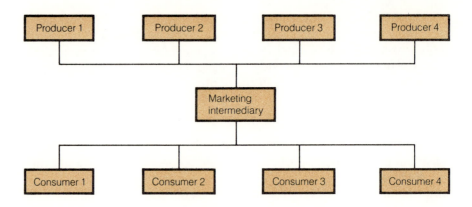

pany-owned organization. Exhibit 13-2 shows how one marketing intermediary can reduce the number of contact points to one for each producer and consumer. For example, let's suppose a supermarket serves as a marketing intermediary. Without the supermarket serving as an intermediate link in the channel of distribution, we often would find it difficult to get the exact brands of food we wanted to buy.

Indirect channels of distribution make it possible to have a wide variety of products available when and where consumers want them in a timely manner. The channels are used to concentrate, sort, and disperse products at points between producers and final consumers. Channels of distribution are an essential part of marketing because they provide shopping convenience to consumers. Without channels of distribution, increased marketing cost and less variety in products would make our nation's standard of living significantly lower. It is important to understand that no single channel is always the best one. Channels of distribution change over time to meet changing consumer needs. This is why Levi Strauss & Co. changed its channels of distribution (see Business Close-Up, p. 274).

Major Channels of Distribution

Various types of channels of distribution are used in the United States. The type of channel used to move products to consumers depends on the product and on how consumers view it. Complex products built to the consumer's specifications require a close link between the producer and the consumer. Channels are different for consumer and industrial goods, as shown in Exhibit 13-3.

CONSUMER CHANNELS   Selling direct from producer to final consumer is the simplest of all consumer channels of distribution (channel 1 in Exhibit 13-3). A *direct channel of distribution* is used for all consumer services and for many consumer products. Companies like Avon Products (cosmetics), Electrolux (vacuum cleaners), and Prestoware (cooking utensils) sell products directly, from door-to-door. A farmer who raises vegetables and fruit and sells them at a farmer's market or roadside stand also uses a direct channel of distribution.

Many producers use a producer–retailer–final consumer channel (channel 2 in Exhibit 13-3) to distribute products. Men's and women's

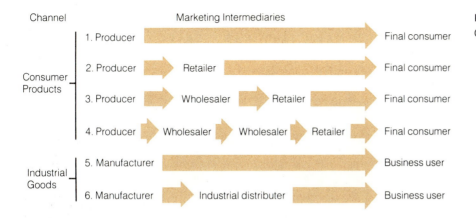

Channel — Marketing Intermediaries

Consumer Products

1. Producer → Final consumer
2. Producer → Retailer → Final consumer
3. Producer → Wholesaler → Retailer → Final consumer
4. Producer → Wholesaler → Wholesaler → Retailer → Final consumer

Industrial Goods

5. Manufacturer → Business user
6. Manufacturer → Industrial distributer → Business user

EXHIBIT 13-3
Channels of Distribution

clothes are often distributed in this manner because retailers buy in very large quantities. Federated Department Stores, a national retail chain, is an example of such a retailer. Meat processors and meat packing houses, which produce perishable products, also use this type of channel. Some producers that have many products use this channel, but the retailer is a company-owned store. Sherwin-Williams (paint) and Singer Corporation (sewing machines) are two companies that use this type of channel. This is also the type of channel Frakes Furniture Company uses in Chicago, New York, and Boston.

On the Job Revisited

Channel 3 in Exhibit 13-3, producer–wholesaler–retailer—consumer, includes two marketing intermediaries. This is the channel of distribution used for convenience goods such as groceries, building supplies, paper products, and tobacco, among others. The wholesaler buys from the producer and sells to the retailer. This channel of distribution is especially useful for smaller producers and small retailers. The wholesaler builds up a product supply from various producers, sorts the supply, and sends it out to retailers. By performing these functions, wholesalers help small producers reach consumer markets that would otherwise be closed to them. Small retailers also benefit because they do not have to store large and expensive inventories.

There are other ways to build channels of distribution. One is to use two wholesalers in the channel (channel 4 in Exhibit 13-3). This channel arrangement is especially useful for very stable products, such as candy, cigarettes, oil products, and fertilizers. Another alternative is to place an agent in the channel. An *agent* is a person with legal power to act for a producer but who does not take title to a product. The agent's main job is to help make products move smoothly through the channel. An example of an agent is a person who matches buyers and sellers for industrial equipment.

INDUSTRIAL CHANNELS The direct manufacturer—business user channel, channel 5 in Exhibit 13-3, is used frequently to distribute industrial products. Industrial sales may involve complex or special-order products that are sold by sales engineers. A large, complex computer installation and a shipyard dry dock are examples of specially designed and engineered

LEVI TRIES TO REVIVE SAGGING JEANS SALES

During the 1970s, Levi Strauss & Co. was one of America's strong growth companies, even though it was part of the cyclical apparel industry. But 1981 proved to be the highmark, and Levi's earnings started to decline after years of steady growth.

Some retailers think that the problem is that the jeans business has matured. In other words, jeans are now in the mature stage of their product life cycle. This supposedly has happened because of an aging population and less consumer interest in the Western look.

Levi executives do not agree with this rather gloomy outlook. In fact, people have predicted the demise of jeans several times since 1962. Certainly Levi Strauss & Co. has learned how to prosper even with these often dire predictions. Flexibility has been a key to the company's prosperity. The company has changed its product offering several times to keep up with consumer changes. But jeans have always been an important part of the product line.

Another recent change was made in the marketing mix that affected their channel of distribution. Levi's traditionally has sold its products through specialty retail stores, high-quality department stores, and small jeans shops. The year 1982 marked a radical shift in this distribution policy. Levi moved to develop channels of distribution that used nationwide mass merchandisers. Two of these national merchandiers included the retailing giants Sears, Roebuck and J. C. Penney.

This marketing decision did not make store owners happy, especially those that had built their business around selling Levi's jeans. However, changing the channel of distribution can help Levi Strauss maintain or possibly increase its share of a market that may be getting smaller. The company plans to revive the jeans business in the 1980s by taking advantage of market changes that are occurring in the retail business.

Adapted from "Levi Tries to Revive Sagging Jeans Business Amid Predictions of Denim Look's Demise," *The Wall Street Journal*, November 18, 1981, p. 25.

products. For these products, the only practical means of distribution is a direct channel of distribution.

But manufacturers of standard machinery parts, heavy equipment, fiberglass, and tools can use indirect channels of distribution like channel 6 in Exhibit 13–3. Industrial distributors are added to the channel to serve the same purpose wholesalers serve in consumer channels. For example, one type of industrial distributor may sell heavy machinery such as stamping presses, rotary lathes, and rock crushers. Another type may sell small power tools such as air screwdrivers and air stapleguns that are used to manufacture furniture. Industrial distributors normally are located in cities, close to large industrial concentrations.

MULTIPLE CHANNELS   A producer may use more than one channel of distribution to sell a product. The type of channel used depends on the market or market segment to be reached. Multiple channels have become common in recent years because products are frequently sold to more than one market segment.

Computer companies like IBM use multiple channels to sell computers. A direct channel is used to sell computers to industrial or business users because large computers like these require extensive engineering and service and are best distributed directly by the producer. However, IBM uses retailers to distribute its smaller personal computers, the IBM PC.

CHANNEL MEMBERS

RETAILER
Any business that does over 50 percent of its total sales to final consumers.

Two marketing intermediaries have been identified so far in our discussion of channels of distribution. First is the wholesaler. A wholesaler buys products from producers and sells them to other wholesalers, retailers, or industrial users. A business is considered to be a wholesaler if over 50 percent of its sales are to other organizations. The second intermediary is the retailer. A **retailer** is any business that sells over 50 percent of its total sales to final users. Retailers buy products directly from either a producer or a wholesaler and sell directly to final users.

Wholesalers

WHOLESALER
A business that buys products from producers and sells them to other businesses. Over 50 percent of the wholesaler's sales are made to other businesses.

INDEPENDENT WHOLESALERS
Businesses that stock a variety of products for resale to retailers.

On the Job Revisited

AGENT WHOLESALER
A business that never takes title to goods but may or may not take possession of products.

Exhibit 13-4 shows the major types of **wholesalers** found in marketing channels. Wholesalers are either independent businesses or owned by manufacturers.

INDEPENDENT WHOLESALERS Private businesses that stock a variety of products for resale to retailers, called **independent wholesalers**, are of two types. *Merchant wholesalers,* who take possession of a legal title to products, are the most important link in the channel between producers and retailers. This type of wholesaler distributes many types of products, including hardware, furniture, lumber, grocery items, candy, nonprescription medicines, and lighting fixtures. Recall that Esther Walters had to ship furniture from Frakes's plant to independent wholesalers in Seattle, Kansas City, and Jacksonville.

Agent wholesalers never take legal title to products, and they may or may not take physical possession of products. Their main function is to help producers distribute products for a commission payment. A broker, who matches buyers and sellers in the marketplace, is one example of an agent wholesaler. This type of wholesaler is important in distributing coal, textile by-products, lumber, produce, home furnishings, canned goods, and heavy industrial equipment. Some agent wholesalers, like auctioneers, do take physical possession of a product.

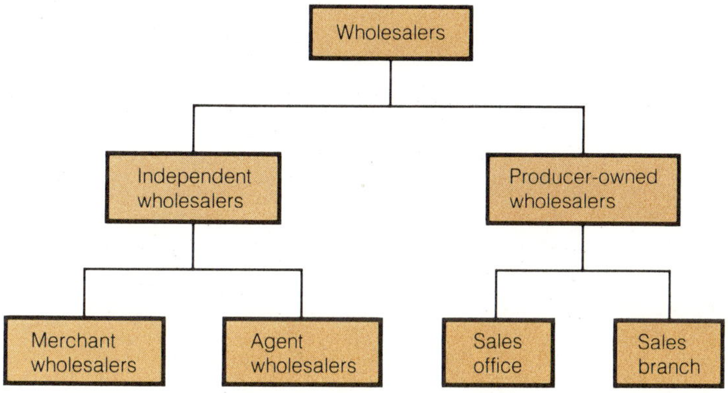

EXHIBIT 13-4
Major Types of Wholesalers

PRODUCER-OWNED WHOLESALERS These "captive" wholesalers, set up by producers to avoid relying solely on independent wholesalers, provide producers with more direct control over the distribution function. Sales offices and sales branches are the major producer-owned wholesalers. Sales offices seldom stock an inventory; they serve as a base of operation for the manufacturer's sales force. After a sale is made, the product is shipped from the closest factory.

A sales branch, which also serves as a salesperson's base of operation, stocks a small inventory of products and repair parts. Installation and repair requests are handled from this small inventory. Organizations that make computers, chemicals, autos, petroleum products, and electrical goods often use sales branches.

Retailers

Retailing is the part of distribution that consumers are most familiar with because retailing is the final link in the channel of distribution. Retailers are the channel members that have more direct contact with consumers. At this point, consumers make buying decisions that determine the success or failure of the marketing effort. A typical retail purchase may be described as a small-value, urgent, customer-initiated sale made with a local merchant.

There are close to 2 million retailers in America, most of which are small to medium-size businesses. But by no means are all retail businesses small or medium-size. Some of the largest businesses in the United States are involved with retailing. For example, Sears, Roebuck's total sales exceeded $25 billion in 1980. The remaining nine of the nation's ten largest retailers, listed in Exhibit 13-5, had total sales in excess of $85 billion.

RETAILING DYNAMICS It is not easy to classify retailers because retailing changes constantly. New stores open for business, and others close; on top of this, the basic nature of retailing changes. One concept used to explain the constant change in retailing is called the **wheel of retailing**. According to this concept, new retailing businesses enter the market with low costs and low prices. Over time, competitors enter the market, hoping

WHEEL OF RETAILING
A concept used to explain the constant change that happens in retailing.

EXHIBIT 13-5
Ten Largest Retailers in America
(Ranked by Sales)

COMPANY	ANNUAL SALES (IN BILLIONS)
1. Sears, Roebuck	$25,194,900
2. Safeway Stores	15,102,673
3. K Mart	14,204,381
4. J.C. Penney	11,353,000
5. Kroger	10,316,741
6. F. W. Woolworth	7,218,176
7. Great Atlantic & Pacific Tea	6,684,179
8. Lucky Stores	6,468,378
9. American Stores Co.	6,419,884
10. Federated Department Stores	6,300,686

Adapted from *The 1981 Fortune Double 500 Directory* (New York: Time, Inc., 1981), p. 64.

to equal the success of the original retailers. As the retailers struggle to be different from one another, business costs rise. Successful retailers expand their services and product lines and cease to look much different from the retail businesses they first challenged. This is exactly the problem faced by K Mart in 1982. Their decision was to add new departments carrying higher priced merchandise like German wines, designer eyeglass frames, and gourmet pots and pans. These now not so low-cost and low-price retailers become targets for new businesses entering the retailing business. Thus, the wheel of retailing turns constantly.

Scrambled merchandising is another reason it is hard to classify retailers. Many retailers have increased the different types of products they sell as one way to increase sales volume. Supermarkets now stock auto accessories, fresh flowers, lawn and garden supplies, and hardware, among other nonfood products. Service stations often sell food, ice, beer, milk, and a few auto accessories. There is a definite trend in the United States toward more scrambled merchandising in the 1980s.

SCRAMBLED MERCHANDISING
A form of retailing where stores carry many different types of products that do not fit well with their traditional product lines.

TYPES OF RETAILERS   One way to classify retail stores is according to the types of products sold. A few retailers carry only one product line, but most carry more than one. Major retail businesses that appear in this classification include department stores (Macy's and Marshall Field & Co.), convenience stores (7-11 Food Stores and U-Tote-M), supermarkets (Kroger and Safeway), and specialty stores.

A second method of classifying retail stores is by the amount of control maintained by suppliers. Some retailers are independent, and others are under the control of a supplier. Independent retailers, not part of a chain or cooperative group, represent about 90 percent of all retail stores. Retailers under some degree of supplier control are chain stores (Western Auto), franchise stores (McDonald's), and cooperative stores (farmers' feed stores).

Retail stores can also be classified by how much they stress price competition, varying from those with low prices (discount stores) to those with high prices (specialty stores). The majority of retailers stress low prices and include warehouse stores (Levitz Furniture Company), discount stores (K Mart), and catalog showrooms (Wilson's and Best's).

Another way to classify retailers is according to their use of the business location. One important system is called nonstore retailing. The largest part of nonstore retailing is done through mail orders handled by such catalog companies as Sears, Roebuck, Montgomery Ward, and J. C. Penney. Another important form of nonstore retailing is done through vending machines. Vending machine retail volume expanded rapidly in the 1960s and will approach the $10 billion level in the 1980s. Products like cigarettes, coffee, soup, apples, sandwiches, and gum are sold through vending machines by such companies as Canteen Corporation and Snappy Snack.

America's system of channels of distribution is very large, consisting of several layers of wholesalers and retailers. The services of these wholesalers and retailers of course are not free. People sometimes raise questions about distribution costs and the number of layers of wholesalers and

**THE COSTS
OF DISTRIBUTION**

SELLING COMPUTERS TO CONSUMERS: A NEW TWIST IN DISTRIBUTION

In 1981, two of America's giant corporations jumped into a market that was new for both of them. IBM and Xerox Corporation introduced a new personal home computer aimed at consumers. Rather than worrying about the product, management's major concern was how to sell it! This was a strange position for these two marketing giants to find themselves in, especially after all their past successes!

The solution to this problem was to use their own sales force as well as a chain of retail stores that sell personal computers. For the first time, independent retailers were helping IBM and Xerox sell their products. This was a drastic change from their past marketing efforts. But it was a necessary change if these companies were to compete in this market. Their direct channel of distribution was too costly for selling products with a retail value under $500. In fact, marketing costs using their established distribution methods would have been more than manufacturing costs.

Finding a new method of distribution for personal computers was important to IBM and Xerox. By 1985, over 10 million of these computers will be sold to consumers. By 1990, personal computers may be as common in American homes as television sets are today. This represents a multibillion dollar market potential for the 1980s. The major hurdle to realizing these sales is a distribution limitation in the industry. Channels of distribution that efficiently move personal computers from producers must be developed. This development will require the cooperation of computer manufacturers, mass merchandisers, independent retailers, and specialty chains. Given the market potential and possible consumer benefits, the chance of these new channels of distribution being developed is very great.

Adapted from "Computer Stores," *Business Week*, September 28, 1981, pp. 76–80.

retailers. There is no simple answer to their questions; the issue of distribution costs is not simple.

Maybe the best way to look at the issue is to ask what would happen to the mix and costs of products if wholesalers and retailers were eliminated from the channel of distribution. Would the product mixes available to final consumers be affected? Would the products be less expensive to final consumers?

The distribution services of wholesalers and retailers must be performed if product availability is to be unaffected. Eliminating wholesalers and retailers does not eliminate the need to distribute products. Producers are unlikely to be capable of picking up the slack in the channel that would be caused by the loss of intermediaries. Thus, the mix of products available to final consumers would be significantly limited.

Suppose producers tried to send a salesperson to visit each store that carried their product. These salespeople can sell only their own product. Imagine what would happen to the price of the different products. The prices would increase very much just to pay for higher direct selling costs.

Wholesalers play a valuable part in America's distribution system. They place fewer but larger orders, which cost less per unit to fill. The producers' salespeople have fewer outlets to contact, so selling costs are lower. And wholesalers have warehouses to prevent perishable products from spoiling, reducing costs to consumers. Wholesalers do add to the cost of selling products and to the prices consumers pay, but they add value to the products as well.

It is unlikely that the distribution costs added to the price of products by intermediaries are as great as they would be if producers had to perform the wholesaler's or retailer's services. Well-stocked, producer-owned distribution centers located in all parts of America would be more expensive to maintain. Getting rid of wholesalers and retailers does not eliminate the need to do their jobs or the costs of doing them.

Physical distribution has been called the other half of marketing because it accounts for about 50 percent of the total costs of marketing. **Physical distribution** is the storage and movement of products from producer to the point of final purchase by consumers. The main purpose of physical distribution is to keep products flowing through the channels of distribution. This involves storing/warehousing and shipping products.

PHYSICAL DISTRIBUTION

PHYSICAL DISTRIBUTION
The storage and movement of products from producers to the point of final purchase by consumers.

Storage of products is an important part of an organization's marketing program. Having the right products in the right place helps producers promptly fill orders and comply with service requests.

Many large organizations have built distribution centers across America to store their products. Distribution centers are warehouses where products are shipped in large quantities, stored, and distributed to retailers and individual customers in smaller quantities. In distribution centers, quantities of products can be built up into large lots and these can be broken into smaller lots for shipment to retailers.

Sears, Roebuck is one example of a business that uses a network of distribution centers. Sears once distributed all its products from its Chicago office. To reduce the time required to fill customer orders and resupply retail stores, Sears built a nationwide distribution network. The company now maintains distribution centers in thirteen major cities, each serving customers in several states. This reduces the time customers have to wait to receive a product.

Storage of Products

A business that transports products or people is called a **carrier**. By law carriers are divided into three types: private carriers, contract carriers, and common carriers. Esther Walters worked closely with both contract and common carriers in shipping furniture from Frakes's plant in North Carolina.

Private carriers transport only their own products. Examples of private carriers are Montgomery Ward (retailer), Exxon (oil products), and U.S. Steel (metals).

Contract carriers are "for hire." They carry products to meet the special needs of other organizations over routes agreeable to both parties. Contract carriers do not keep regular schedules, and they may refuse to carry the product of a company. Flying Tiger Airlines is one of the best known contract carriers in the United States.

Carriers

CARRIER
A business that transports products or people.

PRIVATE CARRIERS
Carriers that transport their own products.

CONTRACT CARRIERS
Carriers that are for hire to carry products for other organizations to meet their special needs.

COMMON CARRIERS
Carriers that must accept shipments from anyone requesting their services.

Common carriers must accept shipments from anyone who requests their services. They maintain established routes granted by government agencies and publish their rates and schedules. There are many types of common carriers in America, representing different modes of transportation. Some common carriers include New York Air, Illinois Central Gulf Railroad, and United Parcel Service.

Methods of Transportation

There are five major types of transportation used in America: railroads, motor vehicles, waterways, airlines, and pipelines. Exhibit 13-6 summarizes the characteristics of these transportation modes.

RAILROADS   Overall, railroads are a very versatile transportation mode, being adaptable to handle many different types of freight with speed and dependability. Even so, the importance of railroads as a freight carrier has declined since 1945. Trying to reverse this trend, railroads have spent billions of dollars in the last several years to modernize their equipment. New equipment includes shipping containers, boxcars that humidify produce, three-level boxcars to carry new cars, and specially cushioned cars to handle fragile cargo. Esther Walters especially likes to use cushioned cars to move large shipments of furniture to the wholesalers because of low damage rates.

On the Job Revisited

In addition to buying new equipment, railroads have developed new customer services including the following:

■ Livestock are fed and watered in transit.
■ "Piggyback" container service includes pickup and delivery of containers at truck terminals. The containers are then loaded onto flat cars and carried by train to their destination.

EXHIBIT 13-6
General Comparison of Transportation Modes

CHARACTERISTIC	RANKING*				
	Rail	**Highway**	**Water**	**Air**	**Pipeline**
Speed (portal-to-portal time)	3	2	4	1	5
Frequency (scheduled shipments per day)	4	2	5	3	1
Dependability (meeting schedules)	3	2	4	5	1
Capability (ability to handle various products)	2	3	1	4	5
Availability (number of geographic points served)	2	1	4	3	5
Cost (total transportation costs)	3	4	1	5	2

Adapted from Ben M. Enis, *Marketing Principles*, 2nd ed. (Santa Monica, Calif.: Goodyear, 1977).
*A ranking of 1 is best; 5 is poorest.

■ Shippers can divert railcars in transit to new destinations without back-tracking.

■ Wheat is unloaded from the railcar, ground into flour, reloaded to the railcar, and hauled to its destination.

MOTOR VEHICLES   The most flexible and second most costly mode of transportation are motor vehicles. Motor vehicles carry slightly less than 25 percent of the nation's total freight, and most of this is carried by truck. Common carriers like Greyhound and United Parcel Service also carry freight, but their freight packages are restricted in size.

Service is the key to the success of motor freight businesses. One carrier (TIME-DC) offers coast-to-coast "yellowbird service" between New York and Southern California in sixty-nine hours. On less-than-carload shipments, Esther uses motor freight lines. They are very useful when smaller shipments are going direct to a retail furniture store. Motor vehicles can serve many small towns because they are not limited by fixed roadbeds and they can carry small loads on short hauls. The two major limitations of motor vehicles are bad weather and limits placed on the total weight carried on highways by state governments.

On the Job Revisited

INLAND WATERWAYS   About 17 percent of all freight in America is carried by barges, freighters, and tankers on inland waterways. Waterways are used mainly to transport bulky goods (sand, coal, and oil) because the rates are low. Barges can carry large loads of freight. One barge may hold the equivalent of over fifty railroad freight cars.

The main advantage of water transportation for shipping is low cost. One tugboat can push enough loaded barges to equal two or three railroad freight trains. Carrying larger loads on water, it is possible to reduce the cost per mile to move bulky goods. The greatest disadvantage of water transportation is that routes—rivers and canals—are fixed. Besides lacking the flexibility of other transportation modes, water transportation is very slow and subject to interruption from bad weather.

AIR FREIGHT   Although it is the most expensive mode of transportation, air freight is the fastest. Air freight usually carries items that are perishable (flowers), of high value (racehorses), or urgently needed (medicine and blood). Less than 10 percent of the nation's total freight is presently carried by air.

The cargo jet placed air freight rates within reach of many businesses and expanded air freight markets for carriers. Most major airports now handle air freight shipments, thereby opening new, nationwide markets for producers or products suitable for air transportation.

The main disadvantage of air freight transportation is that direct shipping is restricted to major cities. Consequently, air cargo shipments to smaller cities may have to be transferred between airlines, increasing handling charges and causing some time delays.

PIPELINES   Pipelines have grown in importance in moving products to markets, carrying about 25 percent of the nation's total freight. They are normally restricted to carrying liquids and gaseous products along fixed routes. For example, natural gas, crude oil, gasoline, and coal slurry are regularly transported by pipelines. Thousands of miles of natural-gas pipelines run from Louisiana and Texas to the northern and eastern parts of America.

Pipelines are often constructed by several companies because of the large expense involved. The newest pipeline is the Trans-Alaska pipeline built jointly by eight oil companies. The Trans-Alaska pipeline is 48 inches wide and runs about 800 miles from Alaska's North Slope/Prudhoe Bay region south to Valdez. Nine years, over 20,000 workers, and more than $9 billion went into building the project. The pipeline, opened in June, 1977, can supply about 15 percent of the nation's oil needs at full operation.

There are several advantages to using pipelines to transport products. One advantage is their low transportation cost per ton-mile shipped and their low maintenance and operating costs. The major disadvantage of pipelines run from Louisiana and Texas to the northern and eastern parts or used to distribute several different products.

SUMMARY

- Channels of distribution are an important part of the marketing mix because they make a large variety of goods available to users and buyers.
- Channels are made up of various marketing intermediaries, including wholesalers and retailers.
- Consumer channels of distribution are normally longer than industrial channels. The standard consumer channel is producer to wholesaler to retailer to consumer.
- Industrial channels of distribution normally use a direct link between producer and business.
- The two major types of wholesalers are independent and producer-owned wholesalers.
- Retailing is a dynamic business because it changes so quickly, with new firms entering and old ones dropping out. The wheel of retailing is used to explain the phenomenon.
- Distribution and marketing costs are often as much as 50 percent of the retail price. Marketing intermediaries can be eliminated, but the functions they perform cannot be eliminated.
- The major forms of transportation are railroads, motor vehicles, inland waterways, air freight, and pipelines. Overall, railroads are the most versatile mode of transportation.

ISSUES TO CONSIDER AND ANALYZE

1. Consumer groups often claim that the "marketing middleman" should be eliminated and the cost savings passed on to consumers. This is supposed to lower the price of goods. Is their claim valid? Is the reasoning correct, in your opinion?
2. Explain what type of distribution channel should be used for the following products:
   a. Gasoline
   b. Fresh produce
   c. Prescription medicine
   d. Hairstyling
   e. New automobiles
   f. Home furniture

3. Explain the difference between agent wholesalers and independent wholesalers.
4. What method of transportation would you use to ship the following products 50 miles and 1500 miles?
   a. Natural gas
   b. New automobiles
   c. Iron ore
   d. Blood plasma
   e. Live beef cattle
   f. Orchids
5. Discuss the advantages and limitations of the five basic methods of transportation.
6. Is there any single mode of transportation that is, in your opinion, superior to all other modes?
7. How does a gourmet restaurant in Denver get fresh, live lobsters daily from Maine?
8. How does a channel of distribution used for industrial goods usually differ from a channel used for consumer convenience goods? Explain your answer.
9. Explain the importance of physical distribution in developing a marketing strategy to serve final consumers.
10. Explain the differences between wholesalers and retailers.

DISTRIBUTION MAKES HITACHI COMPETITIVE

CASE FOR ANALYSIS

When a business is one of the world's largest manufacturing companies, it has to work hard to stay competitive. This is because the channels of its distribution stretch across the world. Hitachi, Ltd. of Japan is aware of the importance of distribution and competition. Hitachi sells a wide range of consumer electronic products throughout America. This is a highly competitive market segment making distribution even more critical.

Bobby Hinamoto is Hitachi's distribution manager for North America, and he is faced with increasing transportation costs on a monthly basis. Hinamoto feels Hitachi must look closely at all aspects of the distribution business including various modes of transportation and the types of distribution channels used.

To evaluate the options for moving Hitachi products, factors like rates, transit times, economics, and service provided by each carrier will be checked. Most of the goods are shipped by motor freight in less-than-truckload lots to large retailers and company distributors. Hinamoto is proposing that the company use computers to evaluate each shipment. Routing guides can be developed to help managers in carrier selection get the lowest shipping costs.

Hinamoto also wants to use private distributors (wholesalers) to supplement the company-owned distribution centers. He thinks private centers will be very flexible and willing to accommodate Hitachi's distribution needs. Senior management in Japan supports the computer application concept but wants to use company-owned distribution centers exclusively.

Adapted from "Effective Distribution Helps Hitachi Compete in U.S. Market," *Traffic Management*, October 1979, pp. 50–56.

QUESTIONS

1. Do you agree with management's view toward using a computer for distribution management? Explain.
2. Explain how a computer might be used to link customer information to the distribution (shipping) network in order to improve Hitachi's distribution system.
3. Do you agree or disagree with Hinamoto's proposal of using independent wholesalers to move Hitachi's products? Explain.

CHAPTER 14

PROMOTING GOODS AND SERVICES

LEARNING OBJECTIVES

After studying this chapter, you should be able to:

Explain the meaning and purpose of *promotion*.

Discuss why promotion benefits both consumers and sellers.

Discuss how marketing communication and promotion are related.

Identify certain methods of promotion used by organizations.

Explain some of the factors that affect an organization's choice of a promotional strategy.

KEY TERMS

Promotion
Communication
Promotion mix
Advertising
Sales promotion
Point-of-purchase
  advertising
Public relations
Publicity
Missionary selling
Technical selling
Pull strategy
Push strategy

GOLDEN STATE ADVERTISING

Uri Cohen has worked in the media department at Golden State Advertising for eight months. This is his first job since graduating from college in 1982. In college, Cohen studied marketing, advertising, and other areas of business administration.

According to the media manager, Rosie Myers, Cohen is ready to begin developing media plans and making media buys. This is an important assignment since media buys may easily involve budgets of several thousand dollars. On this assignment, Cohen must decide what advertising media are best suited for his client, the large Mexican restaurant chain El Felix, based in California. The basic question he must answer is how to use a limited budget in order to get the most impact for his client's dollar. Here impact means getting customers into El Felix's various restaurant locations.

Cohen has reviewed the previous media plan and restaurant location sales. After considering advantages and disadvantages of various media, he has decided to drop local radio spots entirely. His new plan includes outdoor signs, local TV spots on new shows, and selected newspaper ads.

Given the client's advertising budget, Cohen thinks his is the best possible media plan. Myers agrees, so media buys for the next eight months will be made in the various markets served by El Felix.

In this chapter, you will learn about promotion, including advertising and personal selling. In particular, you will read about the various types of media that can be used to carry or project advertising messages to consumers. You will also discover how other forms of promotion can be used to help advertising reach customers.

In a marketing economy like America's, successful producers do not trust to luck that consumers will buy their goods and services. Mass production depends on mass consumption, and people must be aware of goods and services before they are likely to buy or use them. This is true even for nonprofit organizations like government agencies. For example, the U.S. Postal Service encourages people to use the mail with their promotion program "Make someone happy today. Write a letter." Consumers seldom will make a special effort to inform themselves of the advantages of new products, services, and concepts.

To overcome consumer inaction, organizations must promote their products. Thus, promotion, the fourth element in the marketing mix, is used by organizations to help reach specific marketing objectives. In this sense, promotion is a very important marketing tool.

PROMOTION

Promotion is the seller's way to inform, persuade, and influence prospective buyers. The promotional message is designed to get consumers to buy a product or to use a service. This is what Uri Cohen was attempting to do by developing a media schedule for El Felix Restaurants. Promotion can also be used to create a favorable image of an organization or to show how important an industry's activities are to a local community or the nation. For example, Columbia Gas, a large gas supplier in the Midwest, has promoted the economic importance of increased natural-gas exploration by means of national television advertisements. From Columbia's viewpoint, increased natural-gas exploration is good for both the industry and the nation. United Energy Resources Company also sponsored a series of ads relating to national energy matters. One such ad focused on developing a substitute for natural gas by using the water hyacinth plant.

PROMOTION
The seller's way to inform, persuade, and influence prospective buyers.

The important point is that all promotional efforts are designed to create favorable consumer attitudes toward goods, the firm, the industry, or some public issue. From a business point of view, favorable consumer attitudes normally result in the sale of a good or service.

Promotion Objectives

The major promotion objectives are informing, persuading, and reminding consumers. The main purpose of all three objectives is to provide information to consumers in order to increase sales. Informing consumers is the first objective because consumers rarely seek out new products and services on their own.

The purpose of persuading consumers is to convince them that a product is better than other available products. Persuasive promotion is used most often for products that appear to be similar, such as aspirin, television sets, and automobiles. When it involves direct comparison of two or more brands, this type of persuading is called *comparative advertising*. Persuasive promotions can often become controversial. Television promotions for Tylenol and Bayer aspirin, for example, involved a series of controversial claims and comparisons made by the producers of both products.

Finally, the purpose of reminding consumers is to keep a product's name before the public in order to get repeat sales. This last objective, like the other two, is consistent with the overall promotional goal of communicating product information to consumers.

The Benefits of Promotion

Both consumers and sellers benefit directly from promotion. For consumers, promotion may have two important benefits:

- *Informing them about specific advantages and characteristics of a prod-uct.* Consumers may want to know about its price, what it will do, styles and colors available, safety features, availability, and the type of guarantee it has.
- *Increasing their need for individual identity and providing a socially acceptable way of satisfying that need.* Promotion can remind con-sumers of what they need, what neighbors have, or what they want.

Sellers benefit in a different way from the use of promotion. As you may recall from Chapter 12, promotion is one of the four controllable variables in the marketing mix. Thus, sellers use promotion mainly to influence the demand for a good or service. The direct benefits a seller receives depends largely on how effectively promotion is used. The major ways that pro-motion influences demand are by:

- *Introducing a new product and telling consumers about its availability and advantages.* For example, the IBM personal computer was adver-tised extensively in business publications like *The Wall Street Journal*. The promotion attempted to create the image of a fast-operating, small personal computer. In the ads, many features of the product were mentioned to stress IBM's image of quality in the computer business.

288

■ *Maintaining or increasing sales of a good or service.* This is accomplished by directing the promotional effort to consumers through special incentive programs, improving the brand or company image with advertising, or focusing on a specific part of the total market. For example, Holiday Inns tried to maintain its image as the world's quality hotel system through the slogan "Holiday Inns welcomes you to the best hotels in the world."

■ *Reversing a decline in sales for a product.* Arm & Hammer baking soda, a well-known consumer product for many decades, had the image of being primarily a baking product. Sales were declining because prepared baking mixes were so widely used in America. So Arm & Hammer began to promote its baking soda as a "new" product that would reduce odors in refrigerators and drains. This promotion breathed new life into an "old" product, and sales increased significantly. The promotion simply found new uses for an old product.

■ *"Demarketing" a good or service because of a change in economic conditions.* Demarketing is an effort to get consumers to use less of a product. Major oil companies such as Shell, Gulf, and Exxon often promote energy conservation through improved driving habits and proper auto care. *The Conservation Bonus Book* (Exhibit 14–1), distributed by Shell Oil Company, is one example of demarketing. Utilities stress energy conservation by encouraging adequate insulation in buildings and homes. As natural resources become more scarce and expensive, demarketing promotions are likely to become more common. Compare the utilities' demarketing efforts with their promotions in the 1950s, when people were encouraged to build all-electric homes.

Neither consumers nor sellers will realize any of these benefits of promotion if the message doesn't get through to the consumer. Baskin Robbins may have the largest and tastiest selection of ice cream in town, but if this information is not communicated to consumers, it won't sell very many ice cream cones for BR. Promotional efforts are usually most effective when they're based on an understanding of sound marketing communications.

Marketing Communication

Communication is what happens when someone sends a message to someone else and it is understood. The hard part of communicating is making sure the message is understood the way it is intended.

Marketing communication is a special type of communication involving only messages between buyers and sellers. These are its basic elements:

■ *Communicator.* The sender or source of the message
■ *Message.* The idea to be communicated
■ *Channel.* The medium or carrier of the message
■ *Receiver.* The audience for whom the message is intended
■ *Noise.* Anything that makes it hard for the message to be understood correctly

These five basic communication elements, plus a feedback element, are combined in the marketing communication model in Exhibit 14–2. Feed-

COMMUNICATION
The process of sending a message to someone so that it is understood by that person.

EXHIBIT 14-1
Promotional Book to Demarket Gasoline
(Courtesy of Shell Oil Company)

back helps the communicator know if the message was received the way it was intended.

In the exhibit, the communicator sending the message is a marketing organization (block 1). Depending on its nature, the message (2) can be put into the form of an advertisement, a public relations message, a sales presentation, or a store display. Typical communication channels (3) include salespeople, advertising media, and public relations people. The

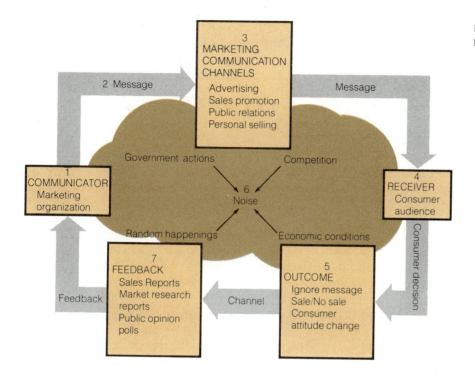

EXHIBIT 14–2
Marketing Communication Model

receiver in the model (4) is the consumer audience, which may consist of many individuals or a small number of businesses. Once a consumer audience receives the message, a decision is made and an outcome is reached (5). The consumer's decision may be to ignore the promotional message, to make a purchase, or to consider some particular product or issue.

Noise may interfere with the communicator's attempt to send a message (6). In marketing, noise may come from several sources, including the promotional messages of the competition, changes in government policy, changes in economic conditions, and personal interruptions during the ad.

It is important to determine whether the promotional message was received correctly. The key to determining the communication's success is feedback (7). Notice that the feedback channel closes the loop. Ways for communicators to obtain feedback include checking sales reports, reviewing marketing research reports, and conducting public opinion polls.

Every well-planned promotional program is based on an organizational goal. The goal may be as simple as getting customers into a department store for the traditional January white sale. Or it may be to build consumer good will toward a company—that's a primary goal of the oil companies when they promote energy conservation.

Refer to Exhibit 14–2 one more time, and look at the four basic communication channels listed in block 3. These four channels may be used separately or in combination to reach a promotional goal. They all are used to communicate with people, but each has different advantages and disad-

PROMOTIONAL METHODS

PROMOTION MIX
Combination of promotional methods used in a promotional program.

vantages. The manager's task is to choose the right promotional methods to do a particular job. The combination of methods the manager chooses is called the **promotion mix**.

Promotional methods fall into two broad categories. Nonpersonal promotion, which includes advertising, sales promotion, and public relations, does not necessarily involve direct seller-to-consumer contact. Personal selling is an example of personal promotion.

Advertising

ADVERTISING
Any form of nonpersonal promotion of products and ideas directed to large numbers of people.

Any form of nonpersonal promotion of products and ideas directed to large numbers of people is called **advertising**. More money is spent on advertising than on any other type of promotion. Most money spent on advertising is used for direct mail, to buy space in newspapers and magazines or time on radio and television, and for outdoor billboards. Advertising is widely used in capitalistic economies, but even countries like the USSR, with a socialistic economy, use some advertising to inform people of the government services available to them.

Advertising may be done on a national, regional, or local basis. Products with broad appeal are often advertised nationally. For example, TV ads for McDonald's and Pizza Hut appear nationwide in newspapers and magazines and on television. Recall that Uri Cohen placed ads for El Felix Restaurants in local newspapers and on local TV shows.

On the Job Revisited

Ads are also run on a regional basis for goods and services that do not have national markets. For example, pesticides used to control insects that attack cotton crops are not advertised to readers in New England, where cotton is not grown. Newspapers such as *The Wall Street Journal* and magazines such as *Time, U.S. News & World Report, Newsweek,* and *Business Week* produce national editions with regional inserts for advertising. These regional inserts make it easier to direct advertising to the proper target audience at a lower cost.

Local advertising is limited in geographical coverage—normally a single county or metropolitan area. Advertisements run in a local market usually promote goods and services sold by local businesses. One well-known form of local advertisement is the large weekly newspaper ads placed by retail grocery stores. These ads promote special buys for major grocery-shopping days in the retail market.

EXHIBIT 14-3

Annual Expenditures on Advertising for Selected Years, 1970–1981

YEAR	EXPENDITURES (IN BILLIONS)
1970	$19,550
1971	20,740
1972	23,300
1973	25,120
1974	26,820
1975	28,160
1976	33,690
1977	37,920
1978	43,950
1979	49,580
1980	54,600
1981	61,650

Advertising Age, September 14, 1981, p. 48.

THE SCOPE OF ADVERTISING   Organizations and industries annually make large investments in advertising programs. For example, the travel industry (airlines, railroads, steamship lines, bus companies, and car rental firms) spent about $700 million in 1980. The total dollar investment in advertising runs into the billions each year. Exhibit 14-3 presents some figures on total advertising expenditures in America for 1970 to 1981. In 1982, total advertising expenditures in the United States may approach $70 billion.

Though these amounts are very large sums of money, remember that advertising is often used in place of personal selling. Considered this way, a large sum becomes quite a small expense for each individual who is reached. In this way, advertising is an economical way to contact millions of potential customers. Without advertising, the promotion of goods and services in America would be much more costly and probably impossible to accomplish. For example, salespeople cannot contact all the potential customers for a particular product. Consumer markets in America are too widespread and diverse *not* to use advertising.

The range of advertisers in America varies from companies like Sears, Roebuck and Ford Motor Company to individuals who spend no more than $3 to $5 on classified ads in local newspapers. Exhibit 14-4 summarizes the advertising expenditures of the nation's largest advertisers in 1980. The first two of these businesses (Procter & Gamble and Sears, Roebuck) spent over $1.2 billion on advertising in 1980. All the businesses listed in Exhibit 14-4 are heavily involved in selling some type of consumer good, which requires reaching many different markets.

Considered by any yardstick, the scope of advertising in the United States is huge. Organizations spend over $300 for every person in the country to promote products and ideas. With expenditures of this size, it is safe to say that every U.S. consumer is directly affected by advertising.

ADVERTISING MEDIA.   No matter how good the advertising message, it must be communicated by the right media for consumers to receive it. The major types of media used by advertisers are print, broadcast, outdoor, and direct mail. The amount national advertisers spent on these different media for 1980 was $15.5 billion. The largest expenditure was for television, particularly national network TV shows.

The two major types of print media are newspapers and magazines. Newspapers serve primarily local markets and reach consumers of every age and income bracket. Newspaper advertisements are particularly useful to retailers because the ads give near total coverage in local markets. This is the reason Uri Cohen used newspapers as one media for El Felix Restaurants. Magazines normally reach consumers in all market segments, especially those with above-average income and good jobs. Magazine advertisements with a long life can be aimed toward specific types of consumers or geographic regions. Over 200 U.S. magazines currently offer a regional advertising insert.

Radio and television are the two types of *broadcast media*. Over 5000

On the Job Revisited

RANK	COMPANY	EXPENDITURE
1	Procter & Gamble Co.	$649,600,000
2	Sears, Roebuck & Co.	599,600,000
3	General Foods Corp.	410,000,000
4	Philip Morris, Inc.	364,600,000
5	K Mart Corp.	319,300,000
6	General Motors Corp.	316,000,000
7	R.J. Reynolds Industries	298,500,000
8	Ford Motor Co.	280,000,000
9	American Telephone & Telegraph	259,200,000
10	Warner-Lambert Co.	235,200,000

From "100 Leading National Advertisers," *Advertising Age*, September 10, 1981, p. 1.

EXHIBIT 14-4
Advertising Expenditures for
the Top Ten American Businesses, 1980

commercial radio stations and 600 commercial television stations operate in America. Many of these stations have formed networks by interconnecting their local facilities for simultaneous national broadcasts. Advertisers use broadcast networks to reach national audiences of millions of people. This type of national advertising is often used to introduce new consumer products.

There are several advantages to using the broadcast media for advertising. TV and radio offer immediacy, so advertisements can be tied in quickly to a current event. Broadcast media are somewhat personal since they rely on the consumer's imagination, and a friendly human voice and appearance. In addition, broadcast media permit the advertiser to zero in on a target audience by choosing the time of broadcast. Consider the ads on Saturday morning television, which are directed toward children. During this viewing time, businesses promote various types of cereals and toys. Although children do not necessarily buy products, they do influence purchase decisions. Broadcast media are expensive, however. Businesses sponsoring a one-hour prime-time national television show can easily spend several hundreds of thousands of dollars on ads. For example, in 1980, a thirty-second ad on the weekly show "60 Minutes" cost $170,000.

Outdoor media are popular in the United States because the population is mobile. The major types of outdoor media are billboards, painted displays, and electric signs. Billboards are the most commonly used outdoor media. Some outdoor media, like the electric signs in New York's Times Square, are very well known.

The main advantages of outdoor media include the length of time they appear in one spot, their ability to be used in specific geographical markets, large physical size, and repeated exposure. In addition, competition is limited because billboards with competing messages tend not to be placed together.

Direct-mail advertising consists of any promotional material sent through the mail. A direct-mail advertising campaign depends heavily on an accurate mailing list. Some businesses specialize in constructing and selling mailing lists that are useful for promoting different types of products, but these cost thousands of dollars. Other sources of direct-mailing lists include state automobile registration lists, business club lists, and trade association lists.

A direct-mail promotion campaign can be highly personal, timely, selective in its audience, and relatively free of direct competition. These advantages make direct mail a very effective advertising medium. Direct mail is used by businesses like insurance companies and auto dealers to obtain sales leads, to deliver complicated sales messages, and to reach specific promotional targets. Other businesses, such as Procter & Gamble, use direct mail to get product samples into the hands of consumers. Most people have, at one time or another, received a free sample of a new soap, shampoo, or other product mailed directly to their home by a manufacturer.

Advertising is an effective and economical way to promote goods, services, and ideas to masses of people. As the cost per individual of personal

MAKING FOLKS HUNGRY

People eat when they are hungry, but there are many choices of foods available in the grocery stores. If you are the Campbell Soup Company, naturally you want people to eat soup, especially Campbell's soup. As a company, Campbell's has about 80 percent of the $1.2 billion annual soup sales. The company is not really interested in increasing its market share. But Campbell's is interested in seeing industry sales grow. For the last ten years, soup sales have not grown much—about 1 percent per year.

To combat this trend of slow growth, Campbell's launched a new ad strategy to get industry sales moving again. This is not an easy job, but Campbell's is trying! The company is spending $23 million to do the job.

The ad campaign slogan "Soup is good food" was pushed nationwide. The media used in the campaign included news magazines, prime-time TV, and regular news sections in papers. This was a new twist in advertising for Campbell's. For many years, the company used women's media like magazines, daytime TV, and newspaper food sections to carry its advertising messages. The results in test markets were very impressive. The new media seem to be working. Maybe people will get hungrier for soup.

Adapted from Bill Abrams, "Campbell's New Ad Strategy: Make Folks Hungrier for Soup," *The Wall Street Journal*, September 24, 1981, p. 25.

selling continues to rise, there is every reason to think that expenditures on advertising will increase significantly. By almost any measure, advertising is an important part of the American economy. However, there are other important channels of communication that can be used to promote a product or idea, including sales promotions, public relations, and personal selling.

Sales Promotion

Sales promotion is difficult to define because it includes many different types of nonpersonal promotion. If a promotional method cannot be classified as advertising, personal selling, or public relations, it is usually called *sales promotion*. Therefore, **sales promotion** is any marketing activity—other than personal selling, advertising, and publicity—that stimulates consumer purchasing and dealer effectiveness. Such marketing activities as displays, shows, and demonstrations are included in this definition.

SALES PROMOTION
Any type of nonpersonal promotion that stimulates consumer purchases and dealer effectiveness.

Sales promotion is normally used with other forms of promotion. In a market economy like America's, often between 20 and 33 percent of all promotional budgets is spent on sales promotion. This translates into billions of dollars in yearly expenditures.

CHARACTERISTICS OF SALES PROMOTION   Regardless of how sales promotion is defined, its main objective is to help "pull" products through channels of distribution. This pull is provided by offering incentives to salespeople to promote specific products and by getting buyers to buy certain products.

One well-known national sales promotion effort is the cash rebate program used by the auto industry in 1973, 1977, and 1981. For example, when the 1973 oil embargo affected the auto industry, Chrysler introduced a plan by which customers received a $200 cash rebate directly from Chrysler no matter what type of deal they made with the local distributor. It did not take long for other auto manufacturers to adopt this promotion plan. The plan was used successfully again in 1977 to reduce the large inventory of General Motors Chevettes, and again in 1981 when auto manufactures tried to improve sales.

SALES PROMOTION METHODS   The sales promotion methods available to business are limited only by creative imagination, as you can see by the various consumer and dealer sales promotion methods included in Exhibit 14-5. The methods of promotion used most frequently include point-of-purchase advertising, specialty advertising, trade shows, coupons and premiums, and special contests. Point-of-purchase advertising and coupons are among the best known methods of sales promotion.

Point-of-purchase advertising (POP) is used to get consumers to buy while they are in the store. Total POP sales in the United States now exceed $3 billion annually. POP advertising is done with displays or actual in-store demonstrations. Standard POP display material includes posters, banners, signs, racks, and streamers. POP demonstrations are used frequently in supermarkets to promote many kinds of food products. For instance, bacon or sausage will be cooked and served to consumers near a special

POINT-OF-PURCHASE ADVERTISING
A form of promotion used to get consumers to buy while in the store.

EXHIBIT 14-5
Forms of Sales Promotion

CONSUMER PROMOTIONS	DEALER PROMOTIONS
Product Samples Giving away product to induce trial	Bonus Extra cash payment for sales
Coupon Certificate that reduces price	PM (Premium or Push Money) Bonus on certain brand
Cents-Off Promotion Reduction in regular price	Contests Prizes to best sales effort in a given period
Premium Small extra "gift" with product	Cooperative Advertising Manufacturer and distributor share advertising costs
Competition Sweepstakes, contests, etc.	Dealer-Listed Promotion Manufacturer's ad that lists distributors
Demonstrations Showing product in use	Consignment Manufacturer finances distributor inventories
Trading Stamps	Point-of-Purchase Displays Countertop racks, posters, mechanized signs

From Ben M. Enis, *Marketing Principles: The Management Process*, 3rd ed. (Santa Monica, Calif.: Goodyear, 1980), p. 464.

display counter. The intention is to get shoppers to buy a package of the meat immediately after eating a small sample. Almost 50 percent of all supermarket purchases are directly influenced by some form of POP advertising in the store.

Probably the best known sales promotion is the use of samples, coupons, and premiums. Free samples of a new product can be sent by mail, distributed door-to-door, or put into packages containing other products. Procter & Gamble introduces new products by distributing millions of samples across America. Health clubs also use free "samples" of the facilities to attract new memberships. People are permitted to use the club's facilities free for a limited number of visits. The objective is to get a certain percentage of these free users as permanent club members. The coupons are distributed by mail, newspapers, magazines, trade journals, and package insertion. Premiums given away free with the purchase of another item serve as an inducement for consumers to buy a good or to use a service. Banks use premiums to get people to open new checking and savings accounts. Fuller Brush salespeople often give the adult answering the door a premium that helps introduce the salesperson to the potential customer.

Public Relations

Public relations is an organization's effort to improve its relationship with the public. The best description of public relations may be that used by *Fortune* magazine: "Good performance—publicly appreciated." This definition refers to the relationship between an organization and its many publics, including employees, customers, suppliers, stockholders, governments, or local communities.

PUBLIC RELATIONS
An organization's effort to improve its relationships with employees, customers, suppliers, stockholders, governments, and local communities.

Most organizations are concerned about public relations. For example, police forces in many large cities, such as Chicago, Dallas, and Los Angeles, have developed programs to better inform the local community about the business of law enforcement. And since the 1973 oil embargo, major energy companies have developed extensive public relations programs.

Publicity, the most direct way to promote good will, is information and news published about an organization but not paid for by that organization. It is free as opposed to public relations programs, which are paid for. Some of the more common forms of publicity are news releases, feature articles in a newspaper, editorials, and press conferences.

PUBLICITY
Information and news about an organization that is published by others and not paid for by the organization.

Personal Selling

All promotional efforts are not impersonal. Impersonal promotion can be directed easily and economically to mass audiences, but often it is necessary to reach fewer people on a personal basis. In this case, personal selling assumes an important role in the promotion mix.

Personal selling—one person selling directly to another person—is the most flexible form of promotion because the salesperson can adapt the message to meet most special situations. This is possible because the salesperson is face-to-face with the prospective customer.

Personal selling in America is not new. Around 1700, Yankee peddlers were selling goods in the eastern part of America. In fact, retail selling in America evolved from these Yankee peddlers. Most personal selling to retail customers now takes place in stores—car dealerships, fur shops, jewelry stores, department stores, and so on. But in-store selling has lost

HERSHEY VS. MARS

For sixty-six years, Hershey Foods spent no money on advertising because it sold all the candy bars it could produce. Hershey was the chocolate champion of the world. As Milton S. Hershey said, "Give them quality. That's the best kind of advertising in the world." That strategy worked for Hershey for over six decades.

Today the candy market is different, and candy bar sales are at their lowest level in forty-three years. Even in the last four years, per-capita candy consumption declined another two pounds. Total industry sales in America are declining toward $4.0 billion per year.

When this declining trend started in 1968, Hershey fought back. In an effort to get a bigger piece of a shrinking pie, Hershey started consumer advertising. Their attempt has paid off. The once chocolate champ now spends over $21 million a year on advertising and now has 30 percent of the market. Mars, which makes M&M's, Milky Way, and Snickers, still has a 36 percent market share, but the battle for the candy market lead rages.

Only recently Mars advertised it was raising the candy bar size 10 percent and holding the price. Finally, Mars had to raise prices, and Hershey countered with ads in 70 local newspapers. The Hershey ad stated "Hershey is holding the line on candy bar prices." There is no end in sight to the Hershey vs. Mars fight for candy market sales. Certainly both companies understand the importance of advertising in their ongoing battle.

Adapted from "Candy and Gum," *Marketing and Media Decisions*, November 1981, pp. 143–156.

some of its promotional importance because of personnel costs. This has resulted in the expansion of the self-service concept to retail stores like Target and K Mart. The self-service concept relies heavily on impersonal promotion, such as advertising and sales promotions, to pull people into the stores.

A second major form of retail selling is door-to-door selling, one of the oldest forms of selling. The importance of door-to-door selling for a wide variety of products has declined. Even so, products like vacuum cleaners (Kirby), encyclopedias (World Book), cosmetics (Avon), household products (Amway), and brushes (Fuller), continue to be sold successfully door-to-door. In fact, Avon has total annual sales of around $2 billion.

Business selling normally offers a good opportunity for a sales career. Products sold by business salespeople range from computers, typewriters, and office copiers to clothes, candy, and toys. The two primary forms of business selling are missionary selling and technical selling.

Missionary selling is used to develop good will and long-term sales for a product. One type of missionary salesperson is the medical detail person, who calls on doctors in their offices to convince them to prescribe the products sold by a pharmaceutical company. For example, Isordil, a medicine used by heart patients, has been promoted through missionary selling since 1959. It now has 46 percent of a $150 million yearly market.

MISSIONARY SELLING
Form of business selling used to develop good will and long-term sales for a product.

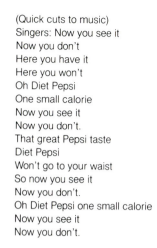

(Quick cuts to music)
Singers: Now you see it
Now you don't
Here you have it
Here you won't
Oh Diet Pepsi
One small calorie
Now you see it
Now you don't.
That great Pepsi taste
Diet Pepsi
Won't go to your waist
So now you see it
Now you don't.
Oh Diet Pepsi one small calorie
Now you see it
Now you don't.

(Sound of hissing steam)
Anncr. (VO): He's the working man
(Sound of sledge hammer striking metal)
Anncr. (VO): Forging dreams with fire
(Sound of hammer)
Anncr. (VO): Building, moving mountains
(Sound of hammer)
Anncr. (VO): Always reaching higher
(Sound of hammer)
Anncr. (VO): He's the wheels that move a nation.
(Sound of hammer)
Anncr. (VO): The stitching in the seams
(Sound of hammer)
Anncr. (VO): He holds it all together
(Sound of hammer)
Anncr. (VO): He wears Levi's jeans
(Sound of hammer)
Anncr. (VO): 'Cause he knows
(Sound of boards going up)
Anncr. (VO): We still build the Levi's jeans
that helped build America.

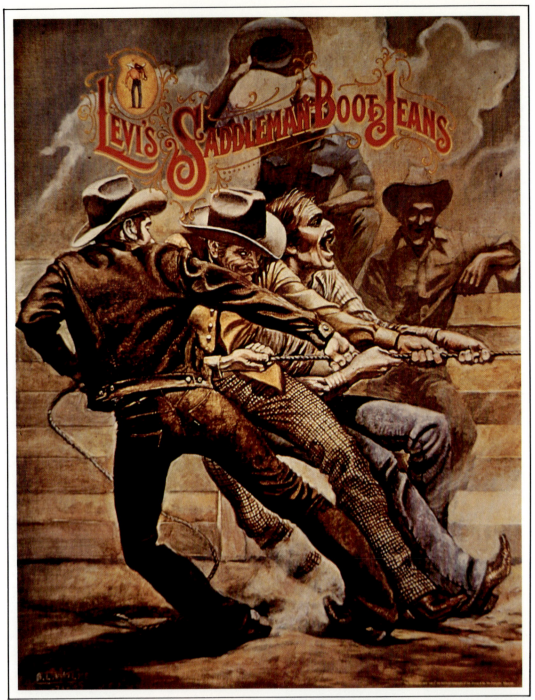

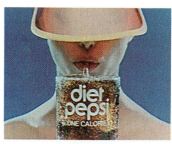

(Quick cuts to music)
Singers: Now you see it
Now you don't
Here you have it
Here you won't
Oh Diet Pepsi
One small calorie
Now you see it
Now you don't.
That great Pepsi taste
Diet Pepsi
Won't go to your waist
So now you see it
Now you don't.
Oh Diet Pepsi one small calorie
Now you see it
Now you don't.

(Sound of hissing steam)
Anncr. (VO): He's the working man
(Sound of sledge hammer striking metal)
Anncr. (VO): Forging dreams with fire
(Sound of hammer)
Anncr. (VO): Building, moving mountains
(Sound of hammer)
Anncr. (VO): Always reaching higher
(Sound of hammer)
Anncr. (VO): He's the wheels that move a nation.
(Sound of hammer)
Anncr. (VO): The stitching in the seams
(Sound of hammer)
Anncr. (VO): He holds it all together
(Sound of hammer)
Anncr. (VO): He wears Levi's jeans
(Sound of hammer)
Anncr. (VO): 'Cause he knows
(Sound of boards going up)
Anncr. (VO): We still build the Levi's jeans
that helped build America.

Technical selling requires that salespeople have a thorough understanding of both their product and the needs of customers. Technical salespeople sell heavy machinery, chemicals, electronic equipment, and other specialized products. They often serve as consultants to many of their customers by trying to apply new uses for their product to meet the needs of customers.

TECHNICAL SELLING
Form of business selling in which the salesperson tries to help customers adapt the product to their own needs.

SELECTING A PROMOTIONAL STRATEGY

An organization can use a number of promotional methods to communicate product information to consumers. Selecting the right combination of methods is not easy because several factors influence the promotion decision.

The product life cycle, discussed in Chapter 12, affects the choice of promotional method. For example, when electronic calculators were in the introduction stage, their promotion centered on the uses of the calculator. While the focus was to develop primary demand for calculators, personal selling and advertising were used. As the public began to accept electronic calculators (growth stage), the promotions began to center on promoting brand names, such as Texas Instruments and Casio. In this stage, national advertising was the major promotional tool, and developing selective demand was the goal.

Budget size also influences the choice of promotional methods. If the budget is limited, then national advertising is normally not possible. However, publicity, personal selling, and selective advertising might be used. Promotion budgets for some businesses, such as Procter & Gamble, exceed $600 million annually. Promotion budgets for small businesses, on the other hand, may total less than $5000 a year and still be adequate.

The nature of the product is a third factor that influences the promotion decision. For example, promoting a widely used popular product such as aspirin depends largely on national mass-advertising campaigns and sales promotion efforts. On the other hand, a specialized industrial product such as the machines used to manufacture aspirin is promoted through personal selling.

The most important factor may be the choice between a push or a pull strategy to move products through the channel of distribution. A **pull strategy** depends on promoting a product to a large audience. The idea is to create a demand so consumers will ask for the product. El Felix Restaurants rely on a pull strategy to get people into the restaurant locations, so Uri Cohen placed ads in three different local media. A **push strategy** requires that salespeople promote a product vigorously within the channel. Personal selling is the single most important promotion method for this type of strategy. In reality, effective marketing requires that both strategies be used to promote most products. What varies is the emphasis. As a rule of thumb, consumer products depend more on a pull strategy, and industrial products more frequently use a push strategy.

After considering the several factors that may affect the choice of an organization's promotional strategy, you can see that selecting a proper promotion mix is not easy. People do not fully understand what one promotional method does for different products. Moreover, it is hard to

PULL STRATEGY
A promotion campaign aimed at a large audience that creates a demand so consumers ask for a product.

PUSH STRATEGY
This requires salespeople to promote a product vigorously within the channel.

PROMOTIONAL METHOD	IMPACT ON INDIVIDUALS	IMPACT PER DOLLAR
Advertising	Low	High
Sales promotion	Low	High
Public relations	Low	High
Personal selling	High	Low

measure the overall results of any promotion mix. Even so, promotion is an essential part of an organization's marketing effort. Business surely knows that people buy more goods and services when their products or services are promoted. A summary of the impact of the major promotional methods is shown in Exhibit 14–6.

SUMMARY

- Promotion is used to inform, persuade, and influence a prospective buyer. Its main purpose is to get prospective buyers to become actual buyers—to make a purchase.
- The three ways that promotion most influences sales are by (1) telling consumers about a new product, (2) maintaining or increasing sales of an existing product, and (3) reversing the decline in sales of an "old" product.
- The major promotional methods include advertising, sales promotion, public relations, and personal selling.
- More total dollars are spent on advertising than any other type of promotion. The dollar expenditures for all businesses run into the billions each year.
- The major types of advertising media are print, broadcast, outdoor, and direct mail.
- Sales promotion includes many types of nonpersonal promotion, including trade shows, demonstrations, publicity, and public relations.
- Selling is the most personal and flexible form of promotion. A salesperson is in a position to adapt the message to meet most special situations with personal selling.
- Several factors influence the choice of a promotional strategy. Some of the important factors are the product life cycle, the budget size, the type of product, and the selection of a push or pull strategy for the distribution channel.

ISSUES TO CONSIDER AND ANALYZE

1. Explain how marketing communications and promotion are related.
2. Discuss the main objectives of promoting goods and services.
3. Why is the choice of a particular promotion mix one of the most difficult decisions an organization must make?
4. Explain the major difference between push and pull promotion strategies.
5. Why do you think the federal government banned cigarette advertising on broadcast media?
6. Why do you think Procter & Gamble spends more money on advertising than U.S. Steel?
7. As a marketing consultant, what form of promotional method, if any, would you recommend for the following organizations?

    a. Supermarket like Kroger's
    b. County government like Cook County (Chicago), Illinois
    c. Professional football team like San Diego Chargers
    d. Local radio station like WNBC (New York)
    e. Medical doctor in Pittsburgh
    f. New car dealer in Boise, Idaho

8. Explain why most businesses use advertising and personal selling as their major methods of promotion.

9. Why is it necessary to use various promotional methods if a well-trained salesperson can perform almost any selling job better than any other promotional method?

10. Explain why national ads appearing on the Super Bowl can cost businesses $360,000 for thirty seconds. Would this be a good buy for a business selling heavy industrial equipment?

McLEMORE CLINIC TRIES MARKETING

CASE FOR ANALYSIS

Lily Johnson is the General Manager of McLemore Clinic, a clinic staffed by twenty-eight doctors in New Orleans. McLemore Clinic has a good reputation in the local community, but the number of patients treated is on the decline. Johnson is concerned, and she blames the decline on too many doctors competing for too few patients. The problem, as she sees it, is that more than one doctor in the market area is looking for the same patient. She cites some data from the Department of Health and Human Services that predicts an oversupply of 70,000 doctors in America by 1990.

Johnson has just returned from a national medical seminar where the subject was marketing medical services. She thought some of the ideas presented by marketing and advertising experts were good. As a result, the Chief of Staff, Dr. Duman O'Meara, called a clinic meeting for the department heads and head nurses.

At the meeting, Johnson outlined some ideas that she thought would help attract and keep patients at McLemore Clinic. Several of her ideas were "new" to the medical field. For example, Johnson suggested the following:

1. Change the clinic hours for the early morning and late evening patients. Also, Saturday morning hours should be set.

2. Publish a medical newsletter on different subjects for distribution to the clinic's regular patients.

3. Check with patients to find out what they like and dislike about the clinic's operation.

4. Send flowers to people who refer a patient.

QUESTIONS

1. Evaluate the four suggestions made by Johnson. Explain why you agree or disagree with each.

2. Can you suggest other possible marketing ideas for McLemore Clinic?

Adapted from Susan Tompor, "Doctors Turn to Marketing to Get Patients," *The Wall Street Journal,* September 1, 1981, p. 29.

MARKETING

In a sense, marketing is the very essence of business. Marketing is everything that happens from the time a product is planned until it is sold. In fact, marketing even continues after the sale because products often require servicing, special maintenance, or warranty work.

Because of the diversity of business activities associated with marketing, a variety of job opportunities are available. Some marketing areas in which you may work are consumer and industrial product sales, sales management, advertising and promotion, and marketing research.

SALES

It has often been said that nothing ever happens in business until the cash register rings. Although the plastic credit card may replace the cash register, the basic idea of this statement is still true. Sales make the register ring, and salespersons are on the front line of the effort to make sales.

Even though selling as a career has a long history and its importance to business is not often questioned, many people do not hold the career in high esteem. This poor reputation is partially the result of the image of the fast-talking, flashy salesperson of past years. Today's salesperson must be well trained because most customers are sophisticated. Even the job title has changed. Salespersons are often called account executives, marketing representatives, sales consultants, sales engineers, or sales representatives.

Selling requires a salesperson to become very familiar with customers in order to properly meet their needs. Thus, career salespeople must work to understand human nature. A salesperson deals with people on a day-to-day basis, whether selling consumer products or industrial products.

The beginning salary of salespeople doesn't always rank as high as other occupations. However, salespeople may be furnished with an automobile and expense accounts, which may be worth an additional $8000 to $9000 per year. After a few years of effective performance, salespeople often find that their salaries increase significantly due to bonus, commission, or incentive plans. It is possible for salespeople to earn over $50,000 annually after five to seven years on the job. Examples of some typical sales jobs are shown in Exhibit IV–A. A person's success in sales depends in large part on his or her ability to communicate, maintain self-discipline, and work hard.

SALES MANAGEMENT

After a person proves his or her ability to sell, a potential career step is to become a sales manager. In this job, the emphasis is directed more toward management than sales. Sales management represents one of the first steps a person may take into the ranks of corporate management. A person often enters sales management as a district sales manager with the responsibility of directly supervising the sales efforts of two or more salespersons. A district sales manager makes sure sales objectives are met and helps the salespeople develop their selling ability.

Exhibit IV–A contains descriptions of two sales management jobs. This important first step into corporate management can lead to several top-level jobs, including national sales manager or vice president of sales. Of course, the possibility to increase your salary improves significantly as you move into higher positions. It is not unusual to find jobs in top sales management paying in the $70,000 to $90,000 range.

ADVERTISING AND PROMOTION

Most organizations use advertising agencies, rather than internal advertising departments, to develop complete promotional programs. Consequently, there are relatively few advertising jobs available for college graduates within most organizations. When internal advertising departments exist, they are typically small.

The most promising opportunities for advertising careers exist within advertising agencies. For example, a person might become a copywriter. The job of a copywriter involves the preparation of the script for ads that appear in books and magazines and on radio and television. Copywriters must be very skilled in using language, be creative, and understand the fundamentals of marketing. Other job opportunities are available in agency production, which makes sure all the groups involved in producing ads do their job properly.

Traffic is a part of agency management that is suitable for people who enjoy facing strict deadlines and having substantial personal contact. In this job, a person plans the flow of agency work to see that an ad is produced on time. The job requires a person to coordinate the activities of several different people within the agency, including copywriters, typesetters, and artists.

Another important job is the account executive. This is the agency person with a direct link to the customer. An account executive's job can be demanding and exciting. First, the account executive must thoroughly understand advertising and the needs of the agency. Second, this person must also understand the nature and operation of the client's business. This means account executives need a thorough

SALES DIVISION

SALES REP This on-the-grow consumer product manufacturer seeks a success-oriented individual to develop new business nationwide. Travel and take advantage of unlimited salary potential—look for minimum earnings of $50,000 within 3 years.

Salary area $27,500 +

INDUSTRIAL SALES

. . . This national manufacturer needs a success-oriented sales rep with proven industrial sales experience. Second year earnings to $29,500.

Salary area $24,200

VP-SALES
Paint or Hardgoods Field

Major paint brush, paint roller, and paint applicator manufacturer with complete and diverse national distribution has an excellent opportunity for an aggressive, strong, shirt-sleeve sales administrator with proven background. Excellent salary and fringe benefits commensurate with experience and background. Please send full resume in complete confidence to:

J. A. Davis, President
AMERICAN PAINT COMPANY
17 N. Walnut
Seattle, Washington 98250

An Equal Opportunity Employer

PHARMACEUTICAL SALES TRAINEE

Just one year of outside sales experience plus a degree could capture this medical field opportunity. Earn while you learn with guaranteed commissions paid monthly. Benefits, expenses and car.

Salary area $15,000

SALES MANAGER
Concrete Forms and Shoring

Our 16-year-old company manufactures a forming system, shoring system and related products for sale and lease to the construction industry. We are entering the U.S. market, with Houston as headquarters. The person we seek will have a successful sales and sales management background in this type of work and will work with us on building up our existing operations in Texas, and then nationwide. This opportunity can rapidly lead to Vice President of Sales for the qualified person. If you are interested in talking with us, call Sam Smith this week at (713) 590–1111 or send your resume to:

Southern Concrete Company
P.O. Box 159
Bay City, TX 77711

EXHIBIT IV–A
Sales Career Advertisements

303

SALES PROMOTION MANAGER

Leading Appliance Manufacturer is seeking a creative person to manage sales promotion activities for its varied housewares line.

Responsibilities will include promotional support for new products, development of promotional tie-ins with other companies, merchandising ideas, and coordination of activities for trade shows and sales meetings. Also the preparation of catalogs, sales literature and point-of-purchase displays, etc.

Qualified applicants should possess 2–3 years applicable experience with knowledge of promotion techniques, graphic arts, printing and production. Must be able to handle several items simultaneously and have good budget controls, planning and supervisory skills. A college degree is preferred but not required.

We offer an excellent salary, attractive suburban Philadelphia location and a comprehensive benefits package including tuition reimbursement.

MANAGER MARKETING RESEARCH
CONSUMER PRODUCTS

We are a major Chicago area consumer product company looking for a Manager of the Market Research Department. It is a unique supervisory position, in that the individual will not only be responsible for all market research activities, but will be directly involved in following through on Research results, developing marketing plans, and seeing that they are implemented.

The successful candidate must have solid marketing research experience and be a self-starter, possessing considerable strength in communicating and interfacing with people. A minimum of 4 to 6 years experience in marketing research and marketing of consumer packaged goods required (MBA preferred). We offer good company benefits; salary will be commensurate with experience and responsibilities.

ACCOUNT EXECUTIVE

Major Southeastern agency has position open for strong, versatile Account Executive for Birmingham office.

Candidate should have 3–6 years agency experience; be capable of handling various accounts including: package goods and financial institutions.

Excellent opportunity to progress with an agency recognized for consistent growth and a strong new business record.

MARKETING RESEARCH ANALYST

We are looking for a professional marketing researcher to join our expanding group.

She or he should have 3–5 years of solid experience including start-to-finish project responsibility in consumer packaged goods MR. The ability to analyze data, and to express the analysis in written report form, is of major importance. Some experience with a research supplier is desirable but not a necessity.

This position is in our corporate headquarters and reports directly to the department manager.

EXHIBIT IV–B
Advertisements for Jobs in Marketing

understanding of business in general and marketing in particular. Life as an account executive can be very rewarding financially but very demanding on a person's time.

Careers in sales promotion involve almost every aspect of promotion except media advertising. The main objective of sales promotion is to increase sales. A person pursuing a marketing career that involves sales promotion must be creative and aggressive, and understand the marketing process. Work in sales promotion might involve appearing at trade shows, running direct-mail campaigns, developing point-of-purchase displays for retail stores, attending company sales meetings to promote new products to a sales force, and developing national sweepstakes and contests. The job involves a significant amount of contact with other people.

Several ads for jobs in advertising and promotion are shown in Exhibit IV–B. There is a wide diversity of jobs and salary ranges available to people seeking advertising and promotion careers.

MARKETING RESEARCH

Marketing research, a specialized area of marketing, involves developing market information and solving marketing problems. Many large organizations maintain an internal marketing research staff, but others use independent marketing research companies.

Marketing research staffs become involved with a variety of specific marketing activities. One area involves research on existing and proposed new products. These types of studies are designed to collect information on consumer opinions of trademarks, brand names, product design, and product quality of an organization's products. This type of research is also used to collect similar information on the competition's products.

Another area of marketing research involves the study of advertising programs. In this type of research, attempts are made to measure consumer recall of advertising, to determine whether consumers remember an advertising message, and to collect consumer opinions of the media used to carry the ads. The purpose of this type of advertising information is to help in planning more effective advertising programs.

Research on sales methods and price policies also is an important area of marketing research. In these studies, company records are analyzed to determine sales performance in various sales regions. Current performance is compared to past performance and the sales potential of each region. This provides sales managers with a strategy to evaluate the performance of their sales force.

Marketing research staffs often prepare sales forecasts for various products. This is important planning information for the management of the marketing department and the entire organization. Preparing sales forecasts requires an analysis of future economic conditions, population changes, economic trends in various sections of the country, and opinions of consumers.

Some of the information used in marketing research studies—including selling costs, customer order size, and frequency of purchase—is available from internal company records. Other information must be collected externally from consumers, usually by mail, telephone, or personal interview using a questionnaire. These data are analyzed, interpreted, and summarized into a written report.

People interested in marketing research careers should have training in statistics, psychology, sociology, marketing, and communications. It is very important to develop the skill of written communication because marketing research involves the preparation of many written reports. Examples of some typical marketing research jobs are shown in Exhibit IV–B.

PROFILE IN BUSINESS

Amadeo Peter Giannini
(1870–1949)

Gabriel Moulin Studios

He drove a cart through San Francisco after the earthquake with $2 million hidden in a pile of vegetables.

Amadeo Giannini's immigrant parents journeyed to California on the just-completed transcontinental railroad in 1869, the year before his birth. Giannini spent his early years in fertile ranch country, then moved to San Francisco when his father was killed by a farmhand and his mother remarried. His stepfather built up a prosperous produce business, which Amadeo joined as a full partner when he was nineteen. At thirty-one, married and comfortably invested in real estate, he sold his produce interests to the firm's employees and retired. "I don't want to be rich," he said. "No man actually owns a fortune; it owns him."

The death of his father-in-law in 1902 drew Giannini into the management of his in-laws' estate, including a directorship in the diminutive Columbus Savings and Loan Society in the Italian neighborhood of North Beach. Most of San Francisco's and Columbus's investments flowed out of the community in large chunks at that time, leaving the little guy around the corner to deal with loan sharks. Giannini tried to alter this policy in favor of small loans to local immigrants. When the controlling faction of the bank spurned his proposals, he resigned to help form the Bank of Italy.

A. P. (as he came to be called) dominated the new bank from the beginning—encouraging small loans to farmers, merchants, and laborers, drumming up business on the streets from people who had never used a bank before, and promoting broad stock ownership. Deposits grew

PART FIVE

FINANCING AND INSURING BUSINESS

steadily. But it was the great earthquake and fire of 1906 that catapulted the Bank of Italy into prominence. As the fire approached his bank building, Giannini drove a vegetable cart through bands of roving looters with $2 million in gold and securities hidden in a mound of produce. A board across two barrels put the Bank of Italy back in business the next day, offering immediate loans to ruined businesses and earning a reputation for resourceful stability. Giannini enhanced that reputation by hoarding gold in anticipation of the panic of 1907, enabling the Bank of Italy to cover withdrawals in hard money while other institutions resorted to clearinghouse certificates.

The panic convinced Giannini that the only truly secure bank was a big bank. He began buying up small banks around San Francisco and farther afield, converting them into Bank of Italy branches and starting the nation's first major program of branch banking. Local competitors and alarmed financiers fought this grass-roots expansion without success. Giannini was careful to keep and encourage local stockholders in each branch and to hire multilingual staffs to serve immigrants. He aligned the Bank of Italy behind California's agricultural interests at the beginning of their phenomenal development. Bank branches spread throughout the state.

To facilitate expansion, Giannini formed the Bancitaly Corporation in 1919 and the Transamerica Corporation in 1928, the latter a holding company for all his banking, insurance, and industrial ventures. In the following year, he took over the Bank of America in New York, consolidating his banks into the Bank of America National Trust and Savings Association. It became the largest bank in the world—but never quite the "transcontinental bank," with branches in every corner of every state to serve small depositors and borrowers, which Giannini had envisioned.

At the time of his death, Giannini was fighting Federal Reserve Board charges that Transamerica had violated the Clayton Antitrust Act with a credit monopoly. The charges stung Giannini's sense of kinship with the common man. He had never been a major stockholder in his own ventures (or any others), preferring to disperse ownership in many hands and to exercise control through his considerable force of personality. Although his financial empire echoed the power and prestige of the House of Morgan, A. P. Giannini left an estate valued at less than $500,000.

CHAPTER 15

MONEY AND BANKING

LEARNING OBJECTIVES

After studying this chapter, you should be able to:

Discuss the characteristics of money.

Identify the different types of money.

Discuss the development of our central bank—the Federal Reserve System.

Understand the structure of the American banking system.

Explain the major functions performed by the Federal Reserve System.

Discuss the different types of financial institutions.

Define electronic funds transfer system (EFTS).

KEY TERMS

Money
Liquidity
Demand deposits
Cashier's check
Certified check
NOW accounts
Credit union share
    drafts
Automatic transfer
    system (ATS)
Money market mutual
    funds
Depository institutions
Time deposits
Certificates of deposit
Traveler's checks
Secured loans
Accounts receivable
Factoring company
Open-market operations
Discount operations
Discount rate
Fractional reserve
    banking system
Reserve requirements
Margin requirements
Electronic funds trans-
    fer system (EFTS)

MOVING INTO THE NEW WORLD
OF DIVERSIFIED BANKING

Greg Preston spent four years studying finance at Eastern Michigan University before taking a position with the City National Bank in Detroit. City National placed him in the training program for operations officers. Because operations officers are responsible for the smooth functioning of branch offices, they must learn all facets of the banking business. Branch management is Greg's present goal because, as he puts it, "I enjoy being with and helping people. The branch operations allow me to meet a number of new people every day, and I enjoy helping them solve their financial problems."

Greg plans to begin his banking career as an assistant operations officer; he then hopes to advance to operations officer at a smaller branch office and eventually to a larger office. Later he may move into regional administration.

The banking system Greg is involved in has been undergoing major changes for several years. Many of these changes will have long-range and profound effects on how people do their banking for many years to come. Greg says, "City National is developing new programs and services for people almost continually. These programs help our customers get better control over their finances. And to be quite frank, such changes are necessary in the highly competitive banking industry of today. For many years the industry has been slow to change; times are different, though. Deregulation in the industry is forcing everybody to keep on their toes and offer more and more services to their customers." Some of the programs Greg refers to are the establishment of remote service units, automatic transfers from savings to checking accounts, and interest-earning checking accounts. Electronic tellers in several local grocery stores will be introduced as well as twenty-four-hour banking services. Finally, Greg's bank is considering helping its customers buy and sell stocks and bonds.

In this chapter, you will explore the rapidly changing banking world that Greg has described. And you will take a closer look at the financial institutions in the overall banking system.

Most business transactions involve the transfer of money from one person or institution to another. Greg, in his position as a small bank branch manager, may handle hundreds of thousands of dollars each day: his customers make deposits, withdraw funds, cash checks, and so on. Greg is part of a banking system in which money plays an essential role. The first question you might ask is, What is money?

On the Job Revisited

The strict dictionary definition of **money** is "any article or substance used as a medium of exchange, measure of wealth, or means of payment." Given this definition, we see that throughout human history different societies have used a variety of items as money, including beads, shells, rocks, and even salt. Money used in modern societies must have certain characteristics in order to remain a circulating means of exchange.

Money must be a durable substance—it has to last for a considerable time. A dollar bill, for example, can be folded thousands of times before it must be replaced, and some coins have lasted thousands of years. Second, money must be produced and designed so that it cannot be easily counterfeited. If this were not the case, money would no longer be scarce, and its value would decline accordingly. Third, money should be relatively easy to divide and carry around. Fourth, money must have the characteristic of **liquidity**; that is, money must be easily converted to other forms of wealth without loss of value. Finally, money must have relatively predictable purchasing power.

Most people think of money in terms of coins and paper bills—what we define as currency, or cash. Money, however, includes currency plus all checking-type accounts. Additionally, money could also include unused credit card balances, sometimes referred to as plastic money.

CURRENCY   All coins and bills are typically referred to as currency, yet currency only constitutes about 20 percent of the amount of money in circulation in the United States today. In 1982, the estimated amount of currency in the economy for every individual in the country was $660. Compare this with just $162 in 1960. During this twenty-three-year period, the number of hundred-dollar bills increased more than eightfold. An incredible 90.6 percent of all hundred-dollar bills in circulation have been hoarded by their owners. In spite of talk about the cashless society, cash is still king.

DEMAND DEPOSITS, OR CHECKING ACCOUNTS   In this country, checks are used as money. Checking account balances, or **demand deposit** balances, are a major part of our money supply. A checking account balance is called a demand deposit because the owner of such an account can demand payment at any time. There are two special types of checks that those engaged in business use frequently: cashier's checks and certified checks. A **cashier's check** results when a bank draws a check on itself. In effect, the bank lends its credibility to the purchaser of the check, thus

WHAT IS MONEY?

MONEY
Anything that is generally accepted as a means of paying for goods and services received.

The Several Features of Money

LIQUIDITY
Moneyness, or the ability of something to be easily converted into other forms of wealth without loss of value. Money is the most liquid of all assets by definition.

Types of Money

DEMAND DEPOSITS
A sum of money a bank sets aside for a customer when it establishes a checking account for him or her.

CASHIER'S CHECK
A check drawn by a bank on its own funds and signed by the cashier.

EXHIBIT 15-1
Examples of Early American Currency

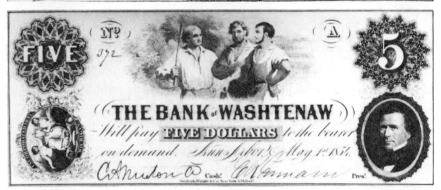

CERTIFIED CHECK
A check certified to be good by the bank on which it is drawn.

making the check available for immediate use throughout the banking system—that check is as good as cash in most instances. A **certified check** is guaranteed by the issuing bank. When a check is marked "certified," a bank promises that it has set aside sufficient funds from the drawer's account to cover the check when it is presented for cashing. The bank cannot deny payment.

OTHER CHECKING-TYPE ACCOUNTS   The money supply once primarily consisted of currency plus demand deposits at regular commercial banks. Since January 1, 1981, the money supply has expanded to include various checking-type accounts; that is, accounts serving the same purpose as

checking accounts but held at institutions other than commercial banks.*
Examples of these are:

1. **NOW accounts.** NOW stands for "negotiable order of withdrawal." A NOW account allows one to earn interest on the account balance and still write checks. NOW accounts were created by mutual savings banks and other financial institutions in an attempt to compete with regular, or commercial, banks for business. Such accounts typically require a minimum balance of $300 to $500, and they pay less interest than regular savings accounts.
2. **Credit union share drafts.** All federally insured credit unions can offer share draft accounts. This means that credit unions can offer a service similar to commercial checking accounts.
3. **Automatic transfer system (ATS).** The use of an automatic transfer system allows a person to earn interest on a savings account that can be automatically transferred from the savings account to a noninterest-earning checking account whenever there is a negative balance.

MONEY MARKET MUTUAL FUNDS   Recently, a large number of **money market mutual funds**—companies that purchase U.S. government and corporate fixed income-earning securities—have begun offering check-writing privileges. In such money market mutual funds, checks normally cannot be written for less than $500 or $1000.

PLASTIC MONEY   Credit cards seem to crop up everywhere. One might think that the money supply is expanding rapidly because people simply use credit cards whenever they want. Such is not the case, however. Only a customer's unused credit line can rightfully be considered part of the money supply. And, surprisingly enough, if we add up all of the unused credit lines available to all credit card holders in the United States, the grand total would add only a couple of percentage points to the stock of money in circulation.

Deregulation has had an impact on the business practices of banks. Greg, in his job as operations manager of a branch bank, sits in on regional monthly meetings where all the branch managers get together. One of their current problems is to decide to what degree their bank should fend off competition from local savings and loans and credit unions. Until recently, Greg's bank didn't even offer interest-earning checking accounts. Greg believed that his bank was losing business and had to meet the competition. He effectively argued that interest should be paid on checking accounts automatically and that a big promotional campaign should be launched.

Additionally, Greg thinks that the bank is going to have to start competing with total money management organizations, such as Merrill Lynch, Kidder Peabody, and other large stock brokerage firms. These firms have

NOW ACCOUNTS
Essentially a checking account that pays interest.

CREDIT UNION SHARE DRAFTS
A checking-type account in which a credit union allows individuals to write share drafts (checks) on their credit union accounts.

AUTOMATIC TRANSFER SYSTEM (ATS)
The use of an automatic transfer system allows a person to earn interest on a savings account from which monies can be automatically transferred to cover overdrafts on a normal, noninterest-bearing checking account.

MONEY MARKET MUTUAL FUND
A mutual fund—investment company—that purchases only U. S. government and corporate fixed income-earning securities.

On the Job Revisited

---

*The Congress passed the Depository Institutions Deregulation and Monetary Control Act of 1980, which allowed for savings and loans, mutual savings banks, credit unions, and other financial institutions to offer various checking-type accounts. Prior to January 1, 1981, there was a limited number of such accounts that were legal in various states.

started to offer what appears to be check-writing privileges, instant liquidity while earning high interest rates in money market mutual funds, the ability to buy and sell stocks and bonds using money in the different accounts, and so on. The higher-up management in Greg's bank is not so certain it is ready to jump into total banking and financial servicing of every individual.

BANKS AND FINANCIAL INSTITUTIONS IN THE UNITED STATES

DEPOSITORY INSTITUTIONS
Any financial institution that can accept deposits, including commercial banks, savings and loan associations, and credit unions.

Businesses can turn to a variety of financial institutions in addition to banks for help with their short-term financing problems. Short-term financing involves borrowing money over a limited several-year period. Financial institutions today are often called **depository institutions** because most of them are authorized to accept deposits from customers and, more important, to allow customers to write checks (or their equivalents) on those deposits. Indeed, the passage of the Depository Institutions Deregulation and Monetary Control Act of 1980 has made the differences among the various types of financial institutions in our country less distinct. Nonetheless, we will offer a short explanation of the main kinds of financial institutions as they now exist.

Commercial Banks

TIME DEPOSITS
Deposits that, in principle, require at least thirty days' notice prior to the withdrawal of funds.

CERTIFICATES OF DEPOSIT
Certificates that are usually sold in units of $1000 or more and that carry fixed maturity dates varying from thirty days to six years or more from the date of issue.

TRAVELER'S CHECK
A check issued by American Express, VISA, or a commercial bank that acts as a substitute for money. The bearer of the check signs once when purchasing the check and countersigns when cashing the check.

A commercial bank is defined as a bank that can offer checking accounts, or demand deposits, to its customers. Until 1981, this was the great distinction between commercial banks and other financial institutions. By law, no other institution could offer true checking accounts. Over fourteen thousand commercial banks participate in the American banking system. Some are chartered by the federal government—national banks—and some by state governments—state banks.

Commercial banks are profit-seeking, privately owned institutions. In addition to checking accounts, depositors can have **time deposits**—savings accounts and **certificates of deposit** (CDS). Time deposits are so called because, in principle, the bank can require thirty days' notice of the owner's intent to withdraw from such accounts. In the case of certificates of deposit, early withdrawal of money results in a substantial interest penalty.

Commercial banks not only accept deposits and make loans to individuals and firms, but they also sell **traveler's checks**, supply bank drafts, certify checks, provide financial advice, supply credit cards to customers, rent safe deposit boxes, act as trustees for both corporate and individual funds, and administer estates.

Savings Banks

Savings banks are the oldest type of savings institution in the country. They were first organized in Boston and Philadelphia to serve individuals looking for a place to deposit their money. Earlier commercial banks did not provide savings accounts. Most savings banks were organized in the early nineteenth century as mutual banks; this means that they were (and still are) owned by their depositors rather than by a group of stockholders. There are approximately five hundred mutual savings banks today, located primarily in the northeastern United States. Only eighteen states and the Commonwealth of Puerto Rico have chartered savings banks. In addition

BUSINESS, BUT NOT AS USUAL

Competition in the banking industry is heating up. Not only are financial institutions like savings and loan associations, savings banks, and credit unions adding many bank services, but many manufacturing companies are also beginning to enter the banking business. Over the past several years, due to changes in the banking industry, several manufacturing companies have been able to get around the Bank Holding Company Act of 1970 that specifically requires all nonbanking companies to get entirely out of banking within ten years.

The question becomes, How are they doing it? The case of Dana Corporation of Toledo, Ohio, is a good example. Dana recently bought the $700 million General Ohio Savings and Loan Corporation through Dana's subsidiary, Diamond Financial Holdings. As David Stevens, president of Diamond, says, "We've been looking for a financial vehicle, and a savings and loan was the most appropriate." This is particularly true since from a regulatory point of view Dana could not own a bank. The rule does not apply to savings and loans, however. Today, of course, savings and loans are becoming more and more like commercial banks, and Dana can now do many of the things it has wanted to in the commercial banking area through its ownership of General Ohio Savings and Loan.

"We started thinking about all this before deregulation was a fact," Stevens said. "We have definite plans for our savings and loan, but we'd rather not discuss the specifics until we've accomplished them." The savings and loan should fit into Dana's other businesses, which include an insurance company, three small reinsurance companies, and a home building firm.

Other large manufacturing businesses that are getting into the banking industry include Gulf and Western Industries, International Paper, and Baldwin-United. Sears Roebuck and Company, a retail firm, has also entered the banking business.

Source: "Banking: New Allies and Competitors," *Forbes*, February 2, 1981, p. 84.

---

to providing funds for the purchase of corporate bonds and government securities, savings banks also offer mortgage money. In general, savings banks are not of primary importance to the business firm, although this could change in the future.

Savings and Loan Associations

Savings and loan associations (called S & Ls) accept time deposits. Though historically limited to loaning money for mortgages on homes and other real estate, savings and loans are allowed to loan money for automobiles and other consumer items. There are about four thousand state chartered and two thousand federally chartered savings and loan institutions in the United States today. Although some of them are mutual companies, most are owned by a group of stockholders that pays interest to depositors.

In 1950, the assets held by savings banks and savings and loan associations were almost equal. By 1973, however, savings and loan associations enjoyed two times the assets of savings banks, and this trend is continuing. The recent deregulation of the banking industry has allowed savings and loan associations to add numerous services—business and personal loans, credit cards, and checking-type accounts.

Credit Unions

Basically, credit unions are savings and loan cooperatives whose members purchase shares. Thus, shareholder-members participate in earnings from loans made to members. Typically, there is a restriction on who can become a member of a credit union. Employees of businesses, government, and some educational institutions are usually eligible to join a particular credit union.

Credit unions often make short-term loans to members for boats, furniture, cars, and other personal needs. Deregulation has allowed credit unions to offer members the opportunity to pay bills with credit union share drafts; these drafts are similar to checks, but they are drawn on the member's interest-paying account at the credit union. Some credit unions now offer credit and/or debit cards. A debit card is similar to plastic money—a credit card—except that the money spent is deducted *immediately* from the customer's account.

Consumer Finance Companies

Companies that specialize in personal, short-term loans for any purpose are called consumer finance companies. Usually, loans of up to $2500 are available, and they are typically repayable in monthly or weekly installments. Consumer finance companies are the largest source of installment-cash loans. Approximately twenty-five thousand are licensed throughout America today.

Sales Finance Companies

A source of credit for many businesspersons is the sales finance company. Such companies finance installment credit for the purchase of automobiles, appliances, furniture, and other durable goods. They provide a vital credit function to dealers who otherwise would not have the financial resources to offer credit to their customers. In addition, many sales finance companies handle installment sales to businesses. If a business can't secure money from a commercial bank, it will often turn to a sales finance company for funds to purchase equipment or store fixtures.

Some of the most well known and largest sales finance companies are the General Motors Acceptance Corporation (GMAC), the General Electric Credit Corporation (GECC), and the Ford Motor Credit Corporation (FMCC). In effect, sales finance companies such as GMAC buy installment credit from retail merchants. This way retailers can transfer the risk involved in lending money.

Commercial Finance Companies and Factoring Companies

SECURED LOANS
Loans that are secured by collateral, such as heavy equipment, inventories, or real estate.

ACCOUNTS RECEIVABLE
Monies owed to a business for goods or services already delivered or rendered but not yet paid for by the customer.

FACTORING COMPANY
A company that buys accounts receivable at a discount.

Commercial finance companies lend money to businesses through **secured loans**. This means that the debt is backed by something tangible, such as heavy equipment or inventories or even by the business's **accounts receivable** (moneys owed but not yet paid by customers). Typically, a firm will go to a commercial finance company only if it can't secure a short-term loan from a commercial bank.

Similar to a commercial finance company is a **factoring company**, which will buy the accounts receivable from a business at a discount. For example, suppose ABC Wire Company has an accounts receivable of $50,000. A factoring company may pay $42,000 for them. ABC's customers will then pay their bills directly to the factoring company (or factor). If a customer refuses to pay, the factoring company must take the loss. Small firms typically use factoring companies more often than larger ones do.

The early history of banking in the United States is characterized by a lack of direction and, at times, general confusion. Since many people were hesitant to grant too much financial power to a central banking authority, it was some time before a national bank was established.

Congress chartered the first National Bank of the United States in 1791 to help stabilize the country's currency, gather gold and silver to mint coins, collect import duties, manage foreign exchange, and sell bonds to finance the government's operation. Although successful in bringing some semblance of order to the banking system, the bank's twenty-year charter was not renewed in 1811.

After severe problems with inflation and financing the War of 1812, Congress once again moved to establish a national bank. In 1816, the second National Bank of the United States was established and given a twenty-year charter. Under the leadership of Nicholas Biddle, this bank was even more successful than the first National Bank. Biddle's bank, as it was called, brought order to the banking system by redeeming state bank notes and issuing national bank notes. It also helped control fluctuations in the national economy. Biddle realized that depression and recovery had a relationship to the supply of money in the national economy. By regulating the amount of money in circulation, he became one of the first economists to try stabilizing the economy through control of the money supply. This is called a *monetary policy* today. In spite of its successes, the charter for Biddle's bank was not renewed in 1836.

From 1836 to 1863, there were no national banks, and "wildcat" banking reached its peak. State banks were chartered with little capital, and almost anyone could go into banking. Because of limited funds, many banks failed, causing financial loss to stockholders and depositors alike.

The turn of the century proved to be a difficult time for the banking system. Many people were suspicious of bankers and felt that they were the ones causing the economic recessions. Following a money panic in 1907, Congress established the National Monetary Commission to study banking reform. The commission's hearings revealed that many bankers were trying to consolidate economic power in an effort to control the American banking system. Because of the commission's findings, Congress passed, and President Wilson signed, the Federal Reserve Act of 1913, which established our Federal Reserve System.

A SHORT HISTORY OF AMERICAN BANKING

Since its establishment in 1913, the Federal Reserve System—called the Fed—has served as the central bank of the United States. Unlike central banks of other developed countries, however, the Fed is not legally an agency of the federal government. Instead, the Fed is owned and managed by its member banks. However, the Fed is a de facto arm of the government.

The Federal Reserve System has divided the United States into twelve districts (see Exhibit 15–2), based on each district's economic activity. For instance, the first district is made up of the New England states; the second is basically the state of New York; in contrast, the twelfth district encom-

THE FEDERAL RESERVE SYSTEM

The Structure of the System

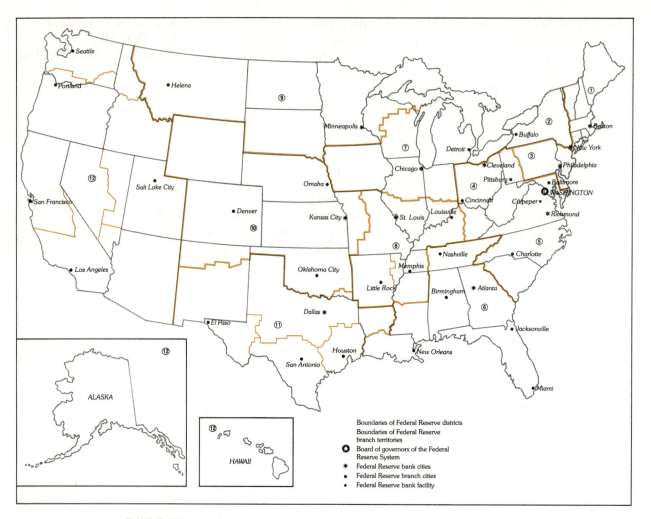

EXHIBIT 15-2

Boundaries of the Federal Reserve
Districts and Their Branch Territories
Source: United States Federal Reserve
System, Board of Governors, *Federal
Reserve Bulletin* 64, April 1978, p. A78.

passes eight large western states. Within each district there is a district
bank, and twenty-five branch banks are scattered throughout the country.
Some districts do not have branch banks; on the other hand, some have as
many as five branch banks. The Fed's main office is in Washington, D.C.

THE BOARD OF GOVERNORS   The Fed is headed by a seven-member board
of governors appointed by the president of the United States and
confirmed by the Senate. Each member is appointed for a fourteen-year
term, and every other year another member retires and is replaced.

   Like the Supreme Court of the United States, the board of governors of
the Federal Reserve System is free from the control of the executive branch
of the federal government. Members of the board of governors cannot be
removed from office except under unusual circumstances, and so are free
to make decisions without political pressure. Nonetheless, conflict
between the Fed and political figures is not uncommon.

FEDERAL OPEN MARKET COMMITTEE   The Federal Open Market Committee assists the Fed's board of governors in setting policy. This committee is composed of twelve members, including the Fed's board of governors plus five members elected from the district banks. One of the five elected representatives is always from the New York Federal Reserve Bank because of New York's position as the leading national and international financial center.

The original purposes of the Fed as expressed by its founders were to give the country an elastic currency, provide facilities for discounting commercial paper, and improve the supervision of banking. From the outset, though, it was obvious that these purposes had even broader objectives. The system was supposed to help counteract inflationary and deflationary movements in the economy. In addition, the Fed was to create an economic atmosphere conductive to a high level of employment, a stable dollar, continuing growth, and a rising level of consumption. Thus, the Fed recognized the relationship between the amount of money in circulation and economic conditions in the country.

The Functions of the System

The Fed controls the amount of money in circulation through what is called monetary policy. In implementing its monetary policy, the Fed uses four tools: open-market operations, discount operations, reserve requirements, and margin requirements.

OPEN-MARKET OPERATIONS   The Fed has responsibility for the purchase and sale of U. S. government securities (bonds) on the open market. These **open-market operations** are directed by the Federal Open Market Committee (FOMC), which is responsible for making the open-market decisions for the entire system. To affect the amount of money in circulation, the FOMC can either sell or buy government bonds on the open market, that is, the competitive securities market.

The purchase and sale of government securities on the open market is made through dealers who buy and sell for their own accounts or for others. When the Fed sells securities, a dealer pays for them by writing a check on a member bank, thus reducing the amount of money the member bank can loan. If a member bank reduces the amount of its loans, consumption is affected. Money becomes harder to get, and businesses and consumers reduce the amount they purchase. When consumption is reduced, production and the level of economic activity decline.

The purchase of securities from dealers has the reverse effect. When the Fed buys securities back, dealers receive money. This money is deposited in the member banks, increasing the amount of money loanable to businesses and consumers. As demand for goods and services increases because of the availability of money, the economy begins to pick up.

The open-market operations are summarized in Exhibit 15–3. The Open Market Committee buys and sells securities in different parts of the country in an effort to keep interest rates fairly equal. It does this by moving money from sections of the country where it is plentiful to sections where money is scarce.

OPEN-MARKET OPERATIONS
Purchase and sale of U. S. government bonds on the open market by the Federal Reserve System.

A RETAILER GETS INTO FINANCIAL SERVICES

The giant retailing concern, Sears, Roebuck and Company, is getting into the banking and financial business. Unable to grow in retailing, Sears is turning to financial services. Not only does Sears want to maintain its number one position in the retailing business, but it also wants to become the leading purveyor of consumer financial services.

The Chicago-based company has a heavy advantage in achieving its goal. Sears is viewed as one of the most trusted of American corporations by millions of households. In addition, Sears has both the means of entering the new markets and the distribution system to make it work.

Sears now offers an impressive array of financial services including: the Allstate property, casualty, and life insurance; mortgage life insurance; a proposal to take over Dean Witter Reynolds Organization, Inc., the nation's fifth largest stock broker; Coldwell, Banker and Co., the largest real estate broker in the nation; a savings and loan operation in California with over $3 billion in assets; and the twenty-five million users of Sears credit cards. In the future, Sears is planning several major additions to its financial services including: money market funds, a Sears debit card (which would put it in direct competition with commercial banks and thrift institutions), automated teller machines in all Sears stores, and a broad move into secured and unsecured consumer loans to rival the finance companies, banks, and thrift institutions.

Even without the addition of these new financial services, Sears is already one of the most profitable financial institutions in the country. The profits from Sears' financial operations rival those of such companies as BankAmerica Corporation, Prudential Insurance Company, and State Farm Mutual.

With the trend toward deregulation of the banking industry, consumers can look forward to more and more financial services being offered over the counter of a Sears store or a related subsidiary.

Source: "The New Sears," *Business Week,* November 16, 1981, pp. 140–146.

DISCOUNT OPERATIONS
Process of loaning funds to member banks by the Federal Reserve System.

DISCOUNT RATE
The rate of interest that depository institutions must pay in order to borrow reserves from the Federal Reserve.

DISCOUNT OPERATIONS   It used to be that one advantage of a commercial bank becoming a member of the Federal Reserve System was its ability to borrow reserves from the Fed. This is no longer the case. All depository institutions that are now required to keep reserves with the Federal Reserve have the right to borrow reserves from the Federal Reserve System. The process of loaning funds to depository institutions is called **discount operations**.

The **discount rate** is the rate of interest that depository institutions must pay to borrow money from the reserve bank in their district. When the Fed decides that there is too much money in the economy, it raises the discount rate so that individuals who borrow from depository institutions will have to pay higher interest rates. At higher interest rates, fewer businesses and consumers borrow. This in turn decreases demand, reduces production, and slows the economy. Lowering the discount rate lowers interest rates and increases borrowing. In turn, demand and production increase and boost economic activity.

320

RESERVE REQUIREMENTS   Ours is a **fractional reserve banking system**. This means that only a small fraction of total deposits are kept on hand to meet the demands of those clients who withdraw their funds on any one day. The rest is used to make loans and earn interest. The Federal Reserve can affect the money supply by changing **reserve requirements**, defined as the amount of reserves that are required to be kept on deposit with the Fed. Prior to 1981, the Federal Reserve required only member banks to keep reserves in district federal reserve banks. The Depository Institutions Deregulation and Monetary Control Act of 1980, however, provides that reserve requirements will now be uniformly applied by the Federal Reserve to all checking-type deposits at *all* depository institutions, whether or not those institutions are members of the Federal Reserve. That means that any depository institution having demand deposits, NOWs, or automatic transfers from savings to demand deposits, and all credit unions, savings and loan associations, and savings banks are subject to the Fed's reserve requirements. In 1980, an eight-year gradual phase-in period started for the reserve requirements of all nonmember banks and so-called thrift institutions. By 1988, all depositor institutions will hold reserves of 3 percent on deposits below $25 million and 12 percent on those above $25 million. The Federal Reserve can vary this latter percentage between 8 and 14 percent.

HOW DOES CHANGING RESERVE REQUIREMENTS AFFECT THE MONEY SUPPLY?   Suppose a bank has $1 million in deposits, and the reserve requirement is 20 percent. That bank can lend out $800,000, and it must keep $200,000 on deposit with the Federal Reserve. Of course, when the $800,000 is loaned out, the money eventually finds its way into other banks. These banks can in turn lend out 80 percent of $800,000, or $640,000. The circle keeps going. The $640,000 eventually finds its way into

FRACTIONAL RESERVE BANKING SYSTEM
A banking system in which banks are required to keep a certain percentage of their total deposits on hand either as vault cash or in reserve at some central bank.

RESERVE REQUIREMENTS
Percentage of demand deposits that member banks of the Federal Reserve System must keep in cash reserves.

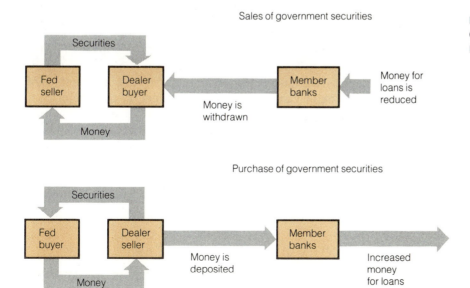

Sales of government securities

Purchase of government securities

EXHIBIT 15-3
Open-Market Operations of the Federal Reserve System

other banks, and so on down the line. What if the Fed raised reserve requirements to 40 percent? (It can't really do that, but we're only looking at a simple example.) The bank with the $1 million deposits would have to have $400,000 in reserves. It would have to call in $200,000 in loans, or at least not renew that amount of loans coming due. This would contract the amount of money in circulation in the economy. Through this method, then, the Federal Reserve can alter the amount of money available. In recent years, however, the Federal Reserve has rarely used changes in reserve requirements to affect the amount of money in circulation.

MARGIN REQUIREMENTS
Percentage of the price that an investor must put down when purchasing stock.

MARGIN REQUIREMENTS   The final tool used by the Federal Reserve System to control the amount of money in circulation is **margin requirements**. Margin requirements specify the percentage of the investor's money that must be put down when purchasing stocks. If the margin requirements are lowered, buyers can borrow more against the purchase price of the stock. Thus, the purchaser is able to buy more stock with less of his or her own money. This increases the availability of credit and makes more money available to businesses and current stockholders. Increasing the margin requirements has the reverse effect. Since 1933, the Fed has been directed by law to restrain the undue use of bank credit for speculation in securities.

A Clearinghouse for Checks

The Fed used to serve as a clearinghouse for checks only for member banks. Now, all depository institutions can use the Federal Reserve as a clearinghouse for checks, but they must each pay the actual cost of check clearing. Indeed, there is a vast number of checks cleared every year in the United States. About 90 percent of all dollar transactions are conducted by check. This amounts to 36 billion checks a year! We show how an out-of-town check is cleared through the Federal Reserve System in Exhibit 15-4.

On the Job Revisited

Greg Preston, the operations officer at City National, has noticed that sometimes checks coming through his bank are not "paid" by the issuing bank for a number of days after Greg's bank sends them through the Federal Reserve check-clearing system for payment. Greg doesn't like the amount of "float" that exists. He thinks that something ought to be done about this situation and has suggested that higher management think about putting in a debit card service for customers. With a debit card, customers could make purchases from specified retailers who in turn would electronically obtain funds from Greg's bank. The customer's bank account would be instantly debited whenever that customer made a purchase. When Greg talked to his superiors, he discovered he needed to learn a lot more about electronic banking. It was fast becoming one of the most important aspects of our banking system, and the pace of developments had become hectic.

ELECTRONIC FUNDS TRANSFER SYSTEM (EFTS)
A system of transferring money with electronic or magnetic signals.

ELECTRONIC FUNDS TRANSFER SYSTEM (EFTS)

Today, much of our normal banking activity is being done electronically through the **electronic funds transfer system**, or EFTS. There are basically three parts to an EFTS—teller machines, point-of-sale systems, and automated clearinghouses.

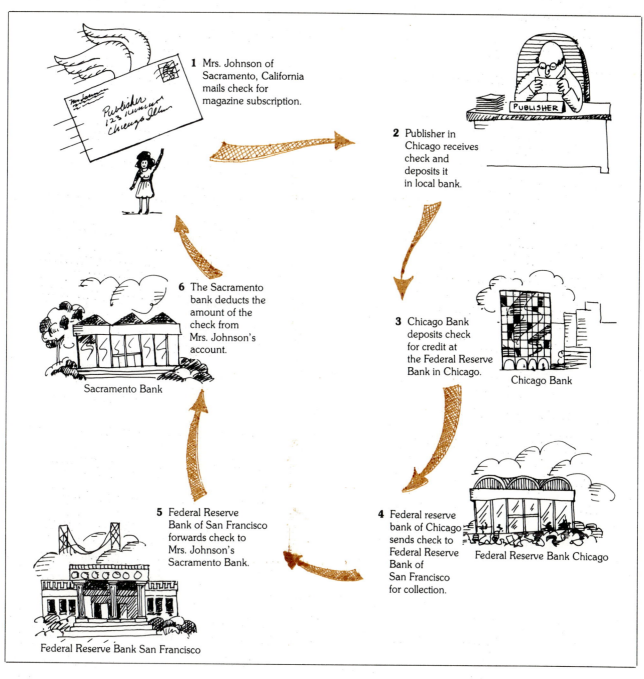

1 Mrs. Johnson of Sacramento, California mails check for magazine subscription.

2 Publisher in Chicago receives check and deposits it in local bank.

6 The Sacramento bank deducts the amount of the check from Mrs. Johnson's account.

Sacramento Bank

3 Chicago Bank deposits check for credit at the Federal Reserve Bank in Chicago.

Chicago Bank

5 Federal Reserve Bank of San Francisco forwards check to Mrs. Johnson's Sacramento Bank.

4 Federal reserve bank of Chicago sends check to Federal Reserve Bank of San Francisco for collection.

Federal Reserve Bank Chicago

Federal Reserve Bank San Francisco

Teller machines. The EFTS development involves teller machines, also called customer bank communication terminals or remote service units. Located either on the bank's premises or in stores such as supermarkets or drugstores, automated teller machines receive deposits, dispense funds from checking or savings accounts, make credit card advances, and receive payments. The device is connected on-line to the bank's computers.

EXHIBIT 15-4
Path of an Out-of-Town Check
Through the Federal Reserve System

Point-of-sale systems. Such systems allow the consumer to transfer funds to merchants in order to make purchases. On-line terminals are located at checkout counters in the merchant's store. When making a purchase, the customer's card is inserted into the terminal, which reads the data encoded on it. The computer at the customer's bank verifies that the card and identification code are valid and that there is enough money in the customer's account to cover the purchase. After the purchase is made, the customer's account is debited for the proper amount.

Automated clearinghouses. Such clearinghouses are similar to ones now used to clear checks between banks. The main difference is that the entries are made in the form of electronic signals—no checks are used. Thus, this is not a system for further automating the handling of paper checks; it is a replacement system. Such systems are especially useful to businesspersons for recurrent payments like payrolls, Social Security payments, or pension fund plans that come up weekly or monthly. The automated clearinghouse is really a glorified processing system.

This system saves customers time, and it saves the banks and companies money. It is estimated that the banking system spends over $6.5 billion annually just to process 36 billion checks. If this processing can somehow be reduced, you as the consumer will benefit. The process might cause some problems but not serious ones. Since most of your fixed expenses, such as for car payments, house payments, and the like, are anticipated anyway, automatic payment is not going to change your behavior. In a cashless, checkless society, you will receive a statement at the end of every month just as you do now; in fact, you will probably always be able to phone in to find out where your finances stand. Since we are all faced with a budget constraint (we know that we cannot for long spend more than we make), checks and balances against overspending will have to be built into any money system. And, of course, that all goes back to formulating a budget and sticking to it.

Protection with Electronic Banking

There are certain rules governing electronic banking, the bulk of which are included in the Electronic Funds Transfer Act of November 1978. In addition to providing a basic framework for the rights, liabilities, and responsibilities of participants in EFTS, the Federal Reserve Board was given the authority to issue rules and regulations to help implement the act. The Federal Reserve Board's implemental regulation is called Regulation E-Electronic Fund Transfers. The board is still writing sections of Regulation E. The rules in effect now, however, are quite important. For example, anyone who finds or steals your debit card—the card that allows you to withdraw cash from your savings or checking account at an automated teller—can loot your account. However, your liability is held to $50 *if* you report the card's loss to the bank within two days. (If you report the theft after two days, your liability is limited to $500.) Additionally, you are now protected against computer foul-ups. If the balance revealed to you in a statement or by an automatic or human teller is less than you believe it to be, the bank has only ten business days to determine the correct balance,

ELECTRONIC BANKING BECOMES A REALITY

In the last month of 1981, key executives from a dozen of the largest United States and Canadian banks flew to a secret meeting at Chicago's O'Hare Hilton Hotel. Why did they meet? They gathered to form a joint venture that would create the first national retail-banking network. This meeting was not particularly special, though. Similar meetings were being held around the country, as worried bankers were beginning to do something about their concerns. They started laying the cornerstone of their strategy to meet the growing challenge from Merrill Lynch, American Express, and Sears. These and other financial service giants have begun closing in on the retail-banking business now that deregulation has become a fact.

In an attempt to build a network for retail banking, groups of banks throughout the country and Canada are forming. They plan to share automated teller machines (ATM) so that customers can obtain cash from any one of them by inserting a debit card issued by each bank for use with its own ATM. The goal is a nationwide electronic network capable of delivering all manner of retail banking services. The name of one particular consortium is First Interstate Group, but it is only one of a dozen contenders in the race to build such a network.

The fact is that the pace is hectic. In the last six months of 1981, greater strides were made in retail electronic banking than during the entire 1970s. The prediction is that by the end of 1983, six national electronic banking networks will be in service. These networks will be far more powerful than Visa or MasterCard—the workhorses of the plastic money game—because they will give each customer access to all of his or her bank accounts. Using an automated teller machine, customers will be able to withdraw cash, make deposits in a checking and/or savings account, and transfer accounts between the two, as well as make inquiries about checking and savings account balances.

Future services for these new networks include electronic funds transfers (EFT) from home and retail point-of-sale terminals. These innovations will allow banks to replace with a simple electronic transaction many of the 36 billion checks now processed each year.

Consider an example: A customer of First National Bank of Dallas is two hundred miles away in Austin, where he can withdraw $100 from his checking acount by using any of the automated teller machines belonging to Austin National Bank. Both banks are members of PULSE, a network that electronically links 400 banks in Texas and Louisiana. The customer need only insert his plastic debit card in the ATM, just as he does in Dallas, and punch in his request and his four-digit identification code. The Austin bank recognizes the correct code and relays the message to the network's Houston switching center. That center routes it via leased telephone lines to the Dallas bank's computer. Once the number is checked out, the Dallas bank's computer sends an approval to the ATM, which then dispenses $100 in cash. The transaction doesn't even take long—only six seconds!

Adapted from "Electronic Banking," *Business Week*, January 18, 1982.

unless it chooses to temporarily credit your account with the disputed amount; then it has up to forty-five days to investigate.

■ Money has several characteristics including the following: It must be durable, hard to counterfeit, easy to divide and carry around, and easily converted to other forms of wealth. These characteristics have been applied by most societies to the specific items they use for money.

SUMMARY

■ In the United States we use several things for money. These include currency (coins and bills), demand deposits (for example, checking accounts), NOW accounts (checking accounts in savings banks and savings and loans), and credit and debit cards.

■ Of the several types of financial institutions in the United States, commercial banks have traditionally been able to offer the widest variety of services, including checking accounts, time deposits, credit cards, and other financial services. With the passage of the Depository Institutions Deregulation and Monetary Control Act of 1980, commercial banks are being threatened by competition from savings banks, savings and loan associations, and credit unions, as well as brokerage firms and money market mutual funds.

■ Numerous depository institutions can offer checking-type accounts. Savings banks can offer NOW accounts (negotiable orders of withdrawal); credit unions can offer credit union share drafts and so, too, can savings and loan associations. Savings and loan associations can also invest money in consumer loans and corporate securities. They can now issue credit cards and issue credit in connection with such cards.

■ The Federal Reserve System was developed in response to a need for a central bank in the United States to control the currency and help finance the operations of the federal government. The bank received its charter in 1913 and has served as the nation's central bank ever since.

■ The Federal Reserve is headed by a board of governors. The most important advisory committee within the Federal Reserve System is the Federal Open Market Committee, which sets policy with respect to the buying and selling of government securities. Ultimately, it is such buying and selling of government securities (bonds) that determine the rate of growth of the money supply in this country.

■ Since 1980, the distinction between member and nonmember banks of the Federal Reserve has become increasingly blurred. By 1988, all depository institutions will have to hold reserves in district Federal Reserve banks. Additionally, all depository institutions can now participate in the check-clearing services of the Federal Reserve System, provided that those institutions pay the actual cost the service entails.

■ A nationwide retail electronic banking system will emerge in the next few years. Such a system will allow customers to obtain cash at different geographical locations and transact other items of business with their banks.

ISSUES TO CONSIDER AND ANALYZE

1. What makes commercial banks so important to business?
2. What are the different forms of money used in the United States?
3. What are factoring companies, and how do they serve business?
4. Explain the difference between sales finance companies and consumer finance companies.
5. Why did it take so long for Congress to establish the Federal Reserve System, and what finally brought about its establishment?
6. What are the functions of the Federal Reserve System?
7. What are the characteristics of money?

A BANKING MERGER

In 1981, Florida National Banks of Florida, Inc., the state's fourth largest bank holding company, entered into an agreement with Chemical New York Corporation with a view toward the New York company eventually acquiring a substantial equity interest in the Florida institution. The investment by the Chemical Bank, the nation's seventh largest, paved the way for a merger between the two banks.

The deal between the two banks was a complicated one that was based on the assumption that interstate banking would soon become a reality. Under the terms of the deal, Chemical and Florida National purchased 2.4 million shares, or about 32 percent, of Florida National stock. In addition, other shares would be purchased over a period of time. The final step, the merger of the two companies, would be taken when interstate banking became legal.

Many critics of interstate banking suggest that if it is legalized, the banking industry in the United States will eventually be dominated by a few large banks. Consequently, many of the small local banks will not be able to compete and will be forced to align themselves with the large bank holding companies, thus reducing competition in the banking industry. Advocates of the plan contend that it will strengthen the banking industry in this country and better enable American banks to compete with the flood of foreign banks that are establishing themselves in the United States.

QUESTIONS

1. Was it a good business decision on the part of Chemical Bank to work out a deal with Florida National?
2. Do you feel that the ban on interstate banking should be lifted?

CHAPTER 16

SHORT- AND LONG-TERM FINANCING

LEARNING OBJECTIVES

After studying this chapter, you should be able to:

Identify the different types of financing used by business.

Identify the major forms of short-term financing.

Understand the difference between equity and debt capital.

Realize the limitations of long-term sources of funds for proprietorships, partnerships, and corporations.

Explain the different types of stocks.

Identify the advantages and disadvantages of debt financing.

Discuss the different classifications of bonds.

KEY TERMS

Trade credit
Open book account
Cash discount
Promissory note
Trade acceptance
Bill of lading
Trade draft
Collateral
Signature loan
Commercial paper
Equity capital
Debt capital
Common stock
Market value
Book value
Par value
Dividend
Proxy
Preemptive right
Preferred stock
Bond

SUE'S SALON

Sue Morris received her degree in retailing from the State University of New York almost ten years ago. Since that time, she has been in the retail business. Her first three years were spent with Sak's Fifth Avenue in New York as a department manager and later as a buyer. She enjoyed her time with Sak's but wanted to own a retail business of her own.

Seven years ago, Sue established Sue's Salon in suburban White Plains. The store took many hours of her time (she often worked eighty hours a week) and most of her money. In addition to her personal funds, Sue borrowed several thousand dollars from her parents in the early days of her business venture. Fortunately, with the success of her business, she was able to repay the loan from her parents. Sue attributes her success to the fact that her store has a unique product mix that appeals to the fashion-conscious women of the area. The store has always carried designer labels but at a reduced price. This combination has attracted a large number of loyal customers who make repeat purchases at her store.

In spite of the success of Sue's Salon, much of Sue's time is spent managing the financial resources of the business. As the owner, Sue believes this task is too critical to delegate. In general, it has been a constant battle to keep the bills paid and to provide funds for the growth of her business. This chapter will discuss some of the sources of funds available to a business like Sue's as well as explore other areas of financial management.

All businesses need money to start and operate. Money finances essentials like machinery, equipment, land, and buildings; it pays for materials, labor, and taxes; and it eases emergencies. The uses for money vary as widely as its potential sources do. Every aspect of business depends on financing; production, marketing, and accounting efforts are impossible unless money is available. In short, no modern business could exist without some type of financing.

Basically, financing is concerned with the efficient acquisition and use of money. Thus, the job of the financial manager is an integral part of a business operation. The financial manager's primary function is to keep funds flowing so that the business can run smoothly. This task is much more complicated than it might seem. The financial manager is constantly confronted with fundamental questions about the operations of the business.

TYPES OF FINANCING

Sources of funds available to financial managers can be divided into two broad areas: *short-term funds* and *long-term funds*. Short-term funds are used to finance supplies, payrolls, and taxes, and are obtained for one year or less. Long-term funds are used to purchase buildings, land, long-life machinery, and equipment.

Sound financial management requires that a funding source be matched to the intended use of the funds. For example, the owner of Sue's Salon would not normally borrow money from a bank on a thirty-day revolving basis to purchase a new building. The potential purchaser of a new home would not normally borrow money from a bank for one year. Rather, a long-term mortgage is traditionally obtained with payments spread over twenty or more years.

Credit from Suppliers

TRADE CREDIT
A form of short-term credit extended to businesses by suppliers; this is the largest source of short-term credit.

On the Job Revisited

The single largest source of short-term financing for businesses is credit from suppliers, more commonly referred to as **trade credit**. Instead of paying cash for a product at the time of purchase, the business delays payment by receiving credit from the supplier. Credit managers estimate that trade credit accounts for about 85 percent of the total retail and wholesale volume of credit.

For example, when Sue Morris orders clothing in June from her New York supplier, Elite Fashions, she receives trade credit. Sue might take delivery of the clothes on October 31 but not have to pay for them until November 30. During this thirty-day period, Sue essentially has free use of Elite Fashions' clothing. In effect, Elite Fashions has helped finance Sue's clothing inventory. Sue will undoubtedly sell some of the clothes during this thirty-day period before paying Elite Fashions. Basically, then, Sue is using credit without having to pay for it explicitly. Essentially, she has a thirty-day open book account with Elite Fashions because of her good credit rating with that company. As we will see below, an open book account is one of the three principal trade credit arrangements available to business people.

The way trade credit is handled depends on the supplier's opinion of the purchaser's trustworthiness as well as the custom in the particular industry.

The three principal trade credit arrangements are open book accounts, promissory notes, and trade acceptances.

OPEN BOOK ACCOUNT
A credit arrangement in which no formal document is drawn up, but the debtor is expected to pay within a few days after the date of the invoice.

OPEN BOOK ACCOUNTS   **Open book accounts** are by far the most popular form of trade credit available in the United States. Under this arrangement, the supplier simply ships the product along with an invoice (bill) to the customer. No formal document is drawn up, but the customer is expected to pay within a few days after the date on the invoice. The length of time allowed for payment varies from industry to industry; however, one of the more common periods is thirty days.

CASH DISCOUNT
A discount, usually 1 or 2 percent, given to a debtor who pays off the amount due either immediately or within ten days after the goods are delivered.

Often the supplier encourages early payment by offering a **cash discount** to its customers. The terms of this discount and the due date are stated on the invoice. The most common terms and due date are 2/10 net 30. This means that if the invoice is paid before the tenth day following the invoice date, a 2 percent discount will be allowed. If the invoice is not paid within the discount period, the entire amount must be paid within thirty days. For example, let's assume Sue purchased $10,000 of clothing from Elite Fashions and the terms on the invoice, dated October 31, were 2/10 net 30. If Sue pays the invoice by November 10, she pays $9,800, or she could wait and pay the full $10,000 on November 30.

On the Job Revisited

PROMISSORY NOTE
A signed written instrument promising to pay a certain sum of money to a payee or a holder on a specified date.

PROMISSORY NOTES   An alternative method of credit that suppliers offer their customers is the promissory note. When one person promises to pay a sum of money to another person at a definite time or on demand, a **promissory note** is used. Promissory notes are used to extend credit in many kinds of businesses. Even in real estate transactions, essentially a buyer executes a promissory note for the unpaid balance on a house, secured by a mortgage on the property being purchased.

In many businesses, the use of promissory notes instead of open book accounts is common practice. They are typically required from customers with unestablished credit ratings. A promissory note does offer one definite advantage: when signed by the maker it acknowledges the accuracy of the debt. We see a typical promissory note in Exhibit 16-1.

On the Job Revisited

When Sue Morris first started buying from Elite Fashions, she ordered only a very small amount of clothing—$5,000 worth—but Elite Fashions required Sue to sign a promissory note agreeing to pay the $5,000 in thirty days, and Sue had to write *"accepted"* on the note itself. This clearly was a more formal procedure than the open book account that Sue Morris now has. When that first promissory note was due, Elite Fashions deposited the note in its bank, and the bank collected the $5,000 from Sue.

TRADE ACCEPTANCE
A time draft drawn by one person and sent to the drawee. When the drawee accepts the draft by signing it, it becomes a trade acceptance.

TRADE ACCEPTANCES   A third means of extending credit to purchasers of goods is the **trade acceptance**. This is a special type of draft that orders the buyer to pay a specific sum of money to the seller at a stated time in the future. The difference between a trade acceptance and a promissory note is that a trade acceptance is an order-to-pay instrument drawn up by the *seller*, whereas a promissory note is a promise-to-pay instrument drawn up by the buyer. A typical trade acceptance is shown in Exhibit 16-2.

EXHIBIT 16-1
A Typical Promissory Note

$ ---3,000.00 ---- Saint Paul, Minnesota April 30, 19 80 Due 6/20/80

-------- Sixty days -------------------------------------- after date,

for value received, the undersigned jointly and severally promise to pay to the order of THE FIRST NATIONAL BANK OF SAINT PAUL at its office in Saint Paul, Minnesota, $ --- Three Thousand and no/100 Dollars with interest thereon from date hereof at the rate of - 15 - per cent per annum (computed on the basis of actual days and a year of 360 days) as indicated in No. 7 below.

- [7] INTEREST IS PAYABLE AT MATURITY
- [8] INTEREST IS PAID TO MATURITY
- [9] INTEREST IS PAYABLE ______ BEGINNING ON ______
- [ ] ______

CANCELLED

The holder of this note may at its option without notice declare this note immediate[illegible] the entire [illegible] principal hereof plus accrued interest hereon upon or at any time after the occurrence of any of the following events: any default in the payment of this note; any default unde[illegible] agreement or other note, obligation, instrument, undertaking or agreement concurrently herewith or heretofore or hereafter given to or acquired and held by the holder hereof to which [illegible] indorser, surety or guarantor hereof is a party; if the holder hereof deems itself insecure; or if there is such a change in the condition or affairs, financial or otherwise, of any maker, co-maker, [illegible] guarantor hereof as in the opinion of the holder hereof increases the risk.

Each maker, co-maker, indorser, surety and guarantor hereof jointly and severally agre[illegible] this note and guarantees payment hereof and waives demand, presentment, protest and notice of dishonor, and consents to any extensions and renewals hereof without notice, and consents to the release by [illegible] holder hereof with or without consideration of any of them, and exonerates the holder hereof from all duty and obligation to make demand on anyone for payment of any collateral now or hereafter securing this note or to give notice to anyone of non-payment thereof or to collect or sell the same and consents to the extension, renewal, exchange, surrender or release by the holder hereof with or without consideration of any such collateral, and agrees that when or at any time after this note becomes due the holder hereof may without notice offset or charge this note against any bank account or other account then maintained by any of them with the holder hereof or then existing between any of them and the holder hereof and to pay any deficiency, and agrees in case of any default to pay all costs of collection, including reasonable attorneys' fees and the maximum interest or late charges permitted by law. The note shall be deemed a contract made under, and this note and the rights, obligations and duties of the parties hereto shall be governed by, the laws of the State of Minnesota.

SIGNATURE Lawrence E. Roberts SIGNATURE Margaret P. Roberts

SIGNATURE ______ SIGNATURE ______

32-364 (8-71)

NO. 096-85-710
OFFICER Clark
BY
ACCRUAL /
[x] NEW [ ] REN'L
[x] SECURED
[ ] UNSECURED

[x] SECURITIES [ ] INSURANCE [ ] SAVINGS [ ] OTHER
[ ] SEC. AGREEMENT 1. INV. & ACCTS. 2. CONSUMER GOODS 3. EQUIP.

Sue Morris has decided to purchase a new line of clothes from Wearever Designers, and she orders $10,000 worth of clothes. Wearever ships the merchandise on November 1, attaching a **bill of lading**, which is a shipping document, and another document called a **trade draft**. The trade draft prepared by Wearever orders Sue to pay the $10,000 owed on the purchases of clothing by November 30. When Sue receives the clothing, she writes "accepted" across the trade draft and returns it to Wearever Designers. The act of signing and returning it to Wearever shows that Sue has formally agreed to pay the $10,000. The signed trade draft is called a trade acceptance.

Wearever now has two choices. It can wait until November 30 to obtain the full $10,000, or it can sell the trade acceptance to a bank or individual for something less than $10,000. The bank or individual will then wait until November 30 to collect the $10,000 from Sue Morris.

On the Job Revisited

BILL OF LADING
A written shipping document given by a transportation company showing the names of the shipper and the party receiving the goods and an itemization of the goods shipped.

TRADE DRAFT
A bill of exchange constituting a written order to pay a third party a certain sum of money on a designated date (time draft) or on demand (sight draft).

EXHIBIT 16-2
A Typical Trade Acceptance

TRADE ACCEPTANCE

Mytown, California March 15 19 80

To The ABC Company

On June 15, 1980 Pay to the order of XYZ Corporation

----- One thousand and no/100 -------------- Dollars ($ --- 1,000.00 -----)

The obligations of the acceptor hereof arise out of the purchase of goods from the drawer. The drawee may accept this bill payable at any bank or trust company in the United States which such drawee may designate.

Accepted at Blackacre, N.Y. on March 15 19 79
Payable at Bank of Blackacre
Blackacre, New York
Buyer's Signature ABC Company
By Agent or Officer Tom Smith/V. Pres.

XYZ Corporation
By Joe Jones/pres.

Commercial Bank Loans

The second most important source of short-term funds for businesses is the commercial bank. In 1982, businesses borrowed billions in short-term loans from the commercial banking sector. In many respects, banks indirectly participate in the management of business because bankers often decide whether to extend short-term financing to people who want to start or expand businesses. Bank officers thereby become partial managers, particularly when deciding to lend on growth concepts.

COLLATERAL
Property or security deposited with a creditor to guarantee payment of a loan.

SIGNATURE LOAN
A loan that is not backed by any specific property; only the good credit rating of the borrower is used.

Two types of loans are available from commercial banks: unsecured and secured. An unsecured loan—one that is not secured by any **collateral**, or security—is sometimes called a **signature loan**. The good credit rating of the borrower is the only assurance the banker has that the loan will be repaid. Typically, banks extend lines of unsecured credit to their better customers, and these preferred customers can draw on their lines of credit up to a specified maximum.

If there is any doubt about the creditworthiness of the borrower, a bank will require security, or collateral, for a business loan. We have already defined collateral as the pledge of specific property to back up a loan in case the debtor does not repay when required. The security will usually be an item whose value can be readily measured, such as stocks, bonds, or inventories. Banks, for example, could loan from 50 to 90 percent of an inventory, depending on what it would cost the bank to sell the inventory to cover the loan should the business default on the loan.

Accounts receivable are also used as security for short-term bank loans. Accounts receivable represent the money owed to a business by its customers. The amount a bank is willing to loan against accounts receivable typically depends on how long the accounts have been outstanding and the credit ratings of the borrower's customers.

Financing from Other Businesses or Investors

COMMERCIAL PAPER
An unsecured promissory note guaranteeing that the person who signs will pay back a certain sum of money by a specific date.

Large, well-known businesses like General Motors, IBM, and Xerox often borrow money for short periods of time by selling commercial paper. **Commercial paper** is an unsecured promissory note guaranteeing repayment of a certain sum of money on a specific date. These notes are generally sold in multiples of $5,000 and range from $5,000 to $1 million. Maturities on commercial paper vary from one month to one year, with an average of five months. Commercial paper is sold to other businesses, insurance companies, pension funds, and banks.

The major advantage of commercial paper is that it has a lower interest rate than an unsecured loan from a bank. The interest rate on commercial paper is usually about 0.5 percent lower than the interest rate charged a bank's best customers, or the prime interest rate.

Another source of short-term financing is a factoring company. As discussed in Chapter 15, factoring is a method of obtaining funds from the sale of accounts receivable to a financial institution, called a factor. Factoring is normally a continuous rather than an occasional process. The seller of the goods receives an order and transmits the order to the factor for approval; upon approval, the goods are shipped and the factor advances money to the seller. Then the purchaser pays the factor when the money is due. Once this routine has been established, goods and money steadily circulate among the factor, purchaser, and seller. The factor performs three functions: checking credit, lending, and bearing the risk of loss.

In addition to short-term financing, businesses need vast amounts of capital to start or expand operations. For example, American Telephone and Telegraph over the last decade has invested over $73 billion to generate sales and profits, create jobs, and satisfy customers. On a smaller scale, the new McDonald's franchise owner needs money for a burger machine, shake maker, and furniture, among other things. Where and how do these businesses raise the funds to finance these projects?

LONG-TERM FINANCING

Several sources of long-term funds are available to the owners of a business. **Equity capital** includes all the funds the owners have invested in the business. In forming a business, owners are normally required to make a substantial commitment of funds. At times, the commitment can include the owners' entire life savings. In order for a business to expand, additional sources of capital are required. There are three possible sources of this capital: (1) more investment from current owners, (2) investment from new owners, and (3) retained earnings of the business. Before seeking out one or more of these sources of equity capital as a long-run source of funds, several factors should be considered.

Sources of Long-Term Capital

EQUITY CAPITAL
Capital invested in the business by its owners.

- There are no fixed interest charges on equity capital; hence, the return to investors can vary greatly from a total loss to a huge rate of return.
- The capital that owners have invested in the business does not have to be repaid.
- Equity financing represents the cushion the business needs to withstand the financial pressures that can arise during a recession or other adverse period. With this capital, which does not require a fixed return every year, the business can withstand losses that might otherwise bankrupt it.
- It becomes easier to secure borrowed funds when the owners of the business have invested a substantial amount of their own money.
- At times, it can be difficult to raise money through equity financing.

DEBT CAPITAL
Funds borrowed from the creditors of a business.

   Debt capital consists of long-term funds borrowed from the creditors of a business. In some instances, it is not desirable or possible to finance the organization's operations through equity capital. When this occurs, the only alternative is debt capital. Before selecting debt financing, the financial manager should consider these factors.

- Debt financing has no effect on management's control of the business.
- Interest must be paid on a regular basis.
- The interest paid on the debt is an expense and therefore lowers taxes.
- The principal must be repaid at a specific date in the future.
- Because the interest must be paid, it can become a significant financial burden during periods of little or no earnings.
- The practice of borrowing money at 16 percent and making 20 percent on it can increase the return to the owners.
- The use of debt financing does not dilute the earnings of owners the way equity financing might. This is because no additional owners have a claim on the earnings.

   Often the choice between equity financing and debt financing is not one that can be completely controlled by the financial manager of a business. In certain situations, even if the business management wishes to obtain debt financing by the sale of bonds, market conditions might be such that the interest the business could offer on the bonds would be prohibitive, that is, unprofitable. Also, even if the financial manager believes that it is appropriate to sell equity to obtain needed funds for expansion of the business, it may be relatively difficult if not impossible to do so. For example, if the business has not done well in the past, it will be extremely difficult to sell equity capital; if it is sold, it will have to be sold at such a low price that the current owners would suffer a substantial reduction in the percent of the business they own and in the value of their share of ownership.

Limitations on Sources of Funds

Making optimal use of the sources of long-term capital poses different problems for the various forms of business. Financial managers must be aware of the limitations imposed by a particular type of business and the use of the funds. There is a substantial difference between the ability of a sole proprietor to raise funds and that of a corporation, and a partnership has its own problems too.

SOLE PROPRIETORSHIPS   Sole proprietors normally are restricted to personal funds and to those obtained from friends, relatives, banks, and other interested parties. Because of the sole proprietor's unlimited liability, the wealthy would probably incorporate to protect the business aginst possible lawsuits. A sole proprietorship, then, usually has limited equity capital.

Because equity capital is limited, the sole proprietor also finds it difficult to secure long-term debt capital. Banks and other sources of long-term debt capital are reluctant to loan funds to sole proprietors, and creditors usually require collateral for the loans, most often in the form of a mortgage on property owned by the business. Limited personal and business assets usually restrict the borrowing power of the sole proprietor.

On the Job Revisited   Take the example of Sue Morris, whose business has been booming. She found a location in another city for a second store and is convinced the new store will bring her even greater profits. Unfortunately, extensive physical improvements are necessary before Sue can begin operations, and she estimates the remodeling will cost at least $65,000. Sue knows that if she borrows short term, she will be financially pressed and perhaps even unable to pay off the loan in less than a year; therefore she is seeking long-term financing. Her operation is too small to incorporate and sell shares; and, so far, Sue has been unsuccessful in getting long-term financing from a bank. Banks know that if Sue's business fails, those so-called lease-hold improvements will be of little value; ultimately there would be no collateral to back up a long-term loan. Sue's only choice may be to bring in a partner who can offer equity capital.

PARTNERSHIPS   From a legal standpoint, sole proprietorships and partnerships are quite similar. Both have a limited life, and the sole proprietor and general partner both have unlimited liability. But the partnership has one major advantage over the sole proprietorship: it has two or more owners. This difference may have a significant effect on the partnership's ability to raise capital.

Instead of having to rely on the wealth of one person, equity financing for the partnership is provided by two or more people. A large number of partners could mean an even larger amount of equity capital.

As the amount of equity capital grows, so does the firm's ability to raise debt capital. Partnerships generally enjoy a high credit rating for two reasons: (1) more equity capital means more collateral for loans; and (2) more people have unlimited liability for the debts of the partnership.

CORPORATIONS Small corporations have many of the same problems that confront sole proprietorships and partnerships. A corporation that is small and family owned has equity limited to the personal wealth of that family. If new shares of stock are sold to others, the ownership and control of the corporation will be distributed among a larger number of people. Several years ago, the Adolph Coors Company faced this type of problem. The government had ruled that the company policy of limiting distribution of its beer to the western United States was a violation of antitrust law, and the government ordered Coors to expand distribution into other states. In order to comply with the government's ruling, Coors needed funds to expand its brewery in Golden, Colorado. These funds were obtained through the sale of equity capital.* In this way, the ownership of Coors was opened to the general public, thus reducing the control of the original stockholders. Today Coors has over ten thousand stockholders.

The availability of debt capital to corporations can also vary widely. For the small, family-owned business, debt capital may be difficult to acquire. Few business assets are available for collateral, and creditors are reluctant to make loans because of the limited liability of the corporation. Thus, at times the owners of small corporations could have to pledge their personal assets as security for business loans. Large corporations do not have this problem, as extensive company assets protect the creditors' interests.

EQUITY FINANCING

Equity capital represents the money invested in the business by the owners. The three main types of equity financing are common stock, preferred stock, and retained earnings.

Common Stock

Common stock is usually the first source of funds for a new corporation and the base for future financing. Common stock, or capital stock as it is sometimes called, is a security that represents the basic ownership interest in a corporation. The common stockholders are the last to share in the earnings of the business, and should the corporation be liquidated, they have last claim on the assets of the company. Clearly, then, it is the common stockholders who assume the greatest risk, exercise greater control, and stand to gain the greater reward through dividends and increases in stock prices. Exhibit 16–3 is an example of a share of common stock.

COMMON STOCK
Security that represents the basic ownership interest in a corporation.

THE VOLUME OF COMMON STOCK   Investors are willing to risk ownership in a corporation because they hope to receive a return on their invest-

*The company issued some nonvoting shares of common stock in order to minimize diluting the control of the then-current owners.

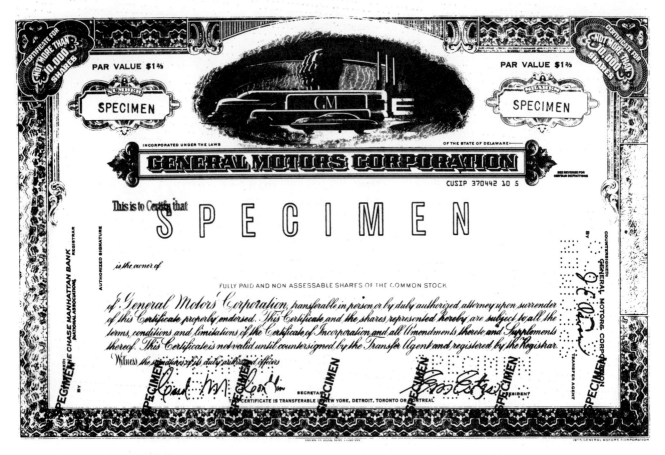

EXHIBIT 16-3

Example of a Share of Common Stock

MARKET VALUE
The current price paid by buyers to sellers of a stock.

BOOK VALUE
The value of a stock on the company's records; can be calculated by dividing the number of shares into the net worth (value of common stock plus retained earnings).

ment, which can come from appreciation in the market price of their stock and/or from the dividends the corporation pays. The **market value** of common stock is the prevailing price buyers pay to sellers of the stock.

The **book value** is the value of the stock on the company records. It is the money left for the stockholders after everything has been sold and all debts paid. For example, if the business has assets worth $20,000, debts of $10,000, and 500 shares of common stock, the book value would be $20 per share.

$20,000 assets − $10,000 debts = $10,000 of book value
$10,000 ÷ 500 shares   = $20 per share book value

Although this value has little or no significant relationship to market value, potential investors calculate book value because it is a rough measure of the value of the stock should the company be liquidated.

PAR VALUE
Arbitrary value of a stock or bond.

The **par value** of common stock is an arbitrary value placed on the stock certificate at the time it is issued. It is used in recording the value of shares on the corporation's records. Because this value is of little use and has little significance in determining the stock's market value, many companies today issue no-par stock if the state in which the business is incorporated permits it.

DIVIDENDS   When you put money into a savings account, you expect to receive a return on your investment in the form of interest. When people invest in a corporation by purchasing stock, they usually expect a return on their investment through dividends. A **dividend** is the return on investment paid to stockholders from the profits of the business.

DIVIDEND
The return paid to the stockholders of a corporation from its profits.

VOTING RIGHTS   Although the rights of the stockholders are determined by the state in which the corporation is chartered, these laws are very similar. They usually grant the stockholders the right to amend the charter, adopt and amend bylaws, elect the board of directors, authorize the sale of manufacturing facilities and similar assets, enter into business combinations, increase the amount of authorized common stock, and approve the sale of preferred stocks and bonds. As individuals, common stockholders also have the right to vote, sell their stock, inspect the corporation's books, share in dividends declared by the directors, and share in the assets if the firm dissolves. In all of this, stockholders generally get one vote for every share of stock owned. Thus, the more stock owned, the greater the number of votes and the greater the control of the individual stockholder.

Before each stockholders' meeting, the current directors send proxies to the stockholders. A **proxy** is a legal document that assigns the right to vote to another person or persons. Returned proxies are voted by the directors as indicated by the stockholder. If a proxy is not returned, it is assumed that the stockholder agrees with the current directors, and they may vote the unreturned and unrepresented proxies at their discretion. Most stockholders do not attend annual meetings or return their proxies. Thus, the existing directors normally reelect themselves and carry on the current policies. See Exhibit 16–4 for an example of a proxy.

PROXY
A legal form that assigns the right to vote to another person or persons.

EXHIBIT 16-4
Example of a Proxy

The Items shown below *are described and page referenced in the Table of Contents (page i) to the Proxy Statement.*   221-771

GM

The Board of Directors Recommends a Vote **AGAINST** *the following Stockholder Proposals:*

	For	Against			For	Against
Item No. 3	☐	☐		Item No. 4	☐	☐

This proxy will be voted "AGAINST" Items 3 and 4 if no choice is specified.

P
R
O
X
Y

You are encouraged to specify your choices by marking the appropriate boxes above but you need not mark any boxes if you wish to vote in accordance with management's recommendations; just sign and date below and return.

PLEASE SIGN, DATE AND RETURN ➤

SPECIMEN

DATE_____1978

(Please add your title if signing as Attorney, Administrator, Executor, Guardian or Trustee.)

THE HOLES PUNCHED IN THIS CARD REPRESENT THE PROXY NUMBER, THUS PERMITTING COMPUTER COUNT OF THE VOTE

PREEMPTIVE RIGHT
This gives holders of common stock the first chance to buy additional issues of common stock on a basis proportional to the number of shares they already hold.

Preferred Stock

PREFERRED STOCK
Equity security providing a claim on the company's earnings and assets ahead of the common stockholders.

PREEMPTIVE RIGHTS   The **preemptive right** provides the holders of common stock with the first opportunity to purchase additional shares of new issues of common stock at a rate equal to their percentage of the business. For example, assume that a company intends to increase the number of outstanding shares by 10 percent. With preemptive rights, each stockholder would receive the right to purchase one additional share for every ten shares owned. If the stockholder does not want to subscribe to the new stock issue or is entitled to a partial share, the rights may be sold to another investor.

Common stock is not the only type of stock that corporations issue. Many companies—especially public utilities like AT&T and Commonwealth Edison, railroads like the Burlington Northern and Southern, and industrial companies like General Motors and DuPont—have chosen to issue **preferred stock** in addition to common stock. Preferred stock has preferential rights over common stock. Preferences vary from corporation to corporation, but, in general, preferred stocks have preference over common stock in two ways:

1. Preferred stockholders receive their dividends before common stockholders do.
2. In case of liquidation, preferred stockholders also receive preference over common stockholders.

Exhibit 16-5 shows a preferred stock.

Preferred stock has features of both debt and equity. It is similar to debt in that it almost always has a fixed dividend payment. The dividends are stated on the stock certificate as a dollar amount or as a percentage of the par value. For example, a preferred stock with a $100 par value could have dividends stated as 10 percent. This means that the corporation would pay $10 in dividends per year to the stockholder. If the stock has no par value, then dividends would be stated as $10. In addition, should the company be liquidated, preferred stockholders are usually entitled to the return of the par value before the common stockholders receive anything.

Preferred stock is similar to common stock in that the company doesn't have to declare and pay dividends. Moreover, failure to pay dividends does not cause default, as it would if bond interest were not paid. Finally, upon liquidation, preferred stockholders receive their equity after all creditors have been paid but ahead of common stockholders. Although preferred stock has some of the features of both debt and equity, most experts feel such stock has more characteristics in common with equity. Thus, preferred stock is normally classified as a type of equity financing.

Retained Earnings

Businesses can do several things with the profits they earn. They can pay the money out in the form of dividends to stockholders, retain the earnings and reinvest them in the business, or some combination of the two. Some corporations pay out a high percentage of profits to stockholders and retain only a small portion for reinvestment in the business. Others believe that the stockholder will earn more if a substantial portion of the profit is reinvested in the business. For example, companies like McDonald's and

EXHIBIT 16–5
Example of a Share of Preferred Stock

Walt Disney Enterprises pay a very small percentage of profits in dividends because they use the money to finance growth. In addition, they often can earn a higher return on the reinvested profits than their stockholders can. The giant Exxon Corporation is another example. In the last few years, Exxon invested $2 billion in oil exploration and development in Alaska and poured $1.4 billion into the development and exploration of North Sea oil. Much of the financing for these projects was obtained by reinvesting the profits of the business. Exhibit 16–6 indicates the percentage of profits that selected companies have paid out in dividends.

Common and preferred stock and retained earnings are equity sources of long-term capital. Debt financing is also available to businesses from individuals, banks, insurance companies, and other financial institutions. Businesses usually borrow money for long-range objectives by issuing corporate bonds.

A **bond** is a certificate of indebtedness given by the issuing corporation to the bondholder. The issuing company promises to pay the bondholders a specific dollar amount of interest from the time the bond is issued until it matures. On the maturity (or expiration) date, the company agrees to pay

DEBT FINANCING: CORPORATE BONDS

BOND
An instrument of long-term debt.

VENTURE CAPITAL INCREASES

In 1980 alone, the venture capitalists invested about $1 billion in new and growing companies. No one connected with the venture capital business expects that the pace of financing these companies will slacken in the future.

The venture capital business is as old as capitalism itself. But organized venture capitalism in the United States has a relatively brief history. After World War II, several wealthy families decided to set up partnerships to finance new companies in electronics, communications, and other fields. Over time, investments in these new and growing firms have ranged from loans to direct stock ownership and control. Today there are approximately 660 venture capital pools in the United States, located in such cities as New York, San Francisco, Chicago, and other major financial centers. These companies are still taking the risks and investing millions in companies based on a good idea that has a possibility for growth.

Does this mean that the heralded "decade of the entrepreneur" is upon us? Are the possibilities for growth or seed money for small businesses unlimited? Venture capitalists point out that venture capital is a highly personal business, where profits are made from correct gut feelings about a company's prospects for success as well as from financial ratio analysis. Because of this, one of the major constraints on the growth of the venture capital business is the lack of experienced venture capital fund managers. Consequently, many people see no increase in the four thousand deals funded each year in spite of the increased flow of money into the field that most observers expect.

Source: "The Billion Dollar Gamble," *Inc.*, September 1981, pp. 57–65.

back the entire loan. Because bonds are a debt of business, the bondholder is a creditor of the corporation rather than an owner. Consequently, bond interest must be paid, and the bondholders have priority over both preferred and common stockholders in case of liquidation. Exhibit 16–7 is an example of a corporate bond.

Classification of Bonds

Although their basic features are similar, there is actually a spectrum of bonds classified in a number of ways: by the assets pledged as security, the method of interest payment, the method of repayment, and the issuing

EXHIBIT 16-6
Percentage of Profits Paid Out as Dividends for Selected Companies

COMPANY	DIVIDEND PAYOUT*
American Telephone and Telegraph	66%
Coca-Cola	58
Digital Equipment	0
General Motors	56
McDonald's	0
DuPont	78
Dayton Power and Light	74
Continental Oil	31

*Calculated by dividing earnings per share by dividends per share.

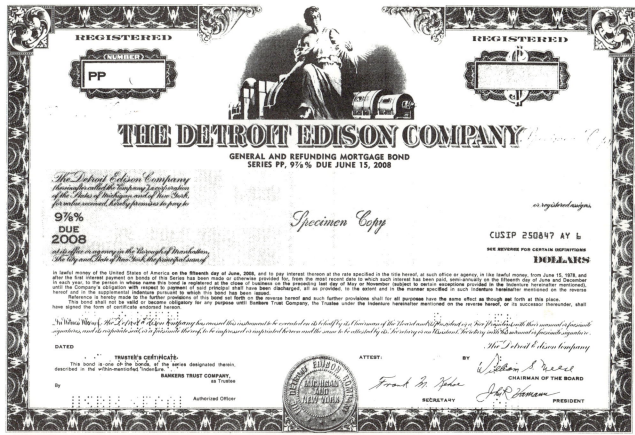

TYPE OF BOND	NORMALLY ISSUED BY	DISTINGUISHING CHARACTERISTICS
Mortgage	Railroads, utilities, and municipalities	Secured by real estate
Equipment trust certificate (not a bond)	Railroads, airlines, and utilities	Secured by movable property (locomotives, airplanes, and so on)
Collateral trust	All types	Secured by stocks or bonds of other companies
Debenture	Industrial companies	No specific assets pledged as security, just credit rating of company
Registered	All types	Issued in the bondholder's name
Income bond or revenue bonds	Businesses in financial trouble and municipalities	Pay interest only if income is earned
Sinking fund	Utilities and railroads	Provide for periodic deposit of money to assure redemption
Convertible	All types of businesses	Allows the bond to be exchanged for common or preferred stock at a specified rate

DISNEY EXPANDS

Epcot Center, Walt Disney Productions' educational and futuristic theme park located next to Walt Disney World in Florida, has run into some thorny problems. When Epcot, the Experimental Prototype Community of Tomorrow, was first conceived in the 1960s, Disney planned to finance almost all of the park internally. It was hoped that with the contributions of the participating corporations and the continued strong earnings of the company, there would be no need to go outside for additional financing. However, high construction costs, ride design troubles, high turnover of key engineers, and the company's decline in profits have combined to deal the project a severe financial blow.

Epcot's original cost estimate of $500 million had gone up 60 percent by 1981. This, coupled with declining earnings, forced Disney into the debt market for more funds and raised fears that the center would not open on time. Corporations sponsoring pavilions have paid in a total of $40 million, and Disney's direct investment had by 1981 totaled more than $450 million. In 1981, Disney sold over $100 million in bonds on the European market and was contemplating drawing on its $300 million line of credit with Bank of America or issuing commercial paper in order to raise the remaining funds. "We are developing a flexible financing strategy," says Michael L. Bagnall, senior vice president for finance. The need to borrow extensively could be reduced greatly if the company became more profitable. All Disney needs to do is introduce a very successful movie, and many of its problems would go away.

Source: "What Is Dimming the Magic of Disney," *Business Week,* November 9, 1981, p. 39.

agency. Exhibit 16–8 summarizes the different types of bonds and their characteristics.

SUMMARY

- All businesses need different types of financing depending upon the intended use of the funds. The two major types of financing are short-term funds, used for one year or less, and long-term funds used for more than one year.
- There are three major types of short-term financing available to businesses: credit from suppliers, commercial bank loans, and financing from other businesses or investors.
- Debt financing means that the business has borrowed money from creditors. Creditors expect the money to be repaid and expect to receive interest payments on time. Equity financing involves raising money from the owners of the business. There is no guarantee that the money will be repaid or that any return will be paid to the investors. Investors, however, have a say in how the business is run.
- The long-term sources of funds for sole proprietorships and partnerships are generally limited to the personal wealth of one or a few people and what the owners can obtain from friends. On the other hand, the corporation—especially a large open corporation—has a wide base of potential investors and creditors to draw from, thus easing the burden of gathering large amounts of long-term capital.

■ There are three types of equity financing available to a corporation: common stock, preferred stock, and retained earnings. Common stock represents ownership in the business. Preferred stockholders receive their dividends and get their money out of the business before common stockholders do. Retained earnings are the reinvested profits of the business.

■ The major advantage in financing a business with debt is that the owners do not give up any control. In addition, the interest payments on debt are an expense to the business and thus reduce taxes. The major disadvantage is that if the principal or interest is not paid, the company is in default.

■ Bonds are classified in a number of ways: by the assets pledged as security, by the method of interest payment, by the method of repayment, and by the issuing agency.

1. What are the sources of long-term funds, and what are these funds used for?
2. What are the advantages of using equity as a source of long-term financing?
3. Each form of business has limitations on its ability to raise capital. What are the limitations of the following: sole proprietorships, partnerships, corporations?
4. Stockholders have preemptive rights. What does this mean?
5. What is a trade credit? Why is it so important to small businesses?
6. Some observers claim that a preferred stock is actually a bond. Do you agree? Why or why not?
7. How do economic conditions affect the process of financial management?
8. What is the relationship between the sources of funds and the uses of funds?
9. Explain the use of the trade acceptance.
10. Why is financing through bonds more expensive than selling common stock?

ISSUES TO CONSIDER AND ANALYZE

AUTOMAKERS IN TROUBLE

CASE FOR ANALYSIS

In the past few years, the U.S. automobile industry has found it rough going trying to compete with Japanese and German car companies. The market share of foreign products has increased from 18 percent in 1978 to more than 27 percent in 1981. The effect of this drastic shift in market share has been felt by the U.S. automakers for the past several years. In the third quarter of 1981 alone, the combined losses of GM, Ford, and Chrysler totaled $970 million, including a staggering $468 million loss by General Motors. Yet despite their losses, U.S. automakers must keep spending money to convert their plants and equipment.

Automakers are roughly halfway through an $80 billion overhaul of plants and products that is intended to win back some of the 2.3 million annual car sales now going to overseas-based competitors. General Motors announced that it intends to spend $40 billion between 1981 and 1985 for new products and facilities. However, this goal is getting harder and harder to reach as auto sales drop off and losses mount. The Japanese have been able to extend their market share due to an estimated $1500 manufacturing cost advantage in 1981, up from $700 just three years earlier. In addition, the Japanese do not have to spend billions to convert their plants and downsize their product line. The U.S. auto industry is in a difficult situation, and the auto companies will have to raise large sums of money to finance changeovers if they are to survive.

QUESTIONS

1. In their attempt to find financing for new plants and product development, would short-term or long-term financing be most appropriate?
2. What sources of long-term financing are available to the auto industry?

CHAPTER 17

THE SECURITIES MARKETS

LEARNING OBJECTIVES

After studying this chapter, you should be able to:

Discuss the objectives of investment.

Identify the factors that should be considered when analyzing a stock.

Discuss the background and purpose of the stock exchanges.

Understand the way in which securities are bought and sold.

Compare national and regional securities exchanges with the over-the-counter market.

Explain the financial pages of a newspaper.

KEY TERMS

Bulls
Bears
Portfolio
Yield
Stockbroker
Market order
Limit order
Floor broker
Specialist
Round lot
Odd lot
Odd-lot broker
Bid price
Ask price
Spread
Margin
Selling short
Closed-end investment
    company
Mutual fund
Load

WHERE IS THE BEST RATE OF RETURN?

Ed Johnson is an investment analyst for a small insurance company in Indianapolis, Indiana. Ed likes his job a great deal, but his current situation was a long time coming. He attended a small regional state university in Indiana and graduated with a degree in business and a major in finance. Shortly after leaving school, he took a position with a local bank as a management trainee.

"The work was fine at first," said Ed, "but I enjoy the investment business much more because it offers greater variety; and we get to make decisions that can mean millions of dollars. That kind of power and pressure is exciting to me. Take, for instance, this week when part of the trust department's portfolio will be reinvested. We will be deciding where we should invest over $20 million. If we invest in the wrong areas, the company could suffer financial ruin. A mistake could mean higher premiums for our insurance clients and could put us at a disadvantage when trying to sell insurance against our competition. If the money is invested in an area with a high return, we stand a greater risk of losing the investment. If we invest in an area with little risk, the return on the investment is usually low. I face a challenge in attempting to balance all these factors when designing the right investment portfolio for our business. We look at stocks, bonds, and notes from a wide range of companies and the government before making the final selection."

During the past hundred years, the average American has devoted an increasing amount of time to the management of personal finances. This is a direct result of the nation's rising income level, which has helped millions of Americans accumulate savings. But, in spite of widespread interest in the stock market by individuals, business investment accounts for about 80 percent of the securities bought and sold in the United States. Banks, insurance companies, pension funds, investment companies, and other businesses all carry on active investment programs.

INVESTING IN SECURITIES

Investors have two basic attitudes toward the stock market. **Bulls** are investors who believe the overall trend of the stock market is upward. Merrill Lynch, the nation's largest stockbroker, advertises that it is "bullish on America," meaning that it is optimistic about our nation's future. Investors who are bullish purchase securities (which include stocks and bonds) on the assumption that stock prices will increase and that they will be able to sell their securities for a higher price than they paid. The name for this kind of investor appears to have come from the way bulls fight, with strong upward thrusts of the head.

Bears are investors who expect stock prices to decline. Bears take action to protect themselves; they either stay out of the market or sell if they own stock. If the stock market is steadily declining, it is called a bear market. Once again the name appears to have come from the way a bear typically fights, pulling its victim down to the ground.

People who are uncertain about the overall trend of the market are said to be sitting on the sidelines, waiting for some sign of the market's direction before they take any action. These individuals are only potential investors.

Exhibit 17-1 demonstrates in general terms how stock prices are determined. When investors feel that the prospects for a company, industry, or economy are good, they purchase the stocks and prices increase. If investors are dissatisfied with the performance or prospects of the company, industry, or economy, they sell stocks and prices decline.

BULL
An investor who believes that the stock market will rise.

BEAR
An investor who believes that the stock market will decline.

THE INVESTOR'S BASIC OBJECTIVES

Investors have three major investment objectives: (1) safety of principal, (2) income, and (3) growth of capital. A retired person is going to be much more interested in safety of principal than growth of capital compared to a highly paid business executive in his or her early forties, who will have different investment objectives. A retired person is also more likely to be concerned with the income from an investment rather than the growth of capital. In any event, one must understand that trade-offs are involved with these three investment objectives, although they are not always mutually exclusive. Generally, the higher the rate of return, the more risk is involved, so that safety of income and of principal are to some extent opposites.

People who speculate in the stock market deliberately select high-risk securities on the chance they can make a quick profit. But speculators also

EXHIBIT 17-1
Why Stock Prices Change
From: *How to Invest*, (New York: Merrill
Lynch, Pierce, Fenner and Smith, 1971).

spend a good deal of time investigating lesser-known companies and special situations in which risks are generally higher before they invest. They take what they feel are reasonable risks. The gambler, on the other hand, accepts risks with no real desire to identify, appraise, or balance them against the opportunities for gain. Gamblers may rely on "hot tips" when selecting stocks, but quite often the only thing they get from a hot tip is burned.

Safety of Principal

Investments in any stock or bond always have some degree of risk. Through the last four recessions, many investors lost a good deal of money on such favorites as IBM, Xerox, and McDonald's. Although risk always accompanies the ownership of securities, this risk can be reduced through careful selection.

How do stocks versus bonds rate on safety of principal? That question is hard to answer, but there is a general pattern. Bonds seem to provide the greatest safety, common stocks the lowest. Preferred stocks fall somewhere between. But these are only general guidelines. The common stock of companies like AT&T and General Motors is much safer than the bonds of some other organizations, such as the City of New York.

Several investment services help measure the risk associated with various investments. For example, both Moody's and Standard and Poor's rate bond issues and provide these ratings to the general public. These investment rating services also rate the risk and desirability of common stocks. Exhibit 17-2 provides the ratings of several issues of common stocks by different investment services. Investors who want to reduce their risk might select companies like Dow Chemical and Union Electric, and those inclined to take a bit more risk might find Coors or Church's Fried Chicken more suitable.

Another way to reduce the risk of stock ownership is to avoid putting all your eggs in one basket. Instead of selecting one company and buying only that stock, a **portfolio** of securities can be developed. A portfolio can be made up of common stock, preferred stock, bonds, or any combination of these. The idea behind the portfolio is to spread the money over a number of securities in order to have *diversification*, or variety. In this way, fluctuations in one security will be offset by the others, reducing the overall risk.

PORTFOLIO
An individual's or institution's holdings of securities; it may include bonds, preferred stock, and common stock of various businesses.

Income

Another investment objective is dividend or interest income. Many investors are looking for ways to increase their current incomes. They will look for common stock that pays a high dividend or a preferred stock or bonds. Bonds generally provide the steadiest interest income, followed by preferred stocks and, finally, common stocks. In many cases, securities pay a higher return on investment than a bank savings account and have greater flexibility.

The return on securities is called a **yield** and is expressed as a percentage. The yield is calculated by dividing the dividend or interest payment by the current market price. For example, if XYZ Corporation pays a dividend of $3 and sells for about $53 per share, then its yield is 5.7 percent.

YIELD
The return on an investment. Calculated by dividing the amount of the return by the amount of the investment.

$$\text{Yield} = \frac{\text{Dividend (Interest)}}{\text{Market Price}} = \frac{\$3}{\$53} = 5.7 \text{ percent}$$

Exhibit 17-3 is a selection of securities and their yields. Of this group, McDonald's is the least likely to appeal to investors interested in high yield. But the other securities on the list would all be prime candidates. Union Electric common stock has a particularly attractive yield.

Growth

Investors interested in capital growth typically have to forego immediate dividends. Growth companies are usually part of a fast-growing industry

COMPANY	VALUE LINE RATING*	MOODY'S RATING†
Dow Chemical	1	High-grade
Coors	3	Medium-grade
Church's Fried Chicken	4	Speculative grade
Union Electric	1	Investment grade

*Value Line rates companies from 1 to 5, with 1 being the highest rating.
†Moody's rates companies in this order: high, investment, medium, and speculative grade.

EXHIBIT 17-2
Ratings of Common Stock

EXHIBIT 17-3
Typical Yields of Selected Securities

COMPANY	TYPE OF SECURITY	MARKET PRICE	DIVIDEND OR INTEREST	YIELD
Union Electric	Common	$ 10.87	$ 1.52	14.0%
General Motors	Common	47.00	2.40	5.1
McDonald's	Common	58.00	1.00	1.7
General Motors	Preferred	40.00	5.00	12.0
Union Electric	Preferred	25.00	4.00	16.0
General Motors	Bond	526.25	80.00	15.0
Union Electric	Bond	620.00	105.00	17.0

like computers, energy, or electronics. The earnings of these companies rise much faster than the average, but to obtain this fast growth, most of them must reinvest the majority of their earnings. The investor expects to benefit in the long run because the retained earnings will help the company grow at an even faster pace. One growth company is Digital Equipment Corporation. Digital pays no dividends and reinvests all its profits. Its earnings have grown from $4.5 million in 1967 to $20 million in 1981. Had you purchased this minicomputer manufacturer's common stock in 1967, you would have paid about $9 per share. A $10,000 investment in 1967 would have been worth $98 in 1982. Spectacular growth like this is somewhat unusual, but the common stock of many companies has increased in price.

On the Job Revisited   Investment analyst Ed Johnson often has to decide between safety of principal or income as well as the growth potential of the investments his insurance company can partake in. Traditionally, insurance companies have been very conservative in their choice of investments. That is to say, they have held security of principal as a primary goal when purchasing assets for investment portfolios. When Ed first took the job, he found that the bulk of the insurance company's assets was in long-term government bonds and highly rated corporate bonds. The climate is changing, however, and Ed is gradually diversifying his insurance company's portfolio. It now includes investments in oil and gas drilling operations, some relatively riskless stocks, and even a few business ventures.

Ed is nonetheless constantly faced with the trade-off between risk and rate of return. Every time he is offered a "great" deal with a high potential return, he ultimately finds that the risk his company would incur would also be great.

THE STOCK EXCHANGES

The stock exchanges are the central markets where the agents of buyers and sellers meet to exchange securities for a price. About 25 million Americans own shares of common stock, and another 80 million, through their pension plans and insurance policies, have a financial interest in the stock market. Exhibit 17-4 identifies the companies with the largest number of stockholders. This trading takes place on the floors of the various stock exchanges.

WALL STREET BLUES

Late in the evening of January 7, Ron Pavlak got the call from his investment advisory service recommending that he sell his securities as soon as possible. He called his broker the next morning even before the market opened to make sure that his PRIME Computer stock would be sold as soon as the market opened. After all, he told himself, he had been paying several hundred dollars a year to receive this advisory newsletter and an even higher premium to get the phone call telling him before the letter got there what it would say. After shelling out that much money, Ron couldn't afford not to take Joe Granville's advice.

The next day on the New York Stock Exchange, the ticker ran a half-hour late all day. Trading in American Telephone and Telegraph, the most widely held stock in the world, failed to open on time. The same was true for General Motors and several other stocks. IBM stock didn't open for trading until 2: P.M. PRIME Computer, one of the volume leaders for the day, opened late in the morning at $32½, down $6⅛ from the day before. By the end of the trading day, over 93 million shares of stock were traded in one of the biggest volume days the stock exchange had ever seen. A similar situation occurred on the American Stock Exchange and in the over-the-counter market. The sell recommendation made by Joseph Granville's investment advisory service had a significant impact on the securities market.

The question that bothers many observers of Wall Street is what would happen if something really bad happened? If a sell recommendation by a smallish investment advisory service could lead to a record trading day, then how much volume would be unleashed if something important happened. That January 7, the market was able to handle the volume reasonably well, but it was not able to handle the massive imbalance of sell orders to buy orders. At first, everyone seemed paralyzed. For many stocks, early price quotations attracted no buyers at all. Later in the day as the first buyers appeared, only a small amount of stock was available for sale, which was sold at successively higher prices. Ron's PRIME Computer stock sold in the morning at 32½. The price had opened 6⅛ lower than it closed the day before. By the end of the day, however, PRIME was selling at $36, up 3½ from the price he sold it for in the morning. Apparently many of the losers were people who paid for and then took Joe Granville's advice.

The major function of the exchanges is to increase the marketability of listed securities. People would be reluctant to buy shares of stock if they weren't sure they could readily sell them for cash. Furthermore, there would be less interest in stock ownership if investors had to wait for only new issues of stock before they could invest. The organized exchanges provide the physical location for the purchase and sale of over 6 billion shares of stock each year, with a market value of over $240 billion. By doing so, the exchanges promote saving and investment, which helps the flow of capital throughout the economy and helps corporations raise money for expenditures like research and development and new plant and equipment. **Stockbrokers** do the actual trading; they are representatives of a member firm of one of the exchanges.

The New York Stock Exchange (NYSE), or the "Big Board," is America's oldest stock exchange. It is where the securities of some of our largest

STOCKBROKER
A registered representative of a stock exhange's member firm.

The New York Stock Exchange

EXHIBIT 17-4
United States Corporations with
Largest Number of Stockholders

CORPORATION	NUMBER OF STOCKHOLDERS
American Telephone & Telegraph	2,934,000
General Motors	1,283,000
Exxon	725,000
International Business Machines	557,000
General Electric	537,000
General Telephone & Electronics	430,000
Ford Motor	341,000

corporations are bought and sold. In order for a company's stock to be traded on the NYSE, the company must meet specific listing requirements. These requirements were initially quite lenient; however, they have since become much more restrictive. The current minimum for becoming listed requires a company to have:

At least a million shares held by the public

A market value for the publicly held stock of at least $16 million

A minimum of two thousand investors, each owning one hundred shares or more

Annual earnings of at least $2.5 million

Net tangible assets of at least $16 million

The American Stock Exchange

The American Stock Exchange (AMEX) is the second largest stock exchange in the country. Companies that have their stock listed on the AMEX are generally smaller and less well known than those listed on the NYSE. The listing requirements are more lenient, which is why smaller companies are listed there. Some of the better known companies listed on the AMEX include the *New York Times*, STP Corporation, Bic Pen, Hartz Mountain, and Gerber Products.

Regional Exchanges

In addition to the New York Stock Exchange and the American Stock Exchange, there are several regional exchanges around the United States as well as international exchanges in the financial centers of the world. Some of the regional exchanges include the Midwest Exchange in Chicago and the Philadelphia-Baltimore-Washington Stock Exchange. There are international exchanges in London, Amsterdam, Paris, Zurich, Tokyo, and Frankfurt. The largest of these is the London Exchange, listing over ten thousand stocks. These exchanges serve the same basic function as the NYSE and AMEX.

How Securities Are Bought and Sold

As stated earlier, securities exchanges provide a place for the agents of buyers and sellers to meet to exchange securities for a price. The steps in this process are not simple, but the regulations and experience that have evolved over the past 175 years make the typical transaction very smooth.

Ed Johnson, the insurance company investment analyst, has decided to purchase shares of stock. His first step is to contact a registered representative, or stockbroker, at one of the exchange's member firms. The stockbroker's primary function is providing information to customers that will help them make a selection.

After some research, Ed decides that American Telephone and Telegraph meets his company's investment objectives, so he wants to make it part of his company's portfolio. His broker informs him that "Telephone" is currently selling at 60¼. Stock prices are quoted in whole dollars and eighths of a dollar. Each eighth is worth $.125. Thus, a stock quoted at 60¼ sells for $60.25.

PLACING AN ORDER   Ed's next step is to order the stockbroker to purchase the stock. He can make one of two basic orders. A **market order** instructs the broker to make the transaction at the best price available at that time. A **limit order** specifies the highest price Ed is willing to pay or the lowest price he is willing to sell for; the broker will not buy or sell beyond these limits.

At this time, Ed places a market order for one thousand shares of AT&T. His order is wired to the floor of the stock exchange, where a clerk receives it and notifies the firm's floor broker that an order exists. The **floor broker** executes orders to buy or sell any listed securities. Each member firm of the exchanges has at least one floor broker.

EXECUTING AN ORDER   Once Ed's order has been received, the floor broker immediately proceeds to the place on the floor where AT&T is traded. The exchange floor has eighteen horseshoe-shaped booths, the trading posts for listed securities. AT&T is traded at post 15. On arrival there, the floor broker is met by other people, among them the **specialist**. The specialist informs the floor broker that the price of AT&T is "60 to a quarter" (that is, someone is willing to pay $60 but the lowest price anyone will accept is $60.25).

Besides the specialist, Ed's floor broker could meet another firm's floor broker who has been ordered to sell a thousand shares of AT&T at market. The two brokers make verbal offers and counteroffers, each trying to do the best for their clients. Once the price is settled on, the final trade information is transferred to the exchange's computer and thus to some 4200 stock tickers across the country.

Exhibit 17-5 shows what the ticker might look like. The ticker automatically displays the symbol for the company, the number of shares traded (in blocks of one hundred shares or, after one thousand, the actual shares), and the price per share. The first symbol on the ticker is the figure T. T is the abbreviation for American Telephone and Telegraph. Below the symbol is the price at which the stock was traded. In this case, Ed purchased a thousand shares of AT&T for $60.25. General Motors was the next stock sold. Three hundred shares of GM were traded at $75.50. The last symbol, MCD, stands for McDonald's, and the numbers show that a thousand shares of McDonald's were sold at $52.50.

All the transactions on the stock exchange are handled in blocks of one

On the Job Revisited

MARKET ORDER
An order to buy or sell a stated number of securities at the current market price.

LIMIT ORDER
An order to buy or sell a stated number of securities at a specified price.

FLOOR BROKER
A member of the stock exchange who executes orders to buy or sell securities on the floor of the stock exchange.

SPECIALIST
A member of a stock exchange who specializes in the purchase and sale of a specific stock or stocks. The specialist has two functions: to maintain an orderly market in the trading of stocks and to assist other brokers with limit orders.

EXHIBIT 17-5
Example of a Stock Ticker

T	GM	DEC	MCD
1000s60-1/8	3s75-1/2	2s57-7/8	1000s52-1/2

ROUND LOT
A unit of trading on the stock exchange; usually one hundred shares.

hundred shares, or **round lots**. An investor who wants twenty shares of stock must buy an **odd lot**, which is handled by an **odd-lot broker**, who brings together several odd lots to make a round lot.

THE OVER-THE-COUNTER MARKET

ODD LOT
An amount of stock less than a round lot or between one and ninety-nine shares.

ODD-LOT BROKER
A member of the stock exchange who buys and sells odd lots of stock.

BID PRICE
The price a broker who has taken a position on a stock in the over-the-counter market is willing to pay for the stock.

ASK PRICE
The price at which a broker who has or will take a position on a stock is willing to sell the stock in the over-the-counter market.

SPREAD
The difference between the bid price and the ask price in the over-the-counter market.

Unlike the NYSE and AMEX, the over-the-counter market (OTC) doesn't have any physical location. Over forty thousand securities are bought and sold through a network of telephone and teletype wires connecting thousands of dealers across the country. The OTC got its name because of the way securities were once sold. In the eighteenth and nineteenth centuries, stocks and bonds were sold over the counters of private banking houses on Wall Street, in much the same way people would buy supplies at the general store. This descriptive name stuck, even though the system of trading has changed greatly.

The way a security is traded over the counter is much different from the auction method used on the floor of a stock exchange. OTC stocks are purchased from a broker who has "taken a position" in the stock. That is, the broker has agreed to hold shares in inventory and to buy or sell these shares at stated prices.

The stocks are quoted at bid and ask prices. The **bid price** is the price the other broker is willing to pay for the stock. The **ask price** is the price at which the broker is willing to sell. The difference between the two is the **spread**. For example, assume Anheuser-Busch has a bid price of $24.25 and an ask price of $24.75. If Ed wants to buy Anheuser-Busch, he would pay $24.75; if he owned the stock and wanted to sell, he would receive $24.25. The exact price at which Ed purchases or sells stock depends on his broker's ability to negotiate a favorable price.

OTHER WAYS OF INVESTING

So far, we have concentrated on the investor who purchases shares of common stock, preferred stock, or bonds for a portfolio using cash as payment. There are, however, other ways of investing and other types of investments, including buying on margin, selling short, and joining an investment company.

Buying on Margin

MARGIN
The percentage that the buyer must put down when purchasing a stock.

Buying on margin permits the buyer to purchase securities with money borrowed from the broker. The buyer puts a specified percentage down and borrows the rest, using the stock as collateral for the loan. The broker charges an interest rate just higher than the bank rate, and the buyer receives the benefit of any appreciation in market value plus dividends declared on the stock. The **margin** is the percentage the buyer must put down when purchasing stock. For example, if the margin requirement is 70 percent, the investor would have to put up 70 percent of the money and could borrow 30 percent from the broker. Margin requirements are set by the Federal Reserve Board and, over the past twenty years, have ranged between 50 and 100 percent. Any investor can buy on margin.

Buying on margin allows the purchaser to buy more shares than would otherwise be possible. If the stock price moves upward, the investor can make a higher profit. If the stock market declines, the losses are greater.

Selling Short

In our discussion of investing, two assumptions have been made: (1) the stock was purchased and (2) the investor hoped the stock's price would increase. It is also possible to make a profit when a particular stock's price is declining. **Selling short** involves the sale of borrowed stock with the promise to return the stock at a later date. The broker loans the customer the stock or borrows it form another customer or broker. The stock is then sold in hopes that its price will fall. The person who sells short speculates that the price of the stock will be lower sometime in the future when the stock is returned.

SELLING SHORT
Selling borrowed stock with the promise to return it at a later date.

For example, assume that Ed expects a severe gasoline shortage in the near future. This, he reasons, would hurt the automobile companies and their stock prices. He instructs his broker to sell short one hundred shares of General Motors. Ed's broker borrows the hundred shares and sells them for $60 per share. The $6,000 is then deposited as security with the lender. If the anticipated shortage develops, and the price of GM stock declines to $40 per share, then Ed would purchase a hundred shares for $4,000 and replace the borrowed stock. The difference between his selling price ($6,000) and his purchase price ($4,000) is a $2,000 profit (not counting the broker's commission). Selling short works to Ed's advantage only if the stock declines, and there is no limit to his losses if the stock rises and he fails to buy in. Consequently, the high risk may be much too high for the portfolio of a conservative insurance company.

On the Job Revisited

Investment Companies and Mutual Funds

Investors who do not have the time or inclination to do their own investment analysis can invest in an investment company, which sells shares of its stock to investors and then uses the money to purchase common stock, preferred stock, bonds, and notes of other corporations and government units. Thus, the individual investor's money is joined with many others and is spread over a number of securities. Some investment companies develop portfolios containing a large number of securities, whereas others select only a few securities for their portfolios. In either case, the effect is to reduce the risk associated with the ownership of securities. With a number of securities, losses on some are likely to be offset by gains in others. The investor thus reduces risk and obtains a professional investment management team.

There are two types of investment companies. The **closed-end investment company**, like other corporations, issues a specified number of shares of common stock. Once these shares have been sold, they are traded in the securities market like other stock. The open-end investment company, or **mutual fund**, gets its name from the fact that it continues to sell new shares

CLOSED-END INVESTMENT COMPANY
An investment company that issues a specified number of stock shares . Once these have been sold, they are traded in a securities market like any other stock. To be contrasted with an open-end investment company, or mutual fund.
MUTUAL FUND
A company that uses its capital to invest in other companies and continues to sell more of its shares of stock as investors demand them.

LOAD
The commission charged by the agent to purchase shares of a mutual fund.

of stock as investors purchase them. In addition, the mutual fund buys back the stock when investors redeem their shares.

There is a wide variety of mutual funds from which to choose. Some charge a sales commission (**load**), and others do not (no load). Some invest only in stocks (stock fund), others only in bonds (bond fund), and still others do a little of both (balanced fund). Some look for appreciation in the price of the securities held (growth fund), and others invest in securities that provide a high yield (income fund). Finally, some mutual funds invest in specific industries, so there are insurance funds, energy funds, and municipal-bond funds. In other words, there is a mutual fund to fit just about any investment objective.

TRACKING
THE INVESTMENT

Once a security has been bought, the investor should keep track of the investment's performance. This can involve reading company reports as well as news stories about the overall economy, the industry, and the company. In addition, most newspapers devote two or three pages each day to the financial news, including the reports of stock averages and stock quotations of the previous day's trading. These figures give precise information on the performance of securities.

Stock Averages

The best known of all the stock averages is the Dow Jones industrial average. The Dow Jones industrial average started in 1897, when it consisted of stock prices for twelve big industrial firms whose shares were traded on the New York Stock Exchange. The average was an index that added up the stock prices and divided them by twelve to obtain an average. The "Dow," as it is called, was expanded to twenty firms in 1916 and to thirty firms in 1928. Today the Dow Jones industrial average is reported hourly as well as at the close of the market on each trading day.

The share prices in the Dow are added up and divided by 1.314. Assume, for example, that the stock prices of the 30 firms included in the Dow add up to $1,314; then the Dow Jones industrial average would be 1,000 ($1,314/1.314 = 1,000). The divisor is less than 30 to adjust for the numerous stock splits that have occurred over the years.

Although the Dow Jones industrial average is a popular measure of the direction of the stock market, it has several limitations. First, it is composed only of large, well-established companies, including Alcoa, AT&T, Bethlehem Steel, IBM, DuPont, Exxon, General Motors, Sears, U. S. Steel, 3M, and General Electric. It can hardly be argued that these companies are average stocks. Second, the stocks are weighted on the basis of price. A $40 stock has four times the weight of a $10 stock. Thus, a 1 percent rise in the $40 stock would have the same impact on the Dow as a 4 percent rise in the $10 stock. Finally, a small percentage change in price can have a substantial effect on the averages. For example, assume the Dow Jones industrials fall from 900 to 892—a drop of 8 points. This sounds like a significant decline, but it would amount to only about 40¢ per share on the average share of stock.

Other stock averages include a larger number of stocks and thus tend to be more representative of the actual price trends. Exhibit 17-6 shows the

EXHIBIT 17-6
Other Major Stock Market Indexes

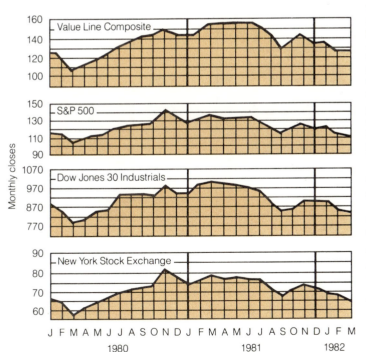

THE VALUE LINE COMPOSITE STOCK INDEX consists of 1,698 stocks, most of them traded on the New York Stock Exchange. Also includes issues from the American Stock Exchange, regional markets, and over-the-counter stocks. The index gives equal weight to each stock.

THE STANDARD & POOR'S 500 is composed of 400 industrial stocks, 40 financial companies, 40 utilities and 20 transportation issues. It is weighted by market value (multiplying the stock price by the number of shares outstanding).

THE DOW JONES INDUSTRIAL AVERAGE consists of 30 blue-chip industrial stocks. It gives greater weight to higher-priced issues. Transportation and utility stocks are not included.

THE NEW YORK STOCK EXCHANGE COMMON STOCK INDEX is a weighted average based on the 1,540 stocks traded daily. Like the S & P 500, it gives greater weight to issues with a larger dollar value of shares outstanding.

other major indexes along with the Dow Jones averages. The Standard and Poor's index includes five hundred stocks from the exchanges as well as stocks traded over the counter. The NYSE index is based on the average of the stocks listed on December 31, 1965, on the NYSE. These indexes have a broad base and thus serve as a useful measure of the direction of the market.

Stock and Bond Quotes

Thousands of different stocks are traded on several exchanges across the country. To avoid the confusion and problems of reporting these prices, a composite quotation was instituted in 1976. The newspaper listing for the New York Stock Exchange now includes trades made on the Midwest, Philadelphia, Cincinnati, and Pacific Coast exchanges. The American Stock Exchange listings include the Midwest, Philadelphia, Boston, and Cincinnati exchanges.

READING THE STOCK PAGE   Exhibit 17-7 represents a partial list of stock quotes on the New York Stock Exchange from a daily newspaper. The stocks are listed in alphabetical order, and when there is a multiple listing for a single company, the common stock is listed first, followed by preferred stocks. Only round lots are listed, so the volume figure is always in hundreds. Stock quoted at 49⅝ actually sells for $49.625.

EXHIBIT 17-7
Quotations from the
New York Stock Exchange

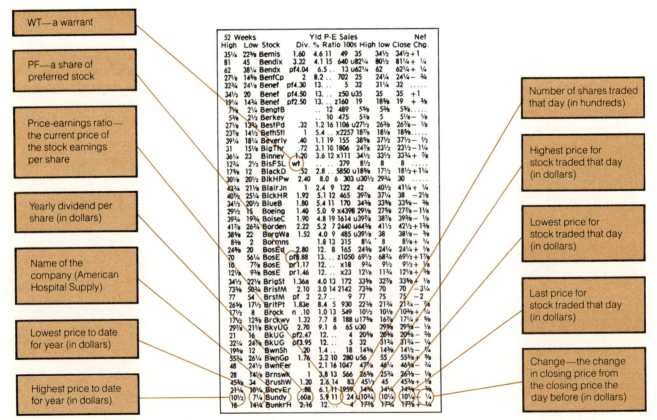

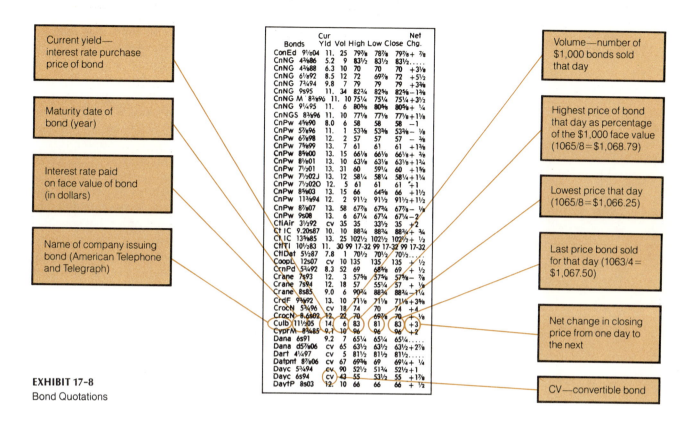

EXHIBIT 17-8
Bond Quotations

READING THE BOND PAGE In addition to stock quotes, most newspapers carry the results of bond trading. Bonds are listed in alphabetical order like stocks, but bond prices are quoted differently. The quotes are a percentage of the bond's face value. The usual face value is $1,000, so a bond quoted at 95⅜ actually sells for $953.75. A bond selling for higher than the face value is said to be selling at a premium, and a bond selling for less than the face value is selling at a discount. Exhibit 17-8 represents a partial listing of bonds traded on the New York Stock Exchange.

- Investors have three basic objectives when investing in stocks or bonds: safety of principal, income, and growth of capital. Although each of these objectives is different, they are not mutually exclusive.
- There is usually a trade-off between principal and income and between income and growth of capital. In other words, you usually can't have two or more of these simultaneously when you invest in a particular stock.
- Typically, one has a portfolio of securities including stocks, bonds, and perhaps other investments. When one has this type of portfolio, one is following the rule of diversification, or variety in investments.
- The income of an investment is given by its yield, which is calculated by dividing the market price of the asset into its dividend if it is a stock or its interest if it is a bond.

SUMMARY

■ Growth stocks are typically issued by those companies that reinvest their profits rather than give dividends to stockholders.

■ The stock exchanges of the world provide a formal way of trading securities. These exchanges promote saving and investment by providing a physical location where stocks can easily be bought and sold.

■ The two largest stock exchanges are the New York Stock Exchange (NYSE) and the American Stock Exchange (AMEX). There are also various regional exchanges in major cities and the over-the-counter (OTC) market, which does not have an actual physical location.

■ The purchase of stocks typically involves using a registered representative, or stockbroker, who places an order through his or her stockbrokerage firm. This order can be either a market order instructing a broker to buy the stock at the best price available or a limit order that specifies the highest price the customer is willing to pay.

■ Prices of securities are determined by the laws of supply and demand. Investors who want to buy or sell securities are represented on the floor of the stock exchange by brokers who negotiate the sales price.

■ The OTC is different from the established exchanges in that the stock purchased on the OTC is bought from a broker rather than another investor.

■ Investors in stocks can purchase stocks on margin; that is to say, they put up only a specified percentage of the total purchase price and borrow the rest from the stockbrokerage firm. Typically, a stock purchaser must put up about 50 percent of the purchase price.

■ An investor who believes that the price of a stock will fall can make a profit by selling short, which involves selling shares of stock that a person does not actually own. The person hopes to purchase those shares of stock at a later date, say, five days later, to make good on the sale, but at a price that is less than what it sold for five days earlier.

■ One way to make an investment in the stock market is through an investment company. An open-end investment company is called a mutual fund. It continues to sell shares of stock as investors purchase them and uses the proceeds to purchase more shares from a diversified group of companies. Investors can redeem their shares in the mutual fund at any time, at whatever the market value of the shares is.

■ The financial pages of the newspaper present a summary of the stock and bond transactions on the major stock exchanges and the OTC.

■ The Dow Jones industrial average, called the Dow, is the best known index of stock prices and is an index of thirty large industrial companies. It is given hourly and at the end of each trading day.

ISSUES TO CONSIDER AND ANALYZE

1. What is the difference between a bull market and a bear market?
2. What is speculation, and how does it differ from investing?
3. Are there ways to make a higher-than-normal rate of return by investing in the stock market? If so, what are they?
4. How does the New York Stock Exchange operate?
5. Compare the New York Stock Exchange with the over-the-counter market.

6. Get a copy of the *Wall Street Journal*. Compare the prices of the stocks listed in Exhibit 17-7 with the day's prices. What has happened to yields and dividends?
7. Do the same thing for the bond quotes presented in Exhibit 17-8.
8. What factors should be considered when evaluating a stock?
9. Describe the purpose of selling short.
10. What is buying on margin?

THE TALE OF THE TAPE

CASE FOR ANALYSIS

Sonny Look and Lowell Douglas manage Softball Country Club (SCC), which is a large sports complex in San Diego. They must decide how to invest $250,000 of SCC's cash assets in the financial market. The two executives have discussed the decision for several days, but they are still not in agreement. The decision about investing cash assets is not easy because Look and Douglas have different ideas about safety and risk.

Douglas wants to invest the cash assets in high-growth common stock paying dividends yielding about 4 percent. He believes that the stock market is entering a major new bull market that will carry the Dow Jones industrial average index to 1500. Douglas supports his prediction on a new single-day record trading volume (132.7 million shares), lower interest rates, and slowing inflation rates. Douglas summed up his feelings by saying, "The tale of the tape is that the stock market has started a new bull market."

Look is not certain this is true. In real terms (adjusted for inflation), he points out that the Dow Jones industrial average is lower than its value in 1949. Look also mentioned that the Dow Jones transportation index and the AMEX index are 60 points below their 1981 highs. To have a new bull market he thinks other indexes besides the Dow must rise. Look wants to invest SCC's cash in a money market fund that buys only federal government securities. He can get annual yields of about 10 percent on this type of investment, but SCC does not get any capital gains on a money market investment.

QUESTIONS

1. If you were to advise Look and Douglas about their investment decision, what factors would you tell them to consider besides safety, risk, and yield?
2. With which executive do you agree and why?

Adapted from Charles J. Rolo, "Anticipating Major Ups and Downs," *Houston Chronicle*, August 29, 1982.

CHAPTER 18

RISK MANAGEMENT AND INSURANCE

LEARNING OBJECTIVES

After studying this chapter, you should be able to:

Illustrate the different types of risk.

Identify and discuss the means of controlling risk.

Explain the four principles of insurance.

Explain the difference between a stock and a mutual insurance company.

Discuss the different types of property and casualty insurance.

Compare the different types of life insurance.

KEY TERMS

Self-insurance
Premium
Principle of indemnity
Subrogation
Stock insurance company
Nonparticipating policy
Mutual insurance company
Participating policy
Extended coverage
Umbrella policy
Term insurance
Whole life insurance
Uniform decreasing
   term insurance
Home protection plan
Renewability
Convertibility
Living benefits
Death benefits
Endowment policy

SPREADING THE RISK

Ellis Lindsay only took one course in insurance principles while in business school. In fact, for a while, his minor in English seemed to interest him more than the courses he was taking for his B. A. in business. His attitude changed, however, when he started interviewing for jobs during his senior year. The economy was in a recession, and companies weren't seeking him out in overwhelming numbers. Ellis finally decided that he did not want an office job just yet, nor was he convinced that he simply wanted to be a salesperson. The insurance industry seemed a good compromise, so he signed on with one of the major life and casualty insurance companies. He was starting at the bottom, but he knew he could easily work his way up.

Ellis did just that. After a couple of years in the field, he was promoted to district supervisor and later to regional supervisor. He then decided to specialize in comprehensive insurance plans for small businesses, in which the entire financial structure of the business, and the owners and employees were taken into account.

Ellis worked on his own to develop a program on the Apple computer he had purchased for his personal financial management. He hoped to figure out a simple, ongoing, cross-checking system that small businesses could use to determine when and for how much people and property were insured and the different kinds of people and property that were covered.

One of the simple truths about being in business is that it is risky. In fact, the definition of an entrepreneur includes the willingness and ability to take risks. What risks are we referring to? The primary risk is that of losing one's entire investment if the business fails. No one can avoid this type of business risk, but numerous business risks and risks related to personal life and property can be covered, or at least reduced. Those risks relate to catastrophic losses from fire or flooding, losses due to theft, lawsuits, the loss of a breadwinning family member, and so on. In other words, there are ways to manage risk.

Risk management is concerned with casualties—those situations in which potential loss does not also involve a chance of gain. It allows a company to protect itself from sudden losses incurred by the kinds of tragedies mentioned above. Risk management deals with risk in five different ways:

RISK MANAGEMENT

1. Avoiding risk
2. Reducing the hazard
3. Reducing the loss
4. Assuming the risk
5. Shifting the risk

How can anyone completely avoid risk? The risk of losing a house to fire can be avoided by not buying a house. You can avoid the risk of being killed in an airplane by not riding in one. The risk of going into business can be avoided by not starting a business in the first place.

Avoiding Risk

If people who own and/or manage businesses tried to avoid all risks, the market would not have any of the products that people enjoy today. Society would be without computers, photocopying machines, instant cameras, video and stereo equipment, and many other products. Taking risks is necessary for the advancement of business and technology.

Many types of risk can be lessened by removing or reducing hazards. For example, good managers conduct training programs to educate employees on the use of equipment. Safety programs are designed to make employees aware of potential hazards. Chemical companies test and monitor products they manufacture to ensure as far as possible that these products will not harm employees, customers, or the environment. In spite of such efforts, substantial risks are sometimes associated with the use or manufacture of many chemicals. For example, even though DBCP, a soil fumigant, was tested before manufacture and monitored during production, it was later proved to cause sterility in male workers.

Reducing the Hazard

Other programs to reduce risk can be introduced by management. Preventive maintenance reduces the chance of machinery failure and prolongs its life. Security guards, guard dogs, employee identification cards, cameras, mirrors, electronic tags on clothing, and many more programs have been designed to reduce chances of theft.

Reducing the Loss

Steps can also be taken to minimize the loss that results when a peril does materialize. The installation of fireproof building materials, automatic sprinkler systems, and fire extinguishers helps reduce losses caused by fires. Designing buildings to withstand the shock of an earthquake and boarding up windows in the face of a hurricane reduce chances of loss. But such precautions cannot prevent the hazard—the fire, earthquake, or hurricane—from occurring.

Assuming the Risk

The assumption of risk is often the path of least resistance when individuals or businesses face uncertainty. For example, families assume the financial loss caused by a member's death when they fail to purchase life insurance. Risk is sometimes assumed through ignorance, too. A homeowner faces a loss from many sources, including fire, wind, hail, explosion, and so on. The homeowner can insure against these risks but might not be aware that he could lose money or his home from a liability suit if someone is hurt while physically on the property. This is one example of how ignorance of potential risks can result in the risk assumption.

In some cases, risks are simply uninsurable—speculative risks are of this nature. People who gamble, race cars, or race motorcycles generally find it difficult to avoid or shift their risks.

SELF-INSURANCE
Assumption of the risk oneself. This occurs when individuals do not buy insurance to cover the risk involved. Self-insurance typically involves setting up a reserve fund to cover potential losses.

Another way of assuming risk is to accumulate funds to cover any financial losses; this is called **self-insurance**. For example, a large chain store operation like Sears may elect to provide its own fire insurance. Because Sears has many stores scattered throughout the United States, the risk of fire can be shared among the stores by establishing a reserve fund for fires. This method is often less expensive than purchasing fire insurance from an insurance company. Self-insurance would not be a realistic choice for smaller companies though. Reserve funds must be large enough to cover potential losses, and a small company would not have the number of outlets necessary to spread the risk.

A large company can also spread the risk of being in business by diversifying into different industries. Should one division of the company do poorly in a given year, the other divisions might be able to pick up the slack.

Shifting the Risk

In all the methods of controlling risk discussed thus far, none involves shifting the burden for risk to someone else. This is accomplished in one major way—insurance. Speculative risk is uninsurable, but pure risk often is insurable. It is impossible to insure against gambling losses (speculative risk) but generally easy to insure against fire and theft. Insurance is a social device for reducing risk by combining a large number of "exposure units" to make the individual losses predictable. The predictable loss is then shared proportionately. In essence, the policyholder agrees to suffer a small loss —a yearly fee—to gain protection from a larger loss, which may or may not occur. The agreement between the insurance company and the insured is spelled out in an insurance policy that states the rights and duties of both parties.

If the risk is spread among a large enough number of people, the **premium**, or yearly fee, which has to be paid will be small compared to the coverage offered. This is typically called the law of large numbers or the law of averages. The greater the number of cases, the closer the actual result will be to the expected result. Using this concept, insurance companies are able to predict with great accuracy things such as how many auto accidents will occur on July 4 or how many houses will burn down in one year in a certain geographic area. They can therefore estimate how much they will have to pay out if they insure a particular group. From this they can predict the premium rates for each member of the group in order to cover the losses and make a profit for the company.

THE PRINCIPLES BEHIND INSURANCE

PREMIUM
The yearly fee paid for insurance.

Insurance companies must apply some principle to prevent individuals from being paid more than their actual financial loss. This is typically called the **principle of indemnity**, which states that the insured cannot be compensated for an amount that exceeds his or her actual economic loss. Most liability and property insurance contracts are based upon this principle. There are several related concepts:

1. Actual cash value
2. Insurable interest
3. Subrogation
4. "Other insurance"

THE PRINCIPLE OF INDEMNITY

PRINCIPLE OF INDEMNITY
The insured may not be compensated by an insurance company for more than his or her economic, or financial, loss.

The principle of indemnity limits the amount a claimant can collect to the actual cash value of the property insured. Actual cash value is most commonly defined as replacement cost less depreciation. Replacement cost could exceed purchase cost, but depreciation schedules are often applied to the actual (historic, or original) purchase price rather than the current purchase price. In any event, under the principle of indemnity, the insurance company is not obligated to pay more than the true replacement cost minus depreciation, which is, in effect, the market value of the item insured.

Actual Cash Value

Consider insurance of personal property such as an automobile. Let's say that you bought a car five years ago that cost you $10,000, and its current depreciated value is listed as $2,500. If the car is destroyed by fire or stolen, your insurance company will only give you $2,500, even though if you tried to replace the car with a new one you would have to pay $12,000 today. In essence, you are allowed costs to replace exactly the same used item, not a newer one. However, you can purchase specific insurance policies that will allow you to recover the price of replacing the lost or destroyed item with a brand new one. Also, as you will see later in the chapter, insurance on real property—houses, apartment buildings, and the like—typically allows the client to receive enough insurance to completely rebuild a damaged piece of property.

In order to insure something, you must stand to lose if that property is destroyed. For example, you can't insure your friend's car because you

Insurable Interest

have no insurable interest in it. If you could insure other people's property, you might have an incentive to let their property become damaged or destroyed because you would always be paid. Imagine that you own a building on which you have full coverage insurance. You sell the building but forget to cancel your policy and continue to pay premiums. If the building is destroyed by fire, will the insurance company pay you because you have a policy in force? No, not under the principle of indemnity: you have suffered no economic loss because you no longer have an insurable interest in the property.

The Right of Subrogation

SUBROGATION
The right of an insurance company to force you to transfer your right to sue another party. If you collect from your insurance company on an automobile accident, you must transfer the right to sue the other person to your insurance company.

The right of **subrogation** allows your insurance company to request reimbursement from whomever caused a loss on which it paid. Alternatively, the right of subrogation allows your insurance company to collect from the negligent person's insurance company. Suppose that your car is wrecked in an auto accident, and the issue of negligence is not clear-cut. Your insurance company may indeed pay to have your car fixed, but then it can also—under the right of subrogation—attempt to collect from the other person's insurance company if it is proved in court that the other person was negligent. Once you receive payment from your insurance company, you subrogate (transfer) your right to sue the other company. In other words, you cannot collect once from your insurance company and again from the other person's company.

The "Other Insurance" Clause

Suppose that you have medical insurance on your automobile policy and health insurance offered by your employer. You are injured in a car accident, and your total medical bills amount to $2,000. You cannot be reimbursed simultaneously by your group health insurance policy and by your automobile insurance policy. Why not? Because most insurance policies have an "other insurance" clause stating that any person with more than one insurance policy on property or health cannot collect more than the total financial loss sustained. Here's another example. You take out fire insurance on your house from two different companies, each policy having a face value of $50,000. Should the house burn down, you won't be paid $100,000 if the replacement value of the house is only $50,000. Each insurance company will pay you a pro rata share of the loss—in this case, 50 percent.

SOURCES OF INSURANCE

The insurance industry today is huge, with almost five thousand companies providing about 2 million jobs and having a responsibility for assets of half a trillion dollars. In addition to these private companies, the government also provides a set of extensive insurance programs.

Government Insurance Programs

At both the federal and state levels, governments provide programs to protect individuals from all types of risks, ranging from unemployment (unemployment compensation) to premature death (Social Security). There are mortgage insurance programs, insurance programs for savings and loan associations, and life insurance programs for veterans of previous wars. Individuals who live in flood-prone areas are able to purchase special flood insurance that they cannot purchase from any private company. Individuals who live in high crime areas can purchase special low-price theft insurance provided by a government agency.

Private insurance companies can be classified on the basis of ownership. There are two types of insurance companies in existence: (1) stock insurance companies and (2) mutual insurance companies.

Stock insurance companies. A **stock insurance company** is owned by its investors, who take the risk of loss and are entitled to any profit. Stock companies sell life insurance at *guaranteed* premium rates—ones that cannot be raised—which are kept as low as possible because of competition. Such coverage is usually called a **nonparticipating policy**. If rates are set too low, the stockholders take a loss; if rates are more than sufficient to cover all costs and claims, the stockholders obtain a profit.

Mutual insurance companies. A **mutual insurance company** is a cooperative association established by individuals to insure their own lives. The policies that are issued are called **participating policies**. There are no stockholders. General mutual company rates are set high enough to cover all contingencies. Participating policyholders in mutual insurance companies typically receive a return of premium "dividend" at the end of each year. This dividend is, in essence, the amount of money left over after the mutual insurance company has paid all of its operating expenses and claims.

In Exhibit 18-1, the ten largest life insurance companies in America are presented. The bulk of these companies are mutuals.

Insurance can cover a wide variety of possible losses. Ellis Lindsay has been working with small to medium-sized businesses for some time, and he has found that most were not as well insured for major risks as they thought. He started an important program for small businesses called keyman insurance, which covers the lives of key executives.

For example, Ellis was recently working with a small computer software company, owned and operated by three partners who had been friends since high school. He pointed out to them in a meeting that if any one of them were accidentally killed or died of natural causes, the other two would suffer tremendous losses. This would be so because each person was in charge of a separate part of the company, and there was little interaction. If one partner died, the other two would be hard pressed to run the business at the same level that it had been running, and they would lose revenues and profits for a while. Ellis convinced the company owners to take out a $50,000 key-man life insurance policy on each of them. The company would pay the premiums and the beneficiary would be the company. In other words, if one of them died, $50,000 would be paid directly to the company. Clearly, the company had an insurable interest in each of its three key executives.

Private Insurance Companies

STOCK INSURANCE COMPANY
An insurance company owned by stockholders who take the risks of any loss and are entitled to a pro rata share of the profits.

NONPARTICIPATING POLICY
The type of policy that a stock insurance company usually offers. The premiums you pay represent the full and actual cost of the policy.

MUTUAL INSURANCE COMPANY
A cooperative association without stockholders.

PARTICIPATING POLICY
A policy in a mutual insurance company in which you become a participant and are given a pro rata return on your premium commensurate with any excess of premiums over payouts and expenses of the company.

On the Job Revisited

RANK		COMPANY	ASSETS IN THOUSANDS	PREMIUM & ANNUITY INCOME		NET INVESTMENT INCOME	
1977	1976			In thousands	Rank	In thousands	Rank
1	1	Prudential (Newark)*	46,423,607	6,742,457	1	2,647,689	1
2	2	Metropolitan (New York)*	39,575,922	5,521,311	2	2,459,595	2
3	3	Equitable Life Assurance (New York)*	24,798,678	3,850,290	3	1,360,609	3
4	4	New York Life*	15,848,213	2,194,734	7	973,431	4
5	5	John Hancock Mutual (Boston)*	15,038,203	2,369,660	6	882,341	6
6	6	Aetna Life (Hartford)	13,620,697	3,272,935	4	916,582	5
7	7	Connecticut General Life (Bloomfield)	9,828,845	2,147,181	8	609,862	7
8	9	Travelers (Hartford)	9,384,343	2,842,468	5	504,141	9
9	8	Northwestern Mutual (Milwaukee)*	9,062,139	986,260	11	550,263	8
10	10	Massachusetts Mutual (Springfield)*	6,949,694	1,119,640	9	421,049	11

*Mutual insurance company.
Adapted from "The Fifty Largest Life Insurance Companies," *Fortune*, July 1982, p. 118.
Reprinted by permission from the 1978 Fortune Double Five Hundred Directory; © 1978 Time Inc.

EXHIBIT 18-1
The Ten Largest Life Insurance Companies

TYPES OF INSURANCE

Businesses and individuals can protect themselves from certain types of pure risk by taking out insurance policies. There are hundreds of different types of insurance policies, but they can be grouped into two broad classifications: (1) property and casualty insurance and (2) life insurance. Exhibit 18-2 indicates the relationships among the different types of risk and insurance.

Property and Casualty Insurance

A number of different types of property and casualty insurance are available, including fire; automobile; burglary, robbery, and theft; workers' compensation; fidelity and surety; credit and title; marine; public liability; and health.

FIRE INSURANCE   Fires in the United States will kill an estimated twelve thousand people this year, with the highest death rates for people under four and over sixty-five. In addition to deaths, fires will cause about $4 billion in damage. In order to protect themselves against losses by fire and lightning, businesses and individuals purchase fire insurance. **Extended coverage** is available, too, and it can provide increased protection to cover losses due to windstorms, smoke damage, hail, water, riots, and explosions.

EXTENDED COVERAGE
A method by which you increase fire insurance protection to cover losses due to smoke damage, hail, windstorms, riots, and explosions.

Fire insurance rates are based on several factors. First, rates are based on the construction of the home or building. Brick houses and buildings enjoy lower rates than frame buildings. Second, distance from hydrants and the fire station can affect rates; the farther the building is from fire service, the higher the rate. Third, the quality of the fire department influences the rates. Finally, the type of roof and the value of the building also influence fire insurance rates.

When fire occurs, a building or house is often only partially destroyed. This has prompted people to insure their buildings for less than their total replacement value, in order to save money on the premiums. For example, a building worth $100,000 might be insured for only $60,000. Any partial loss would then be covered; but if the building were completely destroyed, the owner would suffer a loss of $40,000.

Insurance companies base their premiums on the entire building, and they often protect themselves from partial insurance by including a co-insurance clause in the policy. This clause requires that the insured carry some minimum amount of insurance, expressed as a percentage of the property's value (80 percent is normal) in order to receive full coverage for any partial loss.

Basically, fire insurance covers the insured only for losses directly attributable to fire damage. But other losses can result from a fire, such as loss of rental income while a damaged building is under repair. These losses, known as consequential losses, can be insured only by adding an extra clause to a standard fire insurance policy or by taking out a special policy.

HOMEOWNER'S POLICY   The homeowner's policy provides protection against a number of risks under a single policy. This allows a savings over purchasing each protection separately. In addition to a standard fire policy, you can also obtain liability coverage. There are basically two types of homeowner's policy coverage:

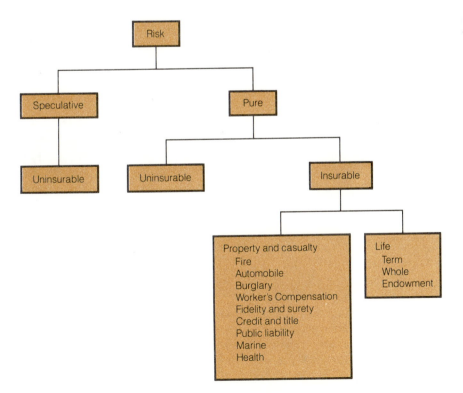

EXHIBIT 18-2
Types of Insurance

1. *Property coverage.* This includes garage, house, and other private buildings on your lot; personal possessions and property, either at home or while you are traveling or at work; and additional living expenses that would be paid to you if you couldn't live in your home because of a fire or some other peril.
2. *Liability coverage.* Basically, this is for personal liability in case someone is injured on your property or you damage someone else's property and are at fault or you injure someone else off your premises (not applicable to auto accidents). Insurance coverage for medical payments for injury to others on your property and for damage to the property of others by you or a member of your family is similar to liability insurance.

FORMS OF HOMEOWNER'S POLICIES   There are basically five forms of home and condominium owners' policies. Exhibit 18-3 describes each type. The basic form covers eleven perils, or risks; the broad form covers eighteen perils, or risks; the special form is like the broad form, except that it does not cover glass breakage and it can exclude specifically mentioned risks on buildings; and the comprehensive form covers those eighteen perils covered by the broad form and all other perils. In addition to the four homeowner's policies just mentioned, there is a special condominium owner's policy that is similar but does not cover glass breakage.

Automobile Insurance

Automobile insurance is the largest single type of protection in the property and casualty business. With a premium volume of approximately $25 billion, it represents 40 percent of premiums paid in the property and casualty areas. There are many different kinds of protection plans for automobiles, but the most crucial is liability insurance.

BODILY INJURY AND PROPERTY DAMAGE LIABILITY COVERAGE   Liability limits are usually described by a series of three numbers, such as 25/50/5; this means the policy will pay a maximum of $25,000 for bodily injury to one person and $50,000 to more than one person, and a maximum of $5,000 for property damage in one accident. Most insurance companies offer liability up to $300,000 and sometimes $500,000. The cost of additional liability limits is relatively small. You should consider taking out a much larger limit than you ordinarily would expect to need because per-

EXHIBIT 18-3   Guide to Package Policies for Homeowners (*on facing page*)
These are the principal features of the standard types of homeowner's insurance policies. The amount of insurance provided for specific categories, such as personal property and comprehensive personal liability, can be increased by paying an additional premium. The special limits of liability refer to the maximum amounts the policy will pay for the types of property listed in the notes. Usually, jewelry, furs, boats, and other items subject to special limits have to be insured separately to obtain greater coverage.

HOMEOWNERS HO-1 BASIC FORM	BROAD FORM HOMEOWNERS HO-1	SPECIAL FORM HOMEOWNERS HO-3	COMPREHENSIVE HOMEOWNERS HO-5	CONDOMINIUM OWNERS HO-6
Perils covered (see key below)				
Perils 1-11	Perils 1-18	Perils 1-18 on personal property except glass breakage; all risks, except those specifically excluded, on buildings	All risks except those specifically excluded	Perils 1-18 except glass breakage
Standard amount of insurance on:				
house, attached structures				
Based on property value; minimum $8,000	Based on property value; minimum $8,000	Based on property value; minimum $8,000	Based on property value; minimum $15,000	$1,000 on owner's additions and alterations to unit
Detached structures				
10% of amount of insurance on house	10% of amount of insurance on house	10% of amount of insurance on house	10% of amount of insurance on house	No coverage
Trees, shrubs, and plants				
5% of amount of insurance on house; $250 maximum per item	5% of amount of insurance on house; $250 maximum per item	5% of amount of insurance on house; $250 maximum per item	5% of amount of insurance on house; $250 maximum per item	10% of personal property insurance; $250 maximum per item
Personal property on premises				
50% of insurance on house	50% of insurance on house	50% of insurance on house	50% of insurance on house	Based on value of property, minimum $4,000
Personal property away from premises				
10% of personal property insurance (minimum $1,000)	10% of personal property insurance (minimum $1,000)	10% of personal property insurance (minimum $1,000)	50% of insurance on house	10% of personal property insurance (minimum $1,000)
Additional living expense				
10% of insurance on house	20% of insurance on house	20% of insurance on house	20% of insurance on house	40% of personal property insurance
Special limits of liability*				
Standard	Standard	Standard	Standard	Standard

Key to Perils Covered:

1. Fire, lightning
2. Damage to property removed from premises endangered by fire
3. Windstorm, hail
4. Explosion
5. Riots
6. Damage by aircraft
7. Damage by vehicles not owned or operated by people covered by policy
8. Damage from smoke
9. Vandalism, malicious mischief
10. Glass breakage
11. Theft
12. Falling objects
13. Weight of ice, snow, sleet
14. Collapse of building or any part of building
15. Bursting, cracking, burning, or bulging of a steam or hot water heating system, or of appliances for heating water
16. Leakage or overflow of water or steam from a plumbing, heating, or air-conditioning system
17. Freezing of plumbing, heating, and air-conditioning systems and domestic appliances
18. Injury to electrical appliances, devices, fixtures, and wiring (excluding tubes, transistors, and similar electronic components) from short circuits or other accidentally generated currents

*Special limits of liability: money, bullion, numismatic property, bank notes—$100; securities, bills, deeds, tickets, etc.—$500; manuscripts—$1,000; jewelry, furs—$500 for theft; boats, including trailers and equipment—$500; trailers—$500.

Adapted from New Jersey Insurance Department. *A Shopper's Guide to Homeowners Insurance,* 1977.

sonal injury suits against drivers proved negligent are sometimes astronomical ($1 million).

Individuals dissatisfied with maximum liability limits offered by regular automobile insurance coverage can purchase separate coverage under an **umbrella policy**. Umbrella limits sometimes go as high as $5 million, and they also cover personal liability in excess of homeowner's liability limits.

MEDICAL PAYMENT COVERAGE   Medical payments on auto insurance policies cover hospital and medical bills and sometimes funeral expenses. Usually you can buy $2,000 to $5,000 coverage per person for about $10 or $15 a year. This insurance protects all the passengers in your car when you are driving.

PHYSICAL DAMAGE COVERAGE, OR COLLISION   This insurance covers damage to your car in any type of collision. Usually, it is not advisable to purchase full collision coverage (otherwise known as zero deductible). The price per year is quite high because it is likely that small, but costly, repair jobs will be required each year. Most people take out $50 or $100 or even higher deductible coverage, which costs about one-fourth the price of zero deductible. This means you pay for the first $50, $100, or whatever deductible amount you have when repairs are needed due to accidents; the insurance company covers the rest.

COMPREHENSIVE   This insurance covers loss; damage; theft; and destruction by fire, hurricane, hail, and vandalism. It is separate from collision insurance. Full comprehensive insurance is quite expensive. Again, $50 or $100 deductibles are usually preferable.

UNINSURED MOTORIST COVERAGE   This coverage insures the driver and passengers against injury caused by any driver without insurance or by a hit-and-run driver. Certain states require that this coverage be included in all auto insurance policies.

ACCIDENTAL DEATH BENEFITS   This provides a lump sum to named beneficiaries if the policyholder dies in an automobile accident. It generally costs very little, but it may not be necessary if you have sufficient life insurance.

On the Job Revisited

The insurance industry has many options to meet the specific needs of individuals and businesses. Ellis Lindsay is trying to figure out the average amount of insurance needed for the typical owner of a small business. Specifically, Ellis wants to know how much and what type of property insurance would be appropriate. He has to look at such factors as the potential loss involved if there were a fire, flood, or other catastrophe. He also has to determine what percentage of the building would still be standing if such a catastrophe occurred. Finally, Ellis realizes that the cost per year per thousand dollars of coverage varies dramatically depending on the amount of deductible his clients are willing to accept. The most expensive casualty insurance involves a zero deductible, where Ellis's insur-

UMBRELLA POLICY
A supplemental insurance policy that can extend normal automobile (and personal) liability limits to $1 million or more for a relatively small premium.

WORKERS GET PAID FOR STRESS ILLNESSES

A successful New York lawyer killed himself a few years ago. He had no history of instability. Rather, a combination of his father's death, hard-to-handle mortgage payments, and, most important, fear that he had made a serious error at work pushed him over the edge. The New York Workers' Compensation Board agreed that he had sustained an accident from pressures on the job, and it awarded his widow weekly disability checks as well as funeral expenses.

Such "stress" claims are a growing phenomenon in workers' compensation offices everywhere in the United States. More than fifteen states have already approved benefits in disability claims stemming from job stress. Many claims have been approved even when it has just been the employee who perceived the job stress.

Let's face it, evaluating stress claims is not a simple task. And what if co-workers rather than company duties cause a person to feel stress? For example, a woman who was transferred from GM's New York office to the company's Detroit headquarters claimed that her insomnia, paranoia, and weight loss resulted from stress caused by co-worker discrimination against her. Why was there discrimination? Because of her New York background, according to the woman.

Mental abuse is a real possibility, and mental illnesses can be just as debilitating as physical ones. But the causes are usually extremely complex, and tracing these problems to job stress is difficult and controversial. Says Alan Tebb, general manager of the California Workers' Compensation Institute, "It is hard to know whether the increases [in stress-related cases] is due more to the diagnostic skills of physicians or of lawyers."

Taken from "Paying for Stress on the Job," *Dun's Business Month*, January 1982, p. 72.

---

ance company pays everything no matter how small the loss. Going from zero to larger and larger amounts, such as $500, $1,000, $2,000, or $5,000 deductibles (and even more for larger businesses), dramatically reduces the cost of casualty loss insurance. He recommends that most of his clients accept the inevitability of small losses by taking large deductibles. This keeps their insurance rates low. After all, figures Ellis, the purpose of insurance is to protect against large, tragic losses that could destroy a business.

BURGLARY, ROBBERY, AND THEFT INSURANCE   Even though burglary, robbery, and theft are all crimes, they are considered different crimes, and the premiums vary depending on the protection provided. *Burglary* is the unlawful taking of property through forcible entry. Forcible entry can be proved by broken glass on doors, marks on windows, and so on. *Robbery* insurance provides coverage for losses resulting from the unlawful seizing of property from a person by force or threat of violence. *Theft* is a general term that covers any type of stealing. Because theft covers such a broad spectrum, it is typically the most expensive coverage. In order to protect against all types of loss, store managers should purchase a special policy that includes protection from loss of stock on the shelves as well as merchandise or equipment.

WORKERS' COMPENSATION INSURANCE   All fifty states and the federal government provide for the cost of medical care, lost wages, rehabilitation, and death benefits for workers injured or killed on the job. Premiums paid by the employer to the state are figured as a percentage of the company's payroll. Rates depend on the hazards of the job and the safety record of the employer. Secretaries, for example, have low premiums, whereas miners and steelworkers have high premiums. The salary benefits are usually set at one-half to two-thirds of the employee's regular pay. An employee who accepts benefits under the program *usually* gives up the right to sue the employer for injuries sustained at work.

PUBLIC LIABILITY INSURANCE   After death or disability, public liability is the biggest risk facing businesses and individuals. When an individual is injured on your premises or by your product or service, two questions have to be answered: Are you responsible? And if so, how much must you pay to compensate for the injury? In recent years, juries and the courts have tended to assume that anyone injured has the right to compensation. Some recent examples of this include a boy whose T-shirt caught fire when he climbed a power pole and brushed a wire, and a factory worker who lost a finger after tying down a strap on his machine. In each case, the manufacturer was forced to pay the claim. Public liability is one of the fastest growing claims areas, and the trend toward increasingly large settlements is beginning to cause concern.

Two types of public liability insurance have received a great deal of publicity in recent years: malpractice and product liability insurance. Malpractice insurance provides various professionals with protection against lawsuits concerning negligence or mistakes. Although malpractice insurance is used in many fields, an increasing number of judgments have hit doctors hardest. Malpractice insurance rates for some California doctors increased by 347 percent in 1976 alone. To reduce settlements, patients in some states are asked to sign waivers before their operations, agreeing to submit claims to a review board. The review board then determines the settlement. Although malpractice suits are a big problem, another type of public liability insurance may cause even bigger problems.

Frederick D. Watkins, president of the Aetna Insurance Company, has suggested that the "malpractice crisis could turn out to be a firecracker compared to . . . product liability litigation." Product liability insurance protects the producer of a product from suits arising from injuries caused by the product. The problems associated with product liability insurance are summarized by T. Lawrence Jones, president of the American Insurance Association: "In essence, the problem is that businesses are now being sued for staggering amounts of money as a result of injuries suffered by people who use the products they make or handle. Economic loss, pain and suffering, punitive damages, and losses for a class of claimants all are being rolled together in giant actions against manufacturers, distributors, and behind the scenes, the companies who insure them." The magnitude

SUING THE BOSS

Most businesses participate in the workers' compensation system, which provides payments to workers for injuries suffered on the job. Consequently, most firms do not carry additional employer liability insurance, but this could be changing.

William Bell was a route salesman for Industrial Vangas, Inc. He was delivering gas to a customer in Fresno, California, when a fire broke out as he transferred propane from his truck to small tanks, and he was badly burned. Bell's only remedy was to obtain a flat payment of up to $30,000 from workers' compensation. The 1911 Workers' Compensation Act specifically prohibits employees from suing employers in the state of California. Comparable laws exist in virtually all states.

Bell sued anyway. He charged that since Industrial Vangas, Inc., had assembled the propane truck, it should be liable—not as an employer but as a manufacturer. The California Supreme Court agreed with Bell's argument.

The court argued that the employer was acting in a dual capacity, both as an employer and as a manufacturer. This California Supreme Court decision is threatening to upset the very foundation of workers' compensation. It could cause California companies millions of dollars by doubling insurance costs for all employers. According to a dissenting judge in the case, the dual capacity logic is simply opening up a can of worms. Companies will now be held liable for injuries attributable to the company in its status as land-owner, motor vehicle operator, or cafeteria proprietor. Several companies are now thinking twice about doing business in California. Bethlehem Steel, Uniroyal, and Ford Motor Company are either considering leaving or have already left the state, naming the California Workers' Compensation system as a partial reason.

Source: "On the Job Injuries: Now, Suits Against the Boss," *Business Week*, January 25, 1982, p. 144.

of these claims was brought clearly into focus by a 1978 product liability judgment against the Ford Motor Company. In that case, the jury awarded Richard Grimshaw $127.8 million for injuries suffered when the 1972 Ford Pinto he was riding in was struck from the rear and burst into flames.

In any event, consumers ultimately pay for all of the claims made against manufacturers and distributors, even when those claims are paid by insurance companies, because the costs of the higher product liability insurance premiums are eventually passed on in the final price that a consumer pays for any product.

HEALTH INSURANCE Programs to pay the cost of hospital and medical expenses are called health insurance. Many companies make this a part of the fringe benefits offered to their employees. This can be an important type of insurance protection because medical costs are very high and increasing faster than most other items. A short stay in the hospital for a simple tonsillectomy can easily run to $2,000. A health insurance program might include coverage for loss of income when due to illness and subsequent unemployment; hospital, surgical, and other medical expenses; eyeglasses; dental expenses; dismemberment; and accidental death.

Recently, the government has become a much more active participant in health care insurance. Through the Medicaid and Medicare programs, as well as the disability benefits of Social Security, the government is reaching an increasing number of individuals. In the past, Congress has considered a national health insurance plan, with the objective of extending health insurance to all Americans. However, there are many differing opinions on the extent of health insurance to provide and on how to provide it. Some plans call for a copayment by the recipient and existing health insurance companies to administer the program. Others are much broader in their coverage and would set up a government agency operated like the Social Security system to provide health insurance.

LIFE INSURANCE

Basically, there are two types of life insurance: term and whole life. **Term insurance** is a form of pure protection—all one is doing is insuring one's life. **Whole life insurance**, on the other hand, combines protection with a type of savings plan. Whole life insurance is sometimes called straight life or cash-value insurance.

Term Insurance

TERM INSURANCE
Life insurance for a specified term (period of time) that has only a death benefit.

WHOLE LIFE INSURANCE
Also called cash value, straight, and ordinary life insurance. It has both death and living benefits. One builds cash surrender value in the policy.

UNIFORM DECREASING TERM INSURANCE
Term insurance in which a fixed premium is paid and the face value of the policy falls throughout its life of, say, twenty years.

HOME PROTECTION PLAN
A type of nonuniform decreasing term insurance where the reduction in the amount of insurance available mirrors the reduction in the amount remaining due (unpaid) on a home mortgage.

RENEWABILITY
A clause in a term insurance policy that guarantees it can be renewed without the insured undergoing a medical exam.

Premiums for term insurance will usually increase at the end of each term (for example, every 5 years), if you wish to keep the same face value on your insurance policy. The increased premium reflects the rising probability of death as age increases. Thus, it will cost you relatively little to buy term when you are 25 years old, but by the time you are 60, your premiums will have risen dramatically. However, by that time you probably will not want as much term insurance because your children will be on the way to financial independence and you will have built up other forms of financial resources for any dependents you still have. An important point to note here is that term insurance is a good way for a young, growing family to carry more insurance at an *affordable price*.

Families often choose insurance with a level premium but a decreasing face value. Such a policy is called **uniform decreasing term insurance**. A similar type of policy is called a **home protection plan**. It is term insurance that decreases at approximately the same rate as the outstanding mortgage balance on a house as payments are made. Thus, if a home protection policy is carried at a face value equal to the mortgage on the home, and the breadwinner dies during the life of the mortgage, the home can be paid off with the insurance benefit.

RENEWABILITY   Standard term insurance is often labeled one-year term or five-year term because those are the interval, or terms, between premium increases. Other periods are also available. A term policy has a **renewability** feature: the coverage can be continued at the end of each period merely by payment of the increased premium and without the need of a medical examination. Renewability, of necessity, increases the cost of the policy, but if you wish to preserve your insurability despite changes in your health, you certainly would want this feature. Term policies are commonly renewable until the policyholder reaches retirement age. All coverage then stops. (Some policies do allow renewal until age 100.)

YEAR	ANNUAL PREMIUM	YEAR	ANNUAL PREMIUM
1	$165.50	11	312.50
2	172.50	12	339.00
3	181.00	13	368.00
4	192.00	14	400.00
5	204.50	15	435.00
6	219.00	16	473.50
7	235.00	17	515.50
8	252.00	18	560.50
9	270.50	19	609.50
10	290.50	20	642.50
20th Year Total	$6,838.50	Total at Age 65	$17,893.00

EXHIBIT 18-4
A Typical $50,000 Yearly Renewable Term Policy, Male, Age 35

CONVERTIBILITY   Often, riders, or supplements, can be attached to term policies allowing you to convert them into other than pure insurance without the necessity of a medical examination. You pay for **convertibility**, however. If you have a convertible term policy, you can convert it into whole life without any problems. The main reason you might want to convert is to continue your coverage after you pass age 65 or 70. After converting the policy, you would pay whole life premiums based on your age at the time of conversion. Most insurance experts recommend that convertibility and renewability be purchased because they provide flexibility at minimal additional costs.

Exhibit 18-4 shows the costs of a $50,000 one-year renewable term policy for a male 35 years of age. If this man keeps $50,000 of term insurance until age 65, he will pay in a total of $17,893. He will have no cash value in the policy, as he would in a whole life policy.

CONVERTIBILITY
A clause in a term insurance policy that gives the insured the option of switching to whole, or straight, life insurance.

Whole Life Insurance

Whole life insurance accounts for a little less than half of the total value of all life insurance in force in the United States. The average payoff value of such policies is around $15,000. Life insurance salespersons often try to sell whole life policies because such policies are more profitable for them and their companies. (It has been estimated that a salesperson earns about nine times more selling the same amount of whole life than he or she does selling term insurance.)

PREMIUMS   Whole life premiums generally remain the same throughout the life of a policy.* As a result, the policyholder pays more than is necessary to cover the company's risk in later years. Exhibit 18-5 gives an example of a $10,000 ordinary life insurance policy with an annual level premium of $222.70 for a male 35 years of age. In the first year, of the $222.70, $205.50 goes to the insurance company to cover insurance costs and $17.20 goes to

*Although the premium *per dollar of protection* rises over time in a whole life policy because the protection declines as the cash value grows.

$10,000 ORDINARY LIFE
DIVIDENDS* TO PURCHASE PAID-UP ADDITIONS
ANNUAL PREMIUM: $222.70   MALE: AGE 35

Year	Deposit to Cash Value	Deposit to Insurance	Total Cash Value
1	$ 17.20	$205.50—	$ 17.20
2	179.71	42.99	196.91
3	190.43	32.27	387.34
4	201.97	20.73	589.31
5	213.47	9.23	802.78
6	225.43	2.73—	1,028.21
7	237.14	14.44—	1,265.35
8	250.35	27.65—	1,515.70
9	262.61	39.91—	1,778.31
10	275.17	52.47—	2,053.48
11	270.17	47.47—	2,323.65
12	282.60	59.90—	2,606.25
13	294.64	71.94—	2,900.89
14	306.82	84.12—	3,207.71
15	320.64	97.94—	3,528.35
16	333.21	110.51—	3,861.56
17	346.11	123.41—	4,207.67
18	360.95	138.25—	4,568.62
19	376.12	153.42—	4,944.74
20	391.60	168.90—	5,336.34

Summary	20th Year	At Age 65
Total cash value	$5,608.97*	$10,566.83†
Total deposits	$4,454.00	$ 6,681.00
Net gain	$1,154.97	$ 3,885.83

*Dividends are neither estimates nor guarantees but are based on the current dividend scale.
†Includes terminal dividend.

the cash value for the purchaser of the policy. By the sixth year, the deposit to cash value is greater than the level annual premium, and it stays greater throughout the life of this particular policy. You can see in the summary of this policy that by the twentieth year—that is, when the policyholder is 55 years old—there is a total cash value in that policy of $5,608.97, after having paid in $4,454.

Take note that the cash value of a whole life insurance policy is not the same thing as a savings account. Insurance industry people often promote whole life as an insurance policy combined with a savings plan. But the cash reserve is not a separate item given to your named beneficiary as a separate payment if you die. Rather, your named beneficiary only gets the face value of the policy. Looking at Exhibit 18–5 again, let's assume you have paid in for ten years. Your total cash value is shown to be $2,053.48.

What if you die at the end of ten years? You have a $10,000 ordinary life policy, and your named beneficiary gets $10,000, not $10,000 plus your cash value of $2,053.48.

Owners of whole life policies often take comfort in the fact that their premiums are level and therefore represent one of the few costs that do not rise with inflation. (However, the real value of the policy, as well as the premiums, declines as the buying power of a dollar falls.) True, the cost is relatively high to begin with, but it gets no higher. The exact level of premiums that you would pay for a $10,000 ordinary life insurance policy as represented in Exhibit 18-5 depends on your age when you buy the policy; the younger you are, the less it will be because the company expects to collect many years of premiums from you. The older you are, the greater the premiums are.

But when one compares whole life with term insurance (already discussed), whole life is relatively expensive because it is a form of financial investment as well as insurance protection. The investment feature is known as its "cash value." In Exhibit 18-5, the cash value at the end of twenty years was in excess of $5,000; at age 65, it was actually in excess of the face value of the policy. You can, of course, cancel a whole life policy at any time you choose and be paid the amount of cash value it has built in. Individuals sometimes "cash in" a whole life policy at retirement when the cash value can be taken out either as a lump sum or in installments called annuities, which are discussed below. These are called the "living benefits" of a whole life policy.

LIVING BENEFITS **Living benefits** are the opposite of death benefits. The **death benefit** of a life insurance policy is obviously the insurance that you have purchased. The living benefit, on the other hand, includes the possibility of converting an ordinary policy to some sort of lump sum payment or retirement income (annuity). In any one year, up to 60 percent of all insurance company payments are in the form of these so-called living benefits. Note that the level premium for a whole life policy is paid throughout the life of the policyholder—unless you reach the ripe old age of, say, 95 or so.

An **endowment policy** offers a combination of temporary life insurance and a rapidly increasing cash surrender fund. It can be considered both a term insurance policy and a growing savings account. If at any time during the specified life of the policy—usually anywhere from ten to thirty years—the policyholder dies, his or her beneficiaries receive the full face value, as with any other life insurance policy. The special feature of the endowment policy is that at the end of its maturity, the living benefit is also equal to the face value. If the policyholder lives to the end of the period, he or she can collect.

Individuals who purchase endowment policies usually want to have a specific amount for a specific purpose at a desired time in the future. Endowment policies have been used, for example, to set up children's college funds. They are a poor way of accomplishing that objective, how-

LIVING BENEFITS
The benefits derived from the cash surrender fund in a whole life insurance policy.

DEATH BENEFITS
The face value of any insurance policy that is paid to the beneficiary upon the death of the insured.

Endowment Insurance

ENDOWMENT POLICY
A policy that combines temporary life insurance and a rapidly increasing cash surrender value.

IS LIFE UNIVERSAL?

Universal life insurance is supposed to combine the best features of whole life and term insurance. It is designed to overcome the drawbacks of whole life—low rate of return and high commission charges—and term insurance—high premiums in later years and no cash buildup. Under universal life, premiums are paid into a cash accumulation fund. The insurance company deducts the amount needed to pay for renewable term insurance from the fund every month. Whatever remains is invested in short-term and medium-term government and corporate securities and earns a return advertised as approaching those paid by money market funds. In addition, the return is tax deferred.

Universal life is more flexible than both whole and term insurance. If the policyholder doesn't pay his or her full premium or skips a premium payment altogether, the insurance company simply deducts the missing amount from the cash accumulation fund. Cash can also be withdrawn, but the face value of the policy is obviously reduced by that amount. There are also some things to note. The advertised interest rate earned on the cash accumulation is figured only on the premiums minus all fees and insurance costs. Moreover, the first $1,000 in the fund earns only 4 percent. Furthermore, the IRS could reverse its ruling that gives tax-free benefits to the policy's investment income. Industry experts say that the concept is a good one, but it's too early to tell how good.

Adapted from "The Ins and Outs of Universal Life," *Dun's Business Month*, January 1982, pp. 110–113.

ever, because they yield a low rate of return. Because an endowment policy builds up a cash value equal to its face value by the end of the specified time period, the premiums on such a policy are even higher than on limited payment whole life.

RETIREMENT ENDOWMENT POLICIES Such policies are designed specifically to accumulate funds for retirement. The difference between a regular endowment policy and a retirement endowment policy is that you continue paying into the latter policy even after the cash surrender value has exceeded the face value of the policy. For example, your cash surrender value could equal $30,000 by the time you reach age 60, but you will continue to pay premiums until age 65. If you die before age 65, your beneficiaries would receive the face value of the policy plus any excess cash surrender value. In essence, after the cash surrender value equals the face value, you are making pure investment.

SUMMARY

■ Risk management involves (a) avoiding risk, (b) reducing the hazard, (c) reducing the loss, (d) assuming the risk, and (e) shifting the risk.

■ Shifting the risk involves purchasing insurance, which is a social device for risk reduction that combines a large number of exposure units to make individual losses predictable.

384

■ The principle of indemnity states that the insured cannot be compensated over and above the amount that exceeds his or her actual economic loss. Typically, an insured item cannot be insured for more than its actual cash, or market, value. The exception to this occurs with specific policies that allow the individual to be reimbursed for the full replacement cost of a new item. Additionally, some homeowner's policies will allow for the rebuilding of a damaged house even if this exceeds the market value of the house before it was damaged.

■ In order to insure someone or something, the beneficiary must have an insurable interest.

■ There are two types of private insurance companies: stock and mutual. In the former, the investors take the risk of loss and are entitled to any profits. In the latter, there are no stockholders, only a cooperative association.

■ Property and casualty insurance includes insurance that covers automobiles, burglary, robbery, theft, workers' compensation, public liability, and fires in dwellings.

■ A typical homeowner's policy covers property damage and liability— being sued by someone who is injured on the premises.

■ A typical automobile insurance policy covers bodily injury, property damage, and liability.

■ Workers' compensation exists in all fifty states. Premiums are paid by the employer to the state. An employee who accepts benefits under a workers' compensation policy usually surrenders the right to sue the employer for injuries.

■ Public liability insurance is of increasing importance as court awards increase; it is not unusual for liability awards of $1 million to be announced in the newspaper. Two important areas of public liability are malpractice and product liability. Ultimately, consumers pay for both types of insurance in the form of higher prices for health care and products.

■ Life insurance is usually either term or whole life. Term insurance is simply pure protection. Whole life has a cash value so that, in a sense, it is protection plus a type of savings account.

■ The premiums paid on term insurance go up at the end of every term, usually at the end of every five years. The premiums paid on whole life, however, remain the same throughout the life of the policy.

1. What is the difference between pure and speculative risk?
2. Explain what indemnity means and how it applies to insurance.
3. Explain the difference between insurable interest and insurable risk.
4. What are the major differences between mutual and stock insurance companies?
5. What can a business do to protect itself from risk?
6. Why would a business use self-insurance?
7. How does coinsurance work?

ISSUES TO CONSIDER AND ANALYZE

8. Distinguish between term insurance and whole life.
9. What distinguishes a participatory policy from a nonparticipatory policy?
10. How is an endowment insurance policy different from term insurance?

CASE FOR ANALYSIS

STOPPING DISCRIMINATION

Paula Dynda, a women's rights activist, was incensed when she discovered that women in her state were having difficulty getting disability insurance. Women were able to get the insurance, but they paid higher premiums than men of the same age and socioeconomic background. Paula felt that the insurance companies should be forced to charge every customer of the same age the same premium, regardless of sex. She pointed out that many of the women needed the disability insurance to protect their families from the potential loss of income. Paula organized the National Organization of Women Against High Insurance Premiums (NOWAHIP) to fight the companies and their discriminatory rates.

QUESTIONS

1. Do you think it is fair for the insurance companies to discriminate between men and women?
2. What principles of insurance might the company use to justify different rates?

FINANCE AND INSURANCE

People who select careers in finance would likely be involved with the efficient acquisition and use of funds in business and government or in financial institutions like banks, savings and loans, investment companies, and stockbrokerage firms. These careers deal with procedures used to allocate the firm's scarce cash resources profitably and to guard against their loss. It is important to ensure that the firm receives the most profitable return from its investments, at an appropriate level of risk, and that it has the ability to meet its current cash expenses.

Because of the wide need for financial services, a large number of positions are open to qualified candidates. For example, if you are interested in a financial career, you could work as a bank officer, loan specialist, teller, securities broker, or financial manager.

BANKING AND SAVINGS AND LOANS

The banking industry is undergoing perhaps its most important change since the formation of the Federal Reserve System in December 1913. Banking is becoming a fully deregulated industry. With the passage of the Monetary Decontrol Act of 1980, the distinction among commercial banks, savings and loan associa-

tions, credit unions, and mutual savings banks is becoming increasingly blurred. Indeed, old-line securities firms such as Merrill-Lynch and Dean Witter have entered the banking business with enthusiasm. Credit card companies such as American Express have begun to offer numerous banking services too. Specialized jobs in financial institutions now number in the hundreds of thousands. About two-thirds of these jobs are clerical; the other third includes officers and professionals, service, and other workers.

Consider the opportunities in a typical depository institution, such as Bank of America, CitiBank, or Chase Manhattan. These banks offer career opportunities in the areas of operations and credit, among others. An operations officer is generally responsible for the smooth functioning of branch offices; operations officers schedule employees' hours, conduct performance appraisals, hire and promote, prepare the office budgets, and handle disgruntled customers. Beginning with operations training, the prospective operations officer might advance to assistant operations and eventually move up to operations officer in a smaller branch office. After these levels, an operations officer can become a regional administrator or advance to credit training and branch management.

In the credit area, one receives initial training and is then placed as a loan officer. The loan officer will first handle smaller accounts and personal loans, and then become responsible for larger accounts and business loans. After advancing to assistant manager for loans, the credit officer can move on to branch manager or assistant branch manager in a larger office. Finally, regional administration in credit is possible. In both operations and credit, training can take as long as a year, although many people finish sooner.

What about those students who end their formal education after two years at a community college? Most financial institutions with deposit capability will start community college graduates as bank tellers, with possible advancement to teller management positions and from there to other branches of the bank. Starting salaries for tellers with associate of arts or associate of science degrees are comparable to many entry-level positions in other industries requiring a bachelor's degree. Nonetheless, the fact remains that advancement in a bank is to a large extent dependent on an understanding of economics, production, distribution, merchandising, and the like.

Through the end of this decade, employment in financial institutions is expected to increase at a faster rate than the average of all occupations. This expected growth is attributed to the deregulation of financial institutions. Starting salaries in the banking industry for those with an associate of arts degree ranged between $10,500 and $12,000 in 1982. Starting salaries for those with a bachelor's degree ranged between $12,500 and $14,000 in that same year. Employees with several years of experience can make two to three times this entry-level salary.

SECURITIES

When investors—large or small—buy or sell stocks, bonds, or shares of mutual funds, they need the services of a securities broker. These workers are also called registered representatives, stockbrokers, account executives, or securities sales workers. In addition to executing purchase and sales orders for customers, stockbrokers may explain market terms, offer financial counseling, devise securities portfolios, and offer advice on the purchase and sale of a particular security. The stockbroker tries to match the needs of individual clients with specific securities. Some clients are interested in long-term growth, whereas others prefer to take higher risks for the possibility of making greater profits in the short run. The securities broker explains the advantages and disadvantages of different investments in an effort to help the customer reach his or her investment objectives.

Almost all states require people who sell securities to be licensed. In addition, sales workers normally must register with the stock ex-

changes where they do business as well as pass the General Securities Examination, which the Securities and Exchange Commission requires.

Most employers provide training to help sales workers meet the requirement for registration. In the larger firms, where most sales workers are employed, the training period is at least four months.

Personality traits are often as important as academic training to the security broker. Employers look for applicants who are well-groomed, ambitious, and able to motivate people. Because maturity and the ability to work independently are important, many employers prefer to hire people who have been successful in other jobs.

Many of the large securities firms offer a tremendous number of professional opportunities for the business-trained student. In addition to trading, they include the following:

Securities research

Operations

Budgets and planning

Accounting

Investment banking and financing

The typical college graduate (two-year or four-year) who enters the area of sales will spend twelve weeks of training at a branch office. The program instruction will acquaint the new employee with the entire business and will provide on-the-job experience with the office manager and other account executives (salespersons). Starting in the thirteenth week, each trainee is required to spend five weeks at company headquarters, reviewing for the general securities examination that one must

pass, learning how to prospect for clients, and sharpening one's selling skills.

Although a college education is not required for employment as a securities broker, it is becoming increasingly important. Courses in business administration, economics, and finance are especially useful. In addition, community college programs in banking can be a great help.

Salaries of securities brokers range from about $1000 per month during the training period to over $200,000 per year. Because stockbrokers are paid on commission, earnings fluctuate from year to year. Commission earnings are likely to be high when there is a great deal of market activity and low when market activity declines. Most firms, however, provide salespeople with steady income by laying a draw against the commissions the firm expects the securities broker to earn.

Job opportunities for securities brokers appear good because larger numbers of people are seeking investment advice. Forecasts suggest that jobs in this area will increase faster than the national average. Unfortunately, because there are only about 100,000 jobs in this area, the total number of new positions will be limited.

INSURANCE

The insurance industry offers many employment opportunities for people

EXHIBIT V-A
(on facing page) Examples of
Advertisements
for Bank Management Jobs

MORTGAGE BANKERS

Income Loan Production & management executives are needed for several mortgage company clients in Pa., Va., Ga., Texas, Calif., & Ill. Positions pay salaries from $25,000 to $40,000 plus attractive incentives and benefits. Respond in absolute confidence:

Banking— Current Openings

We need qualified people for our clients in the M.W. Please call or send resume to Tom Roberts in strick confidence. Company pays fee.

Legal Counsel	45 M
Foreign Exch.	25 M
(Trader/Mgr)	
Controller	35 M
Auditor	25 M
CPA/Accounting	25 M
Latin Amer Rep	25 M
Marketing Dir	30 M
Personnel	23 M
Cash Mgt	20 M
New Busn Sales	20 M
Financial Analyst	18 M
Coll Mgr	17 M
(Coml/Mort/Instl)	
Coml Mort Mgr	35 M
VP Consumer Banking	30 M
Correspondent Loan	25 M
Loan Review	25 M
VP Coml Loan	25 M
Coml Loan (6)	25 M
Syst. Anal Mgt	25 M
Supv-Re Analysts	21 M
Mgr Credit Card	20 M
Branch Mgr	18 M
Farm Mgr	17 M
Prog/Anal (Many)	15–20 M

LENDING OFFICERS VICE-PRESIDENTS

Bank Hapoalim is a leading Israeli International bank with $19 billion in assets and over 330 branches worldwide. Due to continued expansion in our Los Angeles branch and the near opening of our San Francisco branch, we are seeking career oriented individuals with strong commercial lending and business development background.

In these high visibility positions, the ideal candidates will enjoy substantial avenues for professional achievements and advancement. We offer an excellent salary and benefits package commensurate with experience and potential.

If you would like to share in our growth and success, send us your resume and salary history today.

COMMERCIAL LOAN OFFICER

This is an exceptional opportunity to join the commercial loan division of one of our St. Louis area banks. We are seeking an individual with 3 to 5 years commercial lending experience with a metropolitan area bank. The position offers the advantage of joining an established loan division that encourages initiative and quickly recognizes contributions made to business growth. To discuss details of the position, please submit a resume or phone

TRUST INVESTMENT OFFICER

Major Peoria, Illinois, Bank with trust assets of $300 million is seeking an individual to fill the No. 2 position in the Trust Investment Department. Experience of 5–7 years in the investment field is desired. Position involves customer contact with emphasis on portfolio management and security analysis. Undergraduate business/economic degree, or equivalent, required. Please submit a resume in confidence, including qualifications and salary requirements to:

TRUST OFFICERS

Through our network of regional offices, conveniently located in the nation's key money centers, we are fortunate to represent some of the nation's finest and fastest growing banks and trust companies.

Currently we are engaged in a number of searches for experienced Junior/Senior Trust Officers, in areas of Administration (Personal, Probate, Pension); Trust New Business (Immediate Fee or Future Will); Trust Investments (Personal or Employee Benefit); Trust Operations/Taxes (Personal or Corp.) These openings, in a wide choice of locales, are from the Assistant Trust Officer to Division and Department Head levels. Starting salaries range $15–45,000+. Send resume in strictest confidence, including geographical and income requirements.

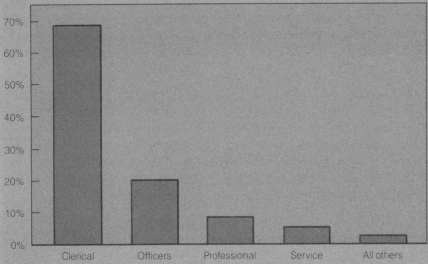

EXHIBIT V–B
Breakdown of Positions in the
Insurance Industry

with associate's and bachelor's degrees. The nation's 1,800 life and 2,800 casualty insurance companies do business in home offices as well as in regional and sales offices. Exhibit V–B shows how the 1.6 million people working in the insurance industry are employed. Clerical occupations in the insurance industry include secretaries, office clerks, claims adjusters, and claims examiners. The salespeople are either agents or brokers who sell insurance to clients. The professionals employed by insurance companies include actuaries and underwriters.

Fair and efficient claim settlement is essential to any insurance company. People who investigate claims, negotiate settlements with policyholders, and authorize payment are known as claims representatives. When a casualty company receives a claim, the claims adjuster determines the amount of the loss and whether or not the insurance policy covers the loss. Adjusters use reports, physical evidence, and the testimony of witnesses when investigating a claim. Finally, if the insurance company is liable, the adjuster negotiates the settlement with the claimant, ensuring that the claim is in line with the real extent of the loss. The claims adjuster's counterpart in the life insurance industry is called a claims examiner.

Salaries for claims adjusters and examiners range from $12,000 to $15,800 per year. Claims supervisors typically earn between $14,800 and $17,100, and many earn more than $25,000 per year. The growth in employment for claims representatives should reflect the national averages throughout the 1980s. The number of insurance claims is expected to keep pace with increases in the population, in spite of the dampening effect no-fault automobile insurance is having on the number of automobile claims.

Insurance underwriters analyze information from insurance applications, loss-control consultants, medical records, and actuarial studies to determine whether the insurance company will accept the risk of issuing insurance. Most underwriters specialize in one of three major categories of insurance: life, casualty, or health insurance. Life insurance underwriters can further specialize in one or more types of life insurance. The casualty underwriter specializes by type of risk, such as fire, automobile, marine, or workers' compensation. The job of the underwriter is important to the insurance company's present and future earnings. If the underwriter appraises risks too conservatively and charges high rates, the company could lose business to competitors. However, if the underwriting decisions are too liberal, the company might have to pay high claims in the future.

For beginning underwriting positions, many companies seek college graduates who have a degree in business administration. College graduates usually start as trainees or junior underwriters and receive on-the-job training as they move up in the organization. A career as an underwriter can be satisfying for people who like working with details and who enjoy evaluating and relating information. Underwriters have to be imaginative and aggressive, especially when their job requires additional information from external sources. Job opportunities in underwriting will increase as fast as the national average. Salaries for underwriters average about $15,500. Senior life underwriters average about $2,500 higher. Underwriting supervisors earn between $19,500 and $24,500 per year.

At times, insurance rates baffle many insurance customers. They wonder how much an insurance policy should cost or why young people pay more for automobile insurance. Such questions are often difficult to answer, but an actuary is a person who tries. Actuaries assemble and analyze statistics on accidents and deaths, and then they calculate the premium necessary for the insurance company to assume the risk. Thus the actuary calculates insurance premiums and policy provisions for each type of insurance offered. Most actuaries specialize in either life and health insurance or casualty insurance.

The minimum background for a beginning position as an actuary is a bachelor's degree with a strong background in math and statistics. It normally takes between five and ten years of on-the-job experience to complete the series of ten exams necessary to attain full professional status. The employment outlook for actuaries is good. Actuarial positions are expected to grow at a faster rate than the average for all occupations. This is due primarily to the growth in demand for all types of insurance coverage and the normal attrition as professionals retire or otherwise leave the field. New college graduates entering the actuarial profession received between $12,500 and $14,500 per year in 1982, depending on the number of professional exams that had been successfully completed and their academic training. Merit increases of $400 to $800 are usually provided by the insurance company each time a professional exam is completed.

There are many positions available in the finance and insurance industries. Employers are looking for intelligent, young, energetic people who like to work with information. If this type of position sounds interesting, you might want to check further into these growing industries.

PROFILE IN BUSINESS

Thomas J. Watson, Sr. (1874–1956)

There is no such thing as standing still.

His father wanted him to be a lawyer, but Thomas Watson enrolled in the Elmira School of Commerce in western New York, where he acquired an immediate and permanent passion for selling. As a teenager, he peddled musical instruments and sewing machines door to door, bartering with farmers for horses and produce. At twenty, he joined the sales force of the National Cash Register Company in Buffalo, where he refined his selling techniques and rose slowly but steadily to become general sales manager.

In 1914, Watson was asked to take over the small, debt-ridden Computing-Tabulating-Recording Company in New York City, which manufactured time clocks, scales, and adding machines. He agreed to a salary based on company income and launched a two-pronged campaign to boost sales and improve and expand the product line; but this required capital investment. With no secure collateral, he obtained a $40,000 loan on the merits of his record at NCR and his fund of enthusiasm—"the hardest sale I ever made in my life." The loan paid for a research and development facility and sales training sessions. CTR's sales force studied the equipment inside and out, but learned to sell services rather than machines. Within two years, the company was in the black.

Watson was constantly alert for

PART SIX

BUSINESS DECISION AIDS

new markets and evolving needs as business accounting grew more complex, and he developed an early line of electric business machines. By 1924, CTR had plants scattered in the United States, Canada, and Europe, prompting Watson to rename the firm the International Business Machines Corporation. When the Great Depression withered IBM's markets, he responded by doubling the sales force and maintaining production levels. Inventories of machines and parts grew to alarming proportions, but Watson insisted they would soon be back in demand, and so they were. IBM filled orders as fast as the business recovery generated them, while competing firms struggled back to full production. The federal government turned to IBM for an army of tabulators to implement its new Social Security system.

At the onset of World War II, Watson's percentage pay scale as IBM president earned him the third-highest salary in the country. He suggested a reduction—and still continued to make more than a thousand dollars a day. During the war, Watson's Depression gamble continued to pay off. IBM's momentum, reliability, and record for prompt delivery brought major government contracts for computing machines, bookkeeping systems, munitions, and coding and decoding devices. But Watson limited the company's wartime profits to less than 1.5 percent.

As Watson's presidency drew to a close, the research and development department he had established when he joined the firm in 1914 was designing prototype electronic computers, IBM's ultimate triumph. His son, Thomas J. Watson, Jr., took over in 1952, a transition that emphasized the elder Watson's paternal style of leadership. He had always presented a firm, personal model to his employees, a code of professional behavior essential to success within the company. He was one of the original corporate sloganeers, posting offices and factories with his favorite dictums: "Think," "Serve and sell," "Aim high and think in big figures," and "There is no such thing as standing still."

CHAPTER 19

ACCOUNTING

LEARNING OBJECTIVES

After studying this chapter, you should be able to:

Illustrate the importance of accounting information.

Explain the accounting equation.

Discuss the components and purposes of a balance sheet.

Understand the objectives and components of an income statement.

Compare the techniques of analyzing financial statements.

KEY TERMS

Accounting
Balance sheet
Income statement
Asset
Current assets
Fixed assets
Liabilities
Current liabilities
Long-term liabilities
Owners' equity
Expenses

FIGURING OUT
CREDIT WORTHINESS

It has been five years now since Marianne Johnson graduated with a degree in accounting from the University of Denver. Marianne has always liked accounting. She says, "A number of my fellow students didn't do well in accounting, but I had little trouble with the subject. I seemed to understand the language of the accountant almost from the beginning. I don't mean to imply that my accounting courses were a breeze; I had to work, but they did seem to come easier for me. My training in accounting has been very useful to me at the bank. I started as a trainee but was able to work my way up to my present position with extra effort and my love of accounting." Currently, Marianne is assistant commercial loan officer at the bank.

"This job provides a great deal of challenge," Marianne says. "We get many customers who come in seeking loans for their businesses, and it is my job to analyze these businesses and determine whether or not the bank should make the loan. We use a number of criteria to judge a customer's ability to repay the loan, but one of the most significant tools we have is the customer's financial statements. We use these statements by applying ratio analysis and comparing the current year's statements with previous years'. This provides us with a picture of the firm's financial condition and helps determine whether it can repay the loan easily." Marianne went on to point out that she had just received an application for a $100,000 loan from Abel & Smith, Inc., a local camera wholesaler. Abel & Smith wants to use the money to construct a new building to expand its storage space. It is Marianne's job to review financial statements and decide upon the loan. Abel & Smith's financial statements are included in this chapter.

In today's competitive world, business people are faced with hundreds of decisions daily. These decisions—if made incorrectly—could lead to the financial ruin of their business organizations. The bankruptcy of W. T. Grant Company is an example of what can happen even to a large retail organization if management makes the wrong decisions. This once vast retail chain was forced to close eleven hundred stores and a new fifty-three story headquarters building, appropriately dubbed "Grant's Tomb" by the employees. In addition, Grant laid off seventy-five thousand long-time employees and owed over $800 million to its creditors. But these figures in no way measure the human tragedy to Grant's employees, managers, stockholders, creditors, and customers.

If a manager knew the outcome of each decision that had to be made, there would be no risk in making decisions, and a manager's job would be fairly easy. But decisions in business are never made with this kind of knowledge; the manager must make decisions with the best data available at the time. Information for decision making comes from many different sources, and one of the most important is an organization's own accounting department.

A satisfactory accounting system is an absolute necessity for a successful business. Practically all business transactions—whether buying merchandise, land, buildings, or equipment, or paying taxes, wages, or expenses—are measured in dollars and cents. The accountant's job is to keep track of these important transactions. Thus, **accounting** involves recording, classifying, and summarizing business transactions and interpreting this compiled information to facilitate informed judgments and decisions. This definition emphasizes the two aspects of accounting: (1) bookkeeping information and (2) analysis and interpretation.

ACCOUNTING
Recording, classifying, and summarizing business transactions, as well as interpreting this compiled information to permit informed judgments and decisions.

For years, accounting has been viewed as simple bookkeeping: the accountant recorded, classified, and summarized transactions. These transactions were recorded in journals and ledgers and then summarized into the major financial statements of the organization. More recently, however, the emphasis in accounting has changed more toward providing useful information for decision making and projecting into the future. Accounting should be viewed as a tool the manager can use to determine what has happened in the organization and to make decisions that chart its future course. Consequently, the information provided by the accountant plays a vital role in determining the success of any firm.

Several groups are directly concerned with the information provided in the financial reports of business organizations. Each has a different motive for seeking this information, but they all are concerned about its accuracy. Unfortunately, accounting data are not always so accurate nor so easy to interpret as one would like.

USERS OF ACCOUNTING INFORMATION

Management

Much of the work of the accounting department is aimed directly at assisting management in the operation of the business. This includes the short-run tactical decisions as well as the long-run strategic decisions that will shape the future of the firm. The following list illustrates the types of questions managers want answered by accounting figures.

How much cash do we have on hand?

How much do the customers owe, and how much do we owe them?

What were sales for the last year, quarter, or month?

What does it cost to produce one unit of a product, and is that cost increasing or decreasing?

What is the profit or loss?

Can we afford to spend money on researching and developing new products?

Owners Potential investors and owners (shareholders or stockholders) of the business also depend on the information contained in financial reports. This is true for all businesses, no matter what size, type, or form (proprietorship, partnership, or corporation). All owners use financial information to measure how effectively the business is being operated. Some of the questions owners ask are:

What is the profit or loss, and what is its trend?

How much money is being made on our investments?

How financially sound is the company?

What items of value does the business own?

The financial reports that are prepared at the end of each quarter and year are the most reliable sources of information on any business. The creditors of a company (those who loan money to the business or grant credit on purchases) make extensive use of these accounting reports to determine the size of any loan, its duration, the rate of interest to be charged, and the security, or collateral, that is necessary. In addition, companies like Dun and Bradstreet, Moody's, and Standard and Poor's, which supply financial information to creditors, use financial statements to determine a company's credit rating. These rating services answer such questions as:

What things of value does the business own that could be used for security on a loan?

How much money has been invested in the business by the owners, and how much by other creditors?

What are the earnings of the business, and are they increasing or decreasing?

SIMPLIFIED ACCOUNTING

BALANCE SHEET
A financial statement that shows the assets, liabilities, and equity of a business.

Companies are assumed to exist for the purpose of making profits. Determining the profitability of a firm, then, is important to those who run it and those who invest in it. We need information provided by accountants to determine the profitability of a firm, which can be learned from two basic financial statements—the **balance sheet** and the **income statement**, sometimes called the statement of earnings. Accountants use these to describe the financial condition of a business. Learning how to analyze these financial statements, which form the basis of a firm's annual report to its stockholders and investors, will help you if you are running a business firm or are thinking about investing in one.

To explain and demonstrate the accounting for financial information, we will closely analyze the balance sheet and income statement for International Business Machines Corporation (IBM). IBM operations are mostly in the field of information-handling systems; its products include data-processing machines and systems, information processors, office systems, electric and electronic typewriters, copiers, dictation equipment, and related supplies and services.

INCOME STATEMENT
A financial statement summarizing all the revenue and expense transactions that result in a profit or loss over a period of time.

THE BALANCE SHEET

Take a look at the IBM balance sheet shown in Exhibit 19–1 and observe that the date, December 31, 1981, is printed so that it appears to be rather important, which it is. The balance sheet is a statement of the financial well-being of a firm at a *specific* point in time. In this case, the balance sheet is a statement of the financial condition or well-being of IBM exactly on that day, December 31, 1981.

Typically, balance sheets are published annually, although there are situations in which a company will publish balance sheets more frequently, particularly if an important event has occurred or if the firm is making a large purchase of another firm and so on.

The Parts of a Typical Balance Sheet

A typical balance sheet is made up of three main sections.

a. Assets
b. Liabilities
c. Owners' equity, more commonly referred to as shareholders' or stockholders' equity.

By definition, assets must equal liabilities plus owners' equity. That is,

Assets = liabilities + shareholders' equity

Assets. **Assets** are those things owned by the company or to which it has property rights. For example, the assets of the company might include cash in the bank, land and buildings, and such intangible things as the rights to patents and the value of copyrights and trademarks.

Current and fixed assets. Under assets, note the subheading "Current assets." **Current assets** are assets that are either in the form of cash right now or will be turned into cash within one year. On the other hand, **fixed assets** include things that have a life longer than one year. IBM lists them as "Rental machines and parts" and "Plant and other property."

Liabilities. **Liabilities** include all debts owed by the company. Examples of common liabilities are debts such as taxes and salaries that the company owes, loans payable to banks, reserves for employee retirement plans, and so on.

ASSET
Something of value owned by a business, including cash, inventory, land, and buildings.

CURRENT ASSETS
Something of value owned by the business that is either cash, will be converted into cash, or will be used up within one year.

FIXED ASSETS
An asset with a degree of permanence (beyond one year); intended for use rather than resale. Also called plant assets.

LIABILITIES
The claims of creditors on the assets of a business.

EXHIBIT 19–1
Balance Sheet: IBM, December 31, 1981
(all figures in millions of dollars)

ASSETS

Current assets:

Cash	$ 454	
Marketable securities, at lower of cost or market	1,575	
Notes and accounts receivable—trade, less allowance:		
1980, $195; 1979, $188	4,382	
Other accounts receivable	410	
Inventories, at lower of average cost or market	2,805	
Prepaid expenses	677	
		$10,303
Rental machines and parts	17,241	
Less: accumulated depreciation	7,651	
		9,590
Plant and other property	12,895	
Less: accumulated depreciation	5,207	
		7,688
Deferred charges and other assets		2,005
		$29,586

LIABILITIES AND STOCKHOLDERS' EQUITY

Current liabilities:

Taxes	$ 2,412	
Loans payable	773	
Accounts payable	872	
Compensation and benefits	1,556	
Deferred income	389	
Other accrued expenses and liabilities	1,318	$ 7,320
Deferred investment tax credits	252	
Reserves for employees' indemnities and retirement plans		1,184
Long-term debt		2,669
Stockholders' equity:		
Capital stock, par value $1.25 per share		4,389
Shares authorized, 650,000,000		
Issued: 1980–584,262,074; 1979–583,973,258		
Retained earnings		
Less: treasury stock, at cost		
Shares: 1981–592,293,624		18,161
		$29,586

Current and fixed, or long-term, liabilities. Current liabilities have the same time framework as current assets. **Current liabilities** are those that must be paid within the following year. Fixed liabilities, or **long-term liabilities**, are those that must be paid sometime after one year or during a period of years.

Owners' equity. **Owners' equity** is the difference between assets and liabilities. That is, whatever is left over after all debts are paid, or at least taken account of, is owned by the stockholders in the company. In the IBM balance sheet, the stockholders' equity was $18,161,000,000 on December 31, 1981. That means that if all debts were paid on that date, the book value of the IBM Corporation would be worth about $18 billion to its owners!

A balance sheet is exactly what it sounds like; it must balance. The two totals on the bottom of each part of the ledger must always be equal. Remember:

Assets = liabilities + shareholders' equity

That means that should IBM borrow to build another plant, the balance sheet for next year would show the value of another plant as an asset, and it would also show a liability equal to the cost of the plant because it would be bought on credit.

The Balancing Act

The income statement for IBM is its "statement of earnings." The income statement focuses on the financial activities of a firm during an entire one-year period. For example, if the balance sheet reports a firm's financial condition specifically on December 31, the income statement will normally report its financial activities between January 1 and December 31 of the previous year.

The statement of earnings reports a firm's revenues, its costs, and its profits during the year. Profit, of course, is the difference between total revenues and total costs. Unfortunately, there may be cases where costs are greater than revenues and when this happens, a negative profit—that is, a loss—results. Losses are represented within parentheses in income statements.

Look at Exhibit 19-2. The first three lines in this IBM income statement, "Sales" and "Rentals" and "Services," represent all the money income received for the products or services sold. In 1981, IBM had a gross income from sales plus rentals and services of $29,070,000,000 or about $29 billion.

THE INCOME STATEMENT

Next on the income statement is a listing of costs. These costs are related to the earning of the revenues from sales and rentals and services. The costs represent the **expense** of doing business or making the product that earned the income.

Costs

Gross Income:

Sales	$12,901	
Rentals	10,839	
Services	5,330	
		$29,070
Cost of sales	5,321	
Cost of rentals	4,152	
Cost of services	2,543	
Selling, development and engineering, and general and administrative expenses	11,027	
Interest expense	407	
		23,450
		5,620
Other income, principally interest		368
Earnings before income taxes		5,988
Provision for U.S. federal and non-U.S. income taxes		2,680
Net Earnings		**$ 3,308**
Per share (average number of shares outstanding: 1981 587,803,373		$ 5.63

EXHIBIT 19-2   Income Statement: IBM, 1981 (in billions of dollars except per share amount)

THE EFFECT OF INFLATION ON ACCOUNTING

Economists and accountants have long known that inflation makes a firm's profits, or earnings, appear greater from one year to the next than they actually are. Consider an example. Assume that Corporation X in, say, 1981, had total sales revenues of $10 and total costs of $8. Profits, or earnings, would be $2. Now suppose that during the following year the price level doubles, and in 1982, Corporation X realizes total sales of $20 and total costs of $16. Total profits for 1982 would be $4, and it seems as if profits have doubled in that year. Of course, only *nominal* profits—those reported on the books—have doubled; *real* profits—profits adjusted for inflation—have remained unchanged.

If you don't take inflation into consideration, *nominal* profits look bigger than profits really are. The maximum distortion would occur if assets were valued at their historic, that is, their original, purchase price. For instance, continuing with our example, suppose Corporation X's productive assets were purchased for $20 in 1981. The ratio of earnings to assets for 1981, in our example, would be

$2 ÷ $20 = 10 percent.

In 1982, if we use the original purchase price as the value of the asset, this ratio would be

$4 ÷ $20 = 20 percent.

But the real value of the assets is their *current* price. Thus, if we did the calculation using the current, inflation-adjusted value of assets, the ratio of earnings to assets would be

$4 ÷ $40 = 10 percent.

This rate is the same as for 1981.

CUBES ARE IN

Rubik's Cube was the hottest new toy since the Hula Hoop for a while. Retailers couldn't keep it in stock, and in Japan, people lined up the night before deliveries were due. But Ideal Toy, the company that makes this best-selling puzzle, posted record losses.

Ideal lost an estimated $19 million on revenues of $135 million. That's roughly as much as the company earned in the entire decade of the 1970s. This loss comes in spite of the $3 million the company made on the cube.

Two major factors led to Ideal's troubles. First, like other toy manufacturers, they were forced to extend credit to their customers for almost a full year—from the Toy Fair in February until after Christmas. Second, Ideal had poured millions into new high-priced electronic games and dolls it was planning to use to lead its product line.

Unfortunately, consumers were unwilling to pay the high prices for Ideal toys. Retailers returned them or didn't purchase to begin with, and Ideal was well on its way to a record loss.

Ideal is currently battling back. The company has cut the average price of its toys and has gone back to some of its old toys for help in the current situation. The company simply can't afford another bad year like the one they had when they introduced the best-selling Rubik's Cube.

Adapted from Jane Carmichael, "Figure This One Out," *Forbes*, April 27, 1981, p. 34.

In short, inflation "overstates" (makes figures appear larger than in reality) the absolute value of profits as well as the ratio of earnings to assets, when assets are valued at their historic (or purchase) value.

Let's return to our loan officer, Marianne Johnson, who has been given a request by Abel & Smith for a $100,000 loan for expansion of one of their plants. On reviewing a financial statement for Abel & Smith, Marianne notes that total current assets are worth $103,000 and total long-term assets, consisting mainly of plant machinery, buildings, and land, are $167,500, for a total asset value of $270,500. On the liability side, Marianne finds out that Abel & Smith has current liabilities of $75,000 and long-term liabilities of $80,000, adding up to total liabilities of $155,000. That leaves a net worth of only $105,500. Based on this information, Marianne is uncomfortable recommending approval of the $100,000 loan. She is not yet convinced that there is sufficient net worth in the business to justify taking such a risk.

These are the types of decisions, based on accounting information, that Marianne must make on an almost daily basis.

On the Job Revisited

Although the balance sheet and the income statement are important sources of information to managers, owners, creditors, and so on about what is going on inside the firm, they only give a general picture of how well a business is being run. In order to tell if the firm is being operated efficiently, it is necessary to analyze the financial information and compare

INTERPRETING FINANCIAL STATEMENTS

it to the company's performance in prior years as well as that of other successful firms.

Comparative Statements

A comparative statement is one of the tools accountants use to aid managers in the interpretation of financial reports. Figures for the current year's financial statements are compared directly with those of one or more previous years. This comparison allows the manager to identify quickly any trends on either the income statement or balance sheet.

A comparative income statement for Abel & Smith is shown in Exhibit 19-3. Notice that a direct comparison clearly shows any changes in the specific expenses and totals. This type of comparison is also possible for

On the Job Revisited the accounts on the balance sheet. Marianne Johnson can use this comparative income statement to spot shifts in Abel & Smith's expenses. Large shifts from one year to the next could mean trouble for Abel & Smith and Marianne's bank if the loan is made.

Ratios

Another tool that is often used for interpreting financial statements is the *ratio*. A ratio is simply the relationship of one number to another. A fraction is a good example of a ratio. The most useful ratios are the current ratio, debt-to-equity ratio, inventory turnover, net profit margin, gross profit margin, and return on owners' investment.

EXHIBIT 19-3
Abel & Smith, Inc., Income Statement
for the Year Ending December 31, 1983

REVENUE FROM SALES	1982	PERCENT	1983	PERCENT
Gross sales	$380,000	(100.00)	$400,000	(100.00)
Less returns	2,000	(.53)	5,000	(1.25)
Net sales	378,000	(99.47)	395,000	(98.75)
Cost of goods sold	200,000	(52.63)	225,000	(56.25)
Gross profit	178,000	(46.84)	170,000	(42.50)
Operating expenses				
Selling expenses				
Advertising	10,000	(2.63)	10,000	(2.50)
Sales salaries	45,000	(11.84)	45,000	(11.25)
Delivery	4,500	(1.18)	5,000	(1.25)
Miscellaneous	5,000	(1.32)	10,000	(2.50)
Total selling	64,500	(16.97)	70,000	(17.50)
Administrative expenses				
Office salaries	40,000	(10.53)	60,000	(15.00)
Taxes	5,000	(1.32)	5,100	(1.28)
Depreciation	6,750	(1.78)	6,750	(1.69)
Insurance	5,000	(1.32)	5,000	(1.25)
Uncollectable accounts	3,000	(.79)	4,000	(1.00)
Total administrative expenses	59,750	(15.72)	80,850	(20.21)
Total operating expenses	124,250	(32.70)	150,850	(37.71)
Net income before taxes	53,750	(14.14)	19,150	(4.79)
Federal income taxes	11,825	(3.11)	4,213	(1.05)
Net income after taxes	41,925	(11.03)	14,937	(3.73)

TYPE OF BUSINESS	CURRENT RATIO
Automobile dealership	1.9
Groceries and meats	2.0
Building materials	2.5
Women's specialty shop	2.5
Department store	3.4
Lumber yard	3.7
Hardware store	3.6

EXHIBIT 19-4
Current Ratios

CURRENT RATIO One of the most common ratios used in the analysis of financial statements is the current ratio, which is found by dividing the current assets by the current liabilities. This ratio is designed to give management an indication of the firm's ability to pay its debts. It is very important to the owners and short-term creditors of the business because it is the current assets that will be used to pay off the current liabilities as they come due. This ratio should indicate whether a company such as Abel & Smith would be able to pay off any current debts it has. But in order to determine if a current ratio is good, it is necessary to have a standard against which to measure the current ratio.

What constitutes a desirable ratio depends on the nature and type of business. A business whose inventory is a high percentage of current assets has a greater need for cash and thus a larger current ratio than a business whose inventory is a small percentage of current assets. Exhibit 19–4 lists the average current ratios from a selected group of businesses. In general, the standard for a current ratio is 2 to 1, or 2.0.

Marianne Johnson took a look at the current ratio for Abel & Smith and found the following.

On the Job Revisited

$$\frac{\text{Current assets}}{\text{Current liabilities}} = \frac{\$103,000}{\$75,000} = 1.37$$

As the standard current ratio is 2.0, Abel & Smith's current ratio falls short. Marianne is concerned about Abel & Smith's ability to pay off its current debts. The $100,000 loan that Abel & Smith has applied for is to be invested in plant, or long-term, assets. That means that Abel & Smith's current liabilities will increase after the loan, but the current assets will remain the same. The current ratio would become:

$$\text{After-loan current ratio} = \frac{\text{Current assets}}{\text{New current liabilities}} = \frac{\$103,000}{\$175,000} = 0.59$$

WORKING CAPITAL Another indication of the firm's ability to meet current debts is working capital. Working capital is closely related to the current ratio, although it is the difference between the current assets and the current liabilities rather than a ratio of the two. Working capital

PLAYING WITH NUMBERS

For those who believe in conventional accounting principles, Centran, Inc.—a Cleveland-based bank holding company with $3.4 billion in assets—made a profit of $9.5 million in 1981. For investors clever enough to look beyond the figures on the income statement and balance sheet, it appeared that the company actually lost $126 million instead of making a profit of $9.5 million. By the end of the fiscal year in June, the company's problems had become painfully clear. The directors had cut dividends, and the stock declined from $22 to $16 in just two days.

Yet in spite of the huge differences noted earlier, Centran didn't violate any accounting rules. The company and its accountants had listed the value of bonds in the bank's portfolio at the price they would be worth when the bonds matured rather than at their current market price, which was substantially lower than the price of the bonds at maturity.

Shortly after Centran completed its financial statements, it was forced to sell the bonds to pay off its short-term debt. Since the bonds were sold at the market price, the bank suffered a loss of $135 million. The result was a quick reduction of the stockholders' equity from $183 million to $13 million.

Adapted from Eammon Fingleton, "Any Warning Would Do," *Forbes*, September 14, 1981, pp. 129–130.

is a measure o the firm's ability to pay for the everyday expenses of running a business or for purchases of material. The working capital for Abel & Smith is:

$$\text{Current assets} - \text{current liabilities} = \text{Working capital}$$
$$\$103,000 - \$75,000 = \$28,000$$

DEBT-TO-EQUITY RATIO The current ratio helps to identify how well a firm can meet its short-term debt. The measure of a firm's ability to pay its long-term debt is the debt-to-equity ratio. The funds invested in the firm's assets come from two sources—creditors (liabilities) and owners (equity). The debt-to-equity ratio shows the relative proportion of funds secured from these two sources. A business that is financed conservatively would have a larger proportion of owners' equity than debt. This allows the owners to absorb a number of years of losses before the firm would become insolvent and unable to pay its bills.

If the debt is greater than the owners' equity, then the business could have problems in the future because the owners can only absorb minor losses before the firm becomes insolvent.

On the Job Revisited   As Marianne Johnson looks further into the financial structure of Abel & Smith, she finds that the debt-to-equity ratio is:

$$\frac{\text{Total liabilities}}{\text{Total equity}} = \frac{\$155,000}{\$105,500} = 1.47$$

Marianne is disturbed with this debt-to-equity ratio of 1.47. She would be more content with a conservative ratio of, say, 0.5. When Marianne takes into consideration the additional $100,000 long-term liability, the debt-to-equity ratio moves up.

$$\frac{\text{New total liabilities}}{\text{Total equity}} = \frac{\$255,000}{\$105,500} = 2.41$$

It doesn't look good.

Profitability ratios indicate how successful a company really is. The three common profitability ratios relate to the profit margin, the return on assets, and the return on equity.

Profitability Ratios

PROFIT MARGINS   There are two types of profit margins: the net profit margin and the gross profit margin. The net profit margin measures the firm's return on sales, or how much it made on every dollar of sales. The formula for this is:

$$\text{Net profit margin} = \frac{\text{Net income}}{\text{Net sales}}$$

The gross profit margin differs from the net profit margin in that it compares gross profit rather than net profit to sales. Its formula is:

$$\text{Gross profit margin} = \frac{\text{Gross profit}}{\text{Net sales}}$$

RETURN ON ASSETS   A return on assets tells how much income the company earned on each dollar it invested. It gives the overall company earnings profitability.

$$\text{Return on assets (ROA)} = \frac{\text{Net earnings}}{\text{Total assets}}$$

RETURN ON EQUITY OR RETURN ON INVESTMENT   The return on equity (ROE), sometimes called the return on investment (ROI), tells the owners the actual, or net, earnings for each dollar of shareholders' equity. Shareholders, of course, are particularly interested in this.

$$\text{Return on equity (ROE)} = \frac{\text{Net earnings}}{\text{Shareholders' equity investment}}$$

In Exhibit 19-5, we show the return on owners' investment for various industries.

Investors, creditors, managers, and others must be careful in using ratios to analyze a business because sometimes a ratio can be misleading. The value of ratio analysis is not in what each ratio says about the company but rather in the overall picture it provides of the company's operations. Each ratio needs to be viewed in light of the other ratios in order for a clear picture to emerge.

Companies like Dun and Bradstreet have made it possible to compare one company with other companies in the same industry by providing

EXHIBIT 19-5
Return on Owners' Investment

INDUSTRY	INDUSTRY MEDIAN	
	1981	1982
Mining	16.3%	16.5%
Pharmaceuticals	16.2	15.8
Chemicals	12.6	14.1
Beverages	14.2	15.4
Food	13.1	12.8
Tobacco	13.5	15.5
Motor vehicles and parts	5.8	13.8
Textiles	5.4	10.7
All industries	11.6	13.3

Adapted from *Fortune*, May 1982.

about twenty ratios in over a hundred different industries. The ratios, a composite of a number of firms in each industry, indicate the average ratio for that industry. Any firm can be measured against this standard.

SUMMARY

■ The accounting equation is: assets = liabilities + equity. The things of value in the business (assets) will always equal the amount of money invested by the creditors (liabilities) and the investment of the owner-shareholders (equity).

■ The balance sheet describes the financial condition of the business. Consequently, it is divided into three areas including the assets, liabilities, and shareholders' equity.

■ The income statement is a summary of the revenue and expenses of the business. The difference between the revenue of the business and the expenses necessary to generate that revenue is the profit of the business for the period in question.

■ Accountants use several tools to analyze financial statements. Comparative statements permit the accountant to compare one year's financial statement with another year's in order to identify areas of major changes. Financial ratios are calculated from the information in the financial statements, and they allow the accountant to compare one business with another. These tools are used to help determine the financial strength and profitability of the business.

ISSUES TO CONSIDER AND ANALYZE

1. Define the balance sheet. Why does it balance?
2. Despite the use of numbers, balance sheets, and income statements, accounting is not precisely accurate. Why is this so? Can you give some examples?
3. What is the difference between current and fixed assets, and between current and long-term liabilities? Why does an accountant or business-person have to make this distinction?

4. Recently the courts ruled that the communication between accountant and client is not considered privileged information, as communication between lawyer and client is. Do you think this is a valid decision? Why or why not?

5. Would you look at the net profit margin or the return on equity to make a decision on whether to purchase an ongoing business?

6. Retained earnings are often thought of as money the firm has but hasn't spent. Why is it incorrect to think of retained earnings this way?

7. Accounting has been called the language of business. Can you explain why?

8. If a current ratio of 2 to 1 is good, then one of 4 to 1 must be better. Why is this statement false?

9. What purpose does the income statement serve?

10. How does the income statement tie into the balance sheet?

DART AND KRAFT, INC.—SHAPING UP

CASE FOR ANALYSIS

Dart and Kraft, Inc., is one of the largest diversified food and package goods companies in the world. It has a strong reputation among consumers because its brand names are widely known and respected. Some product examples include Kraft food products, Tupperware, Duracell, and West Bend appliances. Another important characteristic of Dart and Kraft is its financial resources. Some of the financial characteristics of the company are shown below.

Balance Sheet	(In Millions)
Assets	
Cash	$ 95
Short-term investment	232
Accounts receivable	829
Inventories	1,646
Total Current Assets	2,802
Property, plant, and equipment	1,379
Other investments	352
Intangible assets	145
TOTAL ASSETS	$4,678
Liabilities	
Accounts payable	$ 513
Short-term loans	131
Income taxes	209
Current portion of long-term debt	13
Accrued expenses	425
Total Current Liabilities	1,291

Long-term debt	540
Deferred taxes on income	135
Miscellaneous liabilities	61
Minority interest in subsidiary	4
Total Other Liabilities	740
Shareholders' equity	136
Capital surplus	330
Retained earnings	2,182
Total Shareholders' Equity	2,648
TOTAL LIABILITIES AND SHAREHOLDERS' EQUITY	$4,679

Income Statement

Net sales	$9,412
Cost of goods sold	8,718
Income from operations before taxes	694
Provision for income taxes	310
Net income	384
Net income per share	7.03

QUESTIONS

1. Calculate the following financial ratios for Dart and Kraft.
   a. Current ratio
   b. Acid test ratio
   c. Net profit margin
   d. Return on equity
2. What conclusions can you draw from your analysis about the financial condition of Dart and Kraft, Inc.?

CHAPTER 20

STATISTICAL ANALYSIS OF BUSINESS DATA

LEARNING OBJECTIVES

After studying this chapter, you should be able to:

Discuss the importance of accurate economic data in making business decisions.

Discuss the difference between internal and external data sources.

Explain some basic aspects of statistics.

Illustrate how to compute the mean, median, and mode for a group of numbers.

Describe the purpose of an index number.

KEY TERMS

Internal data
External data
Primary data
Secondary data
Direct observation
Sample survey
Census
Mail interviews
Personal interviews
Mean
Median
Mode
Index number

THE RESHAPED CONSUMER MARKETS

Jackie Green is a statistician for Thomasville Furniture Industries (TFI), a job she has held since graduating from college where she majored in business. The marketing vice president at TFI has assigned Jackie to an important marketing research project. She has to collect information and statistics that will show how two-income families are likely to reshape consumer markets by the mid 1980s. Jackie also has to find out how much consumers will probably spend on furniture as well as the furniture styles they will want to buy.

To complete this job, Jackie found many important statistics in government reports, and she bought other statistics and information from private businesses. From one set of statistics she discovered that *real* family spending should grow by an average of 3.7 percent a year through the 1980s, total family spending should be around $1.3 trillion by 1989, nearly 40 percent of the 67 million American families will earn over $25,000 a year (1977 dollars), and over half of these 67 million families will have two wage earners.

To complete the second part of her assignment, Jackie did a sample mail survey of seven hundred female homemakers. The women included in the sample survey revealed some important information: for example, they wanted furniture that required little dusting and easy care. In a word, these homemakers wanted convenience. The women also wanted smaller furniture made of real wood done in a casual or contemporary style.

Many business decisions about what to make and sell require different types of information, and much of the needed information comes in the form of original data that is collected firsthand. Other business data can be collected from secondary data sources including government publications. No matter what the source, most of the data must be summarized in various ways using different types of statistics. Several of these statistical methods are illustrated in this chapter.

412

Making decisions and operating a business are two important management jobs. Controlling a business is a practical way to see how well management decisions are working and to make changes if necessary. To make good decisions and decide if plans are working, a manager needs the following: (1) performance standards and (2) accurate management data or information. Performance standards are set by managers, but management data must be collected so that the data are timely and accurate. In addition, data must be summarized so it can be used by managers.

In Chapter 21, we discuss the role of management information systems (MIS) in collecting timely and accurate data, but there are ways to collect managerial data other than through an MIS. Some of these ways are discussed in this chapter. No matter how management data are collected, the data must be summarized and studied, a job done using various types of statistical methods, which are also covered in the chapter.

INTERNAL DATA
Obtained from records within a business that relate to the operation of that business.

EXTERNAL DATA
Data obtained from sources outside the business.

PRIMARY DATA
Data collected to solve a specific problem or as part of an ongoing report.

SECONDARY DATA
Published by other businesses, trade associations, and governments.

SOURCES OF MANAGEMENT DATA

Management data can be obtained from both internal or external sources. **Internal data** are obtained from records within a business that relate solely to the operation of that business, for example, the cost of making a sale or producing a part. Data that come from outside a business are called **external data**. Data from governments and trade associations that report on the operation of several businesses are examples of external data.

Internal Data

The sources of internal data include accounting records, inventory records, and personnel files. Accounting records provide information on many aspects of a business, such as accounts receivable, total assets, total liabilities, cash on hand, marketing expenses, advertising expenditures, production expenses, and profitability by product line. These types of internal management data are usually collected on a regular basis, stored for a low cost, and quickly recalled in computers.

Not all management data relate to a business's financial records, however. For example, marketing data can contain information on such customer characteristics as age, income, education, occupation, and types of products and services bought. These are the types of data that Jackie Green collects to find out how consumer markets will be reshaped in the 1980s. Inventory records reflect the stock level of various parts, reorder points for parts, and the quantities of finished goods in the warehouses.

On the Job Revisited

External Data

External data can be obtained in two different ways. First, data can be collected to solve a problem or to answer a specific question. This type of information is called **primary data**, and it can be collected by either direct observation or from a sample survey. Another approach is to collect **secondary data** from materials published by government and private organizations.

Direct observation means watching and recording the behavior of people. For example, suppose a grocery store manager wants to know if customers prefer to buy tomatoes from an open bin or in prepackaged

DIRECT OBSERVATION
A way to collect original data by observing, measuring, and recording people's behavior.

containers. By offering customers a choice between both ways of buying in several stores, the manager can watch for customer preferences. "Nose counting" is likely to provide the manager with more accurate data than by asking the customers about their preferences.

It is not always practical to use direct observation, however; especially for large numbers such as the general public. Then the only practical approach is to use a sample survey. A **sample survey** is conducted by choosing a number of people and asking them a series of questions. If people within the group to be sampled have an equal chance of being chosen, then the survey is called a *random sample survey*. One example of a random sample is a national political poll of voters regarding how they plan to vote in a presidential election. Two of America's most famous polls that make use of sample surveys are the Gallup Poll and the Harris Survey. Another example is the energy survey conducted by the National Family Opinion Poll (Business Close-Up). The results of surveying a few hundred households showed that over 10 million American homes are without any attic insulation.

When information is collected from all people, all customers, or all businesses, this is called a **census**. The United States government conducts a census of the nation's population (all people) every ten years and a census of American business every four years. Unless the total number of people, businesses, or customers in a population is small, the census method is too costly to use. For example, the government spent over $1 billion to collect the 1980 national population census.

Data Collection

Once a sample is selected, data can be collected by one or more interview methods: direct-mail interviews, telephone interviews, or personel interviews. **Mail interviews** are conducted by sending questionnaires to people in the sample and asking that they fill them out. Mail questionnaires seem like a simple and inexpensive way to collect data; but unfortunately, this is not always true. First, the cost per completed mail interview can be high if the number of people completing a questionnaire is small when compared to the number of people receiving a questionnaire. Second, people who fill out and return a questionnaire could be different from those who did not complete it. They could be different in age, income, race, sex, and, most importantly, in their opinions. Even so, mail interviews are widely used by both businesses and governments. This is the way Jackie Green collected information from the seven hundred homemakers she interviewed, for example.

When they can be used, telephone interviews are the quickest and least expensive way to collect data. They are conducted by talking directly with people selected for the sample. This is the method most often used in political polls such as the Gallup Poll. The major limitation of telephone interviews is that the interview cannot last too long, usually no more than ten to twenty minutes. There are exceptions to this rule of thumb, particularly if the interview topic is current and interesting.

Personal interviews involve face-to-face meetings between people. This direct, personal contact can provide a wide variety of detailed data. The

SAMPLE SURVEY
A method of collecting original data by selecting a number of representative people and recording their answers to various questions.

CENSUS
A survey of all people or customers in a category.

MAIL INTERVIEWS
A way to conduct surveys by mailing questionnaires to a population sample.

On the Job Revisited

PERSONAL INTERVIEW
A face-to-face conversation between interviewer and survey sample.

SKYROCKETING ENERGY COSTS

The cost of energy is important to everybody's household budget, especially since the large 1973 oil price increases. Many items on the "Most Wanted List" of home energy wasters add to the total home energy bill. The most important items on the list include underinsulated attics, uninsulated walls and floors, lack of storm windows, and improperly adjusted furnaces. Finding these problem items is fairly easy, and applying commonsense solutions can help cut energy costs.

The number one energy waster is the uninsulated home attic. A National Family Opinion Poll revealed that over 10 million American homes are without any attic insulation.

Also, another 22 million homes do not have enough insulation. According to the U.S. Department of Energy, a family's yearly energy cost can be reduced between 18 and 23 percent by having proper home insulation. Projected energy costs through 1990 give American homeowners good reasons to try to cut energy costs. Based on a consumer energy price index, home energy costs will skyrocket. For example, a $100-per-month home energy bill in 1970 will probably be over $730 by 1990. In 1983 the bill could be $400, representing a 400 percent increase since 1970.

Adapted from the *Steele, Missouri, Enterprise*, August 12, 1981.

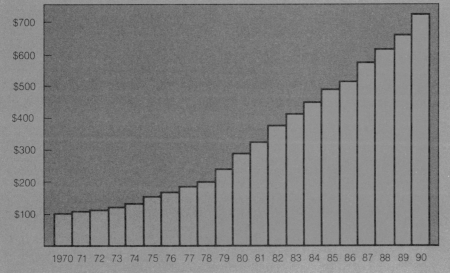

EXHIBIT 20-1
Projected Energy Costs through 1990 for an American Home.

interviewer can also explain confusing questions, which helps keep unanswered or incorrectly answered questions to a minimum. The key to successful personal interviews is a well-trained interviewer, and this interviewing method is the most costly. Even so, the quantity and quality of information that can be obtained from personal interviews are often worth the cost.

Secondary Data

On the Job Revisited

It is not always necessary to collect primary data. Useful information can be found in secondary data sources, but they are frequently overlooked. This is unfortunate for two reasons: secondary data usually cost less to collect and also require less time to collect. Thus you should always start with secondary data sources to see if the information that you need is available. Secondary data sources provided Jackie Green with information about how much family spending will grow in the 1980s. It is important to realize that secondary data are not always suitable because the exact type of data required may not be available in published sources. In this case the only alternative is to collect primary data if possible.

Secondary data are published by both private and government sources. The following list includes only a few of the many types of secondary data available from private sources:

Dun and Bradstreet Marketing Identifiers. This marketing information service on businesses in the United States and Canada is updated daily.

Nielson Retail Index. This is a sample survey taken of twenty-five hundred retail merchants every two months. Data are collected on product turnover, store displays, prices, and promotional activity.

MRCA Consumer Panel. This is a panel of seventy-five hundred scientifically selected households that represent the total United States population. The respondents, or panel members, use a diary to record information about their purchases of groceries and personal-care products. The panel is conducted by the Market Research Corporation of America.

Other useful private publications and marketing guides include *Fortune Directory*, *Handbook of Economic Almanac*, *Economic Statistics*, *Commodity Yearbook*, *Moody's Manuals*, *Rand McNally Commercial Atlas and Marketing Guide*, and *Sales Management Survey of Buying Power*.

The United States government is the largest producer of secondary data, and much of its data is either free or available at a small charge.

Census Data. The Bureau of the Census publishes data collected from a series of censuses taken at regular intervals. Examples include data on population, housing, business, manufacturers, mineral industries, agriculture, government, and transportation.

County Business Patterns. This source contains data on the number and type of businesses, employment, and payroll size by county for every state.

Survey of Current Business. This publication, available monthly, contains a complete summary of data on the national income and product accounts. It also reports data on such items as foreign trade, real estate activity, personal consumption expenditures, general business indicators, and construction activity.

Other important government publications are *Statistical Abstract*, *U.S. Industrial Outlook*, *Federal Reserve Bulletin*, *County and City Data Book*, and *The Economic Report of the President*.

Statistics are useful in many areas of business. For example, businesses usually deal with thousands of consumers, any one of whom could buy any number of goods and services at different times. This erratic pattern makes it impossible to predict exactly what specific product a person will actually buy. But if the purchases of thousands of people are analyzed, a stable buying pattern may be found. This situation is well illustrated with the home computer. When home computers were introduced, Apple Computer could not predict which specific households would buy a computer, but the company could make a reasonable prediction about the percentage of total households that might buy a home computer. Businesses are more interested in analyzing the "typical" behavior of large numbers of people than the specific behavior of a single individual.

Another example of how combining individually unpredictable events can produce stable events is found in the life-insurance industry. It is impossible to predict when a specific person will die, but if thousands of ten-year-olds are taken as a group, it is possible to predict how many of them will probably survive to age forty or age eighty.

Both of these examples depend on the use of large amounts of data because this avoids mistakes created by focusing on the erratic behavior of any one person or household. Large amounts of data are usually stable, so it is possible to measure and describe the characteristics of a population using sample data. The phrase *large amounts of data* does not always mean that thousands or even hundreds of people or businesses are represented in the sample. Large is relative to the population total. For example, if there are only ten thousand people in a city, a properly selected sample of one hundred people could be adequate. Many samples are small because, if properly selected, the samples accurately represent their populations.

Cost data, employment records, sales figures, and other important information collected from samples can be most accurately and effectively presented to managers by using basic statistical methods.

Visual Analysis

When preparing statistical reports of business and economic data, visual presentation and analysis can be effective. Different forms of visual presentation include line charts, pie charts, bar charts, and pictographs. How inflation has shrunk family income is shown in Exhibit 20-2. This *line chart* shows that although family income has doubled, families have about the same buying power as they did in 1970.

The *pie chart* in Exhibit 20-3 shows the type and value of goods exported to the USSR by the United States. For example, $938.3 billion of food and feed grains were exported by America.

The energy status of the United States in 1980, according to the government, is shown in Exhibit 20-4. Using a *bar chart*, the percentages of energy provided by oil, natural gas, coal, and nuclear power are compared with the reserves of these resources. Note that coal, which represents 90 percent of the nation's energy reserves, accounts for only 18 percent of our current energy supply.

In Exhibit 20-5, a pictograph represents how the American economy has

EXHIBIT 20-2
Shrinking Family Income

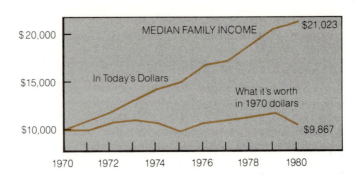

grown since 1960. Each dollar sign in the pictograph represents $500 billion of GNP. For example, in 1980 the GNP of the nation was approximately $2.5 trillion.

Computing Averages

MEAN
A statistical measure used to describe the "typical" value of a set of sample data. Also called the arithmetic average.

MEDIAN
The middle value in a list of numbers.

MODE
A number in a list that occurs most frequently.

EXHIBIT 20-3

American Exports to the USSR, 1980

International Letter, Federal Reserve Bank of Chicago, January 1, 1982, p. 1

USSR TOTAL $1,509.7 MILLION

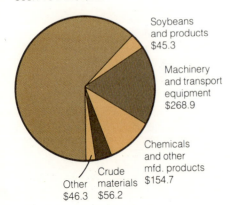

Soybeans and products $45.3

Machinery and transport equipment $268.9

Chemicals and other mfd. products $154.7

Crude materials $56.2

Other $46.3

Averages are used to describe the "typical" characteristics of large amounts of data. Averages are called measures of central tendency because averages describe a number located near the center of sample data. This means that the numbers in the sample data tend to "cluster" around this central or typical value. There are three important and frequently used types of averages—mean, median, and mode. In computing a typical value from a set of sample data, you can choose from among these three types of averages. However, the meanings of these averages are all different and, except in one case, their values will be different.

The mean is the most commonly used of the three averages. When people speak of the average price or average cost, they are usually referring to the mean. The **mean** is computed by adding a group of numbers and dividing their total by the quantity of numbers in the group. The mean is also called the *arithmetic average*.

This type of average can be misleading, however, because the mean does not always reflect a typical value of the numbers in the group. This point is well illustrated by the New York Stock Exchange price data in Exhibit 20-6. The stock price data are presented in a list of numbers arranged in numerical order from low to high. Adding this list of fourteen numbers gives a total of $415.11. Dividing the total by fourteen yields an average (mean) price of $29.65. But no single stock price on the list is close to $29.65. The value of the mean is distorted by the three high-priced stocks at the bottom of the list. Because the mean misrepresents the typical value of the stock prices, either the median or mode may give managers a more typical stock price.

The **median** is the middle value in a list of numbers. Half the numbers lie above and half lie below the median. In Exhibit 20-6, simply count halfway down from the top to locate the median. The median value lies between $17.25 and $18.12, or at $17.68. This is a more typical value of the list of stock prices than the mean of $29.65.

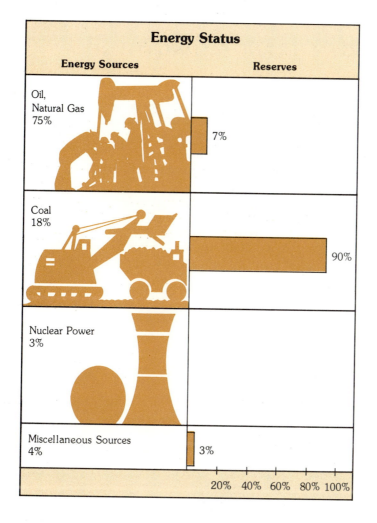

Energy Status

Energy Sources	Reserves
Oil, Natural Gas 75%	7%
Coal 18%	90%
Nuclear Power 3%	
Miscellaneous Sources 4%	3%

20% 40% 60% 80% 100%

EXHIBIT 20-4

United States Energy Sources and Energy Reserves

EXHIBIT 20-5

American Economic Growth Measured by GNP

1960	$
1970	$ $
1980	$ $ $ $ $
1982	$ $ $ $ $ $

$ equals $500 billion of GNP

From United States Department of Commerce, Bureau of the Census of Population, 1980 (Washington, D.C.: Government Printing Office, 1980)

EXHIBIT 20-6

New York Stock Exchange Price for Selected Common Stocks

CORPORATION	STOCK PRICE
Farah	$10.00
Chock Full O'Nuts	11.00
Equimark	13.88
American Airlines	14.12
Black and Decker	15.12
LTV	16.75
Revere Copper	17.25
Daniel Industries	18.12
Pepsi Cola	35.12
Columbia Pictures	38.88
General Motors	38.88
IBM	55.50
Delta Airlines	62.50
Cox Broadcasting	68.00

Adapted from *The Wall Street Journal*, October 9, 1981.

The **mode** is the number in the list that occurs most frequently. The mode stock price is $38.88. This value is not an especially typical average value of the stock price list, however.

The mean, median, and mode do not always vary this much. Often their values tend to be close together, but seldom are they exactly equal. The important points are that the mean value should not be used if numbers cluster on both ends of a list. The median should be used when numbers in a list vary over a wide range. The mode is chosen if it is important to know what value in a list occurs most often. It is good business practice to compute all three averages.

An alternative to using a list is to classify data according to the numerical value of a particular item. This permits a manager to find out how often each number appears in a list by creating a *frequency distribution*. Family income data from a real estate survey is classified in a frequency distribution and shown in Exhibit 20-7. Here the family income of the survey

RUNNING FASTER AND FALLING BEHIND

Large price increases or inflation have been a serious national problem for over ten years. Politicians have made many attempts to bring inflation under control but with limited success. It is not an easy job since there is no single solution that is acceptable to a majority of people. But people are aware of the problem because they see it every time they make a trip to the grocery store.

Even so, many families are really unaware of just how much inflation has hit their pocketbooks. During the 1970s, median family income more than doubled, rising from $9,867 to $21,023. But due to inflation, family purchasing power rose only $40 since 1970! This means that inflation has put millions of families on an economic treadmill.

Even though people are running faster and falling behind, it is possible for them to do certain things to help survive inflation. One thing is to get more education because it pays off. According to U.S. Department of Commerce statistics, education can boost your income by large amounts. The table below shows how much.

FAMILY HEADS OVER TWENTY-FIVE YEARS OF AGE	MEDIAN FAMILY INCOME IN 1980
College graduate	$32,469
Some college	24,866
High school graduate	21,845
Some high school	16,203
Finished grade school	14,115
Did not finish grade school	10,836

For example, a person who graduates from college is likely to head a family that has about three times more income than a person who did not finish grade school. This conclusion is based on data collected from a large group of people in each category. Education does pay according to the data shown above.

Adapted from *U.S. News & World Report*, August 31, 1981, p. 8.

respondents is tabulated into various incomes brackets. For example, 30.3 percent of the respondents reported a family income between $20,001 to $25,000. The same data can be described graphically by means of a *histogram*, as shown in Exhibit 20–8. The histogram, a helpful way to summarize data, also indicates that the largest number of respondents in any one category of this survey was the $20,001 to $25,000 family income group.

Index Numbers

INDEX NUMBER
A relative measure computed by dividing a series of numbers by one number or a combination of numbers from the series.

Index numbers help managers understand the typical changes in volumes of data. Without index numbers, it would be very difficult or even impossible to learn about changes over time in an economic variable like consumer prices. An **index number** is a relative measure computed by dividing a series of numbers by one number or combination of numbers from the series. For example, a series of index numbers permits you to answer the question, "What has been the change in the cost of housing during the last ten years?"

One of the most frequently used indexes is the Consumer Price Index (CPI), which is published by the Bureau of Labor Statistics. The CPI summarizes changes in retail prices for a large number of consumer goods and services purchased by people. A summary of the numerical values of this

FAMILY INCOME	NUMBER OF RESPONDENTS	PERCENTAGE OF RESPONDENTS
Under $10,000	10	1.6%
$10,000–$15,000	49	7.7
$15,001–$20,000	145	22.8
$20,001–$25,000	193	30.3
$25,001–$30,000	106	16.6
$30,001–$35,000	87	12.9
$35,001–$40,000	34	5.3
Over $40,000	18	2.8
Total	637	100.0%

EXHIBIT 20-7
Family Income for Real Estate Survey Respondents

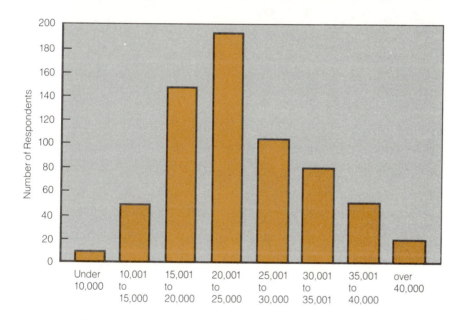

EXHIBIT 20-8
Frequency Distribution for Income Data

index for all goods and services for the years 1967 through 1980 is shown in Exhibit 20–9. The base year for the index is set at 1967. In this base year, the CPI equals 100 percent. From these numbers, you can see that consumer prices rose about 80 percent from 1967 to 1977. In addition, most of the increase occurred after 1973. This illustrates a major advantage of index numbers. Trends up or down over a period of several years are easy to spot by looking at the values of different index numbers.

Other different statistical methods can be used to analyze managerial data, but most of these are more complicated than the basic methods just described. Correlation analysis, regression analysis, time series analysis, and analysis of variance are a few techniques that can help managers understand the relationships that often exist in business and economic data. These statistical methods are best explained in a course devoted to the study of statistics.

Other Statistical Methods

EXHIBIT 20-9
United States Consumer Price Index

YEAR	CPI
1967	100.0%
1968	104.2
1969	109.8
1970	116.3
1971	121.3
1972	125.3
1973	133.1
1974	147.7
1975	161.2
1976	170.5
1977	177.1
1978	195.3
1979	217.4
1980	245.7

Adapted from selected issues of
the *Survey of Current Business*,
published monthly by United
States Department of Commerce.

SUMMARY

- Management data can come from sources both inside and outside the business. Internal data are obtained from company records. External data come from sources other than the business.
- The two major types of external data are original data and secondary data. Original data are normally collected for specific problems. Secondary data come from different published sources.
- The three ways to collect sample survey data are mail surveys, personal interviews, and telephone interviews.
- Statistics uses various techniques to summarize information into numbers that are representative of large amounts of data.
- Two basic ways to present data to managers are by visual analysis and averages.
- Three important averages are mean, median, and mode.
- Index numbers are used to show average changes over time in some economic or business variable like the consumer price index.

ISSUES TO CONSIDER AND ANALYZE

1. Explain why secondary data sources should always be checked before making a decision to collect original data.
2. Suppose it is necessary to collect impressions of the images of five banks from six hundred people in a local market within two weeks. What survey method should be used to collect the opinions of the public? Explain your answer.
3. A great value of statistics is that it permits managers to determine what is typical in a set of data. Discuss this statement.
4. Explain the major purpose of using sample surveys to collect managerial data.

5. Why is the mean not always a good measure of typical value for a list of numbers?

6. The following average prices show the cost of buying a home in seven major cities.

San Francisco	$133,900
Los Angeles	120,100
Washington, D.C.	100,900
New York	93,600
Houston	90,200
Minneapolis	82,300
Milwaukee	78,200

a. Compute the mean sales price.
b. What is the median value of sales price?
c. What is the mode?

7. What is the main reason for using index numbers to analyze economic data?

8. These pie charts summarize the Honsju Company's total business activity. Complete the following calculations.

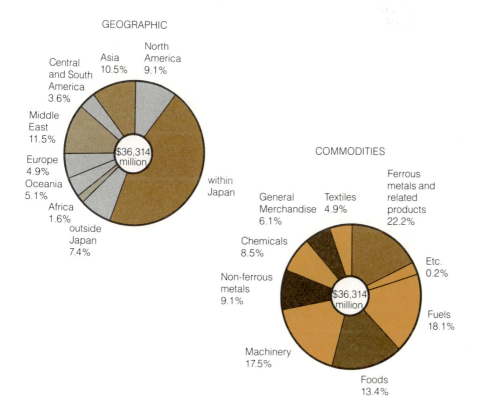

GEOGRAPHIC

Central and South America 3.6%
Asia 10.5%
North America 9.1%
Middle East 11.5%
Europe 4.9%
Oceania 5.1%
Africa 1.6%
$36,314 million
within Japan
outside Japan 7.4%

COMMODITIES

General Merchandise 6.1%
Textiles 4.9%
Ferrous metals and related products 22.2%
Chemicals 8.5%
Etc. 0.2%
Non-ferrous metals 9.1%
$36,314 million
Fuels 18.1%
Machinery 17.5%
Foods 13.4%

a. What percent of sales occurred within Japan?
b. Compute the dollar value of sales by geographic region.
c. Compute the dollar value of sales by commodity.
d. Prepare data lists for the values computed in b and c on a high-to-low basis.

9. The following data show the residential electric costs for various cities in the United States. The costs are measured in cents per kilowatt-hour.

New York, New York   16.47¢
Honolulu, Hawaii   11.53
Boston, Massachusetts   10.18
San Diego, California   9.33
Oklahoma City,
    Oklahoma   5.21
Columbus, Ohio   6.70
Cincinnati, Ohio   5.21
Dallas, Texas   7.27

a. What is the mode value for this list of costs?
b. What is the mean value for the costs?
c. What percent of the average cost is the cost of electricity in Cincinnati?

10. Look at the statistics shown in Exhibit 20–7 and answer the following questions.
a. How many families were included in the sample survey?
b. What income bracket had the largest number of families? What percentage of the total sample does this bracket represent?
c. What percentage of the families made between $10,000 and $25,000 per year.

CASE FOR ANALYSIS   OSHMAN'S SPORTING GOODS

The president of Oshman's Sporting Goods, Al Lubetkin, is planning to expand the company into several new markets located in the Sun Belt. The company currently operates stores in Houston, Dallas, Northern California, Los Angeles, and San Diego. Lubetkin has identified several factors that influence the purchasing of sporting goods equipment. Three of the most important are (1) life style, (2) population, and (3) household income.

No data exist on life-style patterns. However, Lubetkin believes that Americans will continue to place an increasing importance on physical fitness, devoting much of their leisure time to exercise and sporting activities. Population growth is a significant factor because it means more people will be available to purchase sporting goods and participate in leisure activities. Rising family income is critical because families with higher incomes spend more on items like sporting goods. Lubetkin has collected statistics on disposable personal income (DPI), population, and retail sales for several Sun Belt cities summarized below. DPI is the amount of income households have to spend on goods and services. Based on these data, he has decided to expand into the Miami, Tampa, and San Antonio markets by 1986.

METRO AREA	DPI		RETAIL SALES		POPULATION	
	Household	% Change	Household	% Change	Total	% Change
1. Houston	$34,104	54.5%	$22,428	54.1%	3,271.0	14.7%
2. Dallas–Ft. Worth	31,746	49.2	16,434	29.1	2,867.1	5.8
3. San Francisco–Oakland–San Jose	32,373	45.2	15,061	38.6	4,958.5	4.0
4. Atlanta	30,253	46.1	16,966	38.6	2,058.1	9.8
5. San Antonio	28,535	53.3	15,559	25.1	1,065.9	4.4
6. Birmingham	27,606	54.6	18,991	52.3	866.0	5.5
7. Miami–Ft. Lauderdale	27,505	47.4	16,710	34.3	2,725.7	14.5
8. Phoenix	27,317	44.3	17,853	54.1	1,550.9	15.7
9. Los Angeles–Long Beach–Anaheim	27,285	37.9	14,940	36.1	11,525.0	6.1
10. San Diego	24,448	33.2	14,442	33.0	1,965.8	10.3
11. Tampa–St. Petersburg	22,082	49.5	14,689	42.4	1,649.6	14.6
Total United States	27,168	45.1	14,967	40.8	230,991.2	5.1

Source: Sales and Marketing Management Survey of Buying Power, Part II, 1979.
Base year for percent change is 1978.

EXHIBIT 20-10   1983 Projections

QUESTIONS

1. Explain why you think Lubetkin considered life style to be an important factor influencing the purchase of sporting goods equipment.
2. Review the table to see if you agree with the selection of expansion cities. If you disagree, explain why.

CHAPTER 21

COMPUTERS AND MANAGEMENT INFORMATION SYSTEMS

LEARNING OBJECTIVES

After studying this chapter, you should be able to:

Explain the importance of computers in the operation of different types of organizations.

Discuss the historical development of computers.

Describe the fundamental components of digital computers.

Describe how a simple computer program is written.

Explain the general concept of a management information system.

Discuss some of the issues facing the development of computers in the future.

KEY TERMS

Computer
Input device
Output device
Central processing unit
Primary storage unit
Secondary storage unit
Control unit
Arithmetic/logic unit
Computer hardware
Computer software
Computer program
Flowchart
Management information system

KATHY'S KRANES CORPORATION

One of the greatest sources of new jobs, economic growth, and new technology in the United States is the number of small businesses; yet the majority of these small businesses fail each year. There are several reasons for these failures, and one is the inability of many small businesses to adapt big business know-how to their operations.

Kathy Anderson is the president of Kathy's Kranes Corporation in St. Paul, Minnesota. Kathy realized that to be profitable she would have to use big business expertise, keep operating costs and overhead low, and increase sales. In 1979, Kathy's Kranes moved into the Control Data Business and Technology Center in St. Paul. This important relocation made big business resources and support services available on a small business budget. For example, Kathy's Kranes developed a strategic business plan, improved its bank credit line, and gained access to a large computer. The computer is used by the company to manage many types of business records including finance, personnel, inventory, and sales. Kathy is even using this big business support system to develop some international business opportunities.

Computers can be used to help make a business grow and become more profitable in many ways. These important uses are explained in this chapter along with a discussion of how electronic computers work. In addition to understanding computer uses and advantages, it is important to be aware of the risks businesses face in using computers. Even by today's standards, computer crime and personal privacy abuses are serious problems that managers have to deal with.

Adapted from *Business Week*, August 31, 1981, p. 33.

428

Computers play an increasingly important role in our lives because organizations—businesses, governments, hospitals, and universities—use computers to keep accurate and timely records of their activities. Keeping these records requires the storage, retrieval, and analysis of large quantities of data, which provide the information managers need to run an organization, plan its future, and provide governments with the information required by law.

Managers have always found it necessary to maintain records, but today they are faced with ballooning information requirements. As a matter of survival, it has become necessary to develop better and more accurate ways to store, retrieve, and analyze this information. The development and practical use of computers provided a solution to this problem. As a potential manager, it is important that you gain a basic understanding of computers.

THE DEVELOPMENT OF COMPUTERS

The word **computer** can be applied to any machine or device that has the ability to calculate (add, subtract, multiply, and divide). In modern usage, the word is often used to refer specifically to an electronic computer. However, many types of "computers" were developed long before electronic computers were.

COMPUTER
Any machine or device that has the ability to add, subtract, multiply, and divide.

Perhaps the first computer was the abacus, a device developed to solve arithmetic problems over three thousand years ago by the Chinese. The abacus, a frame containing many wooden beads, is still used in certain parts of the world, especially in Asian nations. The first mechanical calculating machine to perform all the basic arithmetic operations was developed by Gottfried Leibniz in 1694 in Germany.

Modern Developments

The general concepts of modern computers were developed by Charles Babbage, an English mathematician from Cambridge University. Babbage's computer, called the difference engine or analytical engine, was conceived around 1835. The analytical engine contained all the essential features of a modern computer. Unfortunately, Babbage's analytical engine was not a success because it exceeded the available technological capabilities of the time. There was as yet no effective way to produce all the parts needed to make the thing work as a computer does today, yet Babbage's idea was conceptually close to today's machines.

The first commercial computer designed in the United States was called UNIVAC 1 and was installed at the Bureau of the Census in the early 1950s. The first business application of the computer was made in 1954 at the General Electric Appliance Park in Louisville, Kentucky. This marked the point at which commercial use of computers became a reality.

Computer Generations

Computers developments since UNIVAC 1 have been so dramatic that growth in the computer industry is classified in generations. The first generation, consisting of computers built in the 1950s, was called the "gee whiz" era. This first generation of computers did not save money but became the symbol of a progressive company.

Second-generation computers, developed around 1958, made about ten times as many calculations per second as first-generation machines could. This generation has been called the "paper pushers." The increase in speed was the direct result of using solid-state (transistor) circuits in the computers. Second-generation computers were also smaller and more reliable because transistors were used. Transistors were not only smaller but also had a longer life expectancy than the vacuum tubes previously used.

In 1966, the third generation of computers was introduced with the delivery of the IBM System/360. Because people could communicate with these computers, this was called the "generation of communicators." These third-generation computers, which could make over a million calculations per second, had even smaller electronic circuits and were more reliable. Their electronic circuits were put on small silicon chips.

The fourth generation of computers appeared in the United States in 1974. They have been called the "information custodians" because they store billions of bits of business information that can be recalled instantly to help managers operate their businesses. This was an important factor in Kathy Anderson's decision to move her business into the Control Data Business and Technology Center. Companies that helped pioneer the use of fourth-generation computers include Zayre (retailing), Weyerhaeuser (wood products), and the Department of Defense (government).

On the Job Revisited

There is as yet no fifth generation of computers; no new and radical breakthrough in computer technology has been accomplished that warrants the phrase. Even so, major refinements and significant improvements in computer technology have taken place in recent years. For example, the introduction of minicomputers in the 1970s opened up the computer field to many smaller organizations that could not previously afford standard computers. It is likely that the fifth generation of computers will not appear until the mid 1980s. Looking more into the future, managers might be using computers that do not run on electricity. Instead, optical computers could operate from light waves making the present-day electronic computers obsolete by the year 2000.

HOW COMPUTERS WORK

No matter how large or small computer installations are, they operate in much the same way. They all have the same basic components, employ logic, and communicate with people through special codes.

Computer Components

Physically, computers can be divided into six basic components: (1) input device, (2) output device, (3) primary storage unit, (4) secondary storage unit, (5) control unit, and (6) arithmetic/logic unit. The relationship among these six components is shown in Exhibit 21–1. To help you to understand this relationship, the figure compares a computer to a stereo system. Babbage had introduced these same components in the analytical engine in 1835.

The input device. To use a computer for data processing, data must be entered into the machine. This means that information contained on a business document like a purchase order must be put in a form that can be used to convert the information into electronic impulses that the

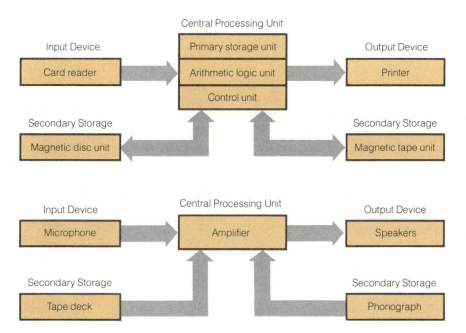

EXHIBIT 21–1
Computers and Management
Information Systems

machine recognizes. Punched cards, on-line typewriters, magnetic tapes, drums, or terminals with television screens are often used for this purpose. An example of a punched card is shown in Exhibit 21-2. Any information on punched cards is transformed into electronic impulses by a card reader (**input device**), shown in Exhibit 21-1, and is placed in a computer storage unit.

The output device. The opposite function is performed by an **output device**, which converts electronic impulses into a form that can be

INPUT DEVICE
A computer component that transforms information into electrical impulses.

OUTPUT DEVICE
A computer component that converts electronic impulses into a form that can be used by people.

EXHIBIT 21–2
Eighty-Column Computer Card

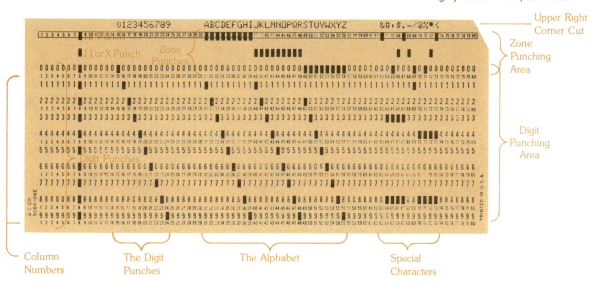

COMPUTER CRIME

Computer technology is often considered the great hope of American business. This is because computers can be used to file large amounts of management information, schedule production runs, prepare payroll checks, and store different types of customer information. Computer technology is generally seen as a way businesses can operate more efficiently in the 1980s.

Future advances in computer technology are likely to be made in quantum leaps. While progress has many potential benefits, new advances also dramatically increase the opportunities for computer crime. More people will have access to business computers, and more people will know how to use computers. Many of these people will be able to outwit computer security safeguards, making computer crime big business.

There are currently many examples of dramatic computer-assisted crime. In 1981, an officer at Wells Fargo Bank, America's eleventh largest, allegedly took $21.3 million. He did this by making fake deposits at one branch using electronic computer transfers. The bank's *own* interbank account settlement program was used to make the internal transfers. For over two years this computer crime scheme went undetected because bogus deposits were "created" by the computer to cover the illegal withdrawals.

There is no apparent easy way to prevent computer crimes, but businesses are trying hard. Methods presently being used include software programs restricting computer access, scrambling data transmissions, and conducting more internal and customer account audits. By 1985, annual expenditures on computer security and crime prevention alone are projected to exceed $500 million. Preventing computer crime, itself, has already become a growth industry.

Adapted from *Business Week*, April 20, 1981, p. 8B.

---

understood and used by operators and managers in their daily work. Output media include on-line typewriters, punched cards, on-line display units, paper printers, or magnetic tape, disks, or drums. A printer is also shown in Exhibit 21-1.

CENTRAL PROCESSING UNIT (CPU)
The computer's brain, divided into a storage unit, control unit, and arithmetic/logic unit.

Storage units. The link between the input and output devices is called the **central processing unit**, or CPU. The CPU serves as the "brain" of the computer. Note in Exhibit 21-1 that the CPU is divided into a storage unit, a control unit, and an arithmetic/logic unit.

The primary storage unit. This does exactly what the name suggests. That is, the **primary storage unit** stores input and output data along with the set of instructions to be executed by the computer. The information is stored internally as long as it is needed and can be recalled at any time by the control unit. In addition, information in the storage unit can be fed through the output device and punched onto cards, printed on paper, or shown on a video display unit.

Secondary storage units. Many business problems require more information than the primary storage unit is capable of storing. **Secondary storage units** can be added to the computer to provide the extra storage capacity. These secondary storage units normally consist of either magnetic tapes or magnetic disk units (See Exhibit 21–1.)

A computer's speed for storing and recalling data is difficult to comprehend. The time gap between when data are requested and when they are available can be as short as one nanosecond (one-billionth of a second). There are as many nanoseconds in a second as there are seconds in thirty years. Some computer operations are performed in picoseconds (one-trillionth of a second). This speed is precisely the characteristic that permits computers to process enormous quantities of data quickly and accurately.

The control unit. Although many people believe that computers think, they do not. Their job is simply to follow instructions and perform routine tasks according to a set of specific commands. The **control unit** gives a computer this important capability. One way to think of the control unit is to consider it the link between people and the machine. In addition, the control unit serves as the nerve center for the internal operations of the computer. As soon as one specific instruction is finished, the control unit searches for the next instruction.

CONTROL UNIT
A computer component that serves as the computer's nerve center.

The arithmetic/logic unit. Data processing requires arithmetic operations and simple decision making. To accomplish these tasks, computers are equipped with an *arithmetic/logic unit*. The arithmetic operations are addition, subtraction, multiplication, and division. To do more advanced mathematics with a computer, these basic operations are merely expanded. The logic operations performed by a computer include comparing two numbers to determine whether one is larger or if one is negative, zero, or positive. In short, the **arithmetic/logic unit** has the capability to compare and rearrange data and to make simple decisions.

ARITHMETIC/LOGIC UNIT
A computer component that has the ability to compare, rearrange, and manipulate data to make simple decisions.

The components described above are electronic and mechanical and are called **computer hardware**. For example, the CPU consists almost entirely of transistors, diodes, and resistors. Input and output devices have both electronic and mechanical elements.

An equally important aspect of computers is the software package. **Computer software packages** are computer programs designed to make computers serviceable to businesses. They are normally available from the manufacturer, and they can accomplish tasks such as scheduling jobs, sorting computer records, and organizing and maintaining internal files.

A **computer program** consists of a series of logical statements or instructions that tell the computer how a job must be done. These logical instructions are read into the CPU and stored in the storage unit, where they remain until the control unit calls them up for a computational job. People write computer programs, their instructions to the machine, in a special language that computers can understand.

To repeat and emphasize: computer programs must contain a series of logical statements. Therefore, people writing computer programs often draw the required program steps in their proper sequence. The **flowchart** that results is a way to visually describe, by means of symbols and lines that connect, the structure and general sequence of operations in a computer program. An example of a flowchart appears in Exhibit 21-3. This particular

Computer Programming

COMPUTER HARDWARE
The electronic and mechanical elements of a computer used to read, store, process, and provide data.

COMPUTER SOFTWARE
Computer programs supplied by a manufacturer to accomplish such tasks as scheduling jobs through the machine, sorting computer records, and organizing and maintaining internal computer files.

COMPUTER PROGRAM
A series of detailed instructions and logical statements that explain how a specific job must be performed.

FLOWCHART
A device for visually describing, by symbols and interconnecting lines, the operational structure and sequence of a computer program.

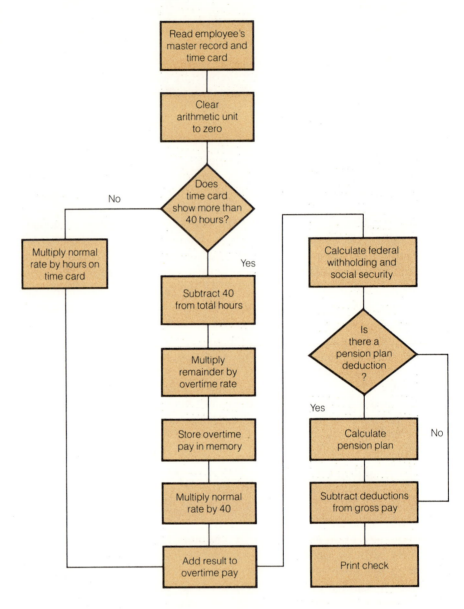

flowchart provides a detailed set of logical instructions for calculating a person's pay and preparing the payroll check.

Computer Languages

People must talk with computers in order to use them, and they can do this by means of special languages that computers can understand. These computer languages are electronic codes. Initially, people had to talk with computers in machine language, a language computers use for internal calculations. Today many of NASA's space shuttle programs are written in machine language because execution time is important. Machine language permits programs to be executed faster, but it is a very difficult language to use. Because of this difficulty, symbolic languages were developed so computers could internally translate instructions into machine language. Two important modern computer languages are Common Business Oriented Language (COBOL) and Formula Translation (FORTRAN).

COBOL was designed to facilitate business data processing in such procedures as cost accounting, inventory control, and payroll jobs. It is a language designed to be used by businesses like Kathy's Kranes Corporation. These types of jobs involve processing large volumes of both input and output data, and COBOL is widely used for this today.

FORTRAN is a scientific computer language. It was first designed to solve scientific and mathematical problems, but FORTRAN has also been used for solving business, economic, and statistical problems. Widely used, it is suitable for any type of problem that can be expressed in mathematical formulas or arithmetic terms. This language is easy to learn and can be used by people with limited understanding of how computers work.

On the Job Revisited

A Sample Business Problem

To understand the usefulness of computer programming, consider the following example. A common problem that banks face is computing the interest charges for business loans. This problem can be easily solved with a computer using a program written in FORTRAN.

The basic mathematical formula for computing interest charges on commercial loans is:

$$I = P \times R \times T$$

I is the dollar amount of interest, P is the dollar amount loaned (or principal), R is the interest rate, and T is the time of the loan (usually in years). Once a FORTRAN program has been written to solve this problem, it can be used to calculate the interest on any number of commercial loans.

Suppose Minnesota NorthSide Bank has made a new construction equipment loan of $100,000 to Kathy's Kranes Corporation. The loan is made at an annual rate of 18 percent for a period of 270 days. This means that the following values must be assigned to the variables in the interest equation:

On the Job Revisited

P = $100,000
R = .18
T = 270 days

The programming objective is to write a computer program that will compute the dollar value of I, or interest, for this loan.

The first step in using a computer is to read the input data and program into the storage unit. Thus, the values of the variables P, R, and T are read into the computer.

P = 100,000
R = .18
T = .75

In this problem, the length of a year is set at 360 days, so T = 0.75 or 270/360.

The program for the actual computation appears in Exhibit 21-4. The three-digit numbers identify specific cards in this computer program. Card

EXHIBIT 21–4
Loan Interest Program

```
C          Program to compute loan interest charge
100        Read (1, 101) P,R,T
101        Format (F6.0, 3X, F3.3, 3X, F2.2)
102        I = P * R * T
103        Write (3,104) I
104        Format (5X, F10.2)
105        Stop
106        End
```

100 is a command to read the values for P, R, and T. The next card, numbered 101, contains the format in which the input data values are punched onto the data card. This means the value for P is punched in the first six columns, as card 101 indicates. The next three columns are blank, indicated by the 3X, and the value of R is punched in columns 10 to 12, indicated by the F3.3. 3X means skip three more columns; then F2.2 indicates columns 16–17 pointed off two decimal places, .75. Card 102 contains the interest equation I = P * R * T, where the FORTRAN symbol * means to multiply. This card tells the computer how to compute the interest charge for the loan. Once the interest calculation is made, it must be printed, so the "write" card, numbered 103, is included in the program. The printed answer (output) is $13,500. Thus, at the end of 270 days, Kathy's Kranes Corporation will owe a total of $113,500 to Minnesota NorthSide Bank. This is the amount of $100,000 principal plus the interest charge. Cards 105 (Stop) and 106 (End) tell the computer that its job is completed. The first card, denoted with a C, is called a comment card and only identifies the program by name.

This computer program is written in FORTRAN language. There are other ways to write the program and obtain the same output—some more efficient. This example was only to illustrate how computers can be used to solve practical business problems. Computer programs become most valuable to businesses when the problem must be solved repeatedly. But solving business problems with a computer always requires an understanding of the problem and accurate information (input). What you get out of a computer is only as good as what you put in!

MANAGEMENT INFORMATION SYSTEMS

Certain information is often critical to the daily operation and long-run survival of business. That is why businesses must be able to store, recall, and analyze information. The W. T. Grant Company, formerly a nationwide retailing chain, is a case in point. Grant failed because important decisions were made with little or poor-quality information. Other factors—like changing the merchandising policy to include expensive consumer durable goods—added to Grant's bankruptcy. But a lack of timely and useful market and financial information was an important factor contributing to this multimillion dollar failure.

COMPUTER SOFTWARE'S MILLION SELLER

The key to unlocking the power of any computer is to have good software—and personal computers are no exception. The three types of computer software programs used by any machine are operating systems (tell how the machine functions), languages (tell the machine what to do), and application programs (direct the performance of complex jobs). The people who write software programs are like song writers in that their work can become a best seller.

Most of the computer software hits are written by two people rather than individuals. Daniel Bricklin and Robert Frankston teamed up to write a software program called VisiCalc. The need for the program occurred to Bricklin when he was a student at the Harvard Business School. Each time he made a mistake on his personal calculator, he would have an entire series of numbers wrong and have to start the calculation again. He says the need for a computer program like VisiCalc that would avoid this problem was the most important thing he learned at Harvard.

In 1978 Frankston and Bricklin pooled $16,000 to start a business called Software Arts. Their product, VisiCalc, has been compared to an automated pencil, paper, and calculator. The software package has sold over one hundred thousand copies, making it the top seller among applications programs. Software Arts is a growing business that now employs over thirty people with sales exceeding $2 million a year. Bricklin and Frankston are not resting on their past successes either. They are now creating a new variation of VisiCalc and also writing completely new software programs.

Adapted from *Fortune*, June 29, 1981, p. 86.

People have a limited capacity to store and accurately recall large volumes of information, but computers can do this at rapid speeds over extended periods of time. On the other hand, computers cannot learn by trial and error nor can they innovate and adapt to special situations. Thinking, reasoning, and creating are human processes that computers cannot yet perform.

By combining the best capacities of people and computers, managers can develop the complete information systems they so vitally need. This type of system is called a **management information system** (MIS). An MIS is what Kathy Anderson needed as a support system in her business as she attempted to reduce overhead and increase profits. An MIS can be defined as a person-machine system that produces timely and useful information that contributes to an organization's overall operation and efficient management. Providing more usable information for management is the key contribution of any MIS. The key words are *planned, timely*, and *useful*. If an MIS provides only untimely and irrelevant information, then it is of no use to management.

MANAGEMENT INFORMATION SYSTEM (MIS)
A planned combination of human and computer resources that produces timely and useful information for the efficient management of an organization.

On the Job Revisited

Many different types of MIS have been designed for specific purposes. Examples include:

Types of MIS

437

■ *Inventory management.* Helps to place orders, maintain the proper types of parts in inventory, and reorders parts automatically.
■ *Manufacturing management.* Focuses on determining the types of components and subassemblies that are needed to produce a product.
■ *Personnel management.* Aids in payroll operations, personnel evaluations, and organizational inventories of personnel skills.
■ *Financial management.* Focuses on cash flow management, budgeting, and capital investment analysis.

Other types of MIS are used by educational institutions (student records), law enforcement agencies (records of stolen autos and arrest warrants), governments (income tax files), and transit authorities (numbers of passengers and mileage totals).

An Application of an MIS

Computers and MIS have been applied in several different types of business organizations. In one case, an MIS was designed for the transit system in Cincinnati. The broad components of the MIS are shown in Exhibit 21-5. The exhibit shows the kinds of information the MIS provides: normal operations, status of new transit programs, and the status of the budget and external funding programs (grants). These different elements, considered together, provide the transit authority management with timely and comprehensive information regarding their entire system.

The actual data collection (input) and management information (output) systems for the Cincinnati transit system are very complex and detailed. There are four types of input data collected for this MIS: data on vehicle servicing, job data, inventory control data, and direct labor data. Each type of datum requires the collection of minute details from each source of input.

The output data for this transit MIS include reports prepared for daily, weekly, monthly, quarterly, and yearly time periods. This is what timely information means. Without computers, it would be impossible to process this volume of input data so regularly. If the reports had to be prepared manually, they would not be timely and so would be of limited value to management. However, control over computer-developed reports is vital to any information system. Without proper control, managers can become swamped with so much information that they cannot use it effectively.

OTHER COMPUTER APPLICATIONS

Many other valuable computer applications are not as detailed as an MIS. Instead of collecting and analyzing data and preparing reports, these applications are more job related.

Ticket Selling

In many cities, tickets to sports and cultural events can be purchased at remote ticket locations in a department store or sporting goods store. This is accomplished by putting remote terminals in stores that can be used to access the main computer memory bank. This means the store computer is in almost instant communication with the main computer. The advantage of remote computer ticket selling is that the best available tickets to an event can be purchased at any moment locally. These tickets are immediately issued by any selling facility.

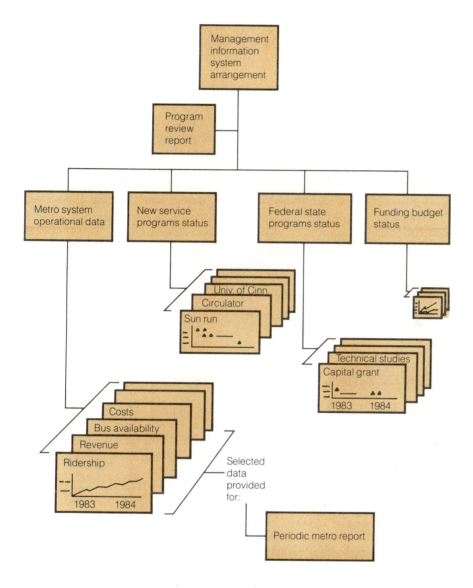

EXHIBIT 21–5
Basic Components of a Transit Management Information System

System developed by Vogt, Sage and Pflum Consultants, Cincinnati, Ohio.

Stock Markets

Computers are used by the New York Stock Exchange (NYSE) to improve communication among stockbrokers, floor traders, and stock buyers. Information concerning buy and sell orders, stock volume, and current sales price is immediately available via a cathode-ray computer terminal (CRT). A CRT is a computer terminal that has a television screen. In addition, the NYSE uses computers to speed up the transfer of ownership on buy and sell orders. This application reduces the volume of paperwork that must be done by people.

Banks

Banks are important computer users. For example, computers are used to maintain current balances on different types of customer accounts. Some banks even prepare comprehensive monthly financial statements on accounts held by each customer. An example of one such financial summary statement is shown in Exhibit 21-6. Note that the customer automatically receives balances on a checking account, passbook savings accounts, certificates of deposit, credit card accounts, and installment and commercial loans.

Banks are expanding their use of computers to include automatic teller machines, which permit a person to complete almost any standard banking transaction twenty-four hours a day. For example, authorized persons can deposit money to checking or savings accounts or make cash withdrawals from the automatic teller. In addition, they can pay certain types of bills at automatic teller machines.

Production

Computer assisted machinery can be used to increase the productive capacity and productivity in manufacturing plants. Often a machine that is controlled by a computer can increase its output three to four times. In addition, one machinist can run two machines at the same time using a computer. For example, a conventional lathe that turns metal castings for

EXHIBIT 21-6
Bank Financial Summary Statement

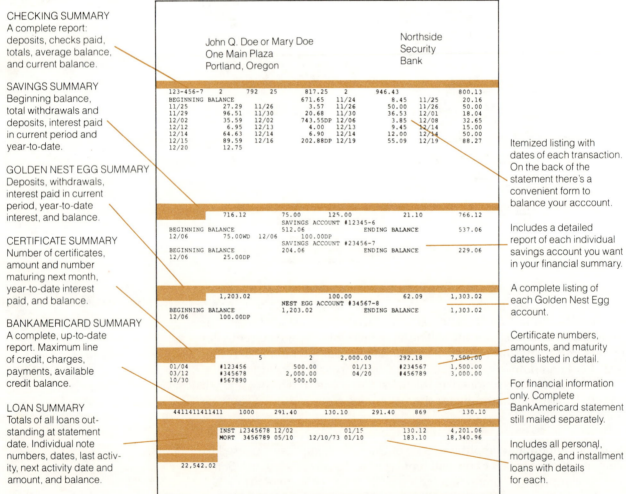

CHECKING SUMMARY
A complete report: deposits, checks paid, totals, average balance, and current balance.

SAVINGS SUMMARY
Beginning balance, total withdrawals and deposits, interest paid in current period and year-to-date.

GOLDEN NEST EGG SUMMARY
Deposits, withdrawals, interest paid in current period, year-to-date interest, and balance.

CERTIFICATE SUMMARY
Number of certificates, amount and number maturing next month, year-to-date interest paid, and balance.

BANKAMERICARD SUMMARY
A complete, up-to-date report. Maximum line of credit, charges, payments, available credit balance.

LOAN SUMMARY
Totals of all loans outstanding at statement date. Individual note numbers, dates, last activity, next activity date and amount, and balance.

Itemized listing with dates of each transaction. On the back of the statement there's a convenient form to balance your account.

Includes a detailed report of each individual savings account you want in your financial summary.

A complete listing of each Golden Nest Egg account.

Certificate numbers, amounts, and maturity dates listed in detail.

For financial information only. Complete BankAmericard statement still mailed separately.

Includes all personal, mortgage, and installment loans with details for each.

pumps can turn one part at a time and requires a machinist to operate it. A computer-controlled lathe can turn four castings at once, and one machinist can operate two lathes. In this type of application, computers can significantly increase the productivity of the lathe operator.

Airlines do not make money when their planes are on the ground. Normal maintenance, which often takes two or three weeks, is costly in terms of both labor charges and lost revenues. Republic Airlines developed a computer system called SCEPTRE that helps company management schedule maintenance so efficiently that most complete airplane overhauls have been eliminated. The SCEPTRE system keeps a running file on all items that affect the maintenance of the airplane fleet. Small overhauls are done once every four or five days, and a plane is normally back in service the next day. Furthermore, these minioverhauls are done after 1 A.M., when few flights are scheduled. Using the computer, Republic has eliminated much unnecessary airplane servicing.

Airlines

Computers are used in many other ways. For example, medical practitioners use computers to help analyze complicated diseases and monitor critically ill patients. At the University of Wisconsin's Center for Health Sciences, people have been examined by a computer that "talks" to them. This computer carries on a question-and-answer conversation through a video tape display. The machine does not diagnose any medical problems, but after analyzing the patient's responses, the computer calculates the odds for good health and long life. It also tells the person how to improve the odds of a long life, thereby contributing to preventative medicine.

Medical Science

There are other computer applications as well, but these listed show the many advantages computers offer to managers. However, computers do have some limitations.

Computers can't do everything—at least not everything some people expect them to do. They can't think; they must be instructed or programmed. Also some jobs are done so infrequently or are so complex that they may be too expensive or too difficult to program. In such cases, it could be less costly to have people do the work. From a practical viewpoint, computers are limited to standard or repetitive jobs. Computers have limited potential for organizations if a specific program must be written each time the computer is used to do a job.

PRACTICAL LIMITATIONS OF COMPUTERS

Another limitation of computers is obsolescence. Often an entire computer system becomes obsolete when a faster and better machine is developed and sold. This was a problem in the 1950s and 1960s when complete computer systems cost millions of dollars. Today, there is a trend to replace some large computer systems with smaller, less expensive and more efficient minicomputers or to lease large computers rather than sell them. Even so, obsolescence remains a potential problem because improved computer hardware is introduced every year. But a computer only becomes obsolete to a business when it can no longer adequately meet the company's needs. A company does not have to buy every new computer that comes out.

Another limitation is that computers frequently do not accomplish all that managers expect of them, and then managers become disenchanted with computers. This problem probably stems from two things. First, managers do not always take the time to become informed about the capabilities and practical limitations of specific computers. Second, salespeople may oversell the capabilities of a computer.

Although a computer has certain limitations, it is a powerful management tool. With increasing technological development and continuing human creativity, the future of computers is open ended. In fact, advances in computer applications during the next ten years will probably exceed the advances made during the past forty years.

COMPUTERS AND THE FUTURE

Future developments in the computer field will probably come in two areas. First, people will find better ways to use existing computers. Second, people will find new computer applications, or uses, which will require the development of new and better computer systems.

The development of new computer applications is limited only by human imagination. As long as individuals have broad and searching minds, new applications will continue to be discovered. The key to developing new computer applications is people's ability to think and be creative.

It's hard to predict how computers will develop. The present trend toward smaller, faster, and less expensive computers will probably continue. Storage capability will become larger, faster, and less expensive. Some new small computers might be able to store over eight billion pieces of information; this approaches the capacity of the human brain for storage. In addition, the speed of input and output information will probably grow even faster.

Computer technology can advance very rapidly. In the 1970s, Intel, a computer manufacturer, developed a complete central processing unit (CPU) on a small silicon chip (¾ by ¼ inch), something that would have seemed impossible only a few years earlier. Developments in the field of microelectronics made this miniaturization possible.

From all indications, the future of computers is unlimited, and projections are that over 1.4 million businesses will be buying computer services and software programs by 1989. Data communications in the next few years will likely be done by ultraspeed computers using lasers and light-wave guides. Systems like these can transmit data about six hundred times faster than present systems can.

COMPUTERS AND PERSONAL PRIVACY

We in the United States believe that an individual's right to privacy is basic to our form of government, and some people regard this right as the cornerstone of our individual freedom. No wonder people object when this right is violated or threatened.

1. **Civil Service:** 14 data systems with 103 million records, mostly dealing with government employees or applicants for government jobs.
2. **Department of Commerce:** 95 data systems with 447 million records, primarily Census Bureau data but including files on minority businesspersons, merchant marine, and others.
3. **Defense Department:** 2,219 data systems with 321 million records pertaining to service personnel and persons investigated for such things as employment, security, or criminal activity.
4. **Department of Health and Human Resources:** 693 data systems with 1.3 billion personal records including marital, financial, health, and other information of recipients of Social Security, social services, Medicaid, Medicare, and welfare benefits.
5. **Justice Department:** 175 data systems with 181 million records including information on criminals and criminal suspects, aliens, persons linked to organized crime, securities-laws violators, and "individuals who relate in any manner to official FBI investigations."
6. **Treasury Department:** 910 data systems with 853 million records that include files on taxpayers, foreign travelers, persons deemed by the Secret Service to be potentially harmful to the president, and dealers in alcohol, firearms, and explosives.

EXHIBIT 21-7
Selected Records Maintained by Government Agencies

A current point of contention is the government's right to collect, store, and use information about people. The extent to which government agencies already maintain files on people is staggering. In the early 1980s, the federal government used over eleven thousand computers to maintain files. A list of some agencies and the types of files each maintains is shown in Exhibit 21-7. The list makes it clear why some people believe that individual privacy can be threatened by computers.

But other groups of people believe that governments must maintain information files on citizens. These groups reason that government planning, if it is to be effective, requires substantial quantities of detailed information. There is no doubt that a government has to maintain some records on its citizens, but how far should the government be permitted to go?

How can we be protected from abuse by computer information files? There is no easy, single answer to this question. We must depend on the good judgment of those who manage computer information files. But this is, in itself, insufficient, so Congress has enacted several laws that specifically address the issue of an individual's right to privacy. These laws include the Fair Credit Reporting Act, Federal Privacy Act, and Family Education Rights and Privacy Act. Even with laws, a person's rights can be abused. Consequently, governments and businesses should be careful about who has access to personal information files. On the other hand, too many restrictions on access to these data could eliminate the potential managerial benefits of accurate information.

SUMMARY

- A computer is any machine or device that can be used to add, subtract, multiply, and divide.
- The first business use of computers was made by General Electric in 1954.
- There are six basic components in a computer: input device, output device, primary storage unit, arithmetic/logic unit, control unit, and secondary storage unit.
- A computer program is a series of logical statements that tells a computer how to do a job.
- Flowcharts are used by programmers to visually describe how a computer program works.
- The two most frequently used computer languages are FORTRAN and COBOL.
- Management information systems are used by business to develop timely, planned, and useful information.
- Computers have limitations that must be recognized. They cannot think, do not work well on many special jobs due to cost considerations, and can become obsolete.
- Even though computers can help managers run businesses more efficiently, safeguards must exist that protect individuals from abuses.
- The government has passed several laws which help to ensure that a person's personal privacy is not violated.

ISSUES TO ANALYZE AND CONSIDER

1. Using Exhibit 21–1, explain how the basic parts of a computer work and how they tie together.
2. Describe the purpose of computer programs. Make a list of five jobs that can be easily done on a computer.
3. What is the purpose of drawing flowcharts for jobs before the computer program is written?
4. Select an industry and develop a brief report explaining how businesses use computers to make day-to-day operations more efficient.
5. Draw a simple flowchart that describes how a student might do a job during a routine day on campus.
6. Management information systems (MIS) are able to store, recall, and analyze large volumes of data. Explain why the quality of data is so important to the practical use of an MIS.
7. List some important factors that can directly affect the quality of data that are put into an MIS.
8. Select a local student organization in your university and develop a list of the major parts of an MIS that could be used by the organization. Now link the parts together in a chart.
9. What are five types of MIS that organizations use? Be sure to explain the purpose of each system.
10. What is the purpose of computer software programs?

TURMOIL IN PERSONAL COMPUTERS

North Star Computers (NSC) is an established company in the personal computer industry. In 1982, total industry sales were around the $2 billion level and climbing rapidly. Some forecasts projected personal computer industry sales to reach $7.5 billion by 1985. Personal computers are going to enter and alter almost every phase of our lives in the eighties. It is possible that two or three personal computers could be in every home along with one on every executive's desk by 1990.

Until 1981, most companies making personal computers managed to prosper financially. The market forgave big mistakes simply because business was so good, but this is rapidly changing. For example, big computer companies like IBM have entered the home computer market. They, too, want a piece of the sales action. The coming years will probably produce turmoil in the industry, with many companies failing.

NSC does not intend to be counted among the failures. Its management is developing a business plan to help guide NSC through the projected turmoil. Four market targets of opportunity seem to be open to NSC. These include hobbyists, professionals, consumers, and small businesses. The opinion of the management at NSC is to direct its marketing effort toward small businesses and executives in big companies. The consumer or home market is considered too tough to crack until around the late 1980s; NSC thinks the price of $3,000 per computer is too high to be accepted by a mass home computer market. Home computers require an expensive line of software to perform a variety of functions. Personal computers will have to become even more flexible and less expensive before they are popular with individual owners.

QUESTIONS

1. Select one of the four market targets and explain the reasons why you think it offers growth potential to NSC.
2. Do you agree or disagree with NSC's management regarding the home market for personal computers? Explain.
3. Is the decision of IBM and other big computer companies to enter the personal computer market important to NSC? Explain your answer.

Adapted from Bro Uttal, "The Coming Struggle in Personal Computers," *Fortune*, June 29, 1981, p. 84.

THE USE OF BUSINESS DECISION AIDS

Business and government organizations accumulate large amounts of financial and other information. They need people to collect the data and, more important, to process and analyze the data.

ACCOUNTING

Accountants normally prepare financial information that managers use in making decisions about the operations of a business or government agency. However, accounting information is only one factor in managerial decision making. Other factors, such as outlook for a product, general economic conditions, and the financial position of the business, should also be considered.

There are three primary accounting fields: public accounting, management accounting, and government accounting. Public accountants own their own business or work for accounting firms, and they often specialize in one particular aspect of accounting, such as tax analysis or auditing. For example, an auditor reviews company records to determine whether they are accurate and reflect the true financial condition of the organization. Some public accountants serve as management consultants to businesses. In this capacity, they develop accounting systems to provide important managerial information.

Management accountants, sometimes called industrial accountants, work for businesses that produce goods and services. About 60 percent of all accountants do this type of accounting work. (The remaining 40 percent are split about evenly between government and public accounting.) Management accountants develop and summarize financial information that managers need to make important business decisions. Management accountants do work in cost accounting, internal auditing, taxation, investments, and budgeting. Internal auditing is an area of accounting that is increasingly important to business. Internal auditors become involved with almost every aspect of a business. For example, they monitor corporate financial systems and management control systems to help keep operating costs at a minimum.

Government accountants work for various government agencies in different types of jobs. For example, government accountants can work as auditors (General Accounting Office), investigators (Federal Bureau of Investigation), tax examiners (Internal Revenue Service), and bank examiners.

Accounting offers many opportunities for women. Currently, almost a fourth of all accountants are women. In addition, women are entering the accounting field at a more rapid rate than men, and there is no reason to expect this trend to change in the near future.

It is virtually impossible to find a good accounting job without a bachelor's degree; indeed, most candidates have master's degrees. Candidates with bachelor's or master's degrees can find opportunities in comptroller's offices and auditing divisions, which usually recruit graduates who have majored in accounting, finance, or computer sciences. Employees in the auditing division of a company will, for example, evaluate the reliability of the accounting data being produced by the corporation. They will review and appraise the administrative and accounting controls and verify the assets and liabilities of a corporation. The typical auditor travels almost 40 percent of the time, going from one corporate location to another.

Virtually all auditors and, indeed, all accountants who have high-level jobs are certified; that is, they become certified public accountants, or CPAs. The CPA certificate is issued by states to individuals who have passed an examination prepared by the American Institute of Certified Public Accountants.

Starting salaries for public accountants in large firms usually range between $18,500 and $20,400,

Houston based Continental Airlines, a leader in the airline industry, is currently seeking aggressive, highly professional individuals to work in the following capabilities:

FINANCIAL ANALYST

The successful candidate will be responsible for work performed in the following areas:

- Analysis of proposed capital projects.
- Preparation and maintenance of the corporate capital plan.
- Preparation of the annual profit plan.
- Analysis of monthly operating performance.
- Periodic forecasts of operating results in response to changing economic/competitive conditions.

Individuals preferred will have 1–3 years financial analysis and/or planning experience and an MBA in finance.

SUPERVISOR OF PAYABLE AUDIT

Responsible for audit of other airlines' billings. Some statistical and financial analysis involved. College degree in Business Administration OR equivalent experience in an airline's revenue accounting environment required. 1–3 years supervisory experience preferred.

Texas International offers a competitive salary, excellent benefits, and travel privileges unique to the airline industry. Qualified individuals should submit their resume and salary history, in confidence, to:

Continental Airlines, Inc.

Employment Dept. 10
Atten: Phil Alexander
P.O. Box 12788
Houston, Texas 77017

We are an EEO/AA employer.

PRICE WATERHOUSE

MANAGEMENT COUNSULTING OPPORTUNITIES

Growth of our management advisory services practice creates career opportunities for professional with private sector experience. Experience with a management consulting firm and/or with Energy Industries is highly preferred.

EDP—design and implementation of mangement information systems, feasibility and evaluation studies of a wide range of systems; effectiveness, application security control evaluations; and minicomputers and word processing evaluation and implementation.

FINANCIAL PLANNING AND CONTROL—requirements definition, design and implementation of "state of the art" financial systems, financial modeling and forecasting, cash and financial management; and strategic planning.

Successful candidates will have at least 4 years experience and a record of accomplishment. Advanced degree is desirable. Excellent technical, communication, and entrepreneurial skills required.

FINANCIAL ANALYST

The Robert A. McNeil Corporation, a rapidly growing national Real Estate Investment company, seeks a highly motivated professional to fill the position of Financial Analyst. Responsibilities include: Budgeting; Monthly Variance Analysis; Management Reporting; Cash Flow Analysis; and Profitability Forecasting. Ideal Candidate should possess a degree in Accounting/Finance (MBA preferred), and have at least 2 years experience in Financial Analysis. If you are interested in this position, please send resume and salary history to: The Robert A. McNeil Corporation, ATTN: Personnel, 2855 Campus Drive, San Mateo, CA 94403.

EXHIBIT VI-A　Advertising for Financial Positions

(Continued on p. 448)

FINANCIAL PROFESSIONAL

DOMESTIC OPERATIONS

Financial career opportunity is available to a highly motivated and successful financial/accounting professional. The initial assignment with the Internal Audit Group (approximately 2 years) will provide a solid overview of the company and an excellent springboard for key positions throughout our worldwide organization.

The successful candidate should be a CPA and have a minimum of 3 years experience with a Big 8 firm (or equivalent). MBA highly desirable. Well-developed communication skills are essential. Approximately 25% domestic travel is involved.

We offer an excellent starting salary complemented by a high dollar value benefits package. For immediate consideration, please forward resume with salary requirements to Mr. E. J. Stoll,

MERCK & CO., Inc.
P.O. Box 2000, Rahway, N.J. 07065

An Equal Opportunity Employer M/F

ATARI
A Warner Communications Company

DISCOVER
How Far You Can Go

. . . in our unprecendented growth momentum and newly established Corporate Internal Audit Department at Sunnyvale Corporate Headquarters on the SAN FRANCISCO PENINSULA. ATARI sets the pace in advanced consumer electronics, providing you an environment of excellence for your financial career.

INTERNAL AUDITORS

Key opportunities exist for Audit Managers and Auditors at various experience levels to perform financial and operational audits. Ideal candidates should have 3–10 yrs. of public accounting (Big 8 an asset) and/or internal audit experience in manufacturing (preferably electronics) and CPA or C.I.A. certification. Travel approximately 10–20%, including some International assignments. Salaries commensurate with experience.

Join ATARI as we continue to grow and expand successfully—send resume with salary history to ATARI, Inc., Professional Employment MS/EO, P.O. Box 427, 1349 Moffett Park Dr., Sunnyvale, CA 94086, or call (408) 745-4164 for more information. Equal opportunity employer m/f/h. No agencies, please.

EXHIBIT VI–A Continued

in medium-sized firms the range is $15,800 to $18,800. Internal general auditing and cost accountants in large firms usually start at $14,700 to $17,200 and in medium-sized firms, $14,700 to $16,600. Accountants who become tax preparers are in especially high demand. It is estimated that during this decade, the growth in tax preparers will increase by 65 percent.

DATA PROCESSING

Even though the field of data processing has grown rapidly during the past thirty years, there should be many new career opportunities during the next decade. These career opportunities will be found in a wide variety of business organizations and government agencies. The future is bright because computers can be applied in many different ways to accomplish jobs and to process needed management information. For example, computers are used to

DATA PROCESSING PROFESSIONALS

We are a religiously affiliated multihospital health system with healthcare centers nationwide. Our headquarters are in a pleasant midwestern college town. Our strategic plan has created multiple career opportunities in a rapidly developing environment. Our hardware is currently IBM 4300's and HP 3000's.

ANALYST PROGRAMMERS

Multiple positions for persons with between 2–6 years programming in COBOL. Our project teams are designing and implementing hospital applications utilizing distributed, on-line, data base and communications techniques.

SUPPORT ANALYSTS

Several positions for persons with between 1–4 years experience in hospitals. Expertise in business office or ancilliary areas is desirable. These positions interface between the hospital users and data processing in developing and implementing applications. Travel is extensive.

TECHNICAL ANALYSTS

Positions for persons with 4–8 years experience in systems software and/or research. Experience with DOS/VSE and CICS and/or MPE/IMAGE is desirable. Ability to perform research and feasibility studies is required.

We offer a competitive salary and comprehensive benefit program.

MANAGER DATA PROCESSING CONTROLS
$45,000 + RANGE

$250 million company with best record in its field, and growing rapidly seeks a "mover and shaker" to:

- Build the Data Processing Controls function
- Identify problems, opportunities and solutions
- Insure that proper Data Processing controls are adequate and functioning in existing systems and sufficiently designed for all new systems
- Insure Data Processing resources are effectively and efficiently used
- Support development of management information systems

Position will have high visibility.

Ideal candidate will be skeptical, hard-driving, self-motivated, self-confident and impatient, ready to work hard in a demanding environment, and have the ability to hire and manage similar people. Candidate must be a take-charge person who can work with a team of aggressive professionals. Minimum 8 years accelerated responsibility with in-depth knowledge of Data Processing systems and controls a must.

National company, midwestern headquarters with exceptional cultural and athletic facilities available. Compensation package tailored to attract the exceptional candidate.

EXHIBIT VI-B
Advertisements for Data Processing Positions

control airline schedules, design bridges, control production systems, and set type for newspapers.

Probably the best-known job in data processing is that of computer programmer. A computer programmer develops and writes a set of instructions (a program) that tells a computer what to do. In order to write programs, a person must be skilled in one or more of the important computer languages, such as FORTRAN or COBOL. There are two major types of computer programmers—systems programmers and applications programmers. Systems programmers usually work for computer manufacturers or at large computer installations. Their primary job is to write the programs used to control the internal operation of the computer. Applications programmers, on the other hand, develop computer programs for specific, practical applications. For example, applications programs are written to maintain inventory records in an auto manufacturer's parts depot, to control traffic flow on a city's expressway system, and to assist police in locating stolen autos.

Systems analysis is one of the most varied and interesting jobs in the field of data processing. Systems analysts develop systematic methods to collect and process large volumes of data that are used to solve problems and manage organizations. For example, a systems analyst can design a student-records data base for your college. To design the data base, the analyst would have to

449

meet with the college deans, the registrar, and the admissions officers to determine exactly how student data should be stored and retrieved. In addition, the analyst would have to determine how the data are to be used in managing student records. Because the work of an analyst is varied and complex, most analysts tend to specialize in different types of business, educational, scientific, or government applications. Organizations that employ large numbers of system analysts include banks, colleges, insurance companies, government agencies, and manufacturing firms.

A third career in data processing involves selling computer systems and associated equipment. A person who sells computers is called a customer service representative (CSR). The CSR serves as the direct link between customers and computer manufacturers. Every computer system is designed to meet the special, unique needs of a specific customer. Thus, selling computers requires a high degree of marketing skill and technical knowledge; this is normally provided by a team of specialists. In such cases, it is easy to see the importance of the role the CSR plays in linking the customer to the computer manufacturer's staff. A CSR often spends the majority of his or her time at the customer's computer installation, making sure that needed services are being provided. A person can become a CSR with a college degree in one of several majors, such as engineering, business administration, economics, or liberal arts. The characteristics of a CSR are the abilities to work with other people and provide leadership to a team of business people and a thorough technical knowledge of computer equipment. Most computer manufacturers send their customer service representatives to company schools for extensive training. This initial training often lasts more than a calendar year. Of course, CSRs must continue training throughout their careers to learn about new computer systems and associated products.

In 1983, starting salaries for those entering the data processing field were reported to range between $20,600 and $23,000. The highest paid jobs were in the manufacturing industries, such as automotive, chemicals, electrical machinery, and petroleum products. During this period, the average starting salary was $22,800. Data processing students with graduate degrees averaged a salary of $27,200.

The future of data processing is extremely bright. The Department of Labor projects that during this decade there will be a 148 percent growth rate in data processor mechanics, 108 percent in systems analysts, and 88 percent in computer operators. There will be a 74 percent increase in the amount of computer programmers and an 81 percent increase in the number of business machine servicers.

RESEARCH AND BUSINESS STATISTICS

Businesses now use quantitative methods more than at any other time. Quantitative analysis is used in deciding what products to market, which prices to set, and so on. Scientific decision making based on accurate data is practiced at all levels of production and distribution. Models are built; computer programs are used; and decisions are made on the basis of projections and statistics.

Management science uses research to a large degree, and market researchers are also in demand in many companies. The ideal candidate for a job in research and statistics, particularly with respect to marketing, has a background in statistics and mathematics, as well as economics, psychology, and sociology. Writing skills as well as quantitative skills are important. The future of marketing researchers without quantitative skills is not very bright. It is necessary to be able to handle the increasing sophistication of the tools available.

B. Artin Haig Studios

The world was ready for his supermarket but not for his concept of computerized shopping.

Clarence Saunders took a job as salesperson for a wholesale grocery company in Tennessee when he was nineteen. Immediately, he began boosting his own sales by advising retailers how they could increase their stores' efficiency and sales volume. He helped a group of grocers form a chain called United Stores which he then supplied.

In 1915, he started his own wholesale grocery business with $23,000 in initial capital. In a year, sales grew to $2 million, but his zeal for volume and competitive pricing distracted him from rising costs. Profits didn't materialize. Saunders responded by opening his own store in Memphis with the whimsically unlikely name Piggly Wiggly, alerting customers to a unique shopping experience. They entered through a turnstile, selected

their food from long aisles of merchandise, brought it in baskets to cashiers, and left through another turnstile—the original supermarket. In 1916, Piggly Wiggly was an instant success, and Saunders, in his drive for volume and economies of scale, quickly multiplied it. Within one year, there were twenty-five Piggly Wigglies. In six years, there were more than twelve hundred, half of them owned by Saunder's Piggly Wiggly Stores, Inc., the other half independently operated with a royalty arrangement for the use of Saunder's patented merchandising methods. Even the turnstile was patented. There was no ready source of equipment for such stores, so Saunders set up his own factory.

In the early 1920s, Piggly Wiggly went public, listing its assets at nearly $100 million. But trouble awaited Saunders on the stock market. The failure of several independent stores in the Northeast prompted rumors that Saunder's bubble was about to burst. Specula-

PART SEVEN

BUSINESS: ENVIRONMENT AND CHALLENGES

tors sold Piggly stock short, driving the price down. Saunders retaliated with $10 million borrowed from southern banks, buying more than a hundred thousand shares in one week. When he had gained control of more than 99 percent of Piggly Wiggly stock (the last corner the New York Stock Exchange would see), Saunders demanded delivery from the speculators who had sold short. A mad scramble ensued, Piggly's price shot up, and the Exchange stepped in to restore order. Piggly Wiggly was dropped from the trading list, leaving Saunders with a pile of unsellable stock and staggering bank debts. He lost control of his organization and sank into bankruptcy.

He never fully recovered, but neither did he stop experimenting with new merchandising schemes. A chain of markets with the defiantly preposterous name "Clarence Saunders, Sole Owner of My Name, Stores" failed in the dark of the Depression. A few years later, he pa-

tented another original marketing system implemented in a futuristic supermarket called the Keedoozle Store. Individual samples of all merchandise were displayed in glass cases with a small slot corresponding to each item. Every shopper received a key and inserted it in the slots of the items to be purchased. The key registered each selection on a central adding machine. Finally the shopper inserted the key in a master keyhole, automatically adding up all purchases and summoning the groceries from a stockroom by conveyor belt.

Keedoozle ("key does all") made the Piggly Wiggly markets look like old-time country stores. Saunders claimed his computerized system would reduce thefts and spoilage and accommodate ten times as many shoppers as the average grocery store, with a skeleton staff. But as soon as the first Keedoozle opened in Memphis, in 1937, there were problems. Shoppers wanted to talk to the butcher. They wanted to change

their minds about selections. There were mechanical errors. Sometimes the wrong groceries came down the conveyor belt. While Saunders tried to work out the bugs, more of the store's operations had to be handled manually. Equipment and retooling costs ate up profits. A second store opened in 1938, but both that and the original closed down by the end of 1940. The Keedoozles were still a few years ahead of the computer technology that could have effectively supported them.

Clarence Saunders never abandoned his automated shopping system. Throughout the 1940s, he modified and refined it, waiting for backers to give it another chance. His plans for a chain of Foodelectric Stores died with him in 1953, but computerized food markets have recently opened in Japan, forty years after the first Keedoozle.

CHAPTER 22

INTERNATIONAL BUSINESS

LEARNING OBJECTIVES

After studying this chapter, you should be able to:

Explain what is meant by international business.

Discuss how specializing in making certain products can help a nation raise its standard of living.

Discuss why American business firms are involved in international business.

Explain why barriers to international business limit the economic growth of nations.

Identify the relationship between a country's balance of trade and balance of payments.

Discuss the importance of multinational businesses in the conduct of international business.

KEY TERMS

International business
Exporting
Importing
Balance of trade
Balance of payments
Rate of exchange
Foreign exchange
　market
Absolute advantage
Comparative advantage
Tariffs
Quota
Embargo
Multinational business

CROWN COLONY IMPORTERS MOVE TO EUROPE

Glenn Wilkerson started to work for Crown Colony Importers during his junior year in high school. Crown Colony operates forty-five import stores throughout America selling high quality merchandise. Most of the imported merchandise comes from the Far East since the business was started in Los Angeles.

Glenn just graduated from college and now works full time for Crown Colony. Because of his part-time work experience for the last six years, he has just been promoted to buyer. Glenn has two important responsibilities in his new job: he must continue buying fine silk and jade items from the Far East, but he must also locate new suppliers of crystal and china from Europe. Crown Colony wants to expand its product line to include fine European china and crystal.

In order to locate suppliers, Glenn flew to Europe to make personal calls on possible suppliers. He was able to locate several suppliers in England, Germany, Sweden, France, and Rumania. There were no import quotas on these products from these countries, but Crown Colony did have to pay revenue tariffs to the American government on all imported items. Glenn also had to visit foreign exchange markets to convert U.S. dollars into local money to pay for the goods. How much local money he received for his dollars depended on the rate of exchange published in the local newspapers. After returning from this buying trip, Glenn realized how important international business is to Crown Colony. He also realized that international business can be more involved than he had previously thought.

In this chapter you will learn about several important aspects of international business—the purpose of tariffs, how foreign exchange markets work, and why some nations are better able to produce certain goods than other nations. You will also learn about multinational businesses and how they influence world trade.

America's economy is large but it is only part of an even larger and complex world economy. Countries are not economic islands because they cannot be entirely self-sufficient. They must buy goods and services from and sell to one another. Thus, the economies of countries are interdependent, although some are more dependent than others. This interdependency develops when one country does not have the resources needed to maintain its standard of living.

Buying and selling or trading among countries, called **international business**, occurs in one of two ways: (1) between businesses located in different countries or (2) between businesses and foreign governments. Glenn Wilkerson was engaged in international business when he went to Europe on a buying trip for Crown Colony Importers to buy china and crystal. However and wherever it occurs, international business is an important part of the world's economy.

INTERNATIONAL BUSINESS
The buying and selling among countries that takes place in one of two ways: between two businesses or a business and a foreign government.

EXPORTING
One nation selling goods to another nation.

IMPORTING
One nation buying goods from other nations.

INTERNATIONAL BUSINESS IS IMPORTANT

The amount of international business or world trade is large, and since 1970, the world trade conducted between countries has grown rapidly. Trade between countries means they export and import goods. When one nation sells goods to another nation that is called **exporting**. The nation buying goods is **importing** them. Exhibit 22-1 indicates that the total value of imports and exports was $580.6 billion in 1970. By 1979, that value had increased over five times, to almost $3.1 trillion. This expansion is likely to continue since the world's economies are tending to become more and more dependent on one another.

Most international business occurs among such heavily industrialized countries as America, West Germany, Japan, and France. Exhibit 22-2 lists some leading countries in imports and in exports and the dollar volume of their international business. These countries account for over 60 percent of the world's total import and export trade. As you can see from the exhibit, America is a dominant force in the world's economy.

With the exception of Saudi Arabia, all of the countries listed in Exhibit 22-2 are considered to be industrialized. Saudi Arabia is the world's largest exporter of crude oil, a raw material (or natural resource) that has assumed an important role in the world's economy. As Saudi Arabia has gained importance in international business, it has also become a major market for goods exported from industrialized countries.

The demand for raw materials (natural resources) from other developing countries in South America, Latin America, and Africa is expanding and this makes these countries more important to the world's economy. For example, some developing countries in Africa, such as Kenya, Nigeria, and the Ivory Coast, are good prospects for increased trade with other industrialized nations.

It is often claimed that industrialized countries import raw materials from developing countries and, in return, sell these countries large quantities of finished goods at high prices. By doing this, some Third World countries suggest the industrial countries are taking unfair advantage of them. However, this claim is not entirely correct because industrialized

International Business Leaders

EXHIBIT 22-1
World's International Business Summary ($000,000)

YEAR	IMPORTS	EXPORTS
1970	$ 296,600	$ 283,400
1971	331,600	317,400
1972	389,200	376,900
1973	536,400	524,400
1974	785,300	774,100
1975	814,100	796,800
1976	923,500	907,100
1977	1,061,800	1,030,900
1978	1,226,800	1,193,300
1979	1,544,800	1,508,200

Source: International Financial Statistics Yearbook, 1980, pp. 63, 67.

		IMPORTS			EXPORTS	
Rank	Nation	1979	1980	Nation	1979	1980
1	America	$218,927	$240,000	America	$181,802	$221,000
2	Germany	159,711	188,001	Germany	102,284	192,930
3	Japan	109,815	140,250	Japan	171,887	129,248
4	France	107,008	134,912	France	100,681	111,251
5	United Kingdom	102,944	120,095	United Kingdom	91,016	115,390
6	Italy	77,962	99,452	Italy	72,233	77,667
7	Netherlands	68,205	76,881	Netherlands	63,669	73,871
8	Belgium	60,393	71,185	Saudi Arabia	59,334	109,111
9	Canada	56,825	58,545	Canada	58,183	64,252
10	Switzerland	29,356	36,356	Belgium	56,249	64,066

Source: International Financial Statistics Yearbook, 1980, pp. 63, 67.

EXHIBIT 22–2
Leading International Business
Countries ($000,000)

countries largely trade among themselves. For example, America trades primarily with Japan, Mexico, and the countries of Western Europe, the most heavily industrialized parts of the world's economy. The same trade pattern holds for the other industrialized countries.

Imports and Exports

International business is less important to America than it is to many countries, such as the United Kingdom, Australia, and Japan. Even so, in 1980, America imported $240 billion in goods from other countries and exported $221 billion in goods. A large amount of this business took place with the ten countries listed in Exhibit 22–3.

America imports both manufactured and agricultural goods from many countries. Many agricultural products, like coffee, copra, tea, spices, cocoa, and bananas, must be imported because they do not grow in America. But the value of these products is only a small fraction of the total dollar volume of America's imports. The largest part of the dollar volume falls to petroleum products, machinery, steel, autos, and other manufactured goods.

America mainly exports grains, cereal products, machine-tool equipment, other manufactured goods, chemicals, and coal. But some other items are a bit more unusual. For example, Pepsi-Cola has "exported" its bottling license to the USSR and Rumania. And Coca-Cola is now made and sold in the People's Republic of China. Foreign licensing of products often proves more practical than exporting the actual product. This is because some nations prefer locally produced products for nationalistic reasons.

PAYING FOR INTERNATIONAL BUSINESS

Very little international business is carried out by bartering, or exchanging goods for goods. Nearly all international business requires that money be exchanged, though one exception was the 1973 Russian-American exchange of oil for wheat. Even so, barter agreements are rare since most countries prefer monetary payments. To explain how countries and com-

AMERICA IMPORTS			AMERICA EXPORTS	
Rank	Nation	From	Nation	To
1	Japan	$30,701	Japan	$20,790
2	Mexico	12,520	Mexico	15,144
3	West Germany	11,681	United Kingdom	12,693
4	United Kingdom	9,755	West Germany	10,959
5	Venezuela	5,297	France	7,458
6	France	5,247	Italy	5,511
7	Indonesia	5,182	Venezuela	4,573
8	Italy	4,313	Brazil	4,343
9	Brazil	3,714	Australia	4,130
10	South Africa	3,320	Argentina	2,625

Source: *Survey of Current Business*, October 1981, pp. 5–19.

EXHIBIT 22–3
United States Trading Partners, 1980 ($000,000)

panies pay for international business, you must understand three fundamental concepts: (1) balance of trade, (2) balance of payments, and (3) foreign exchange markets.

Balance of Trade

The **balance of trade** is the difference between the money value of a country's imports and its exports. When a country exports or sells more than it imports or buys, that country has a favorable (surplus) balance of trade. On the other hand, a country has an unfavorable (deficit) balance of trade if it buys more than it sells.

BALANCE OF TRADE
The difference between the money value of a nation's imports and its exports.

The data for America's balance of trade in Exhibit 22–4 show both surpluses and deficits. Before 1968, America's balance of trade was favorable. Since that time, the country regularly began to import more goods than it exported; and in 1979, the unfavorable balance stood at about $36.1 billion. This large unfavorable balance of trade reflects to a large degree the sharp price increases for imported crude oil. But the value of the American dollar, relative to other currencies, also declined significantly in 1978. This made American goods less expensive in foreign markets. As a result, the dollar volume of exports increased, leading to a somewhat more favorable balance of trade for America.

Balance of Payments

The **balance of payments** is a country's annual accounting of all its trade transactions. The balance of payments is defined as the money value of all the international business activities occurring between one country and the rest of the world. This represents the flow of money into and out of a country and, in an accounting sense, is like the business income statement.

BALANCE OF PAYMENTS
The money value of all the international business activities occurring between one nation and the rest of the world.

Countries, like individuals and businesses, must find a way to pay for all the goods and services they buy (import). Several factors besides imports affect a country's balance of payments. In addition to imports, money spent for travel and transportation abroad, military transactions, foreign aid, and money spent on the purchase and sale of foreign stocks and bonds all affect the balance of payments. These factors, called "outpayments," have a negative impact on the balance of payments. The china and crystal

JAPANESE ROBOTS ON THE EXPORT OFFENSIVE

Japan currently makes about 45 percent of all the world's robots. Most of these robots are sold in Japan to automate its own manufacturing plants. Robots are important to Japan's continued economic growth. These electronic workers are crucial because robots are the most economical way to make goods in a time when short product life cycles are getting shorter. Changeovers in production runs that are needed for products with short life cycles are less expensive when robots are used. Rather than buying new equipment and machines, the computer software that controls the robots is changed. The altered robots are then able to make the new product. Robots are also cheaper than workers because workers' wages and benefits are rising faster than robot prices. These lower labor costs will help Japan export even more goods to its trading partners in the 1980s.

To put the robots on the export offensive, Japan's government is spending $140 million to help develop "intelligent" robots that can assemble entire products—like cars. Some of the robots will even be able to see and feel objects. Making and selling robots is, in itself, big business. For example, by 1990 some predict that just America's market for robots could exceed $9 billion. Certainly the international business stakes in the robot industry are high, and Japan has plans to dominate the business.

Adapted from "The Push for Dominance in Robotics Gains Momentum," *Business Week*, December 14, 1981, p. 108.

On the Job Revisited

bought by Crown Colony Importers affected America's balance of trade because American money was spent in foreign countries. Also, Glenn Wilkerson had to spend money for travel to and from foreign countries. All of these expenditures are "outpayments." "Inpayments," which have a positive impact, include such factors as exports, foreign money invested in a nation, and all money spent by foreign tourists. For example, Arab nations make significant inpayments to America in the form of large capital investments in hotels, banks, real estate, and farmland.

Exhibit 22–5 reports America's balance of payments for the years 1967 to 1979. During 1968 and 1969, the balance of payments was positive, indicating that America maintained a surplus payment position. But note that the country had a deficit position (minus sign) in its balance of payments in most of these years. During deficit years, more was spent by America than was received from other countries.

By definition, the balance of payments account must balance. Any international business deficit is covered by the transfer of gold and financial claims between trading countries. The country's trade position appears to be improving because the prices of American exports have been falling relative to the prices of other countries' exports. This makes American products more attractive in foreign countries since the products are relatively less expensive. However, it is unlikely that America's trade position in international business will ever again be as consistently strong as it was during the 1950s.

EXHIBIT 22-4
America's Balance of Trade ($000,000)

YEAR	EXPORTS	IMPORTS	BALANCE OF TRADE
1960	$ 20,601	$ 16,367	$ 4,234
1961	21,037	15,939	5,098
1962	21,714	17,779	3,935
1963	23,387	18,816	4,571
1964	26,650	20,304	6,304
1965	27,530	23,185	4,354
1966	30,430	27,744	2,686
1967	31,622	28,744	2,878
1968	34,636	35,319	-683
1969	38,006	38,314	-308
1970	43,224	42,429	795
1971	44,130	48,342	-4,212
1972	49,758	58,862	-9,104
1973	71,339	73,575	-2,236
1974	98,507	107,996	-9,489
1975	107,592	103,389	-4,103
1976	114,992	129,565	-14,573
1977	120,164	156,695	-36,531
1978	143,660	183,090	-39,430
1979	181,802	218,927	-36,130

Source: International Financial Statistics Yearbook, 1980, p. 433.

EXHIBIT 22-5
U. S. Balance of Payments ($000,000)

YEAR	BALANCE OF PAYMENTS
1967	$ -3,418
1968	1,641
1969	2,739
1970	-9,840
1971	-29,739
1972	-10,313
1973	-5,356
1974	-8,822
1975	-4,711
1976	-10,468
1977	-35,314
1978	-32,410
1979	-11,090

Source: International Financial Statistics Yearbook, 1980, p. 433.

Businesses, like people, must pay for the goods they buy and collect for goods they sell. However, exchanging money between businesses located in different countries is not as easy as paying off a local bill. A local business firm is paid with money that can be spent anywhere within the country.

Because countries use different types of money, a rate of exchange must be established. A **rate of exchange** is the price at which one country's currency is exchanged for that of another. For example, assume that one American dollar is equal to about 2.4 German marks, meaning each German mark is equal to about 42¢ in American money.

The actual conversion of marks into dollars takes place in a **foreign exchange market**. Foreign exchange markets exist in such places as New York City, Chicago, Houston, London, Moscow, and Tokyo, among other major world cities. Through these markets businesses are able to make and receive payments for international business. Recall that Glenn Wilkerson had to go to a foreign exchange market to convert American dollars into local money in order to pay for the china and crystal he bought in Europe. In one case, Wilkerson had to convert dollars into British pounds at a London foreign exchange market.

A highly simplified example can show you how foreign exchange markets work. Suppose U. S. Steel has contracted to sell Mercedes-Benz $1 million worth of a special rolled steel. The rate of exchange between the two currencies is 2.4 marks for each American dollar. At this rate, Mercedes-Benz owes U. S. Steel 2.4 million marks.

Foreign Exchange Markets

RATE OF EXCHANGE
The price at which one nation's currency is exchanged for that of another.

FOREIGN EXCHANGE MARKETS
The place where the actual conversion of one currency for another takes place.

On the Job Revisited

1. Mercedes-Benz sends a check for 2.4 million marks to U. S. Steel in Pittsburgh.
2. U. S. Steel cannot pay its bills with German marks; it must use dollars. So the check is sold to a New York bank that has a working relationship with a German bank.
3. U. S. Steel now has a $1 million deposit in the New York bank, which can be used to pay its debts.
4. The New York bank deposits the Mercedes-Benz check in a German bank and now has a claim to 2.4 million marks.

In this exporting example, a demand for American dollars was created. In an importing situation, the process is reversed, and a demand for foreign currencies is created. This is because American businesses must purchase foreign currencies to pay for what they have bought from foreign businesses.

THE REASON FOR INTERNATIONAL BUSINESS

The benefits countries get from trading with other countries are basically the same ones individuals receive. By doing what they do best, or specializing, people can become more productive on the job. Trading lets a country specialize in producing goods that it produces well. These goods are then traded with other countries for goods the other countries are best able to make, and everyone benefits.

Countries are able to specialize in making certain goods because they have different types and quantities of economic resources. For example, Kuwait has oil, America has vast quantities of coal, and Taiwan has a large labor force. This imbalance of natural resources, capital, and labor provides the basis for national specialization and international business. Taiwan, with few natural resources, has specialized in manufacturing complex electrical equipment. The country's labor force has been trained to assemble the electronic components in color television sets and electronic calculators. Assembly costs are thus likely to be lower in Taiwan than in many other nations.

Kuwait could build a television assembly plant and produce its own television sets, but because of its readily available natural resources, Kuwait has concentrated on producing oil. This gives it the money to buy televisions from Taiwan. By specializing in what it does best, each country is able to enjoy a higher standard of living than if each tried to meet all its needs and wants internally.

Some fortunate countries, such as America and Canada, have sufficient quantities of several natural resources, skilled labor, and capital. Because of their abundant resources, these countries can produce agricultural goods, high-technology products, and a large variety of consumer goods, which combine to offer a high standard of living. But these unusual situations are not likely to last forever; a country's resources and technological levels change. Thus, over a period of time, the pattern of international business changes.

Two economic concepts, absolute and comparative advantages, play an important role in explaining how countries can use product specialization to improve their economic well-being. When a country can produce a good at a lower cost than other countries, that country is said to have an **absolute advantage**. But it is unrealistic to expect one country to maintain an absolute advantage in world trade for two reasons. First, few countries happen to be the only ones capable of producing a specific product. Second, world economic conditions change, which directly affects the cost of producing a good.

The concept of comparative advantage offers a more realistic explanation of how specialization affects world trade. A country has a **comparative advantage** if it can produce a good relatively more efficiently and at a lower cost than it can other goods. So long as a country maintains a comparative advantage in producing some goods and a comparative disadvantage in other goods, it can benefit from specialization and international business.

To understand how comparative advantage works, consider America, which has a comparative advantage in the production of such goods as soybeans, wheat, and coal. America sells or exports these items to other countries in large quantities. The comparative advantage in these goods is largely due to the country's abundant supply of natural resoures, its rich farmland, and large coal deposits.

On the other hand, America buys other goods (imports them) from other countries. For example, Taiwan has a comparative advantage in producing sweaters and Italy in shoes because their labor costs are low compared to America.

Although countries can benefit directly from specialization and international business, not all choose to do so. Some countries try to be economically self-sufficient, primarily for military and nationalistic reasons. The USSR is one example. For years it tried to avoid any significant international business with the industrialized Western World. It was not until the 1970s that the USSR expanded its trade with the West. The problems with a national economic policy of self-sufficiency are similar to those that face individuals who want to do everything for themselves. In the long run, countries that adopt this economic policy suffer a lower standard of living than countries that freely engage in international business.

The ideal situation is to have international business conducted on an open and free basis, which means unrestricted buying and selling among nations. This is the type of buying and selling Americans are familiar with. For example, if you live in Kansas City, Kansas, and go shopping in Kansas City, Missouri, most goods purchased in Missouri normally can be taken into Kansas without paying special taxes.

Even though economic advantages are associated with free and open

COUNTRIES SPECIALIZE

ABSOLUTE ADVANTAGE
An advantage one country has when it can produce a good at a lower cost than other countries.

Comparative Advantage

COMPARATIVE ADVANTAGE
The ability of a nation to make a product relatively more efficiently and at lower costs than other goods.

Self-Sufficient Markets?

BARRIERS TO INTERNATIONAL BUSINESS

international business, trade between countries is often not free and open. In some instances language, local customs, and geography create natural barriers. Landlocked nations like Mongolia engage in little international business. Most barriers to free trade, however, are not natural but are created by governments. Governments create trade barriers in several ways in order to raise money and to make it easier for their own producers to sell goods.

Tariffs

TARIFFS
Taxes placed on imported goods and services.

Taxes on imported goods and services are called **tariffs**. Glenn Wilkerson's Crown Colony Importers had to pay tariffs on the china and crystal it imported from Europe. Tariffs may function to raise government revenues or to protect local businesses. Revenue tariffs are designed primarily to raise money for a government. America used this type of tariff in its early history to raise money for the new government.

Protective tariffs put imported products in an unfavorable price position relative to domestically produced products. For example, suppose a person wants to buy a car. A German-made car may sell in America for $11,000, whereas a comparable auto produced in America may sell for $11,300. To protect the domestic auto manufacturer, the American government could impose a 20 percent import tariff on the German auto, which would raise the retail price of the German auto to $13,200. The American consumers may then buy the domestic auto because it costs $1,900 less. The only purpose of protective tariffs is to restrict imports by raising their retail prices.

Several reasons are often given to support import tariffs on foreign goods sold in America: (1) industries need protection from foreign competition; (2) American markets should be reserved completely for domestic producers; (3) importing goods made with "cheap" foreign labor takes jobs away from Americans; and (4) we need specific industries in the event of war (national defense). The third reason is often expressed through "Buy American" bumper stickers. The important point is that the logic underlying the first three reasons is nationalistic and is hard to support under any form of economic analysis that has a world perspective. Of course it is equally important to realize that a worldwide economic perspective is not usually a major consideration in national political decisions.

Quotas

QUOTA
A definite limit on the quantity of a good that can be brought into a country.

Governments can also place quotas on imported goods. A **quota** is a limit on the quantity of a good that can be brought into a country. Quotas have proven to be less popular with governments than tariffs, although America has used quotas on selected products. For example, quotas have been used to restrict imports of sugar, cattle, sheep, and crude oil. It was in 1973 that an oil import quota was lifted by President Nixon at a time when the country faced a serious gasoline shortage due to the Arab oil embargo.

The push for quotas still exists. Some unions and businesses would like to set limits on the amount of a product that can be imported. Two prime examples are the automobile and steel industries; they would like to have restrictions placed on imports in their areas.

AMERICAN STEEL GOES FOR QUOTAS

America is often considered one of the world's champion promoters of free trade. International business has helped make America's economy the largest in the world, and America's steel industry has benefited from free and open international business. Yet in 1982, the steel industry launched a campaign against what the industry termed "unfair" foreign imports. The problem was that eleven foreign nations subsidize their steelmakers, which supposedly gives these foreign steelmakers an unfair price advantage in competition with American steel. To prevent this situation, American steelmakers sought blanket quotas on imports of all European steel. This was counter to the free-trade position of the Reagan administration.

Many economists and executives felt the steelmaker's request for import quotas on European steel was bad for America. Protectionism is an "ancient problem" that has never helped an economy in the long run. Executives against the quotas said the real problem with America's steel industry was the industry's low productivity and high labor rates. For example, in America labor costs per ton of steel were roughly twice those in Japan's steel mills. Granting quotas on imports from Europe "would likely have created more problems in the long run than they would have solved in the short run. Becoming more competitive in a strong world economy based on free and open international business offers the best long-term hope for any industry including America's steel industry."

Adapted from "Steel's Subtle Goals for Quotas," *Fortune*, February 8, 1982, p. 46.

An **embargo** prohibits either the import or export of goods by means of a complete ban. Embargoes are placed into effect for health, moral, political, or other reasons. For example, America placed an embargo on trade with the People's Republic of China during the Truman administration which remained in effect until President Nixon removed it in 1971. President Kennedy ordered a complete trade embargo on Cuba in 1962 as a result of the Cuban missile crisis. Under the Carter administration, America enacted a ban on the export of wheat to the USSR in response to that country's invasion of Afghanistan. In 1982, the Reagan administration imposed restrictions on the transfer of American technology to build the new gas pipeline from the USSR to Western Europe.

Fortunately for international business, total embargoes are the exception rather than the rule. Most governments promote trade because of its benefits, and many developing countries encourage international business and business investments in their countries. This is an effective way to attract new foreign investment capital to a developing country. In addition, countries with limited natural resources, such as the island nations of Great Britain and Japan, have developed economically mainly because of their governments' active and longtime support of international business. In these situations, international trade becomes a part of the country's foreign policy.

Embargoes

EMBARGO
A ban that prohibits the import or export of certain goods.

MULTINATIONAL BUSINESS

Many countries, particularly those in the Western world, actively encourage the development of international business. The majority of this international business is conducted not by governments but between large businesses whose transactions are watched by their own governments. Consequently, it has become increasingly difficult to understand the world's economy without some appreciation of the role and scope of these international businesses because they influence both the economic and political worlds.

There is more than one acceptable definition of the term *multinational business* (MNB). One definition states that a MNB must operate in at least six countries and have sales exceeding $100 million annually. If this definition is used, possibly half of the world's multinational businesses are American. For our purposes, we use a broader definition. A **multinational business** is a business headquartered in one country but maintaining production and marketing facilities in one or more foreign countries. In this sense, a multinational business views the world as its market. This means that the distinguishing element of a MNB is that its operations are global in scope.

Many MNBs operate around the world, including IBM, Exxon, McDonald's, RCA, Mobil Oil, Holiday Inn, and Coca-Cola. An advertisement announcing the opening of a new McDonald's in Hong Kong appears in Exhibit 22-6. But all MNBs are not headquartered in the United States. A

MULTINATIONAL BUSINESS
A business headquartered in one country that maintains production and marketing facilities in one or more foreign countries.

EXHIBIT 22-6
McDonald's Kui Mo Ba

Better 'n Kai Yick?

Take your pick: McDonald's, called Kui Mo Ba by the Chinese in Hong Kong, can mean either "food of the heroes," "champion fighter," "kung fu fighter" or "invisible hero." McDonald's doesn't seem to mind any of the translations as its profits keep sizzling.

C'mon over on Sunday, September 26 at 11:30 a.m. for the Grand Opening of our First Store in Kowloon.
九月二十六星期日十一時半油蔴地麥當勞正式開幕

McDonald's

Address: Nathan Road, Yaumati, Kowloon. (near Wing On)
地址： 九龍油蔴地獨教道恒成大厦 （永安百貨公司鄰近）

RANK 1981	RANK 1980	COMPANY	HEADQUARTERS	SALES ($000)	NET INCOME ($000)
1	1	Exxon	New York	108,107,688	5,567,481
2	2	Royal Dutch/Shell Group	The Hague/London	82,291,728	3,642,142
3	3	Mobil	New York	64,488,000	2,433,000
4	4	General Motors	Detroit	62,698,500	333,400
5	5	Texaco	Harrison, N. Y.	57,628,000	2,310,000
6	6	British Petroleum	London	52,199,976	2,063,272
7	7	Standard Oil of California	San Francisco	44,224,000	2,380,000
8	8	Ford Motor	Dearborn, Mich.	38,247,100	(1,060,100)
9	12	Standard Oil (Ind.)	Chicago	29,947,000	1,922,000
10	9	ENI	Rome	29,444,315	383,234
11	11	International Business Machines	Armonk, N.Y.	29,070,000	3,308,000
12	10	Gulf Oil	Pittsburgh	28,252,000	1,231,000
13	16	Atlantic Richfield	Los Angeles	27,797,436	1,671,290
14	14	General Electric	Fairfield, Conn.	27,240,000	1,652,000
15	17	Unilever	London/Rotterdam	24,095,898	800,379
16	38	E. I. Du Pont de Nemours	Wilmington, Del.	22,810,000	1,401,000
17	15	Française des Pétroles	Paris	22,784,032	175,807
18	18	Shell Oil	Houston	21,629,000	1,701,000
19	•	Kuwait Petroleum	Safat (Kuwait)	20,556,871	1,690,312
20	22	Elf-Aquitaine	Paris	19,666,141	682,316

Adapted from "The Largest Industrial Companies in the World," *Fortune*, August 23, 1982. p. 181.

EXHIBIT 22-7
The World's Largest Industrial Companies, 1981 (ranked by sales)

review of the MNBs listed in Exhibit 22-7 shows that many international firms are located in Japan, Germany, England, and France. However, of the twenty largest MNBs, twelve are headquartered in America.

America is an attractive foreign market for MNBs, and many companies from other countries have built large plants here. Volkswagen (Germany) and Olivetti (Italy) have located in Pennsylvania; Bowater Paper Company (England) constructed a mill in South Carolina; and Bekaert Steel Wire (Belgium) built a plant in Arkansas. The impact of these plants on the American economy is significant because they provide about 1.5 million jobs. The Volkswagen plant alone provides jobs for about 4,000 Americans. The main reason foreign investment flows into America, despite rising labor costs, is the stable political climate and the prospect for a comparatively healthy economy.

Why Do MNBs Exist?

Companies tend to become MNBs for economic reasons primarily. For example, the imbalance of economic resources has had substantial impact on the development of MNBs. Low-cost labor in Taiwan influenced some American consumer electronic companies to build assembly plants in Asia. Also, as the economic size of the world shrinks due to growing communications and rising incomes, companies learn more about what people in other countries need and want. Market informaton permits a MNB to initiate actions that satisfy consumer needs and wants.

Most MNBs make capital investments for one of three basic profit-seeking reasons: (1) to secure natural resources, (2) to manufacture finished goods, or (3) to enter into some type of service industry. Anaconda Copper, U. S. Steel, and Standard Oil of New Jersey are examples of MNBs that have invested billions of dollars in efforts to locate and extract raw materials (copper and oil).

Other companies have invested in the construction of manufacturing plants in foreign countries. American companies that have large foreign manufacturing factories include General Motors, Ford Motor Company, IBM, General Electric, RCA, Du Pont, Kraftco, and Coca-Cola. There are many reasons why companies desire to build plants in other countries. Several of these reasons are summarized in Exhibit 22-8. Meeting the demands of an expanding foreign market and trade restrictions were reasons given by 77 percent of the MNB managers as the primary reasons for a foreign investment decision. Low-cost labor was cited by only 5 percent as the prime factor in their foreign investment decisions.

Finally, some MNBs develop because of opportunities in the service industry, which are the direct result of foreign manufacturing investments by MNBs. Business service areas where MNBs are an important factor include law, banking, advertising, and insurance. For example, banks cannot provide needed international financial services to other MNBs without foreign branches. American banks with substantial foreign operations include the Bank of America, Chemical Bank, Citibank of New York, and First National Bank of Chicago.

Possibly the best reason for the existence of MNBs is the potential for profit. MNBs see foreign investment as a way to help provide profits to the business. But profitable MNBs provide thousands of jobs to people in other countries and increase the number of jobs at home by increasing the level of trade.

The Environment of MNBs

Several factors influence decisions that must be made by the managements of MNBs, including different cultural environments, different economic systems, various local customs, unequal technological levels, and different political systems. MNB decision making is complicated by the need to operate in several countries at once.

Consider the situation faced by American companies making business deals in some Middle Eastern countries. The idea of making direct pay-

EXHIBIT 22-8
Why MNBs Build Manufacturing Plants

MAJOR REASON	NUMBER	PERCENTAGE
Meeting market demand	42	57%
Trade restriction	15	20
Investment regulations	8	11
Low-cost labor	4	5
Other reasons	5	7
Totals	74	100

Adapted from *The Role of the Multinational Corporation in the United States and World Economies* (Washington, D. C.: Emergency Committee for American Trade, 1972), p. 16.

ments to important people who can influence trade decisions is an accepted way of doing business in these countries. But in America, this practice is often illegal and is almost always considered unethical. When some American companies were discovered to be making such payments in foreign countries, the American public objected loudly. A list of companies accused of making questionable payments in order to do foreign business is shown in Exhibit 22–9. Similar arrangements in Japan, when discovered, brought on an investigation and trials by the Japanese government.

These differences in cultures, local customs, and political systems often cause foreign governments to restrict the operations of MNBs. Some countries insist that the majority ownership of a foreign-based business be held by local interests. Some countries, such as Canada and Nigeria, require that foreign-owned subsidiaries employ large numbers of local workers. Australia places a limit on the amount of local capital a foreign company can borrow, so when a business decides to locate in Australia, it must bring a substanial amount of its own investment capital. This policy leads to large infusions of direct foreign investment that substantially improves Australia's balance of payments. In the USSR and other Communist countries, some MNBs have accepted a guarantee of fixed income in exchange for not admitting that the MNB is actually foreign owned. This type of arrangement is largely the result of the foreign country's political system.

The important point to understand is that MNB decisions can be complex and politically sensitive due to differing national environments. All management decisions must take American regulations as well as local customs and laws into consideration or run the risk of damaging both the profit potential and the future of the MNB.

COMPANY	PAYMENTS
Lockheed Aircraft	Gave $202 million in commissions, payoffs, and bribes to foreign agents and government officials in the Netherlands, Italy, Japan, Turkey, and other countries, $22 million of which went for outright bribes
Northrop	Paid $30 million in commissions and bribes to government officials and agents in Holland, Iran, France, West Germany, Saudi Arabia, Brazil, Malaysia, and Taiwan
Exxon	Paid $740,000 to government officials and others in three countries; Italian subsidiary gave $27 million in secret but legal contributions to seven Italian political parties
Gulf Oil	Paid $4 million to South Korea's ruling political party; gave $460,000 to Bolivian officials—including a $110,000 helicopter to the late president—for oil rights
Merck & Company	Gave $3 million, largely in "commission-type payments," to employees of thirty-six foreign governments between 1968 and 1975

EXHIBIT 22-9
Questionable Corporate Payments

The Future of the MNB   In spite of often-difficult management problems and government trade restrictions, the future of MNBs appears bright. It is very likely that MNBs will continue to play a major role in business because this form of business is so important to the economic development of many countries. Some economists have estimated that MNBs could account for over 25 percent of the total industrial production in the Western world and Japan during the 1980s. Indeed, the future of MNB and world trade is bright if companies can find ways to accommodate different political and economic environments, exert a positive influence on the local economy, and at the same time make a reasonable profit.

SUMMARY

- International business is the buying and selling or trading that takes place between countries.
- America's economy is a dominant force in the world's economy because of its size.
- Most international business is conducted between industrialized nations like Japan, America, Canada, and Western European countries.
- America mainly sells (exports) grains, cereal products, chemicals, coal, and manufactured goods to other countries.
- Petroleum products, steel, autos, and machinery are the main products bought (imported) by America.
- America's balance of trade, the difference between its imports and exports, has been in a deficit for many years. We buy more than we sell.
- The rate of exchange is the price at which one country's money is exchanged for another's money.
- Countries can raise their standard of living by specializing in producing certain products and then trading with other countries. Countries normally trade goods they can produce with a comparative advantage.
- Governments can set up several barriers to international business. Examples of barriers include protective tariffs, revenue tariffs, quotas, and embargoes.
- Multinational businesses, which are an important part of world trade, are businesses headquartered in one country that maintain production and marketing facilities in other countries.

ISSUES TO CONSIDER AND ANALYZE

1. What would happen to the economies and standards of living of Great Britain and Japan if world trade were restricted for a long period of time?
2. Explain the relationship between the balance of trade and the balance of payments.
3. What is multinational business?
4. Why do multinational businesses make capital investments in foreign countries?
5. What is the purpose of foreign exchange markets?
6. Explain the purpose of tariffs and discuss two specific types of tariffs.
7. What is meant by the term *comparative advantage*?

8. Go to *International Financial Statistics* and prepare a list of the world's ten largest importing and exporting nations. Compare this list to Exhibit 22–2. Are there any significant changes? If there are, give some reason for the changes.

9. Do industrialized nations have any obligation to help smaller countries develop their economies? Is it to the industrialized nations' advantage to do so?

10. Why do industrialized nations tend to trade among themselves rather than with developing nations?

SILICON VALLEY CHIPS MOVES TO JAPAN   CASE FOR ANALYSIS

For years America's auto industry has not sold a high volume of cars in Japan. In 1981, only 7,700 American cars were sold in Japan, while the Japanese sold 1.8 million cars in America. Some company officials say the real problem is a "closed market" in Japan. Others say it is the "left-hand-drive syndrome" that is killing American sales in Japan. Japanese drive on the left-hand side of the road, and American cars are made with the steering wheel on the left (the wrong side for Japan). American companies say the low sales volume does not justify producing right-hand-drive cars.

Silicon Valley Chips (SVC) is building a plant in Japan and wants to avoid the "left-hand-drive syndrome." Mitchell Adams, executive vice president of SVC, laid out the company's plans for entry into Japanese markets. The strategy is to build a laboratory in Japan to work on problems unique to Japan. Also, very high quality control standards will be stressed in the chip manufacturing process. The market program will feature product quality in chips designed for Japanese needs. Adams said, "We're going to apply the marketing concept and build products to meet Japanese needs." The idea of selling the Japanese a "left-hand-drive" chip will not be considered at SVC.

QUESTIONS

1. Do you agree with the position of the American car manufacturers that they cannot afford to produce right-hand-drive cars? Explain.
2. Is Silicon Valley Chips applying the marketing concept in their entry into the Japanese markets? Explain.

Adapted from "The Left-hand-drive Barrier to U. S. Sales," *Business Week*, February 15, 1982, p. 60.

CHAPTER 23

SOCIAL RESPONSIBILITY, ETHICS, AND BUSINESS LAW

LEARNING OBJECTIVES

After studying this chapter, you should be able to:

Discuss the arguments for and against corporate social responsibility.

Understand the concept of business ethics.

Identify several codes of ethics.

Distinguish between constitutional, common, and statutory law.

Define white-collar crimes and give examples.

List the ingredients necessary for a promise to become a contract.

KEY TERMS

Business ethics
Law
Constitutional law
Common law
Statutory law
Forgery
Robbery
Burglary
Larceny
Embezzlement
White-collar crime
Tort
Strict liability

BEING SUED

Clifford Preston wasn't satisfied with his job as financial manager of a medium-sized Midwest corporation, so he decided to study law at night. After five years of night school, he received a J.D. degree from a respected local university. Clifford's current employer chose not to offer him a different position. Forced to go into the job market, he decided to present himself as a "jack-of-all-trades." Clifford understood the financial management of a medium-sized corporation, and he was certain he could apply his legal training to the legal, social, and ethical issues that face corporations today.

Clifford's job search ended in a dissatisfying six-month stint as comptroller and assistant to the president of a small manufacturing firm. But then he met the chief executive officer of a large competitor at a local luncheon of the Economics Society. They seemed to hit it off well, and soon Clifford was offered a job as a member of the legal staff of the company. He immediately found himself embroiled in lawsuits ranging from employees suing for back wages on the basis of unjust firing to consumers suing for damages incurred through use of products the company sold. He was also assigned to a discrimination case filed by the local Human Rights Commission against a number of businesses in the community because of alleged unfair practices with respect to employment opportunities for women.

Clifford was now right where he wanted to be.

Business does not exist in a vacuum today. The business world is governed by a set of laws designed to ensure fairness and equity in our society. Moreover, the business environment includes numerous external forces that influence business decisions. Exhibit 23-1 shows some of these forces.

Business owners seek the highest possible rates of return on their investments, and the profitability of corporate investment is extremely important to them. Employees seek "high" wages, safety, equal treatment, and good working conditions. Consumers want a safe product and the right to choose among numerous products; and they insist on the right to be informed. The government, acting as a voice for employees and consumers (society as a whole), wants business to conform to the laws of society, to keep the environment clean, not to discriminate unfairly against employees, to provide safe products— the list seems to expand endlessly.

In principle, then, for businesses to respond to all of these groups, business managers must engage in socially responsible actions. That raises many important issues to which we now address ourselves.

SHOULD BUSINESS BE SOCIALLY RESPONSIBLE?

In 1882, William Vanderbilt, president of the New York Central Railroad and one of the richest men in the country, addressed the question of social responsibility for business with his statement, "The public be damned!" However, business in the United States has always exercised some degree of social responsibility. Throughout the years, business leaders and their families such as the Carnegies, Rockefellers, Morgans, Mellons, and Fords have donated billions of dollars to libraries, the national park system, art institutes, and numerous universities. This represents only a small part of corporate philanthropy over the past hundred years.

However, times have changed. Today, American corporations are managed by a new type of individual—the professional manager. For the earlier

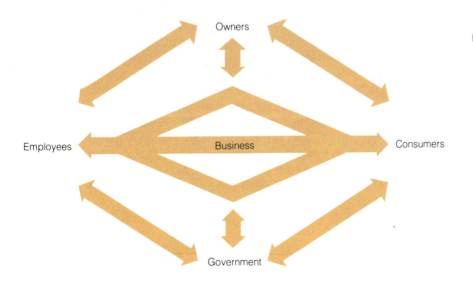

EXHIBIT 23-1
Business and Its Environment

owner-managers, a decision to give money for social projects was a decision to spend their own money. But today's professional manager is responsible to stockholders, who require an adequate return on their investment. Thus, contemporary managers often see a conflict between their responsibilities to owners and their responsibilities to the general public.

Arguments against the Concept of Socially Responsible Businesses

Professor Milton Friedman of the University of Chicago has suggested that the only responsibility a business has is to manufacture and distribute goods and services at a profit. In doing this, the business employs land, labor, and capital as efficiently as possible and generates products, jobs, and tax revenue that can be used for social programs. The choice of which social programs will be sponsored is left to the government (publicly elected officials), which can best determine where the money should be spent. Friedman considers business one of the most powerful elements in our society, but he argues that its power should be applied in commerce and industry rather than in the area of social issues. He feels business can make its greatest contribution to society by doing what it does best.

Another argument centers on the assumption that socially responsible businesses are at a disadvantage because competitors are free to operate without such restraints. Businesses that voluntarily clean up the environment or train the hardcore unemployed have higher costs and, therefore, higher prices. The socially responsible firm may be asking for a slow but certain economic death.

Finally, because the primary task of business is to provide goods and services at a profit, this should be done as efficiently as possible. Anything that distracts business managers from their primary objective reduces the efficiency of their businesses. Business has the responsibility of increasing the nation's wealth, which in turn provides a means for solving social problems.

Arguments for the Concept of Socially Responsible Businesses

Proponents of social responsibility in business acknowledge that business is a powerful aspect of American society. Indeed, they contend that many business decisions have a lasting impact on the environment. Therefore, industry cannot ignore the undesirable results of the production process; the success of a business cannot be measured by profits alone. Business must also be concerned with the quality of life in the United States. Success is limited if products must be used in a badly polluted environment by employees suffering from emphysema or cancer.

Many professional managers feel that business should turn an increasing share of its profits and the talents of its managers to solving social problems. People in business have special talents that can be used effectively in finding solutions to society's problems.

In addition, it may not be wise to allow the government to make all the decisions on social issues. Input is needed from a variety of sources. Our society encourages people to join together to solve problems. If business fails to participate, its interests may not be represented.

Finally, business cannot afford to let other groups turn public opinion against it. Recent opinion polls have indicated that public confidence in

ONE COMPANY'S URBAN COMMITMENT— SOCIAL RESPONSIBILITY IN ACTION

Ralston-Purina Company is a $5 billion agribusiness giant. It decided that part of its social responsibility was the transformation of the area surrounding its St. Louis headquarters from a slum into a well-manicured community of new homes and refurbished old townhouses. The area also contains apartments for the elderly, low-income housing, and churches as well as commercial and light industrial facilities.

Was it an easy task? Not at all. It took twice as long as planned, and the costs were substantial. Ralston-Purina paid over $1.1 million to the city government to qualify for urban renewal money (matching funds). The company also paid $2.5 million for the acquisition of land and improvements to existing structures and almost another $1 million for studies and surveys involved in the planning project. Ralston-Purina expects to recover only $2 million from the sale of refurbished buildings to private developers.

Why did Ralston-Purina do it? Because it believes the project has an excellent long-term investment potential. It also believes that it creates an image for Ralston-Purina as a model corporate citizen. There were two reasons to build up the area. One was corporate responsibility, and the other was that no one wanted to work in a slum. Once the decision was made to stay in the St. Louis area, something had to be done to improve the surrounding area.

Not content with resting on its laurels, Ralston-Purina is continuing its involvement with the project. It oversees its management, security, and maintenance. Corporate executives continue to attend community group meetings. Ralston-Purina also maintains contact with other companies in St. Louis, trying to interest them in similar projects. Ralston-Purina is the model.

Taken from "Ralston-Purina's Urban Commitment," *Dun's Business Month*, January 1982, pp. 97–100.

business is at its lowest level since the Depression of the 1930s. This mistrust of business could lead the public to adopt an extremist position, which may hurt the operation of business in the future. In the long run, it is in the best interest of business to present its side and move toward solutions that will benefit the entire society.

Clifford Preston was recently made head of his company's corporate contributions division. Virtually every major corporation in America today employs someone to oversee donations to worthy causes. At first Clifford was ecstatic about his additional responsibilities. (He still had all his other work to do.) It didn't take him long, however, to find out that the job was no picnic. An assistant was assigned to do a preliminary pass-through of the fifty to ninety applications and requests for money that the company receives per month! She weeded out the obvious "no goes," but Clifford still had to read at least a dozen—and then there were the phone calls. But perhaps the biggest problem he faced was making a decision about where corporate donations should go. On the one hand, he believed strongly in the free enterprise system and wanted to donate to academic and research organizations that show how government intervention hurts rather than helps society. But he also knew that his corporation was expected to help the poor, the disadvantaged, and minority groups in his city. And to top it

On the Job Revisited

off, quite a bit of pressure came from the CEO's wife to give more money to the arts.

Corporate social responsibility wasn't easy for Mr. Preston.

BUSINESS ETHICS

BUSINESS ETHICS
The proper corporate and individual conduct in business situations, determined in large part by the values that society has at a particualr time.

The term *ethics* is derived from the Greek word meaning custom. In a broad sense, ethics is concerned with what is considered right or wrong behavior in a given set of circumstances. In other words, society has established written and unwritten guidelines defining acceptable behavior in given circumstances, and it is up to the individual to conform to these guidelines.

Business ethics concerns itself with proper corporate and individual conduct in business situations. However, because ethics depend on a personal interpretation of society's standards, it is difficult to establish a code that all members of a firm or industry can agree to. Incorrect choices of ethical standards can bring dire consequences to the individual and the business, but unethical behavior does not necessarily mean illegal behavior. An act may be legal yet quite unethical. A truly ethical person doesn't try to justify his or her behavior by arguing that it was legal.

The dean of Stanford University's business school and former president of the Ford Motor Company, Arjay Miller, has suggested a simple test to measure if a particular act is ethical. He asks, "Would I feel comfortable reporting my actions on TV? " It would undoubtedly be difficult for some people to pass this ethical test.

Over the past few years, business conduct has been questioned in a number of instances, including illegal political contributions, exaggerated advertising claims, price fixing, and inaccurate company financial records. For example, the Great Atlantic and Pacific Tea Company (A &P) was found guilty in 1974 of fixing prices of fresh meat at the retail and whole-sale levels. The managers at A&P knew their actions were both illegal and unethical, but they continued to fix prices in restraint of trade. A&P paid a judgment of $9 million to six cattle raisers who had filed the suit. As a result of this case, another suit was filed. Sixty-three cattle-feeding firms filed suit against A&P, Kroger, and Safeway Stores, charging the three food chains with using their membership in the National Association of Food Chains to fix prices.

Business Week magazine reported that price-fixing agreements among businesses are more widespread than most business people believe. In addition, price fixing increases during periods of recession when profit is squeezed. But to suggest that all or even many business managers are unethical would be a gross exaggeration.

Codes of Ethics

Business has for years attempted to establish codes of ethics for business managers. One of the earliest attempts was made by *Printers Ink*, a widely known advertising and marketing publication. This magazine developed an ethical code that could be used by any state to regulate and control false advertising claims. Forty-four states and the District of Columbia later enacted codes based on the model provided by *Printers Ink*. Several professional business associations have also established codes of ethics for their members, including associations in the areas of accounting, management, marketing, and finance.

Perhaps the strongest code of ethics is that of the certified public accountant. Just as with medicine and law, the history of accounting reaches back hundreds of years, but the accounting code of ethics is only about eighty years old. In the late 1890s, the state of New York passed the first law establishing the designation "certified public accountant" (CPA). Today, the CPA's code of ethics is strongly enforced by the members of the profession.

First, CPAs are restricted in the way they advertise their businesses. Second, they are forbidden to violate the confidential relationship that exists between the CPA and the client. Third, the accountant's professional judgment must not be influenced by the personal interest of the accountant or the client. Finally, the CPA must not allow his or her name to be associated with any business forecast that suggests the accountant is guaranteeing the forecast. The accounting profession has grown strong and is well respected because of its members' vigorous enforcement of this code. However, in spite of all these efforts, the accountant has come under increasing pressure to behave in even a more ethical fashion.

Better Business Bureau

The Better Business Bureau (BBB) is an outgrowth of attempts by business to regulate ethical practices. Better Business Bureaus exist in many cities across the country. Their major emphasis is on building public confidence in business by helping to establish and enforce codes of ethics for their members. The BBB has sponsored numerous public service messages in an attempt to help consumers spot unethical business practices, but it has had only limited success. It has proven difficult to force the minority of businesses that violate the code to conform. Fortunately, most business managers recognize the need to raise the standards that govern their actions. Higher ethical standards benefit not only the consumer but also the investor and the ethical business manager.

On the Job Revisited

One of the subsidiaries of Clifford Preston's corporation manufactures steel. Even though the corporation made certain that the steel mill conformed to Environmental Protection Agency air standards, a local environmental group claimed that the citizens of the county in which the steel mill is located are due some money. Money for what? Money for past damages including, but not limited to, respiratory diseases, lost days of work due to such diseases, increased deterioration of homes and cars in the area, and mental suffering. Clifford attempted to counter their arguments by maintaining that wage rates at the steel mill and in surrounding areas during the prior twenty years were, on average, 30 percent higher than in cities where there was no pollution. In other words, people were paid higher wages to compensate them for any ill effects of the pollution in the area. He also pointed out that when the steel mill was put into operation, the population was one-tenth the size that it is today, and some of the pollution came from increased automotive traffic.

The environmental group pressing the charges wasn't convinced.

THE LEGAL ENVIRONMENT OF BUSINESS

Ethical standards and corporate social responsibility are the unwritten rules of business behavior. The written rules of business behavior involve business law. Law is simply defined as that body of principles and rules that courts apply in deciding disputes. The study of business law is therefore the study of these rules as they apply to the business community.

Types of Law

Business behavior is governed by three types of law: constitutional, common, and statutory.

CONSTITUTIONAL LAW
Written law found in constitutions either at the national or the state level.

Constitutional Law. The Constitution provides for rights that everyone has, including businesspersons and corporations. For example, the Constitution provides for freedom of speech. Recently numerous cases have shown that freedom of speech applies to commercial speech—advertising.

COMMON LAW
The body of law developed in English and American courts that is not attributable to legislative statutes.

Common Law. Common law is sometimes called decisional law because courts must decide any dispute brought before them. If there is no constitutional law or statute (discussed below), common law provides a rule that the court can apply. What it does is follow the appropriate process that courts in other English-speaking countries have used for centuries. The idea is to base decisions on the outcome of past disputes. If facts are similar to those in an earlier case, a judge will follow the decision set down by the previous judge. Over the centuries, during which thousands of disputes were settled, a large body of law has developed in this way. This body of law was adopted by the American colonies when they won their freedom from England. Many of the laws that pertain to business relationships come from common law.

STATUTORY LAW
That body of law made by legislators at the state or federal level.

Statutory Law. Statutory law is law handed down by legislators at state or federal levels. It is explicitly written out. All the laws pertaining to how businesses must label their products, clean the air, and so on, are statutes.

IMPORTANT AREAS OF THE LAW

Businesses are concerned, at the minimum, with the following areas of the law.

- Criminal law
- Contract law
- The law of sales
- The law of torts
- Bankruptcy law

Criminal Law

Businesses are the targets of criminals, but businesses are also the perpetrators of so-called white-collar crimes. The most important crimes against business are the following.

1. *Forgery.* This involves fraudulent alteration of documents or products that changes the legal liability of another. Forged checks are the most common crime in this area, but forgery also includes changing trademarks, counterfeiting, and falsifying public records. Today, a special statute called the credit card statute covers the illegal use of credit cards.

COMPUTER CAPERS

Films are now made about computer crimes. TV episodes casually talk about fourteen-year-old kids connecting home computers to a telephone line and tapping into the computer at the neighborhood bank. What do the fourteen-year-olds do? They regularly transfer money into their personal accounts. These may be fictional tales, but they are no longer futuristic fantasies. In 1981, the Wells Fargo Bank discovered that an employee had used its computer to embezzle $21.3 million. In Miami, seven workers at a state welfare office were convicted a few years ago of stealing, at a minimum, $300,000 worth of food stamps by falsifying data fed into the agency's computers. A clerk at the People's Savings Bank in Bridgeport, Massachusetts, was arrested at about the same time for using the bank's computer to credit money to three of her own accounts. How much did she take? Almost $40,000.

Nobody really knows how much computer crime there is, but the United States Chamber of Commerce thinks that it is at least $100 million a year and rising. Others put the figure much higher. The FBI wants to do something about it, and so five hundred of its agents have taken courses in electronic crime detection. Computer manufacturers, on the other hand, are waging a publicity battle to tell their customers that the machines are not at fault. IBM put a computer in a lineup and pitched the story that the machines don't commit crimes, people do.

Finally, a whole new industry is springing up. Its goal is to make a profit by helping corporations protect the information stored in their computers. At least a quarter of a billion dollars has been spent on safeguards every year, and that figure is expected to reach a trillion dollars within a decade. For example, the Security Pacific National Bank in Los Angeles uses over 50 people and spends over $1.5 million to protect its computers.

Adapted from "Crackdown on Computer Capers," *Time*, February 8, 1982, pp. 60–61.

2. *Robbery.* Robbery is formally defined as the forceful entry and unlawful taking of something that belongs to someone else. Pickpocketing is not robbery because the action is unknown to the victim.
3. *Burglary.* Burglary is breaking and entering a dwelling with the intent to commit a crime. Typically when burglary involves the use of a deadly weapon, a greater penalty is assessed against the perpetrator.
4. *Larceny.* Many business-related crimes entail larceny, which is defined as fraudulent conduct such as stealing computer programs and trade secrets. Stealing the use of telephone wires by the device known as a "blue box" is subject to larceny statutes. So, too, is the theft of natural gas.
5. *Embezzlement.* This action usually involves an employee who fraudulently appropriates money. Banks face this problem all the time, but so do other businesses.

White-Collar Crimes

One area within criminal activity has been named white-collar crime. White-collar crime is defined as any illegal act or series of acts committed by an individual or corporation by nonviolent means to obtain personal or business advantage.

One of the newest white-collar crimes involves computers. Clearly a temptation exists to manipulate computers for personal or business gain, and detection is often difficult. It has not been uncommon for companies or the government to discover a multimillion dollar theft a long time after it has taken place.

Another white-collar crime involves the bribery of foreign officials. In the 1970s, there were scandals involving payoffs to government officials in other countries in order to obtain contracts. Now the Foreign Corporate Practices Act (passed in 1977) clearly states that any offer to give anything valuable to a foreign government official to influence that government's acts for business purposes is illegal. Fines of up to $1 million can be applied.

Contract Law

Contract law governs the relationships between people and those to whom they make promises. A contract is simply a legally enforceable promise or set of promises. The importance of such promises has been recognized for thousands of years. Not all promises are contracts, however. In order for a promise to be a contract, it must meet the following specified requirements:

1. *Agreement.* There must be an agreement, an offer and an acceptance. One party must offer to do something, and the other party must agree to the offer.
2. *Voluntary.* The agreement must be a voluntary one. There can be no force used to make someone enter into such an agreement.
3. *Contractual capacity.* The parties must have contractual capacity. Each party must possess characteristics qualifying them as competent parties. They must be of legal age, not mentally insane, nor grossly drunk when they enter into the agreement.
4. *Consideration.* Subject to some exceptions, any promise made by the parties must be supported by legally sufficient consideration, defined simply as something of value. Legal consideration exists when something is intentionally exchanged for something else. Take an example where consideration does not exist. Smith says to his son, Smith, Jr., "In consideration of the fact that you are not as wealthy as your cousins, I will pay you $10,000." This is not an enforceable promise. It is not a contract. No consideration was given. Smith simply stated his motive for giving a gift to Smith, Jr.
5. *Legality.* Contracts must be made to accomplish some action that is legal. Any contract that requires either party to commit a crime is not enforceable.
6. *Absence of fraud.* There has to be a genuine acknowledgment and understanding of the terms of the contract. If fraud or gross misrepresentation occurs, the contract is not enforceable.

The Law of Sales (Commercial Law)

In the United States today, business transactions are covered by what is known as codified commercial law in the form of the Uniform Commercial Code. Usually referred to as the UCC, it takes the view that the entire commercial transaction of the sale and payment for goods is a single legal occurrence having numerous facets. Consider a consumer who buys a

SIGNING ON THE DOTTED LINE
MAY NOT MATTER

Contract law is one of the most important areas of business law for a businessperson to understand. There is one rule of thumb, however. A contract may be absolutely perfect in its form and substance, but if it runs counter to public policy it is void—the court will simply refuse to enforce the questionable clauses. Recently that is exactly what happened to a university dental school. The school tried to fight a malpractice suit by citing a document that all patients sign before undergoing treatment. That document states that patients "expressly waive and relinquish any and all claims of every nature" against the dental school. Assuming that professionals have a legal duty to practice with care and skill, the Supreme Court of Georgia wasn't about to let the dental school get away with such a contractual clause. Society would be injured if doctors, dentists, or other professionals were allowed to contract away that obligation. The clause was deemed to be against public policy and therefore void.

stereo from a local appliance store and agrees to pay for it on the installment plan. Different articles of the UCC cover the contract of sale, the processes of the check given as a down payment, and the store's extension of credit to the customer while retaining a right in the stereo (called collateral for the loan). If the appliance company obtains the stereo from a manufacturer's warehouse, several other articles come into play. Virtually all dealings involving the sale of goods are covered by the Uniform Commercial Code, and any person doing business must have at least minimum knowledge of its provisions.

A **tort** is defined as wrongful conduct by one individual that results in injury to another. Two notions—wrongs and compensation—serve as the basis of all torts. A tort is a civil action in which one person brings a suit of a personal nature against another. Business people have to worry about torts because they can be sued for negligence if someone is hurt while on their property, if an employee is hurt while doing his or her job, if a product they sell causes injury, and so on.

The areas subject to torts that concern business people are expanding. Business torts involve such vague categories as unfair competition, interfering with the business relations of others, infringing on trademarks, and disparagement of property or reputation.

Finally, there is an expanding area of tort problems involved with the notion of strict liability. **Strict liability** involves liability without fault. Under the theory of strict liability, liability for injuries is imposed for reasons other than fault. Most manufacturers are held liable even if it was not their fault that someone was injured using their product. For example, in one lawsuit, a couple recovered damages for facial burns their child suffered when the child crawled out of a crib and pulled over a hot water

The Law of Torts

TORT
Civil wrongs (as opposed to criminal) not arising from a breach of contract; a breach of a legal duty owed by the defendant to the plaintiff. The breach must be the proximate cause of the harm done to the plaintiff.

STRICT LIABILITY
Liability regardless of fault. Under tort law, strict liability is imposed on any person who introduces into commerce any good that is unreasonably dangerous when in a defective condition.

483

vaporizer because its electrical cord had been strung across the room. Clearly, it was the fault of the parents for having strung the electrical cord. Nonetheless, the manufacturer of the hot water vaporizer was held strictly liable.

Bankruptcy Law

When a business is no longer able to pay its bills, it may be forced into bankruptcy by its creditors. The United States Constitution provides that Congress shall establish uniform laws on the subject of bankruptcies. Therefore, federal law dictates how creditors may force companies into bankruptcy, how bankrupted businesspersons must act, and how potentially bankrupt businesses can voluntarily seek the aid of the courts in satisfying creditors' demands.

Bankruptcy law is designed to protect debtors from frivolous suits by creditors. It is also designed to provide a fair means of distributing a debtor's assets among all creditors. Thus, bankruptcy law establishes priorities among creditors and does not allow a debtor to favor one creditor over another.

Prior, during, and after bankruptcy proceedings, an area of criminal law called bankruptcy fraud can be a problem.

On the Job Revisited

Clifford Preston's corporation provided $84,000 worth of parts it manufactured to a buyer nine months ago, who then refused to pay, claiming that he did not have the funds. Clifford conferred with the other attorneys in his section and, while he didn't like doing it, he filed a petition with the federal bankruptcy court to force the debtor into involuntary bankruptcy. By the time all the information was made available to Clifford and the court, the debtor company showed virtually no assets. Clifford smelled a rat. He hired a private investigator to find out what had happened.

What he discovered was bankruptcy fraud. Because the owner of the debtor company knew he was going to be forced into bankruptcy, he started selling many of the assets of the company to friends and relatives at ridiculously low prices. His intention was to buy them back personally at just a hundred dollars more than the corporation had been paid. In one instance, the corporation sold a corporate car at 20 percent of its book value.

Now Clifford had to negotiate with the owner of the debtor firm. Clifford had every intention of going to the state attorney general's office to ask for criminal prosecution if the owner did not cooperate. By law, the owner had committed the crime of bankruptcy fraud.

SUMMARY

- Proponents of corporate social responsibility maintain that corporations should do more than simply make a profit. They point out that business managers have special expertise that can be applied to social problems.
- On the other hand, critics of the concept of corporate social responsibility contend that corporations should maximize growth in the economy; this would generate the most products, jobs, and tax revenues, which could then be used for social purposes. Social concepts should be left to publicly elected officials, according to these critics.

■ It is difficult to accurately define the concept of business ethics. One simple definition is that an act is ethical if the businessperson doing it would not be afraid to report his or her actions on a TV show.

■ Many professions have codes of ethics that establish the way in which members should act toward fellow members and clients.

■ The legal environment of business involves constitutional, common, and statutory law.

■ Businesses are concerned with criminal law in the sense that they are targets of criminal activity involving forgery, robbery, burglary, larceny, and embezzlement. Additionally, businesses are the perpetrators of white-collar crimes that involve illegal acts committed by individuals in a business capacity by nonviolent means in order to obtain personal wealth.

■ The elements necessary for a contract to be binding are: (1) an agreement; (2) it is voluntary; (3) the parties have contractual capacity; (4) consideration; (5) legality, and (6) absence of fraud.

■ A tort is a private wrong done by one individual against one or more other individuals that results in an injury.

ISSUES TO CONSIDER AND ANALYZE

1. Why is it important for businesses to continually alter their operations and perspectives to accommodate society's changing values?
2. Explain the differences between commercial law and criminal law.
3. What are businesses' costs and benefits of being socially responsible?
4. The text summarizes the pro and con arguments concerning the issue of business and social responsibility. Explain your position on this debate.
5. What requirements must a "promise" fulfill to be classified as a legal contract?
6. Why is it so difficult for an industry to establish an effective code of ethics?
7. The text mentions pollution and ethics as two vital areas of social responsibility for business. Suggest other important areas in which the public expects business to be socially responsible.
8. How does constitutional law affect businesses?
9. Is it possible for a business to be too socially responsible? Explain your answer.
10. What purpose and functions does the Better Business Bureau serve?

CASE FOR ANALYSIS

FIRESTONE: WAS THE COMPANY RESPONSIBLE OR IRRESPONSIBLE?

In 1978, the Firestone Tire & Rubber Company, the industry's second largest firm, reached agreement with the federal government to recall several million Firestone 500 tires sold on or after September 1, 1975, and manufactured before May 1, 1976. The recall allowed for free replacement of the Firestone 500s and remounting with the newer, safer, and better quality Firestone 721s. Firestone also voluntarily agreed to give customers a 50 percent trade-in value on six million Firestone 500s sold before September 1975. The cost to Firestone was estimated at $135 million.

The recalls were the result of extended efforts by the National Highway Traffic Safety Commission and others to convince Firestone to recall the tire. Records, analyses, and data collected showed that 41 deaths and 65 injuries were allegedly caused by blowouts or failures of the Firestone 500. It was disclosed that Firestone had specific test data in 1975 that indicated that some of the steel-belted tires did not measure up to standards after a year or two of storage. These tests were kept secret by Firestone.

Because of the recall, Firestone's production of 721s was strained to keep up with the demand for replacement tires. It was necessary to produce about 400,000 tires a month just to replace recalled tires. Also, in order to offset some of the negative public reaction to the recall, Firestone decided to extend its warranty on 721 tires from one year to two years.

Firestone found that contacting customers eligible for the recall was difficult. Car owners who had bought the tires as original equipment received letters from Firestone. Newspaper advertisements were placed in the Sunday editions of 242 major papers, and spot broadcasts about the recall were made on television. As of October 31, 1979, only about 25 percent of the recalled tires had in fact been replaced. The recall period officially ended in April 1980.

Firestone was concerned about cheating on the recall. The firm instructed dealers to interact directly with owners, have the owners sign a form verifying the replacement, and cut the serial numbers out of the exchanged 500s to eliminate retrading.

QUESTIONS

1. Do you feel that Firestone acted responsibly in this case? Why?
2. Some critics claim that Firestone was hypocritical in that it wanted to guard against cheating when in fact it had cheated. What do you think?
3. Should managers be held responsible for the deaths and accidents allegedly associated with defective tires?

Adapted from "Firestone Recall," *New York Times*, November 25, 1979, p. 49, and Mark N. Dodosh, "Big Firestone Recall Changes Used Tires into Collector's Items," *Wall Street Journal*, October 30, 1978, p. 1.

CHAPTER 24

BUSINESS: TRENDS AND CHALLENGES AHEAD

LEARNING OBJECTIVES

After studying this chapter, you should be able to:

Discuss the major issues surrounding the depletion of natural resources.

Explain the myths associated with women workers in the labor force.

Illustrate the role of government in the future business environment.

Define what is meant by increasing social responsiveness, and describe the work that a department of social responsibility does in a business firm.

Identify some examples of the competitive challenge being faced by American businesses.

KEY TERMS

Demographics
Social awareness
Quality of work life
Productivity

More than a decade ago, Alvin Toffler published his best seller, *Future Shock*. The author forecast, in 1970, that Americans would suffer stress and disorientation because they were experiencing too much change in too short a time span. Then, as if life imitated Toffler's predictions, the 1970s swept in, and change, disorientation, and stress were facts of life. Even Toffler, however, missed predicting:

- Student rioting and shootings at Kent State and Jackson State
- The recognition of Red China
- Watergate and the resignation of a president and vice president of the United States
- New York City and Chrysler on the brink of bankruptcy
- Inflation
- The decrease in American productivity
- Unemployment at 9.8 percent—the highest in thirty-five years
- The significant increase in the number of bankruptcies

Attemping to predict the future even by those who study it, like Toffler, is a tricky business. One of the trickiest sets of forecasts to make involves business: what will business be like in the 1980s and 1990s? Despite the problems associated with prediction, business managers and organizations must look at the future and consider its implications in order to make business decisions.

The one thing that is obviously part of the future is change. Managers and organizations will have to face and cope with change in order to survive. If they don't, they face financial losses and the eventual end of their businesses. The failures at Laker Airlines, Penn Central Railroad, and Rolls Royce illustrate this point. Managers and organizations as well as all the rest of us can profit from looking at these changes. As Mark Twain once remarked, "I am concerned about the future because I am going to spend the rest of my life there."

THE PAST TWENTY-FIVE YEARS

The last quarter century has seen significant changes in our society brought about by technological advances, social modifications, economic conditions, and political pressures. Some of the more publicized changes are listed in Exhibit 24-1. Many of these changes were not even imagined fifty years ago, but they will undoubtedly affect the direction society takes as it moves toward the twenty-first century. Changes have side effects that influence our life style and the quality of life now and in the future. Some of the side effects of recent changes are declining productivity, inflation, the depletion of natural resources, increased social awareness, rising educational levels, concern about the quality of work life, the increasing involvement of women and minorities in business organizations, government regulation, and the increase in international business responsibilities.

These and other side effects certainly have implications for business decisions.[1] Business leaders will have to respond to these effects, developing procedures to reduce unnecessary and wasteful energy depletion, to search for and implement challenging jobs, to integrate more women

EXHIBIT 24–1
Changes in the United States
from 1958 to 1983

Technological

- Computerized sales scanners in supermarkets
- Microsurgical equipment
- Bone-growth stimulators
- Over a 1 million-fold increase in computer power
- Astronauts on the moon
- Supersonic transportation
- Weather-detection space satellites
- Diesel passenger cars
- Personal home computers
- Speaking electronic scanners in supermarkets

Social

- Growth of suburban shopping malls
- Increased consumer awareness and pressure for better products and services
- Increased influx of Cuban, Haitian, Vietnamese, and Polish immigrants
- Acceptance of the philosophy that education is a lifelong process
- Declining birth rate
- Significant increase in the number of women and minorities in the labor force

Economic

- Devaluation of the dollar
- Multibillion dollar national government budget deficit
- Over twelve million Americans unemployed
- Increase in the standard of living for most people
- Significant expansion of a checkless or credit-card society
- Influx of international capital and managerial expertise into the United States
- Significant increase in the price of gold
- Rapid economic growth of Japan and West Germany

Political

- Medicare for the aged
- Severed relations with Iran
- Resignation of a president and a vice president
- Signing of the Panama Canal and Strategic Arms Limitations treaties

and minorities into the organizational mainstream, and to cope effectively with government regulations and procedures. The reactions of many business managers have been commented on throughout the book. The remainder of this final chapter calls attention to what the future may hold for business organizations, and the future is taken seriously by most businesses. The Business Close-Up shows how four prominent firms are preparing for the future.

THE WORK TODAY OF FOUR FIRMS LOOKING AT TOMORROW: BRISTOL-MYERS, KOPPERS, CROWN-ZELLERBACH, AND DART AND KRAFT

Bristol-Myers is a multibillion dollar pharmaceutical firm that is looking to the future. Some of the products being prepared for this future at Bristol-Myers are:

- Acne therapy drugs
- Hypertension medication
- Analgesic compounds to treat arthritis pain
- Infant formulas to improve nutrition
- Oral antibiotics

Koppers is a multibillion dollar firm involved in the synfuels industry, genetic engineering, coal industry, engineering construction, forest products, and road materials. To prepare for the 1990s, Koppers is working in these areas:

- Increased exploration of uses for coal, oil, and gas. The firm expects to produce 10 million tons of coal per year from their properties by 1990.
- Support of research projects at eight universities studying materials-processing techniques and energy sources with a view to the employment of advanced technology for the specific development of new products.
- Spending over $750 million on new facilities and equipment.

Crown-Zellerbach is one of the largest forest products and paper companies in the United States. It owns twenty-two corrugated container plants and eight high-technology facilities. There are more than thirty thousand employees in thirty-eight states and Canada working for Crown-Zellerbach (C-Z). The C-Z management team has a view of the future as witnessed by these actions:

Source: Company annual reports for 1981 provided this information.

- Capital investments of $2.1 billion from 1979–1984. The key to these investments is to increase productivity. This is a stated objective in C-Z's modernization plans for plant and equipment.
- Plans to increase substantially the firm's use of energy from renewable sources. Power-generating boilers capable of burning renewable fuels are operating at fourteen facilities, with plans to convert all C-Z facilities.
- Increasing international operations. Expansion of facilities in Canada and increased marketing to mainland China, South America, Central America, and the Middle East.

Dart and Kraft is a manufacturer, marketer, and distributor of brand name food products, specialty chemicals, and plastics. Some of the Dart and Kraft products you have probably seen or used include Philadelphia cream cheese, Cracker barrel cheese, Velveeta, Miracle Whip salad dressing, Breyers ice cream, Duracell batteries, and Tupperware. The company has paid particular attention to the social responsibility area. Dart and Kraft sees its future in the community. Some of the firm's involvement has included:

- Providing scholarships and fellowships to students pursuing careers in nutrition and its effects on good health.
- Cosponsoring state and national 4-H health awards, which involve over five million young people annually.
- Continued funding of the University of Southern California's Center for the Study of Private Enterprise, which explores the impact of private enterprise on the American economic system.

TODAY'S TRENDS

Current trends set the tone for the future. Thus it is important to understand some of the current developments in our society. In general, these developments are side effects of the industrializaton we experienced earlier in this century.

Natural Resources

Although it is a fact that the world's resources are limited, our society has acted as if this were not the case. Today, however, most business managers

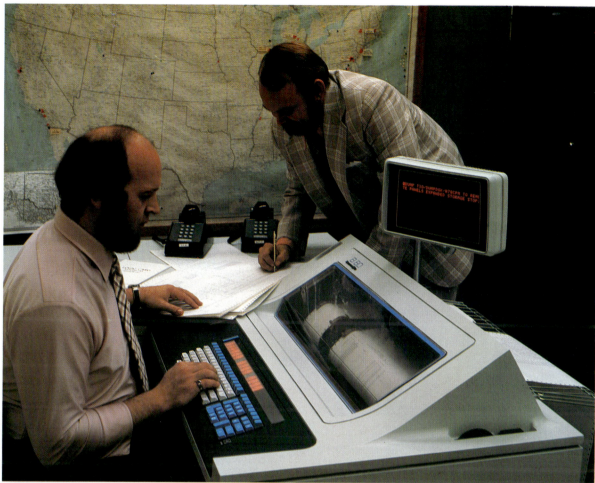

are aware of shortages in world resources and the consequent skyrocketing prices for these resources. Products such as sugar, coffee, paper, and petroleum have undergone significant price increases in world markets, and there are no signs that such dramatic increases for goods in short supply will end. Americans must, therefore, reorient themselves away from wasteful consumption and toward an intelligent *conservation of natural resources.* This, of course, will have an effect on business strategy, pricing, profit margins, and business responsibility.

If resources existed in unlimited amounts, there would be little need for efficient management. But as gas supplies dwindle, as coffee crops are damaged through patterns of soil erosion, as water supplies become unfit for human consumption, and as many other natural supplies change, better management of resources becomes increasingly important. Business, government, unions, and citizens all have a shared personal stake in the efficient management of scarce, valuable resources.

The development of alternative sources of energy—nuclear, solar, and oil shale—through new processes like offshore drilling and gasification—will take a decade or more as well as changes in national policy. The Congress has yet to act forcefully on these issues because of the complexity of energy problems and the controversy surrounding them. But the problem isn't the government's alone. In order to achieve steady economic growth with full employment, we must help. Nearly half of all the energy consumed ends up heating or cooling the outdoors—a total waste. Thus the cheapest source of new energy for the United Sates is *conservation energy,* the energy produced by cutting waste. On the whole, people have been reluctant to conserve energy, but they must be convinced that the energy shortages facing the world are genuine. We have already lost valuable time in the fight to conserve our dwindling resources.

Demographics

The picture emerging from the 1980 census portrays a dynamic, fast-changing America. **Demographics** are statistics that describe populations.[2] A look at the demographics of the United Sates indicates shifts in the rural makeup of the country, life-style changes, and a population that on the average is growing older. Demographics also indicate that the most population growth in the United States will be in the southern and western regions, there will be an increase in the proportion of college-educated adults, and the number of working women will increase substantially in the decade ahead.

DEMOGRAPHICS
Statistics that are used to describe a population with reference to age, gender, education level, birth rate, geographical distribution, and so on.

Exhibits 24–2 through 24–5 present some of the demographic trends that will affect each of the areas of business covered in this book. An awareness of such trends is essential to business managers who must make timely and on-target decisons about finances, marketing, management, and government matters.

For example, population size, gender, and age have several implications for marketing decisions. The slow growth rate of the population means that businesses must work to extend further into existing markets, and management must realize that sales growth has to come from superior products and services. Marketing managers can also see that babies, the early middle-aged, and senior citizens will be major groups to focus prod-

CHARACTERISTIC	1960	1970	1980	1990	2000
Population size	180,671,000	204,878,000	221,651,000	243,004,000	259,869,000
Rate of population increase over prior decade	18.5%	13.4%	8.2%	9.6%	6.9%
Annual number of births	4,257,850	3,731,386	3,575,000	3,868,000	3,676,000
Percent males	—	48.7	48.7	48.7	48.6
Percent females	—	51.3	51.3	51.3	51.4
Life expectancy of males	66.6	67.1	69.4	69.7	70.0
Life expectancy of females	73.1	74.6	77.3	77.8	78.3
Median age of population	29.4	27.9	30.2	32.8	35.5

Source: Current Population Reports (Washington, D.C.: U.S. Bureau of the Census), Series P-25. Projections are based on Series II assumptions.

EXHIBIT 24-2   Selected Characteristics of United States Population, 1960–2000

EXHIBIT 24-3

Distribution of United States Population by Geographic Regions, 1970–2000

Source: U.S. Bureau of the Census, *Current Population Reports*, Series P-25, No. 460 and Series P-20, No. 324. Projections based on Series II assumptions.

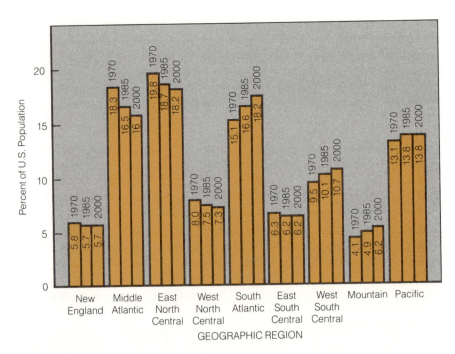

KEY OF REGIONS
New England: Maine, New Hampshire, Vermont, Massachusets, Rhode Island, Connecticut
Middle Atlantic: New York, New Jersey, Pennsylvania
East North Central: Ohio, Indiana, Illinois, Michigan, Wisconsin
West North Central: Minnesota, Iowa, Missouri, North Dakota, South Dakota, Nebraska, Kansas
South Atlantic: Delaware, Maryland, District of Columbia, Virginia, West Virginia, North Carolina, South Carolina, Georgia, Fiorida
East South Central: Kentucky, Tennessee, Alabama, Mississippi
West South Central: Arkansas, Louisiana, Oklahoma, Texas
Mountain: Montana, Idaho, Wyoming, Colorado, New Mexico, Arizona, Utah, Nevada
Pacific: Washington, Oregon, California, Alaska, Hawaii

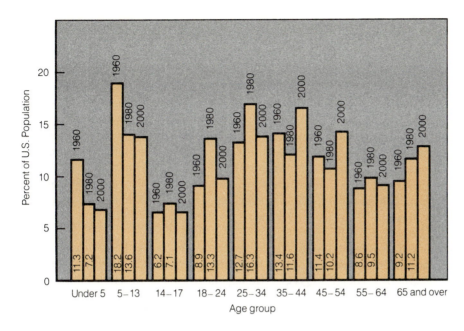

EXHIBIT 24-4

Age Distribution of United States
Population, 1960–2000

Source: U.S. Bureau of the Census,
Current Population Reports, Series P–25,
Nos. 310, 311, 519, 704, 721.
Projections are based on Series II
assumptions.

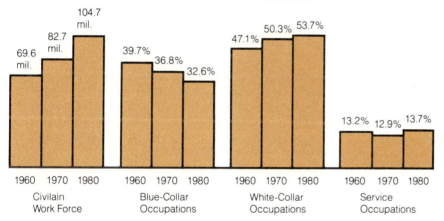

PROPORTION OF NONFARM JOBS IN–

EXHIBIT 24–5
The American Workforce

Between 1960 and 1980, the number of white-collar jobs increased 78 percent to 51 million and service jobs grew 62 percent to 13 million. But blue-collar jobs only gained 28 percent to 31 million.

uct and service attention on. Personnel and corporate managers can see from the trends in the workforce that growing attention must be paid to white-collar and service occupations. Developing and implementing motivational programs that work with employees in these occupations will become important.

The 1960s and 1970s were characterized by a steadily increasing **social awareness**. The media directed attention to well-known business organizations and their efforts to improve the quality of their products and

SOCIAL AWARENESS
An awareness, beyond immediate profits, of such social concerns as pollution, product quality, employment discrimination, safer products, and employee safety.

Social Awareness

services, reduce prices, eliminate employment discrimination, and increase the corporate role in communities. The available evidence suggests that this pressure and concern for social well-being will continue and probably increase.

Concern for the environment, fair value, and product and service quality will eradicate some of the planned obsolescence and product frills—such as the "extra three cubic feet" of trunk space in an automobile—that have been in effect since the early 1950s. The importance of less expensive, safer, and more durable products will replace many of the inefficient products presently available. In addition, the production, distribution, and use of products will have to meet the test of environmental acceptability. *Social awareness* means that people in every age group voice their environmental concerns.

Quality of Work Life

QUALITY OF WORK LIFE
A managerial program that increases outcomes such as productivity or performance by better management of jobs, people, and working conditions.

The **quality of work life** (QWL) has become the focus of growing concern in the past few years, not only in the United States but throughout Western industrialized society. **QWL** is the approach to a work environment that increases outcomes like performance by better management of jobs, people, and working conditions. As people become more educated, they become more concerned about adequate and fair compensation, the safety of the work environment, the development of their skills, psychological growth, and workers' rights and privileges.

The quality of the work life seems to influence the workers' response to the job. Improvements in this quality can lead to increased (1) job satisfaction, (2) job performance, (3) personal development, and (4) organizational effectiveness. Because these are such potentially important consequences, managers will examine strategies for improving the quality of work life more closely. Of course, any managerial action in this area has to be balanced with such forces as rising inflation, increased foreign competition, depletion of natural resources, and increased governmental intervention in business activities, as well as with other work programs.

Women and Minorities in Business

Racial, ethnic, and sexual job discrimination has had a long history. Until the middle of the twentieth century, many businesses specified the desired sex and race when advertising for employees. But recently businesses, as well as many citizens, have tried to minimize discrimination in employment.

Fortune once listed 379,000 black managers in American businesses.[3] Yet many black business managers still feel they are not doing meaningful jobs. Integrating more black managers into the business mainstream is a continuous task that more companies will work on—some in response to government pressures but many just to provide more challenging opportunities for blacks.

Spanish-surnamed people, American Indians, and Orientals make up 5 percent of the population of the United States. All of them have experienced the kinds of employment discrimination that blacks have suffered. The educational levels of Spanish-surnamed people and American Indians have been lower than the average population, which has hindered them from getting important, high-skilled jobs. But Orientals, who have high educational levels, have moved into an increasing number of white-collar and skilled occupations in the past twenty-five years. However, there is still much work to be done. For example, the American Indian is found in greater numbers in labor-type jobs than whites; blacks hold fewer professional jobs and fewer managerial jobs than whites.

It appears that the movement of these minority groups into business will be difficult even with government intervention. Differences in customs, values, and accents will slow down their integration into the mainstream, but business management can take a leadership role in overcoming employment discrimination.

Despite such legislation as the Equal Pay Act of 1963 and the Equal Employment Opportunity Act of 1972, discrimination against women in employment is still a difficult problem. Although equal pay for equal work is the law, such jobs as secretary-stenographer, bookkeeper, school-teacher, and household worker have developed lower pay ranges than comparable jobs traditionally done by men. Even today, American women working full time earn only about 60 percent of what men earn. In an effort to close this earnings gap, there is and will be a growing movement to have the widely accepted concept of equal pay for equal jobs expanded to include equal pay for comparable jobs.[4]

There are many myths associated with women workers, including the following:

- Women take jobs away from men.
- Women don't have to work.
- Women don't work as long as men.
- Women don't want job responsibility.

These myths are not supported by studies of men and women employees, and therefore steps must be taken to minimize the effects of these myths on employment decisions.

One survey indicated that in the United States women represented 3.5 percent of the lawyers, 6.5 percent of the physicians, 2.1 percent of the dentists, 2.0 percent of the judges, and 1.2 percent of the engineers. Women in the Soviet Union at about the same time made up 36 percent of the lawyers, 75 percent of the physicians, 83 percent of the dentists, 30 percent of the judges, and 28 percent of the engineers[5] These discrepancies are the result of differences in opportunity rather than differences in the intelligence, skills, or abilities of American and Soviet women.

Full and effective use of women's talents is not yet a fact in this country. Attitudes and expectations are changing slowly, however, and they will continue to change as women continue to prove their abilities.

Government and Business

Since the early 1930s, the government's role in business has increased markedly. The government has been actively involved in Social Security programs, environmental pollution controls, equal opportunity legislation, standards for mergers, price and wage controls, education, and health care. No available evidence indicates that this trend will be reversed by the twenty-first century. The Reagan administration has reduced some government involvement, but business still has to deal with a variety of policies, laws, inspections, and programs emanating from Washington, D.C., or some state capital.

During the 1970s, government was the fastest growing sector in our economy. Local, state, and federal governments will probably continue to be involved in such areas as banking, housing, transportation, medical services, human rights, environmental quality, and international trade. In fact, additional legislation seems to be coming in the areas of welfare, health care, environmental quality, and human rights. The growing role of government in business was evident in the creation of Amtrak and the financial support given New York City and Chrysler as well as the breaking of the Professional Association of Air Traffic Controllers Union in the summer of 1981.

Worldwide Business Responsibilities

Business transactions among nations have been conducted for thousands of years; however, the multinational business is relatively new. A multinational business (MNB) is one that operates in many countries, that carries out research and manufacturing in those countries, and that has a multinational management team and a multinational group of stockholders.

The reasons for trade among countries were cited in the discussion of international business in Chapter 22. A country is assumed to be better off concentrating on the goods it can produce most efficiently and economically and then trading those goods for goods produced efficiently in other countries. But there are other reasons for investment abroad, including reducing transportation costs because the market is closer, using local raw materials, tapping new markets, and controlling the manufacturing process more closely.

In many countries, the relationship between the multinational company and the host country's government is tense. The host country may complain about such irresponsible actions as:

■ Failure to train competent nationals to take over managerial positions
■ Lack of concern for the country's social customs
■ Absorption of local savings that could be invested in national business
■ The hiring away of the most talented local personnel
■ Exhausting the country's natural resources

Such major companies as IBM, Exxon, and Singer earn more than half of their net profits from foreign operations so they have every reason to be concerned about host countries' complaints. Management should be more concerned in the future about developing programs that reduce these potential tensions. Of course, Japanese, West German, British, and other multinational firms operating in the United States also have to show more responsibility in this country.

As American firms venture into the international marketplace, they encounter such giants as Siemans of Germany, Phillips of the Netherlands, and Mitsubishi of Japan. For example, Mitsubishi is involved in making over twenty-five thousand different items from salt to television sets to airplanes.[6] The company is already doing a $16 billion annual business in the United States. These and other multinational firms do more than transport goods and services into and money out of a host country; they also bring jobs and products to the local economy. For example, ITT

THE 1980s MAY SPAWN THE FIRST WORLD ECONOMIC WAR: THE UNITED STATES VERSUS JAPAN

American business leaders claim that worldwide business can be expanded in the future if barriers imposed by foreign governments are relaxed. The Japanese are notorious for raising such barriers, which are expected to continue until the United States government and business present a united front. Here are some examples of the barriers (for example, red tape, special taxes, tough inspections).

Sporting goods. The American inventor of aluminum baseball bats was forced by regulators in Japan to stop selling in that country because the bats used the wrong kind of aluminum.

Volleyball, soccer, and handball leagues permit use of Japanese-made inflatable balls only

Agriculture. Quotas limit the amount of leather goods and beef, oranges, fruit juices, milk and cheeses that can be imported despite the fact that Japan has signed treaties agreeing to bar these trade restrictions.

Cars. Autos exported to Japan (for example, an Oldsmobile or Chevrolet) require six volumes of documents on standards and testing for each model, adding as much as $500 to the retail price.

Auto inspectors are so strict that defects are found 80 percent of the time, and long waits are required before retesting is completed.

Health care. Pharmaceuticals and medical equipment are hard to sell in Japan. A manufacturer seeking to sell a product there must first turn it over to the government for a safety inspection. Product testing takes months—even years. In the meantime, Japanese producers are given samples of the item by the government and have time to produce their own imitations of the product before the American version is allowed on the market.

(manufacturer of telephone systems and telecommunications equipment) regards the four hundred thousand jobs it provides around the world as its greatest contribution to global well-being.

The move into Japanese markets is still frustrating American business leaders. The Business Close-Up spells out some of the difficulties that will probably be facing business for years to come.

The job of running a business is quite difficult as it is. With the social changes we have just contemplated and the others that will undoubtedly occur, the managerial job will become even more complex, challenging, fast-paced, and rewarding.

The United States is experiencing major changes: from cheap to expensive energy, from an era of single-digit to double-digit inflation and high interest rates, from regulation to deregulation, from one technological change to another. In addition, world events in the Middle East, Central America, Europe, and Asia affect American business decisions. We are also faced with a dismal record of productivity. In simple terms **productivity** is the relationship between the output of goods and services and the input of

BUSINESS IN THE FUTURE

Productivity

PRODUCTIVITY
The relationship between the output of goods and services and the input of labor and other resources used to produce the outputs.

labor and other resources used to produce the outputs. From 1880 to the early 1950s, the United States annual growth and productivity was about .7 percent higher than in any other leading country. This was a small but a decisive difference. Since the early 1950s, this difference has been reversed.

Opportunities to turn our productivity rate upward exist, but one challenge is that we must learn how to measure productivity.[8] Task forces within organizations will be needed to study, measure, and experiment with productivity. What is not measured can't be controlled or improved. When United States productivity figures are published, they only represent the output of the manufacturing sector and occasionally that of agriculture. The data must be extended to include service-sector productivity (for example, insurance, medicine, accounting, research and development). The business community will have to work more at measuring productivity in their sector of the economy. Productivity can't be ignored, and in the next two decades it will have to be studied more by individuals who understand statistics, measurement, economics, and human behavior.

The Economy

Whatever happened to that American dream of owning a home? Only ten years ago, a family's house payment averaged a little more than about twenty-five cents out of every dollar earned. Today it takes about forty-four cents out of every dollar. Fewer than one out of eleven families can afford to buy their first home. In addition to individual dreams and hopes that are unattainable, the nation is now faced with sagging productivity. We must increase productivity, make it possible to modernize plants, and use the technology that is available. This means reducing unemployment, improving worker efficiency, bringing government spending back within government revenues. These challenges will face many readers of this book in the future.

Since 1960, the United States government has spent 5.1 trillion; the national debt has grown to over $648 billion, and prices have skyrocketed by over 178 percent.[9] Are we better off? The facts add up to a fundamental truth: there are problems today in the United States because the economy is not productive enough to do all the things that we demand of it. Creative and enthusiastic leaders in business, labor, health, law, and the government will be needed in the next decade more than at any time in the history of the United States. Unless the economy is improved significantly, there will be more and more business disappointments and failures.

Competition

The competitive challenges to business leaders in the future will intensify. Domestic competition will remain at about the same level because the number of firms will be fairly stable. In some industries, like transportation and oil and gas exploration, competition will increase as a result of government deregulation. Air fare and gasoline pricing wars are examples of this.

The impact of foreign competition will continue to grow. In the United States today, foreign businesses are now capturing large market shares—28 percent of the automobiles, 30 percent of sports and athletic goods, 34 percent of microwave ovens, 90 percent of both CB radios and motorcycles, and almost 100 percent of video cassette recorders.[10] Radial tires, calculators, cameras, premium beers, digital watches, and outboard motors are also imported in large numbers. The successes of foreign businesses are based on quality control, somewhat lower production costs, good promotion, and innovation.

American business leaders must seek out innovations, reduce the time necessary to respond to market conditions, and upgrade quality control. Even before wooing foreign markets, businesses must reestablish the "Made in the USA" label among American consumers. Again, leadership by business managers will be needed to turn things around.

Market Patterns

A society such as ours, suddenly faced with the reality of limited resources, must shift its philosophy from one of abundance and waste to one of scarcity. To the manager educated under the philosophy and practice of abundance, the issue of scarcity may be difficult to accept and put into practice. Yet managers in all functional business areas must play a more dominant role in conserving resources. For example, the role of the marketing manager will come to involve promoting intelligent product use rather than stimulating overconsumption through advertisements.

From a managerial perspective, it is possible to tone down wasteful consumption. In the future, business will derive profits from selling smaller quantities of higher-priced products. This will mean automobiles that go farther on less gas and that require less maintenance, appliances that can easily be repaired, buildings that are better constructed, and furniture that lasts longer.

As a current example of conservation, consider the products available in the tire, battery, and auto accessory field. Top-line automobile tires once lasted for about 15,000 miles. Today, many companies guarantee their tires for 40,000 miles. Pricers are higher, but the consumer is being educated on how to get the best performance from them. Similarly, automobile batteries, which once lasted for two years, can now last for the life of the car. This type of engineering and marketing is consistent with intelligent conservation.

Another important shift in market patterns involves the changing nature of our population. Presently, the Census Bureau is forecasting an additional 50 million Americans by the year 2000. This means that there will be about 275 million Americans. But the average age of the population will increase dramatically. The number of children, teenagers, and young adults under thirty-four will increase by less than 40 percent. The challenge facing managers is to determine the needs of an older population and then shift resources into areas to fill those needs so that their companies can make profits. The use of statistics, computers, and marketing research tools will be important in meeting this challenge.

The shift in population patterns is accompanied by changing values. The trend today in most age categories is away from the Protestant work ethic and toward more pleasure, leisure, immediate gratification, and sexual freedom, and away from worry about the long-term or the future. Changes in values pose many problems for managers, who will need to become more behaviorally oriented. That is, they will need to learn about employee values by being good listeners, asking questions, and observing people more carefully. Managerial practices that worked in the 1970s may not be appropriate for employees with the different values reflected in the 1980s.

A business organization's survival will always depend on the effectiveness of decisions—what products to offer, where to offer them, and at what price. But business leaders of tomorrow must cope with limited resources, an older population, and changing values. Understanding and being able to implement major concepts of business and the economy, organization and government, management, finance, marketing, and analysis and control are necessary if the right decisions are to be put into action in the future.

Job Design

Rising educational levels and employee concerns with improving the quality of work life will require managers to consider building challenge, autonomy, and personal development into jobs. Business managers will have to provide opportunities for workers who want these types of enriched jobs. Managers who fail to provide such opportunities in the form of redesigned jobs will be faced with high turnover and the necessity of hiring and even rewarding marginal performers.

The creative business manager will be able to find ways to make jobs more gratifying, but other managers will have to undergo training to improve their redesign skills or else face the possibility of working with frustrated, hostile, and dissatisfied workers. Such unpleasant conditions could result in higher levels of stress, which in turn could lead to high turnover among the poorly prepared managers. Creative managers will be needed in every business function, from production to accounting.

Although future employees will be better educated, have higher aspirations, and be prepared to take on greater job responsibilities, they will make greater demands on managerial time. Redesigning jobs is a significant challenge, especially because not all workers want such changes. The business manager must walk a very narrow path, enriching jobs for some without alienating others.

Social Responsibility

Business is allowed to operate by the people of the United States. So long as society wants business to continue to exist, it can move forward. Thus, the organization must be responsive to the society it operates in and do business in a responsible manner. Business organizations must also be responsive to the needs and desires of stockholders, employees, suppliers, and consumers. Even small organizations must address issues of social responsiveness on a regular basis. In the next twenty years, managerial attention to *social responsiveness* will probably become more intense.

In order to be responsible, it appears that business firms need to develop a systematized program of social responsiveness. Some business organizations have already established departments of social responsibility, and more organizations will probably develop such departments. A social responsibility department is typically charged with handling consumer issues, government relations, public relations, community affairs, contributions, and academic relations. The managers of the unit must continually monitor the social environment to pick up warning signals of problems. This type of monitoring will probably be done by well-trained professional managers who serve as contact persons with the greater society.

The public expects business to show leadership in such areas as controlling air and water pollution, rebuilding cities, eliminating economic depressions, and eliminating racial discrimination. These expectations are difficult to meet without a systematic program. One such program exists at Prudential Life Insurance Company. Prudential has a special department focusing on social responsibility, working on such problems as investment policy and how to make it more socially responsive, urban problems, and equal employment opportunity and minority assistance.[11]

Prudential's forward-looking approach appears to be more effective than a crisis-oriented approach. In the crisis approach, an organization only reacts to problems such as pollution or alleged discrimination in hiring minorities when there is a community complaint. But such a reactive program has little continuity or long-run commitment; at best, it's a patchwork approach. In order to respond on a continual basis, more businesses will incorporate a full-time unit charged with addressing in a proactive way the firm's social responsibility. This means social responsiveness will have to be measured and evaluated over time—no easy task. For years businesses have tried to develop performance measures in production, marketing, and finance. There is every reason to believe that social responsibility measures can be developed that are as good and as valid as other traditional measures. However, it will take commitment and work to come up with them.

Organizations are already trying to assess their social responsibility under the label of the "corporate social audit." More organizations will become involved in such efforts to pinpoint their successes and failures in responding to social needs in such areas as ecology, urban growth, and employment.

Admittedly, major problems are associated with these structural changes and performance measurements. Any firm that addresses social responsibility will have to cope with attendant financial matters. What is the proper balance between earning a satisfactory profit and contributing to society? These two activities, both important, can compete for the resources of a business. For example, the dollars Shell Oil gives to academic institutions are not available as dividends to stockholders. The hours a Xerox executive donates to a group of minority small-business owners, helping them solve problems, cannot be spent on solutions to excessive production costs in the corporate business. These efforts pay off in a better educated, aware, and stimulated society that is more productive and involved in business. Thus, these programs have value for both the firm and society as a whole.

These considerations bring up a final question: who must pay the costs of being socially responsive. Customers can pay in the form of higher prices; employees can pay by not receiving the wages they believe are fair; owners can pay by receiving lower dividends. An important part of future strategies will be to work out equitable plans for sharing these costs. The only way that a fair sharing program can be developed is by measuring social responsiveness. Cost sharing, planning, and the development of performance measurement will consume many executive hours in the future.

CONCLUSION

Change is always difficult to predict. The suggestions in this chapter are an attempt to discuss the kind of changes that may influence the business world in the next two decades. One certainty seems to be that business organizations will be held responsible for their actions now and in the future. These responsibilities will involve tackling the productivity problem, facing increased foreign competition, wisely using limited resources, manufacturing and marketing safe and durable products, hiring and promoting more women and minorities, redesigning jobs for more satisfaction, and conducting more business in foreign countries. The implications of these and other future responsibilities are significant for business managers because it is management that must respond creatively to the changes in our society. Managers will need the knowledge, skills, tools, and attitudes discussed and presented throughout this book to meet the problems changes will bring. Indeed, many of the managers who will meet these challenges have just finished reading this book. You are the future of American business.

The fate of American business will eventually be in your hands. This fate is convincingly portrayed by the comments made by John K. Collings, Jr., vice chairman of the Coca-Cola Company:

> The stamp "Made in America" no longer identifies those products bought in and outside of this country. Our angel at the top of the tree has dimmed its light. This country is no longer in a prosperity position of being competitive. The leadership of American business must pull tightly on the reins to secure a sound direction for the future. . . . America is beautiful. America can be successful once again. But the blinders that have discouraged its growth and forward thrust must be removed so that prosperity and a fine competitive edge can once again be part of this great country's calling card. It is time to revitalize American business.[12]

ISSUES TO CONSIDER AND ANALYZE

1. Select a business such as a grocery store, a gasoline station, or a fast-food restaurant and ask the manager or owner what changes he or she has seen in the business during the past ten years. You should try to find a business in which the manager or owner has at least ten years of experience.
2. One expert claims that in the next decade two hundred thousand energy auditors will be needed in the United States. These auditors would identify the profitable conservation potential in homes and buildings for clients, customers, or organizations. Is this an occupation that you think is needed and will become important? Why?
3. Why have Japanese and West German business organizations been so successful in United States and Canadian markets?
4. What are companies in your city or town doing to reduce or eliminate sex, race, age, and handicap discrimination? Provide some examples.
5. Why must productivity be improved before the United States economy becomes healthy?
6. Why would business managers be interested in the demographics of the United States?

7. Some people believe that we must sacrifice some of the growth rate in our standard of living to improve the quality of life. What does this mean?
8. How can the government become more effective in working with business organizations in the future?
9. Can American business be revitalized in the future? How?

QUBE: A SYSTEM FOR THE FUTURE

CASE FOR ANALYSIS

Columbus, Ohio, is a city with a metropolitan population of about 1,100,000. The people in this area have an opportunity to participate in the Warner Communications/American Express' Qube cable television system. Qube is an experimental system aimed at determining viewer opinions about products, services, people, political figures, the economy, and even business in society. The system is called interactive—people communicating with a computer.

Qube's main innovation is a set of buttons in Columbus homes that feed yes-no answers from viewers of a television screen to a central computer network. By interacting (the viewer feeds answers into the computer), political polling, marketing research, and overall public opinion responses can be collected. This kind of interactive technology is said to be the wave of the future.

Predictions are that ordinary newspaper advertisements and video catalogues will be coded on television screens, thus enabling subscribers to order department store merchandise from their homes. Bank-at-home systems are now being tested. In one experiment, viewers are able to read their bank statements from television screens and pay their bills without leaving home. Loan applications are filled out at home, and loans or withdrawals are made at automatic cash machines in banks or stores.

The Qube type of interactive communication is compatable with trends in society. Energy shortages and conservation are now important issues. By staying at home instead of traveling by automobile to and from banks and stores, energy can be conserved. The growing demand for leisure time is met through use of the time-saving Qube system. Social responsibility goals can be partially met by companies using Qube systems to inform users of product safety features. Working women and dual-career families (husband and wife) would find the Qube system useful because they could sit in their living room and make business transactions that are difficult because of time constraints.

QUESTIONS

1. Do you believe that Qube type systems will be widely used by the end of the 1980s? Explain your answer.
2. What other uses of Qube do you forsee?
3. Would you subscribe to a Qube system? Why?

Based on Edward Meadow, "Why TV Sets Do More In Columbus, Ohio," *Fortune*, October 6, 1980, pp. 67-68, 71–73.

CAREER PACKAGE

Career planning is an individual process. Each of us has a unique set of values, interests, and work and personal experiences. Understanding how this unique set of factors blends is an important part of career planning, but it is also necessary to understand the requirements of various jobs so that your own personality and intellectual abilities can be matched with a job. Your career decision will shape your life style.

This book points up career opportunities in economics, government, management, finance, marketing, accounting, statistics, and management information systems. In the future, many similar opportunities will exist for those college graduates (four and two year) who have been personally and educationally prepared for careers. This appendix focuses on the activities the about-to-graduate person follows in deciding on and starting a career. The emphasis is on prior planning. A person who plans systematically can develop a program of action that will achieve her or his goals.

In order to achieve some degree of job satisfaction, each of us needs to find a job that uses our skills, aptitudes, and potential. An important first step in finding this kind of employment is to assess your own skills, interests, attitudes, and goals.

SELF-ANALYSIS

Answering some basic questions is a part of self-assessment. A personal evaluation of these and similar questions is a worthwhile exercise. These questions may help you develop a job or career identity.

Who Am I?

Many people start to think about a career as teenagers. Dr. Eli Ginzberg has proposed an interesting theory of vocational choice that helps explain the forces that influence a person's career selection. He suggests that individuals go through a fantasy stage (before age eleven), during which they assume that they can become anything they desire—a firefighter, a professional basketball player, a doctor, or president of the United States. Next they enter a tentative stage (ages eleven to seventeen), in which values and interests develop and change. In the final stage, the realistic stage, the person tries to integrate interests, skills, values, and goals.

According to Ginzberg, the career choice eventually involves a compromise. We try to choose a career that fully uses our skills and aptitudes and also satisfies important needs and goals. The person who has conducted an honest self-assessment is on the right road to making the best and most realistic career choice.

Professional Help for Self-Assessment

Professional counselors can help you decide which career path to take. Most high schools and colleges provide free counseling services where trained professionals help a person perform a realistic self-assessment.

WHO AM I EVALUATION WORK SHEET

The following are some of the things you should consider in your own self-evaluation. Make your answers honest. They are meant to help you and should not represent a "good" or "bad" value judgment.

1. What are the things I do best? Are they related to people, data, or things?

   _____ related to _____

   _____ related to _____

   _____ related to _____

2. Do I express myself well and easily?
   Orally: Yes _____ No _____ In writing: Yes _____ No _____

3. Am I usually a leader of a group or team? Yes _____ No_____
   Am I an active participant of a group or team? Yes _____ No_____
   Do I like to work on my own? Yes _____ No _____
   Do I like supervision? Yes _____ No _____

4. Do I work well under pressure? Yes _____ No _____
   Does pressure cause me anxiety; in fact, is it difficult for me to work well under pressure? Yes _____ No _____

5. Do I seek responsibility? Yes _____ No _____
   Do I prefer to follow directions? Yes _____ No _____

6. In the future, which of the following things are most important to me:
   a. Working for a regular salary _____ b. Working for a commission _____
   c. Working for a combination of both _____

7. Do I want to work a regular schedule (e.g., 9 A.M. to 5 P.M.)? Yes _____
   No _____

8. Am I willing to travel more than 50 percent of my working time? Yes _____
   No _____

9. Do I prefer an urban environment (population over a million)? Yes _____
   No _____
   or population between 100,000 to 900,000? Yes _____ No _____ or
   do I prefer a rural setting? Yes _____ No _____

10. Do I prefer to work for a large organization? Yes _____ No _____

Vocational tests are often used to verify one's self-analysis and to reveal any hidden personal characteristics. This test information is then explained and interpreted by professional counselors. No one test or battery of tests can make a career choice for you, but tests can supplement the information you're reviewing as you mull over career opportunities and personal characteristics. Your college placement office has counselors who can recommend which tests are most appropriate for you.

In addition, the counselor can help you with your self-assessment by providing publications discussing career opportunities. Some widely publicized and frequently used publications include:

■ *College Placement Annual*, College Placement Council, Inc., P.O. Box 2263, Bethlehem, Pa. 18001—published annually. This annual provides information on current job openings in companies. It also provides suggestions on preparing resumes and interviewing for jobs.
■ *Occupational Outlook Handbook*, U.S. Department of Labor, Government Printing Office, Washington, D.C.—published annually. This handbook lists all major occupations with a brief description of job requirements, opportunities available, and future job prospects.

Self-assessment, help from a professional counselor, and career publications can provide the necessary background information to properly plan your career. But in the final analysis, you alone must make the career decision and seek appropriate job opportunities. A counselor, parent, or friend cannot make a career decision for you.

THE JOB SEARCH: A PLAN

In school, you prepare for examinations by organizing your notes and planning. In searching for a job, you also need to organize and plan. The first job after graduation can affect your entire career, so a plan is a must. Without a plan, you will lose valuable time and experience unnecessary frustration.

There is no single best job-search plan, but there are some basic principles. Because your time is limited, you must use some systematic procedure to narrow the number of job possibilities. Each company offers different conditions, opportunities, and rewards to its employees. Here are some important questions to ask about the firms you are considering:

■ Does the company have opportunities for a person with my skills, aptitudes, and goals?
■ What kind of job security will I have in this company?
■ Does the company usually promote from within?
■ What type of professional development is available for new employees?
■ What kind of working environment exists within the company?
■ What is the future growth potential for the company and the industry?

Answers to these kinds of questions will enable you to narrow the available job opportunities. Answers can be found in such sources as company annual reports. *Standard and Poor's Corporation Records*, and *Dun and Bradstreet's Reference Book of Manufacturers*. Another source is the company's employees. If you know some employees, ask them for firsthand information.

Most companies furnish brochures on career opportunities. These sources are impressive, but they often give a totally positive picture of the company. Consult your school's placement officer to learn more about each company and to determine the accuracy of the company brochures.

There are two other sources you should consult— newspapers and professional magazines. The classified ads, especially in the Sunday or weekend editions, provide a lot of job information. These advertisements usually provide information about job vacancies, the type of people the company is looking for, and the person or post office box to contact if you are interested. An outstanding listing of job opportunities appears in the *Wall Street Journal*. It lists jobs at the highest management level as well as openings at the supervisory level.

Professional magazines, such as the *Personnel Journal, Training and Industry, Personnel Administrator,* and *Nation's Business*, often list vacancies. These advertisements are for both recent graduates or people with work experience. If you are interested in a particular occupation, consulting the professional magazines in that functional area can be helpful.

The job-search plan can also include using public or private employment agencies. Some agencies locate jobs in specialized areas, such as personnel, financial control, or statistics. The employment agency will try to market your talents to organizations interested in hiring. In doing so, employment agencies incur expenses. They must cover these expenses and also earn a profit. In some cases, as much as 10 percent of a person's first-year salary is the charge for locating the job. Thus, it is important to determine at the outset who will pay the search and placement fee—you or the company you join.

Public employment agencies also provide job-search and placement services. These state agencies are not usually consulted by most college graduates, because they are identified more with processing unemployment compensation for noncollege employees than with locating jobs for accountants, financial managers, or industrial sales engineers. However, a complete job-search plan should include the public agency, because it has lists of professional managerial and lower-skill level jobs.

PERSONALIZING THROUGH A RÉSUMÉ

After personal and professional self-assessments and a job search via newspapers, professional magazines, and employment agencies, the next step is to personalize your campaign. This means that you must communicate to others who you are. The basic devices used to communicate are the résumé, letters, the telephone, and the personal interview.

A résumé is a written summary of who you are. It is a concise picture of you and your credentials for a job. A résumé should highlight your qualifications. achievements, and career objectives. It should be designed to present you as an attractive candidate for a job.

There is no generally accepted format for a résumé. Its purpose is to introduce you to the employer and to get you an interview. Few, if any, employers hire college graduates solely on the contents of a résumé. In most cases, you can attract attention with a one-page résumé. Longer résumés are for people who have had extensive professional experience.

Employers like résumés that read well and look good. Résumés read well if they are concise and easy to follow. Résumés look good if they are reproduced on an offset press on high-quality paper. There are companies that prepare professional résumés for a fee. The yellow pages of the telephone directory can provide names of firms that sell this service.

Other elements found in good résumés are personal data (birth date, address), job objectives, educational background, college activities, work experiences, and references. The arrangement of these elements is a personal decision. But keep the résumé uncluttered and neatly blocked to create an attractive and informative résumé with eye appeal.

Exhibits A–1 and A–2 present two slightly different résumé formats, but both are succinct summaries of the candidate's qualifications. Dan's résumé is concise and informative, but it fails to list his career objective. It is what is called a *chronological résumé*. It lists the most recent events first. However, it is important for an employer to know about his professional objectives. Therefore, in his cover letter for the résumé, he should list his career objective.

Jill's résumé uses a slightly different format and is called a *functional résumé*. Jill's résumé focuses on the functional skills or aptitudes or talents she believes she has that can be applied on a job. She includes a concise career objective—communication and motor skills—but she doesn't include a list of references.

It may be necessary to prepare a different résumé for each employer so that your credentials can be slanted for the job openings. Whether you think a different résumé for each company can do the job is a decision that only you can make.

Just as important as the points to include are some points to avoid in preparing your résumé. *Don't*

- State what salary you want
- Use a lot of dates or numbers
- Use negative words
- Send a résumé with false information
- Send a résumé that is sloppy and contains typographical errors
- Clutter your résumé with unnecessary information
- Inform employers that you will accept only a certain kind of position
- Use fancy colors or gimmicks to sell yourself

A cover letter should accompany the résumé. The objective of the cover letter is to introduce yourself. It can also encourage the employer to read your résumé and meet with you. The cover letter should not duplicate the more detailed résumé. Instead, it should add to what is presented in the résumé and show that you are really interested in working for the company. The cover letter also reveals how well you can communicate. This clue is often used by employers to put prospective employees into one of two categories: a good communicator or a poor communicator.

Employers receive cover letters and résumés from many more job applicants than they could ever hire or even interview. Therefore, they screen

RÉSUMÉ FOR
DAN M. DANTE

17113 Wilcrest Lane
Chicago, Illinois 60616

PERSONAL DATA: Single   Age: 22
Height: 6'4"   Born: Washington, D.C.
Weight: 195 lbs.   March 18, 1962

EDUCATION: Notre Dame University 1979–1983
B.S. Business Administration
Major: Accounting
Minor: Computer Science

EXPERIENCE: Summers   Bilko Fast Food Emporium—kept
1982–1983   accounting books for three restaurants in
Chicago area.

Summers   Murphy Accountants, Ltd.—worked on pre-
1980–1981   paring tax forms for small businesses.

Summer   Jason Stock Brokerage Firm—worked as
1979   assistant to department manager for
preparing accounting forms.

INTERESTS: President of Notre Dame Glee Club
Member of South Bend, Indiana, Scuba Diving Team
Served as Big Brother to an orphaned boy for two years

REFERENCES: Don Kindle   Dr. Martin Galton
President   Department of Accounting
Bilko Fast Food Emporium   Notre Dame University
9873 Exchange Avenue   South Bend, IN 46516
Chicago, IL 60617

whatever letters and résumés they receive. Screening is often accomplished rather quickly, so it is better to present your story and objective concisely and neatly.

The number of letters and résumés you send depends on your strategy. Some people narrow down their list of organizations to the ones they really would like to work for and prepare a personal cover letter to accompany each résumé. Other candidates use a "shotgun" spproach. They mail numerous letters and résumés to any company with an opening in a particular area of interest. The newspapers, professional magazines, listings in the placement office, telephone directories, directories of organizations, and tips from friends are used to develop a potential list. Then perhaps as many as two hundred letters and résumés are sent out.

RÉSUMÉ OF
JILL M. MURPHY

Campus Address until June 1   *Home address* after June 1
Russell Arms Center   913 Bellea Fonda
4986 Creling Drive   Seattle, WA 98101
Seattle, WA 98114

Single   5'9"   Excellent Health
Born 12/1/62   130 pounds

CAREER OBJECTIVE

Interested in beginning a career in finance by joining a bank management training program in a large urban bank. Eventually would like to become a chief executive officer of a prominent bank.

EDUCATION

University of Washington 1981–1983
North Seattle Community College 1979–1981
Will earn a B.A. degree in economics. Earned a 3.9/4.0 overall grade-point average.

SKILLS

A. Communication
- Able to communicate effectively verbally and orally
- Attentive listener

B. Mathematical
- Am able to work with numbers easily and make very few mistakes
- Like to do detail work challenged by working with data and information

WORK EXPERIENCE

Worked for past four summers at First City National Bank in trust, loan, and estate planning departments. Also worked in computer center at bank programming accounts.

CAMPUS ACTIVITIES

President of Chi Omega Sorority
Chairperson of Student Scholarship Committee
Wrote columns in student campus newspaper that focused on social responsibility and corporations during junior and senior years

REFERENCES

Academic and professional references will be furnished on request.

An example of a cover letter appears in Exhibit A–3. Note that it is concise and written in the candidate's personal style. It conveys the impression that Jill Murphy is sincerely interested in the company. It also shows that Jill is confident and knows what kind of career she wants. But Jill's confidence is not overdone. Finally, she asks for a meeting with Mr.

EXHIBIT A–3
Sample Cover Letter

Russel Arms Center
4986 Creling Drive
Seattle, WA 98114
(206–431–0019)
January 2, 1983

Mr. Robert Renson
Personnel Director
First City National Bank
4389 Purdue Blvd.
Indianapolis, Indiana 46200

Dear Mr. Renson:

Dr. John Carlson, professor of Money and Banking at the University of Washington, suggested that I write you concerning any openings in your bank management training program. I will earn my B.A. in economics in June and would like to begin my career in an urban bank.

During the past four summers, I have worked as a college trainee at the Chase Manhattan Bank. This experience enabled me to work in different departments within the bank and stimulated my interest to become a banker. I have been given major projects to complete and have been told that my determination and willingness to accept responsibility are characteristics that have resulted in my being considered a high performer at Chase. In fact, the bank's chief executive officer, Mr. Paul Spencer, and the director of the college trainee program have asked me to work permanently at Chase. However, I believe that gaining experience in another bank and geographical location will benefit my career path more in the long run.

My attached résumé highlights my experience and education. I am anxious to talk with and meet you because I feel that I can contribute to your bank. If you need additional information, please call or write me.

Sincerely yours,

Joyce L. Lowe

Enclosure

Renson so that her knowledge of banking and her qualifications can be presented firsthand. With a good cover letter, an informative résumé, and a job-search plan, your chances are improved of being invited to interview with a company representative.

An outstanding cover letter, résumé, and job-search strategy are not enough to get you the job you want. You must also perform well at the interview, which is an oral presentation with a representative of a company. A good recruiter is interested in how a job candidate expresses himself or herself. The interviewer is both an information source and an information prober. As an information source, the interviewer provides you with knowledge about careers in the organization and the company in general. As a prober, the interviewer wants to determine what makes you tick and what kind of person you are.

In searching for job openings, it is necessary to have a plan. This is also the case in having a successful interview. In order to do a good job at the interview, you must be thoroughly prepared. Of course, you must know yourself and what type of career you want. The interviewer will probe into the areas you covered in your self-assessment and in developing a career objective. During the interview, you must make it clear why a person with your strengths and objectives should be hired by the company.

The preparation for answering the question "why you" involves some homework. You should gather facts about the employers. Annual reports, opinions from employees of the firm, brochures, up-to-date financial data from the *Wall Street Journal*, and recent newspaper articles can be used. Exhibit A–4 identifies some of the information that can be used to prepare for the interview. Whether the initial interview is on the campus or in the office of the president of the company, prior preparation will impress the interviewer. This preparedness will allow you to explore other important areas about the company that you don't know about. It will also allow the interviewer to probe into such areas as your grades, motivation, maturity, ability to communicate, and work experience. This information is impor-

THE INTERVIEW STRATEGY

An Interview Plan

Location of headquarters, offices, plants
Officers of the organization
Future growth plans of the company
Product lines
Sales, profit, and dividend picture
Price of stock (if available)
Competitors of the company
Organizational structure
Kind of entry-level positions available
Career paths followed by graduates
Union situation
Type of programs available for employees (stock option, medical, education)

EXHIBIT A–4
Homework Information for the Interview

tant for the company in making a decision whether to have you visit for a second, more in-depth interview.

Interview preparation also involves your personal appearance and motivational state. There isn't enough space here to focus extensively on dress, hair, and value codes. The next best advice is to be yourself and to come prepared to meet with a representative of the organization. If you are to work as an accountant for some firm, then you must comply with standards of performance as well as dress and appearance codes. Use your own judgment, but be realistic. Some employers don't like shoulder-length hair on a male salesperson or barefooted production supervisors. These biases will not be corrected in an interview so don't be a crusader for a cause. The interview is not the best place to project a personal distaste for or discomfort with dress or hair-length standards.

Interviewing makes most people slightly nervous. But if you are well prepared and really motivated to talk to the representative, the interview will probably go well. Consider the interview as a challenge you can meet because you are interested in succeeding. An alert candidate with modest confidence has a good chance of impressing the interviewer.

The Actual Interview

The interview has been called a conversation with a purpose. During the interview, the company representative and the candidate both attempt to determine if a match exists. Are you the right person for the job? The attempt to match person and job follows a question-and-answer routine. The ability to answer questions quickly, honestly, and intelligently is important. The best way to provide a good set of answers is to be prepared.

Exhibit A–5 provides a list of some commonly asked questions. The way you answer these and similar questions is what the interviewer evaluates. Remember that the company representative is trying to get to know you better by watching and listening.

One effective way to prepare for the interview session is to practice answering the questions in Exhibit A–5 before attending the actual interview. This does not mean to develop "pat" or formal answers but to be ready to intelligently and enthusiastically respond. The sincerity of the

EXHIBIT A–5
Some Questions Frequently Asked by Interviewers

Why do you want to work for our company?
What kind of career do you have planned?
What have you learned in school to prepare you for a career?
What are some of the things you are looking for in a company?
How has your previous job experience prepared you for a career?
What are your strengths? Weaknesses?
Why did you attend this school?
What do you consider to be a worthwhile achievement of yours?
Are you a leader? Explain.
How do you plan to continue developing yourself?
Why did you select your major?
What can I tell you about my company?

response and the intelligent organization of your answer must come through in the interview.

Most interviewers eventually get around to asking about your career plans. The purpose of asking these kinds of questions is to determine your reasonableness, maturity, motivation, and goals. The important point is to illustrate by your response that you have given serious throught to your career plans. An unrealistic, disorganized, or unprepared career plan is one way to fail in the interview. Interviewers consider a candidate immature if he or she seems to be still searching and basically confused.

At various points in the interview, it may be appropriate to ask questions. These questions should be important and should not be asked just to appear intelligent. If something is important in evaluating the company, ask the question. It is also valuable to ask a question that is meaningful. But don't ask so many questions that the interviewer is answering one after the other. Some frequently asked questions are summarized in Exhibit A-6.

The majority of interviews last between twenty and thirty minutes. It is best to close on a positive and concise note. Summarize your interests and express whether you are still interested in the company. Interviewers will close by stating that you will hear from the company. You may want to ask if he or she can give you an approximate idea of how long it will be before you hear from them. Typically, an organization will contact a candidate within four or five weeks after the interview.

One valuable practice to follow after the actual interview is to write down some of the points covered. List the interviewer's name, when the company will contact you, and your overall impression of the company. These notes can be useful if you are called for a later interview. Any person talking to ten or more companies usually has some trouble recalling a particular conversation if no notes are available.

One issue that may or may not come up during the interview is salary. Most companies pay a competitive starting wage. Therefore, it is really not that important to ask what your starting salary will be. Individuals with similar education, experience, and background are normally paid the

How is performance evaluated?
How much transfer from one location to another is there?
What is the company's promotion policy?
Does the company have development programs?
How much responsibility is a new employee given? Can you provide me with some examples?
What preferences are given to applicants with graduate degrees?
What type of image does the company have in the community?
What schools provide the bulk of managerial talent in the company?
What are the company's policies for paying for graduate study?
What social obligations would I have?
What community service obligations would I have?

EXHIBIT A-6
Some Questions Frequently Asked
by Job Candidates

same. Instead of asking about salary in the initial interview, do some checking in the placement office at your school or with friends working in similar jobs.

Should you send a thank-you letter after the interview? This seems to be a good way to refresh the interviewer's memory. The follow-up letter should be short. Expressing your appreciation for the interview shows sincerity, and it also provides an opportunity to state that you are still interested in the company.

Interviewers are important processors of information for the company, so it is important to impress them at the interview. Unfortunatey, not every candidate can win (winning means that the candidate will be asked to visit the company or to undergo further interviewing). Why was I rejected? is a question everyone has to ask at some point. Exhibit A-7 lists some of the reasons why candidates are not successful in an interview.

VISITING THE COMPANY AND THE JOB OFFER

If you are fortunate enough to be invited for a company visit, consider yourself successful. The letter of invitation or telephone message will specify some available dates. If you are still interested in the company, you must send a formal acceptance. Even if you are not interested in visiting, a short note thanking the company displays your courtesy.

In some cases, your visit will be coordinated by the interviewer you already met. However, it may be the personnel department or management development officer who handles the details. The important point is really not who will be coordinating but that you must again prepare for a series of interviews. During this series, you should be asking specific questions about job duties, performance expectations, salary, fringe benefits, and career paths. It is at this phase of the career and employment decision process that you need this kind of information.

One of the main reasons for inviting candidates to visit the company is to introduce them to managers and the organization. These introductions will be brief, but they are important. It is reasonable to expect to meet five or more individuals during the company visit. In some cases, you will be given a tour of the plant, office, or laboratory. A wide array of people will be asked to comment on your employability after you leave, so consider

EXHIBIT A-7
Some Reasons for Not Winning

Disorganized and not prepared
Sloppy appearance
Abrasive and overbearing
Unrealistic goals or image of oneself
Inability to communicate effectively
No interest shown in the type of company interviewed
Not alert
Poor grades
Only interested in money
Provided contradictory answers to questions

every interview important, and remember to act alert, organized, and interested. You may be bored because many questions are repeated by different managers, but remember that sincerity and interest are variables that these managers will each be asked to comment on.

During the company visit, you will probably not be given a job offer. In most situations, a week to two weeks may pass before the company contacts you. If you are successful, you will receive a formal job offer. After receiving the offer, make an immediate acknowledgment. Thank the employer and indicate an approximate date when you will furnish a decision.

Whether you accept or reject an offer, you must write a formal letter. Your written acceptance of a job offer is a contract and should be considered a serious obligation. A rejection should be courteously and concisely conveyed. An example of an acceptance letter is shown in Exhibit A-8.

EXHIBIT A-8
Example of an Acceptance Letter

Mr. John Rocco
Personnel Director
Manning Public Accounting Associates
419 Parker Road
Richmond, Virginia 23215

Dear Mr. Rocco:

I wanted to sincerely thank you for the time afforded me on April 6 by everyone I met at Manning. Everyone's courtesy and warmth certainly made me feel welcome.

After careful consideration, I wish to accept your offer as an accounting trainee in the audit department of Manning at a salary of $20,400 per year. I understand that this is contingent upon my passing a routine physical examination.

If it is possible, I would like to report to work on June 1. Please let me know if this is an acceptable starting date.

I plan to be in Richmond during the week of May 7 so that I can locate housing. Any advice that you can provide on this matter would be appreciated.

I am looking forward to joining the Manning team and working with the outstanding people in the company.

Best regards,

Dan M. Dante

A CONCLUDING NOTE

This Career Package has focused on planning. Self-assessment, seeking professional help, the job search, personalizing your job campaign, interviewing, and visiting companies all involve prior planning. The person who plans her or his campaign to find a worthwhile and satisfying job will be more successful than the disorganized person. Thus the most important principle in finding the best job for you is to work hard at planning each stage.

There is no such thing as a dead-end job if you decide to help yourself or seek help from experts. A few examples of moving from seemingly dead-end jobs to successful careers are these:

Abraham Lincoln (sixteenth president of the United States) was a dirt farmer and a hired hand on a flatboat.

Carl Sandburg (poet and biographer) was a dishwasher.

Loretta Lynn (singer) picked strawberries for twenty-five cents a day.

Alvin Toffler (author and futurist) drove a truck.

GENERAL REFERENCES ON BUSINESS CAREERS

General Career Information

The American Almanac of Jobs and Salaries by John W. Wright.
New York: Avon Books, 1982.

Careers in Business by Lila Stair.
Homewood, Ill.: Richard D. Irwin, 1980.

Human Resource Planning by J. W. Walker.
New York: McGraw-Hill, 1980.

Accounting

Accounting Career Council
National Distribution Center
P.O. Box 650
Radio City Station
New York, NY 10019

American Institute of Certified
Public Accountants
505 Park Avenue
New York, NY 10019

Institute of Internal Auditors
170 Broadway
New York, NY 10038

National Association of
Accountants
505 Park Avenue
New York, NY 10022

National Society of Public
Accountants
1717 Pennsylvania Avenue, N.W.
Washington, D.C. 20006

Advertising, Marketing, and Sales

American Advertising Federation
1225 Connecticut Avenue, N.W.
Washington, D.C. 20036

American Association of
Advertising Agencies
200 Park Avenue
New York, NY 10017

American Marketing Association
230 North Michigan Avenue
Chicago, IL 60601

Association of Industrial
Advertisers
41 East 42nd Street
New York, NY 10017

Direct Mail Advertising
Association
230 Park Avenue
New York, NY 10017

Industrial Marketing Associates
520 Pleasant Street
St. Joseph, MI 49085

Marketing Research Association, Inc.
P.O. Box 1415
Grand Central Station
New York, NY 10017

National Association of Wholesale Distributors
1725 K Street, N.W.
Washington, D.C. 20006

National Consumer Finance Association
1000 16th Street, N.W.
Washington, D.C. 20036

National Retail Merchants Association
100 West 31st Street
New York, NY 10017

Sales and Marketing Executives International
Student Education Division
630 Third Avenue
New York, NY 10017

Economics

American Bankers Association
1700 Pennsylvania Avenue
Washington, D.C. 20006

American Economics Association
1313 21st Avenue South
Nashville, TN 37312

Financial Analysis

Financial Analysts Federation
219 East 42nd Street
New York, NY 10017

Financial Executives Institute
50 West 44th Street
New York, NY 10036

Financial Executives Research Foundation
50 West 44th Street
New York, NY 10036

Financial Institutions

American Bankers Association
Personnel Administration and Development Committee
1120 Connecticut Avenue, N.W.
Washington, D.C. 20036

American Savings and Loan Institute
111 East Wacker Drive
Chicago, IL 60601

Federal Deposit Insurance Corporation
Director of Personnel
550 17th Street, N.W.
Washington, D.C. 20029

Mortgage Bankers Association of America
1125 15th Street, N.W.
Washington, D.C. 20005

National Association of Bank Women, Inc.
111 East Wacker Drive
Chicago, IL 60606

National Consumer Finance Association
1000 16th Street, N.W.
Washington, D.C. 20036

Information Systems and Statistics

American Federation of Information Processing Societies
210 Summit Avenue
Montvale, NJ 07645

American Statistical Association
810 18th Street, N.W.
Washington, D.C. 20006

Association for Computing Machinery
1133 Avenue of the Americas
New York, NY 10036

Data Processing Management Association
505 Busse Highway
Oak Ridge, IL 60068

Society for Industrial and Applied
  Mathematics
33 South 17th Street
Philadelphia, PA 19103

Systems Analysis American
  Federation of Information
  Processing Societies
210 Summit Avenue
Montvale, NJ 07645

Insurance

American College of Life
  Underwriters
270 Bryn Mawr Avenue
Bryn Mawr, PA 19010

American Institute for
  Property and Liability
  Underwriters
Providence and Sugartown Roads
Malvern, PA 19355

Health Insurance Association
  of America
1701 K Street, N.W.
Washington, D.C. 20006

Institute of Life Insurance
277 Park Avenue
New York, NY 10017

Insurance Information Institute
110 Williams Street
New York, NY 10038

National Association of Life
  Agents, Inc.
96 Fulton Street
New York, NY 10038

International Business

National Foreign Trade Council
10 Rockefeller Plaza
New York, NY 10020

Trade Relations Council of the
  United States
122 East 42nd Street
New York, NY 10017

Labor-Management Relations

American Federation of Labor and
  Congress of Industrial
  Organizations
815 16th Street, N.W.
Washington, D.C. 20006

International Brotherhood of
  Teamsters, Chauffeurs, Warehouse-
  men, and Helpers of America
25 Louisiana Avenue, N.W.
Washington, D.C. 20001

National Federation of
  Independent Unions
910 17th Street, N.W., Ste. 553
Washington, D.C. 20006

National Labor-Management
  Foundation
1629 K Street, N.W., Ste. 553
Washington, D.C. 20006

United Automobile, Aerospace,
  and Agricultural Implement
  Workers: International Union
8000 East Jefferson Avenue
Detroit, MI 48214

Management (General)

Administrative Management
  Society, World Headquarters
Maryland Road
Willow Grove, PA 19090

American College of Hospital
  Administrators
840 North Lake Shore Drive
Chicago, IL 60611

American Institute of Management
125 East 38th Street
New York, NY 10016

The American Management Association
135 West 50th Street
New York, NY 10020

Hotel Managers and Assistants
American Hotel and Motel
  Association
888 Seventh Avenue
New York, NY 10019

International City Management
1140 Connecticut Avenue, N.W.
Washington, D.C. 20036

Society for the Advancement of
Management
1412 Broadway
New York, NY 10036

Society of Professional
Management Consultants
150 Broadway
New York, NY 10038

Personnel Management

American Society for Personnel
Administration
19 Church Street
Berea, OH 44017

The Information Center
Public Relations Society of
America, Inc.
845 Third Avenue
New York, NY 10022

International Personnel Management
Association
1313 East 60th Street
Chicago, IL 60637

National Employment Counselors
Associations
1607 New Hampshire Avenue, N.W.
Washington, D.C. 20009

Public Personnel Association
1313 East 60th Street
Chicago, IL 60637

Production Management

American Apparel Manufacturers
Association
16111 North Kent Street
Arlington, VA 22209

American Iron and Steel Institute
150 East 42nd Street
New York, NY 10017

American Society for Quality
Control
161 West Wisconsin Avenue
Milwaukee, WI 53203

American Society of Traffic and
Transportation, Inc.
22 West Madison Street
Chicago, IL 60602

Grocery Manufacturers of America
1425 K Street, N.W.
Washington, D.C. 20005

Motor Vehicle Manufacturers
Association of the United
States, Inc.
320 New Center Building
Detroit, MI 48202

National Association of
Manufacturers
277 Park Avenue
New York, NY 10017

National Association of Purchasing
Agents
11 Park Place
New York, NY 10007

READINGS

Colvin, Geoffrey. "International Harvester's Last Chance." *Fortune*, April 19, 1982, pp. 102–108.

Hitchcock, Terrance S. *American Business: the Last Hurrah?* Homewood, ILL.: Dow Jones–Richard D. Irwin, 1982.

Lipset, Seymour Martin. *The Confidence Gap: How Americans View Their Institutions.* New York: Macmillan, 1981.

Steckmest, Francis W. *Corporate Performance.* New York: McGraw-Hill, 1982.

Wreston, Walter B. "The Consent of the Governor: Add Your Own Two Cents Worth." *Enterprise*, February 1981, pp. 1–9.

CHAPTER 1

"Communism: The Great Economic Failure." *U.S. News & World Report*, March 1, 1982, p. 33.

"Reaganomics: Making It Work." *Time*, September 21, 1981, p. 38.

Rudnitsky, Howard. "The Flight of the Bumble-bee." *Forbes*, June 22, 1981, p. 104.

Simis, Konstantin. "Russia's Underground Millionaires." *Fortune*, June 29, 1981, p. 36.

Smith, Lee. "The Freelance Inventor Lives." *Fortune*, June 29, 1981, p. 74.

"Striking It Rich." *Time*, February 15, 1982, p. 36.

Viorst, Milton. "Hyper: The World's Worst Case of Inflation." *Across the Board*, May 1981, p. 6.

CHAPTER 2

Aaker, David A., and George S. Day. *Consumerism: Search for the Consumer Interest.* New York: The Free Press, 1974.

Bork, Robert H. *The Antitrust Paradox.* New York: Basic Books, 1978.

Commoner, Barry. *The Closing Circle: Nature, Man and Technology.* New York: Knopf, 1971.

Kneese, A. V., and C. L. Schultze. *Pollution, Prices, and Public Policy.* Washington, D.C.: The Brookings, Institution, 1979.

MacAvoy, Paul W. *Regulated Industries and the Economy.* New York: Norton, 1979.

Needham, Douglas. *Regulation: A Broader Perspective.* Cambridge, Mass.: Winthrop, 1981.

Shepherd, William G., ed. *Public Policies Toward Business*, rev. ed. Homewood, Ill.: Richard D. Irwin, 1979.

Simon, Julian L. *The Economics of Population Growth.* Princeton, N.J.: Princeton University Press, 1977.

Stelzer, Irwin M. *Selected Antitrust Cases*, 5th ed. Homewood, Ill.: Richard D. Irwin, 1976.

Thurow, Lester C. *The Zero-Sum Society.* New York: Basic Books, 1980.

Weidenbaum, Murray. *Business, Government, and the Public*, 2nd ed. Englewood Cliffs, N.M.: Prentice-Hall, 1981.

CHAPTER 3

Carter, Malcolm N. "Getting a New Venture off the Ground." *Money*, January 1981, pp. 44–49.

Moskowitz, Milton, Katz, Michael, and Levering, Robert. *Everbody's Business 1982 Update*, New York: Harper .. Row, 1982.

Pakowski, Marianne. "Stiflng the Yawn: Annual Reports Awaken to New Audiences." *Industrial Marketing*, March 1981, pp. 66–70.

Steckmest, Francis W. *Corporate Performance.* New York: McGraw-Hill, 1982.

Thomas, Stephen G. "Why Partnerships Break-Up." *Inc.*, July 1981, pp. 67ff.

CHAPTER 4

CHAPTER 5

Brown, Deaver. *The Entrepreneurs Guide.* New York: Macmilliam, 1980.
Kamoroff, Bernard. *Small-Time Operator.* Laytonville, Calif.: Bell Springs, 1981.
Shook, Robert L. The Entrepreneurs. New York: Barnes & Noble, 1980.
Tarrant, John J. *Making It Big on Your Own.* New York: Playboy Press, 1981.
Van Voorhis, Kenneth R. *Entrepreneurship and Small Business Management.* Boston: Allyn and Bacon, 1980.

CHAPTER 6

Donnelly, James H., Jr., Gibson, James L., and Ivancevich, John M. *Fundamentals of Management.* Dallas: Business Publications, 1981.
"Executives under Stress," *Newsweek,* August 24, 1981, p. 53.
Gibson, James L., Ivancevich, John M., and Donnelly, James H., Jr. *Organizations: Behavior, Structure, Processes.* Dallas: Business Publications, 1982.
Louis, Arthur M. *The Tycoons.* New York: Simon & Schuster, 1981.

CHAPTER 7

Cleland, David I. "The Cultural Ambience of the Matrix Organization." *Management Review,* November 1981, pp. 24–28.
Duncan, Robert. "What Is the Right Organization Structure? Decision Tree Analysis Provides the Answer." *Organizational Dynamics,* Winter 1979, pp. 59–80.
Jelinek, M., Litterer, J. A., and Miles, R. E. *Organizations by Design: Theory and Practice.* Plano, Texas: Business Publications, 1981.
Webber, R. "Staying Organized." *The Wharton Magazine,* Spring 1979, pp. 16–23.

CHAPTER 8

DuBrin, A. J. *Contemporary Applied Management.* Dallas, Texas: Business Publications Inc., 1982
Flamion, A. "The Dollars and Sense of Motivation." *Personnel Journal,* January 1980, pp. 51–53.
Herzberg, F. "Herzberg on Motivation for the 1980s." *Industry Week,* Summer 1979, pp. 58–63.
Mazique, M. "The Quality Circle Transplant." *Center for Creative Leadership,* May 1981, pp. 1–4.
Odiorne, G. S. "An Uneasy Look at Motivation Theory." *Training and Development Journal,* June 1980, pp. 106–112.
Rice, Berkeley. "The Hawthorne Defect: Persistence of a Flawed Theory." *Psychology Today,* February 1982, pp. 70–74.
"The New Industrial Relations." *Business Week,* May 11, 1981, pp. 85–98.

CHAPTER 9

Arvey, Richard D. *Fairness in Selecting Employees.* Reading, Mass.: Addison-Wesley, 1979.
Baird, Lloyd S., Beatty, Richard W., and Schneier, Craig E. *The Performance Appraisal Sourcebook.* Amherst, Mass.: Human Resource Development Press, 1982.
Decker, Robert L. "The Employment Interview." *Personnel Administrator,* November 1981, pp. 71–73.
Hagstrom, Paul E. "The Older Worker: A Travelers Insurance Companies' Case Study." *Personnel Administrator,* October 1981, pp. 41–46.
Henderson, Richard I. *Compensation Management* (Reston, Va.: Reston Publishing, 1979).
Hoy, Frank, Buchanan, W. Wray, and Vaught, Bobby C. "Are Your Management Development Programs Working?" *Personnel Journal,* December 1981, pp. 953–957.
Ross, Joyce D. "A Definition of Human Resources Management." *Personnel Journal,* October 1981, pp. 781–783.
Rumack, F. W., and Gravitz, D. H. "New Opportunities in Compensation and Benefits under the 1981 Tax Act." *Management Review,* November 1981, pp. 8–12.
Schuster, Fred E., ed. *Contemporary Issues in Human Resources Management* (Reston, Va.: Reston Publishing, 1980).

CHAPTER 10

Burck, Charles G. "What's in it for Unions." *Fortune,* August 24, 1981, pp. 88–91.
Foulkes, Fred K. *Personnel Policies in Large Non-Union Companies.* Englewood Cliffs, N.J.: Prentice-Hall, 1980.
"Hard Times for Big Labor." *Newsweek,* September 7, 1981, pp. 61–62.

Herriman, Tom. "A Union at J. P. Stevens.;; *AFL-CIO American Federationist,* December 1980, pp. 1–7.

Hill, Charles A., Jr. "The Void in Collective Bargaining: Professional Employees." *Personnel Administrator,* August 1979, pp. 51–57.

"Hospital Staff Finds Strike Ineffective." *Dallas Morning News,* May 16, 1981.

Imberman, Woodruff. "How to Enjoy Not having a Strike." *Management Review,* September 1981, pp. 43–47.

"Eight Who Innovate." *Inc.,* August 1981, pp. 40–42.

Buffa, Elwood S. *Modern Production Management,* 5th ed. (New York: Wiley, 1977).

"How Japan Does It." *Time,* (March 30, 1981, pp. 54–63.

Medows, E. "How Three Companies Increased Their Productivity." *Fortune,* March 10, 1980, pp. 92–101.

Morris, Roger. "Energy and the Environment." *Context,* Volume 6, 1977.

Velocci, Tony. "Rearming: Can We Do It in Time." *Nation's Business,* July 1981, pp. 25–32.

CHAPTER 11

"End of Youth Boom." *U.S. News World Report,* November 9, 1981, pp. 66–67.

"Generic Goods Aren't Selling as Fast." *The Wall Street Journal,* November 12, 1981.

"Houston's 'P. T. Barnum of Opera' Thrives by Emphasizing Marketing, Bottom Line." *The Wall Street Journal,* March 9, 1982.

Kiechel, Walter, "Two-Income Families Will Reshape the Consumer Markets." *Fortune,* March 10, 1980, pp. 110–120.

"Not by Jeans Alone." *A Guide to Enterprise,* 1981, pp. 26–27.

"Small Cities Have Big Stake in Being Defined as SMSA's." *The Wall Street Journal,* November 17, 1981.

"Who's Afraid of MA Bell's Baby?" *Industry Week,* August 24, 1981, pp. 54–60.

CHAPTER 12

"American Hospital's Buys Get Credit for Turning Distribution into Service." *The Wall Street Journal,* September 1, 1981.

"Federal Express Rides the Small Package Boom." *Business Week,* March 31, 1980, pp. 108–112.

"K Mart, Beset by Steady Drop in Earnings, Tries to Attract Higher-Income Shoppers," *Wall Street Journal,* August 10, 1982.

Kotler, Philip. *Marketing Management,* 4th ed. (Englewood Cliffs, N.J.: Prentice-Hall, 1980), Chapters 16 and 17.

"We Will Ship No Wine after Its Time." *Distribution,* February 1981, pp. 73–76.

CHAPTER 13

Poe, Randall. "Narrowcasring." *Across the Board,* June 1981, pp. 6–24.

"Santa's Mail-Order Elves." *Fortune,* November 16, 1981, pp. 131–142.

Waldholz, Michael. "Marketing Often Is the Key to Success of Prescription Drugs." *The Wall Street Journal,* December 28, 1981.

"100 Top Industrial Advertisers." *Industrial Marketing,* June 1981, p. 57.

"1981 Income Tops $5 Billion. "*Advertising Age,* March 24, 1982, p. 1.

CHAPTER 14

Fisher, Douglas. *Money, Banking, and Monetary Policy.* Homewood, Ill.: Richard D. Irwin, 1980.

Hutchinson, Harry D. *Money, Banking and the U.S. Economy,* 4th ed. Englewood Cliffs, N.J.: Prentice-Hall, 1980.

Kamerschen, David R. *Money and Banking,* 7th ed. Cincinnati, Ohio: South-Western Publishing Co., 1980.

Kaufman, George G. *The System: Money, Markets, and Institutions.* Englewood Cliffs, N.J.: Prentice-Hall, 1980.

Light, Jay O., and White, William L. *The Financial System.* Homewood, Ill.: Richard D. Irwin, 1979.

Welshans, Merle, and Melicher, Ronald. *Finance, An Introduction to Financial Markets and Institutions,* 5th ed. Cincinnati, Ohio: South-Western Publishing Co., 1980.

CHAPTER 15

CHAPTER 16

Block, Stanley B. *Foundations of Financial Management*, rev. ed. Homewood, Ill.: Richard D. Irwin, 1981.

Jones, Jr., Ray C., and Dudley, Dean. *Essentials of Finance*. Englewood Cliffs, N.J.: Prentice-Hall, 1978.

Joy, Maurice. *Introduction to Financial Management*, rev. ed. Homewood, Ill.: Richard D. Irwin, 1980.

Neveu, Raymond P. *Fundamentals of Managerial Finance*. Cincinnati, Ohio: South-Western Publishing Co., 1981.

Van Horne, James C. *Fundamentals of Financial Management*, 4th ed. Englewood Cliffs, N.J.: Prentice-Hall, 1980.

CHAPTER 17

Engle, Louis. *How To Buy Stocks*. New York: Bantam, 1977.

Loll, L. M., and Buckley, J. G. *Over the Counter Securities Markets*, 4th ed. Englewood Cliffs, N.J.: Prentice-Hall, 1981.

Sharpe, William F., *Investments*, 2nd ed. Englewood Cliffs, N.J.: Prentice-Hall, 1981.

Widicus, Wilbur, and Stitzel, Thomas E. *Personal Investing*, 3rd ed. Homewood, Ill.: Richard D. Irwin, 1981.

CHAPTER 18

Bickelhauyst, David L. *General Insurance*, 9th ed. Homewood, Ill.: Richard D. Irwin, 1974.

Greene, Mark R. *Risk and Insurance*, 3rd ed. Cincinnati, Ohio: South-Western, 1973.

Heubner, S. S., and Black, Kenneth. *Life Insurance*, 8th ed. Englewood Cliffs, N.J.: Prentice-Hall, 1973.

Mehr, Robert I., and Cammock, Emerson. *Principles of Insurance*. Homewood, Ill.: Richard D. Irwin, 1972.

Williams, C. Arthur, and Heins, Richard M. *Risk Management and Insurance*, 4th ed. New York: McGraw-Hill, 1981.

CHAPTER 19

Anthony, R. N., and Welsch, G. A. *Fundamentals of Management Accounting*, 3rd ed. Homewood, Ill.: Richard D. Irwin, 1981.

Edwards, J. D., and Bergold, L. *College Accounting Fundamentals*, rev. ed. Homewood, Ill.: Richard D. Irwin, 1981.

Johnson, G. L., and Gentry, J. A. *Finney and Miller's Principles of Accounting*. Englewood Cliffs, N.J.: Prentice-Hall, 1980.

Pyle, W. W., and Larsen, K. D. *Fundamental Accounting Principles*, 9th ed. Homewood, Ill.: Richard D. Irwin, 1981.

Welsch, G. A., and Anthony, R. N. *Fundamentals of Financial Accounting*, 3rd ed. Homewood, Ill.: Richard D. Irwin, 1981.

CHAPTER 20

Huntsberger, D. V., Croft, D. J., and Billingsley, Patrick. *Statistical Inference for Management and Economics*. Boston: Allyn and Bacon, 1980.

Levin, Richard I. *Statistics for Management*. Englewood Cliffs, N.J.: Prentice-Hall, 1981.

CHAPTER 21

"Computer 'Architects' Trying to Expand Limits of Design," *The Wall Street Journal*, August 28, 1981, p. 17.

"Japan Starting 10-Year Effort to Create Exotic Computer," *The Wall Street Journal*, September 25, 1981, p. 25.

"Office of the 80s," *Business Week*, February 18, 1980, p. 2.

"Technologies for the '80s," *Business Week*, July 6, 1982, p. 48.

Uttal, Bro. "The Coming Struggle in Personal Computers," *Fortune*, June 29, 1981, p. 84.

"Uncle Sam's Computer Has Got You," *U.S. News & World Report*, April 10, 1978, p. 68.

Burck, Charles G. "Can Detroit Catch Up?" *Fortune*, February 8, 1982, p. 34.

"Canada's Mining Firms Turn to Arctic Islands, Site of Rich Resources," *The Wall Street Journal*, February 5, 1982.

"Mexico Limits U.S. Makes of Computers," *The Wall Street Journal*, January 29, 1982.

"The Chinese Fake the Pepsi Challenge," *Business Week*, December 14, 1981, p. 44.

"Why the U.S. Can't Compete in Japan," *Business Week*, December 14, 1981, p. 44.

Wergland, Robert E. "International Trade Without Money," *Harvard Business Review*, November-December 1977, p. 28.

CHAPTER 22

Carson, Robert B. *Microeconomic Issues Today, Alternative Approaches.* New York: St. Martin's Press, 1980.

Clarkson, Kenneth W., and Miller, Roger Leroy. *West's Business Law.* St. Paul, Minn.: West Publishing Co., 1980.

Meiners, Rober E., and Ringleb, Al H. *The Legal Environment of Business.* St. Paul, Minn.: West Publishing Co., 1982.

CHAPTER 23

Buehler, Vernon M., and Shetty, Y. Krishna. *Productivity Improvement.* New York: AMACOM, 1981.

Communications and the Future. Bethesda, Md.: World Future Society, 1982.

Hayes, Robert H., and Abernathy, William J.. "Managing Our Way To Economic Decline," *Harvard Business Review*, July–August 1980, p. 68.

Ross, Irwin. "The New UAW Contract: A Fortune Proposal," *Fortune*, February 8, 1982, pp. 40–45.

Steiner, George A. "Can Business Survive Its New Environment?;; *Business,* January-February 1980, pp. 13–19.

Terkel, Studs. *American Dreams: Lost and Found.* New York: Ballantine Books, 1980.

Toffler, Alvin. *The Third Wave.* New York: Morrow & Co., 1980.

"Unemployment on the Rise." *Time*, February 6, 1982, pp. 22–29.

Weidenbaum, Murray L.. "The True Obligation of the Business Firm to Society." *Management Review*, September 1981, pp. 21–23.

CHAPTER 24

GLOSSARY

ABSOLUTE ADVANTAGE An advantage one country has when it can produce a good at a lower cost than other countries.

ACCOUNTABILITY Requirement that a person with authority and responsibility be held accountable to a person above him or her in the mangerial hierarchy for any actions.

ACCOUNTING Recording, classifying, and summarizing business transactions, as well as interpreting this compiled information to permit informed judgments and decisions.

ACCOUNTS RECEIVABLE Monies owed to a business for goods or services already delivered or rendered but not yet paid for by the customer.

ADMINISTRATIVE LAW That body of rules and regulations set down by administrative agencies, such as the Federal Trade Commission, the Interstate Commerce Commission, and the Food and Drug Administration. Law that is generated by agency rulings rather than by the legislature.

ADVERTISING Any form of nonpersonal promotion of products and ideas directed to large numbers of people.

AFFIRMATIVE ACTION PROGRAM A program in which an employer specifies how the company plans to increase the number of minority and female employees.

AFL-CIO The merged body of the American Federation of Labor (craft union members) and the Congress of Industrial Organizations (industrial union members).

AGENCY SHOP A company where all employees pay unions dues, whether or not they are union members.

AGENT A person with legal power to act for a producer but who does not take title to a product.

AGENT WHOLESALER A business that never takes title to goods but may or may not take possession of products.

AGGREGATE PRODUCTION PLANNING Planning by business to determine total production requirements for a specific time period.

ANTITRUST LEGISLATION Statutes and laws designed to protect the public from the evils of monopolization; legislation that makes it illegal for firms to collude.

ARBITRATOR Third party to a labor dispute who makes the final binding decision about some disputed issue.

ARITHMETIC/LOGIC UNIT A computer component that has the ability to compare, rearrange, and manipulate data to make simple decisions.

ARTICLES OF PARTNERSHIP A written contract that specifies the names, rights, duties, shares, and responsibilities of each partner.

ASK PRICE The price at which a broker, who has or will take a position on a stock, is willing to sell the stock in the over-the-counter market.

ASSET Something of value owned by a business, including cash, inventory, land, and buildings.

AUTHORITY The right to use resources to encourage people to perform and accept orders.

AUTOMATIC TRANSFER SERVICES (ATS) The use of an automatic transfer service allows a person to earn interest on a savings account from which monies can be automatically transferred to cover overdrafts on a normal, noninterest-bearing checking account.

BALANCE OF PAYMENTS The money value of all the international business activities occurring between one nation and the rest of the world.

BALANCE OF TRADE The difference between the money value of a nation's imports and its exports.

BALANCE SHEET A financial statement that shows the assets, liabilities, and equity of a business.

BASIC GOODS Goods that enter directly into the production process, such as raw materials, semimanufactured goods, and component parts.

BEAR An investor who believes that the stock market will decline.

BEHAVIOR MODIFICATION Application of learning principles, called operant conditioning, to motivation. Behavior depends on its consequences—if consequences are favorable, the behavior will probably be repeated.

BENEFITS Financial payments (e.g., insurance premiums) made by an employer over and above the base wages and salary.

BID PRICE The price at which a broker who has taken a position on a stock in the over-the-counter market is willing to pay for the stock.

BILL OF LADING A written shipping document given by a transportation company showing the names of the shipper and the party receiving the goods and an itemizaton of the goods shipped.

BLIND ADVERTISEMENT A job advertisement that does not include the company name.

BOND An instrument of long-term debt.

BOOK VALUE The value of a stock on the company's records; can be calculated by dividing the number of shares into the net worth (value of common stock plus retained earnings).

BOYCOTT A bargaining tactic whereby the union attempts to get people or other organizations to refuse to deal with the employer.

BROADCAST MEDIA Radio and television stations licensed by the Federal Communications Commission.

BULL An investor who believes that the stock market will rise.

BUSINESS The means of exchanging goods, services, or money for a profit.

BUSINESS ENTERPRISE An organization involved in exchanging goods, services, or money to earn a profit.

BUSINESS REPRESENTATIVE A union official who is responsible for negotiating and administering the labor agreement and for settling problems that may arise in connection with the contract.

BUSINESS TRANSACTION Exchanging a product for money.

BUSINESS TRUST A business that holds title to securities for investors.

CANCELLATION PROVISION The contract provision given a franchisor the power to cancel an arrangement with a franchisee.

CAPITAL GOODS Goods used to manufacture a product that are not part of the final product.

CAPITALISM One type of economic system, often called free enterprise or private enterprise. It is characterized by private ownership or capital and competition among businesses seeking a profit.

CAPITAL RESOURCES Goods produced for the purpose of making other types of goods and services.

CARTEL A group of firms joined together by a collusive agreement in order to restrict output and raise prices to increase the profits of the member firms.

CASCADE APPROACH A method of setting objectives from the top level of management down to lower-level managers.

CASH DISCOUNT A discount, usually 1 or 2 percent, given to a debtor who pays off the amount due either immediately or within ten days after the goods are delivered.

CASH-FLOW BUDGET Statement of what cash will be needed to pay expenses and where the cash will come from.

CASHIER'S CHECK A check drawn by a bank on its own funds and signed by the cashier.

CEASE AND DESIST ORDERS Orders from a government agency that require a firm or firms to immediately stop a particular action. Usually cease and desist orders are applied to so-called unfair methods of competition and commerce.

CENSUS A survey of all people or customers in a category.

CENTRALIZATION All, or nearly all, of the authority to make decisions retained by a small group of managers.

CENTRAL PROCESSING UNIT (CPU) The computer's brain, divided into a storage unit, control unit, and arithmetic/logic unit.

CERTIFIED CHECK A check certified to be good by the bank on which it is drawn.

CERTIFICATES OF DEPOSIT Certificates that are usually sold in units of $1,000 or more and that carry fixed maturity dates varying from thirty days to six years or more from the date of issue.

CHANNEL OF DISTRIBUTION The path a product and its title of ownership take in moving from producer to final consumer.

CHARTER A state's written agreement giving a corporation the right to operate as a business.

CIVIL RIGHTS ACT OF 1964 An act that makes various forms of discrimination illegal. Title VII of the act spells out the forms of illegal discrimination.

CLOSED-END INVESTMENT COMPANY An investment company that issues a specified number of stock shares. once these have been sold, they are traded in a securities market like any other stock. To be contrasted with an open-end investment company, or mutual fund.

CLOSED SHOP A company that hires only workers who are members of the union; illegal under the Taft-Hartley Act.

COLLATERAL Property or security deposited with a creditor to guarantee payment of a loan.

COLLECTIVE BARGAINING Negotiation of a labor contract by union and management. The parties sit down, discuss, debate, and sometimes threaten in an attempt to get a final contract favorable to their side.

COLLUSIVE CONTRACTS Agreements among firms that in some way restrict the free flow of commerce. Collusive contracts may involve restricting output or setting minimum prices.

COMMERCIAL PAPER An unsecured promissory note guaranteeing that the person who signs will pay back a certain sum of money by a specific date.

COMMON CARRIERS Carriers that must accept shipments from anyone requesting their services.

COMMON STOCK Security that represents the basic ownership interest in a corporation.

COMMUNICATION The process of sending a message to someone so that it is understood by that person.

COMMUNISM A type of economic system in which the government run by a single political party controls all of a nation's economic resources.

COMPARATIVE ADVANTAGE The ability of a nation to make a product relatively more efficiently and at lower costs than other goods.

COMPUTER Any machine or device that has the ability to add, subtract, multiply, and divide.

COMPUTER HARDWARE The electronic and mechanical elements of a computer used to read, store, process, and provide data.

COMPUTER SOFTWARE Computer programs supplied by a manufacturer to accomplish such tasks as scheduling jobs through the machine, sorting computer records, and organizing and maintaining internal computer files.

COPMPUTER PROGRAM A series of detailed instructions and logical statements that explain how a specific job must be performed.

CONDUIT The manager's role as a link in the managerial hierarchy.

CONSUMER Buyer, whether an individual, business, nonprofit organization, or government.

CONSUMER MARKET People who buy goods and services for their own use.

CONSOLIDATION A combination of two or more corporations to form a new corporation.

CONTINGENCY APPPROACH A leadership approach that attempts to determine which style of leadership will work best in a given situation.

CONTROL UNIT A computer component that serves as the computer's nerve center.

CONTRACT CARRIERS Carriers that are for hire to carry products for other organizations to meet their special needs.

CONTROLLING The management function of checking to determine whether employees are following plans and whether progress is being made, and of taking action to reduce discrepancies.

CONVENIENCE GOODS Goods bought with little shopping effort.

CONVERTIBILITY A clause in a term insurance policy that gives the insured the option of switching to whole, or straight, life insurance.

COOPERATIVE A business in which a group of owners or buyers join together to operate the business.

CORPORATION A business that is a legal entity separate from its owners.

CRAFT UNION A union in which all members belong to one craft or to a closely related group of occupations.

CREDIT UNION SHARE DRAFTS A checking-type account in which a credit union allows individuals to write share drafts (checks) on their credit union accounts.

CURRENT ASSETS Something of value owned by the business that is either cash, will be converted into cash, or will be used up within one year.

CURRENT LIABILITIES Business debts that will come due within the next year.

DEATH BENEFITS The face value of any insurance policy that is paid to the beneficiary upon the death of the insured.

DEBT CAPITAL Funds borrowed from the creditors of a business.

DECENTRALIZATION When a significant amount of the authority to make decisions is delegated to lower-level managers.

DEMAND DEPOSITS A sum of money a bank sets aside for a customer when it establishes a checking account for him or her.

DEMOGRAPHICS Statistics that are used to describe a population with reference to age, gender, education level, birth rate, geographical distribution and so on.

DEPOSITORY INSTITUTIONS Any financial institution that can accept deposits, including commercial banks, saving and loan associations, and credit unions.

DIRECT CHANNEL OF DISTRIBUTION Selling direct from the producer to the final consumer.

DIRECTING The management function of initiating action.

DIRECT LOAN A loan made to a small-business owner entirely from SBA funds.

DIRECT-MAIL ADVERTISING Promotional material sent to consumers through the mail.

DIRECT OBSERVATION A way to collect original data by observing, measuring, and recording people's behavior.

DISCOUNT OPERATIONS Process of loaning funds to member banks by the Federal Reserve System.

DISCOUNT RATE The rate of interest that depository institutions must pay in order to borrow reserves from the Federal Reserve.

DIVIDEND The return paid to the stockholders of a corporation from its profits.

DOUBLE TAXATION Taxing a coporate owner's money twice by taxing it as income of a corporation and as dividends of the individual owner.

ECONOMICS The study of how a society chooses to use scarce resources to produce goods and services and physically distribute them to people for consumption.

ECONOMIC SYSTEM The process by which labor, capital, and natural resources are organized to produce and distribute goods and services.

ELECTRONIC FUNDS TRANSFER SYSTEM (EFTS) A system of transferring money with electronic or magnetic signals.

EMBARGO A ban that prohibits the import or export of certain goods.

ENDOWMENT POLICY A policy that combines temporary life insurance and a rapidly increasing cash surrender value.

ENTREPRENEUR A person who takes the risks necessary to organize and manage a business and receives the potential financial profits and nonmonetary rewards.

EQUAL EMPLOYMENT OPPORTUNITY ACT OF 1972 A law that has specific provisions about equal opportunities for employment.

EQUAL EMPLOYMENT OPPORTUNITY COMMISSION A government commission that enforces laws that attempt to provide equal opportunities for employment without regard to race, religion, age, creed, sex, national origin, or disability.

EQUITY CAPITAL Capital invested in the business by its owners.

EXCLUSIVE HANDLING A form of control in which a franchisor requires the franchisee to purchase only supplies that are approved by the franchisor.

EXPENSE The cost associated with the operation of a business.

EXPORTING One nation selling goods to another nation.

ESTEEM NEED The need for self-respect and respect from others.

EXTENDED COVERAGE A method by which you increase fire insurance protection to cover losses due to smoke damage, hail, windstorms, riots, and explosions.

EXTERNAL DATA Data obtained from sources outside the business.

FACTORING COMPANY A company that buys accounts receivable from a business at a discount.

FAIR-TRADE AGREEMENTS Agreements by which the manufacturer specifies a minimum, or fair-trade, price, below which all retailers cannot sell the product. Another name for a fair-trade agreement is a resale price maintenance agreement.

FIXED ASSETS An asset with a degree of permanence (beyond one year); intended for use rather than resale. Also called plant assets.

FIXED CAPITAL RESOURCES Long-life capital resources that are used repeatedly in the production process.

FIXED-POSITION LAYOUT Plant layout that requires all the production materials to be brought to one location.

FLOOR BROKER A member of the stock exchange who executes orders to buy or sell securities on the floor of the stock exchange.

FLOWCHART A device for visually describing, by symbols and interconnecting lines, the operational structure and sequence of a computer program.

FOREIGN EXCHANGE MARKETS The place where the actual conversion of one currency for another takes place.

FORMAL STRUCTURE Specified, on-paper pattern of organizational positions and their accompanying responsibilities and authority.

FRACTIONAL RESERVE BANKING SYSTEM A banking system in which banks are required to keep a certain percentage of their total deposits on hand either as vault cash or in reserve at some central bank.

FRANCHISEE The independent owner of a franchise outlet who enters into an agreement with a franchisor.

FRANCHISING A system for selective distribution of goods and/or services under a brand name through outlets owned by independent business owners.

FRANCHISOR The licensing company in the franchise arrangement.

FREEDOM OF CHOICE People's right to select the type of work they do or the way they invest their money.

FREEDOM OF ENTERPRISE A right under capitalism by which people and businesses may enter whatever legal venture they wish.

FUNCTIONAL AUTHORITY Authority to take action in limited areas.

FUNCTIONAL STRUCTURE A structure with units or departments arranged so that each has a different set of activities and responsibilities.

GENERAL PARTNER Owner in a partnership with full rights and responsibilities whose actions are legally binding on all partners.

GENERAL PARTNERSHIP A partnership in which at least one partner has unlimited liability; a general partner has authority to act and make binding decisions as an owner.

GRIEVANCE Complaint about a job that creates dissatisfaction or discomfort, made by an employee or the union.

GROSS NATIONAL PRODUCT GNP represents the total money value of all goods and services produced by a nation during a specific time period.

GUARANTEED LOAN A loan to a small-business owner by a commercial bank but guaranteed up to 90 percent by the SBA.

GUARANTEED ANNUAL WAGES A plan that guarantees an annual wage or employment for members that negotiated the plan. The objective of the plan is to provide economic security.

HAWTHORNE STUDIES A series or experiments at a Western Electric plant from 1927 to 1932. The studies found that work groups significantly affected the way workers behave and perform.

HOME PROTECTION PLAN A type of nonuniform decreasing term insurance where the reducton in the amount of insurance available mirrors the reducton in the amount remaining due (unpaid) on a home mortgage.

HOT-CARGO AGREEMENT Agreement between management and union that workers may avoid working with materials that come from employers that have been struck by a union; a form of boycott; illegal except in the clothing and construction industries.

HUMAN RESOURCE PLANNING The steps taken in estimating the size and makeup of the future workforce.

IMPORTING One nation buying goods from other nations.

INCOME STATEMENT A financial statement summarizing all the revenue and expense transactions that result in a profit or loss over a period of time.

INDEPENDENT WHOLESALERS Businesses that stock a variety of products for resale to retailers.

INDEX NUMBER A relative measure computed by dividing a series of numbers by one number or a combination of numbers from the series.

INDUSTRIAL MARKET Market for goods that are used to produce other products for resale.

INDUSTRIAL UNION A union in which all members are employees in a company or industry regardless of occupation.

INFLATION The rise in the average level of prices for all goods and services in a particular time period.

INFORMAL ORGANIZATION A network of personal and social relationships that emerge when people work together.

INFORMAL STRUCTURE Organizational pattern that develops as employees interact on the job.

INJUNCTION Court order that prohibits the defendant from engaging in certain activities such as striking.

INPUT DEVICE A computer component that transforms information into electrical impulses.

INTERLOCKING DIRECTORATES A situation in which the same individual serves on two or more boards of directors of corporations that are competitive.

INTERNAL DATA Obtained from records within a business that relate to the operation of that business.

INTERNATIONAL BUSINESS The buying and selling among countries that takes place in one of two ways: between two businesses or a business and a foreign government.

INVENTORY CONTROL Maintaining adequate supplies for production while keeping the costs of carrying inventory down.

JOB ANALYSIS The procedures for determining the tasks that make up a job and the skills, abilities, and responsibilities an employee needs to do the job.

JOB DESCRIPTION A statement that furnishes information about a job's duties, technology, conditions, and hazards. Data for preparing the description come from the job and analysis.

JOB ENRICHMENT An approach that involves redesigning a job to increase the satisfaction and motivation of workers. It incorporates variety, feedback, and autonomy in the job.

JOB EVALUATION SYSTEM A process used to determine the relative value of jobs within the organization.

JOB SPECIFICATION A statement derived from the job analysis about the human qualifications needed to perform the job.

JOINT VENTURE Similar to a partnership except that actual management is delegated to one person and the venture usually lasts for only a short time.

LABOR RESOURCES A nation's human talent; people making up the labor force.

LANDRUM-GRIFFIN ACT Labor law passed in 1959 that requires unions and employees to file financial reports with the secretary of labor and that requires certain activities to ensure that the union is operated democratically.

LEADERSHIP The process of influencing the activities of an individual or group toward accomplishing objectives.

LIABILITIES The claims of creditors on the assets of a business.

LIMIT ORDER An order to buy or sell a stated number of securities at a specified price.

LIMITED PARTNERSHIP A partnership with at least one general partner and one or more limited partners who are liable for loss only up to the amount of their investment.

LINE AUTHORITY Unquestioned authority to make decisions and take action.

LIQUIDITY Moneyness, or the ability of something to be easily converted into other forms of wealth without loss of value. Money is the most liquid of all assets by definition.

LIVING BENEFITS The benefits derived from the cash surrender fund in a whole life insurance policy.

LOAD The commission charged by the agent to purchase shares of a mutual fund.

LOCKOUT Management pressure tactic that involves denying employees access to their jobs.

LONG-TERM LIABILITIES   Liabilities that have a maturity, or due date, of more than one year from the date they are incurred.

MACHINE LANGUAGE   The language that a computer uses to make internal calculations.

MAIL INTERVIEWS   A way to conduct surveys by mailing questionnaires to a population sample.

MANAGEMENT   The process of planning, organizing, staffing, directing, and controlling an organization's human, financial, and material resources to accomplish its goals. The process itself is carried out by a team of managers who get things done through other people.

MANAGEMENT BY OBJECTIVES (MBO)   A popular motivational technique that involves superiors and subordinates setting objectives for the subordinate that will cover a specified period of time. The emphasis is on results accomplished.

MANAGEMENT DEVELOPMENT   The process of educating and developing selected personnel so that they have the knowledge, skills, attitudes, and understanding needed to manage in the future.

MANAGERIAL HIERARCHY   The levels of management in an organization. Typically there are three distinct levels—top, middle, and supervisory.

MANAGEMENT INFORMATION SYSTEM (MIS)   A planned combination of human and computer resources that produces timely and useful information for the efficient management of an organizaton.

MANAGEMENT PRINCIPLE   A guideline that serves to help managers make decisions.

MARGIN   The percentage that the buyer must put down when purchasing a stock.

MARGIN REQUIREMENTS   Percentage of the price that an investor must put down when purchasing stock.

MARKET   A group of people or organizations that buy a particular good, service, or concept.

MARKET ORDER   An order to buy or sell a stated number of securities at the current market price.

MARKET SEGMENTATION   The process of dividing a total market in similar groups.

MARKET SHARE   The ratio of customers to total number of people in a market.

MARKET VALUE   The current price paid by buyers to sellers of a stock.

MARKETING   The exchange among individuals and organizations that attempts to satisfy both the needs and wants of people and the organization's objectives.

MARKETING CONCEPT   A business philosophy that consumer preferences for goods and services are important in determining what is to be produced.

MARKETING ENVIRONMENT   The complete environment—consisting of competition, regulation, technology, and social forces—in which marketing occurs.

MARKETING INTERMEDIARY   A person or organization that helps the movement of products between producers and consumers.

MARKETING MIX   The combination of elements—product, price, promotional activities, and distribution channels—that affects the selling of a product.

MARKETING STRATEGY   The blueprint a business uses to compete in its various target markets or market segments.

MATRIX STRUCTURE   Arrangement of activities in both function and product (or project) units. There are both functional and product managers, with varying degrees of authority over the work performed by the same people.

MEAN   A statistical measure used to describe the "typical" value of a set of sample data. Also called the arithmetic average.

MEDIAN   The middle value in a list of numbers.

MEDIATOR   Third party to a labor dispute, who tries to get union and management to reason and works at improving communication between them.

MERCHANT WHOLESALER   A business that takes legal title to and possession of products from producers.

MERGER   The joining tgether of two firms into one firm.

MESBIC   Acronym for minority-enterprise small-business investment company. Such a company is owned and operated by established industrial or financial concerns, private investors, or business-oriented economic development organizations.

MISSIONARY SELLING   Form of business selling used to develop good will and long-term sales for a product.

MODE   A number in a list that occurs most frequently.

MONEY   Anything that is generally accepted as a means of paying for goods and services received.

MONEY MARKET MUTUAL FUND   A mutual fund—investment company—that purchases only U.S. government and corporate fixed income-earning securities.

MOTIVATION   The way drives or needs direct a person's behavior toward a specific goal. It concerns the level of effort one puts forth to pursue the goal.

MRP   A computer-based method that develops schedules for the inputs needed to produce a product, the amounts of inputs needed, and the dates when orders for inputs should be placed.

MULTINATIONAL BUSINESS   A business headquartered in one country that maintains production and marketing facilities in one or more foreign countries.

MUTUAL FUND   A company that uses its capital to invest in other companies and continues to sell more of its shares of stock as investors demand them.

MUTUAL INSURANCE COMPANY   A cooperative association without stockholders.

NATIONAL LABOR RELATIONS BOARD NLRB)   A group that investigates cases of alleged unfair labor practices by employers and unions and holds elections to determine whether groups of employees want to be unionized.

NATURAL RESOURCES   Economic resources provided by nature in limited amounts. They must be processed before being used to produce goods and services or being made into a product.

NEED HIERARCHY   A motivational explanation offered by the psychologist Abraham Maslow. He proposed that people have five needs arranged in a hierarchy from the physiological to the self-realization.

NEEDS   Goods and services people must have to exist.

NEGATIVE REINFORCER   A method to discourage certain behaviors; for example, reprimand for not finishing a job on time.

NONPARTICIPATING POLICY   The type of policy that a stock insurance company usually offers. The premiums you pay represent the full and actual cost of the policy.

NOW ACCOUNTS   Essentially a checking account that pays interest.

OBJECTIVE   A specific result or target to be reached by a certain time.

OCCUPATIONAL SAFETY AND HEALTH ACT (OSHA)   An act to protect the health of employees. Employers must furnish work places free from recognized hazards to life and health.

ODD LOT   An amount of stock less than a round lot or between one and ninety-nine shares.

ODD-LOT BROKER   A member of the stock exchange who buys and sells odd lots of stock.

OPEN BOOK ACCOUNT   A credit arrangement in which no formal document is drawn up, but the debtor is expected to pay within a few days after the day of the invoice.

OPEN-MARKET OPERATIONS   Purchase and sale of U.S. government bonds on the open market by the Federal Reserve System.

OPEN SHOP   A company in which employees don't have to join a union or pay dues, but can decide without pressure whether to become union members.

OPERATING BUDGET   A budget that allows the owner of a business to compare budget activities with actual costs.

OPERATING EMPLOYEE   An employee who isn't performing managerial duties.

ORGANIZATON CHART   A map of positions, people, and their formal authority relationships in the organizaton.

ORGANIZATION STRUCTURE   The arrangement of work to be done in a business.

ORGANIZING   The management function of grouping people and assignments so that the job tasks and the mission can be properly carried out.

OUTPUT DEVICE   A computer component that converts electronic impulses into a form that can be used by people.

OWNER'S EQUITY   Things of value that the owner or owners have invested in a business.

PARTICIPATING LOAN   A loan made to a small-business owner with SBA funds and funds from private sources.

PARTICIPATING POLICY   A policy in a utual insurance company in which you become a participant and are given therefore, a prorata return on your premium commensurate with any excess of premiums over payouts and expenses of the company.

PARTNERSHIP   A business owned by two or more people.

PAR VALUE   Arbitrary value of a stock or bond.

PATRONAGE DIVIDEND   Dividends paid to members of a cooperative in proportion to the amount of goods each has bought or sold through the cooperative.

PERFORMANCE APPRAISAL   A procedure used by managers to assess performance and inform the employee of their expectations and opinions.

PERSONALITY   The way a person acts, feels, and responds to people and situations.

PERSONAL INTERVIEW   A face-to-face conversation between interviewer and survey sample.

PERSONAL SELLING   Activity of a person who sells directly to another person.

PERSONNEL/HUMAN RESOURCE MANAGEMENT   The process or accomplishing organizational objectives by acquiring, retaining, terminating, developing, and properly using the human resources in an organizaton.

PER SE VIOLATION   An action that in and of itself is a violation of a particular antitrust law. In other words, even if the action does not lead to monopoly, the action itself is per se considered a violaton.

PHYSICAL DISTRIBUTION   The storage and movement of products from producers to the point of final purchase by consumers.

PHYSIOLOGICAL NEED   Biological need for food, air, water.

PLANNING   The management function of establishing objectives and developing plans to accomplish them.

PLANT LAYOUT   Process of arranging machines, determining where people will work, and arranging service facilities so that a plant may produce products.

POINT-OF-PURCHASE ADVERTISING   A form of promotion used to get consumers to buy while in the store.

PORTFOLIO   An individual's or institution's holdings of securities; it may include bonds, preferred stock, and common stock of various businesses.

POSITIVE REINFORCER   Something preferred by a worker, such as praise for a job well done.

PREDATORY PRICE CUTTING   Reducing prices even below actual average per-unit costs in order to drive rivals out of the marketplace.

PREEMPTIVE RIGHT   This gives holders of common stock the first chance to buy additional issues of common stock on a basis proportional to the number of shares they already hold.

PREFERENTIAL SHOP   A company that recognizes the union and gives some preference to union members in hiring in some areas.

PREFERRED STOCK   Equity security providing a claim on the company's earnings and assets ahead of the common stockholders.

PREMIUM   The yearly fee paid for insurance.

PRICE   The exchange value of any product to buyers where the exchange value is converted into money.

PRICING OBJECTIVE   Goals for the business or product that affect the manager in setting the price for a product.

PRIMARY DATA   Data collected to solve a specific problem or as part of an ongoing report.

PRINCIPLE   A guideline that managers can use in making decisions.

PRINCIPLE OF FUNCTIONAL SIMILARITY   The principle that work should be arranged on the basis of similarity.

PRINCIPLE OF INDEMNITY   The insured may not be compensated by an insurance company for more than his or her economic, or financial, loss.

PRINCIPLE OF SPAN OF CONTROL   The principle that limits the number of subordinates reporting to a supervisor.

PRINCIPLE OF UNITY OF COMMAND   The principle that no member of an organization should report to more than one superior.

PRIVATE CARRIERS   Carriers that transport their own products.

PROCESS LAYOUT   Plant layout used for products that can be made in a series of separate steps.

PRODUCER   Manufacturer of a good, a wholesaler or retailer, a service business, or a nonprofit organization.

PRODUCT   A good or service that satisfies consumers.

PRODUCT LAYOUT   Plant layout used for products that are produced in large volumes or made in a continuous process.

PRODUCT LIFE CYCLE (PLC)   Evolutionary stages of a product in the marketplace, from introduction to withdrawal.

PRODUCT MARKETS   Places where consumers and businesses buy the output of businesses.

PRODUCT STRUCTURE   An organization structure in which a manager is placed in charge of and has responsibility for a product or product line.

PRODUCTION   Process of changing inputs into goods and services that people want.

PRODUCTION CONTROL   Activities that support the production process through aggregate production planning, production scheduling, and inventory control.

PRODUCTON MANAGEMENT   Activities concerned with the efficient use of economic resources and their conversion into finished goods and services.

PRODUCTION SCHEDULE   A production timetable for doing certain jobs and using specific materials and machines.

PRODUCTIVITY   A measure of the relationship between what is produced and what is ued to produce it (output/input).

PROFIT   The difference between business income (revenue) and business expenses (costs); what is left after all costs of making and selling a product, including taxes, are subtracted from its selling price.

PROFIT MOTIVE   The willingness to risk time and money in business ventures with the hope of making a profit.

PROMISSORY NOTE   A signed written instrument promising to pay a certain sum in money to a payee or a holder on a specified date.

PROMOTION   The seller's way to inform, persuade, and influence prospective buyers.

PROMOTION MIX   Combination of promotional methods used in a promotional program.

PROTECTIVE TARIFFS   Tariffs placed on imported products to put them in an unfavorable price position relative to domestically produced products.

PROXY   A written statement signed by a stockholder of a corporation allowing someone else to cast his or her number of votes.

PUBLICITY   Information and news about an organization that is published by others and not paid for by the organization.

PUBLIC RELATIONS   An organization's effort to improve its relationships with employees, customers, suppliers, stockholders, governments, and local communities.

PULL STRATEGY   A promotion campaign aimed at a large audience that creates a demand so consumers ask for a product.

PUNISHMENT   Providing an undersirable consequence (taking away some pay) for a particular behavior (reporting to work late two times within a month).

PUSH STRATEGY   This requires salespeople to promote a product vigorously within the channel.

QUALITY CIRCLES   Teams of eight to twelve employees and supervisors who meet on company time to solve work-related problems. Everyone in the circle has equal say and the same vote in solving problems.

QUALITY CONTROL   Process by which business assures both management and customers that its products have been designed, produced, and marketed to meet high standards.

QUALITY OF WORK LIFE   A managerial program that increases outcomes such as productivity or performance by better managememment of jobs, people, and working conditions.

QUOTA   A definite limit on the quantity of a good that can be brought into a country.

RANDOM SAMPLE   Survey of a group selected by chance.

RATE DISCRIMINATION   Discrimination in railroad rates in which the per-pound, per-mile charge differed according to whether competition existed on a particular route. Also, rate discrimination sometimes involved charging different prices to different companies for the same service.

RATE OF EXCHANGE   The price at which one nation's currency is exchanged for that of another.

RECRUITMENT   Steps taken to staff an organization with the best qualified people.

REINFORCER   A consequence of behavior that improves the chances it will occur again or, in the case of a negative reinforcer, will not.

RENEWABILITY   A clause in a term insurance policy that guarantees it can be renewed without the insured passing a medical exam.

RESPONSIBILITY   Obligation of a subordinate to perform duties required by an immediate superior.

RESERVE REQUIREMENTS   Percentage of demand deposits that member banks of the Federal Reserve System must keep in cash reserves.

RESOURCE MARKETS   Places where economic resources are bought and sold.

RESTRAINT OF TRADE   Any action that impedes the free flow of commerce, such as an agreement among producers to restrict output or to split up geographical sections of the country in which each of them will sell the particular product.

RESTRICTED SHOP   A company whose management tries to keep a union out without violating any labor laws.

RETAILER   Any business that does over 50 percent of its total sales to final consumers.

RETAIL SALES   Consumer purchases of goods and services

REVENUE TARIFFS   Tafiffs designed primarily to raise money for governments.

ROLE   A set of expected behaviors. A manager has three major roles as a conduit, processor, and decision-maker.

ROUND LOT   A unit of trading on the stock exchange; usually one hundred shares.

RIGHT TO PRIVATE PROPERTY   People's right to own private property, the most basic right of capitalism.

RIGHT-TO-WORK LAWS   State laws requiring that two people doing the same job be paid the same wages, whether or not they belong to the union.

SAFETY NEED   Workers' need to be financially secure and protected against losing their jobs.

SALARIES   Compensation based on time, but the unit of time is a week, a month, or longer.

SALES PROMOTION   Any type of nonpersonal promotion that stimulates consumer purchases and dealer effectiveness.

SAMPLE SURVEY   A method of collecting original data by selecting a number of representative people and recording their answers to various questions.

SAVINGS AND LOAN ASSOCIATION   A business in which savers and borrowers are members. Most of the business's money is invested in local home mortgages.

SCALAR PRINCIPLE   The principle that authority and responsibility should flow in a clear, unbroken line from the highest to the lowest manager.

SCRAMBLED MERCHANDISING   A form of retailing where stores carry many different types of products that do not fit well with their traditional product lines.

SECONDARY DATA   Published by other businesses, trade associations, and governments.

SECURED LOANS   Loans that are secured by collateral, such as heavy equipment, inventories, or real estate.

SELF-INSURANCE   Assumption of the risk oneself. This occurs when individuals do not buy insurance to cover the risk involved. Self-insurance typically involves setting up a reserve fund to cover potental losses.

SELF-REALIZATION NEED   The highest need in the Maslow hierarchy; the need to maximize the full range or one's potential and skills.

SELLING SHORT   Selling borrowed stock with the promise to return it at a later date.

SERVICES   Nonmonetary programs provided by companies to employees (e.g., gymnasium facilities.).

SHOPPING GOODS   Goods for which consumers normally compare price, quality, and style.

SIGNATURE LOAN   A loan that is not backed by any specific property; only the good credit rating of the borrower is used.

SILENT PARTNER   A limited partener who does not participate in the management of the partenership.

SMALL BUSINESS   One that is independently owned and operated and not dominant in its field of operation.

SMALL BUSINESS ADMINISTRATION (SBA)   An independent agency of the federal government, created in 1953 for the purpose of protecting the interests of small-business owners.

SMALL-BUSINESS INVESTMENT COMPANY (SBIC)   A privately owned and operated company licensed by the SBA to furnish loans to small firms.

SOCIAL AWARENESS   An awareness beyond immediate profits of such social concerns as pollution, product quality, employment discrimination, safer products, and employee safety.

SOCIALISM   A type of economic system that stresses government ownership of economic resources sand coordinated economic planning.

SOCIAL RESPONSIVENESS   Attention to the needs and desires of stockholders, employees, suppliers, and consumers.

SOCIAL NEED   The need to belong and to interact with other people.

SOLE PROPRIETORSHIP   A business owned and managed by one individual.

SPAN OF CONTROL   The number of subordinates who report direct to a manager.

SPECIALIST   A member of a stock exchange who specializes in the purchase and sale of a specific stock or stocks. The specialist has two functions: to maintain an orderly market in the trading of stocks and to assist other brokers with limit orders.

SPECIALTY GOODS   Goods with unusual characteristics that are usually expensive.

SPREAD   The difference between the bid price and the ask price in the over-the-counter market.

STAFF AUTHORITY   An advisory type of authority in which a person studies a situation but has no authorized authority to take action.

STAFFING   The management function of selecting, placing, training, developing, and compensating subordinates.

STOCKBROKER   A registered representative of a stock exchange's member firm.

STOCK INSURANCE COMPANY   An insurance company owned by stockholders who take the risks of any loss and are entitled to a pro rata share of the profits.

STRIKE   A union weapon used to get management to make concessions. It involves withholding employee services from the employer.

SWEETHEART CONTRACT   Agreement between union leaders and management to terms that work to their mutual benefit but maintain poor working conditions for other employeees.

SYNDICATE   A business that engages in financial transactions. Members can sell their ownership interest to buyers of their choice.

SUBCHAPTER S CORPORATION   A corporation with ten or fewer owners; files an income tax return as a partnership to take advantage of lower tax rates.

SUBROGATION   The right of an insurance company to force you to transfer your right to sue another party. If you collect from your insurance company on an automobile accident, you must transfer the right to se the other person to your insurance company.

SUPPORT GOODS   Goods consumed in the operation of an organization that are not part of the final product, such as supplies and maintenance items.

TAFT-HARTLEY ACT   A labor law, passed in 1947, that prohibits the closed shop, requires unions to bargain in good faith, and makes it illegal for a union to discriminate against employees who don't join the union.

TARIFFS   Taxes placed on imported goods and services.

TECHNICAL SELLING   Form of business selling in which the salesperson tries to help customers adapt the product to their own needs.

TECHNOLOGY   New ideas and inventions and their applicaton to increase America's production and productivity.

TELEPHONE INTERVIEW   A way to conduct surveys by calling people included in a sample.

TERM INSURANCE   Life insurance for a specified term (period of time) that has only a death benefit.

TERRITORIAL STRUCTURE   The organization structure in which units are divided on the basis of territory or geographical regions.

THEORY X   Managerial assumptions that employees dislike work, responsibility, and accountability and must be closely directed and controlled to be motivated to perform.

THEORY Y   Managerial assumptions that employees want to be challenged, like to display creativity, and can be highly motivated to perform well if given some freedom to direct or manage their own behavior

TIME DEPOSITS   Deposits that, in principle, require at least thirty days notice prior to the withdrawal of funds.

TRADE ACCEPTANCE   A time draft drawn by one person and sent to the drawee. When the drawee accepts the draft by signing it, becomes a trade acceptance.

TRADE CREDIT   A form of short-term credit extended to business by suppliers; this is the largest source of short-term credit.

TRADE DRAFT   A bill of exchange constituting a written order to pay a third party a certain sum of money on a designated date (time draft) or on demand (sight draft).

TRAINING   A continual process of helping employees to perform at a high level. Training may occur on the job or at a special training facility.

TRAVELER'S CHECK   A check issued by American Express, VISA, or a commercial bank that acts as a substitute for money. The bearer of the check signs once when purchasing the check and countersigns again when cashing the check.

TRUST AGREEMENT   An agreement to form, in effect, a monopoly by putting control of all the major companies in an industry in the hands of a single group of trustees.

TRUST CERTIFICATE   A share in a business trust showing that the holder has transferred funds to a trustee and has the right to benefit from the success of the trust investments.

UMBRELLA POLICY   A supplemental insurance policy that can extend normal automobile (and personal) liability limits to $1 million or more for a relatively small premium.

UNIFORM DECREASING TERM INSURANCE   Term insurance in which a fixed premium is paid and the face value of the policy falls throughout its life of, say, twenty years.

UNION SHOP   A company that requires employees to join the union after being hired.

UNION STEWARD   Person who represents the interests of local union members in their on-the-job relations with managers.

UNLIMITED LIABILITY   Obligation of investors to use personal assets, when necessary, to pay off debts to business creditors; a disadvantage of sole proprietorships and partnerships.

UTILITY   The ability of a product or service to satisfy consumer wants or needs.

WAGES   Compensations based on the time an employee works or number of units produced.

WAGNER ACT   A law that made collective bargaining legal and required employers to bargain with the representatives of the employees. The law is also referred to as the National Labor Relations Act.

WANTS   Goods and service people would like to have but do not need for survival.

WHEEL OF RETAILING   A concept used to explain the constant change that happens in retailing.

WHOLE LIFE INSURANCE   Also called cash value, straight, and ordinary life insurance. It has both death and living benefits. One builds cash surrender value in the policy.

WHOLESALER   A business that buys products from producers and sells them to other businesses. Over 50 percent of the wholesaler's sales are made to other businesses.

WORKING CAPITAL RESOURCES   Goods produced for the purpose of making other types of goods and services but that are used up in the production process.

WORK MOTIVATION MODEL   A model proposed by social psychologist Frederic Herzberg. He found in his research that a set of job factors, which he called hygienes, were essential to maintain high job satisfaction. These factors included salary, job security, and working conditions. Another set of factors, called *motivators*, included recognition, responsibility, and advancement opportunities.

YELLOW-DOG CONTRACT   A statement signed by an employee promising that he or she will not form or join a union.

YIELD   The return on an investment. Calculated by dividing the amount of the return by the amount of the investment.

ZERO POPULATION GROWTH (ZPG)   A situation in which the average annual increase in the population is zero. This will occur when every child-bearing couple has exactly 2.1 children.

NOTES

CHAPTER 1

1. John Kenneth Galbraith, "Galbraith's Age of Uncertainty: A Quick Look," *The Detroit News Sunday News Magazine*, September 18, 1977, p. 32.
2. Cecil Woodham Smith, *The Great Hunger: Ireland, 1845–1849* (New York: Harper & Row, 1963), pp. 410–411.
3. John Peterson and Ralph Gray, *Economic Development of the United States* (Homewood, Ill.: Richard D. Irwin, 1969), p. 398.

CHAPTER 4

1. The discussion of Frank Gorell is based on "The Sweet Sound of . . . ," *Forbes*, June 1, 1977, p. 72.
2. Currently, ten states have not adopted the Uniform Partnership Act: Alabama, Florida, Georgia, Hawaii, Iowa, Kansas, Louisiana, Maine, Mississippi, and New Hampshire.
3. "Deals of the Year," *Fortune*, January 25, 1982, pp. 36–40.
4. "The New Urge to Merge," *Newsweek*, July 27, 1981, pp. 50–58.

CHAPTER 5

1. U.S. Statistical Abstract, U.S. Department of Commerce, 1981, p. 401.
2. "A National Rollout for Hair-Care Buyout," *Venture*, January 1982, p. 10.
3. Charles G. Burck, "Franchising's Troubled Dream World," *Fortune*, March 1977, p. 117.
4. "There's More to Eat Than Big Mac and Chicken," *Fortune*, March 1977, p. 213.
5. U.S. Department of Commerce, *Franchising in the Economy, 1980–1982* (Washington, D.C.: U.S. Government Printing Office, 1982), p. 12.
6. Robert M. Rosenberg and Madelon Redell, *Profits from Franchising* (New York: McGraw-Hill, 1969), p. 41.
7. Rosenberg and Redell, p. 12.
8. *Restaurant Business*, March 1, 1979.
9. Shelby D. Hunt, "The Trend Toward Company-Operated Units in Franchise Chains," *Journal of Retailing*, Summer 1973, pp. 3–12.
10. Rosenberg and Redell, p. 105.
11. U.S. vs. Arnold Schwinn and Company, 388 U.S. 365 (1967).
12. Mike Fernisilber and William B. Mead, *American Averages* (New York: Doubleday, 1980), p. 299.

CHAPTER 6

1. Peter F. Drucker, *Management: Tasks, Responsibilities, Practices* (New York: Harper & Row, 1973), pp. ix–x.
2. Irwin Ross, "Chyrsler on the Brink," *Fortune*, February 9, 1981, pp. 38–42.
3. Anthony P. Raia, *Managing by Objectives* (Glenview, Ill.: Scott, Foresman, 1974).
4. "GM Provokes Battle in Industry as It Bids to Raise Market Share," *Wall Street Journal*, January 7, 1976, p. 1.
5. Fred E. Fiedler, "The Leadership Game: Matching the Man to the Situation," *Organizational Dynamics*, Winter 1976, pp. 6–16.

CHAPTER 7

1. James L. Gibson, John M. Ivancevich, and James H. Donnelly, Jr., *Organizations: Behavior, Structure, Processes* (Plano, Texas: Business Publications, 1982), p. 350.
2. Peter Drucker, *People and Performance: The Best of Peter Drucker on Management* (New York: Harper's College Press, 1977).
3. Arthur H. Walker and Jay Lorsch, "Organizational Choice: Product versus Function," *Harvard Business Review*, November–December 1968, pp. 129–138.
4. E. Raymond Corey and Steven H. Star, *Organization Strategy: A Marketing Approach* (Cambridge, Mass: Division of Research, Graduate School of Business Administration, Harvard University, 1970).
5. Clayton Reeser, "Some Potential Problems of the Project Form of Organization," *Academy of Management Journal*, December 1969, pp. 459–467.
6. Harvey F. Kolodny, "Evolution to a Matrix Organization," *Harvard Business Review*, May–June 1978, pp. 131–142.

CHAPTER 8

1. Peter Drucker, *Management: Tasks, Responsibilities, Practices* (New York: Harper & Row, 1974), p. 504.
2. Abraham H. Maslow, ed., *Motivation and Personality*, 2nd ed. (New York: Harper & Row, 1954).
3. Abraham Maslow, "Self-Actualizing People: A Study of Psychological Health," in Abraham H. Maslow (ed.), *Motivation and Personality*, 2nd ed. (new York: Harper & Row, 1954).

539

4. Douglas McGregor, *The Human Side of Enterprise* (New York: McGraw-Hill, 1960).

5. Frederick Herzberg, Bernard Mausner, and Barbara Snyderman, *The Motivation to Work* (New York: Wiley, 1959).

6. "Hawthorne Revisited: The Legend and the Legacy," *Organizational Dynamics*, Winter 1975, pp. 66–80.

7. William F. Whyte, *Money and Motivation* (New York: Harper & Row, 1955).

8. See J. R. Hackman and J. E. Suttle, eds., *Improving Life at Work: Behavioral Science Approaches to Organizational Change* (Santa Monica, Calif.: Goodyear, 1977).

9. Peter Drucker, *The Practice of Management* (New York: Harper & Row, 1954).

10. B. F. Skinner, *Contingencies of Reinforcement* (New York: Appleton-Century-Crofts, 1969); and "An Interview with B. F. Skinner," *Organizational Dynamics*, Winter 1973, pp. 31–40.

CHAPTER 9

1. W. F. Glueck and J. M. Ivancevich, *Foundations of Personnel/ Human Resource Management* (Plano, Texas: Business Publications, 1983), p. 1–15.

2. Note to come.

3. A. Anastasi, *Psychological Testing* (New York: Macmillan, 1982), p. 12.

4. Michael Beer, *Organizational Change and Development* (Santa Monica, Calif.: Goodyear, 1980).

5. Douglas Bray and Joseph Moses, "Personnel Selection," *Annual Review of Psychology* (Palo Alto, Calif.: Annual Reviews, 1972), pp. 545–576.

6. Wage and Hour Division, *Equal Pay* (Washington, D.C.: U.S. Department of Labor, 1974), p. 3. Also see Michael F. Carter, "Comparable Worth: An Idea Whose Time Has Come?" *Personnel Journal*, October 1981, pp. 792–794.

CHAPTER 10

1. William F. Glueck, *Personnel: A Diagnostic Approach* (Plano, Texas: Business Publications, 1982), pp. 574–576.

2. John G. Kilgour, *Preventive Labor Relations* (New York: AMACOM, 1981).

3. Mark N. Dodosh, "Companies Increasingly Ask Labor to Give Back Past Contract Gains," *Wall Street Journal*, November 27, 1981.

4. Micheline Maynard, "UAW Panel Approves Pact to Save GM $3 Billion," *Houston Chronicle*, March 26, 1982.

5. Arthur A. Sloane and Fred Witney, *Labor Relations* (Englewood Cliffs, N.J.: Prentice-Hall, 1981), pp. 233–234.

6. Herbert E. Meyer, "The Decline of Strikes," *Fortune*, November 2, 1981, pp. 66–70.

7. "Unions Move into the Office," *Business Week*, January 25, 1982, pp. 90–92.

8. William E. Holley and Kenneth M. Jennings, *The Labor Relations Process* (Hinsdale, Ill.: Dryden Press, 1980), p. 230.

CHAPTER 24

1. Terrance S. Hitchcock, *American Business. The Last Hurrah?* (Homewood, Ill.: Dow Jones-Irwin, 1982).

2. Walter Guzzardi, Jr., "Demography's Good News for The Eighties," *Fortune*, November 5, 1979, p. 92.

3. Juan Cameron, "Blacks Still Waiting For Full Membership," *Fortune*, April 1975, p. 165.

4. Michael F. Carter, "Comparable Worth: An Idea Whose Time Has Come?" *Personnel Journal*, October 1981, p. 792.

5. Cynthia F. Epstein, *Woman's Place: Options and Limits In Professional Careers* (Berkeley: University of California Press, 1970), pp. 12–13.

6. "Mitsubishi: A Japanese Giant's Plans for Growth In The U.S.", *Business Week*, July 20, 1981, pp. 128–32.

7. "Trade Barriers: Japanese Style," *U.S. News & World Report*, February 1, 1982, p. 52.

8. Joel E. Ross, *Productivity, People, and Profits* (Reston, Va.: Reston Publishing Co., 1981), p. 42.

9. Hitchcock, p. 159.

10. Jeremy Main, "The Battle for Quality Begins," *Fortune*, December 29, 1980, pp. 28–29.

11. Daniel S. MacNaughton, "Managing Social Responsiveness," *Business Horizons*, December 1976, pp. 19–24.

12. Hitchcock, p. 179.

INDEX